EUROPEAN COLONIAL RULE, 1880-1940

Contributions in Comparative Colonial Studies
Series Editor, Robin W. Winks

Empires in Collision: Anglo-Burmese Relations in the Mid-Nineteenth Century
Oliver B. Pollak

Social Engineering in the Philippines: The Aims, Execution, and Impact of American Colonial Policy, 1900-1913
Glenn Anthony May

The Politics of Dependency: Urban Reform in Istanbul
Stephen T. Rosenthal

Rhodes, The Tswana, and the British: Colonialism, Collaboration, and Conflict in the Bechuanaland Protectorate, 1885-1889
Paul Maylam

Between Black and White: Race, Politics, and the Free Coloreds in Jamaica, 1792-1865
Gad J. Heuman

British Rule in Malaya: The Malayan Civil Service and Its Predecessors, 1867-1942
Robert Heussler

Economic Control and Colonial Development: Crown Colony Financial Management in the Age of Joseph Chamberlain
Richard M. Kesner

Constraint of Empire: The United States and Caribbean Interventions
Whitney T. Perkins

Toward a Programme of Imperial Life: The British Empire at the Turn of the Century
John H. Field

EUROPEAN COLONIAL RULE, 1880-1940
The Impact of the West on India, Southeast Asia, and Africa

Rudolf von Albertini
with Albert Wirz

Translated by John G. Williamson

CONTRIBUTIONS IN COMPARATIVE COLONIAL STUDIES, NUMBER 10

GP

Greenwood Press
WESTPORT, CONNECTICUT • LONDON, ENGLAND

Library of Congress Cataloging in Publication Data

Albertini, Rudolf von.
European colonial rule, 1880-1940.

(Contributions in comparative colonial studies, ISSN 0163-3813 ; no. 10)
Bibliography: p.
Includes index.
1. Asia—History. 2. Africa—History—1884-1960. 3. Colonies. I. Wirz, Albert. II. Title. III. Series: Contributions in comparative colonial studies ; no. 10.
DS33.7.A4313 909′.09719 81-4264
ISBN 0-313-21275-9 (lib. bdg.) AACR2

Library of Congress Catalog Card Number: 81-4264
ISBN: 0-313-21275-9
ISSN: 0163-3813

First published in 1982

Greenwood Press
A division of Congressional Information Service, Inc.
88 Post Road West
Westport, Connecticut 06881

Printed in the United States of America

10 9 8 7 6 5 4 3 2 1

CONTENTS

List of Maps ix
List of Tables xi
Series Foreword xv
Translator's Note xvii
Preface xix
Abbreviations xxxi

Part I: ASIA 1

1. British India 3
   Administration & Civil Service 13
   Population Movements 21
   Famine 23
   Irrigation 25
   Agrarian Structure and Farm Production 27
   Railroads 44
   Industry 48
   The "Drain of Wealth" Thesis 62
   The Work Force, Working Conditions, and the Trade Union Movement 65
   Indian Nationalism and the Stages of Political Emancipation: Until 1914 67
   Indian Nationalism and the Stages of Political Emancipation: 1914-1939 78
2. Burma 116
3. Ceylon 131
4. Malaya 145

5. The Netherlands Indies 160
Administration 164
Economy 167
National Liberation 178
6. France in Vietnam 193
Administration 196
Economy 202
Vietnamese Nationalism 212

Part II: NORTHERN AFRICA **225**

7. The British "Protectorate" over Egypt: Until 1922 227

8. France in the Maghreb 256
Algeria as an "Integral Part of the National Territory" 257
Indirect Rule, French Version: Tunisia and Morocco 261
Land Acquisition and Agriculture 266
Communications, Mining, and Industry 278
Nationalism 282

Part III: SUB-SAHARAN AFRICA **303**

9. British West Africa: Nigeria and the Gold Coast 305
Indirect Rule 309
Cocoa, Palm Oil, and Peanuts 319
Self-Government: When and How? 328

10. French West and Equatorial Africa: From Senegal to the Congo 343
Administration: Central and Direct 346
Economic Development 353
Evolués, Assimilation, and Integration 361

11. The Belgian Congo 374

12. The German Colonies in Africa, by Albert Wirz 388

13. Portugal in Africa, by Albert Wirz 418

14. British Settlers in Central and East Africa 444
Land and Labor 448
Kenya 448
Uganda 457
Tanganyika 462
Rhodesia 467
Northern Rhodesia 471
Protest Movements and Proto-nationalism 476

15. A Summing Up: Some Reflections on Colonialism 488

Maps 519
List of Works Cited 541
Index 565

LIST OF MAPS

1. India: Annual Rainfall
2. India: Population Density, 1941
3. India: Princely States and British Provinces, 1941
4. India: The Economy, ca. 1930
5. India: Hindus as a Percentage of the Total Population, 1931
6. Ceylon
7. Burma
8. Malaya: Political Divisions, 1909-1941
9. Malaya: The Economy, ca. 1940
10. French Indochina
11. Netherlands Indies
12. Egypt
13. Africa: Political Divisions, 1939
14. Maghreb: Annual Rainfall
15. Maghreb: Agriculture and Industry
16. West Africa 1 (primarily British)
17. West Africa 2 (primarily French)
18. Southwest Africa
19. Rhodesia and Mozambique
20. East Africa

LIST OF TABLES

1.1	Population of India	22
1.2	Productivity of Land in India, 1901-1941	42
1.3	Cotton Production in British India, 1891-1939	43
1.4	Growth of Cotton Industry in India, 1880-1914	50
1.5	Growth of Jute Industry in India, 1885-1939	53
1.6	Value of Total Indian Foreign Trade, 1914-1937	62
1.7	Indian Balance of Trade, 1913-1914 and 1938-1939	64
2.1	Production of Rice in Lower Burma, 1830-1935	120
2.2	Ownership of Land in Burma, 1921-1931	122
3.1	Civil Service Appointments in Ceylon, 1920-1950	133
3.2	Administrative Personnel in Ceylon, 1907-1946	134
3.3	Production of Tea in Ceylon, 1882-1914	136
3.4	Tea Industry in Ceylon, 1885-1896	142
3.5	Tea Export from Ceylon, 1913-1937	142
4.1	Production of Tin, 1871-1940	149
4.2	Malayan Population by Nationalities, 1911-1938	153
4.3	Rubber Plantations in Malaya, 1932	158
4.4	Western Investment Including Colonial Loans in Malaya, 1914-1937	158
4.5	Malayan Civil Service Positions	159
5.1	Indonesian Sugar Growing Areas and Sugar Exports, 1865-1929	168
5.2	Exports from the Netherlands Indies, 1840-1951	170
5.3	Land Rents and Wages Paid in Indonesia, 1930-1938	173
5.4	Weaving Looms in Use in Indonesia, 1930-1941	175
5.5	Indonesian Imports and Exports, 1881-1939	177
5.6	Foreign Investment in Indonesia, 1900-1937	177

5.7	Foreign Investment in Indonesia, 1937-1938	178
5.8	Graduates of Middle Schools in Indonesia, 1910-1939	181
5.9	Personnel Positions Held in Indonesia in Terms of National Origin, 1928-1938	182
5.10	Population and the Economy of Java, 1928-1940	190
5.11	Income and Income Taxation in Indonesia, 1936	191
5.12	Indonesians in Dutch Language Schools, 1900-1940	192
6.1	Rice Production and Consumption in Vietnam, 1931	221
6.2	French Proportion of Indochinese Foreign Trade, 1889-1932	223
6.3	Membership of the Vietnamese Nationalist Party, by Profession, 1929	224
7.1	Productive Agricultural Land in Egypt, 1835-1916	237
7.2	Growth of Population in Egypt, 1800-1957	237
7.3	Changes in the Distribution of Landed Property in Egypt, 1896-1916	238
7.4	Cotton Farming in Egypt, 1883-1913	242
7.5	Egyptian Grain Imports and Exports, 1885-1914	243
7.6	Production Indices for Individual Crops in Egypt, 1821-1878	252
7.7	Indices of Agricultural Growth in Egypt, 1895-1939	252
8.1	Real Property Ownership in Algeria, 1930	269
8.2	Land Planted in Vineyards in Algeria, 1878-1938	271
8.3	Real Property Ownership in Tunisia, 1921	274
8.4	Acquisition by French Colonists of Land in Morocco, 1913-1953	276
8.5	Ownership of Cultivated Land in Algeria	295
8.6	Real Property Ownership in Tunisia, 1937	296
8.7	Acreage and Yields in Tunisia, 1921-1935	297
8.8	Grain Yields in Morocco, 1921-1940	298
8.9	Total Industrial Production in the Maghreb, 1880-1955	298
8.10	Farm Yield Per Capita, Algeria and Morocco, 1911-1950	299
8.11	Population Growth in the Maghreb, 1876-1956	299
9.1	Export Tonnage of Cocoa in the Gold Coast and Nigeria	320
9.2	Production and Export of Palm Products in Nigeria, 1900-1939	323
9.3	Peanut Exports from North Nigeria, 1900-1939	325
9.4	Student Enrollment in Nigeria, 1913-1959	338
10.1	Export of Agricultural Products from French West Africa, 1845-1939	355
10.2	Education in French West and Equatorial Africa, 1938	363

13.1 Civilizados in Portuguese Africa, Native and Non-native, 1940 428
13.2 Moçambique's Foreign Trade, 1910-1940 433
14.1 Agricultural Production in Uganda, 1923-1935 484
15.1 Index of Export Values, 1913 514

SERIES FOREWORD

It is with exceptional pleasure that I include this translation of Professor Rudolf von Albertini's magnum opus in the series on Comparative Colonial Studies. Dr. von Albertini teaches at the University of Zurich, where he has established himself as one of Europe's leading students of modern imperialism. His massive work on decolonization, first published in 1966, roams across the entire spectrum of its subject, examining in detail Great Britain and France, and concludes with an explicit chapter of comparative conclusions. Henri Brunschwig wrote in *Annales* when *Decolonization* first appeared that it was assured of becoming a classic, and in the years since it has clearly done so.

Professor von Albertini joined with Dr. Heinz Gollwitzer to edit the highly regarded *Beiträge zur Kolonial- und Überseegeschichte*, producing volume after volume of colonial and imperial history. During this time Dr. von Albertini was also at work on his major volume, *Europäische Kolonialherrschaft, 1880-1940*, a grand synthesis in the tradition of William L. Langer, Parker T. Moon, and Mary E. Townsend, but suffused with the rich insights of the great burst of literature on imperialism that has appeared in the last three decades. Published in 1976 in Zurich, *Europäische Kolonialherrschaft* immediately established itself as the most authoritative and thorough survey available outside the English language. At once many readers in the United States and Britain asked for an edition they could use, either as text for their students or as a basic reference work for themselves. The first general survey of its kind, Professor von Albertini's volume was pressed into service wherever one might reasonably expect students to read German.

We were fortunate from the outset that von Albertini saw his own work as clearly comparative in its intentions, and that he wished his volume to appear in this series. An able and gifted translator, who holds a doctorate in German history, John G. Williamson, agreed to work with von Albertini in preparing the English-language edition. The result, *European Colonial Rule*, is a distinguished addition to the Greenwood series; it will dependably serve as the encompassing basic work for many years to come.

Robin W. Winks

TRANSLATOR'S NOTE

I would like to point out a number of things about this translation. First, both authors know English well and have read my version carefully. I did not always accept their suggestions for alternative wordings, however, and it may also be that on occasion I have not hit upon the most apt English equivalent for specialized terms. Such lapses are obviously not to be held against the authors, as the responsibility for them is clearly mine. Another problem is the transliteration of names and terms from the Arabic. Here I can only say that I have done my best, and that inconsistencies are accidental and not deliberate; my sins result from ignorance of Arabic rather than malice. On the matter of italicizing Arabic and other foreign words, I have generally italicized the word the first time it appears only, with the English equivalent in parentheses, and not thereafter.

Second, I have attempted to format the monographic citations in the notes as they will be found in the catalogs of large American research libraries. This accounts for an occasional variation in spelling between text and notes (for example, "Mouzinho" in the text and "Mousinho" in the notes). Whether the librarians or the historians were correct seemed less important in individual cases than providing name entries in the form in which they will be found. I have simplified standard catalog formats somewhat (and have not included series information) and have not been able to track down everything, but my hope is that the citations will be found more usable than those one generally encounters. I have also changed the format of journal citations to conform to American practice, for which the authors supplied the requisite additional information. With a few exceptions, however, I have not otherwise checked the journal citations.

Third, the bibliography of the German original was ordered alphabetically by region. Although the authors wished to retain this arrangement, the consensus on this side of the water was that including all works cited in one overall alphabetical list, not broken down by format, would serve the reader's purposes better. To economize, this list is a short-title list, giving only the author's name or main entry, short-title, and a reference, in parentheses, to the first full citation in the notes; for example, Bearce, G. D., *British Attitudes Toward India* (*BI* n4). The capital letters preceding note numbers refer to chapter abbreviations which have been provided in the beginning of the List of Works Cited.

My intent, then, was to render the text as accurately as possible, while at the same time strengthening the bibliographic apparatus, with the overall end of making a magisterial synthesis more useful still. In conclusion, I would like to acknowledge the encouragement and support the administration of St. Mary's College provided for this project and more specifically, the successful efforts of my faithful secretary, Mrs. Pollyanna Melin, in reducing my rather eccentric typescript to legible copy.

John G. Williamson

PREFACE

This book presents the colonial histories of most present-day Asian and African states with a colonial past. To attempt this, and within a relatively limited compass, is a presumptuous undertaking. It calls for some justification. My decision flowed naturally from several years' studies of modern colonial history and the fact that no such general account exists. My original interest lay in European history. The impact during the late 1950s, however, of the Vietnam and Algerian wars and of black African independence movements led me to believe that the Third World, a concept then coming slowly into use, would eventually assume major political significance. European recovery from the ravages of World War II was complete, an economic boom was under way, and the cold war fronts were stabilized. It was only natural and proper that we Europeans were, as historians, primarily concerned with our own past and future, but I believed that the framework within which we considered these matters had become too narrow. The "world history of Europe," to use the sociologist Hans Freyer's happy phrase, had ended. Political, economic, and military power had shifted from the European center to the two great powers on the periphery of Europe, and within a relatively short time the Asian and African peoples had freed themselves from colonial or semicolonial dependency. As independent states they faced the daunting tasks of achieving their own national identities, catching up economically and technologically with the industrial nations, and assuming their places in the community of nations. I still continued to study the questions of development policy and assistance, but came to view the problems confronting the former colonies as staggering if not indeed insoluble. It thus seemed reasonable to predict that the Third World and the whole complex of the problems of underdevelopment would more fully engage our interest sooner or later. Indeed, what lay in the offing seemed to me of greater urgency and importance for our future than the ephemeral "politics of the day" in the historically stabilized and prosperous nations of the West. As a historian, I first directed my attention to decolonization, which was then nearly complete. I then began, however, to treat various aspects of colonial policy in my seminars and lectures. My aim in part was to shatter the national, Europe-centered framework of traditional historiography and to confront the students with the problems of non-European lands. Some of the results are summarized here and presented as an account of European colonialism for the nonspecialist, with the narrative centered on the individual regions.

Until now, such an account has not existed. In international scholarship interest centered first on the breakup of colonialism, the time immediately before and after World War II, and then on an analysis of the internal and external forces that led to independence. Political scientists principally explored concepts such as "nation building," "integration," and the "search for national identity" during the first years of the new states. Sociologists studied the transformation of elites under the impact of "modernization"; colonial administration and economy were treated but briefly, as background matters. German scholars were only on the outer fringes of this effort. Dietmar Rothermund's book on the formation of the Indian political mind, which also treated the nineteenth century, Franz Ansprenger's *Politics in Black Africa*, and Bernhard Dahm's book about Sukarno were praiseworthy exceptions.[1] Ansprenger's *Auflösung der Kolonialreiche* ("*Dissolution of the Colonial Empires*") also provided a summary account of decolonization in the German paperback series (DTV), "History of the Twentieth Century."

There has also been a renewed and increasing interest in the study of imperialism both in a narrow and in a broader sense. In the narrow sense the old question of the drives and motivations behind the post-1870 expansion are being reconsidered. Robinson and Gallagher's concept of "free trade imperialism" and their book *Africa and the Victorians* were the most important impulses behind this renewed interest, which has greatly increased our knowledge of individual areas, particularly of black Africa, but also of Malaya and Vietnam.[2] Discussion has centered on the question, hardly new, of whether the real driving force was essentially political or economic. An unprejudiced observer would have to say it hardly permitted of any novel answer and had to be stated as "both-and" or "it varied according to the locale"; during the imperialist phase, 1870-1900, separating economics and politics is hardly possible. Hans-Ulrich Wehler's concept of "social imperialism" provided a new impetus to the discussion. His concept, developed using Germany as the example, could also be applied, though with considerable limitations, to the other Great Powers.[3] At the same time, the importance of the "local factor" (the pressures on the periphery making for expansion) has been reemphasized, mainly by Anglo-Saxon historians. In German we have comprehensive accounts by Fieldhouse and Mommsen.[4]

In a broader sense, the discussions of American foreign policy also enlivened imperialism studies. The Open Door concept, developed around 1900 regarding American relations with China, has been interpreted by the Williams school as the particular form of an American imperialism directed in the main toward winning markets not only in Latin America but indeed characterizing American foreign policy in the twentieth century, if not since the Civil War.[5] This open door imperialism in good part provoked the cold war after 1945 and because of its claim to domination ultimately led to war in Vietnam.

About this same time, Latin Americans and specialists in Latin America were analyzing the role of North American monopoly capitalism in Latin America. They developed a model for the "dependency" between the metropolis and the periphery to explain the present-day underdevelopment of these countries. From this a general theory of underdevelopment was deduced: it results from integrating the peripheral economies into the capitalist, world economic system and cannot be overcome so long as this system and these dependencies exist. As developed by Paul Baran and André Gunder Frank, this concept has been highly refined. Many consider it a suitable key to understanding the intractable problems of Latin American, Asian, and African underdevelopment.[6] Johan Galtung's "structural imperialism" has much in common with the dependency theory, since it also proceeds from the interaction between the metropolis and the periphery and attempts to show that the benefits flow mainly in the direction of the former. His concept of "bridgeheads," or specific interest groups in the periphery countries, brings into the picture the internal social forces which participate in the exploitation of the periphery by the metropolis and have a vested interest in continuing dependency.[7] These dependency theories were mainly intended to deal with relationships between formally independent states but can naturally be applied easily enough to direct colonial rule.

The study of colonial history in the traditional sense does not exist any longer. My undertaking, to write a history of European colonialism, may thus appear questionable. Today, one is no longer a "colonial historian," but rather a historian of Southeast Asia, or India, or of the Arab countries, or of the Maghreb, or of black Africa. And it is, in fact, no longer possible to investigate the activities of the European powers in their colonies or the activities of individual governors in a manner which treats "natives" as, at best, the objects of colonizing activities. What is now required is rather more a history from within, that is, an Indian, Egyptian, or African history which studies the colonial influences on precolonial societies and places in the foreground their confrontations with European power and civilization. Specialized research has taken great strides in the last few years, especially by integrating ethnological and sociological techniques into methodology. Interest has shifted to individual regions, provinces, and tribes, however, because only at this level is refined socioeconomic analysis possible. This research is not very accessible to the outsider, though the more recent country and regional histories provide valuable assistance. Examples are Michael Crowder's *West Africa under Colonial Rule* and the Oxford *History of East Africa*, but we still have no recent account of India under British rule.[8]

Research into German rule in Africa has started. We have excellent studies by Helmut Bley, Karin Hausen, Rainer Tetzlaff, and Albert Wirz.[9] Still, the interest of German historians and social scientists has remained largely fixed in imperialist researches taken from a European perspective or the limited and special field of the sociological and economic ramifications of development policy. Genuine interest in the history and the problems of the non-European peoples seems not only to be lacking but is accompanied by a lamentable grasp of the facts. There is much theorizing and talk of dependency and exploitation, but if one points out, say, that in the interwar period a tariff-protected cotton industry developed in India that largely displaced British products, the response is incredulity. There is also much theorizing about monoculture and the encouragement of cash crops at the cost of foodstuffs. Such theorists usually believe that cash crops came mainly from European plantations. Or hazy knowledge of the role played by large Latin American landholders is generalized without further ado into a model of colonial agrarian structure. Matters such as land per-capita ratio, the yield per acre, land erosion, and fertilization are not even considered.

What follows is a concise account of European colonialism from the onset of European rule until 1940. Insofar as is possible, my desire is to fill the gap between Mommsen's *Imperialismus* and Ansprenger's *Auflösung der Kolonialreiche*. In each chapter, an introductory account of the establishment of colonial rule is followed by information about the creation of the administrative structure, the development of the economy, and the growth of the national liberation movement. This loose organization is entirely pragmatic. It is thus open to the criticism that the actual tasks and functions of colonial rule—to exploit resources and create markets—are the proper starting place. Administration should accordingly be interpreted as a function of economic exploitation. This objection may have some theoretical validity, but it overlooks the relative independence of the administration, which followed particular models in its development and was determined by the force of particular events. Separate treatment thus seems justified. A further objection to my study can be raised: namely, that my interest in the beginnings of the liberation movement concentrates too exclusively on the new Western-schooled elite with the repressed masses hardly being considered; indeed, ethnological research ought to have been more fully incorporated than I was able to do. Still, I think I have been able to say some useful things about the masses.

My principal intention, then, is to provide basic information which, these days, leaves me open to the fashionable reproach of being a positivist. Theoreticians of underdevelopment, however, all too often feel they can simply ignore the latest historical research. They have, for example, a wearisome tendency to support their thesis that colonial powers expropriated the "economic surplus" by using the example of late eighteenth- and early nineteenth-century India. Besides Marx's famous articles they use sources which even Indian historians hardly accept today without severe reservations.[10] Accordingly, I find it legitimate and necessary to start by setting down the facts and by inquiring about why those on the spot acted as they did. By proceeding in this way, divergent interests are made apparent and the process of interaction can at least be sketched out. Economic exploitation will be outlined with numbers and concrete data. This in no way implies a legitimization of colonial rule, even though the neo-Marxists claim that only they have an accurate perception of the interests that really determine things. One need not use a loaded word like *exploitation* on every page to establish oneself as anticolonial and anti-imperialist. On the other hand, no methodological excursions are needed to make it clear that I too am guided by certain perceptions of interests and cannot proceed without a certain amount of methodological speculation.

I also believe that colonial history can today only be studied within the larger framework of European imperialism and within the scope of Third World underdevelopment. Defined by Rupert Emerson as "the establishment and maintenance, for an extended time, of rule over an alien people that is separate from and subordinate to the ruling power," colonialism means rule.[11] One starts from there. As a historian, I was interested in how this rule was established and maintained. What did the apparatus of colonial rule look like, and what impact did it have on the authority structures of the colonized society? How was the country opened up economically, and how was the colony integrated into a world economic system dynamized by industrialization and centered on Europe? What was the particular impact on rural society? What social mutations were initiated by the colonial power, and which forces gradually formed themselves into a national liberation movement?

Dependency has rightly been emphasized as an important constituent of colonial rule. In 1952 Georges Balandier introduced the concept "colonial condition" into scholarly ethnological discussions of the structure and changes of traditional societies. These were being conducted entirely in terms of endogenous factors and without regard for the colonial context.[12] The "colonial condition" was characterized by the rule of a foreign minority against which the repressed majority reacted. The behavior of both rulers and ruled was determined by this colonial context and could as a consequence be understood only in reference to it. I consider this concept very useful and employ it often.

The dependency specialists and representatives of the idea of structural imperialism, however, interpret the dependency of the periphery, including the colonies, on the metropolis as a function of a world economy dominated by the industrial countries. For them, underdevelopment is everywhere, and not merely in Latin America, and this underdevelopment is a function of this dependency: "capitalism, both world and national, produced underdevelopment."[13] About that, I have the following reservations.

First, a concept of "underdevelopment" is being employed or implicitly assumed which differs considerably from the usual meaning of the word. Underdevelopment is usually taken as equivalent to an extremely low living standard for the majority of a country's inhabitants. On closer examination, the concept really subsumes several relevant factors and indicators. The low per-capita income that expressly marks the difference between the rich and the poor countries has led to the grouping of the twenty-five poorest countries. This criterion remains important.[14] But manifestly—when one considers the oil producers—it is too imprecise. Low productivity and technological level, little or no industry, low literacy levels, lack of trained personnel, modest sanitary services, and low life expectancies must also be used as determinants, as must the unemployment and underemployment of much of the labor force.[15] In this the usual sense, countries like Nepal, Afghanistan, Yemen, Ethiopia, and Chad are not only underdeveloped but are more underdeveloped than, say, Ceylon, India, Egypt, or Ghana. It is ridiculous to make capitalism responsible for the underdevelopment of such states.[16]

Second, those starting with the dependency concept are forced to distinguish between undeveloped and underdeveloped.[17] Undeveloped means that a traditional society remains wholly or largely unintegrated into the monetary economy or world trade and has barely confronted the problems of the modernization process. Furthermore, the sociocultural effects of dependency are not to be seen at all or are visible only at the local level. Underdevelopment, in contrast, implies a pervasive economic, social, and cultural change in the periphery as a result of a dependency relationship with the metropolis. The perverting character of this social transformation, the external determination of the economic development, and the loss of autonomous power of decision are taken to be characteristic. This distinction between *un-* and *under*development may be useful, but because it differs from the usual connotation, the word *underdevelopment* can also lead to misinterpretations and misunderstandings. To give one example, the sultanate of Oman, until a few years ago almost completely isolated and beyond doubt *un*developed, now has the oil revenues to build harbors, roads, hospitals, and schools. It is therefore proceeding gradually toward *under*development!

Finally, underdevelopment in the sense meant by the dependency theory—that is, development induced in the periphery as a result of colonial or postcolonial dependence—makes it impossible any longer to compare the developing countries and preindustrial Europe[18] That may be helpful or perhaps even essential, because simple analogies conceal rather than reveal the particular problems and especial difficulties of the late starters. The per-capita income of the leading states of western Europe was higher by the end of the eighteenth century than that of present-day developing countries. Another important difference was that the intellectual and social foundations of the technological-industrial revolution reached far back in time, whereas the developing countries have been drawn directly into this modernization and Westernization process without such preparation. Quite aside from the specific effects of dependency, they hence have difficulty achieving modernization unassisted. Nonetheless, I do employ the analogy between the preindustrial West and the Third World somewhat.[19]

Lately, critics have asserted that our usual concept of development and modernization implicitly or explicitly has a Western stamp and is thus to be rejected as ethnocentric. There is doubtless justice in this charge. We were, and still are, inclined to understand development in the sense of a complete transformation of a society: as a belated catching-up with the Western industrialization process and all the social and cultural assumptions and implications that that implies. Modernization is thus made equivalent to Westernization and underdevelopment is understood to be a "shortfall in Western modernity."[20] In the discussions of development and modernization of the 1950s, a capitalist-democratic model with an American flavor was advanced without much reflection as the only possible one. The one-party state, for example, was thus dismissed out of hand as the wrong approach to development.

The tendency to make such judgments is with us still, even in the East bloc, where the Soviet-East European path to socialism is pictured as the only one and other countries' own ways encounter mistrust. It has proved easy enough to expose the ethnocentric content of our own concept of modernization and development, but alternative methods are difficult to formulate. Not only have the elites of the developing countries accepted our concept, but the concept of development as such, in the sense of a deliberate attempt to overcome poverty, raise living standards, and increase social equality, dates from the Enlightenment and thus comes from the West. Models of a non-Western way have to be taken seriously and will become increasingly important, but there is no escaping the fact that they, too, in the last analysis are anchored in Western civilization, which today is a part of world civilization. The "breakout to modernity" took place in the West first, and despite the fact that the "backward" countries cannot merely copy the Western model, they do want to "modernize." In the economic sphere, this means increasing production and productivity, technological progress, the accumulation of capital, and at least partial industrialization. In the noneconomic sphere, the requirements are things such as a capable civil service, an organized system of law, social differentiation and mobilization, a primary school system, a management cadre, new forms of political participation, and national solidarity.[21] This creates a dilemma for the colonial historian, who perforce must judge positively the modernization and Westernization that went with the colonial system, despite the distortion and occasionally destructive results that also were a part of cultural contact and the process of acculturation.

The brilliant formulation, "the development of underdevelopment," meaning the integration of the periphery into a world economic system dominated by the metropolises, suggests two conclusions: first, that precolonial society was either destroyed or decisively altered, and second, that dependency may indeed lead to quantitative growth (increasing production and foreign trade) but not to development in the sense of a total societal transformation and the increased capacity to cope with problems that must follow. Because of its all-or-nothing character, this thesis seems to me to miss the mark. I also consider mistaken the implicit or explicit assumption that in the absence of colonial exploitation and distorted development the non-Western nations would have become modern industrial societies on their own. Japan is naturally used to demonstrate the proof of this assertion and is contrasted with British India and semicolonial China. In the case of India, China, and perhaps even Egypt, this proposition can be discussed with some point (though Marx was convinced that Asia lacked the necessary presuppositions for an unassisted breakthrough to modernity). As a general proposition, to be applied to other Asian countries and black Africa, it seems absurd.

To cite other countries and peoples that were never, or only briefly, under colonial rule may seem unfair but not unjustified. I believe that not only growth but also development occurred within the particular context of the colonial condition and that colonial rule, however defined, unleashed the process of modernization.

Exploitation occurred, but colonial rule was based on other things besides exploitation. The former colonies are not poor today because they were exploited by capitalist colonial powers. Instead of harping on the expropriation of surplus value, distinctions must be made and historians must describe and analyze in a way that answers the following questions. What development impulses came from the metropolis, and when and how did these take effect? In what manner was potential for development, in the sense of overcoming poverty through one's own efforts, increased, or, as the case may be, decreased? What did the colonial power accomplish that enabled the former colony to move more easily along the road to modernity in all its creative possibilities and destructive potential, which Europe's capitalist industrial revolution has vouchsafed to the rest of the world? What sorts of distortions and deformations resulted that reduced the potential for development or blocked it altogether? Positive and negative consequences of dependency must be demonstrated. I accept the dependency theory to this extent for its suggestive power, although it reveals less about colonial societies than about the relations between independent states, as for example, in Latin America. Older concepts such as "dual economy" (the coexistence of a subsistance sector beside a modern, capital-intensive, market-oriented sector), "enclave sector" (for example, plantations or mines, with their limited economic impact on the economy of the colony as a whole), and "lopsided economic growth" themselves contain the factor, dependency. Despite the criticisms already mentioned, it still seems to me useful to deal with specific aspects of the colonial economy in order to clarify the aforementioned ambivalence between growth and development. Among matters I shall also consider is the so-called native policy, both as a stabilizing and as a liberating factor, the structure of the colonial schools, and the often hesitant and obstructed bringing of the colonials into the administration, a process which I call "localization."[22] All of these matters are discussed in detail in the chapters on each area, with the more general aspects of colonialism being discussed in the conclusion.

Some additional considerations about the organization of the book follow. First, the decision to go back to the beginning of European rule requires less explanation than the *terminus ad quem* 1940, because the Second World War meant the beginning of the end of colonialism only for South and Southeast Asia but not, however, for Africa. For the latter, the years 1945-1960 are of great interest, because the contest between the national movements and the metropolises rapidly escalated in a sort of dialectical process described by Rothermund as "movement and constitution," on the one hand, and on the other, the colonial economies were given new impetus by financial assistance from the metropolis (such as the Colonial Development Fund, and FIDES). I have nonetheless limited myself to the classical period of colonialism because I can entrust the reader to Ansprenger and my own book, *Decolonization*, and because even a rather summary account would have expanded this book beyond the limits of a single volume.[23]

Second, I have considered each important colony separately and have felt justified in giving India expanded coverage, as it was in a sense both the beginning of the European colonial world and the center of it. Some areas, unfortunately, as for example the Arab mandates, the Sudan, the Italian colonies, Madagascar, and the Antilles could not be covered at all. Third, the ordering of the account by colonies had the disadvantage of making unavoidable a certain amount of repetition and overlapping. Fourth, it is obvious that for the most part I had to depend on the secondary literature. It was supplemented by the more important contemporary sources, books, and articles. Unpublished material was utilized in some cases, but this was more a matter of happenstance than from deliberate researches. Finally, mistakes were hardly to be avoided, particularly since the specialized accounts and the data often differed, and it was difficult to tell which author deserved the more trust. As is usual with surveys of this sort, the notes have a rather arbitrary character, since every fact and figure clearly could not be footnoted.

I should like to thank the following persons. First, my students, whose work I have occasionally pillaged to make my own. Second, my friends and colleagues who have read parts or all of the manuscript with a critical eye: Charles-Robert Ageron (Tours), Henri Brunschwig (Paris), Bernhard Dahm (Kiel), Heinz Gollwitzer (Muenster), Peter Hablützel (Zurich), Dietmar Rothermund (Heidelberg), Emanuel Sarkisyanz (Heidelberg), Alexander Schlölch (Essen), Hansjörg Siegenthaler (Zurich), Jean Stengers (Brussels), and Hans-Werner Tobler (Zurich). I should also like to thank the Schwieizerischer Nationalfond zur Förderung der Wissenschaften for its magnanimous support and Volkart-Stiftung in Winterthur for a publication subsidy.

NOTES

1. Dietmar Rothermund, *Die politische Willensbildung in Indian 1900-1960* (Wiesbaden: Harrassowitz, 1965); Franz Ansprenger, *Politik in Schwartzen Afrika: Die modernen politischen Bewegungen im Afrika französischer Prägung* (Cologne: Westdeutscher Verl., 1961); Bernhard Dahm, *Sukarnos Kampf um Indonesiens Unabhängigkeit: Werdegang und Ideen eines asiatischen Nationalisten* (Frankfurt am Main: Metzner, 1966).

2. See below the notes for the chapters on these areas.

3. Hans-Ulrich Wehler, *Bismarck und der Imperialismus* (Cologne, Berlin: Kiepenheuer & Witsch, 1969).

4. David K. Fieldhouse, *The Colonial Empires: A Comparative Survey from the Eighteenth Century* (London: Wiedenfeld & Nicolson, 1966); in German, 1965. The title notwithstanding, about a third of the book is devoted to the *ancien régime*, and the remainder sketches the expansionist phase rather than events after the establishment of colonial rule. Wolfgang J. Mommsen, *Das Zeitalter des Imperialismus* (Frankfurt am Main: Fisher Bucherei, 1969). *Der*

moderne Imperialismus, ed. Wolfgang J. Mommsen (Stuttgart: W. Kohlhammer, 1971), with contributions from Helmut Böhme, Karl Rohe, Wolfgang Schieder, Hans-Ulrich Wehler, and Gilbert Ziebura.

5. William Appleman Williams, *The Tragedy of American Diplomacy* (rev. ed., New York: Dell, 1962).

6. Paul A. Baran, *Über die politische Ökonomie der Rückständigkeit* (1952), excerpted in Michael Bohnet (comp.), *Das Nord-Süd Problem: Konflikte zwischen Industrie und Entwicklungsländern* (Munich: R. Piper, 1971); André Gunder Frank, *Capitalism and Underdevelopment in Latin America: Historical studies of Chile and Brazil* (New York: Monthly Review Press, 1967); idem, "Die Entwicklung der Unterentwicklung," in *Kritik des bürgerlichen Anti-Imperialismus; Entwicklung der Unterentwicklung. 8 Analysen zur neuen Revolutions-Theorie in Lateinamerika* (Berlin: Wagenback, 1969). See also Dieter Senghaas (ed.), *Imperialismus und strukturelle Gewalt: Analysen über abhängige Reproduktion* (Frankfurt am Main: Suhrkamp, 1972); Dieter Senghaas (comp.), *Peripherer Kapitalismus: Analysen über Abhängigkeit und Unterentwicklung* (Frankfurt am Main: Suhrkamp, 1974); Ronald Chilcote, "Dependency: A Critical Synthesis of the Literature," *Latin American Perspectives* (1974). Finally, see Franz Nuscheler's excellent sketch with critical comments in *Handbuch der Dritten Welt*, ed. Dieter Nohlen and Franz Nuscheler (vols., Hamburg: Hoffman und Campe, 1974), I.

7. Johan Galtung, "Eine strukturelle Theorie des Imperialismus" in Senghaas, *Imperialismus*.

8. Michael Crowder, *West Africa under Colonial Rule* (London: Hutchinson, 1968); *History of East Africa*, ed. Roland Oliver et al. (3 vols., Oxford: Clarendon Press, 1963-1976).

9. On German colonial rule see Chapter 2 below. and the Bibliography.

10. For example, Conrad Schuler, "Zu den Ursachen des 'rückständigen' Systems gesellschaftlicher Arbeit in der Armen Welt" in Bohnet, *Nord-Süd Problem*, 79; Paul A. Baran, *Politik und Ökonomie des wirtschaftlichen Wachstums* (1971), 240 ff: in English, *The Political Economy of Growth*, 2d ed. (New York: Prometheus Books, 1962). Also based to a considerable degree on Baran is Ellen Brun and Jacques Hersh, *Der Kapitalismus im Weltsystem* (1975), originally published as *Kapitalismensudviklingssystem: Laerebog om i-og ulande* (Copenhagen: Gyldendal, 1972), which puts it concisely enough: "No one denies that the English industrial revolution rested on the ruins of the Indian," 45. Brun and Hersh naturally parade Romesh Chandra Dutt, *Economic History of India* (2 vols., 2d ed., New Delhi: Government of India, 1906) and cite Brooks Adams, *Law of Civilization and Decay: An Essay on History* (New York: Macmillan, 1895).

11. Rupert Emerson and D. K. Fieldhouse, "Colonialism," in *International Encyclopedia of the Social Sciences*, ed. David Sills (17 vols., New York: Macmillan and Free Press, 1968), III, 1.

12. Georges Balandier, "La situation coloniale: approche téoretique," *Cahiers internationaux de Sociologie* (1952). For a German version, see Rudolf von Albertini (ed.), *Moderne Kolonialgeschichte* (Cologne: Kiepenheuer & Witsch, 1970).

13. See Frank, *Capitalism and Underdevelopment*, vii., "My thesis is that these capitalist contradictions and the historical development of the capitalist system have generated underdevelopment in the peripheral satellites whose economic surplus was expropriated, while generating economic development in the metropolitan centers which appropriate that surplus," 3. Or Senghaas: "Underdevelopment is a result of dependency.... Underdevelopment [is] here defined, first, as the structural heterogeneity of societal formations in the peripheral states induced by the dominant mode of capitalist production within the context of an international division of labor; and, second, as the blocking of the autonomous development of productive forces that result"; Senghaas, *Peripherer Kapitalismus*, 15, 24.

14. See, for instance, the survey in Bruno Fritsch, *Die Vierte Welt: Modell einer neuen Wirkichkeit* (rev. ed., Munich: Deutscher Taschenbuch Verl., 1973), 32-33.

15. For a detailed examination of the indicators question see *Handbuch der Dritten Welt*, 15.

16. See the trenchant remarks of Alec Nove: "The underdevelopment of Zambia, Saudi Arabia and Ceylon, are due to capitalism. Surely, even the most radical reader will demur. The

few sectors that are developed are capitalist sectors, enclaves which create problems or lopsided development, dual economy, etc. But it is plainly ludicrous to suggest that, were it not for the activities of foreigners in developing copper, oil and tea respectively, the countries concerned would be *more* developed" ("On reading André Gunder Frank," *Journal of Development Studies*, 10 [1972], 445).

17. For example, Hartmut Elsenhans: "Underdevelopment is not coterminous with nondevelopment, but the result of the unfolding of capitalist methods of production," *Handbuch der Dritten Welt*, 163.

18. "The present-day developed countries were never underdeveloped, even though they may have been undeveloped" (Frank, *Entwicklung der Unterentwicklung*, 31); "The dependency model distinguishes underdeveloped Latin America from precapitalist Europe. It does not view underdevelopment as an original condition, but instead assumes that nations may once have been undeveloped but never underdeveloped" (Chilcote, "Dependency," 12).

19. On this analogy, see also Knut Borchardt, *Europas Wirtschaftsgeschichte, ein Modell für Entwicklungsländer* (Stuttgart: W. Kohlhammer, 1967), 8, who also notes: "In important respects the conditions in preindustrial Europe are comparable to conditions in present-day developing countries.... This similarity is in the last analysis attributable to the technological and economic bases of these societies being the same," 15; Simon Kuznets, "Underdeveloped Countries and the Preindustrial Phase in the Advanced Countries," in Amar Nain Agarwala and Sampat Pal Singh (eds.), *The Economics of Underdevelopment; A Series of Articles and Papers Selected and Edited by...Agarwala and...Singh* (New York: Oxford, 1958).

20. Manfred Mols, "Zum Problem des westlichen Vorbilds in der neueren Diskussion zur politischen Entwicklung," *Verfassung und Recht in Übersee*, 8 (1975), 7. See also Nuscheler's subtle treatment in the same vein; *Handbuch der Dritten Welt*, 19f, and his essay in the *Handbuch*, "Bankerott der Modernisierungstheorien," 195ff. In the foregoing Nuscheler reminds us of Marx's famous aphorism: "the industrially developed country...merely shows the less developed a picture of its future."

21. See, in this connection, Wolfgang Zapf (comp.), *Theorien des sozialen Wandels* (Cologne: Kiepenheuer & Witsch, 1969). In addition to the introduction, see in particular the essays by Talcott Parsons, Shmuel N. Eisenstadt, and Reinhard Bendix.

22. I borrow this concept from Richard Symonds, *The British and Their Successors: A Study in the Development of the Government Services in the New States* (London: Faber, 1966).

23. Rudolf von Albertini, *Decolonization; The Administration and Future of the Colonies, 1919-1960*, trans. Francisca Garvie (Garden City: Doubleday, 1971).

ABBREVIATIONS

Journal titles were abbreviated only if they were generally familiar (for example, AHR), used frequently in one of the longer chapters (for example, JHSN), or used fairly frequently over the course of several chapters (COM).

AHR	American Historical Review
CSSH	Comparative Studies in Society and History
COM	Cahiers d'Outre-Mer
EcHR	Economic History Review
IESHR	Indian Economic and Social History Review
JAH	Journal of African History
JAS	Journal of Asian Studies
JEH	Journal of Economic History
JHSN	Journal of the Historical Society of Nigeria
JMH	Journal of Modern History
JSEAH	Journal of South East Asian History
MAS	Modern Asian Studies
MES	Middle Eastern Studies
RFHOM	Revue Français d'Histoire d'Outre-Mer
RH	Revue Historique
SA	South Asia

PART I

ASIA

1

BRITISH INDIA

The British East India Company was chartered in 1600 as nothing more than a trading company. This company, nonetheless, conquered and organized a state on the subcontinent which became the "handsomest jewel in the British crown" and the keystone of the empire. With the settlement colonies of Canada, Australia, and New Zealand, it symbolized Great Britain's status as a world power.

For the first century and a half of its existence, however, the company merely engaged in trade from its coastal factories. It did not aspire to territorial rule and, accepting the sovereignty of the Mughal emperor in Delhi, traded under the sanction of treaties with the Indian princes. The company was initially merely one of a number of European companies which penetrated India's internal trade from their stations on the coast or, acting on their own or as middlemen, opened up trade with China and the Malay Archipelago. In the mid-eighteenth century, however, the companies shifted, rather unwillingly, indeed, and without deliberate forethought, to a policy of military engagement and the gradual development of the administrative apparatus within and beyond their factories. In historical retrospect, this all appears inevitable. After the death of Emperor Aurangzeb (1707) the individual provinces of the empire had made themselves virtually independent. At the same time, France and England were engaged in a worldwide contest for colonial and maritime hegemony. In India, the French were vying unsuccessfully for mastery by expanding outward from Pondicherry by means of raising Indian troops and through treaties. For their part, the British defeated the nawab (governor) of Bengal at Plassey in 1757 and again at Baksar in 1764. Consolidating Britain's position in the north, these victories were made possible in no small measure by the Afghans, who had pushed into the Punjab in 1738, plundered Delhi, and in 1761 inflicted a severe defeat on the Marathas. The latter had built up an extensive territory in the western Deccan and the Bombay hinterland.[1]

In 1765 Robert Clive accepted the *diwani* for Bengal from the Mughal emperor. The *diwani* was the right to collect taxes in the stead of the nawab and in the emperor's name. The plunder of Bengal began. It took the form of forced levies, corruption of company officials, and forcibly depressed prices for cotton and silk destined for export. No takeover of the administration was initially contemplated, but in time it proved unavoidable if the chaos was to be mastered. As early as 1772, Warren Hastings, who "steadily built up an administration in Bengal which in a few years' time was to convert the robber State of Clive into a powerful and organized government," took in hand the tax administration in Bengal and Bihar.[2] He did so by installing British "collectors" subordinate to the board of revenue. Under Lord Cornwallis, governor from 1786 to 1793, police and justice were also removed from company jurisdiction. The India acts of 1773 and 1784, themselves the results of sharp criticism in Parliament and the country at large of company methods of administration and exploitation, also strengthened parliamentary control and largely transferred executive power to the British government. A board of control was established whose consent was required for directives sent to India; and the president of the board sat in the cabinet.

Thus did England, in the guise of the company, become a colonial power in India. No further territorial expansion was contemplated, either by the company or the British government. Wars cost money, and the company stood on the verge of bankruptcy. But British territory gradually expanded, all the same. The "local factor" played in India, as elsewhere, a decisive role. Reports took months to travel to London and back. Decisions had to be made. London could warn, raise objections, condemn actions, but in the end had to accept most faits accomplis. How, indeed, were the frontiers to be best secured? The hegemony of the company still seemed in no way assured. A coalition between Maratha and Mysore had to be blocked. One had to negotiate, make treaties. Some governors were advocates of a "forward policy," others held back, but expansion continued willy-nilly. External dangers (or those imagined) also contributed. At first it was Napoleonic France, then Russia, with its gradual push southward, which came to seem a threat to the British position in India because of Russia's influence in Persia and Afghanistan. The company's directors might show no interest in expansion, but the Industrial Revolution and the consequent rapid increase in British trade nonetheless all but forced it.

War against a strong Mysore between 1790 and 1799 brought the south coast under direct British rule and created the basis for the Madras presidency. What was left remained a princely state under a Hindu dynasty. The nizam of Hyderabad had to accept a so-called subsidiary alliance, in which England guaranteed the independence and protection of the princely territory and stationed troops there under British command. Though paid by the prince, they could be employed both to hinder rebellion and to squeeze their paymaster. Other subsidiary alliances followed, among them one with the nawab of Oudh in 1799. Further wars with Maratha between 1800 and 1803 and in 1818 led to the annexation of Delhi and the upper Ganges valley, Orissa in the east, and the Bombay hinterland. An aggressive thrust toward Kabul ended, indeed, in a spectacular defeat in 1841. The English nonetheless occupied and annexed Sind, until then Afghan territory. Two wars were waged between 1845 and 1849 against the Sikhs, originally a

Hindu sect, who had established a kingdom in the Punjab earlier in the century. The result? Kashmir was carved off and given a Hindu ruler and the Punjab annexed.

"Looking back over this period, it almost seems that the British succeeded in dominating India by a succession of fortuitous circumstances and lucky flukes. With remarkably little effort, considering the glittering prize, they won a great empire and enormous wealth which helped to make them the leading power in the world."[3] Or such was Jawaharlal Nehru's view. He also mentions some of the underlying causes for this relatively rapid and simple conquest of the Indian subcontinent, notwithstanding occasional English reverses: the chaos following the dissolution of the Mughal empire; the rivalries between Indian princes and the countless struggles over the succession in many territories; and the absence of an Indian "nation," which could have stood united against its European conqueror. Even the Marathas had more of a sense of being Maratha than any sort of community feeling based on India as a whole. They had come as conquerors, and their defeat was greeted with relief far and wide in the land. The feudal lords of the Rajput preferred British to Maratha rule. While the Marathas, Rajputs, Sikhs, and Gurkhas of Nepal fought bravely enough, their armies were essentially medieval in character. In the end they were simply no match for a modern army like the English. The ranks of the latter were, indeed, manned largely by Indians, and the Sikhs never forgot that they had been defeated by Muslim troops from Oudh and the Punjab.

I shall later discuss in detail administrative, tax, land, and educational policies in the early nineteenth century, but some information about such matters must be provided here in order to understand the impact of the Mutiny of 1857. In 1813 the company lost its Indian trade monopoly and, in 1833, that for China. It remained responsible for administration, however. This appears rather a paradox when one recalls that sovereign functions had originally appeared to be only subsidiary obligations of a corporation mainly concerned with trade.

A series of outstanding governors and soldiers—Lord Cornwallis in Bengal, Sir Thomas Munro in Madras, Mountstuart Elphinstone in Bombay, and the brothers John and Henry Lawrence in the north, who also have the respect of Indian historians—set the style for government during these years.[4] Fundamental inroads into the Indian social order occurred, especially in tax policy, which the administration took over almost completely. Still, Burkean conservative attitudes remained dominant. Rule was still incompletely consolidated, the language of administration remained Persian, and a communications system did not exist. Along with the regulation of taxes, securing law and order remained the principal problems. Rule was understood to mean reform, the fight against arbitrary conduct and corruption, and the improvement of the lot of the peasant masses. Anglicizing Indian law and institutions was seen as necessary, at least to a degree, as was leveling obstacles to English trade. But these reforms were all to take place over a period of time, and preferably in a way that created an Indian elite ready to accept elements of Western civilization and yet without forcing it to break with its own culture and society. "Let us therefore proceed calmly on a course of gradual reimprovement," was how one administrator put it. Or as Munro said: "I have no faith in the modern doctrine of the rapid improvement of the Hindoos, or of any other people."[5] But it was also Munro who in Parliament, while not denying Western superiority in learning and technology, underlined the positive aspects of Hindu culture and provocatively noted that if civilization became an object of trade, he was convinced that "this country [England] will gain by the import cargo."[6]

This conservative attitude was opposed by both missionaries and British Liberals. The latter were guided by Benthamite Utilitarianism, which combined Enlightenment thought with the ideas of 1789 and now stood beneath the sign of the Industrial Revolution. Utilitarianism was progressive, rationalist, optimistic, and, above all, individualistic, with a belief in personal initiative and free and open social, economic, and intellectual competition. James Mill expressly stated this credo in 1817 in his *History of British India*. Any basis for any insight into Hindu civilization was eliminated. The "tyrannical" system of the princes and Brahmins was founded on a religious system "built upon the most enormous and tormenting superstition that ever harassed and degraded any portion of mankind." In mind and body, Hindus were "the most enslaved portion of the human race."[7] There was no place for temporizing and caution. Abuses were to be remedied, and Westernization was to be pushed ahead ruthlessly and energetically.

The Liberals came to power with Governor-General Lord William Bentinck in 1828.[8] Their position in London was further secured through the Whig victory in 1830 and the Reform Bill of 1832. In 1829, the burning of widows was forbidden. In 1833, English, Urdu, and Hindustani replaced Persian as languages of administration. In 1835, the struggle between Orientalists and Anglicizers in educational policy—which had gone on for years over the questions of whether the classical languages should be taught and whether instruction should be in the native languages or solely in English—was decided in favor of the latter. Thomas Macaulay's famous "Minute on Education" of 1835 provided the justification:

> The question now before us is simply whether, when it is in our power to teach this language, we shall teach languages in which, by universal confession, there are no books on any subject which deserve to be compared to our own; whether when we can teach European science, we shall teach systems which, by universal confession, whenever they differ from those of Europe differ for the worse; and whether, when we can patronize sound philosophy and true history, we shall countenance, at the public expense, medical doctrines, which would move laughter in the girls at an English boarding school—history, abounding with kings thirty feet high, and reign thirty thousand years long—and geography made up of seas of treacle and seas of butter.[9]

Missions, admitted to India only in 1813, received more freedom to found schools, plus some financial support. In 1856 the Widow Remarriage Act was passed, enabling Hindu widows to remarry. It was violently opposed and led to

Indian demonstrations, in which the Brahmin upper classes naturally played a major part.

Aggressiveness was also the watchword in political matters. Lord Dalhousie was a governor-general (1848-1856) of the later Lord Curzon's stamp. Though fundamentally conservative, he was as convinced of the superiority of Western civilization as any radical; "a paternalist who believed in steam engines."[10] He not only pushed ahead with railway construction and set up a public works department but as a representative of the "forward school" also returned to a policy of territorial annexation, though by means of incorporating princely states rather than by war. Another symbolic act was the informing of the aged Mughal emperor that his title would lapse upon his death. In 1856 Oudh, the greatest of the still independent Muslim states, was annexed. Wretched misgovernment provided the desired excuse. The administration declared war on the tax collectors and rural aristocracy, the zamindars and the talukdars, as "useless drones on the soil." The idea was to reduce the burden of the peasants, but the nexus of loyalties within the traditional agrarian society was not sufficiently reckoned with.

The Liberal reform and annexation policy did more than estrange the ruling classes and orthodox Brahmin circles. It also allowed the impression to arise that England had declared all-out war on the Hindu religious and social order and intended to uproot any developing Indian local or national feeling. The mutiny of Indian troops in May 1857 (40,000 soldiers were from the newly annexed Oudh, and Rajputs and the Brahmin caste were heavily represented) thus rapidly widened into a rebellion that for a time seriously threatened English rule and was finally repressed only in 1858. Massacres of Europeans were followed by an extraordinarily bloody repression that cost the lives of thousands of Indians and was accompanied by an orgy of hatred on the part of the British. But the revolt was not national. Both Bengal and the Madras presidency remained quiet, and even the Punjab (including the Sikhs, who had been defeated only shortly before) participated in the struggle against the rebels. Prominent representatives of the new educated class in Bengal also declared their loyalty. Neither Nehru nor present-day Indian historians accept nationalist interpretations of the rebellion. They see the mutiny as an uncoordinated lashing out against British rule by those most directly affected by it and as a defensive action to maintain or restore the endangered old order.[11] For colonial historians, the rebellion shows all the earmarks of a "post-primary" resistance action.[12]

The mutiny altered the British attitude toward India in no fundamental way. It nonetheless left a lasting mark on both the style and the ideology of British rule. The liberals had believed that the introduction of British law and education, Western technology, and the principles of liberal Western economic policy could "modernize" Indian society in a relatively short time. They also believed that the gratitude and appreciation of the ruled would create fertile ground for Anglo-Indian collaboration. These beliefs had proved to be illusions. Occidental and oriental civilization seemed separated by an abyss. It had proved risky to disturb a foreign world and threaten its fundament by well-meaning reforms. Indian society had proved more foreign and more conservative than originally assumed or hoped. "Oriental stagnation" now became a stereotype that symbolized fundamental differences—and also helped to legitimize one's rule.[13] Racism of contemporary pseudoscientific theories combined with the traditional European feelings of superiority: was it not natural law that destined the white European races and Britons as a nation (the British race) first of all, to rule over the Indians, members of an inferior, colored race? England was destined to rule India, found its mission there, and saw its own greatness therein confirmed. This was henceforth the ideological basis of the British raj. Although the other things the English brought India—domestic peace, a unified legal system, and modern administration—were also considered to legitimize British rule, the implicit or stated conviction remained, that India now "belonged" to England and that Indians were incompetent to rule themselves or manage their own affairs; as indeed were all nonwhite races.[14] Rule with such an ideological basis was autocratic and could hardly be anything else, if it was not to call itself into question.

> It is essentially an absolute Government, founded, not on consent, but on conquest. It does not represent the native principles of life or of government, and it can never do so until it represents heathenism and barbarism. It represents a belligerent civilization, and no anomaly can be so striking or so dangerous as its administration by men who, being at the head of a Government founded on conquest, implying at every point the superiority of the conquering race . . . and having no justification for its existence except that superiority, shrink from the open, uncompromising, straight-forward assertion of it, seek to apologize for their own position, and refuse, from whatever cause, to uphold and support it.[15]

"Distance" had to be maintained between ruler and ruled, and distance became one of the earmarks of British ruling style. Speaking polemically but with inherent justice, Nehru compared this attitude with that of an English landed aristocrat managing his estate, exhibiting benevolence toward his tenants and workers and concerned for their material welfare, but taking his superiority and right to do as he pleases as a matter of course.[16] Personal contact remained at a minimum. The viceroy or governor-general might invite members of princely families or local notables to official receptions and exchange a few friendly words with them, and the businessman trafficked with his opposite numbers, but distance was maintained, and the gulf remained. Indians did not belong in Society, nor to the clubs in which the Victorian Englishman so gladly spent his free hours. To stick with one's own in foreign surroundings was natural enough per se, but Nehru rightly remarks that the social distance of the Briton in India nonetheless all too often, only too clearly, bore the mark of racial discrimination.[17]

The Mutiny of 1857 increased this distance. Improved communications with England, making regular home leave possible, and more English women, accompanying their husbands to India for at least a few years, also did their part in estranging British and Indian society and assuring that their contacts remained few. Although the number of lower-class whites remained as small in India as elsewhere in the empire (compared with, say, the French colonies) they did not, unlike the senior cadres, parade their racial superiority, particularly when alcohol had removed their inhibitions. "England in the east is not the England that we know," wrote Charles Dilke in 1869. As late as 1924, in *Passage to India*, E. M. Forster depicted the rulers' distance, insensitivity, and humiliation of the ruled and the simultaneous psychological dependence of the ruled on the rulers. But he also exposed the peculiarities of the colonial situation and the European society which wrapped up the newcomer, who usually arrived full of interest and open to the human side of the new world, and stamped upon him the stereotyped attitudes of racial distance and disdain.

The mutiny shook the confidence of the British. No less a man than G. O. Trevelyan, a representative of Liberal reform around 1860, noted: "[It] irresistably reminded us that we are an imperial race, holding our own on a conquered soil by din of valour and foresight." And great was the disappointment and the hatred in the officer corps as local troops suddenly mutinied. The Indian army was immediately reorganized.[18] The main measure was a drastic alteration in the ratio between Englishmen and Indians. The number of Indian soldiers was reduced from 238,000 to 140,000 (in 1863), and the number of Europeans raised from 45,00 to 65,000. Indian artillery units were broken up and heavy weapons were henceforth manned only by British. Garrisons were always to include both British and Indian troops.

Recruiting policy also reflected the new need for security. Instead of drawing from Rajputs and Brahmans from Oudh, the other provinces in the northwest, and the Deccan, recruiting shifted to the Punjab, bringing in particularly Sikhs and also Pathans and Gurkhas from independent Nepal. In 1930 62 percent of the army was still from the Punjab. One spoke of the "martial races," which, in contrast to, say, the Bengalis, produced particularly able soldiers. The Indians could nonetheless point out that the Marathas and the men of Oudh and Agra had proved at least as warlike, and that in reality the British were merely following a policy of *divide et impera*. In the army itself, caste and clan loyalties were strictly observed, in part to reduce internal tension but also to prevent the development of any national solidarity within the Indian army. The officer corps, the king's or queen's commissioned officers, remained British until the First World War. After 1880 there was some sentiment in favor of a limited Indianization of the officer corps. But that was mainly to keep on the good side of the aristocracy during the disputes just beginning with the new, largely bourgeois, educated class. As the India minister put it in 1897: "If we can keep the affection of the fighting races and higher orders of society in India, we can ignore the dislikes and disaffection of intellectual nonfighting classes, the baboos, students and pleaders."[19] Only World War I changed the situation. Hundreds of thousands of Indians were recruited and sent to the war zones of Europe and the Near East, and Indians received commissions in the army and air force. During the interwar period, Sandhurst was opened to Indian officer candidates. In 1922 the Military College was established in India to prepare young Indians academically and linguistically. Still, Indianization was slow. In 1939 only 316 of 7,200 officers were Indian.[20] Lord Rawlinson, the senior commander, stated the dilemma clearly enough: "We must either trust the Indians or not trust them. The schemes have got to be carried out in their entirety, with the view to eventual self-government, or else we must return to the old method of ruling India with the sword. There is no halfway house."[21] In practice however, the opposition of the British officer corps, supported by retired officers in England, was difficult to overcome. The prospect of having to obey Indian superiors was simply intolerable; by extension, it was also argued that the "martial races" like the Sikhs would regard Indian officers from Bengal as a bit much. Accordingly, from 1923 on, completely Indian units were formed. This opened England to the nationalist reproach of inaugurating a policy of segregation. Slow Indianization, expensive British officers, and other defense costs in the Indian budget were, in any case, already irritants. World War II pushed Indianization forward rapidly, however, so that by 1947 a qualified officer corps was available to both India and Pakistan. During the bloody weeks of the partition the Indian officer corps kept its head well enough, a success some booked to Sandhurst.[22] General Ayub Khan, Pakistani chief of state, was said to bear the mark of Sandhurst: outwardly correct in bearing, measured in speech, desirous of efficiency, and patriotic, yet not without pride in having belonged to the British-Indian officer corps.

Did British rule rest on the army and the police, meaning force? The question cannot really be answered yes or no. With some justice, British historians still point out that the army and police were small in relation to the size of the Indian population; that in countless districts, areas of several hundred square miles, no troops were quartered and the police was almost entirely Indian;[23] that the army was concentrated in the Punjab and on the northwest frontier; that Indian troops were used outside India to conquer Burma, Africa, and in both world wars; and that Gandhi supported British recruiting as late as 1918. The fact yet remains that after the mutiny both British and Indians knew the army was a key element in the apparatus of rule, and that open rebellion was unthinkable so long as England controlled the army and the police. Gandhi's passive resistance and his policy of noncooperation can be interpreted as a tactic to undermine the army and police, and it is hardly an accident that Lord Louis Mountbatten was authorized to offer the Transfer of Power on short notice, in part because of signs of mutiny in the Indian army and fleet in 1946 and 1947.

It was natural that the Mutiny of 1857 led to much criticism of the aggressive Liberal reform policy of the Bentinck-Dalhousie era. The conservative "school" and the opponents of annexation seemed to have been proved correct. In August 1859, India Minister Sir Charles Wood explained to Parliament:

> We must be very careful not to give to the Natives of India any reason to believe that we are about to attack their religious feelings and prejudices... No doubt in the recent case

there was no just cause for suspicion; but they entertained that belief. We have seen the consequences, and if we hope to retain India in peace and tranquillity we must take care so to govern it as not only to consult the interests, but the feelings of the Native population.[24]

Thus was the course set for the years to come: no more overt actions against the Indians' "immoral customs"; in place of missionary zeal, a prudent biding of one's time; a regard for the inherent conservatism of the Orient; and tolerance, if one can call it that, for Indians' private concerns, though not because of fellow feeling or belief in the right of the ruled to their own opinions, but merely as a means of securing British rule. There were, indeed, for decades to come no further prohibitions comparable to that of 1829 against burning widows. The influential Henry Maine, Law Member of the Indian government, wrote in Burkean terms:

The usages which a particular community is found to have adopted in its infancy and in its primitive seats are generally those which are on the whole best suited to promote its physical and moral well-being; and if they are retained in their integrity until new social wants have taught new practices, the upward march of society is certain.[25]

And the learned Governor Alfred Lyall declared: "All the English need do is keep the peace and clear the way."[26] In other words, no reform policy from the ruling power, only stability and efficiency.[27]

This reserve undoubtedly paid off for the British. The important Brahman caste was effectively neutralized as a possible source of religious-political opposition, and the peasant masses were never offered any provocation which might have simplified nationalist agitation in the countryside. The new educated class faced a dilemma. They could indeed accept the critical British appraisals of obsolete Hindu institutions and tabus; and some native reformers did in fact demand or at least accept reform legislation. On the other hand, they thought it incumbent upon themselves to defend the civilization bequeathed them against inroads by the colonial power. A good part of the new leading class anyway was from the ruling castes and was hardly enough of one mind to band together in support of reform laws, to say nothing of acting against the dictates of their castes. None of this prevented the nationalists, both before independence and after, from accusing the British of having stabilized the traditional order with its multiplicity of groupings; indeed, of having consciously encouraged them in order to prevent the rise of national solidarity for the sake of their own rule.

Liberal hopes had been disappointed. Forced Westernization through technology, schools, and English law, in combination with measures against the native ruling class, had not anchored British rule and brought the colonial power the support of the masses. The change of course after 1857 thus implied future reliance on "natural leaders," meaning the traditional ruling class, either by conceding their existing positions of power or by granting new privileges. By demonstrating a painstaking regard for their interests, the colonial power hoped to bind them to itself.[28] What that meant in terms of land and tax policy will be discussed below. One can note briefly, however, that all attempts to protect renters and indebted peasants largely failed because the interests of the landowning class could not be very seriously impinged upon if the "natural leaders" were not to be estranged.

For the moment, only the princely states will be considered in this regard. Dalhousie's policy of annexation had driven them into revolt, and some of the princes, having played leading roles, had to be defeated in the field. Despite this, or perhaps because of it, the English forswore further annexations. In the Royal Message of 1858, it was stated that the British "desire no extension of [our] present territorial possession and would respect the rights, dignity and honour of the native princes as our own." States and territories, large and small, that had come under British rule during the expansionist phase as a result of protectorate and subsidiary treaties, retained the same status.

According to official figures, there were 562 such states, making up about two-fifths of the territory under British rule. They had about 90 million inhabitants in 1939, ranging from Hyderabad with its 18 million to ministates with a few villages only. They were scattered over the entire subcontinent and were not a part of British India per se. They were directly ruled by the Crown, or, in practice by the viceroy, represented in the princely states by a "resident." Their foreign relations were naturally entirely in the hands of the Crown, which in return pledged protection against domestic and foreign enemies. In matters such as customs and transport policy, the princes had to accept what was decided for the rest of India, but in other matters they were largely autonomous. They had their own governments and officials and stood outside the legislative competence and jurisdiction of British India. In the case of flagrant mismanagement, the Crown had the right to intervene, but this right was to be exercised only in dire emergency.

> I should let any ruler do nearly what he liked within his own state. If the condition of his territory affects that of his neighbors, he becomes a public nuisance and we should interfere. So perhaps if a long state of anarchy and bloodshed prevails, but I would not interfere for mere family quarrels.[29]

This was also the rule in the years following. The resident functioned largely as an ambassador and, while he gave advice, his functions at the princely court were largely representational. The administrative model of British India, including cabinet system and land and tax policy, was adopted in part. Some states, Baroda, Travancore, and Mysore, were well and successfully managed, others very badly.[30] The popular picture of the maharajahs reveling in luxury, with their palaces, elephants, harems, splendid weddings, and festivals, dates from the days of British rule, which made possible this "oriental ostentation." Unfortunately, there has not been much research into whether any sort of modernization had begun in any of the princely states and, if so, whether it occurred within the framework of traditional institutions and values, and without the disruptive consequences that accompanied social change in British India.

In the interwar period, the princes came under increasing fire from the nationalists. Even the Congress party, which hardly sought social revolutionary ends, necessarily saw the princely states as British collaborators standing in the way of a modern united India. The princes had never created any representative bodies. Their states thus were more backward than British India and offered the Congress limited scope for agitation. Dependent on British protection, they proved loyal friends of the British Crown, which for its part considered them valuable supports for its rule and not to be estranged. Working out an Indian constitution in the 1930s was accordingly made more difficult. How were the autocratic princely states, which fell back on their bilateral protectorate treaties with the Crown, to be integrated into a unified India, if the latter was gradually to receive self-government at both the provincial and national level? Responsible British politicians ready for reform complained about the rigidity of the princes and were ready to exert pressure but could go no further. The result was a federal solution that pleased no one and deepened the gulf between the Congress party and London. Only an independent India could force a radical solution to the problem of this unique division of the subcontinent into a British India and princely states, which in good part originated with the Mutiny of 1857 and much delayed national integration.

ADMINISTRATION AND CIVIL SERVICE

In 1853, the East India Company's charter was once again renewed for a short term. The mutiny was more occasion than cause for the Crown's taking over the administration of India. The rule of the East India Company, which had won England a world empire, ended in 1858. The break was mainly formal, however, for, after Pitt's India Act of 1784, the influence and control of the Crown over Indian administration had grown steadily.[31] The duties of the president of the board of control, who already sat in the cabinet, were transferred to the secretary of state for India, the de facto India minister. The latter was responsible to Parliament, the supreme authority in imperial matters. Parliament had been involved in Indian activities since the days of Clive and had increasingly acted as the company's supervisory agent. Investigating commissions had exposed insufficiencies and abuses, and the company had occasionally been subject to severe criticism, though the latter admittedly came from interest groups with rather diverse motivations. The renewal of the charter had also given Parliament periodic opportunities for direct or indirect intervention. After 1858, paradoxically, Parliament troubled itself but little over India. Men with experience or interest in India, indeed, sat in both Lords and Commons, and the Indian minister had to report annually and answer questions in Commons, but India itself was not a party question and interested only a minority of the members. The governmental changes between Liberals and Conservatives, and, after the First World War, the rise of Labour, were sometimes reflected in the choice of viceroy, but in the parties themselves it was mainly outsiders who specialized in India and the colonies. Specific matters, Lancashire's concerns about duties, for example, were taken up directly with the administration, and pensioned Indian officials blew off steam in the letters columns of the *Times*.

Parliament obviously did have to be brought into the alteration of the constitution, particularly when a representative assembly was being created for India. This business, which dragged on for years, and resulted in the constitution of 1935, naturally took up hundreds of pages in *Hansard*. Like the English colonies, however, India had "legislative powers," laws for India being developed through close consultation between viceroy and India secretary. The India secretary had an India council to advise him, and official correspondence—dispatches—with the viceroy required its consent. Consisting mainly of former Indian officials, the council proved a conservative body, delaying decisions and watering down reforms or vetoing them altogether. A self-confident and masterful viceroy like Lord Curzon recoiled violently against the India council.[32] In general, however, India policy was discussed and established through personal correspondence between viceroy and India secretary. Whether India was ruled from Calcutta or London is hard to say. After the cable connection was completed (1865-1868), the India secretary could interfere to a much greater degree in the decision-making process, and viceroys were occasionally reminded that they were, in fact, subordinate to cabinet and Parliament.[33] In practice, however, whether a viceroy was able to exploit to the full the potential of his position and get his way in London depended a good deal on his personality.

The governor-general and the viceroy "ruled" in India with the splendor and ceremony of oriental potentates.[34] The durbars in particular, festive receptions when the princes appeared at "court," became symbols of British rule, designed to impress the multitude with the power and the greatness of British rule. Yet the office of viceroy was not the final step in an official career in India. On the contrary. Too strong an identification with India and its civil service, which might seem to threaten London with loss of administrative control, was to be avoided. Most viceroys came from the Anglo-Scottish aristocracy. Leading politicians were only occasionally chosen (Curzon, Edward Wood, later Lord Halifax) and soldiers only during World War II (Lord Archibald Wavell, Lord Louis Mountbatten). Their knowledge of India was usually modest. To assist him, the viceroy had an executive council, consisting of at first three, later six, and finally, fourteen chiefs of the administrative departments. The governmental system resembled, however, the American more than the British. The viceroy was not bound by majority decisions, the council basically confirming decisions already taken between the viceroy and the department head concerned. Nor was he bound by the decisions of the legislative council, about which more below. Important decisions, on the other hand, could only be taken in consultation with the India office.

The administration of British India was not only autocratic, but was centralized until 1919-1920, when provincial governments with limited responsibility toward elected parliaments were established. Provincial governors still retained much of the freedom of action received in 1861, when the provinces had also received legislative powers. Financial competence had also been decentralized in stages, which is to say that control of certain incomes and expenditures were given the provinces. All the same, central control remained tight. Rule came to have an increasingly impersonal character because of the growing importance of several technical administrative functions but also, regrettably, because of the mountain of regulations, intended to curb arbitrary behavior, that set narrow limits upon administrative initiative.

The actual administrative units were the 240 districts, the borders of which were largely coterminous with those of the Mughal Sarkars, yet another indication that England was the legatee of the Mughal emperors. The districts varied in population and area, but were all very large and contained hundreds of villages. The districts, in turn, were divided into subdistricts and *tehsils* in the north or *taluks* around Bombay and Madras. The key figure in the British administration was the district officer, an "all-purpose local agent of the Government" (S. P. Sen). His first duty was collecting taxes. In a larger sense, however, he was responsible for law and order, roads, schools, and hospitals. The district officer and his subdivisional officers, mostly young probationary officials, did not reside in the capital but had roving commissions. Travelling first by horse and later by car, they checked tax registers, heard complaints, and adjudicated disputes. The job appealed because the British official received executive power while still young, stood in contact with the people, and was largely left to his own devices, far from the larger towns.[35] They were called "sun-dried bureaucrats," sometimes in praise, sometimes in condemnation. Although the superintendent of the police and later an increasing number of officials from the technical services (agriculture, public works), served along with the district officer, the political officer always retained pride of place. From early days, there were complaints that the district officers were overworked, being buried in paper, and instead of being able to ride around and talk to people, were forced to write reports and get up the statistics demanded by the secretariats of the governor and the viceroy.

The size of the districts and the astonishingly small number of district and subdivisional officers must also be kept in mind. The meshes of the administrative network were uncommonly coarse, if less so than in Mughal days, and government was more efficient. Like the Mughals, the British mostly limited themselves to gathering taxes. It was hardly chance that in the areas of Permanent Settlement, mainly Bengal and Bihar, where the tax contribution was fixed once and for all, administrative penetration was significantly less than in other provinces, where assessment of taxes was regulated directly with the peasants and villages. As we will see, the British did not interfere much with the village life and made no attempts to force modernization or Westernization. Nonetheless, they were unable to prevent social crisis, or, indeed, the partial disintegration of the traditional village structure. The simple fact that the traditional village officials (*patwaris*) were reduced to being the lowest executive agents in the hierarchy was bound to reduce their autonomy—however questionable that of the now celebrated panchayats may have been—and encourage passive attitudes in the peasantry.

Another point: however loose the British administrative net was, the British could not have gotten by without Indian officials, and not only in the secretariats as auxiliary personnel, but also as tehsildars, who had several villages under them and trafficked directly with the peasants. An intermediary Indian class with rudimentary English schooling thus arose that had a great many opportunities for personal enrichment and abuse of power.[36] Dependent on the support of the colonial power, it itself became an important support of British rule. The district officer might see himself as the "father and mother" of his district and make personal efforts to keep in contact with the people, but in reality he was heavily dependent on information provided by his Indian subordinates.

Executive and judicial functions were not clearly separated. Cornwallis had in 1793 separated the office of collector from that of judge and had given the latter some police functions. In so doing, he was attempting in part to maintain continuity with the Mughal administration. He was also convinced that the office of collector required continuing oversight. This separation of powers worked poorly. Levying taxes, maintaining law and order, and the settling of disputes among the Indians all called for a concentration of authority in the executive. Rather complex judicial procedures added to the confusion of both Britons and Indians. In Punjab, on the other hand, the office of tax collector and judge had remained unified. After the mutiny, a sort of compromise solution was adopted for all British India. The district officer combined the administrative authority for both tax collection and magistracy. He thus possessed limited police and judicial power, while the real judicial power was lodged in a district judge. His decisions could be appealed to the high court of the province. The Punjab system worked, serving in the following period as a model for the other part of the empire. The combining of administrative and magistrate functions corresponded to the manifold duties of the district officer, particularly in maintaining public order. It permitted him to act quickly and settle disputes personally, and, as he was seen by the people as the man who gave the orders, surrounded him with the necessary prestige. The representatives of the new educated classes and, later, the Nationalists did indeed demand a clear separation of powers. After long years of preparation, a unified Indian Penal Code and the Indian Civil and Criminal Codes of Procedure were introduced between 1859 and 1861.[37] In private law, the personal status and the traditional law of the religious communities was maintained.

As autocratic and bureaucratic as British rule was, it rested on a very small cadre of officials, the thousand-odd members of the Indian Civil Service (ICS).[38] Cornwallis had in 1793 separated trade and administration within the company. Those electing to go into administration had to make "covenants" pledging not to engage in private trade. In return they got—and it was a great innovation—a relatively good salary and promise of an orderly upward career. This laid the groundwork for a British-Indian civil service, and in a relatively short time the flagrant abuses were, in fact, ended. In 1800-1801 Lord Wellesley established a college to prepare administrative candidates, who came out to India between the ages of fifteen and twenty for their work. In 1806 this school was moved back to England. The young official received two years of instruction in Oriental languages and was introduced to law and economics (Malthusian and otherwise) at Haileybury College. No very thorough preparation, perhaps, but enough so that it soon instilled in its graduates an *esprit de corps* that left its mark on future administrative styles and moral standards.[39] Mill's *History of India*, with its negative appraisal of Hindu civilization, was one of the standard texts, which, as the great Indian scholar Max Müller confirms, was necessarily influential.[40] Such was also true of the teaching of laissez-faire economics. Entrance into the so-called covenanted service, which included the more highly paid positions, still remained a matter of patronage, in that the directors could propose their own candidates—just as in England itself.

In the course of his reforms, Cornwallis also removed Indian collectors and judges from office and replaced them with Britons. The Mughal rulers had employed Muslim Indians and in the important Bengal area even Hindus in their administration, though they were subordinate to their own chief officials of Turkish-Afghan and Persian origin. The erection of an orderly British administrative system, by contrast, resulted in the expulsion of Indians from the leading positions. The substitution of British for Muslim law and the subsequent abolition of Persian as the administrative language particularly hurt the Muslim upper class. This exclusion was sharply criticized by the conservative school. Munro, in particular, farsightedly suggested that a "spirit of independence" would be the inevitable reaction to the "unnatural" foreign rule. He also warned of the perverse effects of Western education when not accompanied by a corresponding role in the government and administration of one's native land, and himself turned clearly against the Utilitarian-Liberal reforms.[41] He was thinking particularly of the Indian aristocracy, who as "natural leaders" ought to be won over and incorporated into the British system. The Charter Act of 1833 did indeed contain a statement that "no native. . . shall by reason only of his Religion, Place of Birth, Descent, Colour or any of them, be disabled from holding any Place, Office or Employment under the said Company." No Indian was, however, admitted to the covenanted service. Patronage appointment stopped it, and more importantly, the attitude of the Liberals. With the scorn for Indian culture embodied in their watchword "good government," they considered Indianization of the administration as at the very least premature. Only the position of deputy collector was opened to Indians.[42]

But it was also the Utilitarians and Liberals who fought the patronage system and in 1854 forced entrance examinations through Parliament. That made entry into the Indian Civil Service (the new name for the covenanted Service) possible for Indians, especially since the Royal Message of 1858 expressly reconfirmed that of 1833. But the entrance examination had its own difficulties. It was in London, which imposed formidable costs on Indian candidates and limited the pool to those from well-off families. More serious were Hindu tabus, which made the sea voyage and stay in England appear a danger to caste purity and could hence bring a young Indian into conflict with his family. In addition, the examination tested the history of English literature, and a Latin or Greek text counted for more points than one in Arabic or Sanskrit. The first Indian to pass, in 1864, was the poet Rabindranath Tagore's elder brother. Four more followed in 1868, among them the later organizer and president of the Congress party, Surendranath N. Banerjea, and the Indian economic historian, Romesh Chandra Dutt (all four were members of the Hindu reform movement, *Brahmo Samaj*). Between 1868 and 1875 eleven of fourteen Indian candidates passed, an astonishing performance, when one considers that, in 1870, 340 candidates vied for 43 slots.

But it is also understandable that the new educated class, drawn from the upper castes in Bengal, appealed against the fantastic disadvantages, amounting to blatant discrimination, which Indians suffered. They demanded in particular that examinations also be given in India. In 1876, however, entrance was made harder rather than easier. Against the advice of the viceroy, the age limit for taking the examination was lowered from twenty-one to nineteen. This hardly gave the Indians enough time to prepare for the difficult examination. It was thus understandable that between 1876 and 1883 only one of twenty-eight Indian candidates passed.[43]

The discussions surrounding the Ilbert bill of 1883 also documented the deep-rooted distrust, if not to say downright hatred, of "educated Indians." The Liberal viceroy, Lord Ripon, was ready to accept a bill proposed by his Law Member, Sir Courtenay Ilbert, which would have permitted Indian judges to sentence Europeans in the rural districts of Bengal. The measure was required in order to remove an anomaly which had arisen because of the relatively rapid Indianization of the courts and the entrance after 1861 of Indians into the high courts. Indians had proved themselves as judges and seemed less likely to endanger British rule than Indians in leading political and administrative positions. All the same, the bill aroused a storm of indignation, particularly from English planters and businessmen. They called for separation from England, and their threats of rebellion are reminiscent of the later conflict in 1923 in Kenya or the protests of the French in Algeria against the reform plans of the Popular Front in 1936. It was obviously a matter of not merely the substantive content of the bill but also, in a broader sense, Ripon's entire program for the liberalization of British rule. A part of this was his attempt to guarantee the new Western-educated class of Indians a consultative voice in the legislative councils and to push forward the Indianization of the ICS.[44] The Ilbert affair led directly to the foundation of the Congress party in 1885.

Ripon had gotten a public service commission established. It was intended to explore the possibilities of meeting Indian demands for more administrative positions. In 1887 the commission proposed the creation of a new Provincial Civil Service (PCS), which would receive 108 former ICS spots, among them a third of the district judgeships, and a tenth of the collectorships. By 1893 this body comprised 1,030 administrative and 797 judicial positions, all filled by Indians.[45] The hope that the PCS would come to have a prestige equal to the ICS was never fulfilled, however. Possibilities for Indians to advance had indeed been created but the key positions remained reserved to the ICS, and the Indianization of the latter remained unresolved.

The motivations for resistance are obvious. The corps was defending itself against the entrance of "foreigners" who threatened its existing life-style and moral code. Then, too, the ICS was an important and highly skilled instrument of rule. The British dared not lose control of it because their rule rested, as Fitzjames Stephen put it in 1878, "not on consent but on conquest." Or, as the influential John Strachey noted a decade later:

> There never was a country and never will be in which the government of foreigners is really popular. It will be the beginning of the end of our empire when we forget this elementary fact and entrust the greater executive powers to the hands of natives on the assumption that they will always be faithful and strong supporters of our government. . . . Our Governor of Provinces, the chief officers of our army, our magistrates of districts and their principal subordinates ought to be Englishmen under all the circumstances that we can now foresee.[46]

It entirely corresponded with notions of an upper class educated at the public schools that they declared character, courage, and correctness to be specifically English qualities and then ideologized them as a credo for rule. It allowed them to dismiss the scorned *baboo* (a Western-educated Indian) as unsuited to assume political and administrative responsibility. What most members of the ICS and Englishmen with Indian interests in the homeland merely thought, Lord Curzon stated in blunt terms:

> The highest ranks of civil employment in India, those of the I.C.S., though open to such Indians as proceed to England and pass the requisite tests, must nevertheless be held by Englishmen, for the reason that they possess, partly by heredity, partly by upbringing and partly by education, the knowledge of the principles of government, the habits of mind and vigour, of character which are essential for the task; and the rule of India being a British rule, and any other rule being in the circumstances of the case impossible, the tone and standard should be set by those who have created and are indeed responsible for it.[47]

In a letter to the India minister, Curzon expressed another British fear when he noted that because of the "superior wits of the native in the English examinations," they would end up with more and more of the top positions.[48] And not only Curzon, but also the Muslims led by Syed Ahmad Khan and even the

Hindus in the north feared competition with English-educated Bengalis. At commission hearings in 1886, these groups rejected simultaneous examinations in London and India and compulsory examinations for entry into the lower levels of the civil service. When Dadabhai Naoroji who had said in 1887 that the holding of entrance examinations in India was "the chief aim of my life," won a seat in the British Parliament at Westminster in 1892 and in 1893 brought in a resolution to achieve this aim, the viceroy blocked it on the grounds of Muslim opposition and differing education levels in various parts of India. One can call this an alibi and an application of "divide and rule," but the danger that the clever Bengalis would achieve undue predominance in the administration at the expense of other regions was real enough.

After the maximum age for examination was raised again in 1892 to twenty-three, the chances for Indians improved, but their numbers in the ICS remained modest; of 1142 members in 1914, only 60 were Indians.[49] Between 1904 and 1913, 501 Britons and 27 Indians were taken on.

Only after World War I did the administration begin to Indianize and even then but tentatively. The 1918 report of Edwin Montagu and Lord Frederick Chelmsford instructed British officials "to do all that lies in their power to fit the Indians to take their places beside them."[50] The "dyarchy" system with its semiresponsible governments in the provinces called for qualified Indians in the top positions. During the war, moreover, few candidates were taken on. After the war, English demand for places declined and candidates had to be selected by appointment. There was a concrete need for Indian candidates. Between 1915 and 1924, 180 Englishmen and 143 Indians were recruited. In 1922 a commission on parities issued a new directive: the cadres for the departments now under the provincial governments had to be reserved for Indians, half of the new entrants into the ICS had to be Indian and some heretofore "reserved places" were to be filled with Indians from the PCS, mainly Muslims. The goal for 1939 was a fifty-fifty ratio, and, in fact, the numbers were 599 Britons and 587 Indians.[51] In the 1930s, moreover, the number of English candidates dropped sharply and the Indians did better on the exams, with the result that between 1932 and 1943, 110 Britons and 246 Indians were taken in . David Potter has recently attempted to show that lack of candidates and declining interest of the British ruling classes in India were important factors in the final Transfer of Power.[52] But the ICS had also lost much of its attraction for educated Indians.

Since before the mutiny, easier access to the top positions had been one of the most important Indian demands, and was repeatedly put forward by the Congress. Biographies and autobiographies of leading Indians of the nationalist era show emphatically what prestige the ICS had and the attraction it exercised.[53] They also reveal the degree of disappointment and frustration that must have existed when one failed despite painstaking preparation. State service and official careers in India as elsewhere in Asia had long stood in high regard. Legal studies which made possible either a career as a lawyer or service as a judge or official in the colonial service were especially favored. British education and life-style were not without their effects, and membership in so exclusive a club as the ICS offered both a chance to share in the administration of one's country and an opportunity to prove one's equality with the foreign ruling elite. Nonetheless, with the radicalization of the nationalist movement under Gandhi and Jawaharlal Nehru, with the noncooperation movement and the open declaration of hostilities against the colonial power, the members of the ICS became open to suspicion of collaboration. They thus faced the dilemma of choosing between the obligations of their offices and the liberation movement. In his autobiography of 1936, Nehru characterized the ICS, in which members of his family served, as an obstacle in the way to a free, self-governing India.[54] This mistrust continued to exist long after 1947. It became apparent all too soon, however, that India, with its internal tensions and the extreme demands planning and development placed on its bureaucracy, desperately needed the ICS.

There can be no doubt that the Indian Civil Service was a cadre of unusual quality: educated, conscientious, and uncorrupt. The same can be said of lower-level cadres, the so-called All-India Services such as the Indian Police, the Indian Agricultural Service, the Indian Medical Service, and others not discussed here. The prestige of the ICS in Victorian England stood high. It reflected the quality of the applicants and the rigor of the selection process. It was, in fact, "the steel frame of the whole structure," as Lloyd George put it. It unified India administratively for the first time and provided a governmental system based on law and institutional norms. Even Indian historians concede these things.[55] But today one can hardly overlook the shortcomings of this elite cadre. Drawn mainly from the upper middle class, a public school and Oxbridge education left such a firm impress upon the cadre that it was in its own way conformist. It was also so convinced of the superiority of its own mode of living and its right as a class to rule that it threatened to lose touch with a changing world. The leisurely pace of Indianization contrasted flagrantly with official declarations and hardly veiled decently what amounted to blatant racial discrimination. It is clear today that the ICS, despite its undeniable services and accomplishments, stood in the path of liberalization of the regime and helped to delay reform. Both Curzon and James Bryce portrayed it as lacking initiative and imagination.[56] It also had little regard for, or interest in, specialized education and technical knowledge. Such views may have accorded with the style and tasks of nineteenth-century rule, but even in the interwar period they were proving unsuited to instituting policies of economic development or social reorganization. Or, in Helen Lamb's striking formulation, British officials "were gentlemen, unrelated to either the mainstream of modern technology or the new urgency toward economic expansion and development whether by private or public enterprise. They were specialists in judicial procedures and government administration, not economic organizers."[57]

POPULATION MOVEMENTS

India's confrontation with British power and the resulting economic and social change must be seen against a demographic background. Otherwise, the Indian

Table 1.1
Population of India (In Millions)

YEAR	NUMBER OF PERSONS	PERCENTAGE INCREASE
300 B.C.	100-140	
A.D. 1600	100	
1800	120	0.09
1834	130	0.24
1845	130	
1855	175	2.97
1867	194	0.86
1871	255	6.84
1881	257	0.9
1891	282	9.4
1901	285	1.
1911	303	6.1
1921	306	0.9
1931	338	10.6
1941	389	15.0

SOURCE: Kingsley Davis, *The Population of India and Pakistan* (Princeton: Princeton University Press, 1951), 25-28.[58]

agrarian situation and its "involution" cannot be understood. There is, however, space for only the basic facts, as shown in table 1.1.

The first Indian census was taken in 1871. Censuses were taken thereafter at ten-year intervals. This was no mean administrative accomplishment, though even specialists have some difficulty interpreting the results. Although one must depend on estimates for earlier periods, the secular trend is clear enough. Whereas the Indian population can be taken as relatively constant for centuries on end, during 150 years of British rule it more than tripled, or, in absolute terms, increased about 270 million. In Europe the population revolution began around 1750 and the curve rose steadily.[59] The Indian "explosion," by contrast occurred in two stages, between 1845 and 1871 and after 1921. How is this to be explained? It would be mistaken to assume a particularly high birth rate, as the latter was around 49 percent between 1881 and 1891 and even fell slightly after 1921.[60] Mortality was what counted. As in prerevolutionary Europe, in pre-British India wars, epidemics, famine, and high infant mortality prevented rapid rise in population. Under British rule, war and brigandage all but ceased as causes of death, though famine and epidemics continued to take a heavy toll. In Orissa alone in 1865-1866, 1.3 million died, between 1898 and 1900 another 5 million, and another 15 to 20 million in the flu epidemic of 1918.[61] Population accordingly stagnated during these decades but rose steadily after 1921. The British administration was thus confronted with an increase of eighty million in the years 1921-1941 even though the yearly rate of increase was normal. The mortality curve dropped, though remaining high enough,[62] as did infant mortality.[63] Although the average life expectancy rose from 24.6 years in 1871-1881 to 31.8 in 1931-1941, it was still extraordinarily low.[64] Measures against epidemics and medical care had improved—the incidence of bubonic plague and cholera dropped sharply—but malaria still killed over a million in the 1930s.[65]

Population density (246 persons per square mile in 1941) was high in comparison with Russia (23), the United States (41), or even China (130), but was low in comparison with industrial countries such as England (718) and Holland (717), and also Japan (496) and Java (964). But one must also take into account sharp regional differences. Bengal had 60 million inhabitants (779 persons per square mile), the United Provinces 55 million (518). Within these provinces the density, even in agricultural areas, sometimes exceeded 1,000. In Rajputana (13.6 million in 1941) the density fell to 103, but even this was rather high, given the climate and the character of the land.[66]

When one keeps these population figures in mind, it can be seen that as late as 1800 India appeared a rather thinly settled continent, where much "waste" land was available. By 1880 British officials were beginning to speak of population pressure on the land. Such expressions should not be trivialized with, say, comparisons to Japan. The changes and problems of Indian agriculture under British rule—rising land prices and rents, splintering of holdings, increasing numbers of landless peasants, and rural misery—do not appear in the right light unless one keeps in mind this enormous, absolute increase in population, which admittedly in percentage terms was no larger than those elsewhere, without land to provide for it.

FAMINE

The monsoon brings India rain and snow. If it fails to come at the expected time or is insufficient, the harvest is in danger and hunger threatens those who live from their own land. From time immemorial India has suffered from famine. In the Mughal era it is reported that certain regions of India regularly lost good portions of their populations through famine, even in instances when harvests were normal in neighboring regions. Insufficient transport prevented the timely import of food. The ruler could temporarily suspend export but otherwise had limited means of assistance. In the villages themselves, the surpluses of good years were stored, which helped to bridge the hungry months. The village community could assist those especially hard hit, the taxes being levied according to the size of harvests. Famine could still not be prevented. In 1769-1770 a third of Bengal's people died of hunger, and the Delhi region was hit in 1782-1783.

In the British period, however, the number of both minor and severe famines seems to have increased, particularly in the second half of the nineteenth century.[67] Beginning with the Orissa catastrophe of 1865-1866, nearly every year saw one or several provinces hit, and the years of 1895-1897 and 1899-1900 were particularly bad. The number of dead ran routinely into the tens of thousands and in individual instances over a million.[68] How frequently irregularities in rainfall occurred in these years is difficult to say. What is important is that India had become more vulnerable to famine and the causes had changed considerably. The construction of railways and the infiltration of a cash economy had led to a commercialization of agricultural products. India began to export rice and wheat. Surpluses from the fat years were no longer, or to a much lesser degree, warehoused, but were brought to market. The dire result was that if the harvest of the following year was bad, or delayed, foodstuffs had to be bought, and if this could not be done expeditiously, hunger was inevitable. The lack of reserves resulting from sales was emphasized in administrative reports as an important cause of famine.[69] The railway network and commercialization did, on the other hand, simplify shipping in food, except to remote districts, but resulted in prices shooting upward. This meant that those who were too poor to buy suffered especially. This category included the rising number of landless workers, village artisans, and petty tenants.

> It will be commonly understood that when wheat is selling at 8 seers a rupee, a man who earns a rupee once a fortnight must be hard pushed for a living. Nor is this all. When prices rise to famine heights the employers of labour contract their expenditure and discharge from work people whom they can no longer afford. Not only is bread dear but there is no money to buy bread.[70]

Not surprisingly, grain traders, who often were also money lenders, speculated on the price rises and despite famine held back supplies. The peasants were forced to accept credit, increasing their dependence. Zamindars also exploited the desperate situation of their tenants. The situation on the land was steadily worsening, in any case. A great part of the the peasants lived on holdings that were too small and were heavily burdened with taxes, rent, and interest. Inadequately nourished, they lived from hand to mouth. This also helped to assure that a failure of the monsoon would have catastrophic results.

What did the colonial administration do? The administration had been surprised by the famine in 1865-1866 and, making false assumptions, had failed to meet the crisis. It accordingly called afterwards for detailed famine reports. These provided vitally necessary information about Indian agriculture and also revealed the causes of the famines. The administration early on organized "relief works" in order to provide the rural laborers, the worst sufferers, with some money. It was done reluctantly, however, because the Indian debt was rising in the 1870s and the budget was in the red. Sometimes loans were made, and in exceptional cases the government bought food and parcelled it out. But laissez-faire ruled. Although the Famine Commission of 1880 recommended state warehousing, especially to prevent price-gouging, the Indian government turned down the proposal. It took the position that "there will always be available in India a sufficient food supply in unaffected tracts." In other words, the problem was one of communications, meaning the expansion of the railway network had to be supported. That was done, and in no small part as a solution to the famine problem. The government considered railways more important than irrigation projects, although it was only the latter that could stop famines. The administration also strictly refused temporary limits on the grain trade, or even export prohibitions. That led in 1873-1874 to the grotesque situation in which the request of the Bengal government for an export prohibition was turned down, though, despite famine, rice was being both imported and exported in sizable quantities.[71] As late as 1896, the Indian government stolidly refused to intervene in the grain trade.[72] In the 1870s taxes were collected in full, famine notwithstanding, and only with great reluctance would the government permit delays in payment. Between 1897 and 1900 Romesh C. Dutt went so far as to assert that the high tax burden and the increase in taxes resulting from new assessments, especially in the ryotwari region, were responsible for the rural crisis and hence for the famines.[73]

After 1900 the danger of famine subsided. Only smaller areas were affected and prices remained relatively stable, thanks to better communications. Temporary migration helped bridge crises and relief works were better organized. The disastrous famine of 1943 in Bengal that killed a million and a half thus came as a surprise. It showed how precarious the Indian food situation remained and how important imports were becoming. The absence of rice imports from Japanese-occupied Burma was the main cause of the catastrophe. Bengal was more or less self-sufficient, if one disregards the chronic undernourishment of a sizeable portion of the population. After 1938, however, harvests were bad, that of 1941 being the worst since 1928. The government deluded itself that reserves were available. It did not respond to the lack of Burmese supplies, and, trusting to the harvest of 1942, did nothing. Hoarding and speculation pushed prices through the roof in 1943. Administration efforts to fix prices and control trade—for the first time—came too late and only made the situation worse. Imports from other provinces were but slowly gotten under way and at first there was no mechanism to apportion them. Only toward the end of the year did the new viceroy, Archibald Wavell, employ the army for the task. The administration had stood idly by far too long and was obviously not up to the job. But the agency mainly responsible was the government of Bengal, which since 1937 had been Indian. It appears this was the principal reason why the viceroy, Lord Linlithgow, stood aside and shoved responsibility off on the provincial government.[74]

IRRIGATION

India's agriculture requires irrigation. Yearly rainfall is low over wide areas, and even where it suffices it depends on the timely appearance of the monsoons. The Himalayas do, however, feed two great river systems, the Indus and Ganges. Canals, man-made ponds, reservoirs, and dug wells were ways of bringing the necessary water to the dry areas or apportioning it better over the course of the year. Irrigation serves to bring new land into cultivation, may make possible several crops every year, or may permit intensive cultivation (sugar, cotton).

Irrigation goes back to pre-British days, and the Mughal rulers also built canals, mainly in the north. Some irrigation works seem, however, to have fallen into decay in the eighteenth century. While the East India Company undertook some repairs, most new construction dates from the reform period and after. The great Ganges Canal was completed in 1854.[75] By 1857, a million and a half acres were already being irrigated in the province of Madras.[76] Governor-General Charles Trevelyan justly noted at the time:

> Irrigation is everything in India; water is more valuable than land, because when water is applied to land it increases its productiveness at least sixfold and renders great extents of land productive, which otherwise would produce nothing or next to nothing.[77]

Under Dalhousie, a public works department was created in 1854. Credits for public works rose from £600,000 in 1848-1850 to £2.2 million in 1856-1857. Hopes for private investment remained unfulfilled. The state had to take over two irrigation companies between 1866 and 1868. The turning point was 1864; new irrigation canals were thenceforth to be built by the state alone.[78]

The famines of 1866 and 1877 proved the urgency of canal construction, and the Famine Commission of 1880 asserted: "The first place must unquestionably be assigned to works of irrigation."[79] London, however, considered railways more urgent, since these also assisted commerce and could be built by private companies, though only with state subvention. Sir Arthur Cotton, the great pioneer of irrigation, pointed out in 1880 the incongruity of the state's having spent to date £125 million for railways and only £12 million on irrigation.[80] The profitability of irrigation works did not seem adequately proved, an important argument when the India government was on short rations. All the same, some canals were built or extended. The area irrigated by canals rose from 10.6 million acres in 1878-1879 to 15.3 million in 1896-1897.[81] The real push came, however, only with the great turn-of-the-century famines. In 1903 the commission established by Lord Curzon reported. It proposed a twenty-year plan and listed the necessary and possible facilities in the various provinces. It also stated that in addition to productivity, more attention ought to be paid to "protectiveness". To supplement the building of canals and levies for year-round irrigation, the construction of minor works such as wells and reservoirs should be encouraged by not taxing away all of the increased yields.

In the years to come, great irrigation systems with levies and canals were built in the Punjab and Sind in particular. They raised the irrigation area in the Punjab alone from 2.3 million acres in 1887-1888 to 10.4 million in 1922-1926, and brought the northwest a relative degree of prosperity.[82] "Canal colonies" were established. These were regulated settlements in the new arable areas. In the long run, they had the negative effect of drawing population from the neighboring areas. Their population rose rapidly and in the interwar period resulted in striking population pressures.[83] The Indus dam at Sukkur in the northern Sind, completed in 1932, helped to water 5 million acres. It was the largest irrigation system in the world. The Sarda Canal in the United Provinces watered 1.7 million acres, and in 1929-1930, the Sutley Valley system was completed in

Bikaner. By the year 1940, irrigated land totaled more than 50 million acres, approximately half of which was fed by canals and the rest by private reservoirs and wells.[84]

Historical judgments of British irrigation efforts differ greatly. Next to the administrative structure and the railways, the British have always regarded the irrigation system as a particular achievement, and Indians have also praised it.[85] Today, however, the achievement is seen as rather modest. The argument runs that the administration spent too little money despite seeing the need for irrigation, especially in comparison to railways.[86] The increase in irrigated areas was none too large, especially since it profited foodstuffs production less than cash-export corps.[87] Improvements at the local level were neglected because of insufficient administrative assistance, excessive taxes and rents, and a system of land law that, despite safeguards for the renter, gave him too little protection. The landlords invested too little, and the lack of a vested interest in improvements prevented the peasant from making them. The latter was in any case not sure that increased yields would actually profit him. In 1926 the agricultural commission determined that yields in areas with "ordinary wells" had not increased. Village councils and cooperative societies should, the commission believed, show more activity.[88] The efforts of postindependence India were, accordingly, directed mainly at the localities.

AGRARIAN STRUCTURE AND FARM PRODUCTION

Historians today are agreed that in pre-British India land was not considered property in the European sense and that the legislative introduction of the concept of real property around 1800 was a measure the seriousness and consequences of which are still difficult to gauge precisely. Neither the emperor nor those to whom he granted privileges, the feudal-aristocratic jagirs or zamindars, nor village community, nor families, nor yet the individual peasant, or ryot, "owned" land. Depending on locale and era, they possessed only a series of rights to a set portion of the product of the land, regardless of later disputes about whether this was to be regarded as taxes or rent. The "King's Portion," the peasant's payment for protection, was the most important state revenue. In the eighteenth century it amounted to between 30 and 50 percent of the harvest. Often paid in gold, it presupposed at least a rudimentary money economy and markets for agricultural produce. The tax, for in fact this is what the payment was, was uncommonly high, and for this reason one ought not to idealize the precolonial period. In practice, the modest profits of the peasants were siphoned off by the state, which used them for paying officials, waging war, and supporting a sumptuous court. It did not reinvest them in the land. The situation recalls ancien régime Europe.[89]

In contrast, however, to British tax policy which fixed levels of tax revenue for years in advance, the precolonial regime was more flexible. Taxes were tied to yields, which in monsoon country fluctuate very widely. Strong rulers like

Akbar attempted to have their officials collect taxes based on cadastral surveys which took into account the quality of land each family held. The village, usually meaning the headman, was made responsible for collection. This naturally offered ample opportunity to push the burdens off on the weaker and poorer villagers or for the old residents to increase the rents levied against settlers on new land.[90] The precolonial village led a largely self-sufficient existence, cut off as it was from the rest of the world beyond its mud walls. But it should not be transfigured into some sort of democratic state of nature, ruling itself through the village council, or *panchayat*. The caste system determined the village hierarchy and personal dependency relationships, in which Brahmins and certain peasant castes, for example, farmed their land with workers, some of whom were slaves.[91] Rights and duties were determined by social origin. Tax questions and disputes were settled within the village. The peasants did not own land but did possess highly divergent inheritable usage rights. The one thing they could not do was to sell land and especially not to an outsider. That blocked the possibility that a peasant could lose his land as a result of nonpayment of taxes or indebtedness to a moneylender. Under British rule all that changed.

The Mughal emperors had granted their subordinate rajahs certain taxes in return for tribute and had also given senior tax officials the taxes from designated numbers of villages rather than the land itself. After the death of Akbar, the emperors also started renting tax-collection concessions. The tax concessionaire (*zamindar* or *talukdar*) was compensated either with 10 percent of the total tax or the entire tax from specified villages. In the latter case, zamindar demands varied according to the locale. This was one of the reasons why the early British official in Bengal had difficulty understanding rural property and tax relationships, particularly since tax privileges were also tied up with many personal-service obligations on the part of peasants. In the crisis decades of the Mughal empire, the situation grew more complicated still. Rajahs and viceroys who were liable for tribute had made themselves largely independent, officials had usurped rights and set themselves up as rajahs, and zamindars with hereditary privileges, themselves ranging from lords of hundreds of villages down to so-called village zamindars, were hardly to be distinguished from the landed aristocracy of ancien régime Europe.

Another factor must be taken into account. The question of who actually owned the land, aside from the fact that it could not be sold, was not then of great importance because land was plentiful. Any villager could go off and seek a new allotment of land if taxes or debts became too burdensome. The existence of open land served in India as elsewhere as a safety valve.

With the assumption of the *dewani*, or the office of tax collector, in Bengal and Bihar in 1765, the British trod the footsteps of the Mughal emperors—to whom they continued to pay tribute. The East India Company thus immediately faced the questions of who was to collect the taxes and what was to be done with the zamindars. Were the latter concessionaires or really landowners? At first the company merely named a vice-dewan and took over the existing system. It soon discovered the bulk of the taxes flowed into the pockets of the zamindars and their subofficials. In 1772 the company took collection into its own hands. Because it could not determine how much the zamindars actually got from the peasants, Hastings auctioned zamindar rights to the highest bidders for five-year terms. Research has shown that Hastings in fact mistrusted the zamindars and wanted to protect the ryots from excessive tax burdens.[92] The result of auctioning off zamindar rights was, all the same, disastrous. The company had not only ridden roughshod over customary rights but had inaugurated a highly questionable social transformation. City businessmen who often had made their money as moneylenders or as intermediaries for the company outbid the old zamindars. Unlike the latter, they had no roots in agrarian society and thus no interest in preserving at least a modicum of welfare among the ryots. It was the beginning of the "parasitic bourgeoisie," as Rothermund has described it, in Bengal, which as a new Indian leadership class was to play such a dominant role operating from Calcutta. The sale to the highest bidder, moreover, led to a considerable rise in taxes, which obviously had to be provided by the ryots and burdened them intolerably.

In the meanwhile, tax and land rights had been investigated. Indian officials and the directors in London came by stages to the realization that some sort of definite regulation of zamindar rights had to be made and the control apparatus of the company simultaneously expanded. On the basis of the India Act of 1784, collectors were established in the provinces in 1786 and subordinated to the board of revenue. After some hesitations, Cornwallis decided on the so-called Permanent Settlement for Bengal and Bihar in 1793. The tax contributions negotiated with the zamindars during the preceding years were declared definitive and unalterable. The zamindars, previously only tax concessionaires, were recognized as landowners. In many cases this made them very large holders indeed. Despite deep-rooted mistrust of the zamindars, there seemed no other solution. Leases for set terms had worked poorly and were confusing. The company lacked the employees to make direct collections itself and thus depended on the zamindars and their people. The company had only them to deal with in the future and had assured itself of regular revenues. Besides, "it is for the interest of the state, that landed property should fall into the hands of the most frugal and thrifty class of people, who will improve their lands and protect the ryots and thereby promote the general prosperity of the country."[93] The assumption was manifestly that, like the improving eighteenth-century English landlords who had brought about a genuine agricultural revolution, the zamindars would now as an owning class try to modernize without burdening their tenants unduly.

These expectations went unfulfilled. The company got regular tax revenues on a basis which made planning possible. At the same time, it gave up any future share in the profits of increased productivity, cultivation of new land, or rising prices. It thus lost control over moneys that might have been reinvested in agriculture. The percentage contribution of taxes to Bengal revenues fell sharply during the nineteenth century. The original ratio of 9:1 in favor of the state had shifted by the interwar period to 4:1 in favor of the landlords, leaving the provincial governments with slim means indeed.[94] In 1950 in Bihar, five-sixths of the peasant burden was rent, one-sixth taxes.[95] Tax burdens under British rule are often overestimated. In the Permanent Settlement areas, rising yields and higher prices benefited the zamindars, not the state (see below p. 44).

Under the Permanent Settlement the rent burdens of the ryots, now reduced from de facto landowners to tenants, were also supposed to be fixed and limited. Cornwallis had determined on the Permanent Settlement in no small measure to prevent a further increase in peasant burdens. These hopes, however, soon proved illusory. The peasants' former rights were difficult to determine, and the zamindars found ways to raise rents and get rid of obstreperous tenants. Cornwallis had also established a clear separation between collectors and judges, in believing that it would provide the peasant additional protection under the law. This expectation also went unrealized. Litigation increased rapidly with complicated British trial procedures proving of not much use to the ryot. On the contrary. Within the villages, ownership rights had been common knowledge, attested to by other villagers. Now, however, it was impossible for a poor, illiterate peasant successfully to carry a complaint, which required written documentation, to a court that was often several hundred miles away. The failure to precede the settlement with a cadastral survey or any registry of existing rights worsened the situation. Even a successful law suit, moreover, was likely to ruin a peasant, though hardly a zamindar. The latter thus could involve a peasant in legal quarrels as a means of forcing upon him a new, short-term, exorbitantly increased lease.

The company wanted taxes paid on time. Zamindars that fell behind on payments were threatened with the auctioning off of their land. Within a generation, one-third to one-half of the land in Bengal changed hands.[96] The new zamindar class, however, was even less interested than the old in agricultural improvements and investment. It became an urban class of large landholders, collecting its rents and attempting to increase them. It did not play the role Cornwallis had foreseen for it. The transfer of the English model to the unsuitable milieu of India proved a mistake, and later liberal critics such as John Stuart Mill could justly compare the situation in Bengal with that of Ireland. A multitude of petty zamindars, indeed, existed, but in 1872-1873 Bengal and Bihar contained 533 estates of over 20,000 acres and 15,747 with between 500 and 20,000 acres.[97] Gathering taxes was left to collectors, often pensioned, petty officials with their own staffs. Personal dependency and feudal ties remained well into the twentieth century. Splendid festivals, with fireworks and all, underlined the "princely" position of the zamindar, even after a B.A. or an M.A. —that is, an advanced Western education—became a status symbol like Western dress and personal contacts with British officials.[98] The Permanent Settlement did offer England one advantage. The newly created landowner class owed its position to the colonial power and thus became a pillar of British rule.

In the Madras presidency, another system of taxation was gradually introduced. Attempts to auction off collection rights were soon abandoned. Thomas Munro first introduced the ryotwari system in a limited area. He systematized existing practice by concluding tax contracts with each individual peasant after clarifying property and yield relationships. The negative effects of the Permanent Settlement in Bengal and a tendency to glorify the peasant led Munro, as governor (1819-1827), to introduce this system into the better part of the Madras Presidency. Mountstuart Elphinstone and John Malcolm also adopted it for Bombay. In place of the zamindar, the ryot was declared the owner, and the tax assessment was set (as a sort of dues to the state as liege lord of the land). Reassessment was to take place only after thirty years.

The expectation was that private ownership would bring the individual peasant prosperity and enable him to invest in improvements. Munro understood that the success of the system depended on the level of taxation. He asked that taxes be cut by 25 percent, but the administration, interested in a high stable income, refused.[99] Tax reductions for bad harvests were also only grudgingly conceded. If the peasant could not pay, his land went under the hammer. The succeeding years were to show that taxes, up to half the harvest, were perhaps no higher than in precolonial days, but that the tax system was much more strictly administered. It must thus be made responsible for the precarious situation of the peasants even in the areas of the ryotwari system. In the early years in particular, assessments were much too high. The administration did attempt cadastral surveys and a more exact assessment of productivity, but the direct assessment by British officials and their Indian assistants led ineluctably to reassessments within the village. A certain leveling may have been sought, but in practice the tension between rich and poor peasants increased. Another important factor was that Munro, Elphinstone, and Malcolm, in contrast to Cornwallis, wanted to hold the village community together or to strengthen it. But by establishing private property and direct state assessment they loosened the ties of a society based on caste and customary law and stripped the village headman of his most important function. Liberals and Utilitarians condemned the Permanent Settlement and approved the ryotwari system because it did not create a landed aristocracy and recognized the ryot as owner and producer. Their acceptance of Ricardo's theory of ground rents, however, worked to the ryot's disadvantage because it justified taxing away that portion of yield which exceeded the peasant's sustenance minimum.

Finally, after 1822, yet another tax assessment was established in the north, the Mahalwari settlement. Here one encountered very close-knit village communities that could be considered as joint owners of the land. Taxes were hence not assessed individually for each peasant but for the village as a whole, and the talukdars and zamindars, if any, ignored. The village remained collectively responsible for paying taxes, and the headman was pushed aside as in the south. The share of the individual peasant was, however, fixed and could be mortgaged and sold.

Superficially, the British may appear to have assumed the inheritance of the Mughals in their tax system, but in reality they established an administrative system based on European assumptions. The old idea that rights to the product of the land were determined by social origin and caste status was displaced by the concept of private property, which "mobilized" the land and permitted it to become a trade good. It heightened rather than reduced inequalities and dependency within the village. Combined with high taxes and rents and a legal system protecting owners, the system encouraged the indebtedness of the renters and ryots and thus imposed a new dependency upon the moneylenders. A real crisis in Indian agriculture was becoming apparent as early as the mid-nineteenth century. The most recent researches at the local level emphasize, indeed, the continuity between the pre-British and British periods, particularly in regard to the extremely complex status of tenants and ryots and the very strong personal ties between landlord and tenant. These things changed very gradually, being in good part based on caste relationships. It should be borne in mind that in nineteenth-century Europe, particularly in the backward east and southeast, increasing indebtedness also constituted a most serious problem. In Asia, too, the problem was by no means confined to India but was one of the more important manifestations of an agrarian crisis that included other Asian colonies and semicolonial China and Japan as well.

The moneylender was there before the British.[100] From time immemorial he gave the ryot credit, whether to buy food and seed in dry years, or for bride price, or weddings and celebrations, or for taxes. Interest was always high because money was scarce, and the lender had little security. Still, the power of the moneylender had certain limits set upon it. He had to follow village custom and had no recourse to the state or the courts to collect his debts. He could assure himself a portion of the harvest, but could not seize the debtor's land or contest the ryot's hereditary right to his land. The village would not allow transfer of land to outsiders, and according to Hindu law the debt could not build up to more than twice the original principal. With the coming of British tax law and land policy, however, mortgaging became possible and with that, a shift in favor of the moneylender in cases of flagrant insolvency on the part of the debtor. Protection of the village community and customary law largely ceased, since the lender could bring an action in a British court. The latter, basing its judgment on the common law of contracts, would protect him. In contrast to Indian law, the entire property of the debtor could be seized in service of the debt. Without the protection of the village, moreover, the peasants were often swindled. They signed contracts containing obligations they had not agreed to; false bookkeeping entries were attested to as correct; and oral agreements were no longer, as formerly, valid. Peasants also lost cases through failure to appear in court. Because the local moneylender was very often the local merchant as well, he could easily collect his interest payments at harvest time. Later in the year, however, when the peasant's supplies were used up, he had to buy foodstuffs from this same merchant at higher prices. Unpaid interest grew over the years into a mountain of debt that bound debtor almost indissolubly to lender. The latter had merely to sit and wait, being mainly interested in the yield from the harvest. "The *sowkar* (moneylender) finds it to his advantage to keep the ryot in nominal possession of the land and to take the difference between what he produces and what is absolutely required for the support of the cultivator."[101] Under threat of being forced from the land, the peasant was ready to accept increases in rent but had no interest in undertaking long-term improvements. Nevertheless, as early as 1853 in the northwest provinces 114,000 acres had come on the market as a result of peasant indebtedness. Ten percent of the land was in the hands of the money-lenders.[102] The Famine Commission of 1880 noted: "One-third of the landholding classes are deeply and inextricably in debt and at least an equal proportion are in debt, though not beyond the power of recovering themselves."[103]

Two features of the indebtedness of the late nineteenth century and the following period were particularly disturbing. Credit went only in small part to raise crop yields, even when the peasant borrowed to buy seed, buffaloes, or plows. It served above all to bridge lean years or the critical months before the harvest and for marriages and other social obligations. Unfortunately moneylenders themselves had little interest in agricultural improvement. The Deccan Commission of 1892 criticized "the transfer of the land in an agricultural country to a body of rackrenting aliens who do nothing for the improvement of the land."[104]

From the mid-nineteenth century on, the British administration was aware of the problem of indebtedness and the signs of crisis within the agrarian society but did not consider it had grounds to act. According to the tenants of laissez-faire it did not seem to be the task of the state to interfere in the free play of forces within the bounds set by the law or to restrict the right to dispose freely of property. The social alterations could be interpreted as an adaption process that served progress by eliminating the weaker peasants in favor of those with capital and, supposedly, initiative. Doubts did occasionally surface about whether the laissez-faire model and analogies with England had any bearing on Indian conditions and about whether increasing peasant indebtedness might perhaps require legislative amelioration.[105] But it was agrarian disturbances and the great famines, supported by the mammoth investigative reports they occasioned, that finally moved the Indian administration to abandon its former passiveness and make efforts to protect tenants and control the moneylenders.

In 1875 disturbances broke out in the Deccan, the hinterland of Bombay. Ryots plundered moneylenders' houses and businesses. Characteristically, they sought the legal papers attesting their debts. For years conflicts within the village had been building between creditors and peasants swindled out of their ryotwari status. These conflicts burst into the open when the administration raised taxes despite falling cotton prices. The rapid increase in the population prevented the villagers from responding to the new assessments by flight as they had been able to do as late as 1830. Poorer land was already coming under the plow.[106] The

Agriculturist's Relief Act of 1879 attempted to redress a balance weighted crassly in favor of the lender. In the future contracts were only to be concluded in the presence of a village official. In cases of dispute new and nearer courts, presided over by a notable, were to render judgment. In addition, the courts were enjoined to examine the origin and content of contracts and to declare those with exorbitant interest rates null and void. The assumption was that "the passing of a bond by a native of India is often of no more value as proof of debt. . . than the confession of a man under torture of the crime he is charged with."[107] This was an important step. The colonial power had grudgingly consented to intervene on the peasant's behalf in a free contractual relationship because ownership changes resulting from debt had not, as Utilitarian theory would have it, created a class of capitalist entrepreneurs but merely an impoverished and discontented peasantry.

The Law of 1879 proved double-edged. On the one hand, the ryot now received a certain protection and the might of the law worked in his favor. Against that, however, the moneylenders held back credit, which was likely to leave the poorer peasants in severe straits. Mortgaged land was in any case still sold off. In 1901 the Famine Commission reported that a quarter of the peasants in the Bombay presidency had lost their land and only a fifth were debt-free. In the Surat District, moneylenders paid 85 percent of the taxes in 1900.[108] It was already clear then that legislative measures alone could not remove the cause of the indebtedness, namely, the need for agrarian credit and the dependence on the moneylender that went with it.

The next important protection measure was the Punjab Alienation of Land Act of 1900.[109] Indebtedness and land sales to moneylenders had commenced in the 1870s in the Punjab after British trial procedures had been introduced and the paternalistic administrative style of the annexation and transition phase had passed on. But these same Punjab officials early called for protection of the peasant, even if it did run counter to prevailing laissez-faire doctrines. A district officer, Septimus S. Thorburn, who had published the *Musalmans and Moneylenders in the Punjab* in 1886, was charged with making a detailed investigation. He exposed the high level of indebtedness and the machinations of the moneylenders.[110] The ethnological makeup of the Punjab was another factor. The peasants were Muslims or Sikhs, but the moneylenders were Hindus of the urban castes (*banias*). The dependency resulting from indebtedness and alienation of land threatened to unleash a communal antagonism which the British had every interest in avoiding. Muslim peasants and Sikhs from the strategically important border province of the Punjab constituted a large part of the Indian army. The law of 1900 forbade sale of land as a result of court judgment and, going further, any transfer to nonpeasants. Whoever did not belong to a peasant caste, meaning Hindu merchants, was in the future to acquire no land in the Punjab. Metcalf commented:

By this act the British in effect repudiated the contractual and legal view of property which they had introduced into Punjab land tenure fifty years earlier. Status was to replace contract as the criterion of landholding; rural society was to be restored to its traditional form and then guarded by a paternal government free of theoretical scruples.[111]

But even this rather far-reaching law to protect the peasants could not, as in the Deccan, prevent new indebtedness. In place of the moneylender appeared the well-off village peasant who understood during the war and after how to lay hands on some cash. An investigation between 1915 and 1919 disclosed an average debt of 463 rupees. Compared with the land tax, which was one-fifth to one-third of net income, the total indebtedness was twelve times as great.[112] By 1928 five million acres in the Punjab were in nonagricultural hands.[113]

Indebtedness rose further in the interwar period and was estimated in 1929 to be £750 million.[114] Only 20 to 40 percent of the peasants were not in debt, and the average debt amounted to approximately a year's income. Nagendranath Gangulee tells of Bengal peasants with 200 rupees of debt. With a rice crop worth 70 to 80 rupees a year, he had to pay interest of 50 rupees, while rent was only 10 rupees.[115] Thus a tax official for Dacca in East Bengal was able to write: "It is not the oppression of the landlord qua landlord, but the onslaught of the moneylender, often the landlord qua moneylender, that is eating into the vitals of Dacca agriculture, and destroying the basis on which a prosperous agricultural population must rest—a free use of and interest in the land with prospects of a reasonable profit."[116] Yearly interest varied according to the province from 20 to 35 percent and also depended on the peasant's status. "Owners or quasi owners received as a consequence of having better security a lower rate than 'tenants at will' and agricultural laborers."[117] With the fall of agricultural prices by about half during the depression, the real weight of the debt doubled. No wonder that in the province of Madras, for example, approximately 40 percent of the land changed hands between 1928 and 1934, half of it falling into the hands of nonagriculturalists.[118] An important investigative report of 1930 states:

Everything is against the peasant. Because he is a cultivator, he must borrow to secure his crop. Because his holding is small and has to support more persons than it can feed, he must increase his borrowing to keep those persons alive while the crop is in the ground. His caste and his religion compel him to borrow a third time to meet the cost of customary festival or customary ceremony. As the debt grows, replacement of it becomes more difficult, until at last some calamity comes upon him, replacement becomes impossible, and he sinks into a state of chronic indebtedness, from which death alone can release him.[119]

Or, to repeat Malcolm Darling's famous formulation: a part of the peasants "are born in debt, live in debt, and die in debt."[120]

The central and provincial governments passed numerous laws in the interwar period to bring the granting of credit by moneylenders under control (such as the Usurious Loans Act, 1918; Punjab Relief of Indebtedness Act, 1934; Debt Protection Act, 1936). Moneylenders had to register, bookkeeping controls were imposed, maximum interest rates were set, and household effects, domestic animals, and other chattels could no longer be seized for forced repayment of the debt. Laws covering nonpayment of rent also had to be passed. All this gave the peasant some protection against bad times, but the need for credit remained. The moneylender thus continued to seem a "necessary evil" (Darling) so long as there was no alternative. In practice this meant credit accessible to the peasant and at lower interest rates.

Great, really too great, hopes were thus placed upon mutual credit associations.[121] In 1881 plans for an agricultural bank had been developed as a supplement to the Deccan Relief Act. Despite support from the Bombay and Indian governments, the secretary of state turned it down on the ground that it committed the state to too much. In the following years the Raiffeisen system of communal self-assistance was much discussed and propagandized by British officials. As the outcome of a report, the Cooperative Societies Act was passed under Lord Curzon in 1904. Villagers were encouraged to open a fund from their own deposits which would be administered by the cooperative and would lend to peasants at acceptable rates of interest. Old debts were to be paid off in this way and if possible land already mortgaged regained. The movement became a sizable one. The number of cooperatives rose from 8,177 in 1911-1912 to 101,000 in 1929 and about 120,000 at the outbreak of the war. The number of members rose from 403,000 to 4 million with a capital of 900 million rupees. Especially the Punjab was strongly represented, and Darling considered it possible to state in 1925 that the power of the moneylenders was finally broken. But while 10 percent of Punjabi peasants were in cooperatives, in Bengal the percentage was only 3.8, in the Central Provinces 2.3, in the United Provinces 1.8, and in Bombay 8.7. Most important, their capital amounted to only 2 to 3 percent of the total agrarian requirement. There were other difficulties. The cooperatives had to proceed cautiously and with due regard for the uses made of their loans. They could thus not really meet the demand for credit which led to the high interest rates in the first place. Their debt collection methods also suffered in comparison with those of ruthless moneylenders. Some coops went bankrupt due to bad management, and others encountered difficulties as a result of price drops during the depression. The Royal Commission on Agriculture had also placed great hopes in the cooperatives, not only as a means of providing credit but also as an instrument for breaking through the lethargy of the peasants and strengthening their will to self-help. Independent India tied into the program with its Community Development Program, with but modest success.

No more successful were those legislative measures designed to provide the tenant a certain protection against arbitrary cancellation of leases and rent hikes. An attempt at this had been made as early as 1859 in Bengal. Peasants who had farmed their land for twelve years and paid the interest on it received a guarantee of possession. The interest was also to be "fair and equitable" and was not to be raised arbitrarily. In cases of dispute, the collector, not the courts, had jurisdiction, the assumption being that he would know more about land and tax matters. The board of revenue and the zamindars, organized as the British Indian Association, protested, but the latter soon found a way around the law. The tenant was simply moved to another parcel before twelve years was up. British tax officials, who, in the area of Permanent Settlement, trafficked only with the zamindars had little interest anyhow in watching them very closely. After difficult negotiations, the peasants were in 1885 conceded the three *F*'s: fair rent, fixity of tenure, and free sale of occupancy rights and compensation if forced off the land.[122] The law brought some security to the better-off tenants, although they remained vulnerable to zamindar threats of legal action.[123] Not until 1938 did the landlord lose his right to cover tax delinquencies by auctioning off land and his right to 20 percent of the sale price when a peasant with good title sold his land. Subtenants, however, who often were the ones actually farming the land, remained "tenants at will," and like "half tenants" and laborers received no protection.[124] A unique, and occasionally grotesque, system of tenants and subtenants between the zamindar and the land did not exactly simplify tenant protection. There could be as many as twenty intermediaries with divergent tenant rights, with the tenant of some parcels subletting them and farming others himself.[125] Some of the intermediate holdings can have brought in little or no income and were manifestly sought as status symbols, but the burden still rested in the end on the actual cultivator.

The example of Oudh reveals how much the landed aristocracy was not only protected but deliberately shored up and laden with perquisites after the mutiny. Directly after annexation, the British had moved strongly against the talukdars and had concluded ryotwari contracts. In the flush of postmutiny conservatism, however, they sanctioned the judicial authority of the talukdars, recognized primogeniture, guaranteed them security against loss in case of tax delinquency, and finally gave them a virtually free hand against tenants. No wonder that in 1873 landlords threatened some 60,000 tenants with expulsion in order to raise rents. One official noted: "The only law guiding the landlord is to get all he can and let the tenant shift for himself." Many of these rajahs hardly ever visited their "estates," which consisted of dozens or even hundreds of villages, and only a few undertook agricultural improvements. Rent was all that mattered. It was collected either by concessionaires or by the landlord's own staff of officials. These staffs constituted a kind of parallel administration to that of the state and rested on a multiplicity of personal ties reaching down into the villages themselves. Village officials were either appointed or bribed by the landlords.[126] A law from the year 1886 gave the peasant insufficient protection. After seven years his lease could be terminated or rent raised by at most 6.25 percent. Only in 1921 was this seven-year clause eliminated, so that the tenant had life tenure. Still, as late as 1946-1947, only 804 landlords paid 30 percent of all land taxes.

The colonial power certainly meant to protect the peasants from crass exploitation on the part of moneylenders and landlords. But it did so only after its dawning realization of the crisis in rural society had shaken its laissez-faire principles, its belief in contracts freely entered into, and hopes that free competition would create an enterprising and able landowning class. Whether it was acting out of an ethical-paternalistic feeling of responsibility or fear of disturbances does not matter. In the end the decisive factor was the unmistakably conservative character of British land policy. After expectations of the transformation along Western European lines had been disappointed, the British concentrated on holding Indian agrarian society together. Measures against the moneylender and for protection of tenants must be seen in this light. After the mutiny, the British feared to make extensive changes in Indian agrarian society. However critical they might be of the zamindars and talukdars, the latter were supporters of their rule, and as such the British dared not estrange them.[127] More than a certain balance between landowner and tenant interests hardly seemed advisable. The rajahs, zamindars, and, in the ryotwari areas, the large peasant and village notable class, were the collaborators upon whom British rule rested. It is also worth pointing out that the Indian educated classes, who as the Congress party shaped the nationalist movement after 1885, violently criticized British tax policy, making it responsible for the poverty of the rural populace. They nevertheless opposed British tenant-protection measures and did not evolve their own agrarian reforms until the 1930s. Even then, only the left wing of the Congress favored moving against the zamindars,[128] whereas the Bengal Land Revenue Commission of 1937 (constituted by a Muslim government) proposed their removal with compensation from the state.[129] This led to the rather modest land reform of postindependence days.

Additional aspects of the Indian agrarian structure must be considered if we are to understand the frightful poverty of the village populations. First, the area under cultivation. In the early nineteenth century, so far as inexact statistics permit determination, cultivated areas rose rapidly at first and then much more slowly. For British India, the area was 188 million acres in 1880, 199.7 million in 1901-1902, and 210 million at the outbreak of war in 1939.[130] The figures for India as a whole were 271.6 million acres in 1901-1902, and 318.5 million in 1939-1940.[131] A very considerable part of the increased area came from opening up new lands by means of irrigation, particularly in the Madras presidency, in the Punjab between 1901 and 1914, and later in Sind. But in densely settled Bengal, the area declined after 1900.[132]

Taken as a whole, the increases kept step with the increasing population until 1921 and then declined, as the following listing shows.[133]

ACRES UNDER CULTIVATION PER CAPITA

1891	1.04
1901	1.03
1911	1.09
1921	1.11
1931	1.04
1941	0.94
1951	0.84

This decline, in itself, would not have been a sign of crisis if an increasing portion of the population had found employment outside agriculture. But in India this did not happen. Although the cities, particularly Calcutta and Bombay, grew and significant industrialization occurred, they could not absorb the population increases. In contrast to Western industrialization, the agrarian population increased in absolute terms and remained a constant percentage of the population as a whole: in 1881, 61 percent, in 1911, 71 percent, and in 1975, 70 percent.[134]

These unadorned figures conceal a most depressing truth, namely, that families had too little land at their disposal. The majority of holdings were too small to assure even a modest level of sustenance. The census of 1921 reveals the following picture:[135]

ACRES PER CULTIVATOR

Bombay	12.15
Punjab	9.18
Central Provinces	8.48
Madras	4.91
Bengal	3.12
United Provinces	2.51

It took ten to fifteen acres of grain and three to five acres of rice to support one family. Statistically, the available land was barely sufficient. Relations within the village, however, must be taken into account. An investigation in the Punjab in 1926 revealed that 76 percent of the holdings were under ten acres and over half were under five:[136]

ACRES	PERCENTAGE
Over 10	24
5-10	20
1-5	33
1 or less	23

Other regions reveal a similar picture.[137] A minority of prosperous peasants stood vis-à-vis a majority with little or no land. (Of these, 15 to 25 percent were agricultural laborers.) They were miserably housed, badly clothed, undernourished, and the victims of famine and sickness in bad years—to say nothing of the burden of debts, rents, and taxes. As population increased and plots were divided in accordance with Hindu and Muslim laws of inheritance, the number of minifarms and landless works grew. In the Shiwandi district for example, the percentage of holdings under five acres increased from 49.1 to 69.1 between 1886 and 1937.[138] William Wilson Hunter put the matter clearly enough, as early as 1903:

In provinces where, a hundred years ago, there was plenty of land for everyone who wished to till it . . . human beings [are] so densely crowded together as to exhaust the soil, and yet fail to wring from it enough to eat. Among a people whose sole means of subsistence was agriculture . . . a landless proletariate [is] springing up, while millions more [are] clinging to their half acre of earth apiece, under a burden of rackrent or usury. . . . More food is raised from the land than ever was before; but the population has increased at an even more rapid rate than the food supply.[139]

Parcels already too small, moreover, were divided yet again. Each heir received a portion of all the parcels of his father, a custom that made sense in terms of land productivity and available water, but not uncommonly resulted in up to twenty miniplots that could no longer be economically farmed. And it happened that the ox was displaced by the hoe.[140] From the interwar period on, consolidation of holdings had been one of the most urgent but also most difficult tasks of Indian agrarian policy.

Raising productivity thus became all the more important. The most recent researches have shown that the yield per hectare during the last fifty years of British rule was extraordinarily low and did not rise.[141] Here, one must differentiate between nonfoodstuffs (which include not only cotton, jute, and tobacco but also tea and sugar), which were mainly destined for export or intended as industrial raw materials, and foodstuffs (wheat, jowar, and rice). The yield per acre fell in the case of foodstuffs (more precisely, it rose in the case of wheat and jowar, but fell in the case of Bengalese rice), whereas in the case of nonfoodstuffs it rose noticeably, particularly in the case of sugar, cotton, and tea.[142] Irrigation, particularly in the Punjab, was the main reason for the rise in productivity, especially in the cases of cotton, sugar, and wheat. New or improved irrigation facilities also permitted double cropping.

Elsewhere, however, the land was worked excessively and sucked dry of its nutrients. Cultivation methods, particularly for food, scarcely changed during the British period. The Indian peasant plowed and sowed using a buffalo pulling a simple wooden plow. He harvested with a sickle and threshed by stamping on the grain, by using a flail, or some sort of buffalo-driven contraption. The lack of fertilization was, and is, another serious drawback. Cow dung was not collected or was used as fuel. Bone meal, which might have served as fertilizer, was exported, in part to Ceylonese tea plantations, mainly because Indian peasants were for religious reasons reluctant to use it. Artificial fertilizer was also used very little in Indian agriculture before World War II. Its price was prohibitive for the ryot. The excessive stock of cattle could also not be exploited. The skinny cows hardly delivered enough milk for daily needs.

The colonial power only troubled itself very late and rather feebly about agriculture.[143] The opposition of Manchesterites notwithstanding, state assistance had been sought even before the turn of the century, mainly for the improvement of communications, irrigation, and experimental stations. Characteristically, however, it was sought for cotton.[144] Only as a result of the work of the Famine Commission of 1880 were provincial agricultural departments formed, and these at first were taken up with surveys and statistics-collecting. Agrarian research really began in 1903 under Curzon. In the following years, experimental stations and agricultural colleges were established, as was an agricultural service for the provinces. Its staff was much too small, however, to cover India's 500,000 villages.[145] Some successes were achieved in the matter of better seed, but not until the 1930s.[146] The administration made no effort to introduce artificial fertilizer. The demonstration effect of model farms was slight, either because they were few and far between or because the peasants feared to take risks. It has been pointed out that even the example of rich village peasants did not incite local imitation and could result in strikingly great discrepancies in yields within a very restricted area.[147] In any event, the yields for both foodstuffs and other crops remained far behind those of other countries, and not only European ones.[148]

Stagnating productivity per land unit combined with rising population could only result in falling per-capita yields. At the local level, this process of impoverishment in real terms and increasing hunger began fairly early and for India as a whole, in regard to foodstuffs, around 1911 (see table 1.2).[149] The regional differences here are striking. Whereas the decline in rice production set in early in Bengal, the Punjab was able to produce surpluses of wheat until about 1923 because of irrigation.

Until about 1920 India exported foodstuffs. This cannot necessarily be interpreted as proof that the Indian population was adequately fed. Regional surpluses may have occurred in good years, but for the country taken as a whole exports were only possible because a great percentage of Indians lacked the money to buy and were actually undernourished.[150] From 1920 on, increasing amounts of food had to be imported, mainly rice from Burma:[151]

YEARS	MILLION TONS
1920-1925	1.6
1925-1930	7.6
1930-1935	12.7
1935-1938	13.8

It is usual today to attribute to the colonial power's forced cultivation of cash crops this deficient production of foodstuffs. While people starved, mountains of nonfoodstuffs were exported. Or, it is claimed that with the expansion of the cash economy and the rail network, the peasants were encouraged (or forced) to raise cash crops and to neglect providing themselves with foodstuffs. The resulting dependence on fluctuating world market prices also serves for some as proof of colonial dependency and exploitation. In my opinion, this picture requires considerable refinement.

England was, obviously, interested in Indian exports. It was for this reason that the East India Company had early forced the cultivation and export of opium, in order to create the means to pay for Indian textiles. A very questionable system of forced cultivation had also been used in the first half of the

Table 1.2.
Productivity of Land in India, 1901-1941

AREA	PERIOD	% YIELD PER CAPITA	% DECLINE PER YEAR
British India	1911-1941	29	1.14
Greater Bengal	1901-1941	38	1.18
United Provinces	1921-1941	24	1.36
Madras	1916-1941	30	1.40
Greater Punjab	1921-1941	18	1.00
Bombay-Sind	1916-1941	26	1.21
Central Provinces	1921-1941	19	1.05

SOURCE: George Blyn, *Agricultural Trends in India*, 1891-1947 (Philadelphia: University of Pennsylvania Press, 1966), 102.

nineteenth century for indigo. Europeans obtained land and forced their tenants to plant a quarter of their land in indigo which then had to be delivered at a fixed price. The risks were very high, but the profits could be fabulous.[152] But indigo soon lost out, and by 1911-1912 only about 300,000 acres were left. The production of tea as a specific plantation product expanded rapidly, production rising from 54,000 tons in 1891 to 183,000 tons in 1931. India's share in world tea exports amounted during the interwar period to about 40 percent, and tea amounted to 9 to 10 percent of Indian exports. Given the recruiting methods used (for a work force of 922,000 in 1930), the low wages, the harsh supervision, and the poor working conditions, one can speak here of exploitation. This is particularly true considering the opulent lives of planters and administrators and tea company profits, which were occasionally very high. The latter flowed back to England and lent the tea plantations the typical character of an enclave economy, as they had an extraordinarily slight impact on the overall Indian economy. The greatest portion of the tea came, however, from the rain forests of Assam. The seven- to eight-hundred-thousand-odd acres of plantations lay on cleared forest land and expanded rather than limited foodstuffs production.[153]

Cotton naturally required much more acreage. It has been mentioned that Lancashire demanded state support of cultivation, in order not to be dependent exclusively on the American South to meet its rapidly rising demand. The American Civil War unleashed a real boom, from which the Deccan peasants profited even though food prices rose and easier credit encouraged indebtedness. For British India, where cotton required about 7 percent of the total arable, the cultivated areas and production are shown in table 1.3. The area may have been considerably higher in certain districts. Land newly won for cultivation through irrigation was, as in the Punjab, for example, used not only for grain and rice but also for cotton. On the other hand, it has been shown that even in the years 1861-1870 the expansion of cotton was a result of expansion of the total cultivated area and did not come at the expense of foodstuffs.[154] No compulsion was used. The peasant grew cotton because it provided him with

Table 1.3
Cotton Production in British India, 1891-1939

YEAR	ACREAGE IN MILLIONS OF ACRES	PRODUCTION IN MILLIONS OF TONS
1891	8.4	1.7
1914	14.1	3.5
1929	15.8	3.6
1939	13.3	3.3

SOURCE: Peter Harnetty, "Cotton Experts and Indian Agriculture," *EcHR*, 24 (August 1971).

additional cash or because the yield was higher than for food crops. We unfortunately lack detailed studies, however, from the cotton growing zone. It should be noted further that while cotton exports indeed did bring great profits, mainly to European firms, an increasing portion of the cotton was worked up by Indian spinning mills. That contributed considerably to industrialization.

The story for Bengal jute is similar. Contrary to the usual view, the amount grown came to about 2.5 to 3 million acres for all of India, which counted for very little. Even in Bengal, it used only about 8 percent of rice land, and thus can in no way be made responsible for the rising rice imports.[155] The yield per acre was double that of rice,[156] and jute thus contributed a small but important supplementary income, particularly when the same family grew both rice and jute.

The area under cane sugar increased from 2.4 million acres in 1910 to 4.5 million acres in 1936-1937 and competed with wheat in northern India. But it was most profitable for the peasants and enabled India after introduction of duties to build its own refineries and free itself from dependence on imports (see p. 56).

Taken altogether, it turns out that specific export products such as cotton, jute, and tea required about 10 percent of Indian arable land, and if sugar and linseed oil crops are counted, about 20 percent.[157] Dharm Narain has shown that in the case of nonfood crops, area under cultivation correlates with market prices. The peasant was not only ready, in other words, to convert to these crops, but thought along "commercial" lines. These rising acreages allow one to conclude that the peasant recognized opportunities for profit and sought to exploit them.[158] The money income from growing cash crops remained modest because of low per-capita yields, but it still seems to me mistaken to attribute the stagnation of Indian agriculture, the poverty of the peasants, and the deficient food production to the growing of export products.

I consider the origins of this stagnation and poverty to lie first and foremost in the lack of good farmland. Given the small holdings and traditional cultivation methods, the land provided per-capita yields that in good years were no more than minimum subsistence levels, and in bad years inevitably brought famine to the majority of peasants. The arable was, indeed, somewhat increased by bringing in new land and by irrigation and was until early in this century able to keep pace with the growing population. But the vicious circle of poverty was never broken. Indeed, it worsened during the interwar period, when the population increased faster than the supply of new land. More labor could not raise productivity; on the contrary, the land was overused and yields often declined. Underemployment and the number of landless peasants increased. The British land and agrarian policy, which originally aimed at creating a progressive gentry (Permanent Settlement) or an independent, enterprising peasantry (ryotwari areas), proved mistaken. It exposed the traditional rural society to an individualization process that led to the creation of a landowner class uninterested in investment. It allowed the great part of the peasants to become tenants and made their indebtedness an increasingly grave problem. "Underemployment of cultivator, agrarian unsettlement, growth of the landless agricultural labourer class, and the increase of agricultural indebtedness—these are some of the inevitable consequences of defective rural economy confused by the prevailing system," was the view of one expert in 1935.[159] The British administration bit by bit attempted to stop this disintegration process and to stabilize rural society. But it formulated no concept of development and hence blocked rather than encouraged the breakthrough to agricultural revolution. State and private investment in agriculture was, with the exception of irrigation, paltry. At the same time, however, capital was continuously siphoned off in the form of rents, interest, and taxes. No wonder the harried peasant was unable to accumulate any savings that might have been employed to improve his cultivation methods.

The level of peasant burdens is much disputed. Nationalist and British critics of the raj have estimated that the burdens were very high and have made them to a considerable extent responsible for indebtedness, famine, and stagnation. Dutt's *Open Letters to Lord Curzon* became famous as did the "Memorial" of British officials, which he also inspired in 1900. In the latter, among the other demands, it was asked that the administration actually stick to its own instruction to take "only" 50 percent of the peasant's net income (income less production costs) and refrain from raising taxes during reassessments.[160] In 1901 William Digby also leveled sharp criticisms in his provocative book, *"Prosperous" British India*, but his figures mostly have to do with rents. He alleges great differences in revenues between provinces.[161] On the other hand those who warn in the most recent literature against the overestimation of the tax burden mostly use examples from the area of Permanent Settlement and hence also provide a false picture.[162] One can conclude with T. M. Joshi roughly as follows.[163] Tax burdens under the British were little higher than under the Mughals, but assessment varied sharply and taxes were administered rather inflexibly. The effective burden was considerable, especially during the 1930s. Taxes can only in a limited way be made responsible, however, for the disquieting indebtedness of the peasant and the signs of crisis in Indian agrarian society.

RAILROADS

It is hardly surprising that in the 1840s, when England itself was seized with railroad mania and had accumulated capital to invest in them, the question also became acute in India. Inland transportation on the subcontinent remained rudimentary, the oxcart constituting the primary means of transport, and troops could be moved from one province to another only with difficulty. In the older literature, the tendency was to place military and political factors in the foreground. The argument ran that England undertook railway construction in order to tie India together better administratively, to be able to push ahead more rapidly with expansion, and to make easier the exercise of sovereignty. Indian nationalists could play down the accomplishment of the colonial power to the extent that railways had served primarily the latter and not India proper. More recently, economic interests have received greater attention, particularly English interest in Indian railways.[164]

Both the London mercantile houses and Anglo-Indian businessmen in Calcutta and Bombay had pressed for the improvement of maritime ties with England in the 1830s. In 1840 the chartering of the Peninsular & Orient Line greatly improved the sea connection. Interest then shifted to railways. Lancashire was the principal source of agitation. It imported its cotton mainly from America, feared becoming dependent on it, and demanded, as earlier mentioned, "internal improvements" from the East India Company. In other words, state assistance to improve communications was sought, laissez-faire notwithstanding. This meant state assistance for improvement of communications, irrigation facilities, and the cultivation of cotton. India was to provide more of the vital raw material than before, and was also to serve as a market for English products. Chamber of Commerce petitions to Parliament, particularly from Manchester and London, press campaigns, public meetings, and Parliamentary speeches all served to launch a campaign which the government and the company were unable to withstand. It was also argued that competition from continental textiles was increasing and that England had a moral and civilizing role to fulfill. The railway was pictured as an instrument of modernization that would shatter the petrified society of India and open it to progressive Western influence. In India itself, Lord Dalhousie campaigned vigorously for railways and in his *Railway Minute of 1853* set down the guidelines for construction.

But who was to finance and operate the lines? The disorder accompanying railway construction in England had gradually led to the conviction that state oversight was essential. Investors, on the other hand, emphasized the risks of Indian railways and the public interest in getting them built. They demanded financial guarantees from the company. As early as 1844, the railway pioneer George Stephenson had proposed that the state or the company ought to assume a guarantee for the interest on invested capital as had been done in France. In discussions of the matter extending over five years, the guarantee idea was accepted, the first contract being let in 1849. Private companies raised the capital and undertook to build and operate the lines. If the profits did not suffice to pay a 5 percent dividend, the Indian government had to make up the difference with subsidies. At the end of twenty-five years, the government had the right to buy the line. The government received extensive rights of direction and control, both for building and operation. The companies, however, had the right to hand over unprofitable lines to the government at any time in return for complete repayment of capital thus far invested. The risks had thereby been successfully unloaded on the Indian government.

The question of whether the 5 percent guarantee was needed to mobilize British capital has been much discussed in the literature. The interest rate exceeded the contemporary rate for government bonds. Because the companies lost money between 1850 and 1900, the Indian government had to spend fifty million to meet guarantee obligations.[165] To the extent that Indian consumers had to come up with the money in the form of duties and taxes this was an economic drain. Others have pointed out, however, that 5 percent was less than other foreign railways had to pay on the London market.[166] Morris D. Morris even speculates that Indian investors would hardly buy Indian railway stocks because other investments, such as moneylending, land, and trade, promised higher gains.[167] In any case, the 5 percent guarantee inaugurated a "large scale movement of British capital." By 1868, £ 80 million had been invested and by 1902, £ 236 million.[168] Although small and medium investors participated, the main share went to banks, which interested the City in no small measure in British rule in India.

The first two lines, which opened in 1853, ran from Calcutta northwest to the coal fields and from Bombay into the Deccan cotton districts. By 1869, 4,000 miles had been built, at the cost to the Indian government of £13.5 million. The bad features of the 1849 arrangements soon became apparent. Insured against loss, the companies did not trouble about economy, either in construction or operation. Viceroys Lawrence and Mayo both advocated about 1868 that the state itself undertake further construction and operation. London, however, accepted a compromise according to which new lines only were to be built by the Indian government. Still, it was an astonishing decision for the laissez-faire era. But governmental financial difficulties resulting from the Afghan War, famine, and the declining gold value of the rupee reduced the state's capabilities, while at the same time the Famine Commission Report of 1880 called urgently for the expansion of the network. The government responded with changes in the guarantee system for private construction but purchased the lines after the twenty-five year period was up. Although operation of the lines was left in the hands of the private companies, the profits went mainly to the treasury after 1900.

The network grew considerably, from 10,000 miles in 1882 to 25,000 miles in 1900, to 35,000 miles by 1914, and 43,000 in the interwar period. Ton-kilometers rose from three billion in 1881 to nine billion in 1909, and twenty-one billion in 1924-1925. Administration of the railways, however, proved to be deficient.[169] The lines were run by thirty-three separate companies. Some however, particularly those of strategic importance, were run directly by the state. A minority remained in private hands, these being concentrated in the princely states. Control by the state railway department was rigid. Railways were integrated into the general budget, which too often had the consequence that the profits got sucked into the treasury and the railways were left with means insufficient for maintenance and improvements and remained undercapitalized. There was no development plan, and annual budgeting complicated the task of creating one.

The troop and materiel movements of World War I imposed excessive burdens on the railways, and repairs and replacements were neglected. After the war the railways were quite unable to meet the demands made of them. Shipments languished on sidings and factories had to cut production. A commission headed by the railway expert William M. Acworth spelled out the crisis in black and white. Some reforms followed. The railway budget was separated from the general budget, planning was to be done on a five-year basis, and an expansion was accepted. A majority of the commission called for complete nationalization, but London refused. The Indian government nevertheless bought additional lines, about half the total, during the following years and ran them itself.

The building and operation of Indian railways, long seen as one of the significant accomplishments of the colonial power, are today sharply criticized not only by Indians but Western authors as well. Some of their arguments must be presented here. Although the British pointed proudly to a network of 43,000 miles, one of the greatest in the world, the Acworth Commission noted its inadequacy, in effect endorsing the judgment of an earlier British committee (1908) that at least 100,000 miles were needed.[170] Wide areas of the country remained isolated from railheads, which delayed development during the interwar period. The railroads, it is also argued, served British rather than Indian interests, insofar as they were oriented (aside from strategic lines) around the four great harbors of Calcutta, Madras, Bombay, and Karachi. They bypassed some older urban centers and failed to encourage interregional trade. The latter characteristic was, in fact, one that Indian railways shared with other colonial railway systems. Individual lines were monopolies and were insufficiently equipped to meet the needs of trade, particularly during the export season. The rates policy was also mistaken. Freight charges were well under English charges, to be sure, but were still too high for Indian conditions. According to Thorner, lower charges for increased amounts of freight would have been proper.[171] Rate policy served British interests by favoring long-haul lines serving the ports against short hauls; this hampered Indian industrialization.[172] Finally, while British capital for railways did flow toward India, it did so on unfavorable terms, and no efforts were made to mobilize Indian capital.

The Acworth Commission also confirmed the charges of Indian nationalists that the companies had culpably neglected third-class cars, in which most Indians rode, even though they provided most of the passenger revenues.[173] The commission also criticized the dilatory Indianization of the railways, though they employed 700,000 Indians. Top positions were reserved almost exclusively for Europeans, who rested "like a thin film of oil on top of a glass of water, resting upon, but hardly mixing with the 700,000 down below."[174] In the following years, Indianization was accordingly begun.

More important still is the reproach that the railways either contributed nothing to industrialization or only very little and very indirectly. The railways opened the country to British trade and permitted the shift to agricultural products for export. On the other hand they also facilitated the import of British consumer goods and thus helped destroy the Indian artisan trades (see p. 49 below). Nor did they, as was true in Europe, the United States, and Japan, simultaneously become a dynamic impulse for industrialization, particularly in steel and capital goods. Although in 1853 Marx considered it certain that a country with iron and coal would necessarily end up building locomotives, his prognosis proved incorrect for India.[175] Rails, locomotives, and cars naturally came from England in the early phases of development. That was unavoidable and cannot be called specifically colonial. But things did not change with time, and both government and private companies continued to supply their needs from the mother country. Indian coal mining profited, because the railways soon became the leading consumer of Indian coal. Numerous workshops arose that played an important role in developing a class of technicians and trained industrial workers. Jamshed Tata's steel works also succeeded because he was able to supply the railways with rail.[176]

In regard to the general supply of technical equipment to the railways, however, the so-called stores policy was very rigidly followed. Companies were, in other words, forced to channel their orders to British firms through the India office. Only in 1901 did Lord Curzon propose that railway materials, including rolling stock, be supplied by Indian firms. Although in 1905 the stores regulations were loosened, only contracts for such things as lightweight bridges were let, despite Indian firms' ability to fill larger orders. Even after London gave instructions to favor Indian firms in 1909, assuming, naturally, that price and quality were equal to imports, orders did not rise significantly.[177] Why no locomotive industry arose under such conditions is obvious. This was a result of colonial dependency and caused Indian railway development to differ from Japan's. In Japan, railway construction received tariff protection, state orders, and other support and importantly affected industrialization because, in contrast to India, it encouraged iron and steel production. Not until the interwar period were modest efforts made to provide Indian industry more business. The government thus paid a premium of 700,000 rupees a year for the production of rolling stock in India. Still, in 1925-1926, 145-7 million rupees' worth of new material was imported, and only 87.3 million was ordered locally.[178]

INDUSTRY[179]

Since the late middle ages, pre-British India had, like Europe, possessed a flourishing handicraft industry. It enjoyed world renown, particularly in the seventeenth and eighteenth centuries. Village women spun thread. A special caste of weavers wove, to a certain extent on order from the village community. They were usually paid in kind rather than in money. The case was similar with the village trades of smith, potter, joiner, silversmith, and oil presser. The village was thus largely independent of urban crafts, which, aside from their own needs, worked largely for the court and the Indian aristocracy. Goods of the highest quality were made: chintz, muslin, and calico from cotton, gold and silver brocade from silk, and kashmir scarves from wool. The technical equipment was extremely simple and changed but little. These luxury goods found their way to Europe and became fashionable around 1700. The East India Company exploited this situation so effectively that very high duties were raised to protect English producers, without, however, helping them much. Company employees were able to raise Indian exports and to intervene in the production process either by themselves putting out work or employing Indian middlemen to do so. The link between administration and trade created a monopoly that allowed the company to fix prices for raw materials and finished products and often to force the production of those desired.

The Industrial Revolution in England and the end of the company monopoly in 1813 fundamentally altered the picture. Machine-made yarn and cotton stuffs competed with Indian handmade products. Indian cotton exports declined rapidly, particularly after 1825, while English exports rose.[180] English import duties as high as 70 percent accelerated the process, particularly since, under pressure from Lancashire, India was ever more clearly seen as a supplier of raw material, especially cotton, and as a market for English products; and as a colony, India could do nothing about it. Other factors entered in. Indian princely courts became less and less important as markets for luxury goods, whereas the new Bengal bourgeoisie came to prefer English to Indian cloth. The result was large-scale destruction of Indian hand weaving. As the governor-general emphatically put it in his oft-cited report of 1834-1835: "The bones of the cotton-weavers are bleaching the plains of India." Although this was at first only true of the coastal regions and Bengal, the construction of railways after 1850 opened the interior to British imports and caused the inland weavers grave difficulties. The town trade—in, say, Dacca—had an especially hard time and millions of weavers were hence forced back onto the land. But the village trades also suffered. Hand spinning in good part disappeared, and the potters, dyers, tanners, oil pressers, and silversmiths faced increasing English competition. That heightened the village crisis, initially brought on by changes in land law, tax policy, and the money economy, though the village trades were not killed completely.

Since the days of R. C. Dutt, the usual picture in Indian historiography is of the "re-ruralization" of India as a consequence of British policies which delivered over a defenseless India to British economic interests.[181] This view was challenged as long ago as 1924 by the Indian historian D. R. Gadgil and more recently by Morris D. Morris. Both argue that cheap machine-made yarn strengthened hand weaving, and internal demand increased. The rising import of metals also permits one to conclude that while adjustments were occurring, one cannot speak of the destruction of the Indian trades or at most can do so in only a limited sense.[182]

In Europe, too, the Industrial Revolution with its shift to mechanized production, particularly in textiles, had either displaced the traditional crafts or threatened to do so. This also released manpower in the villages and to that extent caused a re-ruralization. Industrialization and the sharp increase in town and city populations that accompanied it, however, absorbed the manpower that had been set free and thus reduced the population pressures on the land. The question then becomes: Did a similar, analogous industrialization process occur in India?

Cotton Industry

A cotton industry arose early. The preconditions existed. Raw material, albeit of rather poor quality, was there in abundance, as was the labor force and, despite the low per-capita income, the markets as well. In 1854 the first Indian spinning mill began production in Bombay. By 1872-1873, seventeen more were in operation, and in 1877 J. N. Tata's very up-to-date Empress Mill began production in Nagpur. Expansion was rapid until 1914 (see table 1.4). These factories, centered around Bombay and Ahmadabad, were almost entirely Indian founded and financed. Many of the founders were from the Parsi religious community rather than being Hindus. Before 1850 the Parsis had entered Bombay's rapidly growing trade as brokers and agents and had shown a particular aptitude for Western education.[183] The profits of the export boom during the American Civil War, the high profits of the companies' early years, and the export of yarn to China after 1880 also had a stimulating effect.

In a certain analogy to Lancashire, where the chief manager was subordinate to the board of directors, in India a unique "managing agency" system of organization arose. The Indian founder and capitalist turned over the day-to-day management to an "agency firm." The latter had a twenty to forty-year contract and received a commission based on production, sales, or profits.[184] The system, which was also adopted in other branches of industry, had some obvious advantages during the very early years. The managing agents functioned as promoters, furnished the vitally necessary management talent, and helped to raise capital. This last was of particular importance, because native Indian capital for industrial investment was so scarce. Many of those with cash reserves preferred to invest in land or to hoard the money. The British banking system, on the other hand, was poorly constituted for financing industry. As time went on, however,

Table 1.4
Growth of Cotton Industry in India, 1880-1914

	1880	1890	1900	1914
Factories	85.0	114.0	194.0	264.0
Employees (in 1000's)	39.5	99.2	156.4	260.8
Spindles (in 1000's)	1408.0	2935.0	4942.0	6620.0
Looms (in 1000's)	13.3	22.1	40.5	96.7
Export of yarn (Mill. lbs.)	26.7	170.5	118.0	198.0

SOURCE: W. A. Lewis (ed.), *Tropical Development, 1880-1913* (London: G. Allen & Unwin, 1970), 323.

the disadvantages of the system came to outweigh the advantages. The agents curbed management initiative without themselves taking an active interest in operations. Normal commissions could not be exceeded but could be manipulated in ways that permitted them to paid even during periods of loss. Agency firms speculated in the stock of their companies and profited from sweetheart contracts, among other abuses. A small number of agencies controlled numerous factories. In family concerns management was hereditary and firings were correspondingly difficult. During the interwar period, the system proved too inflexible and management too stodgy to meet Japanese competition effectively. The system doubtless delayed the rise of an entrepreneurial class not tied to trade.

Customs protection was not granted the Indian textile industry. In the early nineteenth century, England had placed almost prohibitive duties on Indian imports. But at the moment the Lancashire manufacturing industry came to depend on the great Indian market, England converted to free trade. It hence regarded mistrustfully the development of Indian spinning and weaving mills. Only machine tool manufacturers offered the latter development some support. In 1869 the Indian government considered duties necessary to combat budget deficits. Led by the Manchester Chamber of Commerce, Lancashire protested and was finally able to block duties higher than 3.5 to 5 percent.[185] In 1882 even this modest duty was removed, again at Lancashire's behest. Viceroy Lord Northbrook resigned largely because of this decision, taken in England's rather than India's interest.[186] When the financial situation again made a general 5 percent duty necessary in 1894—"for revenue purposes only"—Lancashire was again able to get the duty for cotton reduced to 3.5 percent. A 3.5 percent excise was also imposed on Indian goods in order to keep the latter from limiting English export potential. In short, it can be said that Indian textiles rose before 1914 despite British policy rather than because of it.[187]

By the outbreak of World War I, India was the fourth largest producer of cotton goods, a noteworthy accomplishment. But Japanese competition was already tangible, and the export of Indian yarn to China and Japan was declining. Indian mills could indeed meet growing inland thread demand almost completely at England's cost, but their possibilities for expansion were already limited and depended on an increase in domestic demand. In weaving, the Indians concentrated on goods of low or middling quality, so that 52 percent of demand was still imported, mainly from England. Only 9 percent of local production was exported, mainly to East Africa, Ceylon, and the Straits Settlements.

The Indian textile industry enjoyed a boom during the war and the years 1919-1923. The main cause was full utilization of plants and rising prices, and fabulous profits were made.[188] Years of stagnation and increasing difficulties followed, however, mainly because of Japanese competition. The Indian textile industry did, finally, receive customs protection; the rate for cotton was 7.5 percent in 1917 and went to 11 percent in 1921. In 1925 the hated excise was finally lifted. In 1930 the duty for British cotton was raised to 15 percent and for non-British to 20 and in 1931 to 25 and 31.25 percent. For non-British goods, the rate went to 50 percent in 1932 and in June 1933 to a striking 75 percent.[189] When Japan replied with a boycott of Indian raw cotton in 1934, the outcome was the Indo-Japanese trade agreement of July 1934 which resulted in cutting the duty to 50 percent. It was supplemented with quantitative Indian import restrictions and a Japanese commitment to accept a certain amount of Indian cotton.

It has been shown that London attempted to restrain the protective trend of Indian duties in the interest of the hard-pressed English textile industry. The Indian government, however, with its eye on revenues and the Indian nationalist movement, did not give much ground. Great Britain had, indeed, to be granted preference, but this did not hurt India much since the duties were mainly directed at Japan.[190] And the result? Cotton production rose rapidly again in the interwar period,[191] and imports declined both relatively and absolutely.[192] The English were the great losers, dropping from 1,456 million yards in 1928-1929 to 376 million in 1931-1932 and 206 million in 1938-1939.[193] In the 1930s England was, in fact, almost completely forced out of the Indian cotton market, a decisive structural change in Anglo-Indian economic relations.[194] Indian exports also declined, the export of yarn being only a fraction of that of the years before 1914.[195] Still, the high duties had reserved the Indian market for its own industry, an example of import substitution in the colonial area.

Japan was nonetheless able to increase its exports to India despite the high duties and thus proved itself clearly superior to the Indian industry.[196] There were many reasons why. Contemporary arguments mainly emphasized longer Japanese working hours (after 1934 the Indian workday was ten hours), greater employment of women and children, allegedly lower wages, dumping, and yen devaluation.[197] But that was not the whole answer, nor was the Japanese two-shift system. The Japanese had equipped their factories with the most modern machines and had thus saved on labor costs.[198] They bought raw materials and marketed more skillfully than the Indians. We can hardly determine here whether the reason for the foregoing was the agency system, Indian industrial overcapitalization, low worker productivity in India, too close imitation of English models, or particular value systems. But clearly neither insufficient customs protection nor British competition really caused the difficulties of the Indian cotton industry during the interwar period.

Jute

India competed with other countries to supply raw cotton, particularly with the United States which supplied a good portion of both British and Japanese demand. As a producer of jute, or burlap, however, India enjoyed the advantages of monopoly. Bengal produced nearly all the burlap, which was used as packing material for tropical products such as cotton, coffee, sugar, wool, and corn. Burlap production and world trade enjoyed a phenomenal rise in the late nineteenth century, in good part because of falling freight rates. This led to rapid expansion of jute cultivation and helped create the Indian jute industry. Bengal hand weavers had been making bags and burlap from jute since the eighteenth century, and it was already being exported to America by the early nineteenth century. Machine weaving of jute began in 1835 in Dundee, and jute slowly displaced flax and hemp. The Crimean War played a major part in this because it cut off supplies of Russian hemp. The jute industry came to India as early as 1854-1857. In contrast to cotton, however, Britons, mainly Scots, rather than Indians, seized the initiative, furnishing both capital and management. The Indian jute industry remained under European control, although more than half of the outstanding stock was in Indian hands by 1930. Table 1.5 shows the expansion which began in the 1870s. Practically all factories were favorably situated in a concentrated area along the Hooghly River not far from Calcutta.

Table 1.5
Growth of Jute Industry in India, 1885-1939

YEAR	FACTORIES	LOOMS	SPINDLES	EMPLOYEES
1885	24	4,900	70,800	27,500
1895	27	8,200	164,200	62,700
1914	64	36,100	744,000	216,000
1919	...	40,000	840,000	275,000
1932	99	60,000	1,200,000	263,000
1939	107	68,000	1,350,000	295,000

SOURCE: Lewis, *Tropical Development*, 324; Buchanan, *Capitalistic Enterprise*, 244f.; Singh, *Economic History*, 266f.; Bagchi, *Private Investment*, 277.

The Indian jute industry at first merely displaced local hand weavers. By the 1880s, however, it was already competing with Dundee and had conquered the important American market. Exports rose between 1885 and 1895 alone from 64 million burlap bags to 168 million and from 7 million yards of cloth to 14 million. S. B. Saul has pointed out that Indian jute exports to the United States were of great importance to the British balance of payments. They enabled India to pay for its imports from England and thus helped to counter the latter's negative balance with the Continent.[199] During World War I, India was able to supply enormous numbers of sandbags, with enormous profit.[200] An export duty on jute and jute products gave the Indian government a considerable income.[201] Jute constituted some 15 percent of India's exports.

Despite India's de facto jute monopoly, exports very much depended on the state of world trade. In contrast to the textile industry, no import substitution was possible, and in the interwar period new packing materials began to compete with jute. Overcapacity which became visible in the 1880s led in 1884 to the Indian Jute Mills Association. It was not only able in the following years to limit new factory construction, but was also able to restrict production through limitations in working hours and the idling of looms. Accordingly, profits remained high even in crisis years.

The Indian jute industry can be characterized as a colonial enclave industry. With the assistance of foreign investment capital, a local raw material was processed in factories. Exports, which at first leaped upward and then grew slowly, were impressive and constituted an important factor in the trade and payments balances. Jute-growing peasants earned cash, and jute factories and overseas shipment employed hundreds of thousands of Indians. But hours were long, working conditions harsh, the wages and living standards at the very edge of subsistance minimums. Profits of the nonorganized jute producers were low [202] The return on capital went to Europeans, a goodly portion of the profits and wages for European personnel returning to England. Above all, the multiplier effect of the jute industry was, and is, slight, particularly since the factories were equipped from Europe.

Coal, Iron, and Steel

An English tax official received the right to mine coal northwest of Calcutta as early as 1774. The quality of this coal, however, was poor. At the beginning of the nineteenth century the company helped to locate other fields, but little was actually mined: only 91,000 tons in 1846. The transportation problem had first to be solved, in order for Indian coal to compete with the much superior British coal. Lacking railways and factories, demand was also low. The first stretch of the East Indian Railway, however, opened up the coal fields starting in 1854-1855. In the 1870s production began to rise rapidly, reaching a million tons in 1880, six million tons in 1900, and sixteen million tons in 1914. After Japan, India was the greatest coal producer in Asia.[203]

The largest consumer was the railways, after the India government loosened its stores policy sufficiently to permit meeting demand from Indian production. Inland shipping and cotton and jute mills also used Indian coal. Even limited exports, mainly to Ceylon and Malaya, occurred after 1900. The war forced a decline in production, which had the consequence, among others, that exports stagnated and in part declined, while at the same time the Bombay region began to favor Natal coal over Bengalese. Production fell between 1920 and 1926, only to rise to 24 million tons in 1930 and then to decline until 1936 during the depression. Export coal received rail rebates, but the industry did not get customs protection. Investigating commissions criticized organization and management. Indian coal, found mainly in Bengal, Orissa, and Bihar, is of poor quality but is relatively easy to mine. It is not too deep and the seams are good. The transport problem, shipment from Calcutta to western India, remained a handicap, the more so because the Bombay textile industry was beginning to convert to electricity and oil.[204] The coal companies were financed from European capital working from Calcutta, and management was European. Technical equipment, particularly machinery, was inadequate, and worker productivity was low. The latter resulted mainly from disastrously bad wages and working conditions. In the best early Industrial Revolution tradition, women and children were used to move coal underground.[205] While productivity rose in Europe, and even more in Japan, it stagnated in India.[206]

India had, however, not only coal but also iron. The necessities for an iron and steel industry were thus at hand.[207] Indian steel weapons had once been famous, and even in the eighteenth century one of the lower castes produced a certain amount of iron and steel in small smelters. Its quality tempted a company official to erect a modern smelting furnace. The Madras government helped with credits, and the enterprise produced 2,150 tons of pig iron in 1855, but at a loss, and went under in 1874. This was the precise moment when Indian demand for iron rails jumped sharply, and in the years following, they had to be imported. The Bengal Iron Works Company, which had opened an iron mine in Barakar in 1875, was also unsuccessful. The attitude of the administration is particularly interesting. Iron duties were reduced from 10 percent to 1 percent in 1863, and the opening of the Suez Canal cut freight rates. The Bengal Iron Works Company several times requested a 5 percent guarantee on its capital, following the example of the railways. The government turned a deaf ear, despite the Bengal government's energetic support of the request. The company went bankrupt in 1879. The stock was bought up by the government in 1881, however, because the new viceroy, Lord Ripon, was convinced of the advantages of an Indian iron industry. As he detailed them in a resolution to London they were: cheaper material for Indian railways, irrigation, and housing construction, reduction of "home charges," and more jobs. Whether out of principle or under pressure of English manufacturers, London sharply refused, and did so despite the Famine Commission of 1880's emphasis on the need for Indian industry. The Barakar Iron Works came under control of the Bengal Iron and Steel Company in 1889, but the latter was already in financial difficulties by 1894. Its request for a government loan was rejected. The most the government would do was give the firm a contract for delivery of 10,000 tons of pig iron to the state railways. Not until the arrival of Lord Curzon were serious attempts made to assist the Indian iron and steel industry. As early as 1899, he altered the regulations for prospecting in order to provide corporations as well as individuals with future prospecting rights. He invited English capitalists to build iron and steel works and guaranteed the Bengal Iron and Steel Works support in the form of state contracts with, it must be said, little success. Sen points out that Curzon was willing to support Tata's plans at least in part because he wished to block increasing American, Belgian, and German steel exports to India.

J. N. Tata's modern Empress Mills in Nagpur had established him as by all odds the most able Indian entrepreneur. Becoming in time increasingly interested in iron and steel production, he discussed the matter in 1900 with the India Secretary, Lord Hamilton, and got Curzon to agree in 1903 that Indian production, price and quality being equal, should receive preferment. European and American exports discovered ore reserves with an iron content as high as 60 percent. After the death of J. N. Tata in 1904, his sons attempted to raise capital in London in 1905 and 1906, but without much luck, as the British held back because of the already stiff competition in the steel industry.[208] Only then did the Tatas attempt to raise capital in India. Their success was stupefying. Within three weeks £1.6 million had been signed for. In 1907 the Tata Iron and Steel

Company was registered in Bombay. Since attempts to obtain the most up-to-date equipment and technicians from England failed, they turned to Germany. In 1911-1912 production began. The Indian government had stated it was willing to accept 20,000 tons of rails a year.

The First World War provided booming markets. Tata delivered the government 1,500 miles of steel rails and 300,000 tons of additional steel products. After the war, the facilities at Jamshedpur in Bihar were gradually enlarged (70 million dollars had been invested by 1925) and reached an annual capacity of 800,000 tons by 1939. The steelworks was among the largest in the empire.[209] The difficulties were great, all the same. After the postwar boom, world steel prices had fallen drastically in 1921 and 1922 and by 1923 were only 25 percent above those of 1914. Prices generally, however, had risen 60 percent. In 1923-1924, Tata paid no dividends.[210] Following tariff board proposals, the Steel Industry Protection Act of 1924 provided the iron and steel industry considerable tariff protection[211] and subsidies for rails and railroad cars. This assistance was continued in varying form throughout the interwar period, with the British receiving preferential customs treatment.[212] Production costs were reduced considerably, pig iron was exported to Japan and England, and the railways were able to meet needs for rails and cars, though not locomotives, from Indian works. In the 1930s, Tata alone met 65 to 80 percent of Indian steel demand[213] and was able to Indianize almost completely by the outbreak of war.[214]

The Industrialization Controversy

Until very recently, the British have booked India's considerable industrialization as one of the successes of their rule. Indians, on the other hand, whether historians, economists, or politicians, have held since the late nineteenth century that the British hindered or actually blocked genuine large-scale industrialization, or in any case, certainly in no way assisted it. They argue that the colonial economic system, flying the banners of laissez-faire and free trade, subjugated India to the needs of British industries and blocked native development. Independent Japan, on the other hand, through calculating employment of its own resources, made the breakthrough to industrial Great Power status relatively rapidly. It did so despite a paucity of raw materials and a more rapidly growing population than India's. This hostile view is still *communis opinio* of non-Indian historians and economists. Reinforcing such interpretations are concepts such as "lopsided economic growth" and "arrested economic development."[215] Now well established, these concepts imply sectorial economic growth but no breakthrough to self-sustaining industrial growth.

It was in fact true that as late as the interwar period Indian industrialization was confined to a few sectors. Some underwent conspicuous expansion, among them cement (from 954 tons in 1914 to 886,000 in 1935-1936), paper, and sugar. Thanks to a 185 percent increase in duties, sugar production rose 50 percent between 1931 and 1937 and the number of refineries from 32 to 140. From being an importer, India thus became an exporter.[216] But even a British economic historian, Vera Anstey, pointed out in 1936 that cottonseed was not made into oil as in the United States, that it was questionable whether the silk industry could survive foreign competition, that bone meal was exported despite need for artificial fertilizer, and that bicycle and automobile industries remained tasks for the future.[217] There were scarcely any machine tool factories or chemical works in India at the outbreak of the war in 1939. A statistical summary of factory workers for the year 1935 makes the sectorial character of industrialization clear enough.[218]

Why did India industrialize in this limited, sectorially restricted manner during the British period? We can only highlight some of the more important aspects of the problem here. Whether the preconditions existed in late eighteenth-century India for an industrial revolution must remain an open question because it is hypothetical. The question may be answered affirmatively by pointing to the highly developed export trades, the existence of an Indian fleet and shipbuilding industry, the presence of a system of credit, and a class of rich and enterprising business men. Irfan Habib, the foremost expert on Mughal economic and social history, has, however, expressed serious reservations.[219] The argument that the British first provided domestic order, internal unity, and modern administration, has been opposed with arguments from Bipan Chandra, among others, about the possibility of regional industrialization in, say Bengal or the Bombay area.[220] Japan's political and social structure permitted feudal elements imbued with notions that the emperor was the embodiment of the nation to impose industrialization from above during the nineteenth century. Conditions in India, however, differed fundamentally. The thesis that without British rule India might have followed Japan's example seems to me extremely doubtful.

One must nonetheless proceed from the concept, "colonial condition," insofar as England regarded India as a supplementary colonial area whose primary function was to provide world markets with tropical raw materials and foodstuffs and simultaneously to serve as a market for British industrial products. During the nineteenth century, India was gradually integrated into the system of world trade ruled by England. Despite laissez-faire principles, the administration abetted this process very energetically, mainly by building railways and irrigation facilities. British capital flowed toward India in sizeable amounts, primarily for investment in railroads and state loans, and secondarily for plantations, mines, commerce, and banking.[221] Export figures rose sharply, and terms of trade were favorable, in the early twentieth century at least. At the same time the industries already discussed developed. In contrast to today's prevailing view, I regard this "opening up" of India in the form of foreign investment and rising exports of cash crops as a precondition for economic development and industrialization and not as a limiting factor. But caveats are still in order. Both investments and exports were small in relation to the size of the population, so that no encouragement of growth comparable to Canada or Australia occurred. Farming methods and productivity changed but little. Trading profits went largely abroad, as did home charges (see p. 63 below). An Indian economic historian was hence recently able to prove that capital was flowing back to England as early as 1914.[222] India was clearly an industrial power by 1914, but the industry had an enclave character and accordingly limited the multiplier effects in the sense of "backward and forward linkages." The latter were bound to remain small so long as the state was unwilling to assume the role, necessary for a late starter, of promoter and provider of industrial orders with deliberate support for industry including at the very least favorable customs treatment. One need only point to the examples of the British dominions, or, above all Japan, where the state was active in the initial phases or at least made a start easier. The British administration did not provide such assistance because Great Britain had no interest in India's industrialization. That was the real burden of colonial dependency.[223]

It was not a question of London or the government of India deliberately blocking or prohibiting industrialization, as many interpretations and accounts suggest. Even at the time, some important men viewed efforts at industrialization as essential, because the agrarian crisis and the stagnation in the artisan trades called urgently for more jobs. Inklings of such views were expressed by old-school imperialists like Lord Mayo and John Strachey, who in contrast to doctrinaire laissez-faire Liberals, called for state intervention in agriculture, industry, and trade. It must be conceded, however, that their attention was directed toward the expansion of communications and irrigation in the interest of the export trade. In 1880 the Famine Commission expressly noted the need for a manufacturing industry and the lack of technical education. Lord Ripon laid out in detail the necessity and usefulness of an Indian iron industry.[224] Between 1903 and 1905 Lord Curzon encouraged technical education, loosened up the stores policy, supported Tata, and created his own department for commerce and industry. But these were no more than opening sallies, and in 1910 the reformer John Morley turned down a request from the governor of Madras to establish a "permanent Department of Industries," because of "doubts about a policy of trying to create industries by State intervention."[225] That statement was made in the teeth of complaints over the years from Indian nationalists, inside the Congress and out, that Great Britain was blocking or delaying Indian industrialization.[226] Valentine Chirol of the London *Times* clearly recognized by 1910 that this point of friction between India and England would become increasingly important and would yet give London plenty to worry about.[227]

The Indian administration's need for industrial products was filled by England, and the provisions of the stores policy were loosened only gradually, even for railways.[228] The coal, paper, and steel industries profited from government orders, but the dreary history of steel shows how modest this help was and how late it came. It also shows that an iron-processing industry could have been built up significantly earlier if the state had reduced the risks for new enterprises with orders and other pump-priming assistance. Railway construction therefore had had little multiplier effect, in contrast to the United States and Western Europe, even for the manufacture of rails and cars. And instead of pushing energetically ahead with the construction of locomotives in India, they were ordered from London and expressly exempted from subsidy provisions. The necessary conditions for an Indian locomotive industry obviously existed, and locomotives were indeed built in India. After the turn of the century, however, London did, in response to American and German competition, force the construction of a so-called standard locomotive designed for Indian conditions and got India to buy it; some English factories delivered 30 to 40 percent of their output to India. Even during the interwar period, the state made no concerted effort to support locomotive construction in India.[229]

The same was true of shipping and shipbuilding. The fact that India built excellent ships as late as the eighteenth century hardly proves in and of itself that an independent India would have successfully made the transition to building steam-driven iron ships, as some Indian historians suggest. There is no doubt, however, that England was able to monopolize both overseas trade and shipping as well. British firms did the carrying to the home country. Under such conditions, an Indian shipbuilding industry with its multiplier effects was impossible, particularly since in the face of British competition state assistance such as Japanese shipbuilders received would have been required. The alternative was arms orders, which gave industrialization a decisive push in France, Italy, and Japan; but such orders went to England.

Customs protection was not granted until 1914. England held fast to free trade and, in contrast to the dominions, did not concede India tariff sovereignty. The value of duties in the industrialization process can easily be overestimated, and protected, higher-cost producers create problems of their own. The conclusion is unavoidable that, fine-sounding phrases to the contrary, the interests of the rulers were preferred over those of the ruled. Indian economists could, and still can, justifiably point to the protectionist measures of France and Germany and even more so to those of the United States, Japan, and the dominions, all of which granted their infant industries development protection against British competition. They thus made it considerably easier to create a capital and consumer goods industry. Protection of infant industries was also an important factor in foreign and domestic capitalists' decisions about whether or not to invest in new industries.

It is thus hardly an accident that during the First World War, which interrupted European deliveries and thus encouraged state orders, Indian industry leaped ahead. Existing factories increased their output and factories for new products were built. After 1919, however, most of the latter proved unable to withstand import competition without customs protection and went under.

But the war did bring about a change in British policy. Appointed in 1916, the Industrial Commission presented its extensive and important report in 1918. It set down in critical detail the modest industrialization of India before 1914 and called for an "energetic interventation in industrial affairs."[230] After the war, state readiness to intervene faded rapidly away, to be sure, and neither the institutional nor the financial means were provided to realize the Industrial Commission's program.[231] In October 1921 the Indian government convened a fiscal commission, which in July of the following year accepted in principle "discriminating protection." They noted: "We found a general conviction that the interests of the country require a policy of protection."[232] London sanctioned customs autonomy for India in 1923. A tariff commission was to examine industry demands and make proposals to the government. Protection, however, was only to be granted industry which had natural advantages, would not otherwise develop or would develop too slowly, and had prospects for being competitive in the future without tariff protection. Cotton, steel, paper, and matches received protection in the 1920s. It enabled them to survive and expand noticeably. Some proposals were, however, refused. The commission worked slowly, and new industries, in particular, could hardly reckon with protection. One can hardly speak of an energetic policy of industrialization. By 1925 the average level of duties exceeded that of 1913 by 350 percent, but was still low and lay, for example, well under Australian levels.[233] Not until the depression, when state income from taxes and duties fell sharply, were duties really boosted. That had the paradoxical effect of creating a new Indian industrial boom in the 1930s, especially in sugar.

Industry ministries were created both at the center and in the provinces. In the latter they were "transferred subjects" under Indian ministers. Industries were supposed to be assisted by subsidies and interest guarantees, among other things. But the provinces had too little money. The Indian government, moreover, tried to maintain a balanced budget. The share of state expenditures in national income remained a low 8 to 9 percent, while in other industrial countries, Japan among them, it rose sharply.[234] Because the budget mostly went for administrative costs, debt service, and the armed forces, only minimal sums remained for industry and agriculture.[235] Nor did government spending provide industrial support in any general sense during the interwar period, because after 1935 the government made no additional loans and began to repay older ones.[236]

Was an adequate market at hand? Although the extremely low per-capita income of most colonies and present-day developing countries has made industrialization more difficult or prevented it altogether, such was only true in a limited sense for India because its large population still offered worthwhile marketing opportunities.[237] These opportunities provided the basis for expansion in cotton and sugar and for other consumer goods, as for example, bicycles. A market for certain capital goods, such as machinery for the cotton and jute industries, might also have existed if starting up had been easier. In other areas, however, market opportunities were doubtless too few even in India, particularly when one balances the presence of cheap labor against the lack of skilled personnel and the need to hire expensive European technicians.

The slow progress of industrialization and its sectorial character are probably not attributable to lack of capital. Both Indian and British capital was available. The Indian landowning class, from the princes on down, either invested their profits in land or spent it on a lordly existence. Agricultural rents remained largely tax free. No attempt was ever made, however, to sop up this income by means of taxes in order to provide the state with revenues it could expend productively. The tradition of hoarding was still strong, indeed, but the unwillingness of Indian capitalists to invest has been overemphasized.[238] The cotton industry, the sale of Tata paper before 1914, the investment in the sugar refineries in the 1930s, and the fact that in the interwar period 50 to 70 percent of the capital in the jute industry came into Indian hands, all prove the contrary. Whether Indian mercantile capital was ready to engage in industrial enterprises manifestly depended to a great degree on the risk and the profits. The risks necessarily appeared too great and the chance of profits too insecure so long as the state did not provide a hand to assist new industrial enterprises during their early years. But it was also no accident that, as mercantile profits decreased during the depression, willingness to invest in industry grew.

It is also asserted sometimes that British or Anglo-Indian capital was disinclined to invest in industries that competed with those of the mother country. But this presupposes a solidarity of interest among English capitalists that in practice never existed. This thesis may have some applicability to the cotton industry, but as the jute industry and the rather unsuccessful efforts to establish an iron industry prove, it does not in general hold good. British mercantile firms had, indeed, very little interest in industry, whether because of tradition, estimates of their own advantage, or their not uncommon ties to industry. But the main obstacle was that British banking was not organized to mobilize British or Indian capital and funnel it into the industrial sector. A dual capital market characteristic of India's colonial condition had arisen, an Indian market resting mainly on the landlords and moneylenders, and a British market oriented from the beginning largely toward trade and finance transactions and restricting itself to short-term credits. In the best conservative fashion, established firms were to be favored, and it was doubtless more difficult for Indians to get credit than Europeans. India received a national banking system only in 1934-1935.

The question of whether an Indian entrepreneurial class existed is disputed.[239] There is little argument that the Hindu upper class, with its heavy percentage of Brahmins, preferred to remain landowners or move into the professions, especially law. The same is true of the Muslim upper class. Indian historians, however, note that British land policy, and the Permanent Settlement in Bengal above all, provoked the transfer of mercantile capital into agriculture and thus indirectly deprived new enterprises of it. The British monopoly on trade with England, combined with British control of shipping, led to a mid-nineteenth-century crisis in the rich, enterprising mercantile bourgeoisie of Bengal and blocked their development as an entrepreneurial class.[240] British-Indian firms were favored in the awarding of state contracts, and, except in Bombay, Indians were badly represented in the chambers of commerce. This led to European firms enjoying de facto local monopolies.

The culpable neglect of technical education in British-Indian education also encouraged the traditional tendency to favor the literary professions, as did the bias against Indians in the technical civil service departments. British firms also engaged in bald-faced discrimination. Few Indians reached leading positions before India's independence. Thus, opportunities for learning in this important area scarcely existed, because they were assumed by the colonial power. The fact that very few Indians sat on the boards of the state banks even in the interwar period confirms the foregoing and doubtless also influenced the credit and finance policies of the banks themselves.[241] The Indian cotton industry, on the other hand, shows that a potential entrepreneurial class was at hand as early as 1850. This class was mainly recruited from the Parsis and trading castes of the Gujurat and Marwaris (Birla). The regional and caste basis of recruitment seems to have broadened only during the 1930s. The management of the Bombay cotton industry, which clearly fell behind the Japanese during the interwar period, does, indeed, raise some doubts about the ability of this entrepreneurial class.

THE "DRAIN OF WEALTH" THESIS

In the early days of the East India Company, the export of Indian textiles and spices to England was balanced by a flow of noble metal toward India. This, in a mercantilist age, was regarded as unacceptable, and there was talk of a drain of wealth toward India. When the tax administration of Bengal was taken over, the picture changed. The company was able to buy its trading goods with tax revenues; or, as has been said, the Indian taxpayer paid for his own exports to Europe. In the first half of the nineteenth century, British exports of cotton goods commenced, but at the same time Indian exports also rose, particularly of grain, cotton, indigo, opium, and, later, of jute, oil seed, and tea. Until World War II the growing Indian foreign trade showed, a few years excepted, a clear surplus.[242] Its foreign trade had a rather colonial look, in that raw materials, foodstuffs, jute products, and an increasing amount of cotton cloth were exported, and finished goods such as cloth, machinery, and consumer goods to meet increasing demand were imported. The balance with Britain, however, was strikingly unfavorable before 1914, although the balance with continental Europe, the United States, and Japan was favorable.[243] In terms of the international economy, this meant England could rectify its otherwise unfavorable trade balance through exports to India.[244] During the interwar period, or, more precisely, during the depression, the situation changed fundamentally as table 1.6 shows.[245]

Table 1.6
Value of Total Indian Foreign Trade, 1914-1937 (in millions of rupees)

	1914	1929	1932	1936	1937
Exports	2442.0	3301.3	1558.9	1605.2	1961.3
Imports	1832.5	2533.1	1263.7	1343.7	1252.2
Exports to Gt. Brit.	573.6	690.4	428.8	504.8	610.6
Imports from Gt. Brit.	1175.8	1132.4	448.1	521.9	480.9

Source: *Economist*, 30 October 1937.

It can be seen that India always had a favorable balance, but that the relationship with England assumed a new cast. As a result of the drastic decline in British exports to India, principally of cotton goods (see p. 52), the English share of Indian imports dropped from 64.2 percent in 1914 to 44.7 percent in 1929 and 35.5 percent in 1932, to rise slightly by 1937 to 38.5 percent as a result of preferential duties. In 1914, 23.8 percent of Indian exports went to England, as late as 1929 as much as 20.9 percent, and much more in 1937, 31.1 percent. The Ottawa System was much criticized, but seems to have helped India, since Great Britain took more raw cotton and began buying pig iron.[246] The balance of payments with England became favorable after 1937, which meant Anglo-Indian relations possessed "a greater degree of bilateral equilibrium."[247] A survey of India's most important trading partners makes this apparent (see table 1.7).

India built up its foreign trade organization during the 1930s. This permitted Indian trading houses to intervene more actively in foreign trade.[248] It was also symptomatic that in 1935 the *Economist* called upon British industry to sharpen up their buying organizations in India and look upon the Indians more than heretofore as partners.[249]

Did the favorable balance of trade profit India? Indian economists have long denied it, ever since Dadabhai Naoroji's *Poverty of India* of 1876 and Dutt's formulation of his economic drain thesis.[250] Indian foreign trade, they argued, showed a typical colonial pattern, with imports presenting a mirror image of the devastated Indian artisan trades, and the export profits from, say, tea or indigo, going mainly to British plantation owners. The balance of payments was unfavorable despite the favorable balance of trade because of the great sums that India had annually to send to England.

The sums were the so-called home charges, which grew from about £ 5 million in 1860 to about £ 29 million in 1934.[251] In 1913, they broke down as follows:[252]

HOME CHARGES	MILLION £
Interest on railway and irrigation debt	9.2
Interest on general debt	2.1
Military expenditures	4.4
Pensions of retired civil servants	2.1
Purchases on commodities	1.6
Leave pay of civil servants	0.5
Miscellaneous	0.2
	20.1

There was, so runs the thesis, no comparable payment in goods or services to balance these charges. They therefore constitute a drain of wealth, which, measured by decades, came to an enormous amount and must thus be held responsible for the growing Indian poverty or at least the lack of economic growth.

Table 1.7
Indian Balance of Trade (in crores of rupees)

	1913-1914	1938-1939
England	−59	+12
Other parts of the empire	+25	−10
Europe	+55	+ 3
USA	+17	+ 4
Japan	+18	0

SOURCE: Singh, *Economic History*, 448, 460.

Neither Naoroji nor Dutt deny that British investment in India and interest payments are correspondingly taken into account; but their importance is minimized by pointing out that the resulting orders went to England, that the railroads were relatively expensive, and that their routing served British ends. The British are also reproached for not having tried to raise capital in India. Military expenditures came in for even sharper criticism, all the more because they not only made up a large share of the home charges but also weighed heavily on the Indian budget, some 20 to 27 percent of the total, or 250 to 300 million rupees, even in 1900.[253] India did in fact pay for the army, which in 1914 comprised 157,000 Indians and an additional 80,000 Britons. Savings, officer pensions, and materiel costs flowed back to England. Although it is conceded that an independent India would also have had to pay for defense, it is argued that the moneys spent would for the most part have remained at home. A source of especial irritation was that, whereas London justified the army in the budget as necessary to defend the country, it was in practice used to defend the empire and, indeed, for imperial expansion, to the degree that Indian troops were employed outside India. The demand that London assume at least a part of the costs of the Indian army came not only from Indian nationalists but also British officials in India, Lord Curzon among them, without much effect.

Another gravamen was payments to pensioned officials. The Indians criticized the high cost of the British administration and insufficient Indianization, while the British naturally emphasized that the exceptional qualities of the cadre richly earned these payments. In addition to the home charges, interest on private investments and the earnings of British and other European firms and plantations, only partially reinvested, were thrown into the indictment, as were also services such as marine freight and insurance, which the metropolis monopolized.[254]

The discussions of the drain-of-wealth thesis continue, and some Indian historians have expressed reservations about it.[255] The value of the thesis is that it highlights the shortcomings of judgments based only on foreign trade figures and export surpluses: a drain of wealth engendered by India's dependency without doubt occurred. Despite all reservations about single-cause explanations, the fact remains that at least as late as World War I India was delivered over, defenseless, as an economically complementary area to England's superior economic might. Nor could the state play the role it did in Europe, Japan, and the dominions with orders and in some cases with state enterprises, subsidies, credit systems, and customs protection. The very Indian shortcomings the British so often point out, the lack of Indian initiative, the limited buying power of the masses, and the rigidity of the religious and social structure, made state intervention and support especially significant. Wilfred Malenbaum also points out an important psychological factor.[256] The state, meaning the British administration, was the embodiment of the ruling power and was, in the last analysis, oriented toward the homeland. It did not radiate the atmosphere of trust in the future that is to be seen elsewhere during the initial phase of industrialization. This was particularly necessary in India if new energies were to be unleashed and the restraints of a traditional society slackened, and especially since the basic social alterations and modernization processes were initiated by a foreign power rather than by the Indians themselves. Industrialization would have gotten under way more quickly and would have amounted to more by 1914 than is admitted by today's typical assessment. Comparisons with the United States, the dominions, and Japan, useful though they are, lead easily to mistaken judgments because special conditions in these countries—and India—are not sufficiently taken into account. The specifically regional and sectorial character of Indian industrialization and the lopsided development resulting from British economic policy in India are also clear enough. Lacking state assistance, the economy missed the opportunities of the key years, the nineteenth and early twentieth centuries: the transition from a "leading sectors" economy to one broadly diversified and capable of "self-sustaining growth" never occurred. The interwar period, during which some deficiencies were remedied, was not only too short but also unsuited for achieving the decisive breakthrough. The world economy stagnated in the depression, British capital did not flow in to the same degree, some indeed being repatriated, Japan entered the arena as a competing power, and the population explosion began.

THE WORK FORCE, WORKING CONDITIONS, AND THE TRADE UNION MOVEMENT

The agrarian hinterland provided the work force for the industrial centers. We know relatively little, however, about the social origins or the caste membership of those who permanently or temporarily shifted into industry.[257] They were for the most part peasants with little or no land and were hence members of the village underclass and of the lower castes. Despite oft-expressed opinions, however, the untouchables constituted an astonishingly small percentage, at least in the Bombay and Jamshedpur cotton industry. That was especially true in the beginning, and untouchables got the meanest and most badly paid work. Hindus and Muslims saved the weaving jobs for themselves.[258] There are other surprises. A good part of the mine workers came from a particular caste, and in 1911 almost half the workers in Bombay came from a narrowly restricted district south of the city.[259]

All reports agree that contact with the village remained unbroken, either because the workers returned home for the sowing season or the harvest, or because they worked in factories for a few years only, or because they sent remittances back home. Only a small portion of the workers was actually born in the city itself, and because of the temporary character of industrial employment, there were more men than women.[260] These ties to the village explain the high turnover and the frequent absences from work, and both have been held responsible for the comparative inefficiency of the Indian work force, particularly in comparison with the Japanese in the cotton industry. Morris has indeed somewhat revised this accepted interpretation by showing that in the year 1927/28, to pick one example, more than 60 percent of the work force had been employed in industry five years or longer and that absenteeism was down to around 10 percent. In interpreting the latter figure, one must take account of the fact that workers changed jobs freely and absence was often due to sickness.[261] Morris also questions the lack of labor emphasized by the Royal Commission on Labour of 1931.[262] Here one ought to point out, however, that what the reports were mostly talking about was lack of *skilled* labor, meaning that employers were continually taking on new hands as yet unaccustomed to factory work.

The recruiting or employment of the worker, his training and factory discipline were all handled by jobbers, who, like the Managing Agency System, represent one of the singularities of Indian industrial organization.[263] Originally English-speaking Marathas, jobbers linked English technicians with Indian workers. They came during the British period to hold key positions in Indian factories and mines. The jobber was a sort of straw boss without further possibilities for advancement, separate from management, but armed with great power because he largely controlled hiring, firing, and promotion. Rather dubious opportunities for enrichment were thus created at the very outset. The jobber had to be bribed or bought with personal service. He favored members of his own village and caste and often profited from rapid turnover. Some accordingly tied the inefficiency of Indian enterprise to the jobber system. Criticism began early, but the system offered the employer some significant advantages and thus remained in being.[264]

On the Assamese tea plantations, the contract system resulted in slaverylike conditions. Otherwise, working conditions and wages in factories and mines can be compared with those of Europe in the early days of industrialization: twelve- to fifteen-hour days, women and children working underground in the mines (as late as the interwar period), wholly insufficient ventilation and sanitary facilities, unregulated breaks for meals, and the lot.[265] A series of factory laws (1881, 1891, and 1911), passed in no small part under pressure from Lancashire (which sought to reduce the competition from cheaper Indian labor) and against the opposition of employer groups and the administration, undertook first to regulate female and child labor. As late as 1932, however, the cotton industry worked a sixty-hour week. Small enterprises also remained unregulated. The Workmen's Compensation Act of 1923 insured the worker against industrial accidents. The Trades Disputes Conciliation Act of 1934 provided a labor office to assist in the settlement of work disputes. With these measures India began to approach the worker legislation of the industrialized countries. The British also pointed out that Japan's failure to adopt such measures was a prime reason why it could compete against India so effectively.

According to A. K. Bagchi, wages in the textiles industry increased after 1900, even during the war years, but living conditions for workers streaming from the villages into the worker ghettos and slums of the great cities remained appalling.[266] Chronic undernourishment, indebtedness, sickness, and wholly insufficient sanitary facilities in worker barracks were indeed detailed in numerous reports.[267]

Union organization of workers began late, even though there had been numerous strikes as early as the late nineteenth century.[268] The First World War, with its price increases, political unrest, and Gandhi's nationalist awakening of the masses, ushered in a veritable wave of strikes between 1914 and 1920 and led to the first All-India Trade Union Congress, attended by Annie Besant, Motilal Nehru, and Mohammed Ali Jinnah, among others.[269] The Trade Union Bill of 1926 legalized unions, but the movement afterwards split into moderate and extreme wings. It thereafter played only a secondary role alongside, or within, the Congress party during the interwar period, numerous strikes notwithstanding.

INDIAN NATIONALISM AND THE STAGES OF POLITICAL EMANCIPATION: UNTIL 1914

Indian nationalism can be defined as a superregional movement which worked within the administrative limits set by the colonial power and which sought to acquire, sooner or later, sovereign power and administrative jurisdiction. Such a movement was hardly visible before the last years of the nineteenth century. For even a sketchy outline of the social and intellectual forces involved, however, one must turn to the early years of the century. The system of colonial rule must also be kept in mind. It set the parameters of the liberation movement, at once making it possible and setting fetters upon it. Once established, it forced the British to react to the demands of the ruled, whether by concessions and reforms or through repression.

The East India Company's takeover of Mughal administration and the dissolution of the company have already been outlined, as has British land policy and the colonial economic system. Together, they resulted partly in the displacing of much of the traditional ruling class and partly in the incorporation of it into the colonial system, creating for it new positions of power and economic opportunity. The company, and later the Indian government, required an ever-larger administrative cadre, particularly in the lower and middle levels of tax and justice administration. Permanent Settlement, individual property rights, and English law created a landlord class that in part was new. It invested in neither agriculture nor industry and favored the professions, particularly law and the civil service. Rapidly rising foreign trade, combined with railways and a money economy, also opened new opportunities for Indian businessmen. But one had to be willing to accept Western education and training. The British educational system anchored British rule, while simultaneously permitting the rise of a modern elite. This elite, carrying on a dialogue with its own society and civilization on the one hand and with the colonial power on the other, became the mainstay of the liberation movement.[270] A look at the educational system is therefore in order.

In his famous "Minute on Education" of 1835, Macaulay provided both justification and guidance for creating a Western-oriented educational system: the English language alone provided access to the modern world; it would permit the rise of an Indian educated class which would give allegiance to England and could assume administrative posts; and this class would in addition—as others noted—take up English habits of consumption and thereby support the marketing of English goods.[271] Financial considerations made it seem prudent to begin with the upper and middle classes of the cities, in the hope that in the course of time their new learning would filter down to the masses. In 1854, to be sure, the India secretary, Sir Charles Wood, tacitly accepted in his "Educational Dispatch" state responsibility for the education of the masses by providing grants-in-aid to mission and other schools. But he also founded three universities in 1857 and introduced a policy of laissez-faire, appealing to the initiative of the Indians by offering the prospect of subsidies for such colleges as they might found. The number of the latter rose rapidly in the years following, from 55 in the year 1873 to 156 in 1893, and testified to the great interest of the Indian upper class in Western education.[272] Problems appeared early, however. The colleges were concentrated in the port cities, Calcutta and Bombay in particular, and the Brahmins and mercantile castes proved best able to exploit the new opportunities. Whether because they as officials, landlords, and members of the intellectual professions could afford to send their sons to schools, or whether because they had an especial interest in higher education and the intellectual professions, they did at any rate maintain or reestablish their social positions by means of the colleges.[273] Their quality left much to be desired. The failure rate was unusually high, a source of frustration that could lead to anti-British attitudes. Primary and secondary education, or in other words, the education of the masses, was neglected,[274] as was training in the natural sciences and engineering. In a manner typical of colonial situations, it was argued on the one hand that too few places for scientists and engineers existed and there hence was the risk of unemployed intellectuals,[275] while on the other hand the dilatory Indianization was justified on the grounds of lack of trained personnel. In 1904 Lord Curzon tried to dam this flow of the half-educated with his Indian Universities Act, which placed the colleges under stricter control (see below, p. 77). He provided the provinces with more money for elementary schools and encouraged technical education. The act also assisted in the foundation of the Institute of Science in Bangalore.

The number of elementary students rose considerably in the years following, reaching 5,188,411 in 1917.[276] The Congress party did not become interested in elementary education until the twentieth century and came around to compulsory free education only by stages. The administration also went at the matter in fits and starts, the necessary laws being passed only after World War I. Funds were increased, but remained insufficient. Teacher education was inadequate, and attendance was poor in rural areas. Much of what was learned was soon forgotten. In 1931, 92 percent of the populace remained illiterate.

The basic structure of Indian education changed but little during the British period and not much for several years thereafter. Emphasis was on higher education, and the emphasis there was too heavily on "literary" knowledge, superficial memorization directed toward the examinations. Scientific and technical education was neglected, either because the administration did not push it much or because the Indians themselves were not much interested in it because of Brahmin traditions.[277] The gulf between the urban, educated class and the peasantry was never bridged, in contrast to Japan, where the state pushed energetically ahead with primary education as an important part of its effort to modernize. The Indian educational system is rather to be compared with that of the Latin-American countries, insofar as it met the social needs of a middle and upper class whose aspirations were directed to the professions, the civil service, and commerce. Like their Latin-American counterparts, they displayed little initiative as entrepreneurs and had no interest in drawing the village population into the modernization process. Indian education also reflected an acculturation problem. The danger existed that in adopting a Western European educational system only Western knowledge, but not the cultural and intellectual bases upon which it rested, would be passed on.

The confrontation with the West was also the beginning of a religious and social reform movement in Hindu society in the early nineteenth century. This movement had connections with the liberation movement and decisively stimulated it. Here, the most important man was the imposing personality, Ram Mohan Roy (1772-1833). Master of numerous languages, he sought truth in the study of Hinduism, Buddhism, Islam, and Christianity. He was by profession an official and was also one of the pioneers of Indian journalism. He was one of the founders of the Hindu College in Calcutta in 1816 and in 1828 founded the Brahmo-Samaj movement. Recourse to the Hindu scriptures and religious-social tradition was linked to Western values. This was the basis for his criticism of specific Hindu dogmas and institutions such as the burning of widows, polygamy, and the more extreme forms of caste exclusiveness. His views explain his interest in Western schools. This "modernist" point of departure, which was analagous with Protestantism in many ways, also characterized other movements. Criticism of ossified Hindu culture was sometimes extraordinarily sharp, accompanied by regionally flavored invective against Brahmin ascendency, whereas the Western intellectual tradition and even British rule were greeted effusively as the hammer by which the encrustations on Indian civilization were to be shattered and the obstacles blocking a return to the sources were to be levelled.[278] All this opened up the possibility of a new consciousness of an Indian or humanitarian mission, either religious and missionary like that of Vivekananda and his Ramkrishna Mission, or national and aimed at political renewal and the end of British rule. Tradition and reason, family and caste membership, and individualism, stood in tension with one another and could lead to conflicts both internal and with one's familiars.[279] But these conflicts released energies discharged in struggles against the colonial power.

The founding of the Congress party in 1885 was preceded by a phase of "voluntary associations." The latter were free associations with very divergent aims.[280] The new elite, mostly graduates of "Western" colleges, came either, to use Rothermund's expression, from the "dominant minorities," such as the Bhadraloks of Bengal. The latter were well-to-do Brahmins, often landowners, who had assumed a colonial English life-style.[281] Or they were the "exposed minorities" such as the Parsis and the Chitpavan Brahmins from Maharashtra recruited to work in Bombay. They had multifarious ties to the religious reform movements and found themselves outside the traditional caste and professional associations. These groups all banded together, at first on the local level, to secure their interests and discuss the problems and concerns of their society. As evidence, a single quotation from the autobiography of the noted Dadabhai Naoroji, a Parsi and then student leader at Elphinstone College, must suffice.

> The six or seven years before I eventually came to England in 1855... were full of all sorts of reforms, social, educational, political, religious, etc.... Female Education, Free Association of Women with Men at public, social and other gatherings, Infant Schools, Students' Literary and Scientific Society, Societies for the diffusion of Useful Knowledge in the Vernacular, Parsi Reform, Abolition of Child Marriages, Re-marriage of Widows among Hindus, and Parsi Religious Reform Society, were some of the problems tackled, movements set on foot, and institutions inaugurated by a band of young men fresh from College.... Such were the first fruits of the English education given at Elphinstone College.[282]

The liberating effect of the Western educational system is manifest here and its attraction clear. It is also understandable, however, that political action soon followed, even if at first it only amounted to articulating demands within the context of the ruling system. In October 1851 the British Indian Association was founded in Calcutta, in order to petition Parliament on the occasion of the renewal of the East India Company charter. Its members were mostly from the Landowners' Society, which represented the interests of the Bengal zamindars as a sort of pressure group. Representatives from trade and the ever-more-important lawyer class also came in. Their spokesman was the *Hindoo Patriot*. Members of the association were appointed to the Viceregal Council and Bengal legislature. Followers of Roy such as Romesh Chandra Dutt and the Tagores, landowners, and wealthy merchants were members. Annual dues were high. The association, more than a simple pressure group of the Calcutta Bhadralok families, had to compete after 1876 with Surendranath Banerjea's India Association. The latter aimed mainly at the middle classes (some of whom were also Bhadraloks) and the dynamic younger generation. It succeeded in appealing to lawyers, journalists, teachers, and students and soon began to found affiliated groups outside the capital. It was in keeping with the interests and social origins of its members for it to agitate initially against the entrance provisions of the ICS and next for the expansion of local government. In order to counter the charge of British officials that the new intellectual elite sought to further its interests alone and was indifferent to the peasant masses, the association sought to acquire a populist hue and intervened energetically in behalf of the Bengal Tenancy Act. That, in turn, led to a break with the British Indian Association. Organizations of a similar sort also arose in western and southern India, as for example, the Sarvjanik Sabha of Poona founded in 1870, the leading figure of which was the Chitpavan Brahmin, M. G. Ranade, or the Bombay Presidency Association of 1885 under Parsi presidency.[283]

The communications between the associations founded in the three presidencies long remained poor, however much one attempted to set a nonregional, national tone with the word "Indian." Even the leading men hardly knew each other. The most pan-Indian of all the groups was the London Indian Association, because to influence Parliament and the English public the value of speaking with one voice was apparent. The group having the most all-India impact in the 1870s was the Brahmo Samaj and after 1879, the Theosophical Society, which settled in India and had a considerable following among the new elite. It should be noted, however, that the north was largely untouched by this early politicization.

The British government itself did much to shake the trust that a Liberal England would grant India justice and gradually lead it down the path to self-government. British acts led to protests in reaction, and these came to be increasingly national in scope. The activities of the viceroy, Lord Lytton, a Conservative who sought support from members of the old Indian aristocracy as the natural leaders of the country, provided occasion enough for protest. Indians were used to achieve imperial expansion during the Afghan War. The Vernacular Press Act of 1878 placed the Indian press under supervision. Reducing the maximum age for the ICS entrance examination was for the Western-educated elite a provocative act, and Bombay businessmen were estranged by the removal of the 5 percent duty on cotton stuffs.

The electoral victory of Gladstone and the appointment of Lord Ripon as viceroy thus raised expectations that could only partially be met. In the existing situation, in which the new educated elite could not be denied much longer, Ripon considered England had two alternatives, which he expressed in arresting terms:

There are two policies lying before the choice of the Government of India; the one is the policy of those who have established a free press, who have promoted education, who have admitted natives more and more largely to the public service in various forms, and who have favoured the extension of self-government; the other is that of those who hate the freedom of the press, who dread the progress of education, and who watch with jealousy and alarm everything which tends, in however limited a degree, to give the natives of India a larger share in the management of their own affairs. Between these two policies we must choose; the one means progress, the other means repression. Lord Lytton chose the latter. I have chosen the former.[284]

Ripon was not only ready to liberalize entrance to the ICS but to provide Indians with freer access to the various councils with the aim of granting a sort of political codetermination. London nonetheless refused a proposed increase in the number of elected, as opposed to appointed, legislative council members. The attempt was also made in 1882 to meet Indian demands at least in the area of local government by providing that a majority of city and district councilors be elected from Indians who were not civil servants. This measure encountered administrative opposition and came to nothing, although even Ripon's finance minister, Evelyn Baring (later Lord Cromer), favored the reforms as a "safety valve."[285] Discussions of the Ilbert bill (see p. 18) raised a storm of indignation and in no small measure created a national consciousness that transcended both region and caste. When Ripon departed from India in 1884, he was demonstratively celebrated as a friend of India.[286]

By then, plans for a national conference were being bruited about. The idea was to transcend regional differences and bring the associations together to agitate at the national level. In December 1885 the national Congress met. A. O. Hume, a liberal but headstrong British official who had quit the service in 1879, contributed largely to its success. Even Lord Dufferin, the new viceroy, gave the Congress his consent.[287] Seventy-two delegates, among them thirty-nine lawyers, one doctor, and nineteen journalists, represented the local associations.

The more important spokesmen for the Muslims, however, refused to collaborate. The reasons were complex. The collapse of the Mughal Empire was particularly hard on the Muslims. The Hindus could regard the establishment of the British in Bengal as being in a sense merely the replacement of the old foreign rule by a new, which made it easier for them to accept positions under the British. For the Muslims, however, it signified the end of their power and endangered their privileged positions in the army and administration. The administrative reforms of Cornwallis displaced them as tax collectors, and the Permanent Settlement ruined a goodly portion of the Muslim landowners. In the later nineteenth century, even in the Bengal districts where Muslims were a majority, the greater portion of the land belonged to Hindus, and the Hindu upper castes had always dominated commerce.[288] The substitution of English for Persian as the official language mainly affected the Muslims, making their traditional school and educational system obsolete. A reorientation toward the new Western education and the English language was hard to accept because, more than was true of the Hindus, it appeared to endanger the religious and social community. Loss of capital and income, on the other hand, made it difficult for the Bengal Muslims to found their own schools or send their sons to Indian colleges, to say nothing of England. The more necessary command of English and the passage of specific examinations became to obtain official posts, the more Muslims were forced out of them. In Bengal in 1872, of the 772 Indians in the higher administrative posts, only 92 were Muslims, despite a 2 to 1 Muslim majority in the general population.[289] As late as 1851 there had been more Muslim attorneys in Calcutta than Hindus or Christians, but between 1852 and 1868 not a single Muslim was licensed to practice before the city's high court.

In the northwest provinces and Oudh, Muslims were better able to assert themselves both as landowners and city notables, especially as lawyers, despite the understandable mistrust the British had shown them since the mutiny. Although a minority, 13 percent, the Muslims as late as the 1880s held 45 percent of the uncovenanted executive and judicial posts. But Hindu competition was increasing.[290] Compared with Bengal, the Western school system was far less complete. The Muslims were, however, educationally in no way inferior to the Hindus. One thus cannot speak of general Muslim backwardness.

In both regions, the Muslims nonetheless saw themselves threatened by the new Hindu intellegentsia and had reason to fear being placed in a hopeless minority position if the Hindus succeeded with their demands for Indianization of the administration and elected representatives to the councils. The Muslim zamindars accordingly joined with the Hindus in the British Indian Association to represent their interests, but refused to collaborate when Banerjea tried to enlist them for his campaign to reform the ICS examinations by holding them in India as well as England. Resistance grew as the question of reform of the legislative council and local government became acute under Ripon, because the proposed census-based electoral law promised to work severe hardship on the Muslims. As early as 1882 Muslim spokesmen in the Bengal legislative council were demanding separate, meaning reserved, seats for Muslims.[291] The National Mohammedan Association, founded earlier, in 1878, attempted to add some weight to this demand and in 1884 called for annual conferences representing all Indian Muslims. The leader of the Muslims was from the north, Sayyid Ahmad Khan (1817-1898). Born into a Delhi court family, Khan had entered company service in 1838. He remained loyal to England during the mutiny and had made his career as a lower-court judge. Confronted with the increasing competition of both local Hindus and the Bengalis who had come north, Khan initiated an Indian Islamic reform movement. In a manner analogous to Roy's, he turned to the Koran and emphasized Islam's rational and progressive elements and, in the face of the hostility of the orthodox ulema, pointed out the need to accept Western education and Western knowledge. Together, they would bring about a rebirth of Indian Islam and assure Indian Muslims an esteemed place in society. The education and modernization process would, however, take time. In 1875, he founded the Anglo-Oriental College in Aligarh. In the meantime, he stated, the colonial power had to be persuaded that Muslims were loyal subjects of the Crown, that the mistrust which the administration had shown since the mutiny was unjustified, and that the ruling power had the duty of maintaining order between the two great religious communities. Herein Khan clearly succeeded. The introduction of the electoral principle and the demand of the Bengali nationalists that university examination be a requirement for the uncovenanted service was refused, because, given the situation in the north, Hindu majorities in the councils and Bengalis in the administration would have forced the Muslims out. For these same reasons, Khan turned down the demand that he participate in the Congress of 1885. He was convinced that the Muslims would remain in a minority in the Indian Parliament that was being discussed, rather like "the Irish at Westminister."[292] Metcalf put it a little differently: "The Muslims, when faced with the spectre of representative government, found they preferred British to Hindu rule."[293]

Muslims attended the Congress of 1885 and the ones following, and in 1888 a Muslim even presided. The claim of the Congress party, however, to represent the Hindus and Muslims on a secular basis, or, in fact, the entire Indian nation, was not accepted. With Khan's calling of the Muslim Education Conference in 1886, a sort of counter-Congress had been created: "I object to every Congress in any shape or form which regards India as one nation."[294] With that statement, made at the very moment when the Congress of 1885 signalled the real beginnings of the Indian liberation movement, the most serious obstacle in the way of India's becoming a nation was made manifest, namely, the relationship between the two great socioreligious communities. It was more than chance that this relationship became a problem just at that time. The end of autocratic-bureaucratic rule in India, formerly Mughal, now British, was beginning to be visible, and the Indian national movement had committed itself to Western-British representative bodies. That immediately raised the question of how much could be expected of the nationalist movement in a society where membership in a religious community appeared more important than common social and regional interests.

The Congress, celebrated in the Indian press as the "birth of Indian unity," met annually after 1885 and with increasing numbers of delegates. But it became a genuine party only slowly. There were at first no dues-paying members nor permanent organization, and it remained unclear how delegates were to be elected. The regional associations gradually reconstituted themselves as local committees of the Congress and received their first statute in 1899. One can rightly speak of a patrician party of Victorian liberals, insofar as the delegates nearly all came from the new elite. A third of the delegates were lawyers. The old aristocracy was not represented but provided some financial support. The political demands were also in keeping with the interests of this class: more elected representatives to the legislative councils, ICS examinations in India, abolition of the India council, and reduction of military expenditures. Loyalty to the Crown was strongly emphasized, both out of sincere conviction and in the hope of a favorable effect on liberal English opinion and consequent concessions from the raj. There was no talk of home rule.

The Indian government honored this moderation with appointments of Congress members to the councils but at the same time forbade its officials to take part in the Congress. It also revealed its disinclination to meet demands for the expansion of representative bodies. The liberal viceroy, Dufferin, sputtered about the "microscopic minority" which the educated classes in the Congress represented, and which supposedly spoke for itself alone and not for the Indian people. This is the usual argument employed everywhere to justify the maintenance of rule as a trusteeship. It certainly came conveniently to hand, however, after the Indian members of the councils voted against both the Bengal Tenancy Act and the Punjab Land Alienation Tenancy Act of 1900, and on top of that, the introduction of a modest income tax in 1886.[295]

Economic policy became, indeed, a matter for discussion after Naoroji published his 1874 polemic, *Poverty and Un-British Rule in India*, and thus raised the issue of economic consequences of colonial dependency. Romesh Chandra Dutt's *Economic History of India* (1901-1903) was a path-breaking performance, noteworthy in particular for its portrayal of the destruction of the Indian artisan trades. M. G. Ranade presented in broader perspective the consequences of British laissez-faire policies.[296] There was certainly enough for even moderate nationalists to criticize: customs policy, especially the turnover tax on Indian textiles of 1894 and the refusal of tariff assistance for accelerated industrialization, the high proportion of the budget taken by military outlays and the tiny amounts available for irrigation in the face of high taxation of the peasants. The colonial fiscal policy gave critics occasion to accuse England of exploitation and to demand an economic policy that promised to inaugurate India's development into a modern industrial state.[297] Questions of social reforms, on the other hand, were pushed under the table, in order not to shake the unstable consensus within the Congress. That occasioned Ranade to found the National Social Conference in 1887; in its turn, it ignored religious questions, and at first concerned itself with improving the status of women. It particularly opposed child marriages and the prohibition against widows' remarrying.[298] The debates between 1889 and 1891 over the Age of Consent bill show how much opinions diverged on this question. The Parsi Malavari's demand for reform was coolly received by the Indian government. The age was raised from ten to twelve, and cohabitation before that age forbidden. Two thousand Indians had petitioned Queen Victoria on the matter, and the Brahno Samaj supported the law, but some of the more radical Hindu nationalists had vehemently opposed it.[299]

In 1892 London took another step toward meeting Congress demands. Both the central and provincial legislative councils were expanded and, for the first time, some members were to be chosen by election. Collective bodies such as city councils and chambers of commerce could name their candidates.[300] The budget could be debated and questions could be put, though resolutions could still not be brought in. Passed by viceroy Landsdowne in the face of resistance from both the cabinet and the provincial governors, this modest reform was intended to channel the movement represented by the Congress and integrate it into the system. This indeed happened. A concession had been given the moderates, and their leader, Gopal Krishna Gokhale, was provided the means to win respect through thoughtfully reasoned stands, which in turn made the Congress a more credible body.

At the same time, however, conflicts between the radical and moderate nationalists were coming into the open. The radical leader, Bal Gangadhar Tilak (1856-1920) was, like Gokhale, a Maratha and a Chitpavan Brahmin, though of modest origins. He had attended the Deccan College in Poona and was at home in Western philosophy. He split with his friend Gokhale and began to preach bitterly against British rule and to promulgate a "national ideology based on a twisted interpretation of the Vedanta."[301] He criticized, among other things, reform laws such as the Age of Consent bill as foreign interference. His allies, indeed, numbered both Hindus and members of militant secret sects, who in 1897 began a campaign of uncoordinated terror with the murder of a British official responsible for quarantine measures. Whereas Gokhale held fast as a liberal to gradual reform and was convinced that self-government was to be obtained through cooperation with the ruling power, Tilak refused any compromise. His slogan was "*swaraj* (self-government) is our birthright," and he was ready to use violence as a tactical means to that end. It should be pointed out, however, that the differences between moderates and extremists cannot be equated to the Right or the Left as we generally employ these words. The rebellious attitudes of these "angry young men" were not really combined with any program of social betterment or even any real challenge to the landowning class. In origin, they themselves came from regional upper castes and had neither the means nor the intent to carry their agitation to the masses. (They later were to reveal little understanding of Gandhi's educational concepts.) Their social isolation led them to secret organizations and individual acts of terror. In the interwar period, it was possible for the Communist party to join with extremist Hindu organizations of a conservative nationalist stamp.

The disputes within the party and outside it flared into the open, however, when Lord Curzon said and did things that antagonized the moderates.[302] Curzon was a fascinating phenomenon. Imbued with a sense of imperial mission as it was understood at the turn of the century, he was convinced even as a young man that he was destined to be viceroy of India. In office, the autocratic proconsul set to work with superhuman energy with reform measures in every department. His aim was so to strengthen the "jewel of the British crown" that it would stand firm within and without and demonstrate to all the might and the greatness of the British Empire. The great durbar of 1901, on the occasion of the accession of Edward VII, paraded the might and splendor of the empire before its Indian subjects and the rest of the world. Curzon's other measures included the repositioning of military forces to secure definitively the northwest frontier, tightening up and modernization of the administration, energetic railway construction, but in conjunction with efforts toward Indian industrialization, and measures to protect the peasant such as the Punjab Land Alienation Act, the construction of irrigation facilities, tax reform, and the Cooperatives Law. The construction of the Victoria Memorial served to glorify the raj, as did the newly created archeological service, which was to preserve the art treasures of ancient India. Curzon also represented India interests in London and would have preferred being free of parliamentary control; but he repelled with equal arrogance and energy the claims of the new Western-educated elite to a voice in government, to say nothing of future self-government. He made it insultingly clear that the levers of power had to remain in British hands and for a long time to come.

The already mentioned Universities Act of 1904 loosed the protests of the Bengal intelligentsia and the bourgoisie, and the partition of Bengal in 1905 raised even more protest. The partition seems to have become necessary for administrative reasons. The province had 78 million inhabitants, and the east was neglected. Although the matter had been under discussion within the administration for some time, the overhasty decision to form a province of East Bengal and Assam could only be interpreted as a means to divide and rule. It wounded Bengali patriotism and impinged upon the concrete interests of the high caste Hindus of Calcutta, whose estates lay in the east. They feared a loss of offices should a province with a Muslim majority be created. In the same way, Hindus from Dacca also feared the loss of their positions in the Bengal administration. Curzon had in fact wanted to break the monopoly position of the Bhadraloks in Bengal with his administrative reform, in order to weaken the Congress.[303]

Reaction was violent. Mass assemblies and protest marches were used to appeal to a broader public and draw it into the agitation, even outside of Bengal. As early as August 1905 an assemblage in Bengal decided to boycott English goods. Under the leadership of Surendranath Banerjea, this expanded into the Swadeshi movement. Indians were asked to buy Indian goods insofar as possible, particularly Indian textiles. Although the factory owners were not among the ringleaders,[304] the textile industry nevertheless profited from the agitation. The agitation could hardly last any considerable time, but all the same spoke to the simple Indian and was later taken up again by Gandhi.

The initial effect of the agitation over partition, however, was to heighten tensions within the Congress, particularly since Curzon resigned that very year because of conflicts with the senior commander, General Horatio Kitchener. Although his successor was a Conservative, Lord Minto, in 1906 the Liberals came to power. John Morley, student of J. S. Mill and biographer of Gladstone, became India secretary. He was ready to make concessions to the educated classes without, however, as he felt it necessary to emphasize, taking steps in the direction of representative government.[305] Behind an outwardly amicable facade, the India secretary and the viceroy struggled over questions of reform. The result ultimately appeared in 1909 as the Morley-Minto reforms. Minto and his advisors in the Indian government were primarily concerned with binding the large Indian landowners, the so-called natural leaders, more closely to the administration, as a counterweight to the nationalist bourgeoisie represented by the Congress. Advisory councils were accordingly considered. Morley, on the other hand, held fast to the principle of elections. He managed to get his way, but at the cost of conceding the principle of geographic representation in favor of the "representation of interests." The Imperial Legislative Council was expanded from 25 to 60 members and its competence was enlarged, but a majority of members remained appointed. Analogous changes were also made in the provincial councils. Two Indians were appointed to the India council and Indians were appointed to the executive councils of the central government (the Bhadralok, S. P. Sinha), and the provinces. The consequences, as it turned out, were not only that representation of interests provided the landowners with a relatively heavy representation, but that a separate electoral body was created for the Muslims. Morley, who had contemplated reserved seats for Muslims, but not communal representation, was outmaneuvered by the Indian government. The question must remain open, however, whether the latter was attempting to build up the loyal Muslims against the Congress party, or whether it was simply acknowledging the existence of a separate Muslim party, as had occurred in 1906 with the formation of the All-India Muslim League.[306] Although it cannot be proved that elections without communal representation would have quickly led to bitter friction between the two religious communities, there can be no denying that the legalization of separate electoral bodies made any sort of accomodation within a unified national movement more difficult, though not perhaps not impossible, and thus constituted the first step toward the partition of the subcontinent that occurred in 1947.

The partition of Bengal, rescinded in 1911, loosed a wave of terrorism in Bengal and the Punjab. Radical-nationalist in character, though with religious trappings, the terrorism reflected in no small measure the impatience of the underpaid, underemployed younger generation of the new elite. The bomb attack of 1912 against the viceroy, Lord Hardinge, was a worldwide sensation. The sedition act which Morley had believed necessary in 1907 had simplified achieving solidarity within the nationalist movement and had simultaneously weakened the moderates. Curzon and the partition of Bengal notwithstanding, the moderates, whose most important spokesmen were Banerjea, Naoroji, and above all Gokhale, continued to push for legal means of change, although the reforms of 1909 did not completely meet their expectations. They placed their hopes on the Liberals, who had come to power in England. They found themselves under increasing pressure from the extremists, however, especially from Tilak. The latter, conscious of the military strength of the raj, advocated passive resistance and noncooperation rather than rebellion. At the annual meeting of the Congress of 1906 it was still possible, although with difficulty, to prevent the party from splitting. The following year, however, at the meeting in Surat, the split did occur, though no radical party was formed. A few months later Tilak was condemned to six years in prison for incitement to murder.[307]

INDIAN NATIONALISM AND THE STAGES OF POLITICAL EMANCIPATION, 1914-1939

Shortly after Tilak, by now a national hero, was released in June 1914, World War I broke out. The Indians, as should not be forgotten today, bore ample witness of their loyalty to the ruling power. Not only did the princes and the "natural leaders" provide troops and cash payments, but Gandhi, too, worked after his arrival in London on 6 August for equipment of an Indian ambulance and supported British recruiting efforts as late as the summer of 1918. He did so at risk of compromising himself with the radicals and the masses.[308] Even Tilak considered it necessary in 1914 to defend himself from the reproach that he was hostile to His Majesty's government.[309] Viceroy Hardinge had worked very adroitly in the prewar years to bring about a good working relationship with Gokhale's moderates in the Congress and had won especial sympathy by taking up the cause of Indians in South Africa in 1913. These efforts now paid off. The Indian intelligentsia was still under the sway of England's Liberal tradition, particularly since the victory of Kaiser Wilhelm's Germany hardly offered prospectives more enticing than those within the British Empire. England pulled almost all of its troops out of India and recruited 1.3 million troops and workers during the war. They were used not only in the Near East and east Africa but on the European front as well. Military and administrative blunders in handling the Mesopotamian Expeditionary Force did, however, compromise the Indian government between 1915 and 1917 and led to the resignation of the India secretary, Austen Chamberlain. Conscription in the Punjab during the last days of the war also contributed to the disturbances of 1919.

Economically, India profited from the war, industrially in particular, because shipments from England ceased and Indian production could be increased. An industrial commission was appointed in 1916. Its report of 1918 inaugurated a new course: the supporting of industrialization, customs protection, and the like (see p. 59 above). Prices were also rising, however, including those for food, which probably explains in part the support the radical liberation movement received from broad segments of the public after the war.

Although Gandhi refused to exploit Great Britain's emergency situation, hoping that the latter would repay India's loyalty after the war, both in the Congress and the country at large events were moving into more radical channels. At first, Annie Besant of the Theosophical Society failed to get a home-rule resolution passed, but with the death of Gokhale in 1915 and the reentry of Tilak to the Congress in 1916 the radicals seized the leadership. At the end of 1917 Annie Besant became president of the Congress. Two home-rule leagues founded by Tilak and Besant were, together with their locals, able to bring off an all-India agitation for the first time.[310] Because the Muslims were unsettled by the British war against their spiritual Turkish overlords (really the Ottoman Empire), the Congress was also able simultaneously to secure Muslim cooperation for a moderate nationalist course. In 1916, the Congress and the Muslim League presented in the Lucknow Pact a draft constitution which accepted the principle of electoral separation by religion and gave existing religious minorities a number of deputies exceeding their percentage of the population. A reform of the executive was purposely not touched upon. It seems, however, that sentiment ran in favor of the American presidential rather than the British parliamentary system.[311]

For their part, the British soon saw that the war called for a reexamination of existing India policy. Hardinge in particular had pointed out the need for reforms and had, among other things, called upon British officials to gear up for a new task, namely preparing India for self-government.[312] It was not clear at first what this might mean, whether dominion status, or domestic autonomy, and the how and when of such reform policies were no clearer. England's critical situation, the Lucknow Pact, and the February revolution in Russia occasioned the cabinet to have the India secretary, Montagu, promulgate on 20 August 1917 the famous declaration of the new aims of British policy in India: Indianization and "the gradual development of self-governing institutions with a view to the progressive realization of responsible Government in India as an integral part of the British Empire."[313] Such a declaration would have been inconceivable at the outbreak of the war. As late as 1912, the India secretary, Robert Crewe, had emphatically declared that any comparison between India and the dominions was quite inadmissable; dominion status was "as remote as any Atlantis."[314] The First World War was thus a palpable factor in hastening the pace of decolonization.

Until the war, official England had claimed with utter self-confidence to be pursuing a benevolent imperialism. After the India Declaration of 20 August 1917, however, it was hardly a question of maintaining this any longer, or even of loosening it a bit to allow Indians a greater voice in government in order to stabilize the situation. The question now was timing, meaning, nailing down the schedule for the progressive steps for reaching the goal. The nationalists pressed for self-rule and fulfillment of the promises within the foreseeable future, but London, while offering the prospect of reforms and concessions, was far from ready to abandon its sovereign powers and hoped to delay self-government indefinitely.

The India secretary, Montagu, went to India during the winter of 1917-1918 and in the summer of 1918 turned in his *Report on Indian Constitutional Reforms*, on which the Montagu-Chelmsford reforms of 1919 were based.[315] Lionel Curtis, labelled a "travelling expert on constitutions" by Rothermund, acted as their advisor. If some step in the direction of representative, to say nothing of responsible, government were to be made, and by now it was hardly to be avoided, a federalist solution presented some very decided advantages. The central government could retain sovereign power and concessions could be confined to the provinces. But elected "unofficial majorities" in the regional legislatures, as the Congress had long demanded, must of needs come in conflict with appointed provincial governments which could not be forced from power. Lord Durham had pointed this out as early as 1839 in his report on Canada. Curtis, however, provided a solution with what he called the dyarchy principle. Some departments (education, local administration, public health, agriculture) were placed under an Indian minister responsible to the legislature, while others such as finance and police remained in the hands of appointed ministers responsible only to the governor. This was also intended to prevent Indian deputies from using the legislatures as mere forums for agitation without having to bear any of the responsibility for government. The franchise was broadened considerably (to roughly 5 million voters), but communal representation for Muslims remained. Indian opinion was split, and, as early as the end of 1918, a group of old moderates had split from the Congress and constituted themselves the Liberal party. Led by Besant and Tilak, the majority, indeed, demanded immediate responsible government in the provinces but in December 1919, after the Amritsar massacres in other words, nevertheless accepted the reforms as a transitional solution and promised their cooperation.[316] In the imperial council, however, the reforms carried thanks only to the "official majority."

In the meanwhile, tensions had increased considerably. On 18 March 1919, the bills named after Justice Rowlatt were forced through the council against the votes of all its Indian members. Intended to fill the gap left by the lifting of war powers, the laws were meant to simplify combatting criminal gangs and subversive and terrorist groups. They permitted, among other things, arrest on suspicion without trial. In practice, the laws were never enforced, but their character, and also the manner of their passage, were necessarily seen as a provocation by the Indian educated classes. They unleashed a storm of indignation, as at the very moment the British government was moving toward Indian self-government, it seemed to be bent on repression.

Gandhi's moment had come. In contrast to the previous leaders of the Congress, Gandhi came neither from the dominant nor the entrepreneural minorities of the Presidencies, but was from a Gujurat mercantile caste. After studying law in England, he had emigrated to South Africa. There he had become a spokesman for local Indians and had achieved his first successes with nonviolent resistance. After returning to India in 1917, although originally close to Gokhale, he had established links with the home-rulers. At the same time, however, he had in 1917 won both fame and followers by his tenacious and skillful defense of the Behar indigo farmers. In addition, he began a calculating rapprochement with the Muslim League and the establishment of a common front with the Pan-Islam protest movement.[317] Gandhi considered the Rowlatt bills a personal challenge:

> To me the Bills are the regulated symptoms of the deep-seated disease. They are a striking demonstration of the determination of the Civil Service to retain its grip of our necks. There is not the slightest desire to give up an iota of its unlimited powers, and if the civil service is to retain its unlimited rule over us, and the British commerce is to enjoy its privileged position, I feel that the reforms will not be worth having. I consider the Bills to be an open challenge to us. If we succumb we are done for. If we may prove our word that the government will see an agitation such that they have never witnessed before, we shall have proved our capacity for resistance to arbitrary or tyrannical rule.... For myself if the Bills were to be proceeded with, I feel that I can no longer render peaceful obedience to the laws of a power that is capable of such a devilish legislation as these two Bills, and I would not hesitate to incite those who think with me to join in the struggle.[318]

On 26 February 1919, he addressed an "open letter to the Indian people," calling on them to demonstrate against the Rowlatt bills with a *Satyagraha* (day of inner contemplation) on 6 April. The home-rule sections and Gandhi's own organization organized agitation and coordinated the Satyagraha throughout India. The result was that on 6 April in countless cities *hartals*, as they were called, took place; or, in other words, businesses remained closed. The driving elements and motives for protest may have differed according to class, caste, and region.[319] The rapid rise in prices had created fertile soil for agitation in the artisan, worker, and petty bourgeoisie classes, and the Muslims were then under the influence of the Pan-Islam movement. Nonetheless, it took Gandhi to exploit the Rowlatt bills, channelling the heightened tension between Indians and British into the first demonstrative movement encompassing broad regions of India.[320]

Although the hartals (work stoppages) of 6 April passed by peacefully, after Gandhi's arrest became known on the tenth, tempers flared and clashes with the police led to large-scale disturbances. In the Punjab, where the authoritarian governor, O'Dwyer, had paraded his disdain for the urban educated class when he took office, a classical case of escalation and repression occurred. When a mob killed four British bank officials in Amritsar, General Reginald Dyer, shortly before entrusted with maintaining the peace, considered that the moment for decisive action had come. On 13 April he ordered his men to open fire without warning on an illegal mass demonstration in the inner city. Between 400 and 600 were killed, and brutal and humiliating repressive measures followed.

Gandhi, who understood Satyagraha as nonviolent demonstrating, was most disillusioned and broke off the action, later calling this his "Himalayan blunder." Still, it was not the Amritsar massacre itself that led Gandhi, now established as leader of the Indian liberation movement, to break for good with the colonial power. It was how the Indian government, London, and British public opinion reacted to Amritsar. Montagu, indeed, condemned Dyer's act, but weeks passed before an investigating commission started its work. Dyer was justified in press and Parliament, and the *Morning Post* even began a fund-raising campaign for Dyer when he was finally, very, very tardily, relieved of his post. The report of the investigating commission (Hunter Report) was published only on 28 May 1920, after the Congress had made an official enquiry about it. It was received with indignation in India, because the "wrongs" in Punjab were not condemned with sufficient vigor and the continuance of wartime legal restrictions was seen as a necessity. Motilal Nehru wrote his son: "My blood is boiling over since I read the summaries you have sent."[321] Gandhi commented:

> I have discovered that the present representatives of the Empire have become dishonest and unscrupulous. They have no real regard for the wishes of the people of India and they count Indian honour as of little consequence. I no longer retain affection for a Government so evilly manned as it is now-a-days.[322]

On 1 August 1920, Gandhi launched his "noncooperation" campaign. His intent was "to paralyze the Government, and to compel justice from it." Gandhi also sought and found Muslim support. They had organized the Khilafat movement to protest Allied treatment of the sultan and the treaty of Sevres. For Gandhi, this was the sought-for opportunity to bring Hindus and Muslims together and to place his agitation on a truly national footing.[323] The Congress, on the other hand, vacillated. Resistance came from established national leaders like Tilak (Maharashtra), C. R. Ram Das (Bengal), and Motilal Nehru (United Provinces), who mistrusted Gandhi's act, doubted the success of the campaign, sought an expansion of representative bodies rather than a withdrawal from offices and councils, and, finally, feared a quasi-revolutionary wave which would lead to repression and possibly endanger their own sociopolitical positions of power.[324] According to Gordon, their stands depended on their views of their electoral chances, noncooperation not having been decided upon out of any feeling that the reforms of 1919 were insufficient.[325] In the end, Gandhi pushed the boycott decision through in Calcutta (September 1920) and Nagpur (December 1920), after Nehru and Das agreed to go along with him and after he, for his part, agreed to certain compromises.[326] The departure of Indian officials from councils, offices and courts, and student school boycotts were intended to cripple the governmental machinery. Gandhi promised "swaraj in one year!"

Thousands of students did indeed leave school for a time, and some officials refused to work, but the majority were not yet ready to risk office and income.[327] Although Gandhi, tirelessly crossing and recrossing the country and speaking to mass assemblies, was welcomed enthusiastically and buried in the good wishes of city councils, he also awakened fears and resistance when the workers and tenants were drawn into the movement. The government, confronted with the most critical situation since 1857, held back, although the army, some of the older provincial governors, and even some cabinet members urged repression. The government recognized that repression would solve nothing and would in fact create a hopeless situation. Due regard had to be shown the moderates in the executive council like Tej B. Sapru who opposed noncooperation, and no martyrs were to be created. Some leaders of the Khilafat movement were arrested, but not Gandhi, even though flaring tempers led to a number of bloody clashes.[328] Gandhi screwed up the tension yet more by an act of civil disobedience, the refusal to pay taxes, which would have forced the administration to resort to mass arrests. When the situation deteriorated to the point of spontaneous violence (twenty-two policemen were massacred in a village in the United Provinces), Gandhi saw as endangered his aim of mobilizing the masses through education in self-governance and broke off the boycott. Only then did the government intervene. Gandhi was condemned to six years' imprisonment.

Despite this failure, the propaganda effect of the noncooperation movement of 1920-1922 was overwhelming. British rule was challenged, and the national movement, still supported only by a narrow, educated stratum, had unloosed a wave of national solidarity which comprehended a much broader grouping, both in class and geographical terms. A willingness to sacrifice had been demanded and demonstrated. Rothermund sums up Gandhi's accomplishment as follows:

The symbolic character of Gandhi's language and his creative interpretation of Hinduism was closer to the religion of the people than the ideologized monism of the radical elements within the older educated classes in Bengal and Maharashtra. It signaled a new road toward identification with the masses of the people. The cult of spinning with distaff and spindle, encouraged by Gandhi in order to encourage the underemployed rural population's efforts at self-help, also found enthusiastic adherents from among the ranks of the educated. Noted attorneys were proud of being able to spin the amount of clean, perfect thread prescribed by Gandhi for members of the Congress.[329]

At this same time the Congress party was reorganized to take account of its new role. It was no longer to be an elite of notables, but was to represent the Indian people in its confrontation with the colonial power, and its administrative structure was tightened up accordingly.[330] Instead of administrative division along province lines, twenty-one linguistic "provinces" were created. That permitted the use of the local vernacular, gave the lower cadres more cohesion, and, in a sense, really made possible for the first time contact with the people. The number of delegates to the annual party meeting was made proportional to population, which underscored the notion of representation and at the same time shifted dominance to the regions at the cost of the heretofore dominant presidencies.

The All-India Congress Committee was expanded to 350 members and at the same time given quasi-parliamentary functions. A Working Committee of fifteen members thenceforth functioned as the cabinet and thus became the most important decision-making body. Thus was created an organization which set itself up in opposition to the ruling power as a sort of "parallel state." It had the task, in Rothermund's words, of "springing the painstakingly laid out framework of British constitutional reform" by boycotting the provincial legislatures and "of nullifying by means of agitational zeal the ground rules established by the colonial power for the formation of political opinion." The sharp increase in Congress members during the noncooperation campaign had also led to a marked shift in weight from the great cities to the country districts. It hence pointed the way to broadening the party base, even though the agitation could still not be made to reach the mass of the poor peasants. Because membership in the Congress committees was at the same time declared incompatible with practicing law or holding civil service positions, the number of lawyers declined sharply and social and professional diversity increased. Still, within the highest leadership groups, the numbers of Brahmins and university graduates remained high.[331] Gandhi also launched a very successful fund-raising campaign. Large contributions came in from the Parsi and Marwari merchants of Bombay and Calcutta. The "bourgeois character" of the party was thus guaranteed, although the mass education programs, the women's organizations, the closely allied trade unions, and finally, Gandhi's campaign for the untouchables and underpriviliged were also supported.

The question of whether, after the "capitulation" and arrest of Gandhi (to which reaction was surprisingly small), the boycott of the new provincial assemblies should be continued divided opinion once again. The majority of the Congress remained opposed to entry into the assemblies. In 1923, however, a Swaraj party gathered under the leadership of Das and Motilal Nehru, themselves under considerable pressure from lower party leaders who were concerned with local problems and had followed Gandhi's call for unity rather unwillingly. Holding that boycotting the legislatures was fruitless, the Swaraj party intended to fight the election against the moderates under the slogan, Noncooperation within the Assemblies. The moderates had run candidates in 1919 despite the boycott (and 30 percent of those eligible had voted) and had accepted ministerial posts. The Swaraj party wanted to cripple the democratized Montagu-Chelmsford constitutional system from within. But there was no break with the Congress party. Gandhi, released in 1924 before his term was up, regarded the parliamentary activity as pointless. He concentrated on social-reform efforts and even left to the Swaraj party the leadership of the Congress. The Khilafat movement also ebbed when Kemal Ataturk abolished the caliphate in 1924. With that movement also went the solidarity with the Muslims that Gandhi had so carefully nurtured. The mistrust between the two communities, indeed, broke out into the open again, reactivated by the various movements and militant organizations on both sides. The result within a few years was bloody disturbances.[332]

The Swaraj party achieved notable successes in the elections of 1924, mainly at the expense of the moderates. It proved possible to block the formation of ministries in some provinces, but only temporarily. Regional, religious, and personal interests surfaced, and coalitions became necessary. There can be little doubt that the prospect of becoming ministers appealed to many deputies. In Madras, however, the Non-Brahmin party rather than the Congress came to power. In the United Provinces a landowners majority formed the ministry, despite about two-thirds of the voters being tenants. Dyarchy proved to be a somewhat problematical solution because the "transferred subjects" got too little money. Still, the parliamentary and administrative learning process was begun and eventually profited independent India. That was also true of the elections, in which, besides the urban bourgeoisie, several groups of peasants and, thanks to reserved seats, even industrial workers had participated. The Swaraj party had won 44 out of 146 seats in the enlarged (in 1919) Central Assembly. Motilal Nehru was its leading speaker. The other leading figure was the Independent party's ever elegantly clad Mohammed Ali Jinnah, who—like Nehru, an able lawyer—had gradually risen to the leadership of the Muslims. Under Nehru's leadership, the two parties mustered a majority capable of making life miserable for the government. This forced the latter into negotiation and compromise. It accordingly went a good way toward meeting Indian demands. Some of the matters favorably resolved were tariff sovereignty, customs protection, abolition of the cotton excise, the ICS examination, Indianization, workmen's compensation for industrial workers, and union organizing rights. The government, however, retained the political initiative, particularly since the manifest crisis within the Congress permitted false hopes that nationalist agitation would diminish.

Lord Reading's successor was Edward Wood (elevated to viceroy as Lord Irwin, and later still becoming Lord Halifax). Confronted at the outset with communal riots, the latter sought earnestly but vainly to reduce tensions.[333] The Commission for Indian Constitutional Questions foreseen in 1919 was, moreover, prematurely convened in November 1927 in a Conservative party attempt to anticipate the acts of a Labour government. Its president was the Liberal, Sir John Simon, and Clement Atlee represented Labour, but there were no Indian members. The result was renewed Indian cries of outrage. The commission was sabotaged, and the divergent groups in the national movement received a renewed stimulus toward solidarity which neither Liberals nor Muslims could withstand. In December, against the will of a subdued Gandhi, the young Jawaharlal Nehru, Motilal's son, wrung from the Congress a resolution stating the aim of the Congress to be "complete national independence." Of itself this was hardly more than a more precise statement of the vague concept of Swaraj and in practice no more significant than dominion status. As a slogan, however, it was well suited to symbolize the break with the colonial power.

In 1926, the young Nehru had attended a Communist-dominated anti-imperialist congress in Brussels and had received some enduring impressions on a trip to Russia. His success was also revealed by the coming to the fore in the nationalist movement of a group of younger men who, though revering Gandhi, believed in socialist ideas. They were influenced by the London School of Economics, and Harold Laski was their intellectual mentor. They not only intended to wage an uncompromising fight for independence, but also introduced class-struggle elements into the agitation, which was increasingly directed at the social underclasses, the tenants and the workers.

As an answer to the Simon commission, a committee comprised of members representing several parties met under the chairmanship of Motilal Nehru and with the active collaboration of the Liberal, Sapru. It presented a draft constitution in 1928 which spoke only of dominion status, but did demand responsible parliamentary government at the center as well as in the provinces. Instead of separate electoral body for the Muslims, reserved seats were envisaged, though only in provinces where they were a minority (thus, not in Bengal). The seats were to be awarded on a proportional basis and for a ten-year period only. This did not mollify the Muslims, however. They held fast to separate electoral bodies and considered them necessary even in the Punjab and Bengal. The measure reawakened the old mistrust of the Congress and led to a break when the Congress failed to accept any of Jinnah's supplementary fourteen points. The latter called for, among other things, one-third of the seats in the central legislature and proportional Muslim representation in the Punjab and Bengal.[334] Even in the Congress itself, conflicts were bridged only by adding a supplementary proviso to the Nehru report to the effect that a campaign of civil disobedience would be commenced if dominion status was not granted within the year.

Irwin reacted with restraint and skill. He maintained contact with Gandhi and took no action against the young Nehru. He seized initiative by obtaining authorization from the new Labour government to issue a statement, made on 31 December 1929, that the declaration of August 1917 signified the "attainment of Dominion status." The intent was to eliminate an existing ambiguity and also to block all Conservative attempts to evade placing India on a par with the colonies of settlement by making talk of dominion tabu; or, in other words, to create a new basis of trust.[335] The viceroy's statement was well received in India, the historian Gopal speaking of a "revival of trust." It was not without impact on Gandhi, since Irwin also announced a round-table conference. He meant to avoid the psychological error of the Simon commission, which was to settle the fate of the country without the collaboration of the Indians themselves. The left-wing of the Congress led by the young Nehru put considerable pressure on Gandhi, however, and led the Congress to accept an "Independence Resolution" on 31 December. It also tied participation in the round-table conference to the condition that a dominion constitution be on the agenda. It knew that the viceroy could not accept such an ultimatum.

The new phase in the agitation opened with an eleven-point program that was intended to give specific content to the Congress's demands for independence. The concerns and interests of the divergent groups were appealed to with considerable skill. That simplified the formation of a common front between middle class and peasants, between traditionalists and left-wing intellectuals. As the starting point for his campaign of civil disobedience, Gandhi selected with masterly assurance the salt tax. Since 1836 the government had had a salt monopoly and had made the traditional private production of salt a criminal act, at first to make possible the import of English salt, later as a revenue source. Unlike the *gabelle* of the ancien régime the tax amounted in practice to a trivial burden.[336] But it especially burdened the peasant population and had long been cast by the nationalists as a symbol of colonial exploitation. It was hence brilliantly suited to create the solidarity necessary for the success of Gandhi's action. Gandhi marched with his loyal followers to the coast in Gujarat and made salt, a symbolic act, and one which had the desired effect. It was illegal and forced the administration to act.[337] The civil-disobedience movement covered wide areas of India, countless persons demonstratively breaking the salt monopoly. Foreign goods were boycotted and hartals organized. Women became politically active for the first time. As had happened earlier between 1920 and 1922, the peasants joined in locally because the national movement provided the opportunity to express concrete grievances in public protests. There is also little doubt that the growing unemployment among the educated classes radicalized the campaign. The administration kept its head, either because at first it did not take Gandhi's campaign very seriously or because it wished to prevent escalation. The tiny police force remained loyal but had its hands full controlling this sort of demonstration without resorting to drastic means. Finally, repressive intervention was no longer to be put off. Gandhi was arrested, and by the end of July, 60,000 Indians were in prison and party offices occupied.

Lord Irwin was interested, however, in bringing the Congress to the negotiating table. He succeeded in obtaining Gandhi's consent to an agreement in which Gandhi consented to break off the disobedience campaign and the British consented to free all political prisoners.[338] The agreement caused a sensation. It opened the way for Gandhi to participate in the second round-table conference in September. Prime Minister Ramsay MacDonald also smoothed the way with a statement amplifying the Simon commission report. Gandhi was, however, rearrested some three weeks after his return from London. Civil disobedience had rather tumultuously recommenced in some areas. Like the disorders of 1920-1922, this campaign failed to force the British government to capitulate. Still, aside from its propagandistic effect, it considerably influenced the constitutional reform then under way. The Conservative-dominated National government and the new, rather reactionary, viceroy, Lord Willingdon, attempted to curb the early willingness to concessions shown by Irwin and the Labour party. The National government was under sharp attack by Churchill's "diehards." The latter were able to drag out parliamentary hearings but could not prevent Commons from passing the India Act of 1935, the most voluminous bill yet passed by the British Parliament.[339] Although Great Britain was still not ready to liquidate its rule in India and grant dominion status as sought by the Congress, the new constitution represented a very extensive reform of the acts of 1919 and signified a major step toward responsible self-government.

More administrative in character was the separation of Burma from India, placing the northwest frontier on equal footing with the other provinces and creating two new provinces, Orissa (detached from Bengal), and Sind (detached from Bombay). The shift from dyarchy to full parliamentary responsibility in the provinces also occasioned little discussion. The governor retained, however, certain reserved powers, which enabled him to act in case of a domestic or external crisis. The franchise, male and female, was widened considerably, to about 30 million, or about one-sixth the number that would have been eligible under universal suffrage. But the latter was not demanded by the Congress, or at least not very energetically. The method of elections, however, led to disputes once again, this time not so much because of separate electoral bodies for Muslims, now accepted willy-nilly, as because of a separate electoral college for untouchables. They were organized by the energetic Dr. Ambedkar, himself a pariah. As the colonial power was eager to assume the role of protector of religious and social minorities, Ambedkar's demands were received willingly enough, particularly because they gave the lie to the Congress's claim to speak for the Indian nation. They also permitted setting limits on Congress power in the elected councils. Gandhi, on the other hand, had already protested energetically against Ambedkar's demands at the round-table conference and then, when the British government announced in the Communal Award the foreseen division of seats, threatened to starve himself to death. He rightly believed that separate electoral bodies for some 35 million untouchables would not only nullify his personal efforts to end Hindu prejudices and place the pariahs beyond the pale for good and all, but would also heighten tensions in the political arena and add yet another burden to the functioning of parliamentary institutions. Dr. Ambedkar finally gave way and satisfied himself with reserved seats for the so-called scheduled castes.

The principle of dyarchy was carried over from the provinces to the central government. With the exception of defence and foreign affairs, all ministries were turned over to Indian ministers responsible to Parliament. Their power was, however, considerably restricted by special finance provisions. The viceroy retained or was given rather extensive safeguarded powers. The long-overdue business of bringing the princely states under the constitution, even if only on a loose federal basis, proved a particularly thorny problem. The special position of the 662 princes had not changed in any important respect since 1858. Administratively sharply separated from British India, they were directly subordinate to the viceroy, whose residents interfered as little as possible, even in cases of crass abuses, in their internal affairs. Nonetheless, they had attempted legally to underpin their autonomy, which supposedly rested on treaties acknowledging their sovereign status. They were most unhappy when a commission report of 1929 rejected this claim, even though the report also emphasized that they could not be integrated into a system with parliamentary institutions without their consent.[340] The maharajah of Bikaner had accepted federation in principle at the first round-table conference, but the other princes insisted on their autonomy. The Conservative British government, despite all criticism and irritation with the princely states, still regarded them as supporters of its rule and partners against the Congress. It was hence not ready to pressure them.[341] The India act foresaw that the princely states would turn control of foreign policy, defense, and communications over to the federation, but at the same time gave them the right to name one-third of the deputies in the lower house and one-fifth of those in the upper. The anomaly of their internal autonomy remained. Entrance into the federation was voluntary, and the new arrangements were to take effect only when half of the princely states (in terms of population) had announced their intent to enter. London had thus left the princes in a very strong position, not in the least because the viceroy was dependent on their support in the contest anticipated with the expected majority of opposition nationalist deputies. Whether this intricate system could have functioned, especially in the face of latent conflict between Hindus and Muslims, is questionable. Since the princes refused to enter the federation in any case, only those portions of the India Act of 1935 applying to the provinces came into force.[342]

As in 1919, the Congress party had to decide whether to participate in the elections and agree to the formation of responsible provincial governments or whether to agitate against the system from without. When Congress party politicians willing to work within the system reactivated the Swaraj party, Gandhi neither opposed it nor withdrew from party politics. Instead he took care to retain leadership in his own hands. He consented to the formation of a parliamentary collegium, but made it follow the instructions of the Congress committee. The Congress received, moreover, a new statute of organization, which provided that the president was thenceforth to be elected by the delegates themselves, while he alone was to name the Working Committee. Three-quarters of the delegates had to come from rural districts, and provincial committees were put under closer control of the Working Committee. Rothermund rightly points out that Gandhi here revealed that he had held fast to the notion of the Congress as a parallel government. It is striking that although after 1892 the trend had been toward decentralization of the Indian government and toward Indian participation at the provincial level, the Congress itself had tightened up and centralized its organization in order to agitate more effectively and to be better prepared to assume power should the chance arise.[343]

Gandhi was able to hold his position of leadership thanks to his great personal prestige and tactical skill but was by no means unchallenged. Opposition came mainly from the Left. In 1934 a Congress Socialist party was founded. It forswore collaboration (even in case of the coming "imperialist" war) and declared war not only on the system of colonial exploitation but on capitalism per se. It interpreted India as a class society and demanded far-reaching social reforms, among them dispossession of the landlords, nationalization of the key industries, and a state monopoly of foreign trade. Although Gandhi was a social reformer and had intervened on behalf of both indigo tenants and untouchables, he rejected class struggle, either for reasons of principle or because he did not wish to endanger the national common front. Under pressure of the depression and Nehru, economic and sociopolitical demands were more sharply articulated in the Karachi Resolution of 1931,[344] but within the Congress itself some regard had to be taken of the zamindars and industrialists, who were as members and providers of funds of no small importance. The bourgeois majority was in any case hardly ready to start wearing social revolutionary colors.[345] It is also worth noting that the party's social and economic plans were mainly directed against the colonial power, and that the concrete interests of India's leadership class were touched upon very tangentially or not at all. Gandhi successfully outmaneuvered the new Left opposition in 1936 and 1937 by accepting Nehru as Congress president. Nehru believed in a sort of secularized socialism, but was not a member of the Socialist party. Gandhi on the other hand forced the resignation of the Bengalese, Subhas Bose, who was president in 1938 and 1939. The latter was thus isolated and forced onto a socialist-nationalist course that ended in collaboration with Hitler's Germany.

The Congress turned down the the new constitution in Lucknow in 1936 but then took part in the provincial elections anyway. The electoral campaign was fought energetically with propagandistic spectaculars and processions and, with an eye to the larger electorate, promises of agrarian reform. The Congress party achieved striking success and thus made good their claim to represent the entire Indian people and not merely the urban intelligentsia, as the Conservatives and administration had been claiming for so long. In five of eleven provinces, it had a clear parliamentary majority, and in two others de facto control. Its one striking failure was in Bengal, where the local leadership was still Hindu-Bhadralok in origin and had protested in vain against the Communal Award, which gave the Muslims more seats than the Hindus.[346] The victor was Fazhul Huq, who had organized the Muslim tenants in his Krishak Praja party and formed a government with a platform of agrarian and educational reform.

The right wing of the Congress pushed to form a government. Gandhi had to accede to its demands because obstructionist tactics would have strengthened the left wing. Ministers had, however, to resign from the Congress party. That reflected the ambivalence within a body that was both an agitation organization and a parliamentary party. It resulted in a certain division between the "organizational" and "ministerial" wings. The parliamentary Central Committee under leadership of Vallabhbai Patel and Rajendra Prasad, the later president of the republic, saw to party discipline, however.

The governmental activities of the Congress ministers have still not been studied sufficiently. The provincial governments concerned themselves above all with education and pushed popular elementary education. Tenant-protection laws were enacted which forbade eviction or made it more difficult, regulated new leases, and provided debt relief. These laws really only supplemented existing ones and did not jeopardize the landholders' positions of power. In Behar, for example, the Congress party sought a compromise with the zamindars.[347] The laws also helped the prosperous peasants, upon whom the power of the Congress would in the future depend, rather than the small peasants and landless workers. Investigations into the lot of the industrial workers were begun, but an industrial disputes bill for Bombay encountered union opposition. Although an impulse toward social reform was certainly present, one ought have no illusions about the bourgeois and generally conservative character of the Congress. Its leadership was still drawn largely from the high-caste upper classes. It had succeeded in neutralizing the social tensions in Indian society in the name of the struggle against British rule waged in common with the lower castes.[348] It was, accordingly, also no accident that, as Rothermund puts it:

> Congress ministers proved in no way anarchistic or fastidious when it came to maintaining law and order. Repressive laws attacked earlier were not only not repealed but were employed with right good will. In Madras, Rajagopalachari had hundreds of demonstrators, who were protesting the use of Hindi as the official language, roughed up by the police and thrown in jail. In Kampur, striking workers creating disturbances were fired upon, and even Nehru defended these measures, to the outrage of his socialist friends.[349]

It also should be pointed out that the British administration did its best to see to it that the experiment in responsible Indian provincial government succeeded. The governors restricted themselves to their new roles as constitutional monarchs, and British officials condescended to serve Indian bosses. In this two-year period countless politicians were taught the realities of governmental responsibility and had the opportunity to learn the true value of the administrative apparatus and its steel framework, the ICS. The British officials on the other hand had the opportunity to see that a transfer of power need not signify the oft-prophesied chaos. That surely made the British withdrawal between 1945 and 1947 easier.

At the same time, unfortunately, the gulf between the Congress and the Muslims widened. Jinnah failed in his attempt on the occasion of the Nehru report to find a modus vivendi with the Congress. He rejected the civil disobedience campaign as he had already done in 1920 and in 1931 even moved to London, where he remained until 1935. The Muslims were disunited during these years. Their leaders were mainly interested in maintaining and expanding their regional positions, particularly in provinces with a slim Muslim majority such as Bengal and the Punjab. The Communal Award met them more than halfway, mainly because the British did not want to estrange them.[350] At the national level, the British encouraged a loose Muslim federation out of fear that the Hindus would win a majority in a central parliament.

The poorly organized Muslim League suffered a striking defeat under Jinnah's leadership in the elections of 1937. They did not get a single seat in the frontier provinces, only three in Sind, in the Punjab but 2 of 86, in the United Provinces 27 of 64, and in Bengal only one-third of the Muslim seats. As a result, the Congress party turned down a coalition government. It believed it had little reason not to do so and cherished the hope that it might eliminate its rival altogether. It did not see itself as a purely Hindu party and had numerous highly regarded Muslims in its ranks. The reserved seats also guaranteed the Muslims places in the provincial governments. What tipped the balance was the situation in the United Provinces. There, the Congress party under Nehru's leadership offered to give a Muslim League politician a ministerial post, but only on the condition that he come over to the Congress party. The degree to which Nehru's animosity toward Jinnah played a part in all this remains unknown.[351] In any case, Jinnah refused this "surrender" and proceeded to build the Muslim League into a tightly organized anti-Congress party within a relatively short time. He did this despite the mistrust with which the Muslim leaders of the majority provinces regarded him, despite the handicap of not speaking Urdu, and despite lacking such charisma as Gandhi had. The league was reorganized and some social-reform planks were adopted. In addition, Jinnah succeeded in incorporating both the Unionist party, which ruled in the Punjab, and Fazhul Huq's Krishak Praja party in Bengal. Waving the banner "Islam in Danger" the nightmare of an India dominated by the Hindu Congress was emphasized. The rather insensitive behavior of the provincial governments and many of the measures and utterances of the Congress seemed to offer ample justification for such fears. By stages, a Muslim nationalism was created which spoiled the possibility for unity in the subcontinent and the rise of an "Indian" nation; and plans for partition were already being discussed.[352] After the outbreak of the Second World War, when the Congress ministers resigned in protest—rather unwillingly, it must be said—about not being consulted about India's entry into the war, Jinnah celebrated the event as being freed from the Hindu yoke. At the party congress of 1940 in Lahore, the famous "Two Nations" resolution was passed. It allowed for scarcely any solution save partition, particularly since the Congress moved over into the opposition and with its "Quit-India" campaign of 1942 forced the Indian government to move closer to the Muslim League and heed the latter's demands in the negotiations over constitutional reform, transition government, and the transfer of power.

NOTES

1. Percival Spear, *India: A Modern History* (rev. ed., Ann Arbor: University of Michigan Press, 1972), is a good survey.
2. Kavalam Madhava Panikkar, *Asia and Western Dominance: A Survey of the Vasco da Gama Epoch of Asian History, 1498-1945* (new ed., London: G. Allen & Unwin, 1959), 80.
3. Jawaharlal Nehru, *The Discovery of India* (Garden City: Anchor, 1960), 181.
4. On this question and for what follows, see Thomas R. Metcalf, *The Aftermath of Revolt: India 1857-1870* (Princeton: Princeton University Press, 1964); George D. Bearce, *British Attitudes toward India, 1784-1858* (New York: Oxford University Press, 1961); and Philip Mason, *The Men Who Ruled India*, by Philip Woodruff (pseud.), (2 vols., London: J. Cape, 1953, 1954), I.
5. Bearce, *British Attitudes*, 132.
6. Metcalf, *Aftermath*, 7; Bearce, *British Attitudes*, 125.
7. Metcalf, *Aftermath*, 8-9.
8. "I know nothing so important to the improvement of their [*i.e.*, the Hindus'] future condition as the establishment of a purer morality, whatever they believe. . . . The first step to this better understanding will be dissociation of religious belief and practice from blood and murder"; cited in Metcalf, *Aftermath*, 26.
9. Bearce, *British Attitudes*, 171.
10. Spear, *India*, 265.
11. Metcalf, *Aftermath*, 59; Tara Chand, *History of the Freedom Movement in India* (rev.ed., 4 vols., Delhi: Publications Division, Ministry of Information & Broadcasting, 1965), II, 106; Nehru, *Discovery*, 237.
12. Eric Stokes, "Traditional Resistance Movements and Afro-Asian Nationalism: The Context of the 1857 Mutiny Rebellion in India," *Past and Present*, 48 (August 1970).
13. Metcalf, *Aftermath*, 390ff.
14. On this question, see among others, Francis G. Hutchins, *The Illusion of Permanence: British Imperialism in India* (Princeton: Princeton University Press, 1967); Allen J. Greenberger, *The British Image of India: A Study in the Literature of Imperialism, 1880-1960* (London, New York: Oxford University Press, 1969).
15. Fitzjames Stephen, letter to London *Times*, 1 March 1883, cited in Metcalf, *Aftermath*, 318.
16. Nehru, *Discovery*, 202.
17. Ibid., 205
18. Metcalf, *Aftermath*, 297f.
19. Symonds, *The British*, 57.
20. H. N. Kunzu, member of the Defence Consultative Committee of the Indian legislature, "Defence of India," *Annals of the American Academy of Political and Social Science*, 233 (May 1944), 6. Symonds says 10 percent of the officers were Indian; *The British*, 60. See also

the documents on army policy in Cyril Henry Philips (ed.), *The Evolution of India and Pakistan, 1858 to 1947: Select Documents* (London: Oxford University Press, 1964), 505f.

21. Symonds, *The British*, 58.

22. Ibid., 61.

23. For example, Mason, *Men Who Ruled*, 179f.

24. Cited in Metcalf, *Aftermath*, 20.

25. Quoted in Donald A. Low, *Lion Rampant: Essays in the Study of British Imperialism* (London: Frank Cass, 1963), 57.

26. Ibid., 54.

27. Ibid.

28. "Dearly bought experience may teach us that political security is not necessarily attained by just laws, equitable taxation, and material progress. . . . If there is a body scattered throughout the country considerable by its property and rank it will for certain exercise great influence whether its position be hereditary or not. If this body is attached to the state by timely concessions . . . and obtains a share of power and importance, it will constitute a strong support to the existing Government. It may be true that such a body may become too powerful or . . . oppress a people not protected by efficient laws. But neither of these evils is more to be feared than that which threatens a foreign rule from the ignorance and indifference of its alien subjects, when unattached through their natural leaders and held in allegiance only by military force"; the secretary of the government of the Punjab to the secretary of the government of India, 30 April 1860, cited in Metcalf, *Aftermath*, 165.

29. Metcalf, *Aftermath*, 227; Philips, *Evolution*, 19.

30. See for example, Lord Irwin to H. Butler, 18 August 1926, in which Irwin noted that the nizam of Hyderabad was now ready to accept "advice"; "his administration really has become a gross scandal, and I was satisfied that we were not justified in standing aside any longer"; Great Britain, India Office, "Butler Collection," Europ. MSS. F. 116/60. Hereafter cited as "Butler Collection."

31. Lewis Sidney Steward O'Malley, *The Indian Civil Service, 1601-1930* (2d ed., London: F. Cass, 1965); Hugh Tinker, "Structure of the British Imperial Heritage," in Ralph J. D. Braibanti (ed.), *Asian Bureaucratic Systems Emergent from the British Imperial Tradition* (Durham, N. C.: Duke University Press, 1966); S. P. Sen, "Effects on India of British Law and Administration in the 19th Century," *Cahiers d'Histoire Mondiale*, 4, no. 4 (1958).

32. In communications to Lord Hamilton, cited in Philips, *Evolution*, 19.

33. For example, secretary of state to the Indian government, 31 May 1876, ibid., 15.

34. The more generally used title of viceroy technically applied only in regard to the princely states.

35. Characterized as "salvaging one's honor" in Mason, *Men Who Ruled*, I, 91f.; Robert Carstairs, *The Little World of an Indian District Officer* (London: Macmillan, 1912).

36. On 6 August 1902, the governor of Madras, Lord Ampthill, wrote the secretary of state: "What happens is this: all the lands on which the crops have failed have to be inspected by subordinate agencies which, as you know, is very amenable to bribery in this country. The consequence is that the well-to-do who can afford to bribe the village officers or revenue inspectors get them to report that his crops are withered or totally lost, so as to entitle him to remission. . . . Again it is by no means infrequent that the remissions never reach the ryots for whom they were intended as the village officers deceive the ryots by telling them that no remissions were granted, collect the full assessment and pocket the money themselves"; cited in David Washbrook, "Country Politics: Madras, 1880-1930," *MAS*, 7 (July 1973), 491.

37. "Under the old Hindu Law, a Brahmin murderer might not be put to death, while a Sudra who cohabited with a high-caste woman would automatically suffer execution for the same offence"; Hugh Tinker, *India and Pakistan: A Political Analysis* (New York: Praeger, 1962), 170.

38. In addition to O'Malley and Tinker, see Symonds, *The British*.

39. See Mason's revealing account, *Men Who Ruled*, I, 279ff.

40. Symonds, *The British*, 28.

41. "We profess to seek [the Indians'] improvement, but propose means the most adverse to success. The advocates of improvement do not seem to have perceived the great springs on which it depends; they propose to place no confidence in the natives, to give them no authority, and to exclude them from office as much as possible; but they are ardent in their zeal for enlightening them by the general diffusion of knowledge. . . . Our books alone will do little or nothing; dry simple literature will never improve the character of a nation. To produce this effect, it must open the road to wealth, and honour, and public employment. Without the prospect of such reward, no attainments in science will ever raise the character of a people"; T. H. Beaglehole, *Thomas Munro and the Development of Administrative Policy in Madras, 1792-1818* (Cambridge: Cambridge University Press, 1966), 123.

42. See Bernard S. Cohn, "The British in Benares: A Nineteenth Century Colonial Society," *CSSH*, 4 (January 1962).

43. Tinker, "Structure," 55.

44. Christine Dobbin, "The Ilbert Bill: A Study of Anglo-Indian Opinion in India, 1883," *Historical Studies, Australia and New Zealand*, 12 (October 1965); Wilfred S. Blunt, "Ideas about India," *Fortnightly Review*, 36 (August, October, November 1884).

45. Tinker, "Structure," 59.

46. Symonds, *The British*, 36.

47. Ibid., 37.

48. Ibid. In a similar vein, see also George Otto Trevelyan, Macauley's nephew, in Parliament in 1868; ibid., 35.

49. Tinker, "Structure," 60.

50. Symonds, *The British*, 40.

51. "Report of the Royal Commission on the Superior Civil Service in India," in Great Britain, Parliament, House of Commons, *Sessional Papers: Papers by Command*, 1924 Cmd. 2128, VIII, 607. Hereafter cited as *Sessional Papers*, with command reference.

52. David C. Potter, "Manpower Shortage and the End of Colonialism: The Case of the Indian Civil Service," *MAS*, 7 (January 1973), 49.

53. For example, Rajendra Prasad, the first president of India, reported in his autobiography that he "began to be obsessed by a new idea: to go to England and somehow pass the I.C.S. examinations"; quoted in Tinker, "Structure," 64.

54. Jawaharlal Nehru, *Jawaharlal Nehru: An Autobiography; With Musings on Recent Events in India* (London: John Lane, 1936), 445f; ch. 54, "The Record of British Rule," 433f., is brilliant. See also Naresh Chandra Roy, "The Indian Civil Service," *Modern Review*, 42 (November 1927).

55. See, for example, Panikkar, *Asia*, 122: "There was thus no alliance between the Civil Service and big business, and the British Indian Bureaucracy was not interested in the exploitation of India. In fact, it could legitimately be said that the services championed 'their India' of the dumb masses against British businessmen and capitalists. . . ."

56. "How often have I not pointed out to you that there are neither originality, nor ideas nor imagination in the I.C.S. That they think the present the best, and that change or improvement or reform sends a cold shiver down their spine. Where would have been any of the great subjects I have taken up—Education, Irrigation, Police, Railways, if I had waited for the local government to give the cue?"; Curzon to Lord Hamilton, 4 June 1903, quoted in Philips, *Evolution*, 73.

57. Helen Lamb, "The State and Economic Development in India," in Simon S. Kuznets (ed.), *Economic Growth: Brazil, India, Japan* (Durham: Duke University Press, 1955), 486.

58. Davis makes painstaking estimates and, except for 1931 and 1941, corrects the census figures; see other figures, 85.

59. See the graph below from Davis, *Population*, 25:

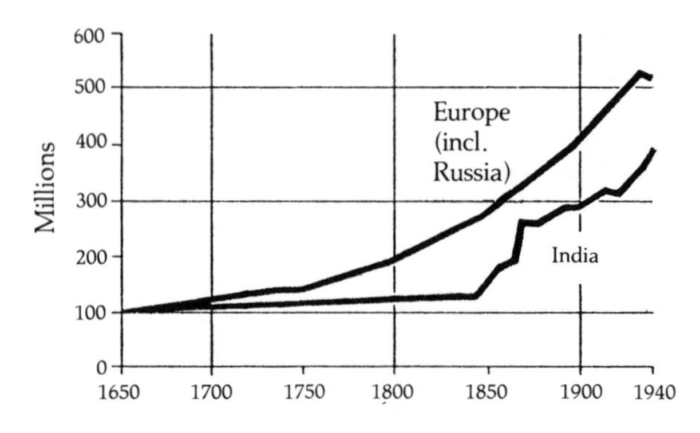

60. Ibid., 69, as corrected, since not all births were announced.
61. Ibid., 33.
62. Ibid., 36, for figures below:

1881-1891	41.3 average death rate
1891-1901	44.4
1901-1911	42.6
1911-1921	48.6
1921-1931	36.3
1931-1941	31.2

63. Ibid., 34-35, for figures below:

1911	205
1921	198
1931	179
1941	158

64. Ibid., 36.
65. Ibid., 43, 45, 53.
66. Ibid., 18-21.
67. This section is based mainly on the fundamental investigation of B. M. Bhatia, *Famines in India: A Study in Some Aspects of the Economic History of India, 1860-1965* (New York: Asia Publishing House, 1963).
68. It is incomprehensible how Spear, *India*, 286, can write: "The series of famines between 1896 and 1900 involved no serious loss of life."
69. Bhatia, *Famines*, 165.
70. Ibid., 79, from a report of 1869.
71. Ibid., 83.
72. "Even in the worst conceivable emergency so long as trade is free to follow its normal course, we should do far more harm than good by attempting to interfere"; "Resolution of the Government of India," 18 May 1897, quoted in ibid., 240.
73. Romesh C. Dutt, "Famines in India and Their Remedy," *Fortnightly Review*, 62 (August 1897), in which government and private famine assistance were praised, along with railways and irrigation, but the unsupportable expenses resulting from expansive imperial policies and taxes were criticised; and Dutt characterized Bengal as favored. In 1900 Dutt agreed to talks with Curzon; Bhatia, *Famines*, 295.
74. Linlithgow noted: "You make various suggestions in your letter as to what the govern-

ment should do. Government in this case is, of course, the provincial government of Bengal and I have no doubt that you have put your suggestions to the ministers, for it is to the provincial government that it will fall to deal with them"; quoted in Bhatia, *Famines*, 339.

75. Bearce, *British Attitudes*, 222. Dalhousie commented: "I shall not be thought vainglorious if I say that the successful execution and completion of such a work as the Ganges canal would, even if it stood alone, suffice to signalize an Indian Administration"; ibid., 223.

76. Vera Powell Anstey, *The Economic Development of India* (3d ed., London: Longmans, Green & Co., 1936), 161; A. V. Raman Rao, *Economic Development of Andhra Pradesh, 1766-1957* (Bombay: Popular Book Depot, 1958), 87.

77. Cited in V. B. Singh (ed.), *Economic History of India, 1867-1956* (Bombay: Allied Publishers, 1965), 164.

78. Bhatia, *Famines*, 142ff.

79. Ibid., 197.

80. Singh, *Economic History*, 165.

81. Bhatia, *Famines*, 198.

82. Great Britain, Royal Commission on Agriculture in India, *Report*... (London: H.M. Stationery Office, 1928), 36. Hereafter cited as Royal Commission, *Report*, 1928.

83. In the district of Lyallpur, for example, the population density rose from six per square kilometer in 1891 to 142 in 1931; Gilbert Etienne, *L'Inde: Economie et population* (Geneva: E. Droz, 1955), 25.

84. Spear, *India*, 285, obviously based on the Agricultural Report of 1928; and Anstey, *Economic Development*, 163; Singh, *Economic History*, gives the following table, 177:

	TOTAL AREA CULTIVATED	IRRIGATION: GOVERNMENT WORKS	TOTAL AREA IRRIGATED
	(millions of acres)	(in percentages)	
1896-1900	179.5	16.0	29.6
1905-1910	204.5	21.2	39.4
1916-1920	203.9	25.9	46.5
1926-1930	209.4	27.2	46.5
1936-1940	212.0	30.5	54.5

The percentage of irrigated areas varied in 1938/39 from 4.5 percent in Bombay and 6.4 percent in Bengal to 42.5 percent in Bihar/Orissa and 88.1 percent in Sind; Singh, *Economic History*, 173.

85. Implicitly, Singh, *Economic History*; Spear, *India*, 285, compares the area with the twenty million irrigated acres in the United States. In 1947 the Punjab had twice as large an irrigated area as Egypt, although Russell Lidman notes—and this is characteristic of the divergencies in interpreting the figures— that Egypt was already irrigating its entire arable area as early as 1911, as compared to only 20 percent in India; Russell Lidman and Robert I. Domrese, "India," in Sir William Arthur Lewis (ed.), *Tropical Development, 1880-1913: Studies in Economic Progress* (London: Allen & Unwin, 1970), 316.

86. Ibid., 317. Dutt raised this complaint in his *Economic History of India*, 174. See also Anstey, *Economic Development*, 162f; and, rebutting Morris D. Morris's essay in the issue cited, Bipan Chandra, "Reinterpretation of 19th Century Indian Economy," *Indian Economic and Social History Review*, 5 (March 1968), 50, 67.

87. George Blyn, *Agricultural Trends in India, 1891-1947: Output, Availability and Productivity* (Philadelphia: University of Pennsylvania Press, 1966), 18, 57.

88. Royal Commission, *Report*, 1928, 34.

89. See, among others, Irfan Habib, "Potentialities of Capitalistic Development in the Economy of Mughal India," *JEH*, 29 (March 1969). B. R. Grove speaks of "private property,"

insofar as the zamindars could mortgage, sell, and pass land on to heirs; "Nature of Landrights in Moghul India," *IESHR*, 1 (July 1963), 15.

90. Dietmar Rothermund, "Die historische Analyse des Bodenrechts als Grundlage für das Verständnis gegenwärtiger Agrarstruktur, dargestellt am Beispiel Indiens," in Albertini, *Moderne Kolonialgeschichte*, 294.

91. This is shown by Dharma Kumar, *Land and Caste in South India* (Cambridge: University Press, 1965), 187f.; idem, "Caste and Landlessness in South India," *CSSH*, 4 (April 1962).

92. H. R. Wright, "Some Aspects of the Permanent Settlement in Bengal," *EcHR*, 7 (August 1954). See also the excellent survey, Giorgio Borsa, "La Proprietà della terra in India sotto il dominio inglese," *Nuova Rivista Storica*, 50 (May-August 1966).

93. Bearce, *British Attitudes*, 45.

94. Bengal, Land Revenue Commission, "Report...with Minutes of Dissent" (Alipore, Bengal: Bengal Government Press, 1940-), II, 5; III, 66; V, 120, 396.

95. Angus Maddison, *Class Structure and Economic Growth: India and Pakistan since the Moghuls* (London: Allen & Unwin, 1971), 46.

96. Borsa, "Propietà della terra," 354 n.52; Bankey Bihari Misra, *The Indian Middle Classes* (London: Oxford University Press, 1961), 132.

97. Misra, *Middle Classes*, 131.

98. Tapan Raychaudhuri, "Permanent Settlement in Operation: Bakarganj District, East Bengal," in Robert Eric Frykenberg (ed.), *Land Control and Social Structure in Indian History* (Madison: University of Wisconsin Press, 1969). Also excellent is Rajat K. Ray, "The Crisis of Bengal Agriculture, 1870-1927: The Dynamics of Immobility," *IESHR*, 10 (September 1973).

99. Beaglehole, *Thomas Munro*, 134, 151; Raman Rao, *Economic Development*, 62.

100. From the more recent literature, see Thomas R. Metcalf, "The British and the Moneylenders in Nineteenth Century India," *JMH*, 34 (December 1962).

101. A British tax collector in the Deccan, as quoted in Neil Charlesworth, "The Myth of the Deccan Riots of 1875," *MAS*, 6 (October 1972), 409.

102. Metcalf, "The British," 393; Ravinder Kumar, *Western India in the Nineteenth Century: A Study in the Social History of Maharashtra* (London: Routledge & K. Paul, 1968).

103. Cited in Akshayakumar Ramanlal Desai, *Social Background of Indian Nationalism* (Bombay: Oxford University Press, 1948), 60. See also Blunt, "Ideas about India."

104. Cited by Desai, *Social Background*, 62.

105. See the evidence in Metcalf, "The British"; and Kumar, *Western India*, 190ff.

106. Kumar, *Western India*, ch. 5, "The Deccan Riots of 1875"; idem, "The Deccan Riots of 1875," *JAS*, 24 (August 1965). Charlesworth, "Myth of the Deccan Riots," as the title implies, writes of "myths" surrounding the events. High existing debts were not the causes of the unrest, nor can one speak of social change. The unrest died down rather quickly and was accompanied by astonishingly little violence. The agitation was directed at nonlocal moneylenders and reflected the loss of authority of the old village elite.

107. Quoted from the justification of the bill in the Imperial Legislative Council, 17 July 1879, by Kumar, *Western India*, 214. Yet another passage may profitably be quoted from this speech: "On the other hand, those into whose hands the land is now observed to be passing are not yearning for it to improve it by their capital or intelligence. With solitary exceptions, the transferees are the professional moneylenders, who have no wish even to hold the status of landed proprietors....Such conditions deprive the transfer of land from distressed to moneyed classes of all the glosses with which political economy would surround it. They show that the noble gift of property in land, made by the British Government to the peasants for their sole benefit, is passing, contrary to their intentions, and in frustration of their objects to a class unfitted to receive it"; ibid., 213. On the background and the effects of the act, see also Dietmar Rothermund, "Freedom of Contract and the Problem of Land Alienation in British India," *SA*, 3 (August 1973).

108. William Digby, *"Prosperous" British India, a Revelation from Official Records* (London: T. Unwin, 1901), 106.

109. Norman G. Barrier, "The Formulation and Enactment of the Punjab Alienation of Land Bill," *IESHR*, 2 (April 1965); idem, *The Punjab Alienation of Land Bill of 1900* (Durham: Duke University Press, 1966); Rothermund, "Freedom of Contract," 74f.

110. See also Digby, *"Prosperous" British India*, 301, 587.

111. Metcalf, *Aftermath*, 216.

112. Malcolm Lyall Darling, *The Punjab Peasant in Prosperity and Debt* (4th ed., Bombay: Oxford University Press, 1947), 3-4.

113. Royal Commission, *Report*, 1928, 136.

114. Darling, *Punjab Peasant*, 19.

115. Nagendranath Gangulee, *The Indian Peasant and His Environment (the Linlithgow Commission and After)*, (London, New York: H. Milford, Oxford University Press, 1935), 20.

116. Quoted in Ray, "Crisis of Bengal Agriculture," 269. The statement dates from 1917.

117. Landowners got mortgages for 9 to 12 percent, tenants and laborers had to pay as much as 300 percent; small wonder that in one village all land had changed hands during the previous thirty or forty years. Moreover, "debt leads directly to agricultural inefficiency"; Radhakamal Mukerjee (ed.), *Economic Problems of Modern India* (London: Macmillan and Co., 1939) I, 170.

118. Maurice Zinkin, *Asia and the West* (London: Chatto & Windus, 1951), 84.

119. Provincial Banking Enquiry Committee, as quoted by Darling, *Punjab Peasant*, 248.

120. Ibid., 179. Gangulee says the normal rate was 36 percent; *Indian Peasant*, 11, 19.

121. Darling, *Punjab Peasant*, ch. 13. "Report of the Royal Commission (Agriculture)," in *Sessional Papers*, 1928 Cmd. 3132, VIII, 9, 444ff.; Singh, *Economic History*, 151ff.; C. B. Mamoria, "History and Growth of Cooperative Movement in India," *Modern Review*, 94 (August/September 1953).

122. Metcalf, *Aftermath*, 187; Mason, *Men Who Ruled*, II, 51.

123. Metcalf, *Aftermath*, 187.

124. Mukerjee, *Economic Problems*, I, 227, 137.

125. "In some districts the sub-infeudation has grown to astonishing proportions, as many as fifty or more intermediary interests having been created, the Zamindars at the top and the actual cultivator at the bottom"; Simon, *Const. Report I*, 340, as quoted in Desai, *Social Background*, 68. See the description in Raychaudhuri, "Permanent Settlement," 167f. "The evils of absenteeism, of management of estates by unsympathetic agents, of unhappy relations between landlord and tenant, and of the multiplication of tenure holders, or middlemen, between zemindar and cultivator in many and various degrees" are noted in *Land Revenue Policy*. . . . (Calcutta, 1902), as quoted in Anil Seal, *The Emergence of Indian Nationalism: Competition and Collaboration in the Later Nineteenth Century* (London: Cambridge University Press, 1968), 54.

126. P. J. Musgrave, "Landlords and Lords of the Land: Estate Management and Social Change in Uttar Pradesh 1860-1920," *MAS*, 6 (July 1972); Metcalf, *Aftermath*, 187ff.

127. "The Taluqdars are the most loyal body in India and a breakwater between trouble in the Punjab and trouble in Bengal. They have always been strong supporters of Government." The reform (Oudh Rent Bill) thus could only be a compromise, Butler noted, and it was good that the taluqdars had supported it; Butler to Reading, 27 June 1921, "Butler Collection," F 116/57. Mr. Wilson, deputy commissioner of Ihelm (Punjab), commented however: "But as the 'Junkers' help to form the Government's body guard on the Council this ever growing latifundia 'which ruined Rome and the Provinces' is not likely to receive any check"; Royal Commission, *Report*, 1928, "Evidences Taken in the Punjab," 809.

128. Walter Hauser, "The Indian National Congress and Land Policy in the Twentieth Century," *IESHR*, 1 (July-September 1963).

129. F. A. Sachse, "The Work of the Bengal Land Revenue Commission," *Journal of the Royal Society of Arts*, 89 (19 September 1941), 666f. On the political situation in Bengal, see J. H. Broomfield, *Elite Conflict in a Plural Society: Twentieth Century Bengal* (Berkeley: University of California Press, 1968), 291f.

130. Singh, *Economic History*, 127.

131. See Table 3 in *Papers on National Income and Allied Topics* (v. I- , New York: Asia Pub. House, 1960-), I, 244.

132. Blyn, *Agricultural Trends*, 133f.

133. Wilfred Malenbaum, *Prospects for Indian Development* (London: G. Allen & Unwin, 1962), 123.

134. Ibid., 128.

135. Darling, *Punjab Peasant*, 253 n.2.

136. Ibid., 3 n.1. In a similar vein, Royal Commission, *Report*, 1928, 13.

137. Bengal before World War II:

ACRES	PERCENT OF FAMILIES
Over 10	8.4
5-10	17
4-5	8
3-4	9.4
2-3	11.2
under 2	46

A 1930 investigation in Sind and Gujurat revealed that in one village holdings were divided as follows:

ACRES	NUMBER OF FAMILIES
Over 30	18
21-30	18
16-20	19
11-15	28
6-10	67
1-5	133
Under 1	143

The average holding was 7.3 acres (it had been 14 acres 25 years earlier). Since 15 to 20 acres was an "economic holding," 87 percent failed to reach that level; Gangulee, *Indian Peasant*, 35. An investigation in Madras revealed that in 1930, 75 percent of the holdings were 5 acres or less. But the average size was decreasing and in 1941 it was 3.7 acres; C.W.B. Zacharias, *Madras Agriculture* (Madras; University of Madras, 1950), 116.

138. Singh, *Economic History*, 137. In one village in the Deccan, the average holding in 1771 had been 40 acres, was still 17 acres in the period 1820-1840, but was only 7 acres in 1915. In the latter year, 60 percent were less than five acres; *Man, Land and Labour in a Deccan Village*, as cited in Anstey, *Economic Development*, 100.

139. As quoted in Daniel and Alice Thorner, *Land and Labour in India* (Bombay, New York: Asia Publishing House, 1962), 110.

140. Mukerjee, *Economic Problems*, I, 116; Singh, *Economic History*, 138. In 1950, in one Bengal district comprising eleven villages, 207 holdings occupied only 820.97 acres, and each holding itself comprised 14.2 plots of an average size of .28 acres; K. M. Mukerjee, "Land Transfers in Birbhum, 1928-1955," *IESHR*, 8 (September 1971), 261.

141. Area and average productivity per acre in India, 1900-1901 to 1939-40 (five-year averages):

Period	Area (million acres)	Value of product (Rps. million)	Average productivity per acre (Rps.)
FOOD CROPS			
1900-1 to 1904-5	221.0	5,602.6	25.4
1905-6 to 1909-10	231.0	5,512.4	23.9
1910-11 to 1914-15	238.3	5,918.6	24.9
1915-16 to 1919-20	239.5	5,992.6	25.0
1920-1 to 1924-5	238.1	5,626.0	23.7
1925-6 to 1929-30	238.1	5,503.2	23.1
1930-1 to 1934-5	247.0	5,702.0	23.1
1935-6 to 1939-40	244.5	5,550.0	22.7
COMMERCIAL CROPS			
1900-1 to 1904-5	55.4	2,033.6	36.7
1905-6 to 1909-10	61.8	2,079.4	33.6
1910-11 to 1914-15	66.5	2,190.6	32.9
1915-16 to 1919-20	62.8	2,272.8	36.2
1920-1 to 1924-5	63.0	2,357.0	36.8
1925-6 to 1929-30	71.7	2,455.8	34.2
1930-1 to 1934-5	71.8	2,607.8	36.3
1935-6 to 1939-40	75.3	2,852.0	37.9
ALL CROPS			
1900-1 to 1904-5	276.4	7,636.2	27.6
1905-6 to 1909-10	292.8	7,591.8	25.9
1910-11 to 1914-15	304.8	8,109.2	26.6
1915-16 to 1919-20	302.3	8,265.4	27.3
1920-1 to 1924-5	302.1	7,993.0	26.5
1925-6 to 1929-30	309.8	7,959.0	25.7
1930-1 to 1934-5	318.8	8,309.8	26.1
1935-6 to 1939-40	319.8	8,402.0	26.3

SOURCE: Amiya Kumar Bagchi, *Private Investment in India*, 1900-1939 (Cambridge: Cambridge University Press, 1972), 95.

142. Blyn, *Agricultural Trends*, 150f.; Bagchi, *Private Investment*, 96. These findings have recently been questioned. Alan W. Heston points out that the statistics are based on data furnished by tax officials and that these data show yields for the period before 1900 far in excess of actual harvests; the picture of generally falling yields is incorrect; "Official Yields per Acre in India, 1886-1947: Some Questions of Interpretations," *IESHR*, 10 (December 1973).

143. See the fine chapter on this in Bagchi, *Private Investment*, 99ff.

144. Arthur W. Silver, *Manchester Men and Indian Cotton, 1847-1872* (Manchester: Manchester University Press, 1966).

145. Royal Commission, *Report*, 1928, 15ff.

146. For wheat in 1926-1927, with a total acreage of 24 million, only 2.9 percent; for rice in 1939, 6 percent of the cultivated area; Blyn, *Agricultural Trends*, 159. Altogether, in 1938-1939, 11.1 percent of the cultivated area; ibid., 200.

147. Malenbaum, *Prospects*, 126f.

148. Singh, *Economic History*, 140. Etienne, *L'Inde*, 54, gives the following figures for 1950:

	RICE	WHEAT	COTTON
India	100	100	100
Egypt	241	—	500
China	243	152	—
USA	161	133	167

149. See also diagrams 5, 3, p. 101. Older accounts, which place the beginning of the fall in output as early as 1900, must now be accounted obsolete. Examples are Singh, *Economic History*, 133f.; and Daniel Thorner, "Long-Term Trends in Output," in Kuznets, *Economic Growth*, and reprinted in Thorner, *Land and Labour in India*.

150. As Singh, *Economic History*, 132, justly notes.

151. Ibid., 134; Etienne, *L'Inde*, 26.

152. Biney Bushan Chaudhuri, "Growth of Commercial Agriculture in Bengal 1859-1885," *IESHR*, 7 (March 1970). An enlightening picture is offered in H. C. Peyer, "Leonhard Ziegler, ein Zürcher in Indien, 1802-1846," *Zürcher Taschenbuch* (Zurich, 1965). As administrator, Ziegler reported: "Day in, day out for nine months I faced the unpleasant duty of punishing Assamis for indolence, recalcitrance, and crop damage—which I usually did with my quirt," p. 47. "The plantation consisted of some 2,000 scattered acres, worked by 5 to 6,000 natives," p. 58. His boss, the planter, lived in a villa and kept a "table which groaned from the weight of dainties and elegant drink from all parts of the world," p. 49.

153. My remarks are based on the comprehensive seminar paper of Max Lemmenmeier. See also Hans Sieber, *Die realen Austauschverhältnisse zwischen Entwicklungsländer und Industriestaaten; eine Verifizierung der These Prebischs* (Tübingen: Mohr, 1968), 124f.

154. Peter Harnetty, "Cotton Exports and Indian Agriculture," *EcHR*, 24 (August 1971).

155. Blyn, *Agricultural Trends*, 92, 254. See also *Papers on National Income*, as cited in n.131 above.

156. In 1929-1930, an acre of rice produced an income of 66.2 rupees, jute, 126.58 rupees; Blyn, *Agricultural Trends*, 251. When the price of rice fell, more was planted. Before 1914, many jute-farming peasants had sufficient rice, but others bought, because even in bad years it paid better to grow jute; James Charles Jack, *The Economic Life of a Bengal District: A Study* (Oxford: Clarendon Press, 1916), 85. Ray, too, writing critically of the impact of colonialism on Bengalese agrarian society, notes: "Jute undoubtedly paid the cultivators better than rice and was on balance beneficial to the peasant economy of East Bengal. Because Bengal had a monopoly of this commodity in the world market, the inflow from this new source of income might conceivably have acted as a stimulus for a much better rate of growth in the agriculture of Bengal, had it not been for the fact that the greater part of this new income was siphoned off to the jute manufactures of Calcutta and Dundee through artificially depressed buying prices of raw jute"; Ray, "Crisis of Bengal Agriculture," 261.

157. For British India in 1911-1912, the figures were:

	MILLIONS OF ACRES		MILLIONS OF ACRES
Foodgrains	183.6	Tea	0.5
Oil seeds	15.3	Opium	0.2
Sugar	2.4	Tobacco	0.9
Orchards	4.4	Spices	1.4
Fodder	4.9	Other non-food	2
Other foodcrops	1.7		235.3
Cotton	14.5		
Jute	3.1	Less double cropping	–32.6
Indigo	0.3		202.7
Coffee	0.1		

SOURCE: Lewis, *Tropical Development*, 314. For India as a whole, see the analogous figures in *Papers on National Income*, as cited in n. 131 above.

158. Dharm Narain, *Impact of Price Movements on Areas under Selected Crops in India, 1900-1939* (Cambridge: University Press, 1965).

159. Gangulee, *Indian Peasant*, xvii.

160. Bhatia, *Famines*, 295f.

161. As a percentage of the "gross produce of the soil," revenue was:

LOCATION	PERCENTAGE
Bengal	5-6
Northwest	10
Punjab	8
Madras	20
Bombay	25

Digby, *"Prosperous" British India*, 366. Lower figures for Bombay and Madras are given in India, Famine Commission, 1878-1880, *Report of the Indian Famine Commission*... (C. 2591, 2735, 3086) (8 vols. in 3, London: HMSO, 1880-1885), III, 393f.

162. See, for example, Raychaudhuri, "Permanent Settlement," 168. For an extreme statement, see Maddison, *Class Structure*, 45, 48, who asserts that in 1947 the land tax was about 2 percent of agricultural and 1 percent of national income. But these figures are for the postwar period. A detailed investigation of the Punjab shows great fluctuations between 1913 and 1942. Tax levels remained relatively constant, while income fluctuated sharply, with taxes exceeding net income in three years; Sarjit Singh and John Landauer, "The Tax Bases of an Indian Land Tax," *IESHR*, 7 (December 1970).

163. Tryambak Mahadev Joshi et al., *Studies in the Taxation of Agricultural Land and Income in India* (New York: Asia Publishing House, 1966), 23, 82-83.

164. Daniel Thorner, *Investment in Empire: British Railway and Steam Shipping Enterprises in India, 1825-1849* (Philadelphia: University of Pennsylvania Press, 1950); idem, "Great Britain and the Development of India's Railways," *JEH*, 11 (Fall 1951); W. J. Macpherson, "Investment in Indian Railways, 1845-1875," *EcHR*, 8 (December 1955); see also Anstey, *Economic Development*, 130ff.; Singh, *Economic History*, ch. 15.

165. Thorner, "Great Britain," 398.

166. Macpherson, "Investment in Indian Railways," 181 n.12.

167. Morris D. Morris, "Values as an Obstacle to Economic Growth in South Asia: An Historical Survey," *JEH*, 27 (December 1967), 598, with reference to Anstey and Daniel Houston Buchanan, *The Development of Capitalistic Enterprise in India* (New York: A. M. Kelley, 1966).

168. Thorner, "Great Britain," 391.

169. Anstey, *Economic Development*, 135ff.; Günther Voigt, "Organisatorische Nachkriegsprobleme der Britisch-Indischen Eisenbahnen," *Archiv für Eisenbahnwesen*, 46 (1923), 444ff.

170. Thorner, "Great Britain," 396; Singh, *Economic History*, 338.

171. Thorner, "Great Britain," 396.

172. Singh, *Economic History*, 337.

173. Income for 1925-1926 was first class: 12 million; second class: 35 million; and third class: 348 million; *Archiv für Eisenbahnwesen*, 51 (1928), 277.

174. Cited in Thorner, "Great Britain," 398.

175. Karl Marx, *Werke, Schriften, Briefe*, ed. H. S. Lieber (Stuttgart: Cotta, 1960), IX, 220f.; article from *New York Daily Tribune*, 8 August 1853.

176. Sunil Kumar Sen, *Studies in Industrial Policy and the Development of India (1858-1914)* (Calcutta: Progressive Publishers, 1964), 65f.

177. Ibid., 84ff.

178. *Archiv für Eisenbahnwesen*, 51 (1928), 277.

179. The most important accounts, some already cited, are: Dhananjaya Ramchandra Gadgil, *The Industrial Evolution of India in Recent Times, 1860-1939* (5th ed., Oxford: University Press, 1971); Buchanan, *Capitalistic Enterprise*; Anstey, *Economic Development*; Singh, *Economic History*; the section on India in Lewis, *Tropical Development*; Lamb, "State and Eco-

nomic Development"; Bagchi, *Private Investment*; S. K. Sen, "Die Investitionen britischer Unternehmer in der Frühzeit der Industrialisierung Indiens, 1854-1914," in Albertini, *Moderne Kolonialgeschichte*.

180. Sen, "Investitionen," 314, gives the following figures:

YEAR	EXPORTS OF COTTON GOODS	IMPORTS OF COTTON GOODS
	(IN MILLIONS OF RUPEES)	
1814/15	8.49	0.05
1819/20	9.03	1.58
1824/25	6.02	5.30
1829/30	0.13	5.22

181. Dutt, *Economic History*, I, 295.

182. Morris D. Morris, "Towards a Reinterpretation of Nineteenth Century Indian Economic History," *JEH*, 23 (December 1963), reprinted in *IESHR*, 5 (March 1968). See, in the same issue, Bipan Chandra's sharp rejoinder, in which he argues that there is so much evidence—for example, Jack, *Economic Life*—that a crisis in the Indian trades can hardly be doubted, especially since British export prices fell sharply over the course of the century and necessarily increased competition. The trades remained in the villages, but wages fell. All of India was not equally affected, and Indians could not afford the finer stuffs. But stagnation surely occurred. In this same issue, however, Tapan Raychaudhuri, citing Gadgil and Nikanth Maheshwar Joshi, *Urban Handicrafts of the Bombay Deccan* (Poona: D. R. Gadgil, 1936), represented the thesis that Indian trades were not displaced; some indeed underwent a crisis, but others adapted, and new ones were created.

183. On the Parsis, see Eckehard Kulke's excellent *The Parsees in India: A Minority as Agent of Social Change* (Munich: Weltforum Verlag, 1974).

184. On this, see Sung Jae Koh, *Stages of Industrial Development in Asia: A Comparative History of the Cotton Industry in Japan, India, China and Korea* (Philadelphia: University of Pennsylvania Press, 1966), 100f.; Anstey, *Economic Development*, 274; Singh, *Economic History*, 231f.; Lamb, "State and Economic Development," 461f.

185. Peter Harnetty, "The Imperialism of Free Trade: Lancashire and the Indian Cotton Duties, 1859-1862," *EcHR*, 18 (August 1965).

186. Lamb, "State and Economic Development," 489.

187. Singh, *Economic History*, 446.

188. Buchanan, *Capitalistic Enterprise*, 209.

189. Singh, *Economic History*, 243ff.; Koh, *Industrial Development*, 153f.; Anstey, *Economic Development*, 263f.

190. Ian M. Drummond, *British Economic Policy and the Empire, 1919-1939* (London: Allen & Unwin, 1972), ch. 4; Bagchi, *Private Investment*, 237ff.

191. From Singh, *Economic History*, 244-45, 238, 247; Buchanan *Capitalistic Enterprise*, 201, 224:

YEAR	FACTORIES	SPINDLES (IN MILLIONS)	THREAD (IN MILLION LBS.)	LOOMS	CLOTH (IN MILLION LBS.)
1919/20	—	—	636	—	1,640
1924/25	—	—	719	—	1,970
1930/31	339	9.3	867	182,000	2,561
1935/36	—	—	—	—	3,571
1939/40	—	—	1,235	—	4,012
1941	390	10	—	199,000	—

192. Anstey, *Economic Development*, 265; Buchanan, *Capitalistic Enterprise*, 222.

193. See the tables in Bagchi, *Private Investment*, 238.

194. The *Economist* of 26 July 1930 provides Manchester's reaction to the 1930 report about the Indian cotton industry: "Nothing short of a miracle will enable Lancashire to recapture her lost trade in piece-goods with India." It was also noted that the Bombay Mill Owner's Association was fighting Japanese competition.

195. 1909-1914, 192.8 mil. lbs.; 1925-1926, 31.9 mil.; 1939-1940, 37 mil.; Singh, *Economic History*, 240, 247.

196. Ibid., 244-45; Buchanan, *Capitalistic Enterprise*, table, 223.

197. On this, see Anstey, *Economic Development*, 268ff.; Buchanan, *Capitalistic Enterprise*, 225f.

198. In the 1930s, Japan needed 6 persons per 1,000 spindles, India, 15, and in 1920, Japan needed 93 workers per 100 looms but by 1931 only 50; Koh, *Industrial Development*, 159.

199. S. B. Saul, *Studies in British Overseas Trade, 1870-1914* (Liverpool: Liverpool University Press, 1960), 62f., 193.

200. Buchanan, *Capitalistic Enterprise*, table, 252, shows enormous fluctuations.

201. In 1926-27, 22.1 million worth of rupees in jute products and 16.8 million in raw jute; *Indian Journal of Economics*, 9 (July 1928-1929), 699.

202. *Economist*, 26 April 1924, 867; Bagchi, *Private Investment*, 284f.

203. Buchanan, *Capitalistic Enterprise*, ch. 12; Singh, *Economic History*, 303f.; see also Sen, *Studies in Industrial Policy*, 28ff.

204. *Economist*, 17 May 1924, 1013.

205. Anstey, *Economic Development*, 239f., was also very critical: "Little can be expected from workers so miserably housed and cared for as Indian miners."

206. Output per capita underground:

COUNTRY	1921 TONNAGE	1932 TONNAGE
UK	178	323
Belgium	143	229
Japan	136	421
India	162	170

SOURCE: Ibid., 240 n.4.

207. Buchanan, *Capitalistic Enterprise*, ch. 13; Singh, *Economic History*, ch. 9; Sen, *Studies in Industrial Policy*, ch. 4; Anstey, *Economic Development*, 242ff.

208. Sen. "Investitionen," 327.

209. Singh, *Economic History*, table 204, gives the following figures:

Year	Tonnage
1916	99,000
1921	126,000
1929	400,000
1939	842,905
1943	1,150,000

210. Anstey, *Economic Development*, 245.

211. Viceroy Reading wrote Butler on 3 May 1924 that Tata was "in a very bad way. . . may crack financially"; "Butler Collection," F116/37.

212. Details are in Anstey, *Economic Development*; Buchanan, *Capitalistic Enterprise*. See also *Economist*, 9 April 1927, 738.

213. William A. Johnson, *The Steel Industry of India* (Cambridge: Harvard University Press, 1966), 12, 14.

214. Ibid., 45.

215. The concepts "lopsided" and "arrested" were used by Sir Basil Blackett, "The Economic Progress of India," *Journal of the Royal Society of Arts*, 78 (31 January 1930), 314, 317. See also Lamb, "State and Economic Development"; Bagchi, *Private Investment*. Krishan A. Saini introduced an additional term in his essay, "A Case of Aborted Economic Growth," *JAH*, 5 (1971).

216. Bagchi, *Private Investment*; Buchanan, *Capitalistic Enterprise*; Singh, *Economic History*.

217. Anstey, *Economic Development*, 292.

218. From Mukerjee, *Economic Problems*, II, 1941:

INDUSTRY	PERSONS EMPLOYED	INDUSTRY	PERSONS EMPLOYED
Cotton (spinning, weaving and other)	516,000	Cement, lime, and potteries	13,000
Jute mills	281,000	Tobacco	12,000
Cotton spinning and baling	180,000	Petroleum refineries	11,000
Railway and tramway works	116,000	Leather and shoe and tanneries	8,000
Rice mills	79,000	Woollen mills	8,000
Sugar factories	73,000	Dyeing and bleaching and indigo	8,000
Tea factories	66,000	Silk mills (including filatures)	7,000
Printing and book-binding, etc.	40,000	Glass works	7,000
Jute presses	32,000	Paper mills	7,000
Matches	21,000	Coach building and motor-car repairing	7,000
Dockyards, shipbuilding and engineering	21,000	Stone dressing	6,000
Ordnance factories	19,000	Hosiery	6,000
Bricks and tiles	15,000	Flour mills	6,000
Oil mills	15,000	Kerosin tinning and packing	6,000
Saw mills	14,000	Rubber	6,000
Rope works	14,000		

219. Habib, "Potentialities of Capitalistic Development."

220. Conversation with the author in Delhi, October 1972.

221. Saini, "Aborted Economic Growth," 102, gives the following figures:

YEAR	MILLIONS OF £s
1860	69
1870	153
1884	255
1897	294
1910	430

For 1910 the breakdown is as follows:

	MILLIONS OF £s
Government securities	158
Railways	194
Plantations, banks, factories, insurance, etc.	15
Mining	11
Miscellaneous	52

SOURCE: Ibid., 106.

222. Ibid., 111.

223. The best account is Lamb, "State and Economic Development."

224. "The Government of India have, for some time past, had under special consideration the importance of developing the iron industry in India. The advantages which such development would afford both the State and the public—by cheapening the cost of railway construction and maintenance, and of works for improving the water-supply; by substituting metal for more perishable materials in buildings; by reducing the home charges and their concomitant loss by exchange; by creating for the population non-agricultural employment; and by increasing the means for profitable investment of capital—are too well known to require lengthened exposition"; Resolution of 4 August 1882, as cited in Sen, *Studies in Industrial Policy*, 47.

225. Morley to viceroy, 29 July 1910, "Despatches Revenue," no. 50, in England, India Office, *Selections from Despatches Addressed to the Several Governments of India by the Secretary of State in Council* ("53rd Series, Part II") (London: HMSO, 1911), 195. On Curzon's attitude, Chatterton's activities in Madras, and the administration's conservative laissez-faire attitudes, the first detailed study is Clive Dewey, "The End of the Imperialism of Free Trade: The Eclipse of the Lancashire Lobby and the Concession of Fiscal Autonomy to India," in Clive Dewey and A. G. Hopkins (eds.), *The Imperial Impact: Studies in the Economic History of Africa and India* (London: Athlone Press, 1978).

226. Bipan Chandra, *The Rise and Growth of Economic Nationalism in India: Economic Policies of Indian National Leadership, 1880-1905* (New Delhi: People's Publishing House, 1966). Ivan Klein, "Indian Nationalism and Anti-Industrialization: The Roots of Gandhian Economics," *SA*, 3 (August 1973), points out the ambivalent relationship between reformers and nationalists. W. S. Blunt also demanded, among other things, customs protection so that "factories could be established in the Indian country towns in which the surplus labour of the ryot would find employment, and so the injury done him be in part redressed"; "Ideas about India," 177.

227. He was less optimistic than Butler: "Crux will surely come when they begin to insist, as I believe they will before long, on a more generous treatment of India in regard both to the financial relations between India and the metropolis and the econom c question, i.e., tariffs and excise duties. You do not mention these points, yet they are the points upon which all the Indians I have met, Mohammedans and Hindus, moderates and conservatives, politicians and others have laid particular stress. Political 'nationalism,' I should say, may in the near future give way to an economic 'nationalism' which will put British statesmanship to a far more severe test..."; Chirol to Butler, "Butler Collection," F. 116/37.

228. Sen, *Studies in Industrial Policy*.

229. Frederick Lehmann, "Great Britain and the Supply of Railway Locomotives of India: A Case Study of 'Economic Imperialism'," *IESHR*, 2 (October 1965). This was criticized by, among others, G. Das Birla, "Industrialization in India," *Annals of the American Academy of Political and Social Science*, 233 (May 1944), 123.

230. India, Industrial Commission, *Report of the Indian Industrial Commission, 1916-18* (Calcutta: Superintendent Government Printing, 1918).

231. This is shown clearly by Dewey, "End of Imperialism," who notes particularly the consequences of the Montagu-Chelmsford reforms, which turned the industry departments over to the provinces. Also interesting is his evidence that the British viewed industrialization as, on the one hand, a means to capture the nationalist opposition, and, on the other, forecast new difficulties as a result of it.

232. *Economist*, 21 October 1922, 653, spoke of a "lamentable decision" and noted: "It is a melancolic Report, written by unhappy men."

233.

AVERAGE TARIFF LEVELS	1913	1925	AS PERCENTAGE
USA	33	29	− 13
Australia	17	25	+ 68
Canada	18	16	− 12
India	4	14	+286
France	18	12	− 66
Great Britain	0	4	+400

SOURCE: William Arthur Lewis, *Economic Survey, 1919-1939* (London: G. Allen & Unwin, 1949), 48.

234. Percentage Ratio Per Capita of Government Expenditure to National Income:

	India	Japan	UK	Germany
1890	8.60	12.1	8.8	13.2
1900	10.35	21.5	14.4	14.9
1913	7.66	29.7	12	14.8
1920	5.56	46.9	26.1	N.A.
1928	7.75	36.7	24.2	29.4
1933	9.81	51.2	25.9	36.8
1938	8.00	56.0	30.1	42.4

SOURCE: Kaipa Narayana Reddy, *The Growth of Public Expenditure in India, 1872-1968: A Secular and Time Pattern Analysis* (New Delhi: Sterling Publishers, 1972), 62.

235. Central and provincial budgets for 1935-1936 show entries for the following amounts:

	Millions of Rupees
Military services	500
Interest on productive debt paid out of the profits of commercial departments	450
Interest on unproductive debt	126
Avoidance of debt—i.e.debt retirement	43
Administration of justice, jails, police	203
Agriculture	27
Industry	9
Scientific departments	7
Medical and public health	55
Education	122

SOURCE: Lamb, "State and Economic Development," 489-90.

236. Bagchi, *Private Investment*, 23, 47, 66.

237. See Sen. "Investitionen," 313, against Nurkse.

238. G. C. Allen, "Industrialization of the Far East," in *Cambridge Economic History of Europe* (7 vols., Cambridge: Cambridge University Press, 1963ff.), VI: 2, 909-16. In 1941, however, Mukerjee also noted: "Indian enterprise and capital are shy of developing on new and untried lines"; *Economic Problems*, II, 62. For an opposing view, see Bagchi, *Private Investment*, 20f.

239. See Amiya Kumar Bagchi's brilliant "European and Indian Entrepreneurship in India, 1900-1930," in *Elites in South Asia*, ed. Edmund Leach and S. N. Mukherjee (Cambridge: Cambridge University Press, 1970).

240. Like Bagchi, Morris emphasizes profit considerations. The Bengalis participated where profits were higher than in industry; Morris, "Values as an Obstacle," 61.

241. Bagchi, "Private Investment, 165f.
242. Anstey, *Economic Development*, 330; Singh, *Economic History*, 444f.
243. Imports, Exports, and Balance of Trade in 1913-1914 (in crores of rupees):

	Imports	Exports	Balance of trade
UK	117	58	− 59
Other parts of the British Empire	11	36	+ 25
Total British Empire	128	94	− 34
Europe	30	85	+ 55
USA	5	22	+ 17
Japan	5	23	+ 18
Other foreign countries	15	25	+ 10
Total foreign countries	55	155	+100
Grand Total	183	249	+ 66

SOURCE: Singh, *Economic History*, 448.

244. See note 199 above.
245. As adapted in Jürgen Wendt, *Economic Appeasement: Handel und Finanz in der britischen Deutschland-Politik, 1933-1939* (Düsseldorf: Bertelsmann, 1971), 378, from the *Economist*, 30 October 1937.
246. Bagchi, *Private Investment*, 88, 95.
247. Ibid., 439.
248. Wendt, *Economic Appeasement*, 378.
249. *Economist*, December 1935; also Blackett, "Economic Progress," 321.
250. On this, see Birendranath N. Ganguli, *Dadabhai Naoroji and the Drain Theory* (New York: Asia Publishing House, 1965). See also Naoroji's own *Poverty and Un-British Rule in India* (London: S. Sonnenschein & Co., 1901).
251. Lamb, "State and Economic Development," 492.
252. Lewis, *Tropical Development*, 332. For 1934, see Lamb, "State and Economic Development," 492.
253. Werner Simon, *Die britische Militärpolitik in Indien und ihre Auswirkungen auf den britisch-indischen Finanzhaushalt, 1875-1910* (Wiesbaden: Steiner, 1973), 32f. K. Narayana Reddy, "Indian Defence Expenditure, 1872-1967," *IESHR*, 7 (December 1970), 471, gives slightly higher expenditures.
254. In his statistical presentation for 1921-1922 to 1938-1939, Banerjee gives the following average values:

Service Balance (in millions of rupees)	
a) Credits	
1. Expenditure of foreign ships in India	3.94
2. Insurance receipts	0.47
Total Credits	4.41
b) Debits	
1. Freights, insurance etc. on imports	15.35
2. Government pensions	8.33
3. Cinematograph royalties	2.19
4. Profits etc. remitted by exchange banks	3.01
5. Tourist account	1.85
6. Insurance remittances	2.54
7. Coastal freights etc.	3.41

8. Interest on sterling public debt	18.07
9. Interest and dividends on other foreign investments	32.21
Total Debits	87.02
Net Debit (b-a)	82.61

SOURCE: From Arun Kumar Banerjee, *India's Balance of Payments: Estimates of Current and Capital Accounts from 1921-22 to 1938-39* (London: Asia Publishing House, 1963), 91. The government of India's transactions in the United Kingdom alone created a net debit of 12.88 million rupees; ibid., 115.

255. Ganguli, *Dadabhai Naoroji*, praises his subject's economic analysis but accepts no responsibility for his figures. See also K. N. Chaudhuri's very critical "India's International Economy in the Nineteenth Century: An Historical Survey," *MAS*, 2 (January 1968), 41f., where he notes the "proportion of invisible and debt servicing charges in the current account of the balance of payments could not have been much more than five percent of India's national income in this period [before 1914]."

256. Malenbaum, *Prospects*, 157.

257. Morris D. Morris, "Caste and the Evolution of the Industrial Workforce in India," *Proceedings of the American Philosophical Society*, 104 (1960).

258. Ibid., 128. Oddly enough, in Jamshedpur in 1951, of 550 workers in "least skilled categories," 21 percent were from twice-born castes; ibid., 129. See also Morris D. Morris, *The Emergence of an Industrial Labor Force in India: A Study of the Bombay Cotton Mills, 1854-1947* (Berkeley: University of California Press, 1965), 74. He gives the percentage of untouchables in the work force as a whole as: 1872, 0.99 percent; 1881, 2.1; 1911, 9.05; 1941, 13.81.

259. Buchanan, *Capitalistic Enterprise*, 295f.; Morris, *Emergence*, 63.

260. Buchanan, *Capitalistic Enterprise*, 298.

261. Morris, *Emergence*, 88-95.

262. Ibid., 38ff.

263. Ibid., 128.

264. "To a large extent the jobbers bring the labor. . . . We think the jobbers are the men most competent to do that under the present circumstances. . . . I do not think otherwise we can fill up the places of our absentees or keep all the machinery going. The jobbers are in touch with the men"; 1926 statement from the Millowner's Association, as quoted in ibid., 136.

265. As late as 1930, 18 percent of those working underground were women; Buchanan, *Capitalistic Enterprise*, 298. In the 1890s in one mine, 151 men, 59 women, and 24 girls and 54 boys between the ages of 9 and 16 worked underground; ibid., 299.

266. See the table in Bagchi, *Private Investment*, 122. For tea workers the index of real wages, with 1914=100, was 195 in 1933, 115 in 1935, and 124 in 1937; Sieber, *Realen Austauschverhältnisse*, 145.

267. "Report of the Royal Commission on Labour in India," in *Sessional Papers*, 1930-31, Cmd. 3883, XI, 571. Buchanan, *Capitalistic Enterprise*, ch. 17. There was on the average less food available than in Bombay's prisons; ibid., 401. In general, see also Murkerjee, *Economic Problems*, II, 107ff. Also excellent is Beryl M. Le P. Power, "Indian Labour Conditions," *Journal of the Royal Society of Arts*, 80 (24 June 1932), 763f.

268. V. B. Singh, "Trade Union Movement," in Singh, *Economic History*; Buchanan, *Capitalistic Enterprise*, ch. 17.

269. Ravindar Kumar, "The Bombay Textile Strike, 1919," *IESHR*, 8 (March 1971).

270. For the following see above all, Seal, *Indian Nationalism*; Misra, *Middle Classes*, chs. 6, 10; Rothermund, *Politische Willensbildung*, ch. 1.

271. The oft-cited portion of the "Minute on Education" reads as follows: "We must at present do our best to form a class who may be interpreters between us and the millions whom we govern—a class of persons Indian in blood and colour, but English in tastes, in opinions, in morals and in intellect"; quoted in Misra, *Middle Classes*, 154. Wood's "Educational Dispatch"

noted that European knowledge "will teach the natives of India the marvellous results of the employment of labour and capital, rouse them to emulate us in the development of the vast resources of their country, guide them in their efforts, and gradually, but certainly, confer upon them all the advantages which accompany the healthy increase of wealth and commerce; and, at the same time, secure to us a large and more certain supply of many articles necessary for our manufactures and extensively consumed by all classes of our population, as well as an almost inexhaustible demand for the produce of British Labour"; quoted ibid., 155.

272. The number of students rose from 4,499 in 1873 to 18,571 in 1893; ibid., 283.

273. Of the students in the colleges in Bombay and Poona, in 1884, 241 were Brahmins, 13 Kshtryas, and 51 Vanis. In Deccan College in Poona 97 percent of the students were Brahmins; Kumar, *Western India*, 282f. For Bengal, see Broomfield, *Elite Conflict*, 7f.

274. In 1893 there were 97,000 primary schools with 2.45 million students.

275. On 18 June 1888, the Indian government stated: "It would be premature to establish technical schools on such a scale as in European countries, and thereby aggravate the present difficulties by adding to the educated unemployed a new class of professional men for whom there is no commercial demand"; quoted in Misra, *Middle Classes*, 286.

276. Aparna Basu, "Indian Primary Education, 1900-1920," *IESHR*, 8 (September 1971).

277. The figures for 1937 were 272 arts colleges, 7 engineering schools, 6 agricultural, and 2 forestry colleges; Ludwig Alsdorf, *Vorderindien: Bharat, Pakistan, Ceylon; eine Landes-und Kulturkunde* (Braunschweig: G. Westermann, 1955), 96.

278. On this point, see Charles Herman Heimsath, *Indian Nationalism and Hindu Social Reform* (Princeton: Princeton University Press, 1964), 10ff. For example, B. K. Chandra Sen a leader of the Brahmo Samaj, noted in 1877: "Who can deny that Victoria is an instrument in the hands of Providence to elevate this degraded country in the scale of nations." He demanded of his educated countrymen that they "be loyal to the British Government, that came to your rescue, as God's ambassador, when your country was sunk in ignorance and superstition and hopeless jejuneness, and has since lifted you to your present high position"; ibid., 21. On the important M. G. Ranade (1852-1904), see also Kumar, *Western India*, 290f.

279. Surendranath Banerjea, *A Nation in the Making: Being the Reminiscences of Fifty Years of Public Life* (London: Oxford University Press, 1928), 25. In 1873 the social reformer Ranade wanted to marry a widow after his own wife had died but gave way to the pressure of his father and married an eleven-year old girl; Heimsath, *Indian Nationalism*, 184.

280. See above all Seal, *Indian Nationalism*, ch. 5.

281. Broomfield, *Elite Conflict*, 5ff.

282. Seal, *Indian Nationalism*, 197. By 1874-1875 there were already sixty-six such associations in the Bengal Presidency; ibid., 205. See also Jürgen Lütt, *Hindu-Nationalismus in Uttar Pradesh, 1867-1900* (Stuttgart: E. Klett, 1970), 124f.

283. On the important role of the Parsis, see Kulke, *Parsees in India*, 160f. On the Chitpavan Brahmins, see Gordon Johnson, "Chitpavan Brahmins and Politics in Western India in the Late Nineteenth and Early Twentieth Centuries," in *Elites in South Asia*. The members of the Sabha were mainly lawyers, teachers, officials, and journalists from Poona, who dominated the Chitpavan Brahmins; ibid., 109. See also Ravindar Kumar, "The New Brahmins of Maharashtra," in Donald A Low (ed.), *Soundings in Modern South Asian History* (London: Weidenfeld & Nicolson, 1968).

284. Cited in Seal, *Indian Nationalism*, 149.

285. Ibid., 156.

286. Developments in Madras have already been analyzed by R. Sunthatlingam, "The 'Hindu' and the Genesis of Nationalist Politics in South India, 1878-1885," *SA*, 3 (August 1972).

287. See Seal's detailed discussion, *Indian Nationalism*, 265ff.

288. Again, Seal is best; ibid., ch. 7.

289. Khalid B. Sayeed, *Pakistan, the Formative Phase, 1857-1948* (2d ed., London: Oxford University Press, 1968), 13. In 1881, the population situation was:

	%Muslims	%Hindus
Bengal	31.2	65.4
Bombay	18.4	74.8
Madras	6.2	91.4
Northwest Prov. and Oudh	13.4	86.3
Punjab	51.4	40.7
Central Provinces	2.5	75.4
Assam	27	62.7

SOURCE: Seal, *Indian Nationalism*, 299.

290. In addition to Seal, see also Metcalf, *Aftermath*, 301f.

291. Seal, *Indian Nationalism*, 311. In 1887 the *Mahomedan Observer* of Calcutta concluded: "To insist upon open competition as the only mode of selection for State employments means the absolute exclusion of the Mahomedans from the public service. To ask for representative institutions, without sufficient guarantees for the representation of the minority means the swamping of the minority by the majority. From every part of Bengal where Local Self-Government has been introduced, comes the cry that the minority is tyrannised over by the majority; from every part of Bengal comes the cry that the organisation of the majority is more solid and stronger than that of the minority. Even in places where the Mahomedans outnumber the Hindus, the representation is entirely in the hands of the latter. What guarantees have the so-called Mahomedan delegates extorted from this irresponsible Congress for the protection of Mahomedan interests? If their political foresight had been keener, they would have seen that though the influence of the majority is predominant even at present in the Councils of the State, which shows at times too great a subserviency to their intelligence, wealth and power of combination, yet there is more hope of a fair equilibrium being maintained from the political wisdom of a neutral Government than from the generous instincts of a majority looking primarily, but naturally, to the interests of its own bulk. The minority have a right to see their interests safeguarded. And we say advisedly that until our people have come abreast with the Hindus in education and political intelligence, political concessions to the majority, without sufficient guarantees for the protection of the interests of the minority, would be destructive to the latter"; quoted in ibid., 315.

292. Ibid., 320. See also among others, Hafeez Malik, "Sir Sayyid Ahmad Khan's Doctrines of Muslim Nationalism and National Progress," *MAS*, 2 (July 1968).

293. Metcalf, *Aftermath*, 302.

294. From a letter of 1888; Seal, *Indian Nationalism*, 324.

295. Viceroy Dufferin to India secretary Northbrook on 16 October 1886: "If it [i.e., the expansion of the legislative councils] could be done, of course it would be an excellent thing; but the more I see of these people the less sanguine I am of reaching a conclusion which will both work advantageously for the country at large and satisfy native aspirations. There would be great difficulty in getting hold of the best men, and then, when we have got them, they represent after all only an infinitesimal section of the people and the interests of a minute minority in reference to a great proportion of the subjects with which legislation deals. All the efforts of the Government of India are principally directed towards the improvement of the condition of the masses. We should be very apt to find ourselves thwarted and opposed by constituencies whose qualifications are simply wealth and education. For instance, all our recent legislation would have been carried with infinitely more difficulty, and against a heavier dead weight of opposition, if more natives had been present in the Council"; quoted in Misra, *Middle Classes*, 349. John R. McLane attempted to present a more differentiated picture. Only in the Punjab did most Congress members stem from the new landowner class. Still, McLane has to concede that "in the case of tenancy legislation, the government seldom received support from members of the Congress party," because solidarity and consensus were deemed higher values; "Peasants, Moneylenders and Nationalists at the End of the 19th Century," *IESHR*,

(July-September 1963). See also C. A. Bayly, "Patrons and Politics in Northern India," *MAS*, 7 (July 1973).

296. Mahadev Govind Ranade, *Essays on Indian Economics: A Collection of Essays and Speeches* (Bombay: Thacker & Co., 1899).

297. Chandra, *Economic Nationalism.*

298. At the Congress of 1886, Naoroji stated that the Congress "must confine itself to the questions in which the entire nation has a direct participation and it must leave the adjustment of social reforms and other class questions to Class Congresses"; quoted in ibid., 359. See also Heimsath, *Indian Nationalism*, 187f., for the details.

299. Ibid., ch. 7.

300. For details see Sarvepalli Gopal, *British Policy in India, 1858-1905* (Cambridge: Cambridge University Press, 1965), 180f.

301. Rothermund, *Politische Willensbildung*, 39.

302. In addition to Curzon biographies, see V. C. Bhutani, "Some Aspects of the Administration of Lord Curzon," *Bengal Past and Present: Journal of the Calcutta Historical Society*, 85 (July-December 1966), 159-81.

303. See Gordon Johnson's excellent "Partition, Agitation and Congress: Bengal, 1904-1908," *MAS*, 7 (July 1973); also, Broomfield, *Elite Conflict*, 25f. For evidence that in addition to administrative considerations Bengali Indian resistance was to be dealt a blow, see Gopal, *British Policy*, 270, and Rothermund, *Politische Willensbildung*, 49.

304. A. P. Kannangara, "Indian Millowners and Indian Nationalism before 1914," *Past and Present*, 40 (July 1968).

305. Manmath Nath Das, *India under Morley and Minto: Politics behind Revolution, Repression and Reforms* (London: G. Allen and Unwin, 1964).

306. Rothermund, *Politische Willensbildung*, 54f.; idem, "Reform and Repression, 1907-1910, the Dilemma of British Rule in India," in his *The Phases of Indian Nationalism and Other Essays* (Bombay: Nachiketa Publications, 1970). For a Muslim interpretation, see Sayeed, *Pakistan*, 28f. For a considered judgment and new material, see Peter Hardy, *The Muslims of British India* (London: Cambridge University Press, 1972), 153f.

307. Besides Rothermund, see Daniel Argov, *Moderates and Extremists in the Indian Nationalist Movement, with Special Reference to Surendranath Banerjea and Lajpat Ral* (London: Asia Publishing House, 1967).

308. Bal Ram Nanda, *Mahatma Gandhi: A Biography* (Boston: Beacon Press, 1958), 168f. In November 1917, Gandhi stated: "Loyalty is no merit. It is a necessity of citizenship all the world over"; quoted in Donald Mackenzie Brown (ed.), *The Nationalist Movement: Indian Political Thought from Ranade to Bhave* (Berkeley: University of California Press, 1965), 147.

309. On 27 July 1914 Tilak stated: "It has been well said that British Rule is conferring inestimable benefit on India [and] not only by its civilized methods of administration"; ibid., 90.

310. H. F. Owen, "Towards Nation-Wide Agitation and Organization: The Home Rule Leagues, 1915-1918," in Low, *Soundings*.

311. Rothermund, *Politische Willensbildung*, 73.

312. S. R. Mehrotra, "The Politics behind the Montagu Declaration of 1917," in Cyril Henry Philips (ed.), *Politics and Society in India* (New York: Praeger, 1963); Albertini, *Decolonization*, 62f. For this and the following see also Robin James Moore, *The Crisis of Indian Unity, 1917-1940* (Oxford: Clarendon Press, 1974).

313. For the text, see Philips, *Evolution*, 264. The initiative was mainly Austen Chamberlain's.

314. Mehrotra, "Montagu Declaration," 78. The shift in British attitudes is tangible even in, say, Valentine Chirol. See his *Indian Unrest* (London: Macmillan, 1910), and *India Old and New* (London: Macmillan, 1921).

315. Sir Sigismund David Waley, *Edwin Montagu: A Memoir and Account of His Visits to India* (New York: Asia Publishing House, 1964). Also good is Shane Ryland, "Edwin Montagu in India, 1917-1918: The Politics of the Montagu-Chelmsford Report," *SA*, 3 (August 1973).

316. As late as 24 December 1919 Gandhi could still write: "This is a document of which the British people have every reason to be proud and with which every Indian ought to be satisfied"; Nanda, *Gandhi*, 179.

317. Judith M. Brown, *Gandhi's Rise to Power: Indian Politics, 1915-1922* (Cambridge: Cambridge University Press, 1972).

318. From a letter to the liberal, Shastri; *Essays on Gandhian Politics: The Rowlatt Satyagraha of 1919*, ed. R. Kumar (Oxford: Clarendon Press, 1971), 2.

319. See regional studies in ibid.

320. For a rather different view, see the provocative essay by Richard Gordon: "Non-Cooperation and Council Entry, 1919-1920," *MAS*, 7 (July 1973). He points out the negative attitude of nationalist leaders like Motilal Nehru and Tilak, who wished to await the detailed provisions of the constitutional reform.

321. This dates from 27 July 1920; quoted in Brown, *Gandhi's Rise*, 244.

322. As stated in *Young India*, 28 July 1920; quoted ibid., 247.

323. Treated in detail in Rothermund, *Politische Willensbildung*, 91f.

324. J. H. Broomfield, "The Non-Cooperation Decision of 1920: A Crisis in Bengal Politics," in Low, *Soundings*. See also his *Elite Conflict*, 224f.

325. Gordon, "Non-Cooperation," 473.

326. Brown, *Gandhi's Rise*, 262ff.; Gordon, "Non-Cooperation," 463f.

327. Details in Brown, *Gandhi's Rise*, 307f.

328. D. A. Low, "The Government of India and the First Non-Cooperation Movement, 1920-1922," *JAS*, 25 (February 1966).

329. D. Rothermund, "Die Rolle der westlichen Bildungsschicht in den politischen Massenbewegungen in Indien im 20. Jahrhundert," in International Congress of Historical Sciences, [12th], Vienna, 1965, *Rapports*, ed. Hanns Leo Mikoletzky (4 vols., Horn, Lower Austria: Verlag F. Berger, 1966-), II, 169.

330. Rothermund, *Politische Willensbildung*, 99f. Gopal Krishna, "The Development of the Indian National Congress as a Mass Organization, 1918-1923," *JAS*, 25 (May 1966).

331. The percentage of lawyers in 1914 was 64.4, by 1923, only 21.3. The percentage of Brahmins in the All-India Congress Committee was 72.5; Krishna, "Indian National Congress," 422, 424.

332. For Bengal, see Broomfield, *Elite Conflict*, 275f.

333. Besides Rothermund, *Politische Willensbildung*, see Sarvepalli Gopal, *The Viceroyalty of Lord Irwin, 1926-1931* (Oxford: Clarendon Press, 1957). Moore, *Crisis of Indian Unity*, 40ff., provides new evidence of Irwin's large-spirited desire for understanding.

334. The Nehru report, Jinnah's attitude, and the refusal of the Congress have naturally been much discussed since in assessing blame for partition. Why did the break occur in the face of not very serious divergences? Was Jinnah truly ready for collaboration? Was the Congress under pressure from its intransigent Hindu wing? For the Muslim view, see Sayeed, *Pakistan*, 79f. For a balanced judgment, Rothermund, *Politische Willensbildung*, 133.

335. For internal British discussions, see Moore's detailed account, *Crisis of Indian Unity*, 51ff.

336. Gopal, *Lord Irwin*, 56f.

337. Rothermund, *Politische Willensbildung*, ch. 8, "The Symbolic Revolution." "By the ritualistic staging of his great 'salt march' to the sea, he determined the reaction of the masses. The Indian people repeated like a gigantic chorus the message handed down by the Mahatma in his making of salt on the strand at Dandi"; ibid., 140. See also Gopal, *Lord Irwin*, ch. 5.

338. Gopal, *Lord Irwin*, ch. 6, and for the text of the agreement, see the Appendix.

339. On the internal British discussions, see Albertini, *Decolonization*, 87f.

340. Gopal, *Lord Irwin*, ch. 7.

341. Rothermund, *Politische Willensbildung*, 153, believes he has evidence that the administration stirred up resistance on the part of the princes.

342. On the position of Viceroy Linlithgow and Interior Minister Zetland on the question of

the princes and the federation, see R. J. Moore, "British Policy and the Indian Problem, 1936-1940," in *The Partition of India: Policies and Perspectives, 1935-1947*, ed. C. H. Philips and Mary D. Wainwright (London: G. Allen & Unwin, 1970).

343. D. Rothermund, "Bewegung und Verfassung: Eine Untersuchung der politischen Willensbildung in Indien, 1900-1950," *Vierteljahreshefte für Zeitgeschichte*, 10 (April 1962).

344. The resolution advocated a right to a living wage, an inheritance tax, a progressive income tax, and state control of basic industries, among other rights; *Indian Annual Register*, 14 (January-June 1931), I, 249. See also D. Rothermund, "Nehru and Early Indian Socialism," *St. Anthony's Paper* 18 (1968) reprinted in his *Phases of Indian Nationalism*. For the provisions of the Faizpur agrarian program regarding taxes, debt moratoriums, etc., see Pitambar Datt Kaushik, *The Congress Ideology and Programme, 1920-1947: Ideological Foundations of Indian Nationalism during the Gandhian Era* (New York, Bombay: Allied Publishers, 1964), 135.

345. That did not, however, stop the landlords from speaking of "Congress-cum-Bolshevik doctrines," nor the governor of the United Provinces, Sir Malcolm Hailey, from calling upon them to organize a party in opposition to the Congress; P. D. Reeves, "Landlords and Party Policy in the U.P., 1934-1937," in Low, *Soundings*, 264.

346. Broomfield, *Elite Conflict*, 289f. John Gallagher, "Congress in Decline: Bengal 1930 to 1939," *MAS*, 7 (July 1973), maintains the Hindu Congress of Bengal was "sacrificed" by the party leadership.

347. Hauser, "Indian National Congress."

348. This is the much discussed interpretation of Indian developments in Barrington Moore, *The Social Origins of Dictatorship and Democracy: Lord and Peasant in the Making of the Modern World* (Boston: Beacon Press, 1966).

349. Rothermund, *Politische Willensbildung*, 180.

350. For the striking stand taken by the viceroy, see Gallagher, "Congress in Decline," 617.

351. Rothermund, *Politische Willensbildung*, 174; B. R. Nanda, "The Indian National Congress and the Partition of India, 1935-1947," in *Partition of India*, 157. The Muslim version is in Sayeed, *Pakistan*, 85.

352. Syed Sharifuddin Peerzada (ed.), *Foundations of Pakistan: All-Indian Muslim League Documents, 1906-1947* (2 vols., Karachi: National Publishing House, 1969-1970) II, xx. See also Ram Gopal, *Indian Muslims: A Political History (1858-1947)* (Bombay, New York: Asia Publishing House, 1964), 269f.

2

BURMA

Burma was of limited importance within the trading imperium of the East India Company. The Indianized kingdom had in fact pursued an active foreign policy, having repeatedly clashed with both China and Siam. But its center of gravity was in northern Upper Burma, and the coastal zones—Arakan, the Irrawaddy delta, and Tenasserim—were inhabited by non-Burmese peoples. Although they paid a tribute to the king of Burma, they otherwise enjoyed a considerable autonomy, which their warlike nature reinforced. Nor were the Burmese mariners. Foreign trade was modest, mainly because exporting rice from the delta was forbidden, in order to safeguard the food supply. In addition, the wars of the eighteenth century had decimated the already sparse population of Lower Burma and had devastated the cities of Syriam and Pegu. And although Burma had accepted Buddhism and Indian Brahmins and astrologers played a considerable role at the royal court, contact with the outside world, even India, remained minimal. British expansion into Burma proceeded from India, and in the end Burma became a province of British India.[1]

The East India Company undertook the conquest of Burma rather in the spirit of establishing a forward defense line. In 1784 the kingdom of Burma had conquered the kingdom of Arakan. Although Arakanese were taken prisoner by the tens of thousands, many fled, mainly to the Bengalese coastal city of Chittagong. Demands for the repatriation of the refugees and border raids led to the initial friction with the British. When Burma occupied Assam in 1819 and began making forays across the Brahmaputra, the company saw military force as the only way to maintain its rule in East Bengal. A British expeditionary force landed on 10 May 1824; on 24 February 1826 the Burmese king signed a treaty forcing him to give up Assam, Arakan, and Tenasserim, and also to pay an indemnity, accept British residents in his capital, and sign a trade treaty. But British economic interest in Burma was still minimal, and even in 1830 the British contemplated the return of Tenasserim. It need hardly be said that relations remained tense. Burmese attempts to impose controls on British ships in Rangoon and Pegu led to the second Burmese war, when Lord Dalhousie, a representative of the "Forward School" in India, responded with an ultimatum. By April 1852, the British occupied Rangoon and by November, Pegu. On 20 December, the governor-general proclaimed the annexation of Pegu, and thus did Lower Burma become British.

The kingdom of Burma remained in existence, however, and under the able Mindon Min (1852-1878) attempted with some success to modernize itself. To strengthen the central administration, senior officials were put on salaries, an income tax was introduced, teak and oil monopolies were established, gold coinage was introduced, river steamers were purchased, and trade encouraged. The army, however, remained weak. The king also had to grant some privileges to the British who already regarded Burma as an annex of British India. They hence followed the king's efforts to establish diplomatic relations with other powers, particularly France, with considerable mistrust. With the financial assistance of the Rangoon Chamber of Commerce, the British were also trying to determine the possibilities of trade with southwest China in a manner analogous to contemporary French efforts to gain access to Chinese markets, first via the Mekong and then up the Red River. Interested groups in Rangoon used succession struggles and mass executions in Mandalay as propaganda to justify aggression, and as early as April 1879 there was talk of a new British ultimatum. Nevertheless, in September, the British residence was closed, the Afghan War and Gladstone's opposition to imperial ventures making at first for caution. In 1883, however, Burma sent a new mission to Paris and on 18 January 1885 concluded a treaty with France that opened the door for French economic activity in Burma. The treaty foresaw a railway concession and a Burmese bank to be financed by French capital and amortized with oil revenues and customs duties. The British interpreted this treaty as a French attempt to establish indirect control over Upper Burma, which would have threatened the British position in Lower Burma and blocked future access to South China. Freycinet, who had succeeded Ferry, who fell as premier of France in March, denied any anti-British intent, recalling the French consul in Mandalay to demonstrate the purity of his motives, and British officials in Burma warned against expansion. Nevertheless, between June and December 1885 the expansionists in the Salisbury cabinet carried the day. On 22 October the British issued a brusque ultimatum offering a protectorate or war. King Thibaw chose war and rallied the populace to resistance. On 28 November Mandalay was taken, and the king was exiled to India with his retinue.

One can hardly speak of a planned and deliberately executed English expansion into Burma. All the same, the British Burma policy was characteristic of imperialist expansion: an intervention supposedly defensive in intent unleashed a process of escalating tensions. The reaction of the local ruler to these external threats, modernization at home, and a search for diplomatic support abroad, was seen by the affected colonial power as a provocation that, in the light of Great Power rivalries, could only be met by further expansion. In addition, British businessmen in the coastal regions initially occupied became, with their growing commercial activity, an important "local factor," closely tied to English chambers of commerce. They worked together to influence the government and gain its support for their joint interests when the time was ripe for action. Moreover, earlier confrontations with Europeans and quarrels over succession weakened native societies and rendered them incapable of sustained resistance. Even limited military actions on the part of the technologically superior Europeans were thus apt to result in sizeable conquests.[2]

Law and order were in no way restored by the British military success and the deportation of the king. On the contrary. Exactly as had happened in Tonkin-Annam, the annexation of Burma, officially proclaimed by Lord Dufferin in February 1886, ushered in a period of guerrilla warfare. Wide areas of Upper Burma, and even Lower Burma, rose in revolt. Military posts were attacked, communications cut. Soldiers from the Burmese army engaged in these activities, as did important members of the traditional ruling elite who refused to collaborate with the British. Their activity was hard to distinguish from that of plundering bands of robbers (*dacoity*) and village militias, who were not above requisitioning foodstuffs by force. Even Buddhist monks took up arms. The British responded with repressive measures—shootings, burning villages—engaging ten to twenty thousand Anglo-Indian troops for several years.

Indirect rule in Burma, advocated by some officials, was out of the question. A suitable pretender was lacking, and members of the royal council were either regarded locally as quislings or had taken part in the rebellion. The royal throne, the symbol of the center of the Burmese universe, was placed in a museum in Calcutta and the palace in Mandalay transformed into a British club. Only in the Shan States did the British depend in the following period on the traditional rulers and allow them some autonomy, in a manner analogous to the treatment of the princely states in India. The British thus exploited the tendency of the ethnic minorities to resist the Burmese. With the exception of the Karens, who in a certain sense were made protégés and later received separate seats on the councils, these peoples lived in the economically less important border regions and could hence serve as buffers between Burma and the outside world. Only the minority peoples, the Shan, Mons, and Karens, were recruited for the army, and not the Burmese. This policy paid off for the British as late as World War II when these minorities provided important assistance against the Japanese. It did, on the other hand, delay national integration, and it left independent Burma with a minorities problem still unresolved today. The "real" Burma received an administrative structure modelled after British-India. Unlike Ceylon, Burma did not become a separate colony but was annexed to India. It was at first administered by a high commissioner and, after becoming a province in 1897, by a governor. British civil servants came from India, were guided by their Indian experience, and reported to London through the viceroy of India.

Even before Upper Burma was annexed, the traditional figures of authority were being eliminated. In Tenasserim, the British had from 1826 to 1852 still attempted to link justice and administration to the traditional order. In Lower

Burma, however, the *myothugyis*, regional hereditary officials enjoying great prestige, had already been replaced by paid, appointed Burman officials (*myouks*), who supervised district tax collectors, police officials (*guangs*), and, at the local level, village chiefs, who served as police informers and executive agents. These were all newly created offices without roots in the traditional society. They received accordingly little regard and their creation marked the onset of social dissolution and an increasingly evident lawlessness. Accentuating this process were immigrants from Upper Burma, who, having themselves escaped from the severe sanctions and customary law of the traditional village community, were bearers of the spirit of individualism. The British reforms of 1887-1889 undertook to strengthen the village chief (*thugyi*) and make him the sole administrative official at the local level. Indeed, whenever possible, the colonial rulers appointed men from the village and decked them out with the trappings of the earlier *myothugyis*. But the traditional hierarchy in Burmese society was largely destroyed, and the village chief was never able to play his foreseen role as representative of the village community. "So the village died and where in Upper Burma it had been able to keep up paths and bridges, a monastery and a monastery school, in Lower Burma whose villages often only grew up under the new regime, only one village in four had so much as a monastery and a monk."[3]

The institutions of justice and Anglo-Indian law heightened the alienation between the governors and the governed in Burma as elsewhere. Before the British came, minor offenses and conflicts had been settled locally without any formal court structure by the *myothugyis* and village chiefs acting in accordance with customary law—with all the shortcomings of that sort of justice. The new system was based partly on the Buddhist law code (*Dhammathat*), which despite the contrary opinion of British judges had not played a very large role in precolonial days, but mainly on Anglo-Indian law. The system remained strange and incomprehensible to the Burmese, the more so because proceedings were carried on in English. Confidence in the system was lacking, witnesses and lower justice officials could be bribed, lying seemed to be in order, and the sanctity of the law disappeared. Litigiousness flourished, to the profit of the lawyers. The elimination of the traditional leaders combined with the artificial character of the new village administration, the new legal system, and the breakdown of the traditional religious sanctions, all combined to produce a rapid rise in crime. This development, noted as early as 1880, seemed irremediable. It became in the following decades one of the most serious problems facing the British administration. It revealed all too clearly the crisis of the traditional society.[4]

This crisis, particularly striking in Lower Burma, reached catastrophic proportions there because an additional factor was at work, a colonial economic system based on laissez-faire. Superficially, the country appeared to be a successful example of opening-up and development. Burma was indeed transformed from a country that was cut off from foreign trade and dependent on subsistence agriculture to one of the world's largest rice exporters. The merits of the West's opening the country and tying it to the international economy with the help of foreign capital seemed definitely established. Rice had been cultivated since time immemorial, particularly in the coastal strips of Arakana and Tenasserim and in the Lower Burma delta, where thick jungle and regular monsoon rains provided excellent conditions. Since export was forbidden, however, there had been no incentive to expand production. The British removed these restrictions, and from 1840 on, thanks to continuous increases in the area cultivated, production and exports rose steadily, first from Tenasserim, then after 1852, from Lower Burma (see table 2.1). New habits of consumption in Europe, the American Civil War which cut off supplies of Carolina rice, the opening of the Suez Canal in 1869, the introduction of faster ships, the activities of European firms, particularly rice mills, and the rising import requirements of India, all provided ample markets. Rapidly rising world rice prices increased the incentive to grow it, though not without some alarming repercussions at the low points in the business cycle.[5]

Table 2.1
Production of Rice in Lower Burma, 1830-1935

YEAR	AREA CULTIVATED (IN THOUSANDS OF ACRES)	AVERAGE YEARLY INCREASE	AVERAGE ANNUAL EXPORT (IN THOUSANDS OF TONS)	EXPORTS TO INDIA IN PERCENTAGES	EXPORTS AS PERCENTAGE OF PRODUCTION
1830-	66				
1851-1852	1000				
1866-1870	1686	40			
1871-1875	2094	82	679	1.2	62
1881-1885	3529	158	946	4.1	53
1891-1895	5062	182	1226	15.2	56
1901-1905	6927	173	1937	15.9	56
1911-1915	8182	84	1970	26.3	62
1921-1925	9058	126	2402	26.2	53
1931-1935	9678	–5	2998	48.1	63

SOURCE: Aye Hlaing, "Trends of Economic Growth and Income Distribution in Burma, 1870-1910," *Journal of the Burma Research Society*, 47 (June 1964), tables pp. 92, 95.

In fact, "when we arrived in 1852 the delta was 'tall jungle and high grass, where the elephant dwelt and the tiger held dominion'. When we left in 1942 it had seven million acres under rice, an unending plain of wet ricefields larger than Wales, nearly three fourths of it grown for export; the needs of the export trade have been dominant throughout."[6] When one considers the social effects, however, the picture is entirely different. Lower Burma is in fact the very model of the contrast between the impressive production and export figures of a one-crop economy on the one hand and, on the other, the process of social disintegration within a precolonial economy and the rise of a plural society in which the gains of economic expansion went primarily to a foreign minority. The British colonial official J. S. Furnivall has explored the latter problem in detail and has in numerous works elucidated the difficulties in which laissez-faire policies placed traditional societies, whose primary values were not economic, by delivering them rudely up to an individualistic capitalistic economic world.

There was plenty of land for colonists in thinly settled Lower Burma. Rice-farming peasants streamed in from Upper Burma after the British had opened up the latter with the trade treaty with King Mindon. It was easy to obtain an occupancy right. Anyone who paid taxes for twelve years on a plot could claim it for his own. As a practical matter, however, occupants could sell the land or mortgage it from the very beginning. A frontier atmosphere prevailed. Given the still haphazard administration, squatters were quite willing to assert their claims by force.

The main problem for the Burmese, however, was indebtedness. Land had to be prepared for cultivation, seeds and tools had to be bought, and food as well, for it took a considerable time before the land produced enough to live on. The squatter obtained credit and then all too often was forced to give up his property rights and move on. Even peasants who owned land and were harvesting rice went into debt to buy more arable, or an ox, or because of illness or bad prices, or for weddings or religious festivities. In this way they behaved in exactly the same manner as Indian, Vietnamese, or African peasants did when they began to produce for the market. As was also characteristic of the colonial society, the traditional society's taboos against "luxury"—formerly certain articles of ornament and dress were restricted to the ruling class—disintegrated. Although Chinese traders, Burmese moneylenders, and European rice firms all gave credit, the peasant's main source was Indian Chettyars, the members of a south Indian trading caste. After 1880 they streamed into Burma in large numbers to exploit the existing opportunities. By the 1920s they controlled the rural credit system through some 1,650 agents and had a capital stock estimated in 1930 at 750 million rupees.[7] Annual interest was 30 percent and more. Were the peasants unable to pay their debts, they lost their land or became tenants subjected to very steep rents. An administrative report from one district noted as early as 1908-1909: "Much of the land is in the hand of moneylenders and traders, who let it out on yearly tenancies.... Indebtedness is general... cultivating owners are often merely creatures of the Chetties."[8] Land became a good that changed hands, new buyers or tenants were found, and they in turn went into debt. In some instances land was even rented annually to the highest bidder. Only a fraction of the land was farmed by the same peasant for a period of years. "A large floating population of tenants [is] constantly on the move from holding to holding."[9] Since land prices and rents rose, while real wages for the growing number of agricultural laborers fell,[10] land was purchased not only by moneylenders and merchants, but also by officials, doctors, and urban businessmen. In the decade 1921-1931 alone shifts in ownership occurred as shown in table 2.2.[11] By 1937 about half the cultivated land in lower Burma belonged to nonagricultural landlords, and a quarter to the Chettyars alone.[12]

Table 2.2
Ownership of Land in Burma, 1921-1931 (in percentages)

	1921	1931
Cultivating owners	50.6	36.9
Tenant cultivators	22.3	23.0
Agricultural laborers	27.1	40.1

SOURCE: J. R. Andrews, *Burmese Economic Life* (Stanford: Stanford University Press, 1949), 40.

The Great Depression was very hard on the peasants. Although the population continued to rise, expansion of the arable ceased, and rice prices fell sharply. The terms of trade, which with the exception of the years 1916-1922 had always been good, worsened.[13] In short, in the face of high rents and usurious interest, a great number of peasant families squeezed by on barely more than a subsistance minimum.[14] The rice mills and the export trade were also in foreign, usually British, hands. The peasants, in debt and in need of cash, had to sell at harvest time or even when the crop broke ground for fixed prices. The merchants, however, could wait, especially since they had a monopoly in Rangoon. During the interwar period, the number of Burmese rice mills did in fact increase rapidly (from 57 in 1911 to 224 in 1921), but they employed relatively few workers and supplied mainly local markets.[15]

The situation in Upper Burma was not as bad. Rice was also cultivated, but it required irrigation and was consumed locally. Besides rice, other crops were increasingly grown. Upper Burma was thus neither so vulnerable to market collapses and meteorological vagaries nor was it so fully enmeshed in the cash nexus. For the most part land remained in peasant hands, and the village community was more closely knit.

Since the end of the nineteenth century, the colonial administration had tried to combat the all-too-evident land crisis in Lower Burma with measures such as tenant protection, the making of land transfers more difficult, and the provision of easier credit. But their hearts were not in it, they moved hesitantly, and their palliatives had even less success than in India.

> It is not that officers in Burma were tender to vested interests: English interests were not involved, there were no English landlords, we had little love for the moneylender, and we were almost sentimentally silly on behalf of the peasant cultivator. But we were dominated by the dogmas of laissez-faire: it was the unspoken major premise of our mind that men are best left to manage their own affairs. Sometimes it was not even unspoken: at one conference, attended by some of the best land revenue officers in the country, the chairman used language worthy of J .S. Mill himself to prove that nothing ought to be done, and I remember the pained silence when the youngest officer present chimed in with "Then we are to do nothing but hold the ring? 'A fair field and no favour', as the elephant said when he danced among the chickens."[16]

When a Burma Tenancy Bill was introduced in 1908, the large landowners, Chettyars, and English economic interests raised such cain both inside the legislative council and out that the bill was withdrawn, despite having the support of the governor.[17] Not until Burma was separated from India in 1937 did the first Burmese government carry a tenancy bill, and only then after administrative reports confirmed the disquieting lot of rice growers in Lower Burma. The Japanese invasion occurred, however, before the law had had much effect. Energetic and effective land reform measures had to await the independence of Burma in 1948.

In addition to rice, the Burmese exported 500,000 tons of teak a year, mainly to India. The teak forests contributed one-fifth of the state income. The forestry concessions were mostly in British hands, the Burmese having been forced out early. Foreigners also owned the sawmills.

The Burma Oil Company was founded as early as 1886. At first buying oil from the natives, it later brought in modern boring and other gear. In 1908 it opened a pipeline from the oil fields to refineries in the port of Syriam. In the 1930s, the company accounted for 0.5 percent of the world's production and most of its production went to India. Although it was the only foreign company to make serious efforts to "Burmanize" its work force—it employed 8,000 workers in the oil fields—it remained nonetheless an enclave. Its profits and a goodly portion of its wages flowed out of the country. And the same could be said of the other extractive industries (such as tin, zinc, silver, wolfram).

The exploitation of Burmese resources called for a modern transportation system. In 1865 the Irrawaddy Flotilla Company was founded to develop transport on that enormous river system. Although the company made the transport of export products to the coast possible, it also put man-powered river boats out of business and hence left thousands unemployed. Railway construction was financed from the budget of British India. The system never exceeded 2,000 miles. The road system remained equally modest.

The colonial character of the Burmese economic system is clear enough. Enterprise and investment were directed toward trade in export goods, the extractive industries, and the transport which served them. In 1940, 1,027 concerns came under the provisions of the Factory Law. Of a population of 16 million, they employed 90,000. Rice mills constituted nearly two-thirds of the total, 673 (employing 41,626), 116 were sawmills (employing 11,579), and 54 were cotton gins (employing 3,766). Industry in the modern sense hardly existed.[18] At the same time, imports severely damaged the Burmese skilled trades, though not destroying them completely. Local salt was replaced by imported salt, village weaving declined everywhere, though managing to hang on in upper Burma (yarn imports increased). In the 1930s, 75 percent of cotton goods were imported, mainly from India and Japan.[19]

Most investment capital, which tripled during the interwar years, came from abroad and from England and India in particular.[20] Foreigners owned and ran virtually the entire modern sector of the Burmese economy. European, Indian, and Chinese firms were generally headquartered in Rangoon, the population of which rose from 176,000 in 1891 to 400,000 in 1931. The situation provided a good example of the shifting of a country's political and economic centers from its inland towns to a colonial port city. Nine-tenths of Burmese exports passed through Rangoon. The balance of trade, with its rising export surplus also had a colonial look to it: in 1938-1939 exports were 485 million rupees (of which 223 million was for rice), imports 215 million (of which only 26 million were capital goods). In the same year, Hlaing estimated that payments abroad totalled 240 million rupees, 94 million of which was sent by European firms, 50 million by Chettyars, 75 by Indians, Chinese, and Europeans. Of the amount remaining, 25 million went for debt service, civil service pensions, and other items.[21] In short, there was a drain of wealth that prevented the genuinely Burmese sectors from profiting from the favorable balance of trade.

This expansion of the export sector would not have been possible without imported labor. The number of Indian coolies rose from a few thousand in 1880 to 150,000 by 1900 and over 400,000 by the 1920s. Most came as seasonal workers or at most for a few years. They worked the rice fields, the rice mills, and in transportation, and for wages and under working conditions that the Burmese were disinclined to accept until the depression. Since the Indians came mainly from the cities, they were better prepared for industrial work and were accordingly favored over the locals. The Indians' position was also established, especially in the great cities, where they constituted as much as 60 percent of the population. In Rangoon, nearly 90 percent of both skilled and unskilled workers were Indians; in transport, there were 100,000 Indians and 90,000 Burmese.[22] The result was friction and anti-Indian rioting, particularly when rice production stagnated and the Burmese streamed into the cities. In 1930 when those Burmese who had been hired to break the strike among Indian dockworkers were fired and jeered at, the acts led to a bloody pogrom in which more than one hundred Indians were killed and a thousand wounded.[23] Another pogrom in 1938 resulted in more Indian dead.

The Indians even dominated the administration, particularly in the technical departments.[24] Building contractors for public works were Indians, and they favored Indian coolies. Hospital personnel from top to bottom were almost entirely non-Burmese. Zinkin mentions vaccination officials who could not even speak Burmese. The post office was the same. The educational system obviously played a part in all this. It was similar to that in India, but developed later and produced relatively few academically trained Burmese. Rangoon College, founded in 1878, was a branch of Calcutta University; Burma received its own university only in 1920. As late as 1937, only 60 of the 178 students standing for examination were Burmese.[25]

The interwar period did, however, witness considerable progress in bringing Burmese into the administration. Although only one Burmese passed the entrance examination for the Indian Civil Service—he was from a prosperous family of Arakan bankers and had had an English education—by 1940 the senior cadre of the Burma Civil Service consisted of 95 Englishmen, 62 Burmese, 14

Anglo-Burmese, and 2 Indians. The cadre analogous to the Indian Provincial Civil Service employed 207 Burmese and 14 Anglo-Burmese.[26]

Burma's colonial situation was characterized by its incorporation into the world economy, the disintegration of the traditional social structure, and the rise of a plural society. In that society the Burmese were relegated to agriculture, while foreigners controlled virtually the entire modern sector and blocked the rise of a native bourgeoisie. That circumstance naturally left its mark on the Burmese liberation movement. It explains why the decisive impulse came from Buddhism and why politicizing monks led in fomenting political demonstrations and forming parties. The British in Burma had, in fact, in contrast to their behavior in Ceylon, acted with brutal lack of regard for basic local political and religious beliefs, which were rooted in Buddhism. They treated the monks, who enjoyed high regard in Burmese society, insultingly. The kingship, guarantor of a world order centered on Burma, was abolished. The British were quartered in monasteries during the pacification. The traditional royal control of the monks ceased. The use of canon law to settle monastic disputes was curtailed. The use of English in the administration and the economy undermined the prestige of the traditional school system and favored secularized, Western-oriented schools.

The first genuine political discussions began in 1906 within the Young Men's Buddhist Association (YMBA; like the YMCA). The Burmese nationalist movement really dates, however, from the end of World War I, when in 1918 the Reform Committee for India refused to discuss Burma ("the desire for elective institutions has not developed in Burma") and sought some special arrangement for it. In 1919 the YMBA organized protest demonstrations and demanded from London not only separation from India but some principle of dyarchy for Burma. The small "new elite," much concerned with finding and hanging onto its identity, was "hypersensitive" (according to Cady) about any sort of discrimination and in this found themselves at one with the traditional forces of the country. In December 1920 they organized a boycott of the newly founded University of Rangoon, the aim of which was to launch a truly national school system. Influenced by Gandhi, they also simultaneously boycotted the elections to the Indian legislative council.

In the years from 1921 to 1923, Burma received a dyarchy constitution like that of the Indian provinces. Seventy-nine of 103 members of the legislative council were elected by a surprisingly democratic suffrage, manifestly because the administration hoped to strengthen its position vis-à-vis the small, educated elite. Among the "transferred subjects," under two responsible ministers, were education, forests, public health, agriculture, and public works. Financial control, however, remained in the hands of the governor. The powers of the native ministers were thus rather restricted, as was also true in India. Participation in the electoral process remained limited, and in party terms both government and opposition deputies were rather loosely organized, so that politics was fought out in terms of personal rivalries. The electoral boycott was continued by the General Council of Burmese Associations (GCBA), which had split off from the YMBA in 1920. The GCBA linked the urban elite and the politicizing monks, the *pongyis*, who were openly hostile to the "heathen" colonial power. This alliance was not without its difficulties for the city people but nevertheless determined the course of politics for the coming years. The pongyis were the representatives of the endangered old order and its fundamentalist, Buddhist mentality. They understood precisely how to mobilize hatred of the foreigners, and their police and taxes. The pongyis also intrigued actively against the village headmen, who had almost completely lost face.

U Ottama was a leader in pongyi activities. As early as 1906 he had celebrated the victory of Japan. During the succeeding years he travelled throughout Asia, returning to Burma in 1921. With his grasp of how to give Buddhism political content, he levelled the barriers preventing the peasant masses from participating in the anticolonial struggle. He clearly had a sort of Burmese Congress party in mind, and he is not unworthy of comparison with Gandhi. Sarkisyanz has also showed how the cosmopolitan prophetic character of the traditional popular Buddhism could be mobilized in the struggle against colonialism through the proclamation of the "ideal ruler."[27]

Saya San, the organizer and leader of the great peasant rebellion of 1930-1932, was another former pongyi.[28] As an active member of the radical group within the GCBA, it was his duty to investigate complaints about taxes, debts, and other matters. He subsequently helped organize local secret societies. His rebellion broke out in the Tharrawaddy district on 28 December 1930, on the very day that the governor had rejected the advice of a study commission to allow the depression-ridden peasants to postpone tax payments. The hour being set by astrologers, Saya San was secretly crowned king as Galon Raja (a mythical beast that destroyed snakes, the symbol of British sea power) and the traditional White Umbrella, a symbol of divine kingship, was held aloft over him. This was a direct appeal to the peasants. Thousands responded. The rising gathered momentum rapidly and soon covered a good portion of Burma. The British were taken completely by surprise. They had to bring in outside troops, and the situation worsened because the rebels believed themselves invulnerable to bullets. The rebel oath revealed very clearly the political-religious character of this pongyi rebellion, even if attacks against the hated forestry administration revealed concrete grievances.[29] Roughly 3,000 Burmese were killed or wounded, 9,000 taken prisoner, 350 arrested, and 128 hanged, including Saya San himself. Whether one emphasizes the "nativist," backward side of the rebellion[30] or the deliberate skill with which Saya San deployed the symbols of popular Buddhism,[31] there can hardly be any doubt that the uprising deserved the label "national" to the extent that it revealed not only the economic-social and psychological crises brought on by the elimination of the monarchy and the penetration of the money economy, but also the distance between rulers and ruled. Saya San's failure was a major impetus to the "modern" liberation movement.

The educated urban classes opted out, viewing the rebellion with considerable mistrust or abjuring it altogether. They had already, in 1925, opposed the tax boycott which the pongyis had organized and had in the same year formed some rudimentary parties (Home Rule party, Swaraj party). They fought elections with these parties and agitated within the bounds set by the colonial power. In 1928, however, the developing question of Indian reform livened things up considerably. Separatists opposed antiseparatists—with the latter victorious in 1932 and 1936—even though both sought responsible government. The Burma Act of 1935 replaced the dyarchy system with a cabinet of nine members, fully responsible to an elected Parliament. The tie with India was cut. The governor remained responsible for foreign policy, defense, and currency and could still employ his reserve powers, but he was instructed to follow the counsel of his ministers.

The first Burmese to become prime minister, in March 1937, was U Ba Maw. He had studied in Rangoon and Cambridge, at Bordeaux had been the first Burmese to become a J.D., and had more recently made a name for himself as Saya San's lawyer.[32] His strongest opponent was U Saw, the son of a landowner who had failed to gain admission to a university either in Calcutta or in England. He had, at least pro forma, identified with Saya San's rebellion and had sent a seditious brochure about the brutal repression of the rebellion to the colonial secretary in London. U Ba Maw's government did what it could about education and hazarded a land reform, without, however, achieving much. A commission of inquiry was supposed to prepare the way for village reform, and another revealed the extent and nature of corruption.[33] But elections, governmental policy, administration, and the unedifying personal rivalries that went with them interested only the small Burmese educated class, mainly located in Rangoon. This class had in good part already lost contact with the mass of the population, mainly because there was no organization like the Indian Congress party to reconcile internal conflicts and bring in other groups by means of local committees. That in turn reflected the general absence of any middle class except for civil servants, lawyers, and journalists.

Although within the Indian Congress party a radical nationalist group espousing a Marxist-Socialist credo fought for leadership of the party in the 1930s, in Burma such groups had hardly any ties with the moderates. In 1935 the "We Burmans Society" was formed. Its members added *Thakin* ("Lord" or "Master") to their names, both an allusion to British rule and a claim for immediate independence. Those so addressed were mostly University of Rangoon students, whose student organizations were forums for discussions and who had proved all the more accessible to radical slogans because only the best qualified had any prospect of getting senior administrative posts. The percentage of dropouts was extraordinarily high. The resulting social frustration could be transmuted easily enough into nationalist protest.[34] Nationalism became tied to the Marxist intellectual heritage, in part through personal ties to England, in part through the Left Book Club in Burma. The social crisis and the dominance of the Burmese economy by British firms made a Marxist interpretation of colonial rule obvious enough, and even Buddhist notions could be made to support it—through the conception of an alleged earlier time when property was held in common and when an ideal society existed as a sort of secular Nirvana in which the consequences of avarice, hatred, and ambition had been eliminated.[35] The few existing communists joined the Thakin party. Its leaders, however, were the Fabian Socialists, U Nu and Aung San, young student leaders who had been much influenced by J. S. Furnivall. In February 1936 they exploited a dispute with the rector to organize another successful boycott of the universities and high schools. Two years later they tried to organize strikes among the Indian dockworkers and Burmese bus drivers. Hammer-and-sickle flags appeared, and in Rangoon resolutions favoring the dictatorship of the proletariat were passed. In January 1939 the Thakin leaders were arrested, and in February the British broke up a pongyi-student demonstration in Mandalay with gun fire; 14 demonstrators were killed and U Ba's government fell. Aung San escaped, seeking aid first in China and then in Japan. He marched back into Burma in 1942 at the head of the Burma Independent Army.[36]

Independent Burma's policy of exclusion, even at the cost of foreign investment and technical assistance, is understandable enough, when one bears in mind the colonial period, with its export orientation, foreign economic domination, and social disintegration. This self-incarceration may appear irrational to the Western *homo economicus*, but it makes very good sense for a society seeking reintegration and its own identity, and oriented toward Buddhist notions of inner accord and social harmony rather than ideals of individual achievement.[37]

NOTES

1. See in particular, John Frank Cady, *A History of Modern Burma* (Ithaca: Cornell University Press, 1958). See also the chapter in Daniel George Edward Hall, *A History of South-East Asia* (3d ed., New York: St. Martin's, 1968). For administration and social and economic development, John Sydenham Furnivall, *Colonial Policy and Practice: A Comparative Study of Burma and Netherlands India* (Cambridge: University Press, 1948), is basic. See also F.S.V. Donnison, *Burma* (New York: Praeger, 1970); Frank N. Trager, *Burma: from Kingdom to Republic; a Historical and Political Analysis* (New York: Praeger, 1966); and Godfrey Eric Harvey, *British Rule in Burma, 1824-1942* (London: Faber & Faber, 1946).

2. The importance of Randolph Churchill, who as India secretary was the driving force, and the significance of the hoped-for access to the South China market has been convincingly established by Peter Staub in a Zurich University *Lizentiat* thesis of 1974.

3. Zinkin, *Asia and the West*, 99. Furnivall, *Colonial Policy*, 74-75, also noted: "By converting the village from the social and residential unit into an administration unit, it cut at the roots of organic social life within the village. . . . They were regarded merely as units of administration and consequently many considerations irrelevant to the life of the community enter into the formation of a village. It may contain one or more hamlets within its borders, or its boundaries may cut with seeming irrelevance through the heart of some large residential unit. The general principles determining its formation are that its area must not be too great for the control of a headman, and the revenues must be sufficient to afford by the commission on their collection an adequate remuneration for its various responsibilities." In a 1932 report, it was also noted that

the village headman discharged his duties "in face of the apathy or opposition of the villagers"; Furnivall, *Colonial Policy*, 75.

4. Cady, *History of Burma*, 173; Furnivall, *Colonial Policy*, 131. See also Harvey's comments based on personal experience, *British Rule*, 341. In addition, see F. Bigg-Wither, "Cleaning up Burma's Murder Zone," *Contemporary Review*, 156 (December 1939); Kyaw Yin, "The Problem of Crime and the Criminal and its Solution in Socialist Burma," *Journal of the Burma Research Society*, 47 (June 1964).

5. Hlaing, "Trends of Economic Growth," provides the best analysis of Burma's colonial economy. See also, in addition to Furnivall, Cheng Siok Hwa, "The Development of the Burmese Rice Industry in the Late Nineteenth Century," *Journal of South East Asian History*, 6 (March 1965); Charles Donald Cowan (ed.), *The Economic Development of Southeast Asia: Studies in Economic History and Political Economy* (New York: Praeger, 1964); and James Russell Andrus, *Burmese Economic Life*, foreword by J. S. Furnivall (Stanford: Stanford University Press, 1949).

6. Harvey, *British Rule in Burma*, 49.

7. Michael Adas, "Immigrant Asians and the Economic Impact of European Imperialism: The Role of South India Chettiars in British Burma," *JAS*, 33 (May 1974).

8. Cited in Cady, *History of Burma*, 160.

9. Burma, Land and Agriculture Committee, *Report. . .1938* (Rangoon: Gov't. Printing and Stationery, 1938-40), 14. Hereafter cited as *Report, 1938*.

10. Hlaing, "Trends of Economic Growth," 122f.

11. Ibid., 127, has somewhat different figures.

12. The following table is taken from *Report, 1938*, 38, 147:

	Occupied area (in millions of acres)	Agriculturalists (in million of acres)	Occupied by	
			Resident nonagriculturalists (in acres)	Nonresident nonagriculturalists (in millions of acres)
Lower Burma	11.2	5.9	989,000	4.3
Upper Burma	8.1	7.0	475,000	0.66

13. Hlaing, "Trends of Economic Growth," Appendix B, 145-146.

14. "Rents [are] too high. . .Tenant must borrow. . .[to] keep the tenant's standard of living down to a bare subsistance level and maintain him in a state of permanent indebtedness from which there is no hope of escape"; *Report, 1938*, 10.

15. Hlaing, "Trends of Economic Growth," 135 n.2.

16. Harvey, *British Rule in Burma*, 52.

17. Cady, *History of Burma*, 165; Furnivall, *Colonial Policy*, 111-12. In connection with the Land Alienation Bill of 1910, which also failed to pass, the same governor wrote, "Gradually, but surely, the Burman is being squeezed off the land and. . .if, as seems likely, the proposed legislation is abandoned, the land will fall into the hands of non-agriculturalists and natives of India. Free trade in land. . .from an economic point of view. . .is probably sound. More rice will be grown for export; more land revenue and customs duty will be garnered. But. . .the standard of living will be lowered. The deterioration of the Burmese race, which will inevitably accompany their divorce from the land, will be a subject for regret when it is irremediable. Similarly, tenants in Burma. . .need protection"; Cady, *History of Burma*, 167.

18. Figures from Andrus, *Burmese Economic Life*, 142; Hlaing, "Trends of Economic Growth."

19. Hlaing makes the necessary distinctions, 103 ff. Based on Hlaing is Stephen A. Resnick, "The Decline of Rural Industry and Export Expansion: A Comparison among Burma, Philippines, and Thailand, 1870-1938," *JEH*, 30 (March 1970), 57.

20. Foreign investments in Burma in 1941 were:

	(in million £s)
Oil companies	16
Other mining companies	15
Teak and lumber companies	3.5
Rubber, tea and other plantations	1.2
Banking, trading and manufacturing	5.5
Communication	6
	47.2

SOURCE: Helmut G. Callis, *Foreign Capital in South East Asia* (New York: International Secretariat, Institute of Pacific Relations, 1942), 105.

21. Hlaing, "Trends of Economic Growth," 117. Callis, *Foreign Capital*, 104, estimates the share of foreign companies even higher at £10 to 12 million or 133 to 160 million rupees.

22. Hlaing, "Trends of Economic Growth," 131; Zinkin, *Asia and the West*, 100; Harvey, *British Rule in Burma*, 69f.

23. "The Burmese proletariat walked with a lighter step. They had shown the Indians their place. This was Burma, a land which had been independent for hundreds of years before it fell to the English. Too many Indians had crowded into it from their starving villages across the bay. They could...undersell the Burmese, and there was a swarm of them too in public services, particularly in the railways and the prison department. Well, they had been taught a lesson"; Cady, *History of Burma*, 305.

24. Hlaing, "Trends of Economic Growth," 133.

25. U Kaung, "A Survey of the History of Education in Burma before the British Conquest and After," *Journal of the Burma Research Society*, 46 (December 1963). Nyi Nyi, "The Development of University Education in Burma," ibid., 47 (June 1964). See also Furnivall's very critical comments, *Colonial Policy*, 202.

26. Tinker, "Structure," 68.

27. Emanuel Sarkisyanz, *Buddhist Backgrounds of the Burmese Revolution* (The Hague: Mouton, 1965), 149f.

28. In addition to Cady, *History of Burma*, 309 and Sarkisyanz, *Buddhist Backgrounds*, ch. 22, see Robert L. Salomon, "Saya San and the Burmese Rebellion," *MAS*, 3 (July 1969)

29. "We are banded together to drive out all unbelievers...till we are free of the rule of the English....Grant to us liberty and to the Galon King dominion over the land"; Cady, *History of Burma*, 311-12. For the entire text, see Salomon, "Saya San," Appendix, 221.

30. "It was a phenomenon of what anthropologists call 'nativistic' response against overwhelming impacts of an alien civilization that had been dissolving traditional society up to its economic foundation and challenging the traditional world conception of Burmese folk Buddhism...a desperate attempt to restore the old symbols of cosmic and social harmony"; Sarkisyanz, *Buddhist Backgrounds*, 161.

31. Salomon, "Saya San," 221.

32. U Ba Maw, *Breakthrough in Burma: Memoirs of a Revolution, 1939-1946* (New Haven: Yale University Press, 1968), Introduction.

33. As with Indian Congress party governments from the period 1937 to 1939, opinions about the quality of this government vary considerably. Harvey, *British Rule in Burma*, 87f., is very critical; Cady, *History of Burma*, ch. 12, is more moderate.

34. Cady, *Burma*, 373f.

35. Sarkisyanz, *Buddhist Backgrounds*, 166ff.

36. For British policy and the role of Aung San during and after the war, see also Albertini, *Decolonization*, 196ff.

37. See Hans O. Schmitt's shrewd remarks in "Decolonization and Development in Burma," *Journal of Development Studies*, 4 (October 1967).

3

CEYLON

Ceylon's location off India's southern tip explains India's formative influences upon it. Its particular geographic situation is also the reason for European interest in it because it provided the desired way station on the maritime route from Europe, the Persian Gulf, and the Malabar Coast to East Asia.[1]

Ceylon's most important population group, the Sinhalese, immigrated from northwestern India in the sixth century B.C. The Sinhalese language is based on an Aryan dialect, and they became Buddhists when Buddhism came from India in the third century B.C. After the second century Dravidian-speaking Tamil Hindus periodically invaded from the North. The Sinhalese kings repelled most of these invasions, waging war from their capital of Anuradhapura in the northern lowlands. In the eleventh century, however, the South Indian Chola kingdom ruled Ceylon for a short time, and in the fourteenth century, Tamil Hindus founded the kingdom of Jaffna at the northern tip of the island. Thus was created the juxtaposition and opposition of these two very different groups, the Buddhist Sinhalese and Tamil-speaking Hindus. These opposing groups still rule the political life of the island, and even today their opposition complicates the task of nation-building.

The Sinhalese had earlier erected a magnificent irrigation system in the arid north in order to grow rice, their main food crop. The irrigation system decayed, however, when they migrated south to escape Tamil pressure and shifted their capital to Kotte near modern Colombo. Their feudal social order was based on an obligation to serve the king and the feudal nobility in return for the right to till the soil; rajakariya, or corvée, provided the means to build levies and pagodas. The export trade in elephants, spices (particularly cinnamon), and precious stones was in foreign, mainly Arab, hands. The Arabs' descendents, along with Malays and Indian Muslims, still constitute the Moor minority—the Portuguese called all Muslims "Moors."

By 1500 the three native rulers of Jaffna, Kotte, and the inland kingdom of Kandy struggled for control of the island. When the Portuguese arrived in 1505, they were sympathetically received as valuable support in these rivalries. A sort of Portuguese protectorate soon became de facto rule, though it was restricted to the western coastal strip. Jaffna was annexed only in 1619, and Kandy remained independent. The Portuguese exploited the royal cinnamon monopoly granted them and proselytized actively, but otherwise left local administration to the Sinhalese nobility, the Mudaliyos. Key positions were filled with Christians, which was yet another ground for both the Sinhalese nobility and ambitious men to convert to Christianity and to assume a Portuguese life style. The Dutch expelled the Portuguese in the seventeenth century, Colombo falling to them in 1656 and Jaffna in 1658. They also ruled through the traditional feudal elite and were in fact mainly interested in the cinnamon monopoly, later a source of great profit to the Dutch East India Company. After the British had occupied Ceylon, the Dutch who remained and adopted English as their language, became known as "Burghers." The Burgher community was very important in the nineteenth century as a modernizing elite, especially in the administration. They still attempt today to maintain their separate identity vis-à-vis the Tamils and Sinhalese.

Clive, to secure the British position in India, required a safe windward harbor at the southern end of the Bay of Bengal. The Dutch-held city of Trincomalee on the east coast of Ceylon seemed just what was required. The British East India Company also wanted to break into the cinnamon trade and sought to break the existing Dutch monopoly by concluding a treaty with the king of Kandy. The French invasion of Holland in 1795 provided the British with the necessary excuse for initiating the Madras government's military operations against Ceylon. When peace came in 1815, the British had no inclination to return to the Dutch such an important base on the sea route to India and East Asia. Earlier, in 1802, the Crown had taken over the government of Ceylon (or, more precisely, the populated coastal strips) from the East India Company because of the latter's mismanagement. The company had also depended on the Sinhalese elite, which had been Catholic under the Portuguese, Calvinist under the Dutch, and under the British had become in part Anglican. Sinhalese names reflect these changes: de Silva, de Souza, Abraham, Christoffel. The British occupied Kandy in 1815 and sent the king of Kandy into exile. Kandy aristocrats and Buddhist priests led two revolts in 1817-1818 and 1848, the British repression of which led to violent criticism in Parliament and recall of the governor.

The British administrative system reached its "final" form in 1833.[2] The coastal areas, Kandy, and Jaffna, were made administratively equal, which facilitated making the island an administrative unity. Five, later nine, provinces, were run by British agents, comparable to the district commissioners in India. The local aristocracy lost most of its feudal judicial rights and was compensated with a fixed stipend. The court system was made independent and administered Dutch (that is, Roman) law. In keeping with the liberal spirit of the day, the rajakariya, or corvée, was abolished. This left the feudal aristocracy very badly off but freed the peasants for, among other things, work on the plantations.

The governor, previously a virtual autocrat, was placed under the supervision of an executive council made up of the heads of the administration. In addition, a legislative council was created. It consisted of fifteen appointed members and six representatives of the Ceylonese upper classes and European business interests. This council could enact laws, subject to the governor's veto, which in practice made it a forum for the representation of interests. The reform of 1833 also had a wider significance, because Ceylon became the administrative model for all parts of the empire, displaying an efficient system of rule for the nonsettlement colonies. Under the leadership of the governor, the Ceylonese "dependency" was assured a certain autonomy, though it was under pressure to become self-supporting. Taxes and duties thus came to be seen solely in terms of their effect on revenue. Still, arbitrary conduct was pretty well excluded, and the natives were allowed some voice in things, which, through later changes in the makeup of the legislative council, could be augmented to permit representative, if not responsible, government.

As in India the civil service was also opened to the Ceylonese in 1833. While liberal in intent, this proviso was also intended to accelerate the Westernization of the local ruling class and to bind it to the colonial power.[3] In the following years, however, only a few Ceylonese were appointed, mainly to the judiciary. The entrance examination, given in London (only starting in 1924 in Colombo) and requiring an English public school or university education, set rather narrow limits on "localization," although at the same time the upper levels of the Ceylonese school system were revamped along English lines. From the 1880s on, one could obtain "external degrees" from the University of London, and the University College in Colombo was tied to London as late as World War II. "This had the customary denationalizing, demoralizing, and intellectually and socially cramping results, but popular opinion hugged the chains because it thought it was getting English standards."[4] Like the Indian Congress party, the Ceylonese elite also clamored for accelerated Ceylonizaton of the administration. London responded to these demands in 1919-1920 by reserving one-third, and later one-half, of the places in the civil service for Ceylonese. The last Briton was appointed in 1937. Table 3.1 shows the civil service composition during the interwar period. The really important positions, however, namely, the government and assistant government agents, remained firmly in British hands.[5]

Table 3.1
Civil Service Appointments in Ceylon, 1920-1950

YEAR	EUROPEANS	CEYLONESE
1920	79	11
1930	83	55
1940	49	81
1950	11	124

SOURCE: Sidney A. Pakeman, *Ceylon* (New York: Frederick A. Praeger, 1964), 89.

The localization of the technical branches of the administration was significantly more rapid. The medical college was established in 1870 and its degree was declared equivalent to an English degree in 1888. In 1925 the public health service was Ceylonized, and the police corps in 1930. By 1907 one-third of the engineers in the public works corps were already Ceylonese, and by the Second World War about one-half. The irrigation department proved the least attractive to Ceylonese, manifestly because it often required work in remote and malaria-ridden areas.[6]

During the first half of the nineteenth century, the governors favored Christian Sinhalese, who were drawn to Colombo from overpopulated Jaffna and sought an English education in order to rise socially. When examinations were introduced, however, the Burghers, by now almost completely Anglicized, and the Tamils gained a number of places quite disproportionate to their representation in the general population, as shown in table 3.2. The Sinhalese began to regain lost ground after 1930 but were still under-represented at the time of independence. That naturally encouraged Sinhalese nationalism. What made the situation worse was that the Sinhalese members of the civil service were mostly from the old ruling class, whose members had often converted to Christianity and who in terms of dress, speech, and life-style were more Anglicized than corresponding Indian groups.The Buddhist Sinhalese middle classes found this frustrating, a feeling the Sinhalese politician Solomon W.R.D. Bandaranaike was able to turn to his advantage in the 1950s.

Table 3.2
Administrative Personnel in Ceylon, 1907-1946

YEAR	BURGHERS	SINHALESE	TAMILS
1907	6	4	2
1925	14	17	8
1946	16	69	31

SOURCE: S. J. Tambiah, "Ethnic Representation," 127, 133.

The British took over the cinnamon export monopoly from the Dutch. In the early years of the nineteenth century, it was the colony's main source of income. It rapidly declined in importance, however, being displaced from European markets by Chinese cassia and less expensive Indian and Javan cinnamon. In 1833 the government lifted its monopoly and removed export duties, too late, however, to make cinnamon a paying venture again.[7] It was coffee, in fact, that was to revolutionize Ceylon's agriculture.[8] Although the Dutch had earlier established some coffee plantations in the lowlands, the most suitable area proved to be the Kandy highlands. The governor personally took the initiative, building the roads necessary to link Kandy with Colombo. After London removed the tariff preference for West Indian coffee in the 1830s, the Ceylonese boom began. Three million pounds was invested in coffee plantations between 1837 and 1845. Exports tripled. Although the depression of 1847 ruined many planters, by 1853 high prices prevailed once again, and the area under cultivation rose rapidly, reaching 275,000 acres by 1878. By the 1870s Ceylon exported nearly a million tons a year. Within a decade, however, a fungus disease had again ruined the plantations. In the meanwhile, "King Coffee" had been responsible for the construction of 3,000 miles of roads, a rail line from Colombo to Kandy (1867), and the establishment of shipping firms, mercantile houses, and banks in the port cities. In 1854 the Ceylon Planters' Group was founded, which in subsequent years was to be the most important local economic pressure group.

After the annexation of Kandy, land for plantations was available, or seemed to be available, on the hillsides, because the peasant villages and rice fields lay in the valleys. In 1840 the administration claimed all uncultivated land for which no title could be established—and who could do that?—as Crown land. It was sold for give-away prices to English planters. Within fifty years, 100,000 hectares of forest had been cut and replaced with coffee bushes. Ceylonese peasants seem only in exceptional cases to have been forced off the land. They did, however, lose the right to cut firewood, to hunt and graze stock, and to clear land by burning, or *chena* rights, as they were called. These are the typical results of colonial land seizure and also occurred in the Maghreb and elsewhere. In the beginning it did not matter much. Later these measures worsened the crisis within the peasant economy and social structure which came when the population increased and land became scarce. Some lowland Sinhalese who had made money in transport or construction were also able to become coffee planters. Little capital was needed, and the techniques required were simple. Even villagers planted coffee as small holders, producing some 25 percent of the crop in 1870. That was not to be the case with tea.

One bottleneck soon proved to be the lack of workers. The villagers were willing to clear the soil—though how much coercion was required is unclear—but were not interested in wage labor on the plantations. The Sinhalese were not so much "naturally lazy," as the planters believed (a belief akin to the African sterotype of the "lazy black"), as they were busy with rice cultivation, which continues over much of the year. Most villagers also owned coconut palms and other plants. Surplus labor thus really did not exist in the villages. According to traditional village views, wage labor also reduced one to virtual slavery. Finally, wages were too low and working conditions too hard to be attractive. From 1828 on, the British therefore brought workers from famine-ridden South India, as the Sinhalese kings had earlier done to work the cinnamon. Coming mostly as seasonal workers, by 1860 eighty to ninety thousand men, women, and children streamed in every year. At first they came south in long marches through malarial regions. Mortality was enormous. The sick were simply abandoned by the wayside. Later they came by way of Colombo, in part by rail. Cheated by recruiting agents and gang foremen, they were exploited and often mistreated on the plantations themselves. These things occurred despite early administrative intervention, in contravention of laissez-faire principles, to impose sanitary rules, to construct rest hostels, and to enact other protective measures. The bureaucracy acted in response to pressure from the planters themselves, who sought to safeguard their labor supply, in response to humanitarian protests by officials and physicians, and in answer to Parliamentary questions at Westminster.[9]

Coffee was later displaced by tea. Although Royal Botanical Garden experiments around 1860 had proved very promising, the planters switched over to tea only after the coffee blight. Tea plantings produce only after three to six years, require careful cultivation, and require factorylike preparation facilities on the plantation; or, in other words, a considerable capital investment. The Ceylon hill country, however, had an ideal climate and soil. The higher the plantation the better the tea. The tropical rainfall, which spoiled coffee, raised the tea yield. Rising English consumption by all classes and a shift in taste to the stronger Indian and Ceylon teas, which sharply reduced the consumption of Chinese tea, brought about a tea boom, as the figures in table 3.3 show.[10] During the interwar period, the area cultivated remained roughly the same as in 1914, but the export value continued to rise until 1927. During the depression, however, prices fell on occasion to less than the cost of production. However, because export volume continued to increase, employment remained surprisingly constant. The Imperial Preference Duty was some help. In 1933 the world's most important tea producers agreed on a quota system, and export values rose once more.[11]

Table 3.3
Production of Tea in Ceylon, 1882-1914

	CULTIVATED AREA (IN ACRES)	PRODUCTION (IN MILLIONS OF POUNDS)	VALUE (IN RUPEES)
1882	15,000	1	592,000
1890	236,000	46	22,900,000
1900	405,000	149	47,611,000
1914	487,000	194	89,726,000

SOURCE: Lewis, *Tropical Development*, 229.

In contrast to coffee, the Ceylonese never gained a foothold in tea, as they lacked both capital and the necessary skills; tea plantations remained in European, and mainly British, hands. After the 1880s, the plantations belonged increasingly to London-based corporations. Managers rather than owners now ran things. Only in the border zones, where rice and tea cultivation were intermingled, did the Sinhalese peasants grow tea as small holders.Their production was, however, only about 10 percent of the total, with 2,362 plantations and 69,916 small holders in 1938.[12]

The labor question remained acute, especially since tea requires more care than coffee and must be picked year round. The tea factories required additional labor. Plantation workers continued to come from South India. In 1911, 366,000 workers of a total of 465,000 were Tamils, and by 1927 there were 720,000 Tamils. Travel advances were booked as debts which bound coolie to employer, and further advances for weddings and festivities increased this debt. This sort of debt slavery was not formally abolished until 1921. In practice it continued after 1921 in one form or another.

On the plantations, dominated on one side by the white overseer's bungalow and on the other by the tea factory, the coolies lived in company houses, or coolie lines. The coolies were physically isolated from the native Ceylonese and were also separated from the latter by language and religion. No ties existed even to the Ceylonese Tamils in Jaffna and other cities. There was always much coming and going between Ceylon and India. Many Indians returned home for a time and married there. Working and living conditions (daily rice rations, sanitary services, schools for the children) seem to have improved in the interwar period. Still, even in 1936 much coolie housing failed to meet government standards. Child mortality remained high, and invalids were often packed off home without further ado. Workers could be fired at any time, and without a discharge certificate work was not to be had elsewhere. Unionization attempts collapsed as a result of planter resistance. Salaries remained low, but were nonetheless considerably above those for agricultural labor in south India.[13]

As in Malaya and Sumatra, rubber production also rapidly increased in Ceylon, once the right varieties and production methods had been discovered. The area cultivated rose from approximately 2,000 acres in 1900 to 200,000 in 1910, to 267,000 in 1920, and to over 500,000 in 1928. The plantations lay in the lower-lying areas in the west and southwest and hence did not compete with tea. Since planting and harvesting were relatively simple and required less capital than tea, Sinhalese as well as Europeans were able to buy or establish plantations. In 1927, 40 percent of the total production came from native plantations, and 15 to 20 percent from small holders. The rubber trees were tapped by the village population, mainly the women, rather than by coolies. The collapse of prices during the depression thus hurt the Ceylonese producers badly, and more will be said of the international producers' agreements below (p. 151). The coconut palm and its by-products was another valuable cash crop. The coconut palm was also cultivated on plantations, mainly on the Colombo coastal strip, the Jaffna peninsula, and the east coast. The million-odd acres of palms were almost entirely in Ceylonese hands, either in plantations or in small holdings within the framework of the village economy. Both the Sinhalese low-country landlord families and the new urban bourgeoisie used this opportunity to produce cash crops. In the crisis years, however, half of the palm land fell into the hands of Tamil moneylenders.[14]

The traditional agrarian sector, however, stagnated. Rice was cultivated in the coastal areas and the high-rainfall, bottom-land areas of the west and southwest. By the interwar period, the cultivated area was reaching the limits of the suitable land and the plantation boundaries, while the village population continued to increase. The consequences were noted in a report of the Kandy Peasantry Commission in 1951:

The village area is comparatively densely populated. The villages are hemmed in on all sides by plantations and are found as a rule in a cluster at the bottom of the hills. Many

> tanks and "pathahas" which provided irrigation for the sowing of paddy, the main item of diet, have been partly silted up by soil erosion or absorbed by estates. The paddy area has not increased with the increase of population. The garden land available is not sufficient to meet other requirements. . . . The peasants are landless and the main problem is landlessness.[15]

The main rice-growing area of Ceylon was, and still is, the relatively dry zone in the north and east. Uncultivated land was still available, but required irrigation. The great irrigation works of the classical period had, as mentioned earlier, fallen into ruin, and lifting of the corvée (1832-1833) by which the state and the villages had maintained the remaining canals and tanks, made things even worse.[16] From the 1850s on, the British saw the need for administrative and financial support of irrigation and in the following years budgeted substantial amounts of money for it. The area under cultivation, 834,000 acres in 1926, increased very little, and the yield was the lowest of any of the monsoon countries. The land was poor, cultivation methods were old-fashioned, fertilizer was seldom used, and the dry zone was malaria ridden because the open reservoirs attracted mosquitoes; and the smallest holders had to pay 40 percent of their crops to the landlords.[17]

Ceylon had occasionally imported rice even in the nineteenth century. As its population rose from 2.7 million in 1881 to 4.1 milliion in 1911 and 5.3 million in 1931, it became increasingly unable to feed itself.[18] Burmese rice covered one-half to two-thirds of requirements and was about 25 percent of the total imports. Ceylon thus offered the classic picture of a cash-crop producing, exporting colony that simultaneously had to import much of its food. Rising English demand for tropical products had encouraged a plantation agriculture which, dependent on the world market, was one-sidedly devoted to export-oriented economic development.[19] Tea, rubber, and coconuts earned 44.5 percent of the national income in 1938 and constituted over 90 percent of all exports. "From 1881 until 1931 exports rose on the average of 53.7 percent per decade, and revenues on the average of 52 percent."[20] The colony enjoyed rather large revenues between 40 and 60 percent of which came from import and export duties. This income permitted construction of a good transportation and school system and provision of sanitary services.[21] Growing, processing, transporting, and shipping the cash crops created many jobs both within and outside the primary sectors of the economy. Employment by European firms enabled many to rise socially. Work on the rubber and coconut plantations or on one's own small holding provided the peasants of the densely settled southwest a better life than that enjoyed by the rice-farming peasants of the dry zone. The living standard was significantly higher than in India. These positive aspects of the export economy must be conceded.

But the dual nature of the colonial economic structure must also be admitted.[22] The tea industry was not only based on foreign capital, owned by foreign firms, and managed by foreigners but also rested on imported foreign labor. It thus formed an enclave with which the native Ceylonese had very little contact.

The Ceylonese did participate in the production of rubber and coconut products, but remained dependent on European—mostly British—mercantile firms, banks, and shipping companies, whose managers were also European. Plantation company profits were reinvested or were repatriated to England.[23] Corporations paid no income taxes. Rising import figures conceal the fact that imports consisted largely of food for Indian coolies, consumer goods for the European and Ceylonese upper classes, and capital goods for the plantations.[24] The export industry did not foster growth in other sectors. Industry remained marginal.[25] It is hardly surprising that toward the end of the 1930s unemployment became increasingly severe.[26] In the neglected traditional sector, with a rising population (1.6 percent a year before 1941, 3 percent today) and declining productivity, a downward spiral began that, when terms of trade worsened rapidly for tea and rubber around 1960, left the entire economic and social structure in very serious straits indeed.[27]

The Crown Colony constitution of 1833, with its "Official Majority" in the legislative council, offered little scope for political action. At first only the planters, who had the right to participate in the setting of the budget, used these opportunities to secure their interests. They criticized the high military expenditures and demanded that railway construction be speeded up. For a time organized as the Ceylon League (1865), the planters believed that their "Unofficial Majority" ought to count as the first step toward responsible government along Canadian and Australian lines. The governor, Sir Henry Ward, turned them down cold:

> In a colony, the population of which consists of seven or eight thousand Europeans, a small though intelligent class of Burghers, and two millions of Cingalese [sic], Tamils, and Moormen...you cannot introduce the principle of Representative or Responsible Government....The Government must for many years hold the balance between European and native interests.[28]

In contrast to India, the new elite—planters, businessmen, lawyers, senior officials, and men with British educations—never organized in the nineteenth century. A few locally based groups formed after the Liberals came to power in 1906 in England: the Low Country Producers' Association, the Jaffna Association, and the Ceylon National Association. They urged the principle of elective government on London in memoranda and petitions, and in 1912 London responded in modest measure to their demands. Six of the ten Unofficials on the twenty-two member council were to be appointed as representatives of ethnic groups, but four were to be elected, two by Europeans, one by the Burghers, and one by the "educated Ceylonese." The latter elected a well-educated Tamil, Sir Ponnambalam Ramanathan. Ceylon was the first colony granted the right to elect a non-European to the legislative council. Although the competence of the council was extended only slightly, the governors nevertheless (following instructions from London) attempted to use the council's small Official Majority of two votes as little as possible, preferring to settle disputes over bills by negotiating and attempting to meet the freely expressed criticisms of the Unofficials by turning matters over to committees.[29]

Several clashes between Sinhalese and Muslim Indians occurred in May and June of 1915 in a small town near Kandy because a Buddhist procession playing music had passed a mosque. The governor, completely nonplussed, responded by invoking martial law and bringing in Indian troops in the mistaken impression that the disturbances were directed against the colonial power. Among other measures, the Sinhalese politician Don Stephen Senanayake, was summarily jailed.[30] In May 1917 the Ceylon Reform League was formed, and in December 1919 the Ceylon National Congress. In the wake of the Montagu-Chelmsford reforms in India, London also acceded to Ceylonese demands in 1920 and granted the Unofficials a majority in the legislative council. The governor did retain, however, sufficient powers to protect himself if he was outvoted in the council. The next step came as early as 1923. Under pressure from the congress, the council was reconstituted as follows. In addition to the twelve civil servants, there were thirty-seven other members, twenty-three chosen on a territorial basis, eleven elected by the minorities, and three appointed, The suffrage was extended to include 204,000, or about 4 percent of the population. The chairman of the council was elected by that body, which received extensive powers over legislation and finance, and the governor lost his veto right.

There were some striking personalities in the council, but only a few representatives of the predominantly urban "colonial bourgeoisie." Their English schooling was outwardly expressed by their dress and life-style, and an abyss lay between them and the Buddhist-educated, more traditionally inclined lower middle class. The fact that the Sinhalese upper class plumped for a territorial rather than communal or ethnic group representation only in a limited sense implied that they subordinated their ethnic interests to the notion of national solidarity or class interests, because modern territorial representation necessarily favored the Sinhalese majority at the cost of educationally and economically advanced minorities. Given the existing system of seats reserved for specific ethnic groups, the minorities were over-represented in the council as it was. As early as 1921, the Tamils had walked out of the congress and formed their own organization, the Ceylon Indian Congress. "As the colonial Government was persuaded to concede power gradually, Ceylonese politicians contended among themselves over the share that communal groups would receive."[31]

Since the days of the Durham Report of 1839, the English had understood that representative government could only be a halfway house. The executive faced an "irresponsible" legislature, in which power was not linked with responsibility. The Ceylonese deputies could thus block legislation and confront the governor with the alternative of either giving in or accepting a stalemate. A study commission headed by the Earl of Donoughmore pointed this out clearly enough as early as 1928.[32] To retreat was impossible, and London was still not ready to concede either responsible government or dominion status. In addition,

Ceylon's plural society, which lacked a national consensus and whose parties were organized along ethnic lines, seemed unsuited for the Westminster model. London therefore accepted the Donoughmore proposals and with the constitution of 1931 tried another approach. A council of state replaced the legislative council. It was composed of seven committees, the elected heads of which were also heads of the administrative departments. Together the heads constituted a ministry, the members of which were individually responsible to the council of state and could be forced to resign by a vote of no confidence in the council. The Ceylonese ministers for the "transferred subjects" received direct executive responsibility. At the same time, communal, or ethnic, representation was abolished and universal suffrage for men—and women! —introduced. For the times, this was a revolutionary step, the intention of which was manifestly to force Ceylonese politicians to pay some heed to the concerns of the lower classes.[33]

In the years that followed, noteworthy efforts were made in education and agriculture in particular (D. S. Senanayake was responsible for agriculture). Ceylonization was pushed, and in 1935 the Bank of Ceylon was founded, in order to loosen the bonds of British and Indian lenders. The expansion of the suffrage (to 2.1 million) did not, however, reduce the power of the Westernized elite.[34] The leading politicians, or, more accurately, political families, constituted a plutocracy. The Senanayakes, and also Sir John Kotelwala, elected prime minister in 1953, owned graphite mines and plantations.[35] S.W.R.D. Bandaranaike came from a well-to-do family that had converted to Christianity and had long-standing ties to the British. He grew up on a great plantation, enjoyed the best Oxford education, and learned Sinhalese only after his return from Oxford in 1930. He then adopted native dress and converted to Buddhism in order to gather around his own party (Sinhala Maha Sabha) a middle-class Buddhist Sinhalese following. In 1956 this following brought their charismatic leader into power under the banner of Sinhalese nationalism.

The Ceylonese criticized the Donoughmore constitution from the very outset. Sinhalese politicians wanted complete domestic autonomy and a cabinet system like the British, while minorities felt shut out, and all the more so because all seven ministers were Sinhalese in 1936. The Tamils boycotted the elections of 1931. The British hope that creation of the council of state would reduce racial tensions went unfulfilled. The system did not permit effective executive leadership and complicated rather than aided the formation of parties. As early as 1938, the governor had begun the constitutional reforms that, though delayed by the war, led to dominion status in 1947. All the same, it should be emphasized that the constitution of 1931 gave the Ceylonese ruling class parliamentary and administrative experience, and that, even before World War II, Ceylon enjoyed a very considerable measure of self-government.[36]

NOTES

1. See Lennox Algernon Mills, *Ceylon under British Rule, 1795-1932; With an Account of the East India Company's Embassies to Kandy, 1762-1795* (London: F. Cass, 1964); idem,

Britain and Ceylon (London, New York: Longmans, Green and Co., 1945); Sidney Arnold Pakeman, *Ceylon* (New York: Praeger, 1964); William Howard Wriggins, *Ceylon: Dilemmas of a New Nation* (Princeton: Princeton University Press, 1960).

2. For a sketch of the administrative structure, see Sir Charles Collins, "Ceylon: The Imperial Heritage," in Braibanti, *Asian Bureaucratic Systems*.

3. "By such an appointment the honourable ambition of the upper class of natives will be safely gratified, and the great man of the people will be bound by ties of affection to a government which ceases to withhold offices of power from its native subjects"; letter to the secretary of state, 1932; quoted in Pakeman, *Ceylon*, 65.

4. Great Britain, Colonial Office, *Report by the Right Honourable W.G.A. Ormsby Gore, M.P. (Parliamentary Unter-Secretary of State for the Colonies) on his Visit to Malaya, Ceylon and Java during the year 1928*... (London: H.M. Stationery Office, 1928), as quoted in Symonds, *The British*, 107. Hereafter cited as Ormsby Gore, *Report*.

5. On the life-style of "white sahibs" in Ceylon before the First World War, see Leonard Woolf's graphic *Growing: An Autobiography of the Years 1911-1914* (London: Hogarth Press, 1967). "We were grand because we were a ruling caste in a strange Asiatic country"; ibid., 24. On the tensions between planters and officials, see ibid., 16f.

6. S. J. Tambiah, "Ethnic Representation in Ceylon's Higher Administrative Services, 1870-1946," *University of Ceylon Review*, 13 (April-July 1955), 125; Symonds, *The British*, 105f.

7. See Mills for details, *Ceylon under British Rule*, ch. 11.

8. Ibid., ch. 12; B. Bastianpillai, "From Coffee to Tea in Ceylon: The Vicissitudes of a Colony's Plantation Economy," *Ceylon Journal of Historical and Social Studies*, 7 (January-June 1964).

9. M.W. Roberts, "Indian Estate Labour in Ceylon during the Coffee Period (1830-1880), *IESHR*, 3 (March 1966).

10. Table 3.4 gives additional data.

Table 3.4
Tea Industry in Ceylon, 1885-1896

YEAR	CONSUMPTION IN THE UK (IN THOUSANDS OF POUNDS)	PERCENTAGE FURNISHED BY CEYLON	INDIA	CHINA
1885	182,409	2	36	62
1890	194,008	18	52	30
1896	227,785	35	54	11

SOURCE: S. Rajayatam, "The Ceylon Tea Industry, 1886-1931," *Ceylon Journal of Historical and Social Studies*, 4 (January-June 1961), 171.

11. Table 3.5 gives further data.

Table 3.5
Export of Tea from Ceylon, 1913-1937

YEAR	VALUE OF EXPORTED TEA (IN MILLIONS OF DOLLARS)	REAL VALUE OF EXPORTS (TAKING TERMS OF TRADE INTO ACCOUNT) (IN MILLIONS OF DOLLARS)
1913	28.5	28.5
1923	57.8	39.3
1925	72.5	48.7
1927	77.6	56.2
1930	65.7	52.6
1932	28.3	33.3
1935	54.4	45.3
1937	64.3	52.3

SOURCE: Sieber, *Realen Austauschverhältnisse*, 141.

12. Mills, *Britain and Ceylon*, 64.

13. Officially, the British declared themselves pleased, noting the planters' "well-deserved reputation for management of Labour"; Ormsby Gore, *Report*, 78. See also the critical remarks in Harold Beresford Butler, *Problémes du Travail en Orient: Inde, Etablissements Français dans l'Inde, Ceylon, Malaisie et Indes Néerlandaises* (Geneva: no pub., 1938), 44f. Of the 70,181 quarters inspected, 21,844 failed to meet standards and 207 of 459 plantations had insufficient sanitary installations. See also Granville St. John Orde Browne, *Labour Conditions in Ceylon, Mauritius, and Malaya: Report*. . . .[Cmd. 6423] (London: H.M. Stationery Office, 1943).

14. Burton Stein, "Problems of Economic Development in Ceylon," in Robert Crane, *Aspects of Economic Development in South Asia; With a Supplement on Development Problems in Ceylon*, by Burton Stein (New York: International Secretariat, Institute of Pacific Relations, 1954), 297.

15. Quoted in Wriggins, *Ceylon*, 216. See also, "Village Surveys," in Ceylon, Ministry of Labour, Industry and Commerce, *Bulletin*, 5-13 (1937-1944), passim.

16. Michael Roberts, "Irrigation Policy in British Ceylon during the Nineteenth Century," *SA*, 2 (August 1972), 48 n.4, casts doubt on this commonly accepted thesis; see also Lewis, *Tropical Development*, 237.

17. Stein, "Problems of Economic Development," 295.

18. According to official figures. Corrected figures are somewhat higher: Angelika Sievers, *Ceylon: Gesellschaft und Lebensraum in der orientalischen Tropen; eine sozialgeograpische Landeskunde* (Wiesbaden: F. Steiner, 1964), 60.

19. On this, see Burkhard Gagzow, *Aussenwirtschaftsorientierte Entwicklungspolitik kleiner Länder: das Beispiel Ceylons* (Stuttgart: G. Fischer, 1969), 79ff.

20. Ibid., 80-81. Amita Dutta, "Interwar Ceylon: Trade and Migration," *IESHR*, 7 (March 1970).

21. According to Ormsby Gore, Ceylon had in 1928 "probably the most extensive hospital system of any British possession"; *Report*,91. In the same vein, see also Orde Brown, *Labour Conditions*, 19. Wriggins also writes of a "relatively high standard of living"; *Ceylon*, 29, 68. On the school system, see Hugh Archibald Wyndham, *Native Education: Ceylon, Java, Formosa, the Philippines, French Indo-China, and British Malaya* (London: H. Milford, Oxford University Press, 1933), ch. 6; and J.C.A. Corea, "One Hundred Years of Education in Ceylon," *MAS*, 3 (April 1969).

22. The dual export economy "was nearly perfect"; Donald R. Snodgrass, *Ceylon: An Export Economy in Transition* (Homewood, Ill.: D. Irwin, 1966), 57.

23. Around 1900 the dividends of twenty British plantation companies averaged 19 percent over the long term and in good years went as high as 50 percent; Gagzow, *Entwicklungspolitik*, 82.

24. For the situation up until 1929, see Snodgrass, *Ceylon*, 57.

25. See Ceylon, Banking Commission, . . .*Report [and Memoranda & Evidence] December, 1934* . . .(Ceylon, *Sessional Paper XXII [-XXIII]*, 1934), (2 vols., Colombo: Ceylon Government Press, 1934), which noted that the existing credit system was ill-suited for encouragement of local capital formation or enterprise, that the unemployed "educated classes" were especially vehement in their demands for industrialization, and that a national bank was a necessity.

26. It "had already become a formidable problem," according to Orde Brown, *Labor Conditions*, 29. Dutta, "Interwar Ceylon," 22, writes, however, of almost full employment.

27. René Dumont, *Paysanneries aux abois: Ceylon, Tunisie, Sénégal* (Paris: Ed. du Seuil, 1972), 72, notes that between 1911 and 1970 the population had tripled, and arable land per capita dropped from 27 to 13.5 acres; at the same time, the buying power of a pound of tea had fallen by half. See also Gagzow, *Entwicklungspolitik*, 129f.

28. Quoted in Pakeman, *Ceylon*, 85.

29. As has been well established by A. J. Wilson, "The Creve-McCallum Reforms (1912-1921)," *Ceylon Journal of Historical and Social Studies*, 2 (January 1959).

30. P. T. Fernando, "The British Raj and the 1915 Communal Riots in Ceylon," *MAS*, 3 (July 1964).

31. S. Arasaratnam, "Nationalism, Communalism and National Unity in Ceylon," in Philip Mason (ed.), *India and Ceylon: Unity and Diversity; A Symposium* (London, New York: Oxford University Press, 1967), 262.

32. On this see Albertini, *Decolonization*, 92ff.; Mills, *Britain and Ceylon*, 35ff.

33. Great Britain, Special Commission on the Ceylon Constitution, *Ceylon: Report* . . .(London: H.M. Stationery Office, 1928), noted it is "our belief that a wide franchise would expedite the passing of such social and industrial legislation as is now in force in every progressive country."

34. The middle and upper class belonged mainly to the Karawa caste, which had early converted to Christianity and turned to administration and commerce. Bryce Ryan, *Caste in Modern Ceylon: The Sinhalese System in Transition* (New Brunswick, N. J.: Rutgers University Press, 1953), 331, estimates that 90 percent of the richest families were Karawa in origin. See also Wriggens, *Ceylon*, 110, 119.

35. Sir John Kotelwala, *An Asian Prime Minister's Story* (London: G. G. Harrap, 1956). His family owned plantations and graphite mines; his father committed suicide when Sir John was eleven. He then studied at the Royal College, and then, after further studies in England, entered the army. He was a member of Stable Court, by 1936 minister, and by 1953 prime minister; he was also related to Senanayake; ibid., 14, shows Kotelwala playing polo.

36. Kotelwala noted: "We were free to criticize the Government and all its work as strongly as we liked"; ibid., 22. He also noted the system "gave us an opportunity for gaining valuable experience in the administration"; ibid., 30.

4

MALAYA

Lying as it does between the Indian and the Pacific oceans and separated from Sumatra by only a narrow channel, the slender Malay Peninsula was exposed to foreign influences from the earliest of times.[1] China, Thailand, Sumatra, and India have all left their impress. Of the four, however, Indian influence, penetrating the northwest first and later the south, made the strongest impact on the sparse Malay population. Hinduism and Buddhism were accepted both as religious and cultural institutions and as administrative and social ones. Malaya itself, however, was less a state than an outpost of states, whose centers of gravity lay elsewhere. A Sumatran prince thus founded the Sultanate of Malacca in the early fifteenth century. Subsequently accepting Islam from India, the city-state of Malacca became a significant economic and political power. In part by employing Javanese mercenaries to do its fighting, it was for some decades the leading power on the peninsula and, indeed, in the entire Malay Archipelago. In 1511, however, the Portuguese conquered the city of Malacca and made it into a heavily fortified way station for the China and spice trades. Under pressure from the Sumatran Sultanate of Acheh and the Malayan Sultanate of Johore (the successor state to Malayan Malacca) and, after 1605, the Dutch, Malacca finally fell to the latter in 1641. The empire of the sultans of Johore, however, also disintegrated in the late eighteenth century. In the northern part of the peninsula, the states of Kedah, Kelantan, and Trengganu fell under Siamese domination. The Sultanates of Perak and Selangor and the loosely organized states of the Minangkabau Confederation all became independent.

At the same time, after eliminating the French as competitors in India in 1763, the British East India Company was paying Southeast Asia increasing attention. The China trade was growing, particularly in tea. During the following years, the British sought a harbor in the Malacca Straights, acting with particular urgency after the Dutch shut them out of Dutch harbors during the American Revolution. In 1785 the British induced the sultan of Kedah to cede the island of Penang. In 1800 the British purchased the adjacent mainland strip, which they named Province Wellesley. After 1805 a young company employee named Thomas

Stamford Raffles succeeded in interesting the governor-general of the company, Lord Minto, in the peninsula. After having governed Java from 1811 to 1816, Raffles landed in Singapore in 1819, and, exploiting tensions within the now-diminished Sultanate of Johore, obtained the island by treaty. Declared by Raffles a duty-free port, Singapore proved with its splendid geographic situation to have uncommon drawing power. By the end of 1820 it already had more than ten thousand inhabitants and by 1825 double the trade of Malacca and Penang combined.

In the following years, the Straits Settlements (Singapore, Malacca, Penang, and Province Wellesley), remained nothing more than coastal outposts for the trade with China and the Malay Archipelago. They "belonged" to the East India Company and were administered from India. The company was not interested in territorial conquest, and the watchword for Malaya was "Nonintervention." In practice, the entire peninsula came to fall within the British sphere of influence. In 1867 administration was transferred from the India to the Colonial Office. Business interests in Penang and Singapore had demanded the transfer and had petitioned Parliament for it. They claimed neglect on the part of the Indian government, which only then had sought to levy an excise tax to cover the chronic deficits of the Straits Settlements. They also claimed that India showed little interest in energetic measures against the pirates, and they hoped through a legislative council to gain influence on the administration of the colony. The opening of the Suez Canal gave Singapore a mighty boost, and the financial situation improved. The Dutch, for their part, extended their rule outward from Sumatra and the French began their Indochinese involvement.

No less important, however, were the changes within the Malay princely states. With the discovery of tin in Perak and Selangor, combined with the rising demand for it in Europe and the United States, the Chinese flowed in, both as laborers and mineowners. When the Chinese fell to fighting among themselves, public order collapsed altogether in several areas. Although Malay rulers and princes had summoned them in the first place, they were unable to control the Chinese, who were organized in secret societies. Tin production suffered accordingly, and the prospect threatened that the troubles would spill over into the Straits Settlements, particularly Penang. The Chinese, many of whom were British subjects, and the Europeans began, as men on the spot, to press the Straits administration to see to law and order in the Malay states; or, in other words, to intervene in some way or other. The situation became yet more complicated when succession struggles broke out in Perak and Selangor and the factions sought support from the governor of the Straits Settlements. The first governor, Sir Harry Ord (1867-1873), sought to mediate in and between the states; his policy was limited intervention.[2] He was, however, recalled by the colonial secretary, Lord Kimberley, in 1869. As late as the fall of 1872, Kimberley rejected these domestic difficulties, now hard to distinguish from civil war, as grounds for intervention: "If we are to annex all the territory in Asia where there is misgovernment we must end in dividing Asia with Russia." On 20

September 1873, however, that same Lord Kimberley in his famous instruction to the new Straits governor, Andrew Clarke, told the latter "to employ such influence as they (HMG) possess with the native princes to rescue these fertile and productive countries from the ruin which must befall them if the present disorders continue unchecked."[3] What caused this change of course remains disputed. Did London give way to pressure from the administrators or economic interest groups on the spot, or did it fear the possibility of foreign intervention?[4] Intervention was, as they say, "in the air," for by 1873 Great Britain was already so firmly committed in Malaya both politically and economically, and expansionist forces were running so high, even in Gladstone's Liberal party, that London, meaning the Colonial Office, could no longer withstand the pressure of the various lobbies and was forced to intervene in the coastal states.

But Governor Clarke exceeded his authority. Rather than simply finding out what was really happening and reporting this to London, he intervened directly in the succession and other princely struggles in Perak by recognizing one of the pretenders as sultan; and to top it off, in the Pangkor Engagement (20 January 1874), he arranged for a British resident. He also seized excuses to intervene in Selangor and Sungei Ujong (a part of the later Negri Sembilan). The appointment of a resident had been suggested for some time by various and sundry and seemed indeed perfectly suited to British interests.[5] No open annexation, no expensive British administration, but still, it was more than a protectorate, at least if it could be assured that the "counsel" of the resident would be accepted in all important matters save those of religion. In other words, residency was an instrument for regulating the internal affairs of the Malay feudal states according to British notions. The system could draw upon the treaties with the Indian princes for precedent, and it became the model for Lord Lugard's Indirect Rule in Africa. It was to prove very successful indeed, though only after the ham-handed acts of the first resident, in Perak, had led to his own murder and British military intervention.

The residents, whom London made responsible in advance for all untoward disturbances, were left largely to their own devices. They established close connections with the sultans and feudal lords, set up modern finance systems—the sultans and Malay officials received salaries instead of the feudal dues paid them heretofore—organized the police, customs, postal, and other services. Income from the tin mines paid for the expansion of navigable waterways, the construction of roads, and the establishment of a rudimentary public health network. The sultans chaired councils of state, which along with the resident also included the most important notables and some Chinese businessmen. The councils had legislative and fiscal competence and provided forums for discussion. But the councils of state served at the same time as a facade which, while proclaiming outwardly the power of the sultans, concealed the fact that real power had been transferred to the British residents and their small staffs: "The British advisor ruled and the Malay ruler advised." A Malay "Eton" was created in 1905 in the guise of the Malay College in Kuala Kangsar in Perak. The college provided the sons of the Malay aristocracy the English education necessary to become administrators. The traditional social structure remained largely unaltered, though slavery was abolished and debt slavery was gradually eliminated.[6] The village chiefs (*penghulu*) also became paid officials and thereby lost to some extent their traditional role as leaders and spokesmen for their people.[7]

Under the energetic governor, Sir Frederick Weld, a representative of the Forward School, the still-independent nine Minangkabau states were brought under control after 1880 and in 1895 were forced to join the Negri Sembilan Federation under a British resident. Between 1887 and 1889 a similar treaty was concluded with Pahang on the east coast. The final push in the latter state seems to have come from fear of French or German infiltration, particularly after the race for tin-mining concessions had begun.[8] London refused for the time being, however, to allow annexation of the northern states, in the interest of maintaining good relations with the buffer state of Siam. Loose ties were established but only in 1909. In Johore a protectorate treaty had been considered enough in 1885, and the sultan, who had with some skill exploited the desire for modernization and had issued a constitution in 1895, had to accept a general advisor only in 1914. What is surprising is that Singapore business interests had been against the naming of a resident, on the assumption that an independent sultan was more likely to grant them concessions. The Colonial Office had in fact attempted to block monopolistic concessions and had even favored Chinese over Englishmen because the former had less political leverage.[9]

It soon turned out that the four states with residents, to whom considerable initiative and independence had been granted, were following divergent courses in matters of taxation, justice, land policy, and agriculture and were escaping from effective control. In 1895 and 1896 they were therefore joined together in a federation under a general resident, who was himself subordinate to the governor of the Straits Settlements (in his capacity as high commissioner of the Federated Malay States). Income from tin exports from Selangor and Perak could henceforth be spent in the less-developed states. Civil service and police were unified as was, later, the land law. The sultans were allowed to retain their existing rights, but in practice the federation tended to develop into a union because there was no boundry set between federative and individual state rights. A new capital city was established in Kuala Lumpur. Not only the residents but also the sultans lost their freedom of decision to the federation administration. The more important technical and economic matters became, the less practical was the mere "advising of the traditional authorities." What the sultans were left with was outward pomp and ceremonial functions which maintained their prestige and the loyalty of the Malay population; but effective power had passed definitively into British hands. It was in good part for this reason that those states entering in 1909 and Johore did not join the federation, and the British did not force them to. The British system of rule in Malaya thus grouped as Crown Colonies the Straits Settlements, the Federated Malay States (Perak, Selangor, Negri Sembilan, and Pahang), and the Unfederated Malay States (Kedah, Perlis,

Kelantan, Trengganu and Johore). The interwar period saw no changes. The trend then, however, shifted toward decentralization within the framework of the federation, in order to give the sultans a stronger position and reduce the difference between federated and unfederated states. The hope was that these changes would create the basis for the unification of all the states. Proposals and reports supporting this measure encountered all sorts of resistance, however.[10] Departments such as agriculture, education, forests, and public works were transferred to the individual states in 1932 and given fixed budgets from the federation treasury. The state councils were also abolished. There was considerable reluctance to take the final step of federation or union for all of Malaya, either because no one wanted to hazard such experiments in such a complicated and problematic plural society or because of fear of offending the sultans, the pillars of British rule.[11] Amalgamation was made the preliminary step for self-government only after 1945.

It was not without irony that Malaya, of all places, the classical entrepôt colony down through the centuries, should in the second half of the nineteenth century transform itself so rapidly into a raw-materials producer and thereafter exhibit to an especially striking degree the characteristic features of the modern colonial economy: orientation toward the world market to meet the needs of European and American industrialization; capital investment in mining and plantations; importation of labor; and the creation of a dual economic structure, neither sought by nor profiting the local population. As is well known, tin and rubber set this revolution in motion.

Tin had been mined and smelted in the precolonial period, and the Dutch East India Company had exported tin. Germany was originally the leading tin user, to be displaced in the eighteenth and nineteenth centuries by England, which depended mainly on Cornish tin until the removal of the import duty in 1853. The tin use increased enormously after 1870, particularly in the canning industry, and as early as the 1880s Malaya had become the world's leading tin producer. (See Table 4.1.) During the interwar period, competition from the Dutch East Indies, the Congo, Nigeria, Bolivia, and other areas reduced Malaya's proportional share.[12]

Table 4.1
Production of Tin, 1871-1940 (in millions of tons)

	1871-1880	1881-1890	1891-1900	1901-1910	1911-1920	1921-1930	1931-1940
Malaya	7	20	42	49	46	51	51
Rest of the world	32	37	38	53	79	100	104

It was not, however, the British but the Chinese that started tin mining in Malaya. By the 1850s, the existence of tin was known, principally in Perak. Malay rulers and aristocrats, seeking additional income, opened the way to

Chinese capital from the Straits Settlements, and since the Malay peasants were not interested in wage labor, Chinese coolies were brought in. By 1870 there were already 40,000 Chinese in Perak, and by the end of the 1880s around 80,000. In Selangor, the number rose from 28,000 in 1884 to 51,000 in 1891. As has been mentioned, a kind of state within the state arose in which the Chinese, organized in secret societies, fought bloody battles among themselves and forced the British to intervene to end the chaos. But the British were able to move into tin mining only very slowly. Numerous Englishmen went bankrupt because they did not undertake adequate preliminary investigations, found costs too high, or could not break the Chinese labor monopoly. Europeans were unable to gain a foothold until dredges came to be used. The British were able to raise capital for such costly equipment more easily than the Chinese. Still, by 1914, only a quarter of the production came from European mines. In the interwar period, the European share climbed to two-thirds (1937), while at the same time the number of Chinese workers declined from 170,000 (1910) to 104,000 (1929) as a result of more capital-intensive technology.

Efforts of the colonial administration to assist European mining interests led during the period 1906 to 1913 to rather extensive state supervision. The state took over unexploited land and only conceded it to those who could prove they had "sufficient capital and could employ labor-saving equipment." The Mining Law of 1935 declared subsurface wealth to be the property of the individual Malay states and required licenses limited to twenty-one years for the exploitation of them. The state also allocated water rights.[13] Income from tin mining—concession fees, rents, and, above all, export duties—provided forty-six percent of state income by 1899 and thus paid for administrative expenses and the "basic infrastructure of modern Malaya."[14]

In the twentieth century, rubber came to be even more important than tin. From the early days, Chinese and British in the Straits Settlements and the Malay states had grown products like pepper, spices, cane sugar, and coffee on plantations. But the scale of all this remained modest in comparison with the rubber boom after 1900. The story has often been told of how Sir Henry Wickham smuggled rubber plant seeds out of Brazil and took them to England. Germinated in the botanical gardens at Kew, rubber plants were later also grown in Ceylon and in the Singapore botanical gardens. The director of the latter seized upon the possibilities for rubber cultivation and played no small part in encouraging the first planters to hazard it. But falling coffee prices certainly made the changeover easier. Still, as late as 1897, only 345 acres were in rubber and only 200 tons were exported in 1905, a very small amount when measured against the 60,000 tons extracted from rubber plants growing wild in Brazil, mainly in the Amazon.[15] Between 1901 and 1910 rubber prices tripled, partly as a result of increasing production of bicycle and auto tires, rubber boots, and other objects, but mainly because the Brazilians began fixing prices. Malayan rubber exports rose from 6,313 tons in 1910 to 174,322 tons in 1920 and 360,000 in 1948. In the interwar period the thousand-odd plantations ranging in size from

100 to 1,000 acres were largely British owned and employed 260,000 workers, mainly Indian coolies. There were also Chinese, Malay, and Indian plantations, but with considerably less acreage.[16] Malay small holders (under 100 acres) were important, however, as was also true in the Netherlands Indies. Small holders cultivated 918,000 acres in 1922 and, by 1940, 1.3 million acres.[17] In 1933 Malays produced 219,000 tons or 47.8 percent of the total exported.[18] The magnitude of the "rubber revolution" is perhaps easier to grasp when one considers that more than half of all land cultivated was devoted to rubber, nearly all of which was exported. Other plantation products such as palm oil, coconuts, sugar, and citrus fruits were of very secondary importance, and it is not surprising that despite the rather modest population of four million, it was necessary to import rice in sizeable quantities.[19]

After World War I, rubber prices dropped sharply, from 85 cents a pound in 1920 to 20 cents in June 1922. Trees planted in the boom period around 1910 were beginning to yield, and, after war production ended, demand dropped. The Stevenson Plan of 1922, which set export quotas for Malay and Ceylonese producers, was supposed to be the answer. Prices did rise again in the following years, but Indonesia, which did not accept the plan, raised its export share from 23.9 percent in 1921 to 38.1 percent in 1927, while Malaya's share dropped from 50.1 percent to 38.1 percent. The main consumers, the Americans, had also established their own plantations in Brazil and Liberia. When prices collapsed once again during the Great Depression (from 34.8 cents a pound in 1929 to 19.33 cents in 1930, 9.96 cents in 1931, and 7.01 cents in 1932), Malaya small holders increased rather than cut yields, tapping trees more vigorously, in order to raise their incomes. An international rubber agreement was not achieved until 1934. Its quota systems affected the small holders more severely than the European plantation holders. That naturally served to feed anti-British nationalism.[20]

Like the tin mines, the plantations were dependent on foreign labor, though in the latter case on Indians rather than Chinese.[21] Based on the close collaboration of the planters and planter organizations on the one side and the local administration, the Indian government, and the Colonial Office on the other, a rather complicated system of recruitment, immigration control, and worker legislation developed after 1890. It assured the provision of a low-cost labor force and was intended to protect it from the more blatant forms of exploitation. Free labor replaced indentured labor in 1910, the truck system was forbidden, and recruitment and transport brought under supervision. Still, until 1941 the institutions of the *kangany* (strawboss-contractor) for the Indians and the contractor for the Chinese remained in being, which is to say that, in the same manner as the jobber in the Bombay cotton industry, they recruited workers, supervised them in the tin mines and on the plantations, and acted as overseers for the employers. This, of course, left the door open for arbitrary behavior, favoritism, and personal aggrandizement, particularly since the ordinances regarding housing, sanitary facilities, and the education of coolie children could be evaded. The larger estates had a better record than the small.[22] Wages were high in the 1920s but fell during the depression about 60 percent, and in 1932 were even said to lie some 25 to 30 percent below those of 1914.[23] An investigating commission under the leadership for the Indian Congress Party leader, Lal Bahadur Shastri, declared itself in 1937 to be satisfied with the general working conditions.[24] Parmer concludes:

> Indian estate laborers were not exploited in the sense that their wages failed to meet the costs of food and other bare necessities. This much the laborers had and sometimes a little bit more. In fact, thousands of Indian lives were undoubtedly made easier, healthier and richer in workday experience by their sojourn in Malaya. But exploitation did occur in the sense that any aspirations, however feeble, to anything more than a simple existence were discouraged. Indeed they were not permitted to rise.[25]

The Indians and Chinese did not form unions until the late 1930s, when there were also strikes. One can hardly speak of the introduction of a modern labor policy, however, before the Japanese occupation.[26]

Tin mines and rubber plantations dominated the colonial economic structure of Malaya and contributed four-fifths of exports. As in the case of Ceylon, the question is what this export-induced growth meant. Did the mass of the population, and the "real" natives, the Malays in particular, profit from it? There is no doubt that the colony had a rather high income, which permitted a large-scale expansion of the road network, school system, and public health services. In Singapore, the rate of mortality dropped from 25.19 per thousand in 1931 to 14.30 in 1947 (in France in 1937 it was 15) and, according to Maurice Zinkin, the federation was comparable by 1935 with southern Europe in the relative numbers of doctors and hospitals. Per-capita income equalled Japan's, and the living standard of the masses was higher than in other areas of South and Southeastern Asia.[27] But there can also be no doubt that the dualistic structure of Malaya was particularly striking, with the tremendous exports profiting principally British and Chinese mining companies, banks, mercantile houses, and shipping firms. Western investment, 70 percent of it British, rose from 150 million dollars in 1914 to 447 million in 1930, falling back to 372 million in 1937.[28] In the latter year, Chinese investment amounted to 200 million. What this meant need not be restated.

A little, however, must be said of Malaya's plural society.[29] Chinese and Indian immigration has already been discussed. There had already been non-Malay traders and artisans in Portuguese and Dutch days and later, of course, in the Straits Settlements. Fifty-four percent of the 100,000 inhabitants of Singapore were Chinese, 11 percent were Indians, and only 26 percent Malays. Tin mining brought in many Chinese and rubber many Indians. Although the Malay sultans allowed and, indeed, abetted this immigration, it was the foreign ruling power that needed foreign labor to open up the colony economically. The British therefore assured free immigration until the depression. An independent Malaya or independent individual states would probably have imposed immigration restrictions as soon as the danger of being swamped by outsiders was recognized.

By 1931 the foreigners (Chinese and Indians) outnumbered the Malays and by 1938 the Chinese alone did so. (See Table 4.2.)[30] One must, to be sure, distinguish between regions. Non-Malays were most numerous in the Straits Settlements—Singapore was 80 percent Chinese—and least numerous in the less-developed Unfederated Malay States. More important than the percentages was the fact that, even leaving out the Europeans, foreign communities controlled every sector of the economy. The Chinese retained much of their leading position in tin mining, and the miners themselves were almost entirely Chinese. Chinese mercantile houses and banks thrived in the port cities, and a good many retailers, artisans, and manufacturers were Chinese. The Chinese also owned rubber plantations, farmed as small holders and truck gardeners, and controlled the fishing industry. The Indians not only constituted the bulk of the plantation workers, but also engaged in trade and moneylending. Indians with English educations, as for example Tamils from Ceylon, worked in the railways, postal service, and fiscal administration. There were also numerous Indian doctors and lawyers.[31] Chinese and Indians remained closed communities that divided Malay society vertically along ethnic lines.

Table 4.2
Malayan Population by Nationalities, 1911-1938 (in thousands)

	1911	1921	1931	1938
Europeans	11	15	18	28
Eurasians	11	13	16	18
Malays	1438	1651	1962	2210
Chinese	917	1175	1709	2220
Indians	267	472	624	744
Others	29	33	56	58
Total	2673	3359	4385	5279

And the Malays? They were and remained primarily peasants and fishermen in the villages outside the plantation economy. In thinly settled Malaya, they were not forced to leave their firmly knit traditional society to seek wage labor when the tin and rubber revolutions occurred. But they were also unprepared to meet Chinese and Indians on equal terms in the colonial money economy. The Chinese and Indians arrived with typically immigrant willingness to save and work, and they understood how to exploit the available opportunities. When the Malays were threatened with loss of their lands, the British intervened with the Land Reservation Act (applying in 1913 to the federation, later extended to the other states), which prohibited non-Malays from acquiring land in wide areas. The prohibition was, however, much evaded. It also could not prevent Malay peasants from falling into debt to Chinese and Indian moneylenders and thus even in relatively prosperous Malaya becoming tenants on their own land.

Between 1913 and 1933 the government attempted to prevent land from changing hands as a result of debt, which naturally occasioned protests from the Chettyars. But Malay landlords also collected high rents (between 25 to 50 percent of the net yield) and in individual cases even rented to Chinese.[32] Most peasant holdings were small in any case, and the familiar course of division and fragmentation reduced productivity considerably.[33] The feudal levies of pre-British days were, however, generally abolished. The British were also able to manage without taxing peasants, in contrast to India and Burma. The Malays mainly grew rice for their own consumption (in 1940, 800,000 acres) but, as mentioned, also farmed rubber trees as small holders. The amount of arable land was increased through irrigation, and an agricultural department was established in 1904. In 1928 the department was still judged hopelessly inadequate and had no agricultural school.[34] During the depression, the colonial administration attempted to make the country less dependent on foreign rice and even attempted to stop the planting of rubber trees. This caused bad feeling because rubber assured the peasant a cash income. Even at the bottom of the depression it paid better to sell rubber and buy rice, quite aside from the fact that tapping rubber is easy work and is spread out over the whole year.[35]

Since the Malays mostly remained outside the modern sectors of the economy and since the British made real efforts to preserve the traditional society, the distintegration of the old order went considerably more slowly than, say, in Java or lower Burma. That can be counted a positive good. Still, it was difficult for the Malays, already forced by their numbers onto the defensive, to assert themselves in the stiff competition with the Chinese and Indians. British educational and administrative policy was also not really designed to overcome Malay backwardness, even though the British gave the Malays preference, either in awareness of a moral obligation to the people of the country, or in an effort to set limits to Chinese influence. Some have remarked on the Malayophilia of the British civil service.[36] The school system for the Malays, which the administration started developing quite early, was deliberately oriented toward peasant needs, with Malay as the language of instruction. It was at first not particularly well received. Modern urban schools were mostly attended by Chinese and Indians, who thus had another leg up when it came to civil service jobs and business employment. After World War I, educational efforts were intensified, but still with the aim of tying the Malays to the land. Thus Malay remained the language of instruction in the Sultan Idris [Teacher] Training College, founded in 1922, with some 400 students. The use of Malay provoked its graduates to reproach the colonial power with blocking their access to the modern world.[37] In 1938 there were 268,000 primary and secondary students, or some 50 percent of those of school age, without doubt a much higher proportion than in India or other Southeast Asian states. Four shillings per capita were spent on education in Malaya, compared with ten pence per capita in Burma.[38] Although the transfer to English schools was hence made easier, urban Chinese and Indians retained their advantage and constituted the bulk of the students in the professional schools, in the Raffles College of Arts and Science, and in the King Edward VII College for Medicine.[39] The Western-educated Malay elite remained very limited. In the 1930s there were still very few English-educated Malay doctors, lawyers, and engineers, in contrast to the numerous Chinese and Indians following such callings.

Localization was accordingly slow. The Malay Administrative Service (corresponding to the Indian Provincial Service) had existed since 1910. It provided posts for the Western-educated Malay aristocracy as high as assistant district officer and in the Unfederated Malay States even as high as district officer (a post held, for example, by the later prime minister and "Father of Malaya," Tunku Abdul Rahman in Kedah). In 1922 a commission called for the accelerated Malayization of the administration, motivated though in good part by fiscal considerations. The percentage of Malays in the Malay Administrative Service rose considerably.[40] Chinese and Indians were excluded from it. They dominated the technical departments, however: in the federation 1,742 Malays stood vis-à-vis 4,838 Chinese and Indians in 1938.[41] Since the small Malay educated class had few opportunities outside the administration it settled for what it could get. There were few Malay firms, and European firms preferred Eurasians, Chinese, and Indians, who in turn hired their countrymen. The bureaucratic character of British rule never loosened significantly. Malayization as the presupposition for self-government was introduced only following World War II.

Malaya's plural society must also be kept in mind in order to understand why a nationalist movement developed so late. Malaya had in this regard a special position in the empire.[42] The Chinese and Indians regarded themselves as Chinese and Indians and not as citizens of Malaya. A minority in the Straits Settlements had indeed long sought to have that state considered their domiciliary residence and to have the status of British subjects, particularly the prosperous "Queen's Chinese." The majority, however, were first- or second-generation immigrants who retained family ties to the provinces of their origins. Chinese remittances were estimated in 1930 at fourteen million dollars.[43] The Chinese were inclined to make the necessary accommodations with local conditions, including the sultans, and while criticizing British rule, they also understood its value: "They felt it had done a good job of holding the Malayan cow while the Chinese milked it."[44] The Malay Chinese provided Sun Yat-sen's revolutionary movement with considerable financial support, and during the interwar period many supported the Kuomintang. Chiang Kai-shek thought it important that the Chinese forswear British citizenship. Chinese schools, whose languages of instruction were Chinese and English and which used Chinese instructional materials, propagated a Chinese nationalism directed against the British and forced the administration to undertake stricter supervisory and repressive measures. From 1931 on, as a result of the depression, the immigration of additional Chinese was sharply restricted. After the Japanese attacked China in 1937 the number of Chinese who either could not or would not return home grew. That increased the mistrust, anxiety, and sense of inferiority which the Malays felt, particularly when the Straits-born Chinese began to regard Chinese exclusion from the civil service as racial discrimination and to demand their rightful share of jobs.

The Malays had come to terms with British rule. The sultans and the traditional ruling classes had, despite the imposition of a bureaucracy, not done so badly, as both their prestige and their share in the economic and fiscal prosperity had been safeguarded. The decentralization policy of the interwar period was also designed to bolster them. The mass of the peasants appreciated the merits of the land reservation policy, the low tax burden, the public health services, and in general followed instructions from above. Their loyalties were to the sultans and the individual states. Islam, life-style, and financial dependence on the foreigner separated them from the Chinese and Indians. Interracial marriages were very rare. The middle level of village chiefs, ulema, rich peasants, and teachers was too weak to escape dependence on the traditional ruling elite. What bound the Malays together was the conviction of being the real rulers of the country. The frustrating fact that foreigners dominated Malay economic and social life, leaving the Malays at best a subaltern role, must be considered the strongest impulse behind the Malay self-determination movement. What it amounted to was maintaining or regaining Malay identity, fostering Malay language and culture, and articulating particularly Malay concerns. It was no accident that the beginnings of the liberation movement developed after 1900 out of the Islamic reform movement and from contacts with the Arab world, most importantly Egypt, but also Sumatra. Aristocrats' sons went on pilgrimages to Mecca and to school in Cairo. The avowal of Islam signified a striving to defend oneself against the overly strong influences of foreign "unbelievers." In the 1920s a native Malay intelligentsia of largely peasant origins grew up centered around the Sultan Idris Training College. Consisting largely of teachers and journalists (between 1920 and 1930 thirty-four new Malay-language magazines and newspapers sprang up, most of which folded almost immediately), in 1938 they formed the Young Malay Union. Lacking a clearly formulated program, they were unmistakably anticolonial and "noncooperative" and against both foreign capitalists and their own ruling elite. The latter, English-educated officials in particular, had also long supported study groups and clubs and in 1937 began to found political-cultural associations. In 1939 the first Pan-Malay conference took place, the motto of which, "Malaya for the Malayans," was not so much anti-British as it was a manifestation of their intent to assert themselves against the Chinese. The expansion of education, accelerated localization, and more extensive advisory powers for the councils were sought, but not self-government or democratization, since the Malayan elite rightly feared that the more numerous and better educated non-Malays would gain the upper hand. Finally, in 1930 the Malay Communist party was founded but remained pretty much the affair of a Chinese minority.

Until 1941 Malay nationalism did not endanger British rule. The three communities lived uneasily together, with the British acting as policemen. The beginnings were in place, but the problem of the future was also clear enough: it was how to constitute a Malay nation in an area which still had no administrative unity and which was burdened with the fetters of a plural society.

NOTES

1. Hall, *Southeast Asia*; Joseph Kennedy, *A History of Malaya, 1400-1959* (New York: St. Martin's Press, 1962); Rupert Emerson, *Malaysia: A Study in Direct and Indirect Rule* (New York: Macmillan, 1937); N. J. Ryan, *The Making of Modern Malaya: A History from Earliest Times to Independence* (Kuala Lumpur: Oxford University Press, 1965); John Bastin and Robin Winks (comps.), *Malaysia: Selected Historical Readings* (Kuala Lumpur, New York: Oxford University Press, 1966); John Michael Gullick, *Malaya* (2d rev. ed., London: E. Benn, 1964).

2. "I should not be disposed to approve of any proceedings which would extend the responsibilities of Her Majesty's Government in the neighborhood of the Straits Settlements"; quoted in Ryan, *Modern Malaya*, 111. See also Cyril Northcote Parkinson, *British Intervention in Malaya, 1867-1877* (Singapore: University of Malaya Press, 1960); Charles Donald Cowan, *Nineteenth-Century Malaya: The Origins of British Political Control* (London, New York: Oxford University Press, 1961).

3. David McIntyre, "Britain's Intervention in Malaya: The Origin of Lord Kimberley's Instructions to Sir Andrew Clarke in 1873," *JSEAH*, 2 (June 1961).

4. See, among others, Parkinson, *British Intervention*; Cowan, *Malaya*; McIntyre, "Britain's Intervention"; see also the selections in Bastin and Winks, *Malaysia*.

5. Bastin and Winks, *Malaysia*, 186, 200, 208, 213.

6. See the excerpts from John Michael Gullick, *Indigenous Political Systems of Western Malaya* (London: University of London, Athlone Press, 1958), in Bastin and Winks, *Malaysia*, 221f.

7. Gullick, *Malaya*, 55.

8. Eunice Thio, "The British Forward Movement in the Malay Peninsula" in Bastin and Winks, *Malaysia*, 227.

9. Keith Sinclair, "Hobson and Lenin in Johore: Colonial Office Policy Towards British Concessionaires and Investors, 1878-1907," *MAS*, 1 (October 1967).

10. Stanley Wilson Jones, *Public Administration in Malaya* (New York, London: Royal Institute of International Affairs, 1953), excerpted in Bastin and Winks, *Malaysia*, 286 ff.; Emerson, *Malaysia*, 153f, 314.

11. Ormsby Gore, political under-secretary for the colonies, held that there were no grounds for forcing the princes into a federation, for "to me the maintenance of the position, authority and prestige of the Malay rulers is a cardinal point of policy"; *Report*, 18. In 1931 the governor, Sir Cecil Clementi, reported confidentially, "The Sultans [were] not an anachronism [but] a buffer between us and the Chinese, a buffer too... between us and events such as have taken place in Ceylon"; quoted in J. De Vere Allen, "Malayan Civil Service, 1874-1941: Colonial Bureaucracy/Malay Elite," *CSSH* 12 (July 1970), 153.

12. Chong-Yan Lim, *Economic Development of Modern Malaya* (Kuala Lumpur, London: Oxford University Press, 1967), 321; George Cyril Allen and Audrey G. Donnithorne, *Indonesia and Malaya: A Study in Economic Development* (New York: A. M. Kelley, 1954), ch. 8; Wong Lin Kon, "Western Enterprise and the Development of the Malaya Tin Industry to 1914," in Cowan, *Economic Development*.

13. "It is interesting to see how tin mining in Malaya is an example to the rest of the world of what can be done in the way of public ownership and control of mineral wealth, even within the framework of the present capitalist system"; David Freeman, "The Present Condition and Future Government of Malaya," in Creech-Jones Papers, 19 March 1935, New Fabian Research Bureau, box 26, file 7, Rhodes House, Oxford University, Oxford, England.

14. Lim, *Economic Development*, 48.

15. Kennedy, *Malaya*, 204; see also Lim, *Economic Development*, chs. 3, 4.

16. The breakdown for 1932 shows the following picture:

Table 4.3
Rubber Plantations in Malaya, 1932

Ownership	No. of plantations	Acreage	Average size
		(in thousands of acres)	
Europeans	977	1398	1.4
Asiatics	1324	480	0.36
Chinese	977	348	0.36
Indians	242	58	0.24
Malays	59	13	0.22
Japanese	36	58	1.61
Others	10	3	0.30

Source: Lim, *Economic Development*, 351.

17. J. Norman Parmer, *Colonial Labor Policy and Administration: A History of Labor in the Rubber Plantation Industry in Malaya, 1910-1940* (Locust Valley, N. Y.: J. J. Augustin, 1960), 8ff.

18. Lim, *Economic Development*, 81, and Appendix 4.3, pp. 328-9.

19. In 1936 the Malay Rice Cultivation Committee estimated, however, that the Malays covered 70 to 80 percent of their own needs, and that the rice imports went mainly to Chinese and Indian laborers; P. T. Bauer, "Some Aspects of the Malayan Rubber Slump, 1929-1933," *Economica* 11 (November 1944), 197.

20. For a full account, see Lim, *Economic Development*, 76ff. See also Bauer, "Malayan Rubber Slump."

21. See Parmer, *Labor Policy*, 3ff.

22. Orde Brown, *Labour Conditions*, 99.

23. Bauer, "Malayan Rubber Slump," 194.

24. Parmer, *Labor Policy*, 67.

25. Ibid., 258.

26. Ibid., 264ff. See also J. N. Parmer, "Chinese Estate Workers' Strikes in Malaya in March 1937," in Cowan, *Economic Development*.

27. Zinkin, *Asia and the West*, 156.

28. If rentier investments (colonial loans) are added, the following data emerge:

Table 4.4
Western Investment Including Colonial Loans in Malaya, 1914-1937 (in millions)

1914	$193.7
1930	$559.7
1937	$454.5

Source: Callis, *Foreign Capital*, 63.

29. M. Freedman, "The Growth of a Plural Society in Malaya," in Immanual Wallerstein (ed.), *Social Change: The Colonial Situation* (New York: J. Wiley, 1966).

30. Erich H. Jacoby, *Agrarian Unrest in Southeast Asia* (2d rev. ed., New York: Asia. Publishing House, 1961), 110; Hall, *Southeast Asia*, 750.

31. Sinnappah Arasaratnam, "Die Inder in Malaya in Geschichte und Gegenwart," *Studien zur Entwicklung in Süd- und Ostasien*, N. F., Teil 4 (1966); idem, *Indians in Malaysia and Singapore* (Bombay: Oxford University Press, 1970).

32. Jacoby, *Agrarian Unrest*, 129.
33. V. A. Aziz, "Land Disintegration and Land Policy in Malaya," *Malay Economic Review* 3 (April 1958), 22f.
34. Ormsby Gore, *Report*, 28.
35. Bauer, "Malayan Rubber Slump," 166.
36. On their origins and attitudes, see Allen, "Malayan Civil Service," 177.
37. William R. Roff, *The Origins of Malay Nationalism* (New Haven: Yale University Press, 1967), 142f.
38. Zinkin, *Asia and the West*, 185.
39. According to Ormsby Gore, *Report*, 34, of the students at the King Edward VII College of Medicine, 37 were Chinese, 34 Indians, 21 Europeans and Eurasians, 7 Malay, and one was Japanese.
40. The size of the Malay Civil Service (with technical services not counted):

Table 4.5
Malayan Civil Service Positions (technical services not counted)

Years	Leading positions	Malays in leading positions
1895	118	4
1905	117	5
1915	236	25
1925	258	58
1935	213	76

SOURCE: Allen, "Malayan Civil Service," 160, 177.

41. Roff, *Malay Nationalism*, 120.
42. Ibid. See also the pieces by Silcock and Aziz in William Lancelot Holland, *Asian Nationalism and the West: A Symposium Based on Documents and Reports of the Eleventh Conference, Institute of Pacific Relations* (New York: Macmillan, 1953); Gullick, *Malaya*, ch. 7.
43. Callis, *Foreign Capital*, 64.
44. Lennox A. Mills, *Malaya: A Political and Economic Appraisal* (Minneapolis: University of Minnesota Press, 1958), 6.

5

THE NETHERLANDS INDIES

In 1602, Dutch merchants and shippers banded together to form the United East India Company (Vereenigde Oost-Indische Compagnie).[1] They sought neither territorial conquests nor colonies of settlement. The Dutch wanted to emerge from the anticipated contest with the Portuguese, English and Spanish with a monopoly of the spice trade. The Portuguese had already conquered the important trading center, Malacca, in 1511 and had entered the Molucca trade. They had done so, however, as current scholarship emphasizes, without endangering the centuries-old Southeast Asian trading system which extended from China to the Persian Gulf.[2] The Indonesian archipelago was part of this system, though it had never formed a political unity. The islands of the archipelago, Sumatra and Java in the west, and Borneo and Celebes in the east, were rather distinct from one another ethnically, culturally, and linguistically. Still, a welter of ties linked them, and they formed an independent territorial entity.[3]

Between the fifth and fifteenth centuries, several Indianized kingdoms rose and fell on Sumatra and Java, the most important of the islands. The principal kingdoms were the Javan interior states of Majapahit and Mataram and the coastal states of Srivajaya on Sumatra and Bantam in north Java. The interior states were agrarian, farming rice in irrigated fields—the *sawah* system. Organized on a feudal-bureaucratic basis, the ruler, the court (*kraton*), the upper nobility (*bupati*), and the aristocratic bureaucracy (*prijaji*, or "younger brothers" of the princes) were confronted by villages (*desa*) with considerable independence. Highly refined in life-style and with a sharply defined sense of social hierarchy, these societies had little contact with the outside world and little interest in trade. Srivijaya and Bantam, on the other hand, were trading states, oriented toward the outer world. They were cosmopolitan and rather egalitarian socially, although the rulers in good part controlled and organized the trading themselves.

In the fifteenth century, Islam spread outward from Malacca, first into Sumatra and the coastal towns and then by stages into the Hindu inland states. It was an Islam, however, that had already been filtered through India and was hence easier to accept. A majority of the Indonesian people in the west eventually accepted Islam and followed its main precepts of prayer, observance of Ramadan, and pilgrimage to Mecca. Nonetheless, Hindu-Buddhist and animist ideas about the world and its values remained alive, particularly in Java. Customary law (*adat*), which still plays an important role in village life, was not the least important of these pre-Islamic survivals.

When the Dutch arrived in Java around 1600, the new and mighty realm of Mataram, which sought to control the greater part of the island from its central Javan heartland, faced the mercantile state of Bantam, which controlled the spice trade through the strait of Sunda. Bantam skillfully played European and native spice traders off against each other, driving prices sky-high. The Dutch, determined to obtain direct access to the Moluccas—the Spice Islands—established a factory at Jakarta, a disputed area between Mataram and Bantam: thus was Batavia (Jakarta) founded. Under the strong Governor-General Jan Pieterszoon Coen, the English were not only beaten and driven out, but Amboina and Ternate were forced under Dutch control. Without seeking territorial rule, the company nevertheless became enmeshed in the rivalries of the Indonesian states. Bantam and Maratam gradually gave up bits of territory, the later finally being divided in 1757. Malacca had been seized from the Portuguese as early as 1641, and Makassar detached from Celebes in 1668. These acts gave the company a spice trade monopoly. In the larger framework of the East Asian trade system nothing had changed all that much, but the achievement still represented a severe blow to the traditional native class of merchants and shippers.

The Dutch position on Sumatra and Borneo remained precarious. Even on Java, the company forswore extensive claims to rule, in good part for financial reasons.[4] The local princes were forced to acknowledge company sovereignty but otherwise retained their autonomy; many had only exchanged rulers. In the eighteenth century, this situation slowly changed. Trading profits were falling despite rising prices for tropical products. The company therefore began to take an interest in their production. Coffee was the main crop, but there were also indigo and sugar. In the beginning, the local aristocrats or "regents" were merely forced to deliver the desired products in the amounts and at the prices the company specified (*verplichte leveringen*). This system of tribute, which could be linked to pre-Dutch payments to the overlord, soon led to more extensive measures. Company employees inspected the farms and gave instructions, which if not followed might lead to the deposition of the ruler; the local nobles were increasingly transformed into company employees. At the same time, company employees accepted bribes to make the regencies hereditary. Protected from above and forced to deliver, the regents became local tyrants who learned very quickly how to enrich themselves: the peasants bore the burden.

Nevertheless, the bankruptcy of the company could not be staved off. Even the renting of whole villages to Chinese did not help. Pirates interfered with "honest trade," and in the end, dividends could only be paid by borrowing. In 1798-1799 rule of the company was transferred to the Batavian Republic. Under

Governor Herman Willem Daendels, an adherent of Napoleon, the administration was reformed to conform with European models. The country was divided in prefectures, to which the regents were directly subordinate. A tenth of the rice harvest was reserved for salaries and the accepting of "presents" outlawed. At the same time, a military road was built at great human cost down the middle of the island.

In 1811 the British took over Dutch territories. Influenced by the liberal ideas of the day and also by British land policy in India, Thomas Stamford Raffles, the later founder of Singapore, ended the system of forced requisitions. He attempted to assure each peasant the right to dispose of his produce by declaring all land Crown property. He retained only the right to collect taxes (the land-rent system), when possible to be paid in coin. His intent was to establish a money economy and thus, he hoped, a market for British goods. The prefects became residents. Paid government officials were to collect taxes, which is to say that the traditional aristocracy was bypassed. The latter retained only limited jurisdictional competence within the administration.

When the Dutch got their colonies back in 1816, they continued Raffles's liberal policy. The results, however, were questionable. Given the lack of accurate land registers and estimates of yield, the land tax was necessarily arbitrary. In order to get cash to pay taxes, the peasant often had to borrow money. He thus fell into the hands of usurers, mostly Chinese. Simultaneously, imported manufactured goods began to displace traditional artisan products. Cotton and indigo fields lay fallow. "What gained was crime. The very areas which Raffles had noted as being free from it became rife with arson, robbery, and murder. His system had, in effect, impoverished the people and subverted their social order."[5]

The gradual elimination of the Javan aristocracy was the cause of the postprimary rising of 1825. Led by a Jogjakartan prince of the blood, it was waged as a *jihad* against the Dutch unbelievers. The fighting devastated large parts of the island and cost 200,000 lives.[6] Afterwards, even rising prices proved no inducement to produce. Supervision and pressure from regents on down to village chiefs was necessary. It was already being suggested that the regents be paid in land, in order to raise production and strengthen the aristocracy. In 1830, however, the new governor-general, Johannes van den Bosch, hit upon what appeared to be a solution. It was the so-called Culture System (*cultuurstelsel*) of forced cultivation. Instead of cash payments for taxes, the products themselves could in the future be provided, a priviso soon made obligatory. A fifth of all village land was to be reserved for such production and sixty-six days of labor were to be furnished state plantations. The next step toward a genuine state monopoly over production and trade soon followed. Not only "taxes" but all remaining products had to be turned over to the administration for fixed prices. The latter established a privileged trading company, the Nederlandsche Handel-Maatschappij, to ship its tropical products to Europe for sale.

The outward success of these measures was striking. In a few years, "Java became one large state business concern."[7] Indigo and rice were cultivated in the irrigated fields, coffee in unirrigated. Between 1830 and 1840, the production of sugar rose from 108,000 pikols (about 132 pounds) to 1,023,000 and coffee from 288,000 to 1,132,000. The administration was not only able to pay off the old East India Company debts it had assumed but also made increasingly large payments to the Netherlands. These helped to return the country, heavily in debt because of the separation of Belgium, to solvency. Whereas before 1830 the abandonment of the colony as a financial burden was seriously discussed, by mid-century it had "become a life jacket that held the Netherlands above water."

Governor-General van den Bosch had hoped that forced cultivation would bring both the state and the Javanese advantages, and in some districts it indeed did so. Furnivall, a man of measured judgments, noted that rising imports revealed increasing cash in peasant hands, because, under the Culture System, the peasants could sell produce in excess of the amount required for taxes. All the same, the system proved ruinous in the end, in good part because of the manner of its execution. Because the officials were compensated by commissions on export crops, contrary to the original instructions, they neglected rice cultivation. Oftentimes one-third, or all, rather than one-fifth, of the irrigated land was used for export crops. Wholly unsuitable land was also devoted to cash crops. And on the state plantations in the dry zone, far more than sixty-six days of forced labor was required. After 1840, production declined and famine occurred.

The Culture System called for a strengthening of the traditional authorities, the regents and village chiefs. Although Raffles's policy had been to bypass the regents and establish direct contact with the peasants, van den Bosch and his successors consistently built up the position and the prestige of the regents. They recognized the hereditary character of the office, which dissolved such obligations of loyalty as remained to existing ruling houses and tied the regents firmly to the Dutch. At the same time, they received land and thus magisterial jurisidiction over its inhabitants. The administration was willing to overlook abuses in the employment of forced labor, personal obligations of service (*pantjendiensten*), and other matters. Integrated by commissions into the export-production system, the regents' prestige nevertheless increasingly declined. The same was true of the village chiefs. The Culture System was a matter for the entire village, because it had to organize the annual reallocation of land and provide enough for the cash crops, along with seeing to cultivation, seed, tools, and harvesting. Although no private property as such had existed earlier, individual and family rights to use land had existed. These rights were now thrown into question by communalization. The village chief was given power, but at the same time became dependent on the colonial administration, which punished or paid him according to the results of the harvest: "In the eyes of the villagers he often became a source of governmental oppression rather than, as previously, the keystone of village solidarity and protection."[8] The traditional authority structures were slowly eroding. The nobility and the village chiefs were tied increasingly closely to the administration and were losing their representative and protective functions. The village inhabitants, too, were being declassed, losing their right to participate in decisions and becoming "administered" producers. This change was characteristic under colonial conditions, both in Asia and Africa.

In the 1850s, a critical reexamination of the van den Bosch system of a monopolized colonial economy began in the Netherlands. In the revolution of 1848, King William IV had had a parliament forced upon him and in 1854 a *Regeringsreglement* created the necessary underpinning for giving the colonial apparatus of rule and the officials' personal power of command a basis in law. In 1864 Parliament received some supervisory power over Indonesian matters because the colonial budget now had to be presented to it. Earlier, in 1860, the novel, *Max Havelaar*, by the former colonial official, Eduard Douwes Dekker (written under the pseudonym "Multatuli," meaning, "much have I suffered"), had created a great stir.[9] It portrayed in drastic terms how the regents, protected from above, enriched themselves and demanded personal services. Although Dekker did not attack the Culture System directly, his novel compromised it nonetheless. It provided a very effective basis for agitation for planter and liberal-capitalist forces in the Netherlands who, under the slogan "free-labor versus forced-labor," opposed the state trade monopoly. As early as 1856, the administration had begun to release land to the planters. Between 1862 and 1866 the cultivation of pepper, cloves, indigo, tea, cinnamon, and tobacco was freed from state control. The Land Law of 1870 and the Sugar Law of 1871 dismantled the Culture System and introduced a plantation system based on private enterprise. Still, for coffee, the state monopoly lasted until 1916.

However loudly liberal critics of the van den Bosch system proclaimed their policy of "welfare for the natives," their main interest was breaking the state monopoly. The colonies continued to be seen as objects for national exploitation, and indeed until 1877 large sums of money continued to flow into the treasury.[10] In the years that followed, the colonial budget ran in the red and by 1898 loans totalled 900 million gulden. The profits from the Culture System were no longer coming in, and expenditures for administration, schools, irrigation, and transportation had risen considerably. Forced labor (*heerendiensten*) was used for public works, the increasing number of which rapidly became a heavy burden for the natives. Forced labor positively cried out for regulation and control but was only abolished in the years from 1890 to 1902. And the obligations for service within the villages (*desadiensten*) continued.[11]

ADMINISTRATION

The administration was expanded and formalized. In the 1850s and 1860s the technical departments were created—finance, public works, education, justice, and the like. The residences were divided into districts (*Afdeelingen*) that corresponded to the regencies. At the head of the new districts stood a Dutch assistant resident, the "younger brother of the *bupati*," as it was quaintly formulated. The regencies themselves were divided into districts more systematically than previously and subdistricts and the native officials organized accordingly. The regent once again lost the power and influence that he had either won back or had been given in the interest of the Culture System. His office remained hereditary, but in 1867 he lost both the part of the produce previously delivered to him and the property given him in payment for his services. With the declaration in 1882 that his right to personal service (*pantjendiensten*) from his subjects was null and void, Dutch officials deprived him of one of the last powers from his feudal past, the embodiment of a personal relationship between ruler and ruled. Both he and everyone else saw his position as much diminished.[12] He retained the right to impose punishments, however, though this had no legislative sanction. Dutch administrative practice called, at least pro forma, for as little interference as possible with traditional structures. The regent and his officials were intended to act as executive agents of the colonial power to supervise matters at the village level. His prestige was further diminished by the *controleur*, successor to the cultivation supervisor, who after 1872 as administrator without direct line authority was supposed to maintain contact between the assistant resident and the natives. The young colonial official began his career as *controleur* "constantly on tour, and mixing freely with the people, not as magistrate, policeman or tax collector, but as confidential friend of all the world. . . a liaison officer between East and West."[13] His de facto authority was considerable and was a hallmark of the Dutch colonial administration, which was much more energetic than the British.

Until the beginning of the liberal era in 1870, the Dutch had been concerned mainly with Java and had paid little regard to the rest of the archipelago. After the Napoleonic Wars, the Dutch and English had demarcated their spheres of interest by treaty, with the boundary running between Malaya and Sumatra. Dutch interest in the latter was confined, however, to the fortified settlements of Padang on the west coast and Palembang on the east. The Moluccas were under direct control, but Bali, conquered in 1849, was administratively still relatively untouched as late as 1885. Rather against their will, the Dutch saw no choice but expansion. The first move was against the Sultanate of Acheh in northern Sumatra, which was plundering foreign vessels in the strait of Malacca. War, declared in 1873, dragged on for years, and ended only when the Dutch followed the advice of the noted expert on Islam, Christiaan Snouck Hurgronje, to join with the traditional *adat* chiefs against the ulema. The ulema, not surprisingly, was later to welcome invasion in 1941.[14]

Between 1890 and 1910, Dutch rule was systematically established throughout the entire Indonesian archipelago, in an effort to beat other powers to the punch. This was a part of the worldwide imperialist expansion movement. The Dutch desired also to secure suitable plantation land and had already discovered oil and mineral deposits. By persuasion and threats, countless Indonesian princes were forced to sign the "short declaration." It gave the Dutch both a loose sovereignty and effective political power, although in the following period Batavia contented itself with indirect rule in the outer provinces (*buitengewesten*).

As England unified the Indian subcontinent despite the dualism between British India and the Princely States, the Dutch too created the necessary basis for the Republic of Indonesia, which comprises virtually the entire archipelago today. Economically, interest shifted from overpopulated Java to the outer provinces.

Around the turn of the century the Dutch seem to have reappraised the purposes of their colonial rule and reoriented their administrative practices accordingly. Javanese production and export figures had increased sharply. European demand had risen, the Suez Canal had reduced export costs, and planters had taken over existing sugar plantations and laid them out more efficiently. The number of Europeans on Java increased from 17,285 in the year 1852 to 62,477 in the year 1900. At the same time, however, the Javanese population had exploded, rising from the 5 million of Raffles's day to about 12.5 million in 1860, 28 million in 1900, and 49 million in 1941. Population densities reached nine hundred to a thousand persons per square kilometer in some districts.

Did the native population profit from the economic expansion of the liberal era? Expansion of the rice areas probably failed to keep pace with the population increase. The liberals assumed that, with the end of the Culture System, the Javanese themselves would become innovators and assert themselves in free competition. By 1900 this assumption had proved false. The Javanese reacted passively rather than actively to the money economy.[15] The Dutch began to worry about reduced standards of living (*mindere welvaart*), and in 1901 even the Batavian Chamber of Commerce felt constrained to comment on the "rapidly sinking buying power of the local populace." Two years earlier Charles Theodor van Deventer had written an article that caused a considerable stir entitled "A Debt of Honor." In it, van Deventer noted that under the van den Bosch system the Netherlands extracted huge sums from the colony. He stated that it was high time this "moral debt" was repaid, at least if the home country's declarations of its civilizing mission actually meant anything.[16] In the queen's speech of 1901, this self-criticism was accepted, and the Ethical Policy proclaimed. Instead of the liberal policy of laissez-faire, a policy of active intervention to secure the popular welfare was to be pursued. In particular, irrigation systems were to be built, and the neglected educational system was to be improved. In October 1902 the government established a commission to study the critical economic and social situation (though its three-volume report was delivered only in 1914). In 1905, 40 million gulden were budgeted for the colonies. From 1912 on surpluses were again available from the colonial budget itself. All Dutch parties supported the new policy, as did liberal economic circles, who saw in a population with increased purchasing power a better market for Dutch goods. Much was indeed accomplished in the years following. Between 1900 and 1910, 7.6 million dollars was spent on irrigation, and between 1910 and 1920, 23.2 million.[17] The energy and initiative of the young Leiden-trained civil servants was famous, the quality of the technical cadres setting an example for the other Powers.

The Dutch attempted to encourage the village communities to take an active role in these modernization policies of the welfare state. Such attempts were in line with the Ethical Policy and were also a practical necessity because even an expanded and relatively elaborate bureaucratic apparatus could not lay hands on each individual inhabitant. Each village received its own treasury. The village chiefs were admonished to keep books for income, expenditures, land division, and other such matters and were taught how to do so. At the same time, the monthly village meetings were to settle not only petty administrative problems but also matters such as renting land to European planters and expenditures for irrigation or clinics. Even the regents were, within the boundaries of decentralization policy, to be given more independence. Much of this turned out to be window dressing. Ethical Policy merely meant that Dutch supervisory and technical officials moved all the more energetically to apply "gentle pressure"—really instructions—to reach the desired aims. What came about from village initiatives and was to be treated as village business was really in practice decided and ordered by the administration. The village, indeed, threatened to become a "Public Company, with large funds which the controleur as managing director could apply to whatever he regarded as desirable for village welfare."[18] This impatient paternalism would not work without gentle pressure. It achieved positive results in the sense of bettering the public welfare as understood in the West, but it smothered, willy-nilly, traditional forms of service and decision making, and it encouraged rather than discouraged, as the Dutch had hoped, an attitude of passive acceptance of instructions.

J. S. Furnivall used Burma and Indonesia as examples to elucidate fundamental divergences between the theory and practice of British and Dutch colonial rule. The former, operating in a laissez-faire tradition, confined themselves largely to maintaining law and order. They ruled rather than administered, regardless of the resulting dislocation of the traditional society. The Dutch, on the other hand, attempted through gentle pressure to bring about modernization while preserving the framework of traditional society. Depressed by the social crisis in Lower Burma, Furnivall manifestly sympathized with Dutch efforts and was willing to accept paternalism as an unavoidable transition stage. He thus implicitly posed the dilemma confronting all colonial administrations and all postcolonial modernization policies: How can the village be drawn into the modernization process without its communal structure being subjected to excessive stresses or without its becoming a mere object of administrative action and thus losing its own sense of initiative?

ECONOMY

Every colonial administration must be considered within the framework of the colonial economy. This is especially true for the Dutch paternalism after the end of the Culture System when the agrarian law of 1870 opened the way to a symbiosis of sugar plantations and village rice growing. In comparison with British and French land and agrarian policy in the colonies, the Dutch system was a special position.

The famous agrarian law was supposed to guarantee, in the conservative sense, native legal claims to the land. But it was also supposed to facilitate a shift from the state's Culture System to plantation farming under private ownership. First, untilled land was declared inalienable state property, and, second, the sale of land to foreigners, Chinese or Europeans, was forbidden. That did in fact block the commercialization of the land and made it possible to prevent much land from falling into the hands of urban owners and moneylenders as happened in India and Burma.[19] But if the purchase or foreclosure of land was blocked, the liberals nonetheless threw open the door for the creation of plantations by permitting the administration to hand out "waste land" to private concessionaires on seventy-five-year leases (the *erfpacht* system). Because irrigated land (*sawah*) was already under cultivation, the plantations (*ladang* land, that is nonirrigated) were established in the Java hill country and, more importantly, on thinly settled Sumatra.

To cultivate sugar on Javanese sawah land, a rather artful strategem was devised.[20] The European planter or, after 1885, the European firms that bought out bankrupt planters, concluded 21.5-year rental contracts with villages or individual peasants for the use of part of the irrigated land for sugar. Village chiefs and desa councils were often bought off. By means of a complicated rotation, rice cultivation alternated with sugar. The van den Bosch system of forced cultivation was thus transmogrified into a private-capitalist contractual system.[21] Geertz compares this system to a centaur. The head was the European-owned sugar mill. Representing a heavy capital investment because of its technical complexity, and managed by a cadre of twenty-odd Europeans, it drew its sugar from an area of some 1,000 hectares. The body was the Javan peasant, who provided both land and labor, and not indeed as a coolie with a fixed term of employment but as seasonal labor, hired for planting, cultivation, and harvest. Around 1930, 180 sugar mills employed on a short- or long-term basis some 800,000 men, women, and children.

What were the results of this symbiotic system, which was neither a real plantation system nor native farming? In the area under cultivation, production and export of sugar rose steadily (see table 5.1), sugar displacing coffee as the leading export of Netherlands India, and reached a figure as high as 78 percent in some east coast villages.[22]

Table 5.1
Indonesian Sugar-Growing Area and Sugar Exports, 1865-1929

CULTIVATED AREA (IN HECTARES)		EXPORT OF SUGAR (IN TONS)	
1865	33,000	1865-1869	153,000
1890	44,000	1890-1894	469,000
1914	147,465	1910-1914	1,400,000
1929	200,000	1929	2,900,000

SOURCE: J.A.M. Caldwell, "Indonesian Export and Production," in Cowan, *Economic Development*, 79-80.

The Javanese villages were drawn into the money economy. The sugar mills paid the villagers substantial amounts in rents and also wages for their labor. The individual received a cash income which enabled him to pay taxes and buy European consumer goods. The sugar mills invested to increase the area irrigated, and fertilizer increased yields, both for sugar and for rice. The Javanese peasant as a rule did not sink into the landless laborer class but remained a property owner within the village community. The latter faced the confrontation with a money economy and production methods dominated by the sugar mills, which initially contracted with the individual peasants but came to prefer dealing with the village as a whole or, in practice, with the village chief. Village land was thus considered as a unit. The result was the growth of a class of larger holders, often the village chiefs, of quasi-parasitic character. The mills did raise the efficiency of the cultivation, but by organizing it themselves, which undermined peasant initiative.[23] Worsening the situation was the fact that, not only were rice and sugar cropped in rotation, but the peasants working the land also varied, which prevented the development of an independent peasant class.[24] A consequence of the sugar cultivation was that faster growing but poorer quality kinds of rice were grown, and the rapidly increasing population was forced to terrace new areas and farm poorer land. Other foodstuffs such as soybeans, corn, cassava, and potatoes were increasingly grown, but farming methods remained old-fashioned and changed very little, each family having typically less than a hectare to farm. In short, economic modernization of the Javanese rice region never began despite, or perhaps because of, the symbiosis with sugar.

Julius H. Boeke described the situation in 1942 as one of "static expansion."[25] Geertz called the process "agricultural involution."[26] It was characterized by a unique linking of traditional agriculture with modern sugar production, resulting in increases in the area under cultivation and in diversification, but scarcely altering the basic structure. It also led to increasingly complicated methods of regulating affairs in the village, in property and rent matters, and in the labor relationships both within the family and beyond it. Thus, in the face of an enormous increase in population, a situation gradually developed in which there was sufficient flexibility to absorb more people, if only at the most minimal level of shared poverty, but at the cost of making a breakthrough to modern agrarian society increasingly difficult. It left independent Indonesia a problem with no obvious solution.[27]

The real plantations were developed on *ladang* land, or nonirrigated land, which, as stated above, was leased by the state or in the outer provinces rented from native rulers.[28] Managed by Europeans, the plantations lay outside the villages and were relatively large. The work force was not peasants, but coolies, who, like the tea workers on Ceylon, lived on the plantations in *kampongs*. The plantations were thus enclaves. They were mainly located in the outer provinces, northeast Sumatra in particular, rather than on Java, which besides sugar mostly grew rice and other foodstuffs. Netherlands India became one of the great exporters of tropical products, as table 5.2 shows.[29] After slavery was abolished in

Table 5.2
Exports from The Netherlands Indies, 1840-1951 (in thousands of tons)

YEAR	INDIGO	COFFEE	SUGAR	TOBACCO	TEA	COPRA	RUBBER	PALM PRODUCTS	TIN	PETROLEUM	KAPOK
1840	1	69	62	—	—	—	—	—	—	—	—
1855	0.4	75	99	—	—	—	—	—	—	—	—
1880	—	85	222	11	—	—	—	—	—	—	—
1890	—	38	367	32	3	—	—	—	—	—	2
1900	—	51	736	52	8	67	—	16 (1901)	—	—	4
1913	—	29	1,471	87	27	229	7	—	21	960	10
1920	—	62	1,514	125	46	182	90	—	22	1,784	13
1930	—	63	2,838	80	82	375	296	49	35	4,021	21
1932	—	112	1,480	73	78	472	238	83	18	3,885	19
1937	—	97	1,110	47	67	495	434	194	38	5,878	19
1948	—	2	71	1	9	207	433	41	31	3,850	6
1951	—	24	83	4	40	227	774	97	31	6,072	5

SOURCE: Allen and Donnithorne, *Western Enterprise*, 292.

1860 and forced labor for indebtedness in 1872, a contract work system developed, as elsewhere, in which breaking the contract—or leaving the plantation, in other words—resulted in criminal penalties. The plantations of east Java drew on Madura for workers. In Sumatra, Chinese coolies were recruited from the beginning, and later Javanese. In 1924 the government declared that punishment provisions should be removed from contracts, but the plantation managers opposed it.[30] The shift to truly free labor began only in 1930, when the United States prohibited the import of goods grown by workers under punitive contracts (particularly tobacco from the Deli region of the east coast of Sumatra). Such contracts finally ended only in 1940.

As important as the plantations were within the colonial economic system of Indonesia, the natives nonetheless gradually began growing cash crops, either by raising them alongside or in rotation with foodstuffs on their small parcels. This was possible for sugar only to a limited extent because the mills blocked independent cultivation fairly successfully. In 1920 a law even forbade the mills' purchasing "freehold sugar."[31] The declining profitability of the coffee plantations in the twentieth century permitted Javanese producers to increase their market share; in 1929 the native share was around 50 percent. Peasants grew the tobacco for the sharply rising internal consumption of cigarettes. Copra, the export of which quintupled between 1900 and 1930, came almost exclusively from small producers, as did pepper, the export of which rose from 25,000 tons in 1910 to 40,000 tons in 1925. In 1926 small farmers delivered a quarter of the tea, which until 1910 had been grown almost exclusively on plantations. Most striking, however, was the shift from plantation to native cultivation of rubber in the outer provinces. Between 1925 and 1940 the area in rubber increased from 300,000 hectares to 1.2 million. In 1938, 800,000 small producers provided about 60 percent of Indonesian rubber exports. Native producers' total share of exports rose from 10 percent in 1894 to approximately 50 percent in the year 1937.[32]

Bernard Schrieke illustrated the social effects of the foregoing as early as 1927 with the Minangkabau region of west Sumatra. On their own initiative, the inhabitants had shifted to the cultivation of coffee, copra, and rubber, and in part had even restricted rotation of food crops and were importing them. An individualist-capitalist class of peasant entrepreneurs developed that produced almost entirely for export.[33] Analogous developments could be cited in other parts of Sumatra, though only in narrowly limited locales. Geertz contrasted the above with the involution that had occurred in Java:

> Thus, as the bulk of the Javanese peasants moved toward agricultural involution, shared poverty, social elasticity and cultural vagueness, a small minority of the Outer Island peasants moved toward agricultural specialization, frank individualism, social conflict, and cultural rationalization. The second course was the more perilous, and to some minds it may seem both less defensible morally and less attractive aesthetically. But at least it did not foredoom the future.[34]

Plantation farming is capital intensive or at least demands outlays that pay off only after some time. Sugar is actually the only crop requiring on-site mechanized processing, but coffee, tea, and rubber can be harvested only after a period of some years. Streets, housing for European personnel, and other things had to be built. A great number of the planters hoped to profit from the end of the Culture System by going into sugar growing and processing. Many did not survive the depression of the 1880s because its impact was sharpened by competition from beet sugar producers and declining yields brought on by sugarcane disease. Banks, trading firms, and plantation syndicates bought up the sugar mills, controlling the business thereafter. Agricultural banks (*cultuurbanken*) specialized in sugar mills. The banks owned plantations, either wholly or in part, provided Dutch capital, offered their services to the export trade and often acted as management agencies, which provided the plantations with technical knowledge and administrative skills. The leader of such banks was the Nederlandsche Handel-Maatschappij (NHM), founded as a shipping company in 1824. It was already investing in plantations in the 1860s—already half bank, half plantation owner—and by 1915 owned sixteen sugar mills, controlled another twenty-two and in addition owned fourteen tobacco, twelve tea, and fourteen rubber plantations. Some English banks had also gotten into the business as early as the 1880s (for example, the Hong Kong and Shanghai Banking Corporation and the Chartered Bank). Twenty-four hundred estates, with a total area of 2.5 million hectares, were in practice controlled by a few great companies.[35]

Although the Indonesians increased their share of cash-crop production, they remained dependent on European and Chinese firms for processing, transport, and marketing. The native small holder also needed credit, mostly provided by European and Chinese buyers, which reduced him to dependency on the latter. This happened despite Dutch attempts, more energetic than those of other colonial powers, to provide the natives with a credit system. As a part of the Ethical Policy, a popular credit system (*volkscredietwesen*) was inaugurated. Rice banks were to help with short-term rice shortages, while *desabanken* were to provide small-loan credits on a mutual-assistance basis. As of 1930, about a million borrowers a year took advantage of these opportunities. The banks were, however, undercapitalized and not well managed. In 1900 the state nationalized Chinese pawnshops and, with the usury law of 1916, believed it had brought the moneylenders under control, but the results of such measures were modest.

The Indonesian plantation economy was especially hard hit by the depression, as prices for tropical products collapsed in a particularly spectacular manner. Because the domestic market for such produce was so small, Indonesia was extremely dependent on the world market. It was thus most sensitive to the import restrictions placed on tropical products by some of its former European and Asian customers. The sugar industry was a disaster. Falling prices from 1926 on signalled worldwide overproduction, caused in good part by state subvention of the beet industry (as in England, for instance). During the depression, inventories rose rapidly, and when China, India, and Japan raised their duties early in 1931, the Indonesians had little choice but to accept the Chadbourne Scheme. The scheme set export quotas and banked land. In 1933 cultivated area was cut from 200,000 hectares to 34,000, and only 45 of 179 sugar mills remained in operation. In 1937 things began to pick up but in 1940 production was still at only 60 percent of 1929 levels.[36]

The effects on the villages were very serious. The land rents paid by the sugar mills declined drastically, as did wages (see table 5.3). The Javanese peasants thus lost the cash income that had come from the sugar industry and were thrown back on a subsistance economy. They proved, however, surprisingly resilient. Rice was grown on again available *sawah* land, and diversification into other foodstuffs continued. The area devoted to such products rose noticeably.[37] Although the Javanese population rose 12 percent between 1929 and 1939, the per-capita consumption of foodstuffs increased 10 percent.[38] For its part, the administration was interested in making Indonesia self-supporting and accordingly levied duties on Thai and Burmese rice. The intent was to allow Java to provide the outer provinces with rice, a positive outcome and important for better integration of the island state.

Table 5.3
Land Rents and Wages Paid in Indonesia, 1930-1938 (In millions of gulden)

YEAR	RENTS	WAGES
1930	25	97.9
1934	6.5	9.7
1936	3.2	7.5
1938	5.6	16.5

SOURCE: Willem H. Van Helsdingen (ed.), *Mission Interrupted* (Amsterdam, New York: Elsevier, 1945), 245.

It was also necessary to restrict production for plantation products such as tea, kapok, quinine, and rubber. An additional special excise was levied against rubber from native small holders.[39] The income from cash crops dropped drastically between 1928 and 1932—by half—but from 1935 on began to rise and by 1940 exceeded the level of 1928; and consumer buying power rose accordingly.[40]

Netherlands India was not only a leading producer of tropical crops but also of tin and oil.[41] Tin, found only on three small south Sumatran islands in the sultanate of Palembang, was already mined in precolonial times, and in 1772 the East India Company sent some tin to Europe. Even then Chinese workers were recruited. Modern production began in the mid-nineteenth century, first as a state and later as a private enterprise. Production rose from approximately 10,000 tons in 1890 to 20,900 tons in 1913 and, after a drastic decline during the depression, to 37,600 tons in 1937, or about half what Malaya produced. Whereas in Malaya hundreds of more or less independent mines operated, in Indonesia two concerns dominated tin production. In the beginning, smelting was done on one of the Dutch islands. It shifted to Singapore in the 1920s and, after 1933, to Arnhem in the Netherlands. In 1939, 40,000 persons were employed, mainly Chinese. Indonesian mining, then, was even more of a colonial enclave industry than Malayan mining. Its production added to both balance-of-trade and balance-of-payment figures but its native Indonesian connections were at best peripheral.

That was also true of oil production, which is another prime example of a capital-intensive Western enterprise in Southeast Asia. The manager of a tobacco firm pioneered as a wildcatter in 1880 in Sumatra. Although he succeeded in gaining a concession from the emir of Langkat, he lacked the capital to exploit it and in 1890 transferred it to the Royal Dutch Company, a financing syndicate formed with the aid of the king of the Netherlands. Finances remained precarious for some years, however, because of the expensive construction required—pipelines through the jungle and the like. Nor did stiff competition with Rockefeller's Standard Oil help. In 1902 pumping began in east Borneo, small firms were bought out, and in 1907, through merger with the English Shell Company, the basis was laid for the rise of Royal Dutch Shell as the dominant Indonesian oil firm. Total production rose from 150,000 tons in 1913 to 7,400,000 in 1938. Capital came from Europe, profits were reinvested or repatriated, and only in the very long run can this industry be said to have contributed to Indonesian economic development, insofar as it constituted the most important source of foreign exchange for the Indonesian republic.

Industrial development as such did not occur before the Great Depression. Coal was mined, but only with difficulty. There was little iron ore, and neither tin nor oil provided a basis for manufacturing industries. Cotton could not be harvested in amounts sufficient to support a native textile industry. The import of cotton stuffs, some from Dutch, rather more from non-Dutch, factories, had been increasing since the early nineteenth century, but there seems to be no evidence, as there is for British India, on how much harm this may have caused the native handloom weavers. A report on the batik industry from 1892 does show that foreign products had displaced local stuffs and that the Chinese had been able to control the trade in such a way as to bring native batik workers completely under their control.[42] The native batik traders' attempts to assert themselves against the Chinese led in 1912 to the formation of the first nationalist organization, Sarekat Islam. Still, village craftsmen made most of the articles in daily consumption. The few attempts by Europeans at the beginning of the century to begin factory production of articles like cement, matches, and silk, heretofore imported, did not enjoy much success.

World War I encouraged industrialization, however. In 1915 a factory commission was appointed and a year later an industry expert. In 1918 an industry section was added to the economics department. With state assistance, some factories were built, among others a paper mill. In 1919 the Textile Institute of Bandung was founded to provide technical education. During the postwar recession, however, many of these factories closed. Protective import duties were not granted. In 1925, however, the first cigarette factory began production, and in 1927 General Motors built an assembly plant. Nevertheless, before 1929 one can hardly speak of industry in any real sense.

What finally led the colonial administration to reverse its policy was the world economic crisis which began in 1929. Between 1929 and 1933, exports dropped 17 percent in quantity but 67 percent in value. Plantation workers declined from 1.2 million to 600,000. As one Dutch expert put it: "The policy toward industrialization is a depression-born phenomenon resulting from the collapse of an economy based primarily on large-scale agricultural production for export."[43] The problem was seen as one of raising the seriously reduced buying power of the masses, getting the unemployed back to work, and improving the balance of trade by reducing imports. The Japanese challenge was also important because the Japanese had been increasing their exports to Indonesia since 1918 and, aided by the declining value of the yen, had largely driven Anglo-Dutch imports from the market. The Japanese did not, however, import Indonesian products. Cheap Japanese goods did to some extent meet the needs of a population with the reduced buying power, but they also freed the administration from any obligation to protect Dutch industry, which had been guaranteed import quotas. The administration hence intervened energetically to assist the native artisan trades and petty industry. A veritable flood of measures followed: import quotas (on textiles, cement, and beer); reduced duties on raw materials and machine tools; higher duties on finished products; easier credit and government participation in factory construction; spread of technical information by such means as exhibitions; strong support of technical education; licensing requirements for factories intended to prevent misguided investment, excess capacity, and competition with petty industry; and successful efforts to create producers' associations in order to reduce middlemen's profits. The measures clearly succeeded. The purchasing power of the peasants rose from 1935-1936 on. A thousand-odd modern weaving mills and fifty-eight factories were established between 1935 and 1940. The result was a decline in the price of sarongs, among other things, and a release of some 10 million gulden of buying power. The number of modern looms rose rapidly, as table 5.4 shows.

Table 5.4
Weaving Looms in Use in Indonesia, 1930-1941

	1930	1935	1940	1941
Hand looms	500	4,000	35,000	49,000
Power looms	40	400	6,000	9,800

SOURCE: Peter H. W. Sitsen, *Industrial Development of the Netherlands Indies* (New York: Netherlands-Indies Council, 1944), 33.

A large number of cigarette factories, ranging from small to rather large, employed in toto 24,000 workers in 1940 to produce cigarettes for local consumption. Such was also true for production of umbrellas, silk, light bulbs, flashlights, batteries, paint, kitchen utensils, and leather goods. A bicycle factory with a monthly output of 2,000 bicycles displaced Japanese imports. International corporations also established plants, among others, Unilever, Bata, and Goodyear. The number of factories with more than twenty workers reached 5,500 by 1940, not counting mines and plantations. Employees numbered 324,000, triple the number in 1935. The entire secondary industry sector employed 2.8 million persons by 1939. Exports began, in particular to the outer islands, and tripled between 1935 and 1941.

Indonesians owned a considerable number of these new workshops and factories, despite sharp Chinese competition, which led to many calls for countermeasures in the Volksraad. A native entrepreneurial class began to form in the years before the war.[44] By 1940 a quarter of the management and three-quarters of the supervisory personnel were said to be Indonesians.[45]

Industrialization efforts between 1935 and 1941 are noteworthy, particularly in the general context of colonial economic policy in the interwar period. The catastrophic collapse of sugar, which had heretofore dominated the Javanese economy, and the price drop for other cash crops during the depression crisis led the Dutch administration to abandon their traditional export-oriented policy in favor of a new policy intended to achieve both self-sufficiency in food production and import substitution through the development of industry. To support this program, the state intervened increasingly in the economy, with favorable results. That contradicted the dominant theories of colonial economic policy, however, which posited a complementary relationship between the cash-crop producing colonies and the finished-goods producing home country. The theories assumed successful development could be measured by export surpluses and that surpluses implied increasing mass buying power and thus increasing mass welfare. Mass buying power at best held even before 1914 despite the Ethical Policy.[46] It also failed to rise in the 1920s despite a world economic boom and rising exports. It first rose, curiously enough, during the crisis years 1930-1934, despite the continuing depression and unfavorable terms of trade. Because food production could be increased sufficiently to achieve a large degree of self-sufficiency, both the nutrition and the purchasing power of the masses improved despite the decline in sugar cultivation. Against all expectations, the depression led to industrialization and employment of increasing numbers of natives. The precondition for industrialization, of course, was the colonial government's abandonment of its export policy and its new support for manufacturing and industry. Import restrictions in the form of duties and quotas were important, but more important still was the colonial administration's moral support, without which neither Indonesian, Chinese, nor foreign concerns could have engaged in the trades or manufacturing. A comparison with British India is instructive: India's industry received customs protection earlier than Java's, but no such calculated support as the Dutch administration provided as an answer to the world economic crisis. In both areas, the depression provided a noticeable impulse toward industrialization, which is to say that India, like Java, moved ahead in a phase when world and colonial trade was not expanding, but contracting, when the colonial administration saw itself forced to loosen the relationship of colonial dependency and to push ahead with integrated economic development.

The question about whether a drain of wealth existed is, because of the Netherlands Indies' dual economic structure and the preeminent importance of the export sector, a particularly acute one. The question can only be raised rather than answered definitively. The export surplus is, however, striking (see table 5.5). It is clear that these enormous exports would have been impossible without foreign investment in plantations, mines, and the infrastructure, as shown in table 5.6. About 80 percent of the funds came from Holland, and according to Kroef amounted to some 20 percent of the total Dutch national wealth.[47]

Table 5.5
Indonesian Imports and Exports, 1881-1939

	IMPORTS	EXPORTS	EXPORT SURPLUS (IN MILLIONS OF GULDEN)
1881-1885 (average)	142	189	47
1901-1905	197	275	78
1911-1915	407	643	236
1921-1925	817	1417	600
1926-1930	994	1501	507
1931-1935	375	540	165
1936	287	590	303
1937	498	999	501
1939	469	740	271

SOURCE: J.H. Boeke, *Netherlands Indian Economy* (New York: Institute of Pacific Relations, 1942), 184.

Table 5.6
Foreign Investment in Indonesia, 1900-1937 (in millions of dollars)

	STATE LOANS	PRIVATE INVESTMENT	TOTAL
1900	18	300	318
1914	68.4	675	743.4
1930	396.7	1,600	1,996.7
1937	825.5	1,411	2,263.5

SOURCE: Callis, *Foreign Capital*, 39.

Interest and amortization charges had to be paid on loans, and private investments had to show profits. The latter were in part reinvested and in part repatriated as dividends, which the positive trade balance made possible. According to Vandenbosch, approximately one-half of the 1929 profits of some 500 million gulden were reinvested, while the state took 60 million in taxes from the 250 million that returned to Holland. The amount came to one-quarter of all direct taxes collected.[48] Berkhuysen made the following calculations regarding the 1924 corporation tax. Profits in the years 1925-1935 amounted to 2,717 million gulden, of which 30 percent remained in Indonesia, with 1,890 million returning home, or on the average 172 million a year. Investments of 2.75 billion gulden in the year 1938 paid approximately 6.2 percent.[49]

In addition to transfers of profits, one must also count, as in British India, interest payments and pensions. The picture for 1937 and 1938 is shown in table 5.7.

Table 5.7
Indonesian Payments Abroad, 1937-1938 (in millions of gulden)

	PAYMENTS ABROAD		REIMBURSEMENTS TO HOLLAND	
	1937	1938	1937	1938
For loans	68	53	52	39
Dividends	89	167	62	117
Payments to relations, etc.	19	19	6	5
Management, incl. bonuses	20	27	14	19
Pensions, insurance, etc.	53	54	45	48
Total	249	320	179	228

SOURCE: Helsdingen, *Mission Interrupted*, 246.

There was thus a return flow matching the extensive foreign, mainly Dutch, investments. Whether one ought to call that a drain of wealth out of hand seems doubtful to me, since the answer depends to a considerable extent on how one assesses the value for development of investments, the performance of the Dutch administration, and the management of the foreign firms.

NATIONAL LIBERATION

As is true of Malaya, one has to start with a plural society and a colonial economic structure centered on the plantations to gain the proper vantage point for an understanding of the Indonesian liberation movement.[50] The particular social and economic structures of Netherlands India made the rise of a new elite and its integration into the colonial system considerably more difficult, in both economic, administrative, and political terms—more so, I believe than in other colonies. The old elite of local aristocrats was by no means wholly eliminated, since the Dutch incorporated the princes of the outer islands into their system of Indirect Rule. They had also been able to integrate regents and their subofficials to a very considerable extent into their own direct rule, but at the cost of reducing them to administrative auxiliaries. The regents stood between the Dutch and the local population, helped to stabilize the colonial rule, and retained considerable prestige. Although the external forms of the aristocratic Javanese life were still cultivated, they too often assumed a degenerate form that stood in crass but revealing contrast to the regents' now much reduced power. As ruling class and political elite, the local aristocracy had been displaced by the colonial power, without a new middle-class elite of educational or entrepreneurial origins having arisen within the colonial system. To the extent that the beginnings of such an elite existed, its access to leading administrative or business positions was largely blocked.

Part of the explanation was that the number of Dutch in Indonesia, particularly in Java, was relatively large. In 1930 there were about eighty thousand, only half of whom were born in the Netherlands.[51] Indonesia was no colony of settlement like Algeria or Kenya, for the Dutch did not till the land, but in contrast to the British in India or Malaya, many Dutch in Java did consider it their home. They filled not only the senior ranks of the administration but the middle and junior posts as well. Their social stratification was also considerably greater than that of the English and can be compared to that of the French in Indochina. This accordingly set narrower limits on Indonesian possibilities for upward social movement than was true for colonials in British colonies. There was no color bar, but distance was maintained, to the limits of open or covert discrimination. Whether this was greater or less in Batavia than in Bombay or Saigon, I would hardly venture to say.

One local peculiarity was the great number of mixed bloods or Eurasians, estimated variously at between 160,000 and 200,000 in 1930. Legally, they were equal to the "pure" Dutch, but were never fully accepted by the latter nor fully integrated socially. Their offspring mostly were employed as petty officials and employees. In 1919 their formation of the Indo-European League revealed their growing group solidarity. Increasingly hard pressed by Western-educated Indonesians and the nationalist movement, some Eurasians took sides with the colonial power (being "more Dutch than the Dutch") and some with moderate groups within the liberation movement.[52]

In the economy, the Chinese were largely able to monopolize retail trade and petty industry. As already mentioned, Chinese traders had even in precolonial times settled in the coastal states. The East India Company had, indeed, claimed a monopoly over foreign and wholesale trade, but had encouraged and assisted Chinese as middlemen, first in the purchase of imported goods, then as buyers of cash crops. Finally, the Chinese rented entire villages, and even districts, along with all the feudal rights necessary to exploit the peasants, and were in addition granted a whole series of revenue monopolies (such as tolls and bazaar taxes). In the nineteenth century, Chinese merchants largely displaced Javanese and were also active as moneylenders. They thus reduced the peasants to dependency and forced them to cultivate specific crops, which they bought at fixed prices. Their only setback was their loss of pawnshops, which the administration nationalized during the Ethical Policy era. They also worked their way into petty manufacturing, many an allegedly Javanese enterprise actually belonging to Chinese. At the same time, the influx of Chinese coolies continued. The number of Chinese rose from 221,000 in 1860 to 461,000 in 1890 and 1.2 million in 1930.[53] Many coolies eventually worked their way into the trades and commerce. A pass system, which placed barriers in the way of their activities in the cities, was dismantled in stages after 1900, although both officials and other experts were very critical of the Chinese. Their energy, thrift, and family solidarity were almost ideally suited to make the most of the opportunities created by the capitalist colonial economy.

The ruling economic positions of the Dutch and Chinese left the Indonesians with rather limited entrepreneurial possibilities. But it is also true that specific Javanese values and concepts of the good life were not very compatible with the requirements of a modern economy dominated by considerations of efficiency. A new middle class did form, nonetheless, both in the private sector and outside it, and was able to grow considerably in the 1930s because of administrative support of industrialization.[54] Still, as late as 1936, few Indonesians paid income taxes exceeding 900 gulden, fewer indeed than the Chinese.[55]

It is manifest that in Indonesia as elsewhere the school system which the colonial power introduced was the main force behind the creation of the new elite. Until 1900 the administration had not actually worried greatly about education. After 1848 a few schools for the education of officials had been created, and in 1851 a teachers' college and a school for medical personnel were established. That same year, the missionaries were also allowed to come in. Pupils came from the *prijaji* class and from regents' families wanting civil service positions. They sought access to Dutch schools because the school system largely separated education for Europeans from that for Indonesians. Despite intentional restrictions, the number of non-Europeans in European schools rose from 226 in 1870 to about 2,000 in 1900.[56] Still, only thirteen Indonesians attended the three college-preparatory high schools in 1900.[57]

The education of the peasant population had scarcely begun. The majority of the village chiefs was illiterate. With the inauguration of the Ethical Policy, the Dutch made greater efforts, because the villages could not be revitalized without a minimum of modern schooling. "Education, emigration, irrigation," was the motto on van Deventer's banner.[58] In theory, special emphasis was to be put on primary education. The village had to furnish the schoolroom, and the administration paid the teacher's salary. It nonetheless took "gentle pressure" to force the peasants to send their children to school, especially if fees were charged; in the Netherlands itself education had long been free. The number of pupils rose from about 100,000 in 1900 to 1.5 million in 1928. All the same, in 1940, 93.6 percent of the population remained illiterate. Instruction was in the local language or in Malay, which was a lingua franca for the entire archipelago. These languages offered no access to the higher civil service positions or the skilled trades, for which Dutch education was necessary. The number of Indonesians attending European schools with instruction in Dutch rose after 1900 but remained small in relation to the size of the population.[59] That was particularly true of middle and high schools, which in the eyes of the administration were primarily for Europeans. A breakdown of those completing middle school, as shown in table 5.8, makes this clear:

Table 5.8
Graduates of Middle Schools in Indonesia, 1910-1939

YEAR	EUROPEANS	INDONESIANS	"FOREIGN ORIENTALS" (i.e., CHINESE)
1910/11	49	4	3
1920/21	141	11	17
1929/30	252	157	53
1938/39	457	204	116

SOURCE: G.M. Kahin, *Nationalism and Revolution in Indonesia* (Ithaca, N.Y.; Cornell University Press, 1952), 32.[60]

Some technical schools were opened after 1900, universities only after World War I: an engineering school in Bandung in 1920, a law school in 1924, and a medical school in 1926. In 1940 only 637 Indonesians were attending a university and only 37 passed their commencement examinations. In addition, after 1900 some aristocrats' sons studied in Holland.

As late as the early years of this century, most students in Western schools were aristocrats. Student origins became increasingly democratic, however, a development characterized as a "small-scale social revolution."[61] High school (Hollandsche-Inlandsche Scholen from 1914 on) and college education permitted the rise of a small class of Indonesians who were qualified for senior administrative positions and equalled the aristocracy in status and prestige and even as marriage partners. Education and profession came to count for more than the hallmarks of ascriptive status. Even the younger aristocrats with Western educations counted less on birth than education. But as small as this Indonesian intelligentsia was, its social and professional opportunities were limited. The spheres of trade and manufacturing were anyhow largely monopolized by the Chinese, as already mentioned, and Dutch firms employed Indonesians in leading positions only in exceptional cases, preferring Europeans, or failing the latter, Eurasians. Even sugar mills in the interior seldom employed Indonesians as technical personnel. Europeans in the cities naturally preferred European doctors, and the number of prosperous Indonesians was too low to provide Indonesian doctors much of a practice. The courts also offered few opportunities, in contrast to the British colonies, since the Dutch policy was to exclude native attorneys as much as possible from "native courts." Limits could thus be set on trial "inflation" and various sorts of lawyer "exploitation," but at the cost of giving the attorneys yet another reason to turn against the colonial system. What remained was the administration, and even here, besides Europeans, Eurasians and Christians from Amboina enjoyed a preferred status.

All the same, localization made noteworthy progress during the depression (see table 5.9). Localization mainly affected the middle ranks. The top positions remained in Dutch hands. In October 1940 there were only 221 Indonesians among the 3,039 senior officials. As late as 1938 it was declared that the colonial power would shift administrative powers, if they did so at all, not to Western-schooled Indonesians but to the traditional *adat* class. But in general the top positions were to be reserved for Dutchmen, who "according to tradition and origin, can guarantee that these lands will continue to be governed in accordance with Dutch principles."[62] More important, however, was the fact that despite localization there were not enough administrative jobs to absorb the rising number of Western-schooled applicants. As early as 1928-1929, a quarter were unable to find positions commensurate with their education, which on Java further encouraged the nationalist movement.[63]

Table 5.9
Personnel Positions Held in Indonesia in Terms of National Origin, 1928-1938 (in percentages)

	1928	1938	1928	1938	1928	1938
	Europeans		Indonesians		"Foreign Orientals"	
Technical	84.77	77.14	14.38	20.12	0.85	2.74
Administrative	77.06	55.81	22.28	41.08	0.66	2.21
Finance	80.45	67.08	18.81	30.46	0.75	2.46
Administrative	93.66	65.18	5.10	32.16	1.24	2.66
Supervisory	92.46	83.97	7.33	15.68	0.21	0.35

SOURCE: Wertheim, *Indonesian Society*, 149.

Space does not permit analysis of the dozens of peasant protest movements of the nineteenth century, today wrongly almost forgotten, or of the West Javan Holy War of 1888.[64] Following precedent, I begin with the Budi Utomo ("pure endeavour," or "noble striving") Union of 1908. Medical school students, mostly sons of teachers and low-ranking civil servants, joined in a "voluntary association," which symbolized their interest in the lower classes, their demands for expansion of the school system, and their support of agriculture, both against the colonial power and the Javanese aristocracy as well. It is said to have gained 10,000 members in a short time, but encountered the mistrust of the regents and lost influence when the upper *prijaji* assumed its leadership. The Indische partij of E.F.E. Douwes Dekker, a Eurasian and the grandnephew of the author of *Max Havelaar*, struck a radical note in 1912 with its interpretation of the colonial system as capitalist exploitation, its demand for racial unity, and, as the first to do so, separation from the Netherlands. It had about 7,500 members when it was banned in 1913.

The Sarekat Islam ("Islamic Union") founded in 1912 became a mass movement. Its core consisted of an association of Muslim merchants formed in 1909 who, hard pressed by the Chinese, appealed for a boycott of Chinese batik traders. That demand led to anti-Chinese disturbances in August 1912. The tiny Indonesian middle class had thus formed a militant pressure group whose initial efforts were directed more against the Chinese than the colonial power. But it soon widened its field of action, by 1912 already reaching 93,000 members, and 336,913 by April 1914.[65] This astonishing success rested in good part on the religious character of the union; or, put another way, Islam tied the group together. It thus became the foundation of an Indonesian liberation movement. By 1900 an Islamic modernism had taken shape, the challenge of a Christian colonial rule summoning forth as in Egypt and India an Islamic renaissance. Simultaneously both antimissionary and anti-Chinese, Sarekat Islam sought to appeal to the urban middle classes and the rural masses alike. In the villages its mainstays were the ulema and the growing number of hadjis, or those who had completed a pilgrimage to Mecca. Bernhard Dahm also believes there is evidence that the striking success of Sarekat Islam rested in part on the venerable Javanese eschatological anticipation of the Messiah (*Ratu Adil*), who would free Java from foreign rule: "And the masses pressed to buy membership cards, in order to assure themselves places in this new kingdom."[66]

The administration gave the movement a certain encouragement. Fearing the "fanatical" Pan-Islamicism that those going to Mecca encountered, it followed the advice of Snouck Hurgronje to use Western education as a means of dissolving the ties of the Indonesian masses to both *adat* and Pan-Islamic conceptions. The Dutch hoped to create the basis for a Dutch-Indonesian "association."[67] Although the Sarekat Islam declared specifically at its first congress of January 1913 that it was not a party and swore its loyalty to the administration, it manifestly did so to avoid the strict prohibitions against political organizations. Its actual aim was, nevertheless, to end colonial rule. The administration feared the consequences of such a prohibition and temporized. In March 1914 it granted the local sections of the Sarekat recognition, but not the central organization (that came only in 1916). But if it thought this would weaken the movement or believed that the Sarekat would peter out because of insufficient means and disorganization, it miscalculated. In the following period, indeed, the Sarekat's strengthened, autonomous local sections became the strongholds of its radical wing.

It is hardly surprising that the Sarekat, which had burgeoned into a mass movement in so short a time, was homogeneous neither in terms of leaders nor of followers. The latter came mainly from the peasantry, whereas the leaders were mainly drawn from the lower *prijaji*, petty officials, and journalists. Tensions developed between the Muslim leaders, who sought to create an Islamic state, and the spokesmen for the secularized educational elite, who mainly saw religion as glue to hold the movement together. And if the middle classes considered the Sarekat Islam their spokesman, the young intelligentsia was following an increasingly anticapitalist, socialist course. That was more or less in the nature of things. Imperialism could be interpreted as a system of exploitation responsible for the poverty of the Indonesian masses. The dualistic, colonial economic structure, combined with a plural society, virtually blocked the rise of an Indonesian middle class alongside of the Europeans and Chinese. This particularly emphasized the character of Dutch colonial rule as class rule, to be thrown off only by social revolutionary means.[68] The still small elite was a "free-floating intelligentsia" without any stake in the colonial economic system. This was in clear contrast to, say, British India where the leaders of the Congress party were landowners, businessmen, or professional men. As such, they had a direct or indirect stake in maintaining the status quo and thus set limits on the impact of socialist slogans.

In 1914, the Indonesian Social Democratic Union (SDV), led by the Dutch socialist Hendrik Sneevliet, was founded. It rapidly gained adherents, subscribed to socialist revolution, and began to undermine the Sarekat Islam. The leaders of the latter had to take a more radical course, expressed at the party congress of 1918 in the demand for independence and the threat of possible violence. Its economic program, however, compromised to meet the interests of its middle-class members through the use of the expression "sinful capitalism," which included only foreign or Dutch capitalism. The social unrest with revolutionary undertones that also gripped Holland after the war stimulated the Marxists in the Sarekat. There were strikes in 1919 and 1920 on the sugar plantations, among other places. They were led by the trade unions which had formed after 1908 (such as the Railway Workers' Union) and had in the meantime acquired a sizeable membership. Internal tensions increased, however, splitting the party in October 1921. A Communist party (PKI) had formed as early as 1920.

The government had earlier attempted to loosen up the authoritarian bureaucratic state as part of the Ethical Policy. It introduced a certain amount of decentralization in the form of municipal, regents, and provincial councils made up of elected and appointed members. This was also intended to reinflate the regents. In addition, it was decided in July 1913 to create a colonial council. The necessary law passed in 1916 and in May 1918, the liberal governor-general, Count Johan Paul van Limburg Stirum, opened it as the Volksraad. The Dutch in Indonesia had also pressed for this measure, the better to articulate their own interests. (The French in Indochina had done the same thing.) Half of the thirty-eight members (after 1921, forty-eight) were to be elected, the others appointed by the governor-general. A complicated, indirect electoral procedure assured that Dutch interests were strongly represented and received a majority; and in the beginning the council had only a consultative role in budgetary questions. The new Netherlands India constitution of 1925 did, however, strengthen the autonomy of the colony vis-à-vis the homeland, transferring both colegislative powers and budgetary control to the Volksraad in 1927. The membership of the council was increased to sixty (thirty-eight elected, twenty-two appointed), and, after 1931, Indonesians held a majority. In 1939, 515 out of 1,452 Indonesian electors were officials, however, and eleven of nineteen elected Volksraad members were active or retired officials.[69] Although it is true that Holland, in contrast to England, guaranteed its officials rather sweeping rights to express their views and to take such stands as they wished, one still can only speak of the Volksraad as a genuine representative body in a restricted sense. The Dutch parliament continued to sanction the budget, and the governor-general retained veto powers. The executive remained Dutch and was directly responsible to The Hague. Only one department, education, was entrusted to an Indonesian. There were yet additional safeguards. Although the article of the 1854 Regeringsreglement forbidding all political activity was repealed, the administration could still banish without trial persons deemed "dangerous to public order and security," and in 1923 "incitement to strike" was also made a criminal act.[70]

It cannot be doubted that the council achieved a certain importance in finance questions and some bills were altered as a result of its intervention. But its real significance lay in its providing a forum for agitation and protest and in bringing together the representatives of the various islands. Once can rank the council roughly midway between the Grand Conseil des Intérêts Financiers in French Vietnam—discussed in the next chapter—and the legislative councils of the British colonies. As in India, the nationalists had to face the question of whether they should participate in the Volksraad, which was naturally far from meeting their expectations, or whether they should proclaim a policy of noncooperation. The latter view carried, with the result that the confrontations between the administration and the nationalists took place outside rather than within the council. Its educational role in teaching the use of Western democratic institutions thus remained small.

While the Communist party first dominated the stage after 1921, it soon lost the masses to the Sarekat Islam. The Communists found themselves in conflict with the religious tradition early on and, following Comintern instructions, concentrated one-sidedly on winning the trade unions. Stalin and the Executive Committee of the Communist International criticized this policy in 1925 and 1926 and recommended collaboration with the national bourgeoisie. The party leaders failed to follow instructions, however, pushing ahead with plans for a rising and finally proclaiming it on 12 November 1926.[71] The government moved at once, arresting some of the workers' leaders and Communists, and the badly prepared revolt collapsed after a few days. The rebellion achieved modest successes early in 1927 only in the Minangkabau region in west Sumatra. Some loyal officials were assassinated, and a sizeable arsenal was later uncovered. In this particular area, Communist slogans had not attracted plantation workers or urban proletarians but traders and peasants who had made the switch from subsistence to cash crops. They had rebelled as much against the *adat*, village, and family chiefs as against the colonial power.[72] The government struck hard: 13,000 were arrested, some of the ringleaders hanged, and thousands jailed or banished to New Guinea. The Communist party was smashed. Leadership of the nationalist movements shifted to the non-Communist parties, where it rested until 1945.

The rising also inaugurated a conservative shift in the administration. Decentralization coasted ahead on its own momentum for a time but was stopped in 1931. While the ideal originally had been to grant a measure of Indonesian self-rule, a reversion to the administrative state now occurred.[73] Liberal colonial experts like Snouck Hurgronje and Cornelis van Vollenhoven became disillusioned with the idea of association and warned about underestimating the liberation movement. A notion of rule came to prevail, however, that allowed for no slightest concession. It was characteristic that Hendrikus Colijn, Dutch premier and colonial minister from 1933 to 1937, as early as 1928 had taxed the Volksraad with being a "tree rotten to the roots which must be bodily uprooted," and sketched a policy of divide and rule, to be achieved by allowing each island its own council and eventually some autonomy.[74]

The modernist Muslim movement, the Muhammadiyah, also deserves mention. It has been described as "the most spectacularly successful Indonesian organization between the 1920's and the end of Dutch colonial rule."[75] Founded in 1912, it was not overtly political, but devoted itself to the founding of schools, hospitals, libraries, and cooperatives. It spoke directly to hundreds of thousands of young Indonesians, particularly in the cities. In political terms Islam was split, but nonetheless in 1937 a loose federation of Muslim associations was formed. It survived Japanese occupation as the Majumi party of independent Indonesia. In the contest with the colonial power, however, the Western-educated nationalist intelligentsia retained the initiative.

A new group of intellectual leaders, the *Perhimpunan Indonesia* (Indonesian Association), was formed from the union of Indonesian students in Holland. Its leading figure was Muhammad Hatta (born in 1902), an economics student at Rotterdam. Somewhat influenced by Gandhi, the party totally rejected collaboration with the colonial power and formed "study groups" in several Indonesian cities. The Partai Nasional Indonesia (PNI) founded 4 July 1927, originated from one such group. The PNI's president was Sukarno (born 1901). His father, a teacher by profession, was from the petty Javanese nobility and his mother was a Balinese. After attending a Dutch primary school, Sukarno lived in the household of the highly respected Saraket Islam leader, Umar Said Tjokroaminoto, and successfully completed the course at the Bandung Technical College between 1921 and 1926. "Possessed of considerable Muslim as well as Western education, he had the unique gift of being able to synthesize Western and Islamic concepts with those of the strongly surviving Hindu-Buddhist-tempered Javanese mysticism and translating this synthesis in terms which the peasant could understand."[76] This ability had enabled him by 1928 to achieve the first of his goals, the joining of nationalists, Marxists, and Muslims under one roof, under the slogan Noncooperation, but at the price of any other clearly formulated doctrines. He had, for example, postulated an Eastern nationalism, which, with its anti-Western, anticapitalist appeal, was sufficiently sweeping to allow the fundamental differences between Islam and Marxism to be labelled "misunderstandings." The notion of *pantja sila*, which was propagated after 1945 as the national ideology, was already visible. Sukarno, a great speaker able to carry away not only his auditors but also himself, according to Dahm, brought ten thousand into his party inside of two years. In comparison to other parties that was a great many but few, nevertheless, in comparison to the huge crowds that streamed to his meetings. The liberal governor-general, Andries Cornelis Dirk de Graeff, stood by for some time before giving into pressure from the resident Dutch, and arrested the leaders of PNI, among them Sukarno, on 29 December 1929. Although no plans for revolution could be proved, Sukarno was condemned to four years in prison.

The Partai Nasional Indonesia was so dependent on one charismatic leader, the veneration of whom was already assuming cultlike forms, that his arrest paralyzed it. It actually dissolved itself, though only to be reconstituted in 1931 as the Partai Indonesia (Partindo), the leadership of which Sukarno assumed upon his early release. In 1932, however, an opposition group was formed, the Pendidikan Nasional Indonesia (Indonesian National Education Association). Its leaders were the young law student, Sutan Sjahrir, and Muhammad Hatta, who had criticized Sukarno's leadership style. In place of mere agitational effectiveness they postulated a systematic process of education of the masses and the creation of a disciplined organization. The concrete situation, they believed, had to be clearly analyzed and priority given to the formation of cadres. Ideologically, the party followed a Marxist-oriented, anticapitalist line.

After 1931 Sukarno also emphasized social revolution more strongly and presented the Partindo as the party of the poor, the peasants, artisans, and fishermen, without, however, breaking with the national bourgeoisie. "National independence was described by Sukarno as a 'golden bridge,' after crossing which it would be possible to reach a social order based on justice: to this he gave the name 'Social-Democracy,' since it was to guarantee the political and economic equality of all citizens."[77] But this time he failed to unify the national movement. The Westerners, Sjahrir and Hatta, stood to one side, and the differences in personalities and doctrines could not be written off as mere "misunderstandings." Superficially, at least, the laurels went to Sukarno and his party, which in 1933 is said to have numbered some twenty thousand. Sukarno gave lip service to Lenin's "democratic centralism," yet in fact he does not seem to have troubled himself much over the formation of a disciplined cadre party or even a mass party. Multitudes thronged his grand happenings and worshipped him as their great leader; but whether the peasants in the villages were really much affected may be doubted. When Sukarno called in 1933 for "Holy War," the colonial power stepped in once again, arrested him on 1 August and exiled him, first to Flores and then west Sumatra. In 1934 it was the turn of Sjahrir and Hatta. All three had to await the Japanese for freedom.

With the elimination of the radicals who had refused collaboration with the colonial power, more moderate groups came to the fore. Noncooperation had not really achieved much, and it seemed appropriate to exploit the opportunities offered by participation in the Volksraad and to seek concessions by evolutionary means. It is also possible that the new economic policy of support for native entrepreneurs strengthened the position of the moderates. New parties were formed (Parinda, the Greater Indonesian Party, the Gerindo movement of the

Indonesian people, and the Indonesian Muslim Party). The membership of these parties and associations was estimated at about eighty thousand. In December 1939 some ninety secular and religious associations joined in congress and reached agreement on an Indonesian national language, flag, and anthem, and in light of the international situation declared themselves ready to collaborate with the Netherlands, though under the condition that the Volksraad be declared an Indonesian parliament.

The colonial power did not exploit this opening, however, and was not ready to accept a policy of a gradual transition to self-rule. Governor-General Bonifacius Cornelis de Jonge (1931-1936) declared in an interview: "I believe that since we have worked in the Indies for some 300 years, another 300 will have to be added before they may perhaps be ready for some kind of autonomy."[78] The Indonesian Dutch in 1929 formed the *Vaderlandsche Club* (Patriotic Club) as an answer to the disturbances of 1926 and 1927, demanded action from the administration against the nationalists, and proclaimed that the tie with the homeland was indissoluble. A prominent member was, for example, to state in 1939 in the Volksraad that the Ethical Policy had had its day, because the Indonesian society could never become economically independent and within an imperial economy would always require firm Dutch leadership.[79] The Indonesian official Soetardja got a petition accepted in 1936, twenty-six votes to twenty, which proposed a conference to work out a ten-year plan for the gradual provision of self-government within the framework of the Dutch constitution. The government, however, turned the request down cold in 1938 and again in 1940 (Wihowo Resolution). Many Indonesians understandably greeted the Japanese as liberators and were ready to collaborate.

NOTES

1. Bernard H. M. Vlekke, *Nusantara: A History of Indonesia* (rev. ed., Chicago: Quadrangle Books, 1960); John David Legge, *Indonesia* (Englewood Cliffs, N. J.: Prentice-Hall, 1964); Bernhard Dahm, *History of Indonesia in the Twentieth Century*, trans. P. S. Falla (London, New York: Praeger, 1971); John Sydenham Furnivall, *Netherlands India: A Study of Plural Economy*, with an introduction by A.C.D. De Graeff (London: Cambridge University Press, 1967); Justus Van der Kroef, *Indonesia in the Modern World* (2 vols., Bandung: M. Baru, 1956); idem, "Dutch Colonial Policy in Indonesia, 1900-1950" (Dissertation, Columbia University, 1959); Willem Frederick Wertheim, *Indonesian Society in Transition: A Study of Social Change* (2d rev. ed., The Hague: W. van Hoeve, 1964); idem, "Social Change in Java, 1900-1930," in his *East-West Parallels: Sociological Approaches to Modern Asia* (The Hague: W. van Hoeve, 1964). See also the useful selections in Ruth T. McVey (ed.), *Indonesia* (New Haven: HRAF Press, 1967).

2. See the pioneer effort of Jacob Cornelis Van Leur, *Indonesian Trade and Society: Essays in Asian Social and Economic History* (2d ed., Bandung: "Sumur Bandung," 1960), and Legge's discussion of it, *Indonesia*, 60.

3. Dahm, *History of Indonesia*, emphasizes both the lack of unity or any common feeling of unity, in opposition to more nationalistic interpretations.

4. Leslie H. Palmier, "The Javanese Nobility under the Dutch," *CSSH*, 2 (April 1960), 205f.; Bertram J. O. Schrieke, "The Native Rulers," in idem, *Indonesian Sociological Studies: Selected Writings of B. Schrieke* (2 vols., 2d ed., The Hague: W. van Hoeve, 1966), I.

5. Palmier, "Javanese Nobility," 213.

6. For the details, see Bernhard Dahm, *Emanzipationsversuche von kolonialer Herrschaft in Südostasien: die Philippinen und Indonesian: ein Vergleich* (Wiesbaden: Harrassowitz, 1974), 89f., who emphasizes the chiliastic aspects as well as the political and economic causes.

7. Hendrikus Colijn, as quoted in Furnivall, *Netherlands India*, 121. On the Culture System, see, in addition to Furnivall, Clifford Geertz, *Agricultural Involution: The Process of Ecological Change in Indonesia* (Berkeley: University of California Press, 1966), 52f. The formulation does, however, provide a misleading picture, insofar as a relatively small portion of the arable was involved; according to Vlekke, *Nusantara*, 292, 3 to 4 percent, and Geertz, *Agricultural Involution*, 53, 6 percent.

8. Robert Van Niel, "The Course of Indonesian History," in McVey, *Indonesia*, 286.

9. Edouard Douwes Dekker, *Max Havelaar, of De Koffij-veilingen der Nederlandsche Handel-maatschappij*, by Multatuli (2 vols., Amsterdam: J. de Ruyter, 1860).

10. As much as 160.3 million gulden (fl.) as late as 1867-1877, and for the period 1831-1877, fl. 832.4 million; Furnivall, *Netherlands India*, 211.

11. Ibid., 186. Personal labor services continued, however, to be exacted, particularly in outlying regions as yet largely unaffected by the cash economy. Such services were cut off completely only in 1941, when taxes replaced them.

12. Palmier, "Javanese Nobility," 218.

13. Furnivall, *Netherlands India*, 194.

14. Discussed in detail in Vlekke, *Nusantara*, 317f.

15. Furnivall, *Netherlands India*, 225ff.

16. "Buying Power," as quoted in Van der Kroef, "Dutch Colonial Policy," 257. Colonial Minister A. W. F. Idenburg, appointed in 1902, explained matters as follows: "During the past twenty years the population (of Java) has increased by 45 percent while the area of sawah land increased only 23 percent (productivity 28 percent).... The average production per person is thus declining. The number of farmers who do not own their own land is increasing. The number of persons seeking their livelihood in other fields of endeavor is increasing, but their average income is declining. All these facts justify the conclusion ... that Java is in a period of transition ... from a pure agricultural community to one in which industry comes forward to take a place next to agriculture.
And when one recognizes this fact as the general cause, then the direction in which one must seek general improvement is obvious.
Under the first rubric of means one will then try to advance industry to the advantage of the native people.
The second category concerns means for enlarging the productivity of agriculture in general; that is, increasing and improving the irrigation works. My attention has been drawn to the trivial amount expended for this purpose during the past ten years. Further there must be more intensive cultivation and curtailment of agricultural usury through the extension of better agricultural credit. Where overpopulation seems to be the chief problem one's thoughts are automatically led in the direction of emigration"; quoted in Robert Van Niel, *The Emergence of the Modern Indonesian Elite* (The Hague: W. van Hoeve, 1960), 32-33. Charles Theodor van Deventer, "Een Eereschuld," *De Gids* (1899), III, 205.

17. Lewis, *Tropical Development*, 264.

18. Furnivall, *Netherlands India*, 386.

19. The so-called *particuliere landerijen* constituted an important exception. These were private holdings which the administration had sold to Chinese and Europeans, mainly in the early nineteenth century. These latifundia amounted to roughly one million hectares in 1915, and their owners held rather extensive powers over the inhabitants. The state began repurchasing these estates after 1910 but as late as 1940, 500,000 hectares remained in private hands; ibid., 313f. See also Sartono Kartodirdjo, *Protest Movements in Rural Java: A Study of Agrarian Unrest in the Nineteenth and Early Twentieth Centuries* (Singapore, New York: Oxford University Press, 1973), 21f.

20. On this matter we now have Geertz's brilliant *Agricultural Involution*. He also provides us with a case study in his *The Social History of an Indonesian Town* (Cambridge, Mass.: MIT Press, 1965). The Western viewpoint, however, had earlier been set down in Julius Herman Boeke, *The Structure of the Netherlands Indian Economy* (New York: International Secretariat, Institute of Pacific Relations, 1942), and G. H. Van der Kolff, "European Influence on Native Agriculture," in Bertram J. O. Schrieke (ed.), *The Effect of Western Influence on Native Civilization in the Malay Archipelago* (Batavia, Java: G. Kolff & Co., 1929).

21. "The sugar cultivation of the estates and the rice and other cultivations of the population are, as it were, co-ordinated in one large-scale agricultural enterprise, the management of which is practically in the hands of the sugar factory"; Van der Kolff, "European Influence," 122.

22. Van der Kolff, "European Influence," 124; Boeke, *Netherlands Indian Economy*, 58, 84.

23. Geertz, *Social History*, 49.

24. Van der Kolff, "European Influence," 123f.

25. Boeke, *Netherlands Indian Economy*, 162.

26. "The result was an arabesque pattern of life, both reduced and elaborated, both enormously complicated and marvelously simple: complicated in the diversity, variability, fragility, fluidity, shallowness, and unreliability of interpersonal ties: simple in the meager institutional resources by which such ties were organized"; Geertz, *Agricultural Involution*, 103.

27. But there is opposition to this critical view: "The conservative influences of the sugar system may be admitted; but it does not follow that had Western Enterprise in this field been absent conditions would then have been favorable to the appearance of peasant proprietors"; Allen and Donnithorne, *Western Enterprise*, 82.

28. Acreages are given in Furnivall, *Netherlands India*, 212.

29. Export values in gulden are given in Furnivall, *Netherlands India*, 337.

30. Van der Kroef, "Dutch Colonial Policy," 304.

31. Geertz, *Social History*, 49.

32. Geertz, *Agricultural Involution*, 113f.

33. Schrieke, *Indonesian Sociological Studies*, I, 99f.

34. Geertz, *Agricultural Involution*, 113f.

35. Allen and Donnithorne, *Western Enterprise*, ch. "Banking in Indonesia."

36. Ibid., 85; Furnivall, *Netherlands India*, 429.

37. Boeke, *Netherlands Indian Economy*, 176f.

38. Table 5.10 gives important economic indicators for the years from 1928 to 1940:

Table 5.10
Population and the Economy of Java, 1928-1940

	1928	1932	1935	1939	1940
Population increase	100	106	110	118	119
Cost of living for worker's family with stable standard of living	100	65	56.5	57	60
Price level of food	100	51.5	43.5	44.5	46
Income from native agriculture exports in units of purchasing power[a]	100	52	64	88	116
Total exports in units of purchasing power	100	59	53	87	97
Income from industry in units of purchasing power	100	165	210	335	370
Total imports in units of purchasing power	100	61.5	48	90	85
Consumption of primary foodstuffs in kilograms per person	100	102	105	112	115
Calorie value of this food	-	-	100	110	112
Consumption of textiles in yards per person	100	-	92	136	?
Number of mechanically operated factories	100	132	134	162	184
Area technically irrigated	100	125	139	164	?

SOURCE: Peter H. W. Sitsen, *Industrial Development of the Netherlands Indies* (New York; Netherland-Indies Council, 1944), 2.

[a] The purchasing power of the income for subsistence of a family with an income of about 360 gulden per annum was taken as the unit of purchasing power.

39. Furnivall, *Netherlands India*, 438f.; Boeke, *Netherlands Indian Economy*, 117.
40. See note 38 above.
41. Allen and Donnithorne, *Western Enterprise*, ch. 9, "Indonesian Mining Industry."
42. Furnivall, *Netherlands India*, 213.
43. Geertrui M. Van Eeghen, "The Beginnings of Industrialization in Netherlands India," *Far Eastern Survey*, 6 (9 June 1937), 129. See also Furnivall, *Netherlands India*, 428f. See in particular Sitsen (who was director of the industry division of the economics ministry), *Industrial Development*. Van der Kroef, "Dutch Colonial Policy," 286f. is also based on Sitsen.
44. See Wertheim, *Indonesian Society*, 111.
45. Sitsen, *Industrial Development*, 58
46. As a result of inquests in 1924 and 1926 into the question of tax burdens, Boeke concluded that "the cultivator eats rather less well than before the war and can obtain less in exchange for his surplus produce, while his emancipation from compulsory service has done so little to improve his economic position that he cannot even pay the tax in money which was substituted for compulsory service"; Furnivall, *Netherlands India*, 403.
47. J. Van der Kroef, "Economic Origins of Indonesian Nationalism," in Phillips Talbot (ed.), *South Asia in the World Today* (Chicago: University of Chicago Press, 1950), 177. "From one-fifth to one-tenth of the entire population of the Netherlands is either directly dependent on, or indirectly interested financially in, the commerce or industries of Netherlands India"; Arthur Keller, "Netherlands India as a Paying Proposition," *Far Eastern Survey* (17 January 1940), 11.
48. A. Vandenbosch, "The Netherlands Colonial Balance Sheet," *Southern Economic Journal*, 4 (January 1938), 329.
49. Arnold P. H. Berkhuysen, *De drainagetheorie voor Indonesie* (The Hague: Techn. Vertaal-en Type-Inr., 1948), 97.
50. In addition to the works of Vlekke, Dahm, Van der Kroef, and Van Niel, see George McTurnan Kahin's important *Nationalism and Revolution in Indonesia* (Ithaca: Cornell University Press, 1952).
51. Callis, *Foreign Capital*, 31, provides a summary by occupation.
52. Van der Kroef, *Indonesia*, 275f.; idem, "The Eurasian Minority in Indonesia," *American Sociological Review*, 18 (October 1953).
53. Furnivall, *Netherlands India*, 243.
54. Wertheim, *Indonesian Society*, 149, attempts to show that before and after 1930 the number of Indonesian retailers rose considerably, that the monopoly position of the Chinese became weaker, and that with increasing social differentiation a middle class was becoming visible.
55. Table 5.11 compares the income taxes paid by different groups in 1936.

Table 5.11
Income and Income Taxation in Indonesia, 1936

	NUMBER TAXED	TOTAL INCOME (IN MILLIONS OF GULDEN)
Europeans	65,000	266
Indonesians	27,000	50
Chinese	37,000	82
Other "foreign" Asiatics	3,000	9
TOTAL	132,000	407

SOURCE: Van Helsendingen, *Mission Interrupted*, 246.

56. Furnivall, *Netherlands India*, 221. On the early school system, see, in detail, Dahm, *History of Indonesia*, 15f.
57. Dahm, *Emanzipationsversuche*, 102.

58. Furnivall, *Netherlands India*, 364.

59. Table 5.12 describes the number of Indonesians in Dutch language schools:

Table 5.12
Indonesians in Dutch-language schools, 1900-1940

YEAR	ENROLLMENT
1900-1904	2,987
1910-1914	23,910
1925	61,425
1928	74,697
1940	88,223

SOURCE: Kahin, *Nationalism*, 31.

60. Between 1917 and 1928, only seventy-eight Indonesians passed the abitur examination; Dahm, *Sukarnos Kampf*, 22.

61. Kahin, *Nationalism*, 32.

62. Ibid., 34.

63. "A matter of ever recurring grievance is the small number of Indonesians who are considered for the higher positions. The Government should have more confidence in the capacities of Indonesian intellectuals"; "Visman Report" of 1940, as quoted in Van der Kroef, "Economic Origins," 190.

64. Covered in detail in Dahm, *Emanzipationsversuche*, 95f.

65. Dahm, *Sukarnos Kampf*, 10; idem, *History of Indonesia*, 40. The two-million member figure often given in the literature was that given by the organization itself and according to Dahm was nothing more than propaganda. The latter gives the figure of 450,000 members for 1918.

66. Dahm, *Sukarnos Kampf*, 13.

67. Harry J. Benda, "Christiaan Snouck Hurgronje and the Foundations of Dutch Islamic Policy in Indonesia," *JMH*, 30 (December 1958).

68. A government report from 1920 stated: "The essence of the native movement is the effort to remove the restrictive competition of non-native capitalist concerns by endeavouring to end the entire non-native domination, politically as well as economically. The core of the nationalist movement is therefore the revolt of the increasing productive powers of an early capitalist native society against the economic and political domination of 'foreign capital' "; quoted in Van der Kroef, *Economic Origins*, 180.

69. Alexandre von Arx, "L'Evolution Politique en Indonésie de 1900 à 1942" (Dissertation, University of Fribourg, 1949), 322; Kahin, *Nationalism*, 40.

70. Dahm, *Sukarnos Kampf*, 69.

71. Kahin, *Nationalism*, 76f.; Dahm, *History of Indonesia*, 58f.; idem, *Emanzipationsversuche*, 123f. On the disputes between the PKI leadership and the ECCI see, in particular, Ruth T. McVey, *The Rise of Indonesian Communism* (Ithaca: Cornell University Press, 1965), 257f.

72. Bertram J. O. Schrieke, "The Causes and Effects of Communism on the West Coast of Sumatra," in idem, *Indonesian Sociological Studies*, I; Dahm, *Emanzipationsversuche*, 227f.

73. Harry J. Benda, "The Pattern of Administrative Reforms in the Closing Years of Dutch Rule in Indonesia," *JAS*, 25 (August 1966).

74. Albertini, *Decolonization*, 493.

75. Harry J. Benda, "Indonesian Islam under the Japanese Occupation, 1942-1945," *Pacific Affairs*, 28 (December 1955), 352.

76. Kahin, *Nationalism*, 90. Dahm, in particular, in his *Sukarnos Kampf*, has shown how his subject reflected traditional Javanese ideas and modes of thought.

77. Dahm, *History of Indonesia*, 69, and in more detail, his *Sukarnos Kampf*, 97f.

78. Quoted in Benda, "Pattern," 591 n.8.

79. Albertini, *Decolonization, 493.*

6

FRANCE IN VIETNAM

The Indochinese Union, as established by France between 1887 and 1897, was an artificial colonial administrative entity. It included Annam, Tonkin, Cochinchina, Cambodia, and Laos. In terms of population, culture, and history, the kingdom of Cambodia and the Laotian principalities had little in common with Annamite Vietnam.[1] The former states fell within the Indian cultural orbit and had had a long history of conflict with Annam. But Indochina was also artificial because Vietnam—a name deliberately not used by the French—was divided into three parts, in order to obliterate the old historical unity. Still, one can speak in only a limited sense of a precolonial Vietnamese nation, with established frontiers and administration, its case being rather like that of medieval European states. From 111 B.C. to A.D. 938, the north was under direct Chinese rule and was to a considerable degree sinicized. Rice cultivation on irrigated land, Chinese writing, the use of Chinese as the administrative language, elements of Taoism and Confucianism, and the mandarinate had all been assimilated. Yet the north never lost its own sense of identity, as several rebellions testify. Although Chinese suzerainty was accepted after 938 and a regular tribute paid, further Chinese efforts to extend their rule southward were successfully opposed.

But the Annamites themselves soon pushed southward as invaders and colonizers. They destroyed the Indianized kingdom of Champa in the fifteenth century, reaching Saigon by 1692, and settled the sparsely populated Mekong delta during the course of the eighteenth century.[2] That may have created subsurface tensions between north and south which took on a new relevance during and after the Vietnam War. What is more important is that by 1800 the Nguyen emperors, who shifted their residence from Hanoi to the more southerly Hué, ruled all of Vietnam. The southern march had been along the coast and through the river deltas. The non-Annamite tribes in the mountainous hinterland (Thai, Moi, Han) were conquered and forced to pay tribute but were otherwise left their autonomy. Vietnam has accordingly been compared with two rice baskets, the Red and Mekong Deltas—later called Tonkin and Cochinchina—suspended from a single slender shaft.

The system of rule and the social structure changed little during the nineteenth century. The emperors resided in Hué in the Chinese Confucian tradition. They legitimized their rule as the mandate of heaven. Rule itself was exercised through court ceremony and a ministerial council (the *co-mat*) made up of mandarins. The latter were recruited by examinations for which they had been especially educated. They stood at the top of a cadre of officials that reached from the center into the provinces down to the village level. Landowners and educated men of lower ranks formed the local notable class. The villages retained considerable autonomy and have been termed small republics. They paid taxes, mostly in rice, to the emperors, and had to provide soldiers and workers for corvée. The villages collected the taxes themselves and managed their own internal affairs. Surrounded by bamboo palings as protection against robbers, marauders, and wild beasts, the villages were the basic units of Vietnamese society, being far more than economic or administrative units. In addition to family shrines, which bound the living to their ancestors, there were also central village shrines where the village deities were worshipped.[3] One should nonetheless not idealize Vietnamese villages, any more than Indian. Some families, indeed, owned land in addition to that held in common, and notables were co-opted. In practice, the structure was oligarchic. A considerable portion of the peasantry had little or no land, and the notables got their way in matters such as apportionment and collection of taxes, cultivation of common lands, administration of justice, and the provision of soldiers and workers. It should be noted, however, that tradition and the restraints of subsistence farming placed sharp limits on internal village stratification and misuse of power. Then too, while the sway of the emperor and his mandarins might stop at the bamboo wall, taxes in the nineteenth century were still high. Along with secret societies, famines, and local rivalries, taxes occasioned numerous revolts and uprisings. These disturbances reveal the tensions within the traditional society, tensions which limited the emperor's ability to resist the French as would-be colonial rulers.

Although French missionaries and soldiers played a considerable role in eighteenth-century Vietnam—the soldiers laying out fortifications in the style of Vauban, the French military engineer—the Nguyen emperors assumed the defensive against Europeans. The emperors achieved some noteworthy accomplishments. The north and south were connected by the *route mandarine*, for example, and colonial settlements were established in Cochinchina. Despite the efforts of some intellectuals to formulate plans for renewal and reform following the Japanese example, little else was done, even the army remaining unmodernized. Instead, Hué preferred seclusion as the means to escape Western influence and political pressure. Between 1825 and 1833 Catholicism was banned, and during the following decades thousands were martyred for their faith. Missionaries were suspected of complicity with European aggressors, and the orthodox at court also feared the subversion of the traditional Confucian order.

The "opening" of China went hand in hand with initial French efforts to establish a foothold in Vietnam. The incarceration of a French bishop led in 1845 to an American ship's landing troops in Tourane (Danang), though they accomplished nothing. Two years later, in 1847, French warships followed, and in 1858 French troops landed. They encountered considerable resistance. In February 1859 the French occupied Saigon and in 1861 the greater part of the Mekong Delta. In 1862 the French forced emperor Tu-Duc (1847-1883) to sign a treaty ceding a part of Cochinchina—the remainder was in French hands by 1867—permitting Catholicism, and opening three ports. Both mandarins and peasants continued to wage guerilla warfare against the French, who responded with repressive measures that dragged on for years.

In the meantime, French interest was shifting from the south to the north. Francis Garnier's mission of 1868-1869 had established that the Mekong did not provide a route to South China. But access to South China was then and remained as late as Paul Doumer's time (1897-1902) the principal aim of France's Vietnam policy. In the quickening rivalry for economic and political hegemony over South China, Tonkin and the Red River became the bridgeheads for a French thrust toward South China. The French envisaged an enormous market there that would enable them to win their own "India" and set themselves up beside England as an Asian Great Power. The Franco-Prussian War delayed things very little. As early as 1874, the French forced upon Hué a treaty which permitted the French governor of Cochinchina to lead an expedition to Tonkin. The treaty also recognized the Vietnamese loss of all of Cochinchina and opened up harbors in Tonkin. Although Vietnam remained formally a sovereign state, a veiled French protectorate already existed. After the consolidation of the Third Republic in 1880, a series of French cabinets continued to interfere in Vietnamese matters, such interference culminating in a military campaign against China which forced the latter to abandon its claims to sovereignty over Vietnam and Hué to accept a French protectorate over Annam and Tonkin.

A variety of motivations and forces, some at cross-purposes with others, lay behind French expansion. In addition to the intangibles of power and prestige, the aggressive and independent behavior of the French in Saigon arose from a number of other factors. An expanding fleet under Admiral Jean Bernardin Jauréguiberry sought coaling stations in Asia. Adventurers like Jean Depuis, who had excellent connections in Parlement and elsewhere, lobbied effectively. Geographic societies also spread the message. Particularly important, however, were the hopes placed in the Vietnamese-South China market, which became yet more tempting during the recession after 1882. The discovery of coal in Tonkin created additional economic possibilities and seemed to justify the expectation that a Vietnamese protectorate would dispose of sufficient revenue to need no subsidies from the metropolis. Parlement was carried along by the nationalist wave, but still feared its foreign policy and financial implications.[4]

Emperor Tu-Duc saw disaster coming. He tried to secure Chinese support and to gain concessions from the French through diplomacy. He also feared war because his own position in Tonkin was none too secure. The French, indeed, spoke of liberation and asserted they were merely freeing Tonkin from Annamite rule. Real resistance began only with the loss of independence in 1884. When the French seized Hué in 1885, War Minister and Regency Counsellor Ton That Thuyet fled with the new emperor and called for open resistance against both French and Christians.[5] Thuyet had made preparations for resistance as early as 1883, and the educated classes and mandarins, supported by a goodly section of the populace, continued it until 1888. Well-organized attacks against French outposts and settlements occurred in several provinces. Numerous gangs, acting as brigands or out of genuine political conviction depending on circumstances, caused trouble into the late 1890s. Supported both by local mandarins and mandarin refugees in China, they operated in the hill country and in the Tonkin delta. The peasants also supported them, not always willingly. Since the guerillas were always able to evade French troops, the latter imposed collective punishment, burning villages and hanging numerous Annamites, mostly without trial. The whole business has become familiar enough: "Every village which had given the brigands refuge or had failed to warn of their passage was liable. The village chief and three or four of the head men were decapitated and the village razed to the ground."[6] The French also had much difficulty with Chinese bands. These were mostly groups of soldiers who had fled south after the Taiping rebellion or deserters who joined them later. Colonel (later general) Joseph Gallieni therefore tried to win the sorely tried local populace to his peace policy.

The character and extent of this "post-primary" resistance was later played down or written off as banditry, the employment of French troops, in contrast, being publicized as a glorious and successful pacification effort. Only the most recent histories have accorded this resistance its due. The failure of the resistance is easy to explain. The colonial power was better armed and controlled the maritime supply routes. The resistance lacked central coordination, the local bands acting entirely on their own. The traditional ruling class split into resisters and collaborators. Finally, the French received valuable assistance from the brutally persecuted Catholics, who were most useful informers, and were also able to play the hill tribes off against the Annamites. Gallieni's "races" policy, indeed, amounted to exploiting the ethnic tensions within Vietnamese society for the benefit of the French. Whether one should speak of national resistance is, as elsewhere, largely a question of definition. Whatever one's view, there was clearly a relationship between this early resistance and the "new" resistance which broke out only a few years after "pacification" in consequence of the Russo-Japanese War.[7]

ADMINISTRATION

In common with most such instruments, the Protectorate Treaty of 1884 had a twofold significance. It not only restricted Vietnamese sovereignty in France's favor, but also provided the means to bring the internal administration under French control. Mandarins were, for example, supposed to administer Annam without French interference—except "in matters concerning customs duties, public works, and, in general, those services which require unified direction or the employment of European agents or engineers." That, of course, covered the entire modern administrative and development sector, which was bound to become more important all the time. In Tonkin, French pretensions were even more blatant. French residents were foreseen for each province. They were not to meddle in the details of administration but were merely "to exercise '*control*'." In French colonial practice, however, "*control*" implied extensive interference. It soon became manifest that the protectorate was only a fiction veiling with "marvelous dextrousness" the total French takeover of the Vietnamese administration.[8] Annam represented a particularly clear case, because its people remained loyal to their emperor and traditional institutions.

The lawful emperor had fled in 1885. The new ruler was a French puppet. He held court in Hué, but soon lost all real power. The best that can be said of him is that he preserved continuity with the traditional Vietnam in the new era of colonial rule. The first resident general, Paul Bert, made conciliatory overtures toward the population to supplement the military and repressive measures of pacification he was taking against it. Half of the imperial treasury was returned, and taxes and corvée services were reduced. He sought above all to win over the mandarins and notables: "With them [on our side] we would be secure. They are the representatives of the Tonkinese bourgeoisie, a kind of third estate made of agriculturists, merchants, and educated men outside the administration."[9] A council of notables was created, in order to establish ties with the population and to give it opportunities to express desires and grievances. The measure was not without success.

At the same time, the French sought to restrict the influence of the mandarinate and to loosen the bonds between Annam and Tonkin. Tonkin thus received its own executive and legislative powers, formally transferred to a newly created viceroy and council (*kinh-luoc*). But the French in fact had greater powers of direct interference than ever. By 1897 Doumer had already declared the council worthless for the work of his administration and had disbanded it. The mandarinate was henceforth directly under control of the resident. Tonkin was withdrawn from Hué's control, the cities of Hanoi, Haiphong, and Danang having already been annexed by the French and accorded special status in 1888.

Paul Doumer had been appointed governor-general in 1897 because the critical financial situation called urgently for administrative reform. The metropolis was unwilling to assume further budget deficits.[10] Although Eugène Etienne had earlier established the Indochinese Union in 1887 and, in violation of the Protectorate Treaty, withdrawn it from Foreign Office control, jurisdictional questions remained to be settled. The Indochinese administration also had no revenues it could call its own. Under Doumer, who governed until 1902, these matters were resolved. The Indochinese Union, which included not only the three Vietnams but also Cambodia and Laos, received its own budget, being supported mainly by customs duties. Direct taxes were turned over to the component states of the union. At the same time the union's central administrative divisions were created: agriculture, commerce, justice, customs, public works, and domestic affairs. It was a strikingly centralized administration. Even before 1914, critics were already accusing it of being unwieldy and cumbersome and of sopping up too much of the budget.[11]

The governor-general was, like his colleagues in French West and French Equatorial Africa, the sole representative of the metropolis. He reported to the colonial ministry (after 1894) and had extensive executive powers. In contrast to English viceroys and governors, however, he had no legislative competence. He directly supervised the *résidents superieurs* in the protectorates (Annam, Tonkin, Laos, and Cambodia) and the governor of Cochinchina, which was formally a colony. The conseil supérieur de l'Indochine and the conseil de protectorat of Tonkin prepared the union's budget, planned the more important public works and had certain other functions, but could make no binding decisions. The two councils were made up of senior administrators, chamber of commerce representatives and a few appointed Vietnamese. In Annam the regency council, which had run things during the emperor's minority, was dissolved and the co-mat reorganized. It was thenceforth presided over by the résident superieur, and its acts required his consent. Appearances may have been preserved, but control was firmly in French hands. In the following period, to be sure, France ruled Annam with a far lighter hand than the economically more important Tonkin, where French administration was largely direct.

The mandarinate continued to be a key problem. It was not united in opposing the French, either in Annam or Tonkin, but it remained the most important opponent of French rule. It remained unwilling to accept its loss of power and it was the conservative guardian of traditional values. What was left of the court constituted another doubtful element, which Doumer mistrusted and sought tenaciously to eliminate. The mandarinate was stripped of its executive powers and incorporated into the colonial administration. Using mandarins as tax collectors compromised them with the population, however, particularly since they had to deliver the taxes to French fiscal officials after 1895. The quality of the mandarinate declined considerably in the following years, moreover, because the traditional administrative career was no longer attractive. France allowed the old mandarin examination system to linger on beside the new school system, abolishing it only in 1915, several years after China did so. The modernized portion of the traditional elite remained small, though it had links to the new colonial bourgeoisie.

The French left the village structure, at least in externals, pretty much as they found it. The village remained, particularly in Annam and Tonkin, a largely closed world. Taxation was more strictly supervised, with such things as lists of inhabitants being demanded. New duties such as protection of the telegraph lines and prevention of alcohol smuggling were also imposed. The village headmen—like African chiefs—thus became quasi-civil servants. They continued to stand between the village population and colonial administration but depended increasingly on the latter for protection and support. Efforts to select the village notables by vote were not a success.[12] In the interwar period, complaints were increasingly heard that the untrained notables were no longer up to their jobs. The cities now offered alternative possibilities for advancement, and the ambitious increasingly sought them in preference to positions as village notables.

In Cochinchina, French rule rested on a system of direct administration, although the admirals who ruled between 1861 and 1879 had attempted to govern through native authorities and had also attempted to acquire a knowledge of local customs and institutions. The mandarins, however, had refused to cooperate or fled outright, and the admirals had had no choice but to run the country with naval officers. The sailors later gave way to civil servants, whose activities reached down to the canton and village level. From the beginning, repression and high taxes compromised the positive activities of French administrators and in part explain why the French were unable to use the traditional ruling class as an instrument of colonial rule. Annamite control of the south was of fairly recent origin and much of the area was thinly populated. The establishment of a colonial economy occurred more rapidly and on a more intensive scale than in the north, with concessions, plantations, and all the rest. The traditional social structure was thus loosened and the village could no longer fill its integrating functions. The notables lost their judicial and police functions to colonial magistrates unfamiliar with either local languages or laws; administering a law unfamiliar to the Vietnamese (the *Code Pénal*, introduced in 1880). Justice hence became "less accessible, less certain and more costly."[13] The colonial administration noted as early as 1900 that the notables no longer had much interest in village matters, being mainly concerned as landowners with their own economic interests. Cochinchinese *administration directe* differed considerably from Tonkin's and even more from Annam's.

Cochinchina was formally a colony and received a civil governor in 1879, in 1881 a conseil colonial and, like the "old" colonies and Algeria, a parliamentary deputy. The conseil consisted of six members elected by local French citizens, two representatives of the Saigon Chamber of Commerce, two appointees of the governor, and six Vietnamese notables. It had budgetary powers, determining both the level of taxation and, initially at least, customs duties. It also decided expenditures. Doumer called this particular assimilatory reform on the part of the metropolis "absurd," since it meant that French officials, some 1,500 of the 2,000 voters, not only determined their own salaries but could also create new administrative posts.[14] Although Doumer was able to set limits both on the conseil and the thirst for autonomy of the Saigon French, the conseil nonetheless was in the future to remain a forum for the articulation of colonial interests and a body which closely scrutinized, and influenced, the governor-general's policies. The deputy elected by the Saigon French not only defended their interests in Paris but was also able to influence the local colonial administration. Since owners or representatives of colonial firms occasionally even became mayors of Saigon, the colonial minority came to enjoy a degree of economic and political power which justifies comparing Cochinchina to Algeria. Like Algiers, Saigon became an economic and administrative city decidedly French in character, in which a man "could really live."

The taxation system in Cochinchina acquired its essential form during the time of the admirals.[15] Doumer then tightened it up and applied it to all of Vietnam. The high cost of pacification and the budget deficits, borne grudgingly by the metropolis, have already been mentioned. Financial reorganization was, accordingly, Doumer's most pressing task. It was decided in Paris in 1900 that the colonies should be largely self-supporting. Colonial loans for railways were to be granted only when the colonial budget was largely in balance and sufficient revenue to amortize the loan was at hand. By raising taxes and imposts and employing ruthless collection methods, Doumer did balance the budget.[16]

As in nearly all European colonies a head tax was first imposed. The French took over the precolonial Vietnamese system without much change. The tax was imposed on an entire village, the number of villages was ascertained with mandarin assistance, and the notables were left with the task of dividing up and collecting the tax. The same system was used with the land tax, which varied according to the fruitfulness of the land. The advantages were obvious. Revenues were stable, and there was no need to set up a complicated and expensive tax administration within the villages. Critics, however, soon discovered the system's weaknesses. The villages were able to complicate ascertaining precisely how many persons lived there and how much land they farmed, and the individual peasants were able to block excessively arbitrary assessments. Fixing taxes once and for all, however, took no account of bad harvests and price fluctuations, nor did it prevent the notables from manipulating the system for their own benefit. The administration was not above squeezing the notables and threatening to use the *force indigène* to enforce tax collection.[17] Accordingly the notables often advanced tax moneys and then compensated themselves by measures such as claiming the entire commons for their use. Pierre Gourou estimated that in 1936 the Tonkinese rice-farming peasant had to pay 12 percent of his modest income in taxes, or considerably more than in precolonial times.[18]

More burdensome yet, however, were the indirect imposts paid the alcohol, salt, and opium monopolies.[19] The admirals had sold the opium trade as a concession to the Chinese, but Doumer reclaimed it for the state. The latter bought opium and retailed it through concessionaires. Thus, instead of stopping opium consumption, the state had a stake in increasing it. Opium was easy to buy and made easier by such measures as peddling it in small packets as a comestible. Plantations provided a daily opium ration. France refused to sign international agreements prohibiting the opium trades. Although most of the opium was probably consumed by Chinese, it is not hard to see why the nationalist opposition was able to claim that the colonial power deliberately sought "to poison the Vietnamese people."

The alcohol monopoly was also evil in its effects. The Vietnamese population drank rice wine, particularly on festive occasions, and also needed it for its family shrines. Although most villages did some distilling, some specialized in it. The by-products were fed to the pigs. The French introduced deliveries at fixed prices and concluded contracts with concessionaires that obligated them to dispose of specified amounts and pay taxes based on these amounts. In 1903 the Société des Distilleries de l'Indochine was granted a monopoly over both production and sales. The administration, interested in maximizing revenues, thus pushed alcohol consumption by measures such as setting minimums for each province and offering premiums to village headmen who boosted intake. An important village industry went under and at the same time, the villagers perforce became moonshiners because religious tradition prescribed that ceremonial spirits had to be distilled from one's own rice. The administration's rice wine also had a considerably higher alcohol content than village rice wine. The result was a veritable orgy of seizures, house searches, and denunciations, the consequences of which the parliamentary rapporteur for the colonial budget for 1909, Adolphe Messigmy, spelled out. "The entire result of this merciless struggle on the part of a pitiless fisc against recalcitrant tributaries was to place on the administration the grave and terrifying responsibility for the violent and callous strategems employed to force this vexacious regime on the Annamites."[20] Many villages had collective punishments levied against them, and the guilty could be sentenced to forced labor. This system of repression and punishment, however, softened with time, and moonshining flourished during the interwar period. The monopoly nevertheless remained a grievance and in retrospect can hardly be judged anything but colonial exploitation in the interests of the administration, and one that gained the monopolists enormous profits.[21]

The same was true of the salt monopoly. After 1903 local salt producers were forced to hand over their salt to the administration which, after upping the prices several times over, then sold it to the populace. This *gabelle* hit the entire population and was in practice an indirect tax. Fishermen, who needed salt to preserve their catches, often lacked the necessary cash to buy it and thus saw their fish spoil. The traditional methods of production declined, unable to meet the competition of modern production. The French system somewhat resembled the system in British India, though the real burdens of the latter were much smaller, and was used in Vietnam as in India to mobilize the masses against the colonial power.

The tax burdens borne by the natives contrasted strikingly with the modest taxes imposed on the French. This injustice was not peculiarly French, but was a general characteristic of colonial systems of rule. Europeans paid an employment tax and most of the customs duties on consumer goods, but neither these nor any other taxes bore any just relationship to the size of their incomes. In 1926 the governor-general, Alexandre Varenne, tried to reform "our archaic fiscal system" as he called it, a system which burdened millionaire and petty employee, rich Vietnamese landlord and poor peasant, at about the same real level. The conseil colonial of Cochinchina, however, opposed Varenne's reforms to a man. He was certainly justified in asking, "is it really asking too much of Europeans and natives that they consent to sacrifice a hundredth of their income?"[22] In 1930 Europeans paid on average ten piasters, or three-tenths of one percent of their income, in direct taxes.[23] A reform was not undertaken until 1939.[24]

ECONOMY

Although the statistics are a bit shaky, the population of Vietnam apparently rose from about 10 million in 1878 to 17 million in 1913 and 23 million in 1937. The number of French also increased, from 23,000 in 1913 to 42,000 in 1939, 4,800 of whom were officials. The situation is thus to be compared with the Netherlands Indies rather than British India. Like the Indies, Vietnam also had a sizable Chinese minority, about 350,000 in 1930, which was mainly engaged in commerce.[25]

Population density was roughly thirty persons per square kilometer, compared with seventy-five in France. This average does not, however, mean much, because Vietnamese demography (like Indonesian, with densely populated Java) is characterized by great regional differences. In 1937, 19 of the 23 million Vietnamese were concentrated in one-seventh of the country's area. In the Tonkin delta 7.2 million lived on 15,000 square kilometers. On the Annamite plain and in central and western Cochinchina, another 4.2 million lived on 36,000 square kilometers. The population density in the Tonkin delta reached the very high figure of 480 per square kilometer, higher than Java (315) and very much higher than highly industrialized urban Belgium (270). In individual provinces, particularly along the Red River, the figure climbed to 600 to 1,000 persons per square kilometer. Similar figures prevailed in the paddy regions of Annam, whereas Cochinchina with 100 persons per square kilometer was appreciably less densely populated. By contrast, the population outside the rice baskets was only about ten per kilometer. The differences are partly explained by the character of the land. The rice-farming Annamites settled mainly in the deltas and left the heavily wooded highlands and mountains to the non-Annamite tribes. The deltas were also largely malaria free, and the bordering hills were not, a surprising fact that in the traditional way of looking at things was attributed to the "evil spirits" of the hills. Also of some importance was the historical factor that northerners had settled Cochinchina relatively recently and it was therefore less densely populated.[26]

The high population density of Tonkin made it appear in colonial times as a labor reservoir, particularly since the plantations in the south had great need of labor. The idea was to interest the Annamite peasant in settling the regions bordering the delta and in the south. The success of such efforts was modest. The Annamite was too strongly bound to his village and his ancestors to migrate in large numbers. Even plantation workers returned to their villages if at all possible. The population increase in any case totally nullified all hopes of reducing the population density in the Tonkin delta by resettlement. The birth rate was 35 per 1,000, the result of early marriages, polygamy, and an intense desire for heirs. Despite the high mortality of the 1930s, the population hence increased at the rate of 13 per 1,000 (in contrast to Japan's 12).[27] The administration had already been admonished about the need for birth control and necessity of propaganda for it if the living standard of the masses was to be raised or indeed maintained.

The historical differences between Tonkin and Cochinchina were reflected in the agrarian structure.[28] Although Tonkinese rice paddies only amounted to a fraction of the Tonkin area, they constituted five-sixths of the land actually cultivated. Rice was, and is, the main foodstuff, and the working of the rice fields determined the tempo of village life. In thickly populated Tonkin delta, rice paddy bordered rice paddy, and only at the outskirts of the village were a few vegetables planted. Although the king was the ultimate landholder in precolonial times, and though land could not, per se, be alienated, in practice each family had rights of ownership in addition to rights to common land. Division of holdings among heirs had since the fifteenth century resulted in an unbelievable Balkanization of plots. Given the extraordinary population density, the result was a very high percentage of very small holders: 586,000 families, or 61 percent, held less than one *mau* (.36 hectares) and 869,000 held less than five mau (1.8 hectares). Since a hectare of average quality would hardly support one family, a great part of the peasantry was thus forced to work for neighbors and, with the exception of a short period immediately after the harvest, was chronically undernourished. Small holdings constituted 36.6 percent of the area in rice and medium holdings (5 to 10 mau) about 26.6 percent. Another 20,000 peasants with more than 10 mau, the *grands propriétaires*, held 16.6 percent of the arable.[29] Large holdings, and to some extent medium as well, were farmed by tenants and day laborers. Truly large holdings seem hardly to have existed, although it is extremely difficult to determine the effective size of family holdings because such holdings might be parcelled out among several villages. In spite of this extreme partitioning, a sizeable section of the population, in some provinces one-half, had no land at all and could at best use the relatively large commons (from one-fifth to one-third of the total land). Basically, however, it was a rural proletariat. The petty holdings had indebtedness latent within them for familiar reasons. If food supplies ran out, money was borrowed against the next harvest. Festivals, marriages, and gambling, important in Vietnam, tempted peasants to assume debt, with the better-off peasants taking on the most. Unrepayable debts forced them to sell land, which did not necessarily prevent the peasant from continuing to work the land as a tenant though still entered in the cadastres as the owner. In colonial times the tendency toward large holdings increased, both because of population pressures and a money economy but also because as in India, French law protected creditors.[30]

The colonial administration expended considerable effort in levee and canal building, continuing the age-old tradition of corvée performed by the villagers. It did so not to reclaim new land but to regulate irrigation and block catastrophies; the last great flood was in 1926. Yields were increased and internal communication improved. An agricultural advisory service (Office du Riz, 1929-1931) was established but accomplished relatively little. The land itself was good, two rice harvests a year being possible in Tonkin. Too many varieties of rice were grown, however, and the quality of the seed was poor.

The administration encouraged diversification, particularly into corn, but since rice was about all the Vietnamese ate, the arable devoted to rice had to be continually increased. Thus the monocultural aspects of Vietnam agriculture increased despite efforts to oppose it. Development, indeed, was retrograde. The amount of common decreased, cultivation was extended into less suitable land, the land was overworked and overpartitioned, fertilizer and modern implements were lacking, land prices were high, wages miserable, and much of the population underemployed for the better part of the year. Nourishment was insufficient,[31] and exports possible at most only during good years.[32] The mass of the population remained locked in a subsistence economy, "at the very limits of dearth and misery," as Gourou put it, and had little extra money for additional food and consumer goods.[33] Although the French owned land in Tonkin, the blame for this deterioration can hardly be laid at the door of the colonial power.

The situation in coastal areas of Annam was roughly the same as that in Tonkin. Cochinchina differed significantly, however, particularly in the southwest, which was more thinly settled than the Red River delta. Even in precolonial times the settlement of this area had been the aim of Vietnamese colonial policy, and colonial villages had been established on the march south. The French continued these settlement efforts, proffering enormous land grants under the terms of French real property law. The flight of the population during the first phases of French conquest provided the initial opportunity for these concessions. The French were already building canals in the admirals' time, though at first mainly to assist in the military subjugation of the inaccessible Mekong region. In the following years a system of main and feeder canals several thousand kilometers in extent was created. It controlled the flow of water during the dry season and opened new land for rice cultivation. The canals also permitted shipment of rice to the Chinese-controlled rice mills of Cholon, a Saigon suburb. The rice area of Cochinchina increased from 522,000 hectares in 1870 to 1.2 million in 1900 and 2.2 million in 1936.[34] In the southwest alone, the area increased from 52,000 hectares in 1869 to 1.1 million in 1929.[35]

In contrast to Tonkin, however, with its splintered holdings, the French system resulted in the domination of large holders. Forty-five percent of the rice area was in holdings of more than 50 hectares, and some exceeded 1,000 hectares. Forty-two percent of holdings were between 5 and 50 hectares, and only 12.5 percent were small holdings of under 5 hectares. There were only 225,000 landholders, while over a million peasants had no land. In one province of the southwest, 7.2 percent of landholders controlled 65.5 percent of the rice fields, and in another 559 large landholders controlled 113,755 hectares, leaving 10,919 peasants to manage on 79,743 hectares.[36] In addition to French concessionaires, a Vietnamese class of large holders, some mandarin in origin, who had been able to profit from the colonial situation, developed. In 1931 there were some 6,300 Vietnamese large holders.[37] They mostly lived in Saigon or in the provincial towns and farmed their land with tenants (*tâdien*).[38] These tenants got five to ten hectares, buffalos, seed, and credit, in return for half the harvest (or in practice mostly about 70 percent). In most cases, tenants had no chance to escape these burdens, amounting to debt slavery, or to become landowners. "Despite his hard work, which every year increases the amount of arable and provides magnificent rice exports, the lot of the Cochinchinese peasant remains a miserable one."[39]

It was indeed true that the expansion of the cultivated area in Cochinchina enabled Vietnam to become an important rice exporter. Rice exports rose from about 800,000 tons in 1900 to 1.9 million in 1931, or some 65 percent of total exports.[40] These imposing figures, however, cannot conceal the fact that, as elsewhere, the mass of the population profited very little from them and, exploited by landowners and moneylenders (including Indian Chettyars), continued to lead a desperate existence. What often made things even worse was that the Vietnamese landowner was often an official who sat in the provincial council and was represented in the conseil. In the southwest, the latifundia had largely escaped administrative control, being themselves responsible for taxes and thus having a quasi-feudal character. It was pointless for a Vietnamese tenant to sue a landowner. No less a man than Inspector General Yves Henry, a respected expert, characterized the situation clearly enough in 1936:

> Our so-called "client policy" in Cochinchina was thought an adroit way to establish our rule through attaching a favored minority to us. This minority received the best land, and credit and influence as well. Our policy failed to consider any alternative to large-scale colonization through rice farming. The result has been the creation of a plutocracy of large and medium holders who control eighty percent of the paddy and face a proletarian mass living on pitiful salaries or subject to the exactions of usurer and landlord.[41]

The class structure in Cochinchina developed, in fact, along the following lines. On top was a narrow class of absentee landlords, who lived from rents and whose Western-educated sons had access to the professions. Their life-style resembled that of the French. A Vietnamese entrepreneur class was only beginning to develop, because the Chinese monopolized milling and marketing. The landlord class was politically represented by Bui Quang Chieu's Parti Constitutionaliste (see p. 215 below). The party demanded reforms of the colonial power, but it generally defended the existing social order.[42] The peasant masses were in fact beginning to stir, as both the disturbances of 1930-1931 and the success of new sects and the gradual progress of the Communist party showed.

Indebtedness was particularly serious in Cochinchina.[43] In 1937 a colonial official described the situation in one province:

> There is no one who is neither borrower nor lender. The *tadiên* borrows from his landlord, and the latter, in case of need, from a greater capitalist. The coolie gets credit from his straw boss, and the latter gets it from his employer. The fisherman borrows from the fishery concessionaire, and the retailer from the wholesaler. Those in more independent occupations, such as artisans and functionaries, contract debts with the local Chinese merchant or a usurer.[44]

The latter was often an Indian Chettyar, who might ask as much as 80 percent interest every three months and was not above cheating small borrowers in other ways. By 1936 a quarter of the rice fields were said to be in Chettyar hands.[45]

The colonial administration made some attempts to fight usury. Before 1914 the first Sociétés Indigènes de Crédit Mutuel were established, backed by the Banque d'Indochine. Members with at least one hectare of arable could borrow a maximum of 8,000 piasters at 8 percent interest. The system was expanded after 1918 but with questionable success. The rather limited credits went to peasants with middle and large holdings, who then often re-lent them at usurious rates. In 1926 a law passed which was meant to end corporal punishment for debtors. In 1927 Governor-General Alexandre Varenne created the Crédit Populaire Agricole, in imitation of Dutch Javanese models. He was, however, unable to eliminate Chinese and Indian usurers. Gourou was thus able to write of *échec complet*.[46] The Popular Front administration finally tried to set limits on interest rates and establish some sort of protection for tenants.

In the years of rising rice prices when capital flowed in from France, the result was excessively easy money that tempted even peasants with middle and large holdings to borrow. In 1934 the rice plantations carried a debt of 65 million piasters. During the depression, the government was forced to intervene to prevent the entire credit structure from collapsing and save proprietors from bankruptcy. In short, efforts to rescue Cochinchinese tenants and small holders from the grips of their creditors failed; they remained bound in the chronic indebtedness that prevented their gaining anything of personal value from the export economy.

In colonial circles people generally understood, a few isolated voices notwithstanding, that Indochina could never become either a settlement colony like Australia or a new Algeria, but was to be seen as a colony for exploitation, like British India. In France, however, colonial policy was always closely linked with *colonisation*. Thus from the very outset land concessions were awarded French settlers and not only for intensive cultivation. Doumer, indeed, pointing out the colonists' lack of capital, limited administrative assistance; it was better, he said, "to be governor of a population of large farmers."[47] Others, like Varenne, wanted to assist the colonization of small and middling farmers.[48] Except for the Annamite settlement zones, new land seemed to be available, both in Cochinchina and the north. Thus, after the conquest of northern Tonkin, delta land abandoned by its owners during the resistance was given settlers, who were often ex-soldiers; France had simply declared "empty" land to be state domain and thus at its disposal. When the original inhabitants returned, they found their lands occupied. Disputes also occurred with the cattle-farming upland tribes. French landownership was, however, concentrated in the south. Frenchmen owned 610,000 hectares in Cochinchina and "only" 110,000 hectares in Tonkin.[49] Besides the great rice plantations, especially concentrated in the western provinces of Cochinchina, 250,000 hectares of which were in French hands, coffee and tea plantations were also established. They never assumed very much importance, however.[50]

Rubber plantations were quite another matter.[51] Although the first plantations were laid out in the late 1890s, the first 298 tons of rubber were not shipped out until 1915. After World War I, a series of factors created a speculative boom. The first was auto industry demand, the second, the Stevenson Plan of 1922, which kept prices artificially high, and the last was the fall of the French franc in 1926. Between 1925 and 1929 alone, 700 million francs were invested in rubber plantations, mainly in the famous *terres rouges* north of Saigon. In Cochinchina, the plantations amounted to 29,000 hectares in 1921 and 97,000 by 1934. Exports rose to 36,000 tons by 1936. Although at first investment mainly came from French businessmen and officials in Saigon, the major rubber companies, including the Société Financière des Caoutchoucs, were the great investors of the 1920s. Twenty-seven corporations owned 65 percent of the plantations, four of which exceeded 5,000 hectares. Land concessions were handed out gratis or for purely nominal amounts. Governor-General Varenne criticized this system in 1927 because it left the bureaucracy with very little control. He attempted to strengthen government control by requiring prospective concessionaires to apply for both preliminary and final concessions, by limiting grants to a maximum of 6,000 hectares, and by government participation in management.[52] During the depression, prices utterly collapsed. Speculative overinvestment and, in some cases, overspending on luxuries left the plantations on the verge of bankruptcy. The planter organizations called for state aid, and received it in the form of tax relief, customs aid, subsidies, and mortgage guarantees. The enclave character of such plantations ought not to be overemphasized, as they only then received tax exemption.

Workers were needed for these rice and rubber agribusinesses. There was certainly no lack of manpower. But in Indochina as elsewhere the problem was how to get people to work for wages outside their own villages. The manpower problem was a continuing concern to the administration and also occasioned sharp criticisms of the colonial system of rule. For work in the localities it was easy enough to tie into the traditional work obligations imposed on the villages. That worked well for maintaining roads and levies; the old corvée was simply interpreted by the administration as a tax. In the 1880s the number of annual work days was fixed, in Cochinchina at five in 1881 and in Tonkin at forty-eight in 1886, and later thirty, the obligation for twenty of which could be met in money.[53] Actual forced labor was a more serious matter. The French resorted to it frequently in the early days, using thousands of laborers as porters during pacification and as railway construction workers during the Doumer era. Badly fed and housed, their mortality was high.[54] France failed to sign the international agreement of 1930 for the abolition of forced labor in the colonies.

Chinese and Javanese coolies were already being "imported" as early as 1900 for work on the Cochinchinese rice plantations, while local *main d'oeuvre* had been granted freedom from taxes in 1896.[55] But control measures were also tightened up, work books being introduced in 1899 because the colons demanded more severe punishments for decamping.

The rapid expansion of Cochinchinese rice farming and, after World War I, of the rubber plantations resulted in a rather unseemly recruiting campaign in the most densely populated areas in Tonkin. In 1927 there were an estimated 27,000 coolies in the south. The number from the north had risen from 3,684 in 1925 to 18,000 in 1927. Most were Tonkinese contract workers who had agreed to remain three years on a given plantation. Breach of contract became a matter for the courts. Both recruitment and working conditions revealed the typical abuses. Recruiters wooed their victims with promises and booze, did not have them medically examined for fitness, and shipped them south packed in like sardines. On the plantations, inadequate food, quarters, and medical care went with long hard days in the fields at starvation wages, which were sometimes withheld. Punishments notwithstanding, the desertion rate was naturally high, as was mortality. For the plantations it was fifty-four per thousand, though for the Cochinchinese population as a whole it was only twenty-three; and the victims were men in the prime of life.[56] Tonkinese workers were also recruited for New Caledonia with similar methods and results.

Journalists brought these methods of recruitment and exploitation to a wider metropolitan public. Their revelations, along with André Gide's Congo report, encouraged anticolonial agitation and led the administration to bring recruitment and working conditions under its control.[57] Varenne established the Inspection Générale du Travail in 1927, state control was imposed on recruiting in 1930, contracts were redrafted and made more specific, and plantations were supposed to be inspected. In 1933 additional regulations laid down working conditions for "free labor," mainly concerning working hours and female and child labor, although no provisions were made for accidents and sickness. The Popular Front government in France issued decrees regulating the latter only in 1936. The demands of the Indochinese Congress and a wave of strikes in November 1936 led on 30 December to another decree, the *Code du Travail*, which, linking up with metropolitan legislation, contained additional guarantees, among them two-week vacations and workmen's compensation. Bernard Fall has pointed out that these measures put France ahead of countries like Japan, which placed no restrictions whatever on hours of male employment, and India, which had a twelve-hour day for both men and women. Young works inspectors saw to it that the law was obeyed.[58] Trade unions remained illegal even under the Popular Front, but they organized clandestinely anyway and staged strikes that forced employers to grant significant concessions.[59]

In the nonagrarian area, the French devoted their initial attentions to railways. "The railway question in the entire Far East is today the first order of business," wrote Paul Doumer, whose name is inseparably bound up with the construction of the Vietnamese railway network.[60] His administrative and financial reforms were in no small measure intended to make possible the borrowing for a modern transport system. Military and political considerations, vague hopes of intracolonial exchange between north and south, and a rising fervor for improvement made a trans-Indochina railway between Hanoi and Saigon seem vitally necessary. The covert aim of a thrust toward South China, in order to assure France its due place when the Middle Kingdom was opened up, also played its part. It was, indeed, first intended to extend the Hanoi-Langson line as far as the Chinese province of Kwangsi, the Chinese granting a Franco-Belgian consortium its consent for this in 1897. Under Doumer, however, interest shifted to Yunnan; a Lyon Chamber of Commerce mission, which had government support, prepared the way. French capital was available. One of the first state-guaranteed loans for eighty million francs was oversubscribed twenty-eight times in 1898. Two years later, Doumer received parliamentary assent to a 200 million franc loan based on Indochinese rather than metropolitan credit worthiness. The argument that the credit would in good part return to the metropolis in the form of industrial orders for rails, bridges, and locomotives made the deputies' decision easier.[61]

By 1914, 1,600 kilometers of railway had been built in Indochina and 464 in China, the latter in the face of great technical difficulties. In 1902 the famous Doumer Bridge over the Red River, 1,680 meters (5,512 feet) long, was opened. Railway construction stagnated in the years after World War I, however, the trans-Indochina railroad opening only in 1936. The building of the 2,400-kilometer-long railway network of Indochina ate up one-quarter of the total investment for public works for the period 1900-1930.[62] Although France was proud of its performance, its forced-draft railway construction was violently criticized. The critics claimed it took a disproportionate amount of revenue and too early on burdened the budget with heavy amortization payments and required heavy taxation of the people without conferring on them corresponding advantages. Paul Bernard pointed out in 1934 that astonishingly little freight was carried, in part because the line paralleled the *route mandarine* and in part because exports, such as rice, corn, and coal, mostly departed by sea. Truck transport was also beginning to compete with railways in the interwar period.[63] As in other colonies, the building and operation of the railways failed to encourage other industrial development.

The question of whether industries should be developed in Indochina was one that exercised the administration and metropolitan Frenchmen interested in Vietnam from the beginning, and particularly because of its impact on customs policy. The aim of the expansion toward Tonkin between 1880 and 1885 was to provide French industry additional secure markets. It was expressly emphasized that Indochina was to be only a colonial complement to the French economy and was not to become a competing economic power. Characteristically, it was Doumer who in his lapidary manner set the course for the future: "The establishment of industries is thus to be encouraged only to the extent that they feed the industries of metropolitan France. The latter ought to be abetted, rather than ruined, by the former. In other words, colonial industry is to be created to produce only what French industry cannot produce. . . ."[64] Customs legislation reserved colonial consumer goods imports to the greatest degree possible for the metropolis. In 1892, the free-trade policy until then in force in Cochinchina was abandoned and all of Indochina brought into line with prevailing French policy. Non-French imports paid duties at metropolitan rates, whereas goods from France and other French colonies were largely duty free. In practice, these provisos one-sidedly benefited the metropolis, because raw materials imported into France were either duty free or taxed at very low rates.[65] France's share in Indochinese imports rose after 1892, but French industry made little effort to meet colonial needs despite non-French imports being roughly 15 percent dearer. The Vietnamese paid the piper, particularly since the non-French imports were cheap Asian products and transport costs made French goods more expensive.[66] In the following period, the colonial administration pointed out the exigencies of Indochina's geographic situation and the especial importance of Chinese and Japanese imports and exports. The administration asked for special customs treatment amounting to customs autonomy but without success. Although the new customs law of 1928 would have permitted such autonomy, special regulations made protection even stronger by protecting Vietnamese industries against cheap Chinese and Japanese imports, naturally at the cost of the masses. Such was the dilemma of colonial industrialization.

French capital naturally flowed mainly into mining and manufacturing based on colonial raw materials. The Fuchs Report of 1882 pointed out the presence of coal in the Quang Yen Basin of northeastern Tonkin.[67] Concessions were granted first by Hué, then by the French administration. Production had already reached 500,000 tons by 1913 and reached 2.3 million tons in the record year of 1937. The Charbonnages du Tonking mined 71 percent of this coal and the Charbonnages du Dong Trieu another 21 percent.[68] Domestic consumption was relatively low, the bulk of exports going to Japan. Worker productivity was low (a quarter that in Japan) despite favorable mining conditions, either because of Vietnamese lack of adaptability and poor physique or because of relative lack of mechanization. Such was also true of zinc and tin mining. The work force in mining was 49,200 in 1937. The working conditions typical of early industrialization (with women and children working underground) seem to have improved in the 1930s. The management and technical cadres were almost entirely French, with some Chinese at the middle levels.

The numerous Chinese-operated rice mills in Saigon-Cholon and the distilleries franchises have already been mentioned. There were in addition sugar mills, cement works, glass factories, sawmills, and paper factories. An early cotton mill, established in 1894 in Hanoi, represented the beginning of the textile industry, which included the Société Cotonnière de l'Indochine, founded in 1913. By 1938, the latter owned several mills employing roughly 10,000 workers. Raw cotton was imported and the yarn worked up in good part by traditional cottage methods, but such production was stagnating and losing importance. Not counting mining, 86,000 worked in industry in 1929. Factories were concentrated in two areas, Saigon-Cholon and rather more in Haiphong, a colonial foundation which became an important port and industrial city.[69]

In the interwar period there was some discussion of whether industrialization was necessary at all and whether it should, indeed, be encouraged. In response to a government questionnaire, the Hanoi chamber of commerce stated that labor-intensive petty industry should be encouraged and that Vietnamese workers should be trained in France, in order to be able to meet Japanese competition in the East Asian market. They thought an Industry Department in Tonkin might serve these ends.[70] When, however, established French interests in Vietnam, to say nothing of those of the metropolis, were at stake, and competition with the metropolis even appeared within the realm of possibility, further industrialization was refused. The Union Coloniale, an interest group comprising industries and commercial houses in the colonial trade, was a particularly tenacious opponent of Vietnamese industrialization.[71] Even a man like Marius Moutet, the socialist colonial minister of the Popular Front government, curiously held that the "industrialization of Indochina" was "sufficiently advanced." He also pointed out that cheap Vietnamese labor might tempt French industrialists to shift their production to Indochina, and noted the political consequences of piling up masses of proletarians in the cities.[72]

However, Paul Bernard, director of a colonial financing company, and Grégoire Khérian, an economist at the University of Hanoi, both experts on the Vietnamese economy, were energetic advocates of industrialization.[73] They pointed out the increasing difficulty of exporting farm products and the increasing population pressures. In fact, during the world economic crisis, the French share of Indochinese foreign trade increased.[74] China's buying power had fallen, Japan and the Philippines were covering their own rice needs, and coal exports had stagnated. At the same time, however, French agricultural interests were agitating energetically and successfully against colonial exports of rice and corn, which supposedly competed with their own grain. Building a colonial economy entirely on the export of food and mining products was thus a dubious proposition. As things stood, Bernard asserted, one "produced to sell and not to buy. But the buyers have all stolen away. The abundance of goods signifies misery." Khérian for his part stated that Indochina's export surplus had to be seen, not as a sign of prosperity, but as an "indication of the primitive state of its economy," inasmuch as interest, service charges, and profits flowed back to the metropolis. What was needed, he thought, was to increase the buying power of the population, while simultaneously reducing underemployment in Tonkin. That could not be done by agriculture alone, however great its exertions, but required industrialization. Both Bernard and Khérian pointed to the example of Japan which, despite its lack of raw materials, had succeeded in coping with an enormous increase in population by industrialization and had also raised national income by a colossal amount. Robequain argued along similar lines in 1939, criticizing the fact that Indochina did not even produce oil and soap from its own copra.[75] None of them said much about how the state was supposed to help; Bernard pleaded for free trade, Robequain for customs protection.

VIETNAMESE NATIONALISM

The French administration was undecided about what to do about the traditional methods of education and the sinicized examination system, and how the educational system might best be made to serve its system of colonial rule.[76] The mandarinate had withheld its collaboration, especially in Cochinchina, and the educated classes remained in good part in opposition. Nevertheless, in the beginning, the French believed themselves dependent on the old ruling class and very much hesitated to decree a new, French-oriented school system.[77] Some reforms were introduced, including the *quoc-ngu* system of writing Vietnamese. Otherwise, the old school system was forced onto the defensive, finally being abolished between 1915 and 1919. In the meanwhile, the so-called Franco-Annamite school system was gradually developing. What this amounted to was a curriculum for the Vietnamese with instruction in both Vietnamese and French. It aimed at producing the trained personnel necessary for the administration and the economy and, more generally, at establishing French cultural influence, whether by assimilation or association. Both Paul Bert and Paul Beau, governor-general from 1902 to 1907, did their best for education. Beau established a "Council for Improving the Education of the Natives" and in 1907 founded a university but it had already closed by 1910. In 1913, 50,000 students were said to be enrolled in village schools. Whether the opportunity for rudimentary education in the villages initially declined under colonial rule because of, among other things, higher taxes, seems to be an open question.

Governor-General Albert Sarraut laid the basis for the school system of the interwar period. In the lowest grades of the village schools, instruction was exclusively in Vietnamese (after 1924). Students progressed to middle and high schools in the main district towns and increasingly employed French as they moved upward. Upon graduation from a Franco-Annamite lycée, one received a *baccalauréat local*, which after 1930 was held equivalent to the French *baccaulauréat*. The number of elementary pupils rose from 62,000 in 1924 to 400,000 in 1937, not all that many for a population of 23 million. The educational pyramid also narrowed very rapidly toward the top. In 1931 there were actually only two lycées, one in Hanoi and one in Saigon. In addition, *écoles normales* trained teachers, having 7,734 students in 1935, and a number of vocational schools trained artisans and lower-level technical employees. The University of Hanoi was reopened in 1919, and had departments for medicine, veterinary medicine, law, and agriculture, among others. Its diplomas were never made equivalent to those of French universities, however. Doctors, veterinarians, and agronomists from Hanoi thus remained assistants, or merely a higher grade of auxiliary personnel. This was a source of grievance for the newly educated class. The French lycées in Saigon, Hanoi, and Dalat were, to be sure, open to Vietnamese, who constituted half the student body, and a considerable number successfully completed studies at French universities. In 1931 a *maison d'Indochine* was founded at the Cité Universitaire in Paris. But the dual character of the colonial educational system was clear enough. It permitted only a small group, at a great financial sacrifice, to provide their sons with university educations.

An academic proletariat formed nevertheless. Its situation was worsened by discriminatory hiring and remuneration practices.[78] The question of localization occupied the colonial administration almost from the beginning. Paul Bert and Paul Beau promised the Vietnamese access to "public office on an equal basis" with French officials, but these promises were not kept. A few graduates from the "great families," among them some *polytechniciens*, were taken into the bureaucracy around the turn of the century, but only in cases where they or their fathers had become naturalized French citizens and thus possessed French civil rights. Lack of citizenship remained the great obstacle down to 1942 and meant the Vietnamese had to settle for lower-level positions. The questions remained of what to do with Vietnamese who had attended middle or vocational schools in Vietnam, or indeed French universities, but lacked French citizenship and were not ready to become naturalized. Governor Maurice Long (1920-1922) thought separate, parallel corps of officials (*cadrés complementaires* and *cadrés lateraux*) were the answer. These were gradually to displace the French from all but the key positions. The idea was a failure because the separation, when combined with bad pay, appeared as discrimination. Varenne undertook the bold step in 1926 of opening the French cadre to the nonnaturalized, but this encouraged violent resistance from the Indochinese French, particularly the minor officials. In 1935 the governor-general asserted boldly that such an opening up of administrative careers to the Vietnamese would necessarily lead to the exclusion of French officials and was thus "intolerable."[79] His own *cadrés de remplacements* amounted to the same thing, but underlined the separation by combining equal educational qualifications with extreme pay differentials.[80] These abortive efforts compromised France's modest efforts at localization and nullified attempts to satisfy the new, educated elite politically by opening civil service jobs to it. The discrimination in pay was especially serious because the French, in contrast to the British, filled civil positions down to the very lowest levels with Europeans.[81] These slights and discriminations against the Vietnamese, quite aside from poor-white presumptuousness and hatred of the natives, were bound to be considered an especial grievance in a country where the official had always enjoyed the highest regard and where loss of face was perceived as particularly mortifying and frustrating.[82]

In 1900 Vietnam could be regarded as "pacified." Primary and post-primary resistance had been smashed, although a few "bands" still gave the administration some worries. There is little doubt that a good part of the population, whose horizons hardly extended beyond the village walls and who had suffered severely at the hands of both guerrillas and the pacification forces, was glad enough to see peace. "They were ready to accept the new ruling order, though passively rather than actively. They mistrusted their new rulers, and were separated from them by the abyss of the colonial situation." Part of the mandarinate was willing to collaborate and took the posts the colonial power offered them.

Other mandarins retreated to the villages. The beginning of "improvements," such as the expanding rice culture of Cochinchina and the new school system, permitted the rise of a new middle class, which was integrated into the colonial economic system and profited from it. This class was also confronted with a whole new world of external stimuli, ranging from French culture and the "ideas of 1789," to the revolutionary-national movements then beginning everywhere in Asia and best symbolized by the military, political, and economic rise of Japan.

Small elite reform groups soon began to form. They no longer looked backwards toward restoring the traditional order, but accepted modernization and postulated an inner renewal of the Confucian monarchy. Their most important spokesman was Phan Boi Chau, a scholar and cofounder of the reform organization, Viet Nam Duy Tan Hoi, in 1906. Chau resided for a time in Japan, his writings being smuggled into Indochina. He acquired considerable influence. A pretender to the imperial Vietnamese throne was smuggled out to Japan and money provided for students to visit him there.[83] Although the group aimed at an armed rising of the people, it had to settle for a few terrorist acts. In addition to Phan Boi Chau, Phan Chau Trinh was an early figure of some importance. Opposing mandarinate and monarchy, he called upon his countrymen, in a widely noted 1906 statement, to accept the French protectorate, but without supporting the colonial power. He also urged them to take the education of the masses in hand and to reduce tax burdens.[84] It was characteristic of the attitudes of this new elite that they sought to encourage specific kinds of economic enterprise (such as trade associations, silk factories, hotels, and textile mills), following either Japanese models or the influences of the Indian Swadeshi movement.

As a result of the arrest of three mandarins, agrarian disturbances broke out in central Annam in 1908. Thousands of peasants protested against high taxes, the corvée, the hated system of monopolies, and mandarin corruption. Shortly thereafter a plot to poison the Hué garrison was uncovered. The colonial power responded with repression. Hundreds were arrested and condemned, among them Trinh, although he had taken no direct part in the rising. Sentenced to life imprisonment, he was released in 1911 and went into exile in France. Chau fled to Japan. A debate in the French Parlement, in which Maurice Violette and Jean Jaurès participated, combined with criticism from the Ligue des Droits de l'Homme and the *Revue Indigène* led in 1911 to the appointment of the radical-socialist Albert Sarraut as governor-general and to modest reforms. Torture was abolished, amnesties were granted, and the Tonkin Chambre Consultative was expanded into a Chambre des Représentants du Peuple.

During World War I, France was able to withdraw nearly all its troops from Indochina, while simultaneously employing more than 100,000 Vietnamese soldiers and workers in the metropolis. In 1916, nevertheless, not only did the inmates of one prison rebel, but several rebellionlike attempts were made to storm other prisons and release their inmates. Fifty-one persons were hanged. In May of the same year, the Viet Nam Duy Tan Hoi attempted to kidnap the young emperor and start a revolt. The undertaking was poorly prepared, however, and failed. The emperor was banished to the island of Réunion. "It was the final defeat for the last of the mandarins."[85]

The end of the war, Wilsonian ideals of self-determination, and the Russian revolution combined to usher in a new phase in the nationalist movement, in Indochina as elsewhere. The principal supporters of this movement were the national bourgeoisie on the one hand and a small but increasingly significant proletariat on the other. Sarraut, named governor-general again from 1917 to 1919, seemed inclined to inaugurate a liberal era: the University of Hanoi was reopened in 1917, the examination system abolished, and expansion of the representative bodies proclaimed. On 27 April 1919, Sarraut declared:

> What has to be done is grant those whom I call native citizens a significant extension of political rights in their native cities. Let me put it more clearly still: native representation in existing local assemblies must be augmented, native representation must be created in those assemblies where it does not yet exist, and the native electorate which choses its own representatives must be enlarged.[86]

In 1917 the *Tribune Indigène*, later the *Tribune Indochinois*, began to appear, and the Parti Constitutionaliste was founded. It represented the new bourgeoisie and particularly those portions of the landlord class and educated elite that sought to work for reforms within the framework of the colonial regime.[87] Its leading man, Bui Quang Chieu (1873-1945) was French educated and had studied agronomy in Paris. He had become an official and had risen to the vice-directorship of the agriculture division. The party sought expansion of education (including the establishment of a full-scale university), justice reforms, easing of naturalization procedures, localization of the administration, and the creation of parliamentary institutions. In 1922 France reformed the Cochinchinese Conseil Colonial, increasing the number of native deputies to ten (out of twenty-four) and expanding the electorate from 1,500 to over 20,000. The new urban elite had thus won a forum for action and agitation. Its attempt to block the grant of a harbor monopoly to a French company failed, however, despite the support the Parti Constitutionaliste received from the lawyer Paul Monin and André Malraux's paper, *Indochine*, which attacked the machinations of Governor-General Gognacq in biting terms.[88]

The electoral victory of the Cartel des Gauches in 1924 seemed to presage a policy of genuine liberal reform. Governor-General Martial Henry Merlin, who had earned the hatred of educated Vietnamese because of his policy of *education horizontal* and his opposition to the expansion of higher education, was replaced by the Socialist Alexandre Varenne. In November 1925 the new governor was given the "*cahiers* of Annamite wishes." It contained the demands of moderate bourgeois nationalists and could have been the basis for a broad-minded policy of reform.[89] Varenne issued a fairly general amnesty, liberalized publication by introducing the French press law of 1881 for French-language publications, took in hand the question of labor legislation, and, as already mentioned, attempted to open the civil service to nonnaturalized Vietnamese. A vehement campaign which sank to slander and libel soon forced the "Communist" Varenne onto the defensive, however. The Parti Constitutionaliste succeeded in electing its ten candidates to the Conseil Colonial in 1926, and Bui Quang Chieu became its vice-president. On 24 March, Trinh's funeral ceremonies revealed the degree to which national expectations had been raised. Ten thousand followed Trinh's coffin in Saigon, and throughout Vietnam students and teachers from elementary to university level wore bands of mourning despite official prohibitions. Chieu went to Paris, where he was most courteously received, but he was unable to gain consent for a Cochinchinese constitution. An attempt to found a Parti Constitutionaliste in Tonkin also failed because of administration opposition, as did attempts to introduce elections for the Vietnamese representatives sitting in the Chambre des Représentants du Peuple, which in any case had only consultative powers. Varenné's fall in 1928 represented a clear victory for the colons and the metropolitan colonial interests. In this same year, however, a Grand Conseil des Intérêts Financiers et Economiques was established. The first body representing all Vietnam, it was composed of twenty-eight French citizens and twenty-three Vietnamese (after 1931 the number was equal) and had advisory powers in fiscal matters. The Grand Conseil never achieved any real significance, however, because it failed to provide those of the elite who were willing to cooperate with opportunities for political participation and a forum for hammering out the political will. The conseil was merely intended, as the name indicates, to represent the most important financial and economic interests, with the French naturally coming first. It thus differed considerably from the legislative councils of India and other British colonies, which were conceived of as being, at least potentially, parliaments. Even in the Volksraad of the Netherlands Indies, Europeans and Indonesians served in equal numbers and political discussions were possible.[90]

It is hard to disagree with those who feel that France missed an important chance between 1926 and 1930 to win the sizeable gallicized Vietnamese bourgeoisie represented by the Parti Constitutionaliste for an evolutionary policy. For a time at least, this group was disposed to collaborate.[91] Still, the fundamental differences between the French and British colonial systems should not be overlooked. Because French policy was not oriented toward the goal of self-government—Varenne's proclamation to that effect was not even backed by the socialists—and because the colons even in nonsettlement colonies were allowed effective representation of their interests, the expedient of transforming representative bodies by stages into parliaments was blocked from the outset. Instead of facilitating political activity within the boundaries of colonial rule, France followed in Vietnam, as elsewhere, a policy of depoliticization, the discussion of political questions being strictly forbidden. But that merely drove politicization into nonparliamentary channels. And the 1930s, indeed, were dominated by revolutionary groups and actions.

These revolutionary groups and sects drew their ideologies variously from the terrorism of the days before 1914, Sun Yat Sen's Chinese revolution, and the Russian revolution. Only two of them, however, ever achieved more than ephemeral significance. The first was the Vietnamese Nationalist Party (the Viet Nam Quoc Dan Dang, or VNQDD), a sort of Vietnamese Kuomintang founded in 1927. It was strongest in Tonkin and recruited its followers from the colonial petty bourgeoisie—lower officials, teachers, military men, and students. It made no particular effort to attract workers and peasants, however.[92] The latter groups, in contrast, were those whom the Communist party did seek to attract. The party had been formed in Hong Kong in 1930 by the merger of three communist-revolutionary groups. Its leader was Nguyen Ai Quoc, more familiarly known as Ho Chi Minh. Ho, born in 1890 in north Annam, after receiving both classical Chinese and French educations, had gone to sea. After living for a time in London, he had moved to Paris during World War I and eked out a living as a photographer. He first established political ties with French socialists, but in 1920 had forsaken them at the Congress of Tours for the French Communist party, in good part because the socialists refused to take sharp measures against colonialism. In 1922 he published the *Paria* as a spokesman for colonial revolutionaries living in Paris. He spent 1923-24 in Moscow and 1925 in Mikhail Borodin's entourage in Canton, where he was one of the cofounders of the Vietnamese Revolutionary Youth.[93]

The depression obviously provided a most favorable opportunity for revolutionary agitation. In 1930 the VNQDD, hard pressed by the splendidly organized Sûrété, went into action. On 10 February the garrison of the isolated outpost of Yen Bay in Tonkin mutinied. The action was a complete surprise. Several French officers and noncoms were murdered and the Red Flag hoisted. Although the mutiny was intended as the signal for a general uprising, the affair was badly organized and the mutiny soon quelled. The leaders were arrested, some being hanged, and the party largely eliminated as a political factor.

The Communists had at first accepted the specific social demands of the peasants and workers and placed their main organizational emphasis on their numerous fellow-traveller organizations. In February and March of 1930, the Communists organized strikes among the coolies on the rubber plantations (including those of Michelin)[94] and the cotton spinners of Nam-Dinh. Mass demonstrations on May Day 1930 were the signal for a peasant rising in north Annam. The success of the Chinese Communists in Kiangsi and Yunnan probably influenced the Vietnamese Communists, who like the Chinese sought to create revolutionary strong points in their own land. Government buildings and police stations were stormed, soviets (*Xo-Viets*) formed, land divided among peasants, people's courts set up, and notables, landowners, and turncoats liquidated. Similar but more poorly coordinated acts followed in Cochinchina. The French suppressed the rebellion quickly with the assistance of the Foreign Legion and the employment of aircraft, but disturbances lingered on for several months. Repressive measures against both rebel leaders and the peasants were extremely severe. Dozens were hanged. In May 1931 the party's central committee was arrested and in June Ho was seized in Hong Kong.[95]

A debate in the French Chambre lasting several days during June 1930 confronted both the government and the public with the "*troubles d'Indochine.*" The Right and colonial interests paraded the "Bolshevist peril," picturing the Communists as the wire-pullers behind the disturbances and demanding sharp repressive measures. The left-wing speakers, among them the later colonial minister, Marius Moutet, on the other hand criticized the form repression had taken, the bombarding of villages, in particular, and pointed out the critical social and economic situation in Indochina.[96] In November 1931 the colonial minister, Paul Raynaud, after travelling over all of Indochina, came out in favor of political modernization. On 9 September 1932 the young Bao Dai, European-educated and dressed, assumed the imperial throne. In the course of shaking up his ministry, he transferred several ministers, the thirty-two-year-old Catholic mandarin Ngo Dinh Diem receiving the interior ministry. Bao Dai clearly hoped to loosen colonial rule by modernizing and reactivating traditional forces, in order to achieve more freedom of movement in domestic matters in the spirit of a genuine protectorate. This reform attempt, however, came to nothing

The revolutionary nationalists reorganized, at first mainly in Cochinchina. In the May 1933 city council elections in Saigon, a Communist and a Trotskyite were elected with the support of the paper *La Lutte*. It was a clear sign that the revolutionary Left had been able to win a sizeable following in the petty bourgeoisie. It was also a sign that, despite the Sûreté and administrative pressure, the elections were not shams and fairly unrestricted politicking was possible. The electoral victory of the Popular Front in France on 3 May 1936 naturally awakened great expectations in Vietnam. The new governor-general, Jules Brévié, did in fact bring about a change in due course. The majority of political prisoners were released (though there were still six hundred in 1938), naturalization requirements liberalized, political parties permitted, taxes reduced, and, as mentioned above, metropolitan social- and worker-legislation introduced.

The Communist party, acting on Comintern directives, took an anti-imperialist Popular Front line, in the sense of working with bourgeois-nationalist groups. Under Communist leadership, Communist and bourgeois groups jointly prepared for a Congrès Indochinois, a sort of Estates-General for Indochina, in which cahiers containing concrete demands were to be presented. More than six hundred Comités d'Action, many of which were Communist cells, went to work. The moderates viewed this with mistrust, and it led the administration, under strong colon pressure, to forbid the congress. The Communist common front, on the other hand, became even stronger when the Japanese war against China began in 1937 and in June 1937 they broke with the Trotskyites. The latter succeeded in electing three deputies to the Conseil Colonial in the 1937 elections, against the opposition of the Constitutionalists and Communists. In Tonkin the Democratic Front achieved clear electoral victories in 1937 and 1938, despite the fact that in Tonkin the VNQDD had been able to reform itself, drawing in a considerable Vietnamese bourgeois following and penetrating even traditionally inclined mandarin circles. With the onset in 1938 of the crisis within the Popular Front in France, repression tightened in Vietnam. Numerous arrests were made, and in September 1939, after the Russo-German Pact of August 1939, the Communist and Trotskyite parties and their fellow-traveller organizations were dissolved.

The situation in the Vietnamese nationalist movement showed many similarities with other colonial areas at the outbreak of World War II. Before 1914 a few individuals had formulated demands for renewal and independence, and small isolated groups had committed terrorist acts. During the 1920s the first parties developed, and during the 1930s the depression created the preconditions for mass parties. Peasants were ready to listen to revolutionary appeals, and the intelligentsia was frustrated by the "colonial situation," in which both the government and the administration closed off its chances to participate in the rule of its own country. At the same time, strikes among the plantation and factory workers helped awaken the political consciousness of the proletariat. A religious movement such as Cao Dai, which in a singular but characteristic way combined elements of both Christianity and Buddhism and constituted itself a church—with 300,000 adherents in 1938—must be understood as a typical manifestation of political awakening and simultaneously as a separatist church. It permitted the socially and intellectually disoriented masses a way to articulate their social and religious needs short of either a return to a traditionalist restoration or total acceptance of the Western cultural heritage. The national liberation movement was, in fact, extraordinarily splintered, and not only in comparison with India. What is clear is that France never succeeded through institutional and political reforms in providing the bourgeois-intellectual leading class, which had been won over to French civilization, with sufficient opportunities for action and advancement to present itself as a plausible alternative to a social-revolutionary liberation movement under Communist leadership.

NOTES

1. Jean Chesneaux, *Contribution à l'Histoire de la Nation Vietnamienne* (Paris: Editions sociales, 1955); Le Thanh Khoi, *3000 Jahre Vietnam*; originally *Le Viet-nam, Histoire et Civilisation* (Paris: Editions de Minuit, 1955); Paul Isoart, *Le Phénomène National Vietnamien: de l'Indépendence Unitaire à l'Indépendence Fractionée* (Paris: Librarie Générale de Droit et Jurisprudence, 1961); Virginia M. Thompson, *French Indo-China* (New York: Octagon Books, 1932, 1968).

2. M. G. Cotter, "Towards a Social History of the Vietnamese Southward Movement," *JSEAH*, 9 (March 1968), speaks of a frontier society in the south, , meaning it was more open in terms of village and family structure than the north.

3. Paul Mus, "Das Dorf im politischen Leben Vietnams," in Albertini, *Moderne Kolonialgeschichte*.

4. I follow here the detailed account of Dieter Brötel, *Französischer Imperialismus in Vietnam: die koloniale Expansion und die Errichtung des Protektorates Annam-Tongking, 1880-1885* (Zurich, Freiburg i. Br.: Atlantis Verlag, 1971).

5. On the resistance, see Isoart, *Phénomène National*, 140f.; Truong Buu Lam, *Patterns of Vietnamese Response to Foreign Intervention* (New Haven: Celler Book Shop, 1967), 19f., 113f.; David G. Marr, *Vietnamese Anticolonialism, 1885-1925* (Berkeley: University of California Press, 1971), ch. 3, "The Con Vuong Movement"; and a fine work from the period, Charles Gosselin, *L'Empire d'Annam* (Paris: Perrin, 1904), 247f.

6. Jean-Marie-Antoine de Lanessan, as quoted in Isoart, *Phénomène National*, 152.

7. On this, see especially Marr, *Vietnamese Anticolonialism*, 77ff.

8. Governor General Pierre Pasquier, "Rapport," in Congrès Colonial, Marseille, 1906, *Compte Rendu des Travaux*, ed. Ch. Depincé (4 vols., Paris: A. Challamel, 1907-1908), II, 525.

9. Joseph Chailley-Bert, *Paul Bert au Tonkin* (Paris: no pub., 1887) 125.

10. Barbara Eli, "Paul Doumer in Indochina (1897-1902): Verwaltungsreform, Eisenbahnen, Chinapolitik" (Dissertation, University of Heidelberg, 1967).

11. As for example, Lt. Col. F. Bernard, "La Réforme de l'Indochine," *Revue de Paris*, 15 (1 October 1908), 660.

12. Mus, "Das Dorf," 168.

13. Milton E. Osborne, *The French Presence in Cochinchina and Cambodia: Rule and Response (1859-1905)* (Ithaca: Cornell University Press, 1969), 110; idem, "The Debate on a Legal Code for Colonial Cochinchina: The 1869 Commission, " *JSEAH*, 10 (September 1969).

14. Paul Doumer, *L'Indochine Français (Souvenirs)* (Paris: Vuibert et Nony, 1905), 72f.

15. Osborne, *French Presence*, 146f.

16. Chesneaux, *Contribution*, 155.

17. "With mandarins properly chosen, not for integrity or competence, but for docility, and with collective communal responsibility, one could squeeze the Annamite to the last sou.... He paid, and kept his mouth shut"; Bernard, "La Réforme," 646. See also Jean Ajalbert, *Les Destinées de l'Indochine: Voyages-Histoire-Colonisation* (Paris: Louis-Michaud, éditeur, 1909), 134.

18. Isoart, *Phénomène National*, 20, based on Gourou, whose works are cited below, notes 26 and 28. Mus, "Das Dorf," 170, gives the figure as 19 percent (based on the 1939 example of an eleven-member peasant family with an annual income of thirty-two piasters, six of which went for direct taxes).

19. Thompson, *French Indo-China*, 184f.; Chesneaux, *Contribution*, 154f.; Isoart, *Phénomène National*, 130f.; Eli, "Paul Doumer," 67.

20. Quoted in Isoart, *Phénomène National*, 204.

21. Roger Lorey, "La Régie de l'Alcool en Indochine," *Revue Indigène*, 2 (March 1907).

22. Alexandre Varenne, *Discours prononcé le 21 octobre 1927* (Hanoi: no pub., 1927), 77.

23. Isoart, *Phénomène National*, 207.

24. "La Réforme des Impôts Personnels," *La Revue Indochinoise, Juridique et Economique* Fasc. 2 (1939).

25. A basic text is Charles Robequain, *The Economic Development of French Indo-China* (London, New York: Oxford University Press, 1944). See also Paul Bernard, *Le Problème Economique Indochinois* (Paris: Nouvelles Editions Latines, 1934); idem, *Nouveaux Aspects du Problème Economique Indochinois* (Paris: Fernand Sorlot, 1937). There is also a good chapter in Thompson, *French Indo-China*.

26. Bernard, *Problème Economique*, 16f.; Pierre Gourou, *L'Utilisation du Sol en Indochine Française* (Paris: P. Hartman, 1940), ch. 4; translated as *Land Utilization in French Indochina* (3 vols., New York: Institute of Pacific Relations, 1945). Citations are to the French edition. See also idem, "La Population Rurale de la Cochinchine," *Annales de Géographie*, 51 (1942).

27. Gregoire Khérian, "Le Problème Démographique en Indochine," *La Revue Indochinoise*, Fasc. 1 (1937).

28. On this, see the magisterial work of Pierre Gourou, *Les Paysans du Delta Tonkinois: Etude de Géographie Humaine* (Paris: Les Editions d'Art et d'Histoire, 1936). See also his *Indochine Française: le Tonkin* (Paris: Protat Freres, Imprimeurs, 1931); and his *L'Utilisation du Sol*.

29. Gourou, *Paysans du Delta*, 357; idem, *L'Utilisation du Sol*, 229. A very careful inquiry revealed that 90 percent of all owners held 0-5 mau; Indochina, French. Inspection Générale de l'Agriculture, de l'Elevage et des Forêts, *Economic Agricole de l'Indochine*, by Yves Marius Henry (Hanoi: Impr. d'Extrême Orient, 1932), 108.

30. Gourou, *Paysans du Delta*, 362; "The majority of land sales, which are numerous indeed, are to settle indebtedness"; idem, *Indochine*, 117.

31. Yves Henry, an agriculural expert, estimated 337 kg. of paddy per capita as the normal ration, but in Tonkin the average came to only 217 kg. Khérian, "Problème Démographique," 19, speaks of "chronic undernourishment."

32. The rice situation in 1931:

Table 6.1
Rice Production and Consumption in Vietnam in 1931 (in tons)

	ANNUAL PRODUCTION	CONSUMED LOCALLY	DISTILLED	EXPORTED
Cochinchina	2,844,700	1,227,345	50,000	1,567,355
Cambodia	799,471	665,586	...	133,885
Annam	642,220	627,640	...	14,580
Tonkin	2,051,270	1,768,065	50,000	233,205
Total	6,337,661	4,288,636	100,000	1,949,025

SOURCE: Khérian, "Problème Démographique," 18.

33. In 1898 Tonkin imported goods valued at 11 million piasters and in 1935 goods worth 25 million. Since the population had doubled and goods had become more expensive, the per capita value had fallen; Bernard, *Nouveaux Aspects*, 43.

34. Gourou, *L'Utilisation du Sol*, 265.

35. P. Brocheux, "Grands Propriétaires et Fermiers dans l'ouest de la Cochinchine pendant la Période Coloniale," *Revue Historique*, 246 (July-September 1971), 61.

36. Ibid., 62 n3.

37. Owners with more than fifty hectares; Henry, *Economie Agricole*, 212.

38. "Etude des Rapports entre les Propriétaires Fonciers et les Fermiers Métayers et Ouvriers Agricoles," *Bulletin Economique de l'Indochine*, 41 (1938). Between 1930 and 1932, only 1.2 percent of the landholders in Tonkin farmed their paddy through tenants and subtenants. In Cochinchina, however, the figure was 35.4 percent; ibid., 746.

39. *L'Asie Française*, November 1927, as quoted in International Labor Office, Geneva, *Problèmes du Travail en Indochine (BIT)* (Geneva: Imprimerie Kundig, 1937), 198.

40. See table 6.1 above, n. 32.

41. "La Question Agraire en Indochine," *La Dépêche Coloniale*, 16 December 1936, as quoted in *Problèmes du Travail*, 199.

42. Brocheux, "Grands Propriétaires," 75; Osborne, *French Presence*, 268, 279f.

43. P. de Feyssel, *L'Endettement Agraire en Cochinchine: Rapport d'Ensemble au Gouverneur Général de l'Indochine* (Hanoi: Impr. d'Extrême-Orient, 1933). There is also a good section in *Problèmes du Travail.*

44. Quoted in Gourou, *L'Utilisation du Sol*, 276.

45. Thompson, *French Indo-China*, 225.

46. Gourou, *Paysans du Delta*, 380. Governor-General Pasquier stated on 25 November 1931 in the Grand Conseil: "If only the better portion of the loans could reach the needy *nhaqué* and the improverished *ta-diên* directly, but they do not. What is disheartening is that the principal credit facilities are useless, both psychologically and economically. It has proved nearly impossible, indeed, to assure that advances reach the small farmers, the *ta-diêns* and *nhaqués*, other than through the middle and large holders as intermediaries"; quoted in Feyssel, *L'Endettement Agraire*, 7.

47. Doumer, *L'Indochine*, 359.

48. Cochin China, Chambre D'Agriculture, *Bulletin de la Chambre d'Agriculture*, vol. 29, no. 210 (1926), 5.

49. Robequain, *Economic Development*, 190.

50. In 1937-1938, 13,000 hectares were devoted to coffee, with a production of 1,500 tons, mostly for local consumption. In 1936, 1,306 tons of tea were exported; *Problèmes du Travail*, 11. See also Robequain, *Economic Development*, 194f.

51. Ibid., 201ff.; Thompson, *French Indo-China*, 130f.

52. Speech of 21 October 1927, as reported in *Bulletin de la Chambre*, vol. 30 (1927), 9. See also Varenne's decrees and his commentary on them in the same issue.

53. *Problèmes du Travail*, 28f.; J. Devallée, "La Main d'Oeuvre en Indochine" (Dissertation, University of Paris, 1905); Thompson, *French Indo-China*, 143ff.

54. "Together, the Lao-Kay line and the line into Yunnan have cost about a hundred thousand Chinese and Annamite lives"; Pierre Duclaux, "L'Annam et nous," *Revue de Paris*, 16 (1909), III, 215. According to Thompson, however, only 80,000 Chinese and Vietnamese coolies were employed, a third of whom died during the course of construction; *French Indo-China*, 208.

55. There were protests in the Agriculture Chamber against a proposal to end this immunity from taxation on the ground that "...if the European colons' labor force were to lose the benefit of this exemption from personal taxes which at least relieves them of taxes levied against their villages, they would have no further reason to remain on the plantations and would desert en masse"; *Bulletin de la Chambre*, 24 (1921).

56. *Problèmes du Travail*, 89. Paul Monet's *Les Jauniers: Histoire Vrai* (Paris: Gallimard, 1930), leaves a striking impression of the plantation workers recruited in the north.

57. *Problèmes du Travail*, 100. See also Departs 1923: 1129; 1928: 3048; and France, Archives Nationales, Section d'Outre-Mer, Indochine, N.F., 1487. Hereafter cited as ANSOM. In addition to Monet, *Les Jauniers*, see among others Andrée Françoise Caroline d'Ardenne de Tizac, *Indochine S.O.S.*, by Andrée Viollis [pseud.], (Paris: Editeurs Français Réunis, 1935). By 1929, even the Hanoi Chamber of Commerce was commenting on a "veritable traffic" in recruiting and its "immoral character"; Hanoi, Chambre de Commerce, *Bulletin*, no. 302 (1929), 4. See also Paul Chassaing, "La Naissance du Prolétariat en Indochine," *Revue du Pacific*, 12 (1933).

58. Bernard B. Fall, *The Two Vietnams: A Political and Military Analysis* (New York, London: Frederick A. Praeger, 1963), 37.

59. The comments of the *Courrier d'Haiphong* of 17 February 1937 rather characterized the situation: "We venture to say it right out loud in the paper: to create unions in Indochina is tantamount to wanting revolution day after tomorrow"; as quoted in Bernard, *Nouveaux Aspects*, 141.

60. Eli, "Paul Doumer," 114ff. Critical of Doumer is Thompson, *French Indo-China*, 206f.

61. "And who then profits from colonial resources, if not the French contractors who collect two-thirds of that sum in return for rails, bridges and other materials of every sort"; quoted in Eli,"Paul Doumer," 128.

62. Bernard, *Problème Economique*, 80.

63. "Our railways haul derisory amounts of traffic and their operation is very expensive"; ibid., 81.

64. Doumer, *L'Indochine*, 360.

65. "Metropolitan industry must certainly have recovered in the form of commercial gain the millions spent by France for the acquisition of its new domain. But it was not asked whether the foregoing was in conformity with the role the colony was supposed to play in Asia, namely, providing by virtue of its location a doorway to the Chinese market. Nor has it been asked whether, in imposing high duties on non-French imports, we are not retarding the enrichment, and thus the accession of civilization, of twenty million Asiatics"; from "Rapport des Congrès Colonial," Congrès Colonial, *Compte Rendu*, 154f.

66. Thompson, *French Indo-China*, 202.

67. Brötel, *Französischer Imperialismus*, 92f.

68. Robequain, *Economic Development*, 255. On coal mining, see Thompson, *French Indo-China*, 114f.

69. Robequain, *Economic Development*, is particularly good on these matters.

70. Hanoi, Chambre de Commerce, *Bulletin* (April 1917), 7.

71. *Quinzaine Coloniale*, 25 April 1935. In 1937 Paul Bernard was asked by the Union Coloniale to report on the need for industrialization efforts. The Syndicat Général de l'Industrie Cotonnière criticized Bernard's positive response, noting the situation in India, where British imports had declined sharply. Union Coloniale Française, Paris, Section de l'Indochine, *Les Problèmes posés par le Développement Industriel de l'Indochine* (Paris: Union Coloniale Français, Section Indochine, 1938).

72. Bernard, *Nouveaux Aspects*, 113.

73. Ibid.; G. Khérian, "La Querelle de l'Industrialisation de l'Indochine," *La Revue Indochinoise*, Fasc. 4 (1938).

74. France's share was:

Table 6.2.
French Proportion of Indochinese Foreign Trade, 1889-1932 (in percentages)

YEAR	AMOUNT
1889-1893	10
1909-1913	23
1929/30	24
1932	37

SOURCE: Bernard, *Problème Economique*, 101, 105.

Between 1924 and 1928, 13 percent of rice exports went to France, and in 1932, 36 percent.

75. Robequain, *Economic Development*, 287.

76. On Vietnamese nationalism, see the good account by Philippe Devilliers in his *L'Asie du Sud-Est* (2 vols., Paris: Sirey, 1971) II, livre 8. See also Isoart, *Phénomène National*; and Chesneaux, *Contribution*, and in addition, the latter's "Entwicklungsstufen der nationalen Bewegung Vietnams, 1862-1940," in Albertini, *Moderne Kolonialgeschichte*; and Ralph Bernard Smith, *Vietnam and the West* (London: Heineman Educational, 1968).

77. See, among others, Wyndham, *Native Education*.

78. Jacques Le Prévost and Henri Meyrat, "L'Admission des Indochinois dans les Cadres des Administrations et Services Publiques Françaises de l'Indochine," *Revue Indochinoise*, Fasc. 1 (1942); Roger Pinto, *Aspects de l'Evolution Gouvernmentale de l'Indochine Française* (Saigon: S.I.L.I., 1946), 16f.

79. "The procedure by which Indochinese have been able to claim equality with Frenchmen in seeking admission into the so-called European cadres was valid only so long as a small minority of Indochinese was able to benefit from it. It became inconceivable from that moment they reached sufficient numbers to satisfy completely the needs of such cadres"; quoted in Le Prévost and Meyrat, "L'Admission," 232.

80. In February 1936, for example, a cadre of Indochinese radio and electrical engineers was created, with a pay between 8,400 and 26,400 francs, as against 12,000 to 42,000 for Frenchmen; Pinto, *L'Evolution Gouvernmentale*, 23 n2.

81. "We have never had the guts to raise the salaries of the purely native cadres, and thus pursue a policy of prevarication. But the two matters are connected. That is why a mandarin of the highest rank in the provincial administration makes 300 piasters a month, or about the same as a European policeman. That is also why a doctor, who has undertaken long studies, is much more poorly paid than a European, or even a Hindu, nurse"; G. Angoulvant, "Des Réformes en Indochine," *Revue des deux Mondes*, 59 (15 October 1930), 915.

82. One more example: An Indochinese who was not a citizen had access to the courts as a

lawyer, but was excluded from the lawyer's professional association; Pinto, *L'Evolution Gouvernmentale*, 21 n3.

83. Marr, *Vietnamese Anticolonialism*, 98f.

84. Ibid., 156f.

85. Devillers, *L'Asie*, 743.

86. Ibid., 747.

87. R. B. Smith, "Bui Quang Chieu and the Constitutionalist Party in French Cochinchina, 1917-1930," *MAS*, 3 (April 1969); idem, "The Vietnamese Elite in French Cochinchina," *MAS*, 6 (October 1972).

88. Walter G. Langlois, *André Malraux: The Indochinese Adventure* (London: Pall Mall Press, 1966).

89. Published in the *Echo Annamite* of Saigon in January 1929. According to the Sûreté, some six hundred Vietnamese, mainly landlords but also some members of the councils, had come to Saigon to transmit the cahiers as a manifestation of their sentiments; Indochina, French. Direction des Affaires Politiques et de la Sûreté Générale. *Contribution [à] l'Histoire des Mouvements Politiques de l'Indochine Français: Documents* (4 vols., Hanoi: Gouvernment Générale de l'Indochine, 1933), II, 16.

90. The response to remarks of Pierre Pasquier, Résident Superieur and later Governor-General, to the Union Coloniale in Paris were characteristic: "Monsieur Pasquier raised a question of principle which is important for the future of Indochina, namely, is it necessary to create an assembly representing all of Indochina? It would tend to strengthen the unity of Indochinese territories, but might one day turn against us. The great problem is creating a non-political assembly. It would seem that the English are not always too happy about having created an all-India Parliament in Delhi"; *La Quinzaine Coloniale*, 25 May 1928, p. 191.

91. Smith, *Vietnam and the West*, 95. Chesneaux does not mention the Constitutionalists in the "stages of development" at all.

92. In February 1929 a number of arrests were made following the murder of a recruiting agent in Hanoi. A breakdown by profession showed the following:

Table 6.3
Membership of the Vietnamese Nationalist Party, by Profession, in 1929

OCCUPATION	NUMBER	OCCUPATION	NUMBER
Secrétaires de l'Administration française	36	Etudiants	6
Agents de l'Administration indigène	13	Publicistes	4
Instituteurs de l'Enseignement public	36	Employés de commerce ou d'industrie	10
Instituteurs privés	4	Commerçants et artisans	39
Professeurs de caractère chinois	2	Propriétaires, cultivateurs	37
		Militaires	40

SOURCE: *Contribution [à] l'Histoire*, II, 13.

93. Jean Lacouture, *Hô Chi Minh* (Paris: Ed. du Seuil, 1967).

94. ANSOM, Indochine N. F. Carbon 225, Dossier 1839. There is also material in this file about new disturbances in December 1932, which were wholly the fault of the plantation management, as the official investigations make unmistakably clear.

95. From the period, see Louis Roubaud, *Vietnam: La Tragédie Indochinoise* (Paris: Valois, 1931).

96. For example, the extremely well-informed Jean Dorsenne commented in "Le Péril Rouge en Indochine," *Revue des Deux Mondes*, 12 (1 April 1932), 556: "In North Annam misery is extreme and famine threatens. . . . It is high time for the metropolis to understand that the soil of our fairest colony is sown with mines." Angoulvant, "Des Réformes," is also good on this question.

PART II

NORTHERN AFRICA

7

THE BRITISH "PROTECTORATE" OVER EGYPT: UNTIL 1922

My interpretation of the confrontation between the colonial powers and non-Western societies rests on the assumption that European influences came to be felt acutely only after colonial rule was clearly established. Once this occurred, the colonial power forced through modernization and Westernization and without the participation, at least initially, of endogenous social forces. Egypt, however, constitutes an exception to these generalizations, as it early went through a revolution from above, in the sense of modernization forced by a ruler using despotic means upon a traditional society. This revolution occurred long before the effective imposition of British rule in 1882. It also predated the informal constraints that the Public Debt Administration (Caisse de la Dette Publique), organized to protect European bondholders, had imposed in 1876. The Egyptian revolution, indeed, was pushed a good way forward, though with very mixed results. Egypt's Mediterranean location and proximity to European countries having a traditional interest in Egypt, whether for strategic, economic, or intellectual reasons, obviously facilitated its strivings toward Westernization. On the other hand, the European powers also meddled in this precolonial modernization process and to a degree prevented it. They were then to continue it themselves within a colonial framework, in accordance with their own rather than Egyptian interests.[1] For this reason, I am devoting more than the usual amount of space to the period before 1880, though I must cover it in a dangerously summary fashion.

Napoleonic rule (1798-1801) was of short duration, and the British were gone by 1803. This incursion from outside nonetheless shook up the ossified Egyptian social and political order. Defeat on the battlefield had not destroyed the power and prestige of Egypt's Mameluke feudal rulers, who were of Turkish-Circassian origin, but defeat had weakened them. Bonaparte had attempted to rally the native Egyptian leading classes, the ulema, the shaykhs (sheikhs), and the local notables, all hard-pressed by the Mamelukes, against the latter in support of French rule. But they were the very groups that led the resistance against the Christian invaders. Some administrative reforms, road-building, arsenal construction, a French institute, and French-language publications opened the country somewhat to Western influences. If that had not happened, Muhammad Ali (1805-1849) could scarcely have inaugurated so fundamental a transformation of his country with his revolution from above.

Muhammad Ali had fought at the head of Albanian auxiliary troops with the Turks against the French. He skillfully exploited the power vacuum left by the departure of the French and the animosity of Egyptians against the Mamelukes and the Ottoman sultan to seize control of the country. The sultan officially sanctioned Muhammad Ali's rule in 1805 by naming him governor. He secured his internal position by calling the Mamelukes to Cairo in 1811 and murdering them all. A new Turko-Circassian power elite nonetheless rapidly re-formed. Muhammad Ali employed the sons of the murdered men as ministers, provincial governors, police prefects, and as his leading justices and generals, while at the same time all but excluding Egyptians from such positions.[2] His autocratic power firmly established, Muhammad Ali began modernizing his state. In a manner somewhat comparable to seventeenth-century European absolute monarchs or the rulers of later Meiji Japan, he aimed primarily at strengthening the power of the state and revamping the army. By implication, however, both the administration and the economy or, in other words, the underlying social structures, were unavoidably affected. Unfortunately, space permits discussion only of the agrarian structure and Muhammad Ali's industrialization efforts.

In the seventeenth and eighteenth centuries, tax farmers *(multazim)* were the de facto owners of the land, though in law it belonged to the state. The multazim collected taxes and other dues from the peasants and in addition could claim corvée and military services. In many cases the multazim were able to establish life or hereditary interests in their holdings. These rights, combined with powers of local magistracy, resulted in the establishment of a class of feudal large landholders that can be compared with the zamindars of late Mughal India.[3] In contast to the British East India Company, which recognized the tax farmers as de jure owners of the land in the Permanent Settlement of 1793, Muhammad Ali had by 1814 confiscated their land, in part by using the proven methods of finagling with and increasing taxes. Similar procedures were applied to the *waqf* land of the religious foundations. In this manner the power of the ulema was undermined. Thus in a short time the state achieved a land monopoly. The peasant *(fellah)* could dispose of the harvest as he wished but had to pay exorbitant taxes. In Muhammad Ali's later years, however, state land became the basis for private ownership in land and a new class of latifundiasts arose. New cadastres at first registered land in the name of the village community and simultaneously made it collectively responsible for payment of taxes. From exploitation rights, full ownership developed in a series of stages after 1858, the holders being either fellahin or the grantees of Muhammad Ali and his successors. As early as 1830, Muhammad Ali had begun to grant large blocks of uncultivated land to his senior officials, with the stipulation that they cultivate it. Increasing tax burdens and military conscription—the army numbered roughly 100,000 in 1830—had led to the abandonment of a large amount of arable land, which in turn resulted in tax arrearages that were uncollectable despite use of the most drastic means. After 1840 Muhammad Ali hence resorted to the expedient of making officials, officers, provincial governors, and notables responsible for making up the back taxes. As compensation, they received villages as *uhdas*, meaning they became tax farmers but could employ corvée labor to till part of the ground for their own account. The local administration for all practical purposes fell into their hands. Ismail's *Muqabala* Law of 1871 had analogous effects, as it provided that the holder of a given piece of land could become the full owner by paying six years of taxes in advance. Finally, the new landowner class was further enlarged by the transfer of state property to the ruler and his family. It began with Muhammad Ali himself. By 1845 members of his family already held some 677,000 feddans of land, a feddan equaling .44 hectares. Muhammad Ali scraped huge estates together, including sugarcane plantations and sugar mills. Until Gamal Abdul Nasser's revolution in 1952, the royal family remained the largest landholder in Egypt.

The landholdings created by Muhammad Ali and his successors were, however, subject to a certain erosion, notably through division upon inheritance, confiscation, and sale.[4] Ismail himself (khedive, 1863-1879) had to part with half his family holdings to provide security for state loans. Tax burdens, corvée, indebtedness, and inheritance law also forced many fellahin to part with their land. The gainers were mainly local notables who served as shaykhs or *umdas* (village headmen). By increasing their own holdings in this manner, many ultimately established themselves as fairly large landholders.[5] The mass of the fellahin had only small or very small holdings.

> The rhythm of their lives was determined by the seasons and the Nile. With anxious eye they marked the rise and fall of the flood gage. Every year they ran the risk of annihilating high waters or floods too small to make a crop. Their houses were mud bricks, and entire villages melted away like ice cream in the sunshine when the levies gave way.[6]

Grain and other foodstuffs were farmed as substance crops, the small surpluses being sold in the local markets. Taxes were heavy, and so were the burdens of military service and corvée.

Dependent on the waters of the Nile, the cultivated area was concentrated in the delta and a narrow strip along the river. Between August and October, the waters were turned into the already planted fields. Only one crop was possible. Acreage devoted to summer crops destined for market, such as sugarcane, cotton, rice, and corn, could not be expanded until a modern canal system based on barrages, levies with pumps, and the like, reduced dependence on Nile flooding and permitted irrigation over the better part of the year. Muhammad Ali began the building of the canal system in 1820—by 1833, 240 miles of new canals had been dug—and hence laid the foundations for the modern cotton farming that was to revolutionize the Egyptian economic structure.[7]

Cotton had long been raised in Egypt. What was new were the long-fibered varieties that the French textile engineer Louis A. Jumel discovered around 1818. Seizing upon the export possibilities at once, Muhammad Ali supported Jumel and led the way in cultivating the new varieties. The state bought cotton from the fellahin at fixed prices and then resold it to European traders for export. The price differential was great and went to the treasury; a tested method for sucking up the agricultural "surplus." A considerable part of the new cotton came from the great estates of the ruling family, where important innovations such as steam pumps were first used. Toward the end of the 1830s, however, Muhammad Ali was gradually forced to give up his trade monopoly, which also included grain, sugar, and most imports. The system which prevailed thereafter was one in which European trading houses in Alexandria bought cotton from Greek and Levantine middlemen and exported it. The system had a colonial look to it, to the extent that the Egyptian peasant farmed a cash crop the price of which depended on the world market. The earlier subsistence-farming economy had been transformed into market farming with a tendency toward monoculture, and the marketing itself was almost entirely in foreign hands. The American Civil War brought boom conditions for Egyptian cotton farming. In 1864 a million feddans were in cotton, or nearly 40 percent of all Egyptian arable. Because prices tripled in a very short time, export income also multiplied manyfold.[8] The fellahin shared these profits although they also had to pay higher prices for consumer goods and to invest some of their profits in draft animals to replace stock decimated by rinderpest. At the war's end, prices fell once again, but European demand remained high. Until 1880 production and exports slowly continued to rise.[9] The lot of the fellahin, however, became increasingly depressing. Growing tax burdens and corvée pushed them hopelessly into debt. In 1876 Wilfred Blunt wrote:

> It was rare in those days to see a man in the fields with a turban on his head, or more than a shirt on his back.... The principal towns on market days were full of women selling their clothes and their silver ornaments to the Greek usurers, because the tax collectors were in their village, whip in hand.[10]

The new laws, sanctioned by the mixed tribunals—courts manned by Egyptian and European judges administering French law—made mortgaging land easier and, as in India, protected the creditor.[11] As early as the 1870s one-third of the population had become landless.

But Muhammad Ali's modernization efforts also comprehended his attempts at state-initiated and state-monopolized industrialization.[12] Machines were imported from Europe, European technicians were hired, and a respectable number of textile (cotton, wool, silk), glass, leather, and paper factories were erected. Arms and munitions factories were also built, and a shipyard in Alexandria. Between 1830 and 1840, these enterprises employed more than 30,000 workers. Import substitution seems to have been the primary aim of these efforts, both in interest of state finances and supplying the army. Yet the attempt failed early on in the reign of Muhammad Ali himself. The impetus which the state provided was not, as was necessary, taken up and carried on by an Egyptian entrepreneurial class. Muhammad Ali sent students to Europe for technical education, but the social basis for the new industries was lacking. So was the work force. Workers were bound over to their jobs and miserably paid, and there was no trained cadre to maintain the machinery. Egyptian products were 20 to 30 percent dearer than corresponding imports. An internal market scarcely existed, even though Muhammad Ali went so far as to forbid the traditional village spinning and weaving in 1823. That act brought on a crisis in the guild-organized trades; or, in other words, it deliberately initiated the chain of events familiar to us from India, events most severely criticized by the colonial power itself. The state was able to assume the role of principal buyer, particularly of military materials, but its hands were tied as far as customs went, because an Anglo-Ottoman treaty of 1809 fixed duties at 3 percent. In combination with other European powers, the English resorted to the provisions of the capitulation treaties, protested Muhammad Ali's monopolistic economic policies, and in an 1838 convention with the Ottoman sultan were able to secure free-trade rights throughout the entire Ottoman Empire. After military setbacks in 1840, Muhammad Ali had to reduce the size of his army, and enterprises running in the red were closed during his own lifetime. His industrialization policy was in many respects like that later followed by Meiji Japan and shares with Stalin's industrialization policy both a similar role for the state and a ruthless exploitation of agricultural surpluses for industrialization at the expense of peasant producers. Charles Issawi attributes its failure, rather too one-sidedly, to Egypt's lack of political autonomy, which the country suffered from even before British occupation. Egypt was thus forced to become an export-oriented economy and a direct transition from a subsistence economy to a "complex economy" was hindered. "Egypt could now be integrated, as an agricultural unit in the world-wide economic system."[13]

Said (khedive, 1854-1863) and Ismail (khedive, 1863-1879) energetically continued Muhammad Ali's policies of Westernization and modernization. Aside from some expensive construction in Cairo in the style of Baron Haussmann, however, these policies were pursued within a context of the expansion of cotton farming and the export-oriented economic structure. Great sums were spent on public works supporting the growth, transport, and shipment of cash crops, both cotton and sugar. Money also went into canals, railways, and the expansion of harbor facilities in Alexandria and Suez.[14] Foreign trade rose from £E 3.5 million (Egyptian pounds) in 1838 to 21.8 million in 1880. Cotton's share in exports fluctuated between 40 and 75 percent.[15] Sugar and grain were also important. Public works, financed in good part by foreign loans, and the rapid increase in foreign trade provided foreigners a rapidly expanding and lucrative field for economic activity. There were about 90,000 foreigners in Egypt in 1864.[16] Most lived in Alexandria, which took on the atmosphere of a Western port city. Capitulation treaties assured foreigners a privileged position, exempt from taxes and the jurisdiction of Egyptian courts. The land law of 1858 and mortgage laws enabled them to buy land, and the mixed tribunal court system of 1875 guaranteed their legal rights in a manner that met European interests in the broadest possible way. In short, the basic institutions for colonial rule already existed before Great Britain assumed formal sovereignty in 1882.

The course of the British takeover need only be outlined. Under Said, indebtedness increased rapidly, and with it, the payment difficulties which finally culminated in state bankruptcy. Egypt became a sort of El Dorado both for existing foreign banks in Egypt such as the private houses of Edouard Dervieu and Hermann Oppenheim and for the international houses of London and Paris, which placed the bonds in the market.[17] The worse the financial position of the rulers, the juicier the terms; interest rates were boosted, along with commissions, and the bonds were issued at well under par. The loans assumed by Egypt up to 1873, worth £E 65 million par, actually brought in only 45 million.[18] Under Said and Ismail, a considerable portion of the money went for public works, some of it in the form of forced loans to the Suez Canal Company. Some went for profligate splendor, an expansive foreign policy, bribes, and increased tribute payments to the Ottoman sultan. These outlays sucked up money at a rate unmatched by state income, which despite despotic tax collection methods, was only seven to ten million pounds a year. In 1873 Ismail made one of his last great loans, through Oppenheim. The par value of the loan was £E 32 million, but Egypt received only 20 million.[19] Two years later foreign debts stood at 91 million, as compared with 3.3 million at Ismail's accession. Ismail had to sell his Suez canal shares (or 44 percent of the capital) for four million pounds to England, though his act failed to stave off Egyptian bankruptcy and suspension of interest payments in 1876. Under pressure from the French, the khedive was forced to accept the formation of the Public Debt Administration. Under the management of representatives of the four most important European creditor nations, the Debt Administration had de facto control of Egyptian finance and directly disposed of two-thirds of state income. But this was not the end. In late fall of 1876, the khedive had the so-called Dual Control thrust upon him. Two financiers, one English and the other French, took control of broad sectors of the administration. "Nominally, Ismail continued to rule as sovereign in the name of the sultan. In practice, however, Egypt was bound over to a kind of bankruptcy trusteeship managed by the English and French, who had exercised their power in behalf of European creditors."[20]

An investigating commission went further still in 1878, proposing a number of reforms in tax collection and demanding ministerial responsibility, or, in other words, the stripping away of Ismail's power, in order to gain direct influence over the government through collaborationist ministers. Accordingly, an Englishman became finance minister and a Frenchman minister for public works.[21] The khedive then used the reduction in the army as a lever against the "European government" that had been forced upon him. Officers threatened with dismissal, whose pay was months in arrears anyhow, demonstrated in February 1879, manifestly with Ismail's tacit consent if not open encouragement. At the same time, Ismail sought to ally himself with the Council of Notables, which he had first convened in 1866, not to share in rule, but to "advise" him as ruling autocrat. Until 1879, as Schölch has shown in contravention of the accepted interpretation, the council attempted to defend the interests of the umdas, businessmen, and landowners, but was permitted no extension of its constitutional powers. Now, however, as the "spokesman of the Egyptian people," it turned against the government. In June 1879 that cost Ismail his throne.

His son Tawfiq attempted to follow an active reformist course, though without provoking the European powers. His aim was both to improve tax collection and to reduce the burden on the fellahin, but he ran into resistance from the large landowners and the Turko-Circassian elite. The latter had been able to safeguard its position in the army and in 1880, indeed, appeared to be readying another effort to suppress the "fellahin," or native Egyptian, officers. Under the leadership of Colonel Ahmad Arabi, himself the son of an umda, the fellahin officers went into action on 1 February 1881, occupying the war ministry, freeing three imprisoned colonels, and forcing the war minister to resign. They were not pursuing political or nationalist aims, and their action was not aimed at the khedive. In their disputes with the Turko-Circassian officers and administrators, the fellahin officers had allied themselves with the provincial notables in the assembly of delegates. On 9 September 1881 they staged two demonstrations, forcing the resignation of the prime minister. The mood began to change. "Arabi became rapidly transfigured from a mutinous colonel to the people's hero, the defender of the fatherland and Islam against the overweening and unbelieving European powers, and the liberator of the people from the Turko-Circassian tyranny."[22] The khedive was forced to give in, and both the sultan and representatives of the European powers became very uneasy. England and France stood behind the khedive in their joint note of 8 January 1882. Their implied threat of intervention amounted to throwing down the gauntlet to the council. In the new government, the Turko-Circassians were for the first time forced from their dominant positions. Egyptian notables took over, Arabi becoming war minister. At this point, the khedive, in league with the representatives of the European powers, most notably the British, pressed the sultan and the powers to intervene and fled to Alexandria and the protection of the British fleet. The latter seized upon a trivial pretext to bombard the city on 11 July 1882. An Egyptian defense committee took over the administration and called on the country to resist, while London decided firmly in favor of military intervention. It probably did so because it feared the nationalist movement threatened its communications with the East and to protect its capital investments in Egypt.[23] On 13 September, Egyptian troops suffered an annihilating defeat. The Arabi movement was neither an expression of Egyptian nationalism, nor did it pursue social-revolutionary ends. Egyptian patriotism had indeed increased in step with increasing European influence, but Arabi saw himself as defender of the fatherland and Islam and had to the very end turned against neither the sultan nor the khedivate as an institution. As a fellahin colonel, he opposed non-Egyptian rule and was prepared to undertake reforms mitigating the exploitation of the peasant masses. He never challenged, however, the claims of the native Egyptian landowner and notable class, from whence he himself had risen, to rule. The autocratic power of the khedive, who had treated the country like his private estate and had depended on the Turko-Circassian elite for support in the army and administration, was destroyed in the years 1878-1882. It was Europeans, however, who initiated this "revolutionary" process rather than the Council of Notables or the fellahin officer corps. It was already too late when the native Egyptian elite began to coalesce in resistance to England's military intervention and the colonial rule that followed.

"We were in absolute possession of the country. We had smashed the de facto government, and the de jure government was a phantom."[24] By the latter, Khedive Tawfiq was meant, who, with his loyal followers and those who had managed to turn their coats and join him in a timely fashion shortly before or after Arabi's defeat, had supposedly won back his autocratic position thanks to British intervention. And what indeed were the British to do, for had one not intervened to expand the bounds of empire? Even within the ruling Liberal party opinions differed considerably.[25] Both to gain time and get a closer look at the situation, the British ambassador to Constantinople, Lord Dufferin, later viceroy of India, was sent to Cairo to report. In his report, a classic expression of political liberalism, Dufferin stated that the Egyptians felt excluded from the senior offices of state but would welcome British "advisors. . . to keep them in the paths of rectitude and duty, and to give confidence to the people that henceforth right and justice would take the place of venality, arbitrariness, and the law of the strongest." He thus recommended against both indirect and direct rule and in favor of advice, as he was "desirous of enabling them to govern themselves, under the uncompromising aegis of our friendship. . . ."[26] Awareness dawned but slowly that the khedive's government was truly a phantom and that disturbances would soon follow upon the withdrawal of British troops. "Advice" soon came to imply force, and management of the fiscal crisis called for a strong hand. The new governmental apparatus legitimized itself with the comforting notions that its reform activities ought not to be broken off prematurely and that the Egyptians were anyhow incapable of self-government.

Alfred Milner had early on (1892) characterized British rule in Egypt as a "veiled protectorate."[27] In constitutional terms the system was unique, because neither Ottoman sovereignty nor the position of the khedive and his government was legally altered. No treaty served as the legal basis for British rule—as was the case with Indian princes or Malay sultans—which in practice was exercised through the British consul general. Dual control ended in 1883, but the capitulation treaties remained in force. The other European powers, particularly

France, hence continued to have an important voice in economic and financial policy. The Public Debt Administration continued to function, and all but the British placed on the payment of interest the highest priority. In 1883 Sir Evelyn Baring, then forty-two, was appointed as the new consul general. Baring, later elevated to the peerage as the Earl of Cromer, came from a banking family and had earned high marks as the private secretary to Viceroy Lord Northbrook (his cousin) in India between 1873 and 1876. From 1878 to 1880 he was the debt commissioner in Cairo, and then became Indian finance minister under the Liberal viceroy, Lord Ripon. Until 1907 he was British "proconsul" for Egypt.[28]

Formally, the Egyptian governmental system remained in being. The consul general was only supposed to "advise" the khedive, and the other key British officials were only supposed to "advise" their Egyptian ministers, whom the khedive continued to name. The financial advisor held the key position. He took part in ministry meetings, and though without formal competence or vote, had what amounted to veto rights that extended far beyond purely fiscal matters. Within the finance and public works ministries, the British also served as division heads of, say, customs, post, accounts, or the important irrigation department. Control of the army and police was also in British hands. Cromer emphasized the differences with the French protectorate in Tunisia, where all important positions were filled by Frenchmen whose competencies were so broadly drawn that one could speak of de facto annexation.[29] In contrast to the French, British officials in khedival service had to proceed with prudence, even if hard cases did get decided by the consul general. Cromer also emphasized that the British confined their activities to the senior administrative levels and were unable to supervise the execution of laws and regulations in the provinces. Cromer wrote in 1887 to Lord Salisbury: "The British officials are occasionally very troublesome, especially the Anglo-Indians who cannot thoroughly realize that Egypt is not India. The latter sometimes get very angry when they cannot get their own way."[30] In the early years, the prime ministers, especially the Armenian, Nubar Pasha, fought against being reduced to puppets and attempted to use the ministry of the interior to safeguard the influence of the Egyptian leading class over the provincial administration. With the appointment, however, of an advisor in interior in 1894 and the resignation of Nubar in 1895, "the system of shared authority and indirect rule came to an end. British powers were increased and introduced into almost every branch of the administration."[31]

The number of British officials was not great, but they filled almost all of the senior administrative posts, especially in the technical departments. Not counting the army and police, about 1,200 Europeans were in Egyptian service in 1890. About half of these, however, served in the internationalized administrations of the Debt Administration and the railways and only about 250 in civil administration. In 1920 the Milner Commission ascertained that Egyptians filled only one-quarter of the higher posts and that their share had fallen from 28 to 23 percent since 1905.[32] And Cromer was the last one to trouble himself about Egyptianization. In response to the question of why more Europeans and Britons had not been replaced by Egyptians, Cromer baldly replied in 1908, "the supply of competent Egyptians is not nearly equal to the demand."[33] But what Egyptian, indeed, did Cromer hold competent to assume responsibility? Education was itself no sufficient qualification. As an administrator, an Egyptian—or indeed any other Oriental— would only do if he had cast aside his Islamic manner of thinking and had assumed a Christian and European one.[34] Adding to the difficulties was the unwillingness of truly self-confident Egyptians to accommodate themselves to a British-ruled administrative system, and the British tendency to pass them over, more or less deliberately, if they did so.[35] In addition, the British official cadre, though an able enough group, kept to themselves socially. Egyptians were almost never invited into their clubs.

The first order of business for the British was setting Egyptian finances in order.[36] The Law of Liquidation of 1880 had posited two sorts of state income. The first consisted of railway profits, harbor dues, customs duties, the taxes from four provinces, and incomes from former lands of the khedive. It went to the Debt Administration and hence served to amortize the debt. The remainder of state income was at the disposal of the administration. After 1883 the paradoxical situation thus occurred that surpluses from the Debt Administration made it possible to start repaying the debt, while at the same time the administration was incurring new obligations despite the most rigorous savings measures. Compensation paid those injured in the course of the Arabi rising only made matters worse. After the most tedious negotiations among the powers, the Conference of London of 1885 came up with a new solution. The interest rate on existing debt was cut, and a new, 9 million pound loan was floated to meet the most pressing of governmental expenses. Surpluses from the Debt Administration could be used to cover state deficits, now limited by statute, and any surplus yet remaining divided between the Debt Administration and the government. After 1888 such surpluses were to go into a reserve fund, which could then be used for capital investments. The vexatious claims of the other Powers were finally terminated with the Anglo-French colonial agreement of 1904.

The state debt, which topped out in 1890 at £E 107 million, placed a heavy burden on British policy. Of the 10 million which the state collected in 1890, 41 percent went towards interest payments. If one adds 5 percent for the army, and 6 percent for the high tributary payment to the Ottoman sultan, the total rises to 52 percent. This percentage declined slowly as income increased, but was still as high as 33 percent in 1913.[37] The British did indeed succeed in staving off the threatened bankruptcy and in clearing up financial miseries dating from Ismail's time, but at the cost of budgets that screwed down to the bare minimum outlays for education, public health, and the like. Egypt's situation, in which a high portion of state income flowed off to Europe, is reminiscent of the plight of today's developing countries, burdened as they are with the amortization of development loans.

The European creditor representatives on the Debt Administration naturally considered economic development expenditures worthwhile, particularly when they promised a rise in production and state income within a relatively short time. This was the impulse behind public works, especially the energetic expansion of irrigation facilities. Here the colonial power, proceeding from its Indian experience and utilizing Anglo-Indian specialists, accomplished a great deal, though it should not be forgotten that it was only continuing work which Muhammad Ali, Said, and Ismail had begun.[38] Between 1882 and 1902, 8 percent of state income was spent on irrigation. The great Nile barrage below Cairo had supposedly been finished in 1862. It had extended summer cropping to the delta region but had proved subject to breakdowns. By 1890, however, it had finally been put in good order. The great Aswan Dam was built between 1898 and 1902 and raised in height between 1907 and 1912. The well-qualified corps of officials running the Public Works Department also took pains to see that water was distributed more equitably.[39]

Table 7.1
Productive Agricultural Land in Egypt, 1835-1916 (in 1,000 feddans)

YEAR	CULTIVATED	CROPPED
1835	3,500	...
1877	4,743	4,762
1897	5,088	6,848
1906	5,403	7,662
1916	5,319	7,686

SOURCE: Lewis, *Tropical Development*, 207.

The area under cultivation, and more importantly the double cropping which irrigation made possible, increased very considerably before World War I as table 7.1 demonstrates. While this was an undoubted success, there is still the matter of its social implications. Did the increase in arable keep pace with population increases? How ought one assess cotton farming in historical terms?

Table 7.2
Growth of Population in Egypt, 1800-1957 (in millions)

YEAR	NUMBER
1800-1850	2.5 to 3.5
1869	ca. 5.2
1882	6.8
1897	9.7
1907	11.3
1917	12.7
1957	26.0

SOURCE: Patrick O'Brien, "The Long-Term Growth of Agricultural Production in Egypt, 1821-1962," in Holt, *Modern Egypt*, 174.[40]

Once again, we must start with the increase in population (see table 7.2). Correlating population and arable shows that 1877 and 1897 arable (see table 7.1) because of irrigation increased faster than the population. Thereafter, however, the per-capita ratio fell, or, in other words, population rose more rapidly than the cropped area.[41] Yields did increase, indeed rather spectacularly between 1821 and 1878—O'Brien speaks of an "agrarian revolution"—and not only for cotton and sugar, but also for grain and other traditional foodstuffs.[42] This improvement continued strongly until 1900 and thereafter rather more slowly until 1914 (20 percent between 1895 to 1899 and 1910 to 1914). Per capita yield remained fairly constant in this period, only to fall sharply during World War I and then to rise again until World War II.[43] Because farm prices rose sharply after the depression of the 1890s, the fellahin enjoyed a period of relative prosperity in the years before 1914.[44]

Ownership and holding size must next be considered. The trend toward large holdings which had set in during the final years of Muhammad Ali's rule was not reversed under the British. The statistics in table 7.3 make this clear.

Table 7.3
Changes in the Distribution of Landed Property in Egypt, 1896-1916

	1896		1906		1916	
SIZE OF UNIT	LANDED PROP. AREA	NO. OF OWNERS	LANDED PROP. AREA	NO. OF OWNERS	LANDED PROP. AREA	NO. OF OWNERS
1 feddan or less	—	—	—	—	429,532	1,006,866
1.1 - 5	993,843	611,074	1,292,786	1,084,001	1,020,928	473,688
5.1 - 10	565,810	80,810	538,111	76,935	528,560	76,641
10.1 - 20	574,084	41,276	512,199	36,951	509,991	36,982
20.1 - 49.9	675,639	22,225	611,669	20,029	607,002	19,852
50 or over	2,291,625	11,878	2,476,007	12,665	2,356,453	12,297
Total	5,001,001	767,260	5,430,772	1,230,581	5,452,466	1,626,326

SOURCE: Hershlag, *Introduction*, 120.[45]

From table 7.3 it can be seen that both the number of landholders with more than fifty feddans, who were commonly considered large holders, and their total holdings increased only slightly. It must be borne in mind, however, that division following sale, inheritance, and the like was balanced by the formation of new holdings. Baer has pointed out that the large holdings particularly profited from the large-scale irrigation projects such as the Aswan Dam. The khedival holdings and state lands sold to cover state debts mostly went to existing large holders or were the foundations of new large holdings. Even Cromer was forced to concede in 1907 that "the recent sales of the daira property have also, in all probability, tended to increase the number of large proprietors."[46] The numerous mortgage banks (such as the Crédit Foncier and the Land and Mortgage Company), operating mainly with French and British capital, played an important part in this, because they would only lend to someone who already had land to offer as security and who used the credit thus obtained to buy yet more land. The British administration and the mixed tribunals served as the required institutional underpinning.[47] The large holdings belonged in part to a few thousand

Egyptian families, including the khedive's connections, who usually lived as absentee landlords in Cairo and Alexandria, in part to land corporations with European capitalization, and in part to a few Greeks and Italians who lived in Egypt. In 1913 Europeans owned 678,000 feddans, or more than 10 percent of the arable, and of this, land corporations owned 250,000 feddans.[48] Europeans and members of local minorities, such as Copts, Jews, and Greeks, administered these estates. Landless laborers or tenants did the actual farming. Since rents more than doubled between 1902 and 1912, cash rents were particularly profitable for the large holders.[49]

Middling holders of five to fifty feddans, who were mostly Muslim Egyptians or Egyptian representatives of other minorities, remained roughly constant in number and in their total share of about 30 percent of the arable. The number of fellahin farming less than five feddans, on the other hand, doubled between 1900 and 1914. Since the amount of arable did not increase in kind, their average holding decreased from one and one-half to one feddan. Three to four feddans, unfortunately, was the amount necessary to feed a family. Although the yields increased during this period, the agricultural crisis brought on by the population increase is manifest.

Fellahin indebtedness before 1882, encouraged by the institutions of private property and the mixed tribunals, has already been alluded to. It increased during the British period. Fellahin lost their lands to Greek and Levantine moneylenders and became tenants. In 1898 a special bank was established to provide agricultural credit, but this experiment, as elsewhere, was a failure. Credit mostly went to middle-sized holders. The bank was also undercapitalized and had difficulty in collecting its loans.[50] It was Horatio Kitchener, successor but one to Cromer, who thought he had found the solution in his famous Five Feddan Law in 1911, which stated that the land, home, and tools of fellahin with less than five feddans could not be seized.[51] Praised by some, damned by others, this peasant protection law had, according to Gabriel Baer, virtually no effect whatever.[52]

It would be mistaken to assert that the British administration deliberately encouraged large holdings after 1882 in order to create a class of landholders on which to base its rule. The ruling ideology and the attitude of the officials who actually trafficked with the fellahin was distinctly pro-fellahin. But a genuine land reform was neither conceivable nor possible in colonial Egypt, any more than it was in India. Aside from the fact that no new course was initiated, the British primarily sought stability and otherwise could at best only attempt to reduce traditional fellahin burdens with individual measures compatible with the existing social order. They also hoped that the fellahin might somehow profit from economic development. But had an independent Egypt led by the landowning class done any more?

This is also the place to comment on the abolition of the corvée. As was generally the case in areas farmed by irrigation, the corvée was an ancient institution, used to maintain the canals and levies. Its potential for abuse, whether by ruler, landowner, or village shaykh, was undoubtedly equally ancient. With the building of canals under Muhammad Ali, corvée reached intolerable levels. Every year hundreds of thousands of fellahin had to spend long periods away from their villages, and with the increase in the summer cultivation area, they were unable to farm their holdings. Forced labor was in any case inefficient, and dredges were increasingly available to do the work. The French fought against abolution of corvée in the interests of its bondholders, but it was nevertheless gradually replaced with wage labor in the 1880s. That reduced fellahin burdens considerably.[53]

Land taxes were enormously high and rose steadily during the nineteenth century. In the Ismail era of burgeoning debt, taxes were literally "whipped out of the fellahin." Dufferin's report had called for a reduction in taxes, which was certainly in accord with Cromer's liberal economic views; low taxes implied peasant initiative and prosperity which in turn implied the prosperity and increased buying power of society as a whole. The fiscal situation, however, permitted no drastic changes. Nonetheless, along with an improved and less corrupt administration, under which collectors received monthly salaries, closer supervision, and more precise procedures, the land tax was actually reduced in 1885. This was done in part, as in heavily taxed upper Egypt, by forgiving arrears, which left the hard-pressed fellahin with no more cash but made it easier for them to escape the toils of the moneylender.[54] Scandalous inequalities also existed between the two land taxes, the *kharaj*, which was high, and the *ushr*, which averaged 40 percent of the *kharaj*. But kharaj land was mostly fellahin land, and ushr land was mainly held by an already privileged landlord class. After 1900 these tax inequalities were gradually removed. Cromer considered a new cadastre necessary, but the resistance of the landlords, "the most important and influential class in the country," came to seem more important still, and the proconsul judged it prudent to dodge the issue.[55] The land tax rose but little between 1881 and 1913, despite expanded acreage, higher yields, and rising prices. As a portion of state income, it fell sharply, whereas duties and a special tobacco excise, mostly paid by the moneyed classes, rose appreciably.[56] Even Jacques Berque has to concede that the British administration reduced the tax burden on the abused fellahin.[57]

The crisis of the village community is another matter.[58] It was certainly not brought on by any deliberate British act, but had been building since the mid-nineteenth century and simply continued under the British. As in other parts of Asia, the land was accounted common property and was periodically redivided among the villagers. The village was a fiscal unit and, as such, responsible for the payment of taxes, the maintenance of irrigation facilities, the provision of workers for other public works and, in time of need, for the army. These village obligations obviously put considerable power in the hands of the village shayks and umdas. Under Muhammad Ali, the umda was also responsible for tax collection and reallocation of land and for providing workers and soldiers in numbers far exceeding those heretofore customary. With the introduction of private property in land after 1855, the first of the umda's important integrating functions disappeared and another with the abandonment of collective responsibility for taxes. Finally, corvée was made in 1881 into an individual obligation and then abolished altogether. By the interwar period, observers were agreed that the Egyptian village was no longer a community of the traditional sort; there existed "no representation of the village community, no council of elders, and no communal assembly." [59]

The revolutionary socioeconomic transformations of the nineteenth century, which can be summarized as the shift to year-round irrigation, the cultivation of cash crops, and social differentiation based on private property in land, led to an atomization of the Egyptian village. The umda or village shayk, named by the government, remained, and his power and prestige were sometimes freely acknowledged as legitimate rather than being attributed to mere appointment.[60] But appointment meant he was no longer seen as a trustee of the peasants against the government. He was simply a village notable, usually a landowner, who had been able to exploit the Egyptian agrarian revolution of the nineteenth century to improve his position and had sought to establish political claims through the Council of Notables during the Arabi years. The British attempted with the Umdah Law of 1895 to bolster the umda's supervisory and appointive powers. The fact remained, however, that he no longer supplied workers for corvée, tax assessment and collection was in the hands of experts, his magisterial powers were attenuated, and other duties had been assigned him. He now registered births, supervised water and canal usage, was responsible for the security of post and telegraph, had some responsibility for law and order, and acted as arbiter in land disputes. "The Umdah has a great deal more to do than heretofore. He is at the beck and call of the inspectors of every Department. He is responsible for execution of a number of regulations, which he often fails to understand thoroughly." [61]

Within the context of traditional societies, the umdas were not to be compared in terms of origins with Asiatic village headmen or African village or tribal chiefs. What is striking is that the socioeconomic changes and the individualization process that occurred within the villages in the nineteenth century, when combined with the demands of the colonial administration, had the same effects as elsewhere. Despite enjoying personal prosperity, the umda's loss of traditional functions and the coercive powers that went with them—the British even went so far as to prohibit the traditional hippo-leather whips—combined with being laden with new administrative tasks, tasks for which he had neither adequate preparation nor adequate authority, resulted inevitably in sinking prestige.

Although irrigation, acreage, property relationships, and the lot of the fellahin have been discussed, cotton farming requires a somewhat fuller analysis (see table 7.4). Year-round and more skillful irrigation, which prevented both excessive dryness and flooding, obviously mainly benefited cotton and indeed would otherwise probably not have been undertaken. The greater acreage in cotton resulted from irrigation, the lower Nile barrage being the key factor in lower Egypt. Upper Egypt, which until 1902 raised only 5 to 10 percent of the total crop, upped its share after completion of the Aswan Dam in 1902 20 to 25

Table 7.4
Cotton Farming in Egypt, 1883-1913

YEAR	NUMBER OF PLANTED FEDDANS	YIELD (IN CANTARS[a]/ PER FEDDAN)	PRODUCTION (IN CANTARS IN THOUSANDS)	PRICE (IN £E PER CANTAR)	EXPORT VALUE (IN £E THOUSANDS)
1883/84	778,000	3.43	2,694	3.0	8,100
1893/94	965,545	5.21	5,033	1.8	9,507
1905/06	1,506,291	4.03	5,960	3.9	17,096
1912/13	1,723,094	4.44	7,499	3.5	26,719

SOURCE: Owen, *Cotton*, 184-86, 191, 197.
[a]One cantar = 99 pounds.[62]

percent. In 1890 cotton required about one-third of Egyptian arable, which is to say that with a three-year rotation virtually the entire arable was used for cotton.[63] After 1900 cultivation was intensified by shifting to a two-year rotation and planting corn instead of leaving the land fallow during the off years. To speak of a very strong tendency toward monoculture is thus justified.

Why the yield per feddan fell, at least temporarily, has been, and still is, the subject of much discussion. New varieties and summer irrigation post-1890 seem to have boosted yields sharply, whereas subsequent overwatering, and possibly the shift to two-year rotation and less careful farming, had negative effects. It was one reason why the Department of Agriculture was established in 1911. In addition to research its other duties were the distribution of better seed and agricultural counselling.[64] Prices depended on the world market. They fell during the depression years of the 1890s and rose again during boom periods; in 1913 they were only 15 percent higher than in 1880.[65] Fortunately, the fall in prices coincided with the expansion in acreage and higher yields, and was hence not much reflected in gross profits. Export values accordingly rose after 1895, and in 1913 exceeded those of 1884 by more than 300 percent.

Did the fellah profit from this boom? Roughly 70 percent of the cotton came from large holdings, half the delta belonging to landowners with more than fifty feddan.[66] In the case of share-cropping tenants, they shared increasing profits, though it should also be noted that as population pressures increased rental terms worsened. Tenants paying cash rents and rural laborers seem not to have gained or to have gained very little. The small cotton farmer apparently suffered compared to the larger holders because he could not, like the latter, deal directly with Alexandria commercial houses. He depended on expensive middlemen and, according to Owen, a poor farmer got only 55 to 65 percent of the export price.[67] When prices were high, as in the years before World War I, the fellah had some cash coming in which, assuming no blighted crops and a holding large enough to live on, enabled him to pay taxes and interest on debts and buy a few simple consumer goods. All the same, the lion's share undoubtedly went into the pocketbooks of the large holders and merchants.

Did cotton monoculture lead to a neglect of foodstuffs? Egypt was in fact transformed from one of the traditional grain exporters into a grain importer as table 7.5 shows.

Table 7.5
Egyptian Grain Imports and Exports, 1885-1914 (in thousands of £E)

	IMPORTS	EXPORTS	NET EXPORTS
1885-1889	770	964	194
1895-1899	1112	847	– 165
1905-1909	3261	760	–2501
1910-1914	. . .	1745	. . .

SOURCE: Lewis, *Tropical Development*, 207, 209.

But these figures still leave the questions unanswered. Since cotton required a two- or three-year rotation, the fellahin continued to grow foodstuffs, being concerned about reserves. Cotton was a supplemental crop, grown to pay rents, taxes, and interest. The acreage in grain did not change much, while that in rice and corn increased, and that in beans decreased. Yields, on the other hand, rose, with 1913 wheat production, for example, exceeding that for 1886 by 50 percent.[68] What was decisive was that the value of cotton was significantly higher than that for other crops. This was particularly true in the pre-1914 era of rising prices. Given the lack of land, economic pressures were all in favor of cotton. "Egypt's soil is much too precious to waste on grains, beyond that which is required by rotations." [69] The problems within the Egyptian agrarian structure were not caused by the neglect of foodstuffs in favor of cotton monoculture. First, they resulted from the fact that arable per capita and later, despite increasing yields per feddan, per-capita output were falling because population was rising so rapidly. Second, they resulted from Egypt's dependence on world market prices, or, in other words, the terms of trade.[70] Third, they resulted from a property structure that favored the large holder and sucked up peasant profits in the form of rents and interest, and, finally, they reflected the fact that the nonfarm sector was growing too slowly to absorb the surplus population from the land.

Even during the reigns of Muhammad Ali, Said, and Ismail, the shift from a subsistence economy to an economy exporting cotton with concommitant expenditures for public works and forced Westernization had drawn European capital to Egypt. That was naturally even truer after 1882. King Cotton dominated the Egyptian economy. It provided 70 percent of all exports, and if cottonseed—from which oil can be extracted—is added in, over 90 percent, about half of which went to England.[71] Irrigation facilities served primarily to expand cotton acreage, as did the communications system. The canal and rail networks were augmented. A special normal-gage line was built by concessionaires working with foreign capital. Like the road network, it was meant to open up the cotton districts and facilitate transport to the coast.[72] In the 1890s a great number of gins were built, but one-third of all ginning capacity had already been amalgamated under one company by 1905. The same was true of baling plants which, equipped with modern machinery, were directly or indirectly controlled by the great export houses.[73] Their purchasing methods did not change much.

They had agents in the hinterland, who made advances to middling and large producers and thus secured direct deliveries.[74] They reached the fellahin, as has been mentioned, through middlemen. If one adds to the cotton exporters the multitude of other businesses in European hands—land companies, mortgage and commercial banks, trade houses, construction, electric, and transport companies—the total foreign investment can be estimated at £E 200 million, and this does not count state loans nor the Suez Canal Company. These firms had a paid-in capital of 100 million, and 92 million of this was foreign. Europeans living in Europe actually held only 71 million pounds of this, the remainder being in the hands of Europeans living in Egypt, some of whom had been there for a long time.[75] Anything having to do with cotton production or trade came first: 72 percent of the capital of foreign companies was in mortgage or land companies and was, given the considerable risks involved, of largely speculative character. Public utility and transport enterprises, in contrast, were mostly concessions.

Hardly any industrialization, such as Muhammad Ali had earlier attempted, occurred before 1914. Some of the enterprises connected with cotton can, of course, count as factories, that is, gins, balers, and cottonseed mills. The sugar industry, so boldly and successfully launched by Ismail, had its problems, however. Two French companies merged in 1897 to form the Société Générale des Sucreries et de la Raffinerie d'Egypte, which in turn swallowed up the state refineries in 1902, only to run into difficulties itself shortly thereafter. By 1914, however, the company was refining imported as well as Egyptian sugar.[76] Greeks established a cigarette industry able to compete abroad, despite an 1890 administrative prohibition for fiscal reasons of tobacco cultivation in Egypt. Other industries were breweries, paper and leather manufacturing industries, and repair facilities for irrigation and canal construction machinery. A Belgium cement works, however, had difficulty surviving import competition. The question is, however, why no textile industry developed as in India, and why firms founded after 1899 either failed or had so much difficulty surviving.[77] Textiles constituted 30 percent of all imports, and grew at the rate of 4 percent a year. In analogy to India, a general import duty of 8 percent was neutralized by an equal domestic turnover tax. Cromer had pushed this through in the face of lively protests in Egypt, first because of his dogged adherence to free trade, and second, to avoid difficulties with Lancashire. Owen has shown that Cromer had no wish in principle to hinder industry, particularly in his later years when he began to see that agriculture could no longer absorb the increasing population.[78] Owen also criticizes Issawi, who attributes Egypt's "lopsided development" to both foreign and Egyptian capital flowing abroad. Owen points out that a very well-heeled group of foreigners, notably the Greeks and the Jews, lived in Egypt. Even if the Egyptian upper class preferred investing in land or the stock of European corporations, and even if they preferred official to entrepreneurial careers, the foreign minorities nevertheless constituted a potential capitalist class. With the improvement in the terms of trade and modest mass prosperity before 1914, the potential buying power to support Egyptian industry existed. But the success of the export sector and the profits to be made in it clearly did inhibit industrialization. The administration, moreover, in contrast to that of Japan, remained passive. It provided neither customs protection nor any other support. Combined with a lack of cheap energy and raw materials, the above grounds were the main reasons why cotton exports were an "engine of growth," but not an "engine of development," at least if one is willing to leave the cultural factors subsumed in the word *Islam* out of the picture. "But in the final analysis," Owen states, "the advantages Egypt gained from cotton far outweighed the disadvantages. Only after 1914 did the latter begin to be of overwhelming importance."[79]

Another area where Cromer proceeded in a rather niggardly fashion was modern education. As already noted, in his pursuit of the "Europeanization of Egypt" Muhammad Ali made a beginning with engineering, agricultural, and medical schools and sent Egyptians abroad to study. Another foundation that was to prove especially important was his "school for translations," which not only made Western technical literature accessible in Arabic but also opened Oriental literature and languages to Europeans. The first half of the nineteenth century saw publication of the first Egyptian newspapers and books, both in Arabic and in European languages. These efforts were resumed under Ismail, only to be cut back once again because of the fiscal crisis. The latter resulted in, among other things, the closing of some newly established technical schools. Nevertheless, by 1880 Egypt had a cadre that had received modern educations, either at home or abroad, most of whom worked as civil servants. But education ran on short commons even after 1882. Until 1900, less than 1 percent of state outlays went for education, though the amount rose to 3 percent in the following decade.[80] The number of pupils in state schools, which in addition to Arabic, emphasized European languages, rose very slowly. In the primary schools, the increase between 1890 and 1910 was from 5,761 to 8,644, and in the secondary schools from 734 to 2,197.[81] For Cromer and the British administration, financial considerations represented only part of the picture, however, the other part being the political need to provide a modern school system in order to create an efficient civil service. This also had its dangers, as Indian experience revealed. Nationalist movements were based on new, Western educated elites: "Whatever we do, education must produce its natural results, and one of these natural results, both in India and Egypt, will be the wish to get rid of the foreigner."[82] This was more apt to be true if too few administrative posts were available for the newly graduated young intelligentsia. Cromer had also linked the bureaucracy and the school system by permitting entrance to the administration only to those who had passed their examinations. In order to reduce the crush, tuition, abolished under Muhammad Ali and Ismail, was reintroduced. This effectively cut the less prosperous off from the modern schools. Without having attended these, however, one could enter none of the higher schools, those for law, medicine, and engineering. Only well-to-do families could afford European private schools and foreign study.

The masses were left with the traditional school system, based on the Koran school (*kuttab*) in the villages. After 1898 these were subsidized if they agreed to accept some supervision, but were otherwise left to themselves. The children memorized passages in the Koran but most remained functional illiterates. Still, some made their way to al-Azhar, the traditional Muslim university in Cairo. Al-Azhar resisted modernization. Instruction was only in Arabic and modern disciplines were largely excluded, which underlined the dual character of the Egyptian school system. State schools of Western stamp were provided for the native upper class, and masses got traditional Koranic education which left them as "unmodernized" as ever.[83] "Thus education, far from stimulating mobility, tended to freeze the existing class structure."[84]

The origins and development of Egyptian nationalism cannot usefully be discussed here, as it is only to be understood within the larger framework of the Islamic reform movement and the development of Arab nationalism.[85] Something must be said, however, of Mustafa Kamil (1874-1908), who belonged to a generation that could neither recall pre-British Egypt nor had had the traditional al-Azhar education. Son of a Cairo engineer, he studied at modern schools and graduated from the University of Toulouse with a degree in law. He stayed in touch with French intellectual circles the rest of his life. As a European-influenced liberal, he believed in the existence of an Egyptian nation which could unite Muslims and Copts—who were Christians—in a single community. Although he encouraged Egyptian patriotism, he also sympathized with the Pan-Islamic movement and expressed his loyalty to the sultan. He was sharply opposed to British imperialism, criticizing the exclusion of Egyptians from senior administrative posts and after 1900 proseletizing in favor of a parliamentary government in his paper *al-Liwa*. His program may not have been especially consistent, but his combining of modernist and traditional ways of thinking and his art as journalist and orator made him the leader of the nationalist movement even before it organized itself in 1907 as the National party. His appeal was particularly effective within the new, largely urban elite of students, officials, and professionals. His funeral in 1908 became one of the first great "popular manifestations of the new national spirit."[86]

Although a Constitutional Reform party was founded, it acquired no importance because it was tainted by being the court party. After Kamil's death, leadership of the nationalist movement passed to the Ummah, or People's party, also founded in 1907. A wealthy landowner, Ahmad Lutfi al-Sayyid (1872-1964), who was also an intellectual and senior official, was the party's leading figure and its secretary. He was politically more moderate than Kamil, aiming more at reform than any very immediate departure of the British. He also, however, emphasized his distance from both the khedive and the Pan-Islamic movement. He secularized the idea of the nation by positing the existence of an Egyptian nation independent of the community of believers.[87] Ahmad Lutfi made a strong impression on the younger generation. His party never won a following equal to the National party but was nonetheless strongly represented in the various representative bodies. It was also the precurser of the Wafd party of the interwar period.

Cromer resigned in 1907, mainly for reasons of health, but also because he had to assume that after the Liberal victory in 1906 he would have to reckon with policies at variance with his autocratic and paternalistic notions of rule. He can in many ways be compared with Lord Curzon. Hardly anyone has gainsaid his administrative ability, particularly in fiscal matters, nor the tenacity with which he represented Egypt's interests against the other European powers and their bondholders. Still, while never actually a part of the British Empire, Cromer's Egypt was a state whose interests and future the British would long continue to control. For Cromer, the Egyptians were no nation but merely a "confused jumble" of disparate religious and social communities, incapable of self-government and therefore destined to be ruled by the British. European-educated Egyptians were needed in the administration, but only in subordinate positions. He made no secret of his scorn for Egyptian politicians, intellectuals, and representatives of Islamic orthodoxy, and was not in the least inclined to allow them effective participation in the government of their country.[88] In 1906 he had had to make a modest concession in the form of naming Saad Zaghlul education minister. Born in 1860, Zaghlul belonged to an older generation than Kamil, whose role as nationalist leader he was to assume after 1914. His father was an umda and a prosperous peasant. At al-Azhar Zaghlul was a student of the important Islamic reformers, Jamal al-Din al-Afgani and Muhammad Abduh. He later became a lawyer and judge, marrying the daughter of the pro-British prime minister, Mustafa Fahmi, in 1906. He thus obtained entrée to the power elite at court. As the first Egyptian minister, he successfully asserted himself against his British advisers and from 1910 to 1913 was a reform justice minister.[89]

Cromer's successor was his financial adviser, Sir Eldon Gorst (1907-1911), who sought both to liberalize and, by making some concessions, to stabilize, Cromer's autocratic system of rule.[90] His method was to provide the Egyptian official class with more opportunities for promotion and to take the first step towards self-government. The provincial councils, powerless under Cromer, received more extensive functions, most notably control over primary education in both government and kuttab schools. The franchise was not, however, widened, meaning that the councils remained nominated by the great landholders. Gorst's attitude toward the nationalist movement was inconsistent. Whereas Cromer had sought to win over or neutralize the moderates of the Ummah party, in particular in appointing Zaghlul in the face of Khedive Abbas II's opposition, Gorst sought a better relationship with Abbas, manifestly in the hope of cutting off the support the khedive provided the National party. Gorst's hope was fulfilled, but at the cost of driving the Ummah party into the opposition. A new press law and a Criminals Deportation Act, supposedly needed to master rising lawlessness, had provocative effects, fomenting nationalism and giving the National party a healthy boost. Under Muhammad Farid, Kamil's successor, the party became more radical, expanding its organization and establishing closer ties with the various secondary-school and higher-school student associations and the nascent trade union movement. Gorst's planned extension of the Suez Canal Company contract in 1908 provided the occasion for vehement protest demonstrations. The assassination in 1910 of the prime minister, a Copt, by a National party Muslim ignited the latent hostility between the two groups. It also set the British on the trail of the numerous clandestine groups with links to the party. The tension these events caused within the party began the party's decline.[91]

Cromer's policies were resumed once again with the appointment of Kitchener as consul general in 1911.[92] The leaders of the National party were placed under arrest or sent into exile, the party itself continuing its agitation from Paris and Constantinople. At the same time, however, Kitchener tried to establish better relations with the Ummah party. He combined the two representative bodies with their modest consultative competence (the legislative council and the general assembly) into a single legislative assembly. In 1913 the franchise's high property qualifications resulted in forty-nine out of sixty-one of those elected being landowners and provided the Ummah party with a majority. Although Zaghlul had still been a minister a short time before and had defended the Suez contract in the general assembly, he now became vice-president and leader of the opposition.

It is tempting to compare the situation in Egypt in the years before World War I with that of India. In both places, after the departure of strong proconsuls, the radical wings of the nationalist movements came to the fore. The radicals were mainly the younger generation of the European-educated urban bourgeoisie, who sought to widen their political base to include the lower classes. Although they organized demonstrations and individual terrorist acts, the violence proved a passing phase because the Liberals made concessions to the moderates after 1906. They were thus able to win them, if not for collaboration, at least for a course of evolutionary change. It probably helped that the landowner class and the urban intelligentsia shrank back before a radicalism that might have endangered their own positions. The Morley-Minto reforms in India and the expansion in Egypt of the provincial councils and legislative assembly showed that autocratic rule had to be loosened and forums granted where the nationalist movements could articulate their desires. At the same time restrictive franchises assured that native landowning classes would be heavily represented. Self-government lay in both places beyond the horizon of British policy. Still, the nationalist movements lacked the character of mass movements, although they were able to broaden both their organizational and agitational bases after 1900. It took World War I to create both in India and Egypt quasi-revolutionary situations and to force the weakened colonial power to grant concessions inconceivable before 1914.

Space permits only a cursory coverage of these developments.[93] Because the Ottoman Empire sided with the Central Powers, the Allies declared war against it on 6 November 1914. On 18 November the British ended Ottoman sovereignty over Egypt by issuing a unilateral protectorate declaration, a document sharply condemned not only in traditional Pan-Islamic circles but also among Westernized Egyptians, who feared that Britain sought to add Egypt to the empire. Khedive Abbas II, accused of collaboration with the sultan, was deposed, the legislative assembly was adjourned *sine die*, and martial law was imposed. The military for all intents took over the administration, which led to considerable frustration among even the pro-British ruling elite and among many Egyptian officials. That was one reason why these groups later approached the nationalist movement.

Egypt was transformed into a military camp. In violation of the promise that Egypt would not be brought into the war against the Turks, England began recruiting a Labour Corps—first voluntary and later by draft—and requisitioning camels, horses, feed, and building materials. This severely burdened the rural population and estranged the fellahin from British rule.[94] The prohibition against the sale of cotton to the Central Powers led at first to a fall in prices, but later, from 1915 to 1919, prices rose sharply. The rise brought landowners and traders huge profits and enabled many fellahin to pay off their debts.[95] At the same time, however, the price of consumer goods rose, both because imports were restricted and because of demand from Allied troops stationed in Egypt. The situation profited merchants, army suppliers, and construction firms, but hurt petty officials, artisans, and workers. The war also created opportunities to manufacture previously imported goods and the necessary spur for the development of an Egyptian entrepreneurial class. The formation of the Committee for Trade and Industry in 1917 was a sign of the times. This new, still limited, financial and industrial bourgeoisie would necessarily be interested in economic and customs autonomy in the postwar period.

Neither London nor Cairo took sufficient account of the degree to which discontent was fermenting, nourished in no small part by the tactless behavior of British officials during the war. Surprise was accordingly great when a full-blown radical nationalist movement appeared directly after the war. Zaghlul took over its leadership, informing the high commissioner, General Sir Reginald Wingate, on 13 November 1918 of Egypt's demands for independence and its wish to send a delegation to the peace negotiations in Paris. The planned delegation (al-Wafd al Misri) received its charge and at the same time stated its claim to represent the Egyptian people. When London rejected these claims, Zaghlul launched a large-scale campaign of agitation, in which individuals, associations, and local councils signed a declaration supporting the nationalist demands of the Wafd. The Wafd executive thus created a ground swell of support and a popular basis of sorts for its power.[96] When Zaghlul was arrested on 8 March 1919 and deported to Malta, disturbances broke out which spread from the cities over much of Egypt. There were demonstrations, acts of sabotage, assaults on British soldiers, other terrorist acts, and strikes. What was important was that peasants as well as notables participated,[97] even though the activities of the former were directed not only against the British but also against the landowners in many localities.[98]

Only then did London see fit to act. Wingate was replaced by General Edmund H. H. Allenby, the victor of Palestine. Zaghlul, now a martyr to the nationalist cause, but upon whom the Egyptian government was unfortunately dependent, was brought back. The British now agreed to the sending of a delegation to Paris and sent Lord Milner to Cairo at the head of an investigating commission. Although the latter was boycotted, Milner nevertheless not only exposed the wartime failures of British policy in his remarkable report but also pleaded for the grant of independence, under the proviso that Great Britain be granted rights to control the Suez canal and to maintain a military presence in the country. Milner later went even farther, concluding an agreement with Zaghlul in London in 1920.[99] Zaghlul withdrew from the agreement, however, and the British government was none too pleased with Milner. In Egypt new difficulties arose between the government and the Wafd, during which Zaghlul upped his demands and loosed a new wave of demonstrations. Allenby shipped him off yet again to Malta, while at the same time urging London most strenuously to give in. On 22 February 1922, the British government issued a unilateral declaration proclaiming Egyptian independence. England retained control of defense and the guardianship of imperial communication routes, the right to protect minorities and foreigners, and control over the Sudan. The constitution of 1923 made Egypt a constitutional monarchy and Fuad the first king.

In good part as a result of the war, British rule, exercised between 1882 and 1914 as a "veiled protectorate," thus ended. Still, one can hardly speak of genuine independence. In the following years, the domestic disputes which now commenced provided England, in the person of the high commissioner, ample opportunity to interfere, quite aside from its control over defense and foreign policy. The most important of these disputes was between the king and the unconciliatory Zaghlul and his Wafd party. Foreigners also retained their privileged position and economic dominance. Egyptian sovereignty was recognized in international law only in 1936, and England retained the right to station troops at the Suez Canal and to intervene in time of war, a right used in World War II to occupy the country during the German advance through Libya. The ruling class of large landowners and rich urban bourgeoisie, which had in 1907 through the Ummah party become the backbone of moderate reform nationalism, fought through to formal independence in 1922 under the leadership of Saad Zaghlul. Thereafter, it controlled Egypt economically and politically through a parliamentary system that in practice worked fairly well.[100] Its power ended only with Nasser's revolution of 1952.

NOTES

1. Panayiotis J. Vatikiotis, *The Modern History of Egypt* (London: Wiedenfeld & Nicolson, 1969); Jacques Berque, *L'Egypte: Impérialisme et Révolution* (Paris: Gallimard, 1967); Gabriel Baer, "Social Change in Egypt, 1800-1914," in Conference on the Modern History of

Egypt, University of London, 1965, *Political and Social Change in Modern Egypt: Historical Studies from the Ottoman Conquest to the United Arab Republic*, ed. P. M. Holt (London, New York: Oxford University Press, 1966); Zvi Yehuda Hershlag, *Introduction to the Modern Economic History of the Middle East* (Leiden: E. J. Brill, 1964); Lewis, *Tropical Development*.

2. On the sociopolitical situation during the reign of Ismail, khedive of Egypt (1863-1879), see, in particular, Alexander Schölch, *Ägypten den Ägyptern! Die politische und gesellschaftliche Krise der Jahre 1878-1882 in Ägypten* (Zurich: Atlantis Verlag, 1972).

3. The basic work on the agrarian structure is Gabriel Baer, *A History of Landownership in Modern Egypt, 1800-1950* (London, New York: Oxford University Press, 1962).

4. Ibid., 25.

5. Gabriel Baer, "The Village Shaykh, 1800-1950," in idem, *Studies in the Social History of Modern Egypt* (Chicago: University of Chicago Press, 1969), 48ff.; Schölch, *Ägypten den Ägyptern*, 42f.

6. Schölch, *Ägypten den Ägyptern*, 46.

7. On this question, see Edward Roger John Owen, *Cotton and the Egyptian Economy, 1820-1914: A Study in Trade and Development* (Oxford: Clarendon Press, 1969).

8. Ibid., 89f. Export net profit was £E 1.4 million in 1861 and £E 15.4 million in 1865.

9. See the statistics in ibid., 123f., 160.

10. Quoted, ibid., 149.

11. Baer, *Landownership*, 35.

12. Hershlag, *Introduction*, 85f.; Owen, *Cotton*, 23f., 45f.

13. Charles Philip Issawi, "Egypt since 1800: A Study in Lopsided Development," *JEH*, 27 (March 1961), 6f.; idem, *Egypt in Revolution: An Economic Analysis* (London, New York: Oxford University Press, 1963), ch. 2, "Integration in the World Economy, 1798-1920."

14. See the tables in Hershlag, *Introduction*, 106.

15. Issawi, "Egypt since 1800," 8; Owen, *Cotton*, 168f.

16. Owen, *Cotton*, 113.

17. Based on Edouard Dervieu's correspondence, David S. Landes, *Bankers and Pashas: International Finance and Economic Imperialism in Egypt* (London: Heinemann, 1958), provides a graphic picture.

18. Hershlag, *Introduction*, 100.

19. According to Wolfgang J. Mommsen, *Imperialismus in Ägypten: der Aufstieg der ägyptischen Nationalbewegung* (Munich: R. Oldenbourg, 1961), 31, the khedive received only eleven million in cash.

20. Ibid., 38.

21. For the events up to the occupation in 1882, I follow Alexander Schölch, "Constitutional Development in Nineteenth Century Egypt: A Reconsideration," *MES*, 10 (January 1974).

22. Ibid., 161.

23. Ronald Robinson and John Gallagher, with Alice Denny, *Africa and the Victorians: The Official Mind of Imperialism* (London: Macmillan, 1961), ch.4; Desmond Christopher St. Martin Platt, *Finance, Trade and Politics in British Foreign Policy, 1815-1914* (Oxford: Clarendon Press, 1968), 154f.; Edward Roger John Owen, "Egypt and Europe: From French Expedition to British Occupation," in *idem* and Robert B. Sutcliffe (eds.), *Studies in the Theory of Imperialism* (London: Longmans, 1972). Whereas Robinson and Gallagher picture the alleged threat to sea communications with India as the ground for intervention, Schölch emphasizes the influence on the British government of British financial and economic interests in Egypt; Alexander Schölch, "The 'Men on the Spot' and the English Occupation of Egypt in 1882," *Historical Journal*, 19 (September 1976).

24. Alfred Milner, 1st Viscount, *England in Egypt* (13th ed., London: B. Arnold, 1926), 25.

25. Robinson and Gallagher, *Africa*, 122f.

26. Ibid., 129f.

27. Milner, *England in Egypt*, ch. 3. "It was a veiled Protectorate of uncertain extent and indefinite duration for the accomplishment of a difficult and distant object"; ibid., 28.

28. For this and the following, see, in addition to Milner, Evelyn Baring, 1st Earl of Cromer, *Modern Egypt* (2 vols., London: Macmillan, 1908), II; and the account in Robert L. Tignor, *Modernization and British Colonial Rule in Egypt, 1882-1914* (Princeton: Princeton University Press, 1966).

29. Cromer, *Modern Egypt*, II, 284.

30. Edward Roger John Owen, "The Influence of Lord Cromer's Indian Experience on British Policy in Egypt, 1883-1907," *St. Anthony's Papers*, 17 (Oxford, 1965), 138, and in German in Albertini, *Moderne Kolonialgeschichte*, 199.

31. Tignor, *Modernization*, 174.

32. The figures vary between those of Tignor, *Modernization*, 190f. and Morroe Berger, *Bureaucracy and Society in Modern Egypt: A Study of the Higher Civil Service* (Princeton: Princeton University Press, 1957), 30f.

33. Cromer, *Modern Egypt*, II, 295.

34. Ibid., 294. Owen, "Influence," is very good on this matter.

35. The remarks of the irrigation engineer William Willcocks were perhaps overly critical: "Throughout his long tenure of office Lord Cromer had sedulously depressed and kept down every independent Egyptian and had filled all the high posts with cyphers, with the result that the natural leaders of the people had no opportunity of leading the people"; Sir William Willcocks, *Sixty Years in the East* (Edinburgh, London: W. Blackwood & Sons, 1935), as quoted in Berger, *Bureaucracy and Society*, 26.

36. The classic accounts are those of Milner and Cromer. See also Tignor, *Modernization*, 74f.

37. Lewis, *Tropical Development*, 201; and the similar tables in Hershlag, *Introduction*, 116.

38. But Tignor, *Modernization*, 114, states, "Egypt's irrigation system was on the verge of collapse."

39. "But the PWD was the first in which English influence became supreme, and the first manifestation of that influence was a rigorous control of the distribution of water. The odium excited by that control among the most powerful natives was, in the beginning, very great"; Milner, *England in Egypt*, 78, 210.

40. See also Lewis, *Tropical Development*, 206.

41. Ibid., 207.

42. Production indices were:

Table 7.6
Production Indices for Individual Crops in Egypt, 1821-1878 (Year 1821 = 100)

YEAR	COTTON	SUGAR	WHEAT	CORN	BEANS	RICE
1821	100	100	100	100	100	100
1872-1878	5,000	785	330	670	219	90

SOURCE: O'Brien, "Long-Term Growth," 179.

43. Agricultural growth was as follows:

Table 7.7
Indices of Agricultural Growth in Egypt (Years 1895-1939 = 100)

YEAR	TOTAL OUTPUT	TOTAL POPULATION	RURAL POPULATION	CROPPED AREA
1895-1899	100	100	100	100
1900-1904	110	108	108	109
1905-1909	116	116	117	113
1910-1914	121	124	125	114
1915-1919	103	132	131	115
1920-1924	113	140	138	120
1938-1939	153	166	156	123

SOURCE: Ibid., 188, table, 189.

44. Lewis, *Tropical Development*, 209. On the relative prosperity of the masses before 1914, see also Issawi, "Egypt since 1800," 11. "The per capita income which had risen fairly rapidly till the First World War is today (1960) certainly lower than it was at that time"; ibid., 16.

45. See also similar tables in Tignor, *Modernization*, 241.

46. Baer, *Landownership*, 97.

47. Ibid., 101.

48. On the land corporations, see ibid., 95, 124f.

49. Owen, *Cotton*, 243.

50. Tignor, *Modernization*, 237f.

51. Kitchener's "Report" of 1912 stated: "The government considered it essential to take measure preventing the wholesale eviction by ruthless creditors of the owners and cultivators of small holdings, an interesting and defenceless class of the community whose expulsion from the small farms from which they and their families alone derive their subsistence is opposed to the best interests in an agricultural state like Egypt"; Baer, *Landownership*, 89.

52. Ibid., 90.

53. Tignor, *Modernization*, 120f.; and on Nurbar's services, see Milner, *England in Egypt*, 117.

54. Milner, *England in Egypt*, 315; Tignor, *Modernization*, 106f.; Owen, *Cotton*, 245f.

55. Tignor, *Modernization*, 108.

56. See the tables in Lewis, *Tropical Development*, 203.

57. Berque, *L'Egypte*, 159.

58. I follow here the brilliant essay by Gabriel Baer, "The Dissolution of the Egyptian Village Community," *Welt des Islams*, 6: nos. 1-2 (1959).

59. Hans Alexander Winkler, *Bauern zwischen Wasser und Wüste: Volkskundliches aus dem Dorfe Kimân in Oberägypten* (Stuttgart: W. Kollhammer, 1934), as quoted in Baer, "Dissolution," 29.

60. Baer, "Village Shaykh."

61. Cromer, in the years 1905, as quoted by Baer, "Village Shaykh," 43.

62. My figures come from various tables in Owen, *Cotton*, of which I present only a summary here.

63. Ibid., 184-87.

64. Ibid., 191-96.

65. Ibid., 197.

66. Tignor, *Modernization*, 234.

67. Owen, *Cotton*, 256f.

68. Ibid., 247-251.

69. Issawi, "Egypt since 1800," 16.

70. World market prices were favorable from 1850 to 1870, unfavorable from 1870 to 1895, favorable until 1913. They fluctuated sharply during and after World War I, were sharply unfavorable from 1925 to 1938, briefly favorable, only to turn negative again in World War II. They were favorable from 1948 to 1951, and very unfavorable after 1951; ibid., 14. Similar figures are given in Sieber, *Realen Austauschverhältnisse*, 149f.

71. Owen, *Cotton*, 198.

72. Ibid., 213.

73. Ibid., 219f.

74. A list of the thirty-five houses with the largest exports appears in ibid., Appendix 4, 386.

75. Covered in detail in Tignor, *Modernization*, 358, who largely follows Arthur Edwin Crouchley, *Investment of Foreign Capital in Egyptian Companies and Public Debt* (New York: Arno, 1977, c. 1936). See also Owen, *Cotton*, 276-94.

76. Owen, *Cotton*, 296. On the company's difficulties, see also Hershlag, *Introduction*, 121.

77. On the textile factories, see Owen, *Cotton* 222-24. On this question, see, in addition to Owen, *Cotton*, 300ff., Tignor, *Modernization*, 363f., Issawi, "Egypt since 1800," 11; Lewis, *Tropical Development*, 211f.

78. Edward R. J. Owen, "Lord Cromer and the Development of Egyptian Industry, 1883-1907," *MES*, 2 (July 1966); idem, *Cotton*, 340f.

79. Owen, *Cotton*, 375. Issawi, *Egypt in Revolution*, 18, argues along similar lines: "In the first phase before 1914, the subsistence economy under which the country had lived for centuries was replaced by an export-oriented economy, the bulk of Egypt's available reserves in land, water and underemployed labour were brought into use and its total output and exports increased several times, with a consequent rise in the real per capita income and in the level of living."

80. Tignor, *Modernization*, 346.

81. Ibid., 323.

82. Cromer to Gorst, quoted in ibid., 320.

83. Milner compared the Egyptian school system to a pyramid stood on its point: The government subsidies went to a few thousand students, "mostly of the well-to-do classes," while 91 percent of the population remained illiterate; Milner, *England in Egypt*, 391.

84. Tignor, *Modernization*, 388.

85. Albert Hourani, *Arabic Thought in the Liberal Age, 1798-1939* (London, New York: Oxford University Press, 1962); Nadav Safran, *Egypt in Search of Political Community: An Analysis of the Intellectual and Political Evolution of Egypt, 1804-1952* (Cambridge: Harvard University Press, 1961); Ibrahim Amin Ghali, *L'Egypte Nationaliste et Libérale, de Moustapha Kamel à Saad Zagloul (1892-1927)*, (The Hague: M. Nijhoff, 1969); Anouar Abdel Malek, "La Formation de l'Idéologie dans la Renaissance Nationale de l'Egypte (1805-1892)" (Doctoral dissertation, University of Paris, 1969). Published under the title *Idéologie et Renaissance Nationale: l'Egypte Moderne* (Paris: Editions Anthropos, 1969).

86. Tignor, *Modernization*, 261f.; F. Steppat, "Nationalismus und Islam bei Mustafa Kamel," *Welt des Islams*, 4 (1956). See also Arthur Goldschmidt, "The Egyptian Nationalist Party, 1892-1919," in Holt, *Modern Egypt*.

87. "I reject most decisively the notion that religion can constitute a suitable instrument for political action in the twentieth century. Our nationalism must rest upon our interests, not upon our spiritual beliefs"; quoted by Ibrahim I. Ibrahim, "Der Aufstieg des Nationalismus," 87-117, in Friedemann Büttner (ed.), *Reform und Revolution in der islamischen Welt: von der osmanischen Imperial Doktrin zum arabischen Sozialismus* (Munich: F. List, 1971), 98.

88. "For many a long year to come the Egyptians will be incapable of governing themselves on civilized principles"; Cromer, *Modern Egypt*, II, 343. Cromer's attitude also emerges very clearly in his "Memorandum on the Present Situation in Egypt" of 8 September 1906, in Great Britain, Public Records Office, F. O. 371/68, in which he argued that the situation, which appeared quiet as recently as the year before, had become rather disquieting because of the Pan-Islamic nationalist movement. English public opinion prevented decisive action, and press censorship seemed ill-advised. "Both the assembly and the Council represent mainly the land's interest. The only people who really take an interest in the welfare of the man of the people are the British officials." The administrative system was a "crazy edifice," and it was surprising that it had functioned as long as it had. On Cromer's nations of rule, see also Tignor, *Modernization*, 271f.

89. On Zaghlul, see Hourani, *Arabic Thought*, 209f. Very critical is Elie Kedourie, "Saad Zaghlul and the British," *St. Anthony's Papers*, 11 (1961), reprinted in idem, *The Chatham House Version and Other Middle-Eastern Studies* (New York: Praeger, 1970).

90. For the following see, Tignor, *Modernization*, 291f.

91. Goldschmidt, "Egyptian Nationalist Party," 326.

92. He was sent with the charge "to use his strength and prestige to restore a deteriorating situation, while continuing a policy of cautious liberalization"; Sir Philip M. Magnus, *Kitchener: Portrait of an Imperialist* (London: J. Murray, 1958), 262.

93. Vatikiotis, *Egypt*, ch. 11.

94. Sir Valentine Chirol, for many years foreign editor of the *Times*, commented: "Confidence of the fellahman in the beneficence of British Control had gone and been turned into hatred by the hardship to which they had been subjected"; *Fifty Years in a Changing World* (London: J. Cape, 1927), 65.

95. Baer, *Landownership*, 83.

96. Marius Deeb, "The 1919 Popular Uprising: A Genesis of Egyptian Nationalism," *Canadian Review of Studies in Nationalism*, 1 (March 1973). Kedourie thinks the evidence proves that the Egyptian ministers supported the petitions agitation and that the latter was by no means entirely Zaghlul's "service"; Kedourie, "Saad Zaghlul," 149.

97. Deeb's thesis, in his own words, is: "The 1919 popular uprising was neither organized nor even a premeditated movement engineered by the Wafd or any other group. It was locally organized and led by members of the effendiyya class, in alliance with the village notables"; Deeb, "Popular Uprising," 115.

98. Peasants attacked the house of a large landlord in Upper Egypt whose son had been exiled to Malta along with Zaghlul. When questioned about this, the peasants allegedly answered: "Has Mahmud Pasha Sulayman distributed bread to the hungry? We want bread!"; Gabriel Baer, "Submissiveness and the Revolt of the Fellah," in Holt, *Modern Egypt*.

99. On the attitude of Milner, the cabinet and the most important advisors, see Albertini, *Decolonization*, 42-46.

100. On the high proportion of large landlords in the cabinet and the two houses of Parliament between 1924 and 1950, see Baer, *Landownership*, 143.

8

FRANCE IN THE MAGHREB

The French expansion in North Africa, which encompassed Algeria in 1830, Tunisia in 1881, and Morocco in 1912, occurred within very divergent domestic and foreign policy contexts. Constitutionally and administratively, too, the areas were treated very differently. Algeria became a part of metropolitan France, while Tunisia and Morocco both remained protectorates. Customs treatment was equally divergent. Algeria, again, was to all intents a part of France. Tunisia received its own dispensation. Morocco, governed by the provisions of international treaties, granted all nations the same rights. In historical retrospect, nonetheless, one can fairly speak of the three states as a unified colonial complex, and not only because all three territories with their Muslim populations were contiguous. Important stimuli leading to the conquest of the two protectorates had come from Algeria, but more important was the fact that the French nation saw them as a unity, both politically and economically. Not only Algeria, but also Tunisia and Morocco were considered areas of settlement, in contrast, say, to black Africa or Indochina. For that reason, the land question, which in practice meant freeing land for colons, remained the key political problem. The colons became, indeed, one of the most important pressure groups both in the colonies and in the metropolis. In both Algeria and the protectorates the colons sought to combine administrative and legal integration with the metropolis and yet have local autonomy. They wanted equality and assimilation with metropolitan Frenchmen to be the aims of French colonial policy, but only for themselves, and not for the "colonized." The latter were to remain forever *sujets* rather than citizens. They were to serve as a low-cost work force in assisting the colons to open up the country agriculturally. A goodly portion of the best land in all three territories indeed ended up in colon hands. They exploited representative bodies and local administrations to secure their interests in justice, land and agricultural policy, and even education. In part, the administration sided with the colons. In the interests of stabilizing French rule, however, it also sought a genuine accommodation between native and colon interests. For these reasons, the national liberation movements came to be directed primarily against the colons.

The latter for their part energetically rejected any sort of reform in the interwar period which sought to provide Muslims with opportunities for political collaboration or self-determination. In what follows, I shall outline both the differences and similarities in the tendencies at work in each area.

ALGERIA AS AN INTEGRAL PART OF THE NATIONAL TERRITORY

The regency of Algiers had been under Ottoman rule since the sixteenth century. It was rather indifferently governed by a small Turkish upper class, who had not impinged very much upon the fundamental religious and social institutions of the rural population. Moors and Jews from Spain controlled the artisan trades and local commerce, and Livorno Jews controlled foreign trade and banking. Anti-Turkish tribal revolts led by marabouts (holy men) and shaykhs of noble blood were a common occurrence. One can thus hardly speak of an Algerian state or nation in the precolonial period.[1]

On 14 June 1830, 37,000 French troops landed along the coast and in Algiers and on 5 July the dey capitulated. No territorial occupation had originally been intended, Marseille being the only city in the homeland showing any interest in a French presence in Algeria.[2] The soldiers in charge, however, found themselves increasingly forced to intervene, sometimes offensively, sometimes defensively; a young marabout from eastern Algeria, Abd el-Kader, had proclaimed holy war against the French and had inflicted some embarrassing defeats upon them.[3] The treaties of 1834 and 1837 (with some appendixes even yet under scholarly discussion)[4] led to a war of "pacification" lasting several years. The war was characterized by razzias and crop destruction that laid waste wide areas and led to social disintegration. With the creation of the Bureaux des Affaires Arabes a kind of indirect rule developed, in which Arabic-speaking officers attempted to establish contact with the local Muslim population by recognizing the positions of the local notables. There was in this, however, a tendency to break up the greater tribal units and to take over the local administration.[5] Considering themselves the "protectors of the natives," these administrators soon found themselves at odds with the colons.

Colonization had begun directly after the conquest. In the Algiers region, Turkish landholders had either fled or been driven out, and the French who had come streaming in, a rather motley assortment, had simply seized the ownerless land or purchased it at less than its real market value. At the same time, the *colonisation officielle*, or state-supported colonization, began. Unoccupied land was declared public domain, and the business of clarifying ownership was initiated. As early as 1842 to 1845, 105,000 hectares had been distributed to new settlers' villages. It was characteristic for the following period—and in general for colonial land sequestrations in settled areas—that the transfer by natives to Europeans of pasture land as "uncultivated land" in practice meant the dispossession of the former.[6] In the 1850s the process became institutionalized as *cantonnement*, meaning that Algerians with *arch* land (tribal lands to which they had the usufruct) were either encouraged, or forced, to turn a portion of it over to the state, in return for recognition of individual or group property rights to the remainder. In practice this device also amounted to an expulsion of the natives, especially because many were then unable to withstand the temptation to sell their land.[7]

With the coming of the February revolution of 1848, the day of the civilians, meaning the colons, had dawned. The republican constitution declared Algeria to be an integral part of French territory, as the constitution of 1791 had earlier done with the old colonies. Algeria was divided into three departments with prefectures and subprefectures. The Algerian French received the existing French suffrage and three parliamentary deputies. French law became valid in Algeria, and the administrative divisions were subordinated directly to the ministries in Paris, an action termed *rattachement* in the jargon of the day. The Bureaux Arabes retained jurisdiction over only the "military territories" in the south. This administrative integration accorded with the credo The Republic, One and Indivisible and its egalitarian and centralizing ethos. It was based on concepts of the Enlightenment and the nationalist equation of French culture with modern civilization. In the old colonies and later in the four communes of Senegal, however, all inhabitants, regardless of race, color, or religion, were declared Frenchmen equal under the law. Colonial policies of assimilation, in other words, implied in principle the promotion of subjects to full and equal citizenship. In Algeria assimilation applied after 1848 only to the French, the Muslims remaining subjects without the rights of French citizenship. That continued to be true under the Third Republic, although the ideologies justifying colonial rule postulated a gradual broadening of the terms of citizenship. The realization of this postulate was to collapse against colon resistance, however.

The Second Empire had no unified Algerian policy. Until 1860 settlement continued to be officially encouraged, and free colonization was made easier. Financial houses were thus granted large land concessions. In a ten-year period, 50,000 hectares were conceded to fifty-one companies, with the Companie Genevoise alone receiving 12,340 hectares, and 250,000 hectares were granted individual settlers, whose numbers had increased to 83,000. The Bureaux Arabes performed the service of limiting the policy of *cantonnement* in their areas, laying out new villages for the natives, and making efforts to improve farming. But the colons protested and, exploiting the widespread dislike of "government by saber," succeeded in pushing through a policy of assimilation between 1858 and 1860. This policy was directed against local Algerian notables and was intended to loosen tribal solidarity. Informed of this situation, however, by the Bureaux Arabes, Emperor Napoleon III visited Algeria in 1860 and inaugurated a complete reversal of policy. In his famous letter of 6 February 1863, he proclaimed: "Algeria is not, properly speaking, a colony but an Arab kingdom." In April 1860, Algerian tribes were made the owners of the lands they exploited. Tribes already dispossessed were to have their lands returned to them, and land law, justice, and education were to be reorganized, not in the sense of assimilation but in that of "association."[8]

With the gradual parliamentarization of the Second Empire, however, the colons were again able to assert their interests. Shortly before the fall of the empire, it was decreed that as yet undivided tribal lands were to be distributed to individual tribesmen. The Muslim leaders took this as a deliberate blow against Muslim society, and it thus became one of the causes of the great uprising of 1871. Under pressure from the colons and in the spirit of the republicanism that had opposed the empire, the national defense government decreed civilian administration. As early as 24 December 1870, the jurisdiction of the Bureaux Arabes was severely limited. At the same time, Algerian Jews received French citizenship en bloc through the *Décret Crémieux*, an important measure years in the planning. The fall of Napoleon, the military defeat of the ruling power, and the civil administration decree, which the Muslims understood as a colon victory with all that that implied, resulted in the uprising of 1871; the hour of liberation seemed to have come.[9] Although peasant leagues formed spontaneously, the actual declaration of holy war, on 14 March 1871, came from the great Muslim chieftans of the Constantine region. They also received massive support from the Kabyles. The number of rebels was estimated at 800,000. There was little coordination, however. Although the Algiers and Oran regions remained quiet, the struggle continued for several months. The repression which followed was extraordinarily gruesome and bore all the earmarks of racist revenge. It was also exploited to seize both money and land.[10] A collective punishment of 36 million gold francs and the loss of 446,000 hectares was imposed on the rebellious tribes.[11] This great rebellion falls within the category of post-primary resistance actions, and has not, I think, been accorded its just due by historical scholarship.

The colons exploited their "victory" to the utmost and ruled in years following virtually without let or hindrance. Administrative integration came in 1881 in the form of *rattachements* placing Algerian affairs directly under the control of the corresponding ministries in the homeland. The colons were represented by six parliamentary deputies. These deputies were members of republican inner circles, and thus obtained ample hearing for their interests. Around 1891, all this began to come in for lively criticism in the metropolis. Jules Ferry led a senate commission to Algeria, held hearings, and then presented an extraordinarily critical report on the Algerian administration and the Muslims' catastrophic situation.[12] The rattachements were cut only in 1896, when a governor was placed in charge of the administration. In 1900 Algeria received its own budget, dependence on the finance ministry not having worked out, and could thus issue its own loans. None of this shook colon dominance. They alone elected deputies and senators and they dominated the finance delegation conceded them in 1898. The delegation, divided into two groups, consisted of forty-eight Frenchmen in one section and twenty-one Muslims (fifteen Arabs and six Kabyles) in the other. Algeria was thus at once a part of the national territory and yet enjoyed the advantages of a certain fiscal autonomy.

The local administration accorded with colon views. The areas of colon settlement were organized as *communes de plein exercice*, which were externally copies of the communes of the homeland. In practice, however, they were instruments for ruling the natives, as only the colons voted for mayor (until 1919). In addition, the neighboring villages, or *douars*, were linked to such communes, to permit exploiting native taxes mainly to serve colon interests. The number of communes rose from 196 in 1881 to 261 in 1900 and 304 in 1932. In 1936, 880,000 Europeans and 180,000 "natives" lived within them. No less a man than Jules Ferry characterized them as "exploitation of the natives to the very limits."[13] Rather larger, reaching one-half million hectares in size, were the *communes mixtes*. Because settlers were only a small minority in such communes (in 1936, seventy-eight such communes were inhabited by 53,000 Europeans and 3.8 million natives) they were run by an appointed administrator who possessed magistrate's powers. They thus had a clearly colonial look. Algerian *caids* as village chiefs administered areas about the size of a French arrondissement.[14] Native interests were probably better safeguarded there than elsewhere, which may explain the tenacity with which they fought against being changed into communes de plein exercice.

Only Frenchmen and naturalized foreigners, such as Spaniards, Italians, and Maltese, enjoyed full rights of citizenship. Muslims, however, did not, their affairs being regulated by a special penal statute, the *Indigénat* of 1881. It provided streamlined administrative punishments for a number of acts, internment, sequestration of property, and collective punishment. The Muslim also had to have a *permis de circulation* to leave his village. The Muslims hence asked early on for the loosening up or the abolition of the discriminatory Indigénat, while the colons tenaciously defended it as an important instrument of French rule. The judicial system was also gallicized. The Muslims retained their own law in civil matters such as marriage, inheritance, and gifts—their "personal status" as Muslims—but had to submit disputes to French arbiters who usually judged according to the dictates of the French code. The caids who traditionally judged such matters were thus eliminated. More important, criminal justice lay entirely in the hands of French juries.

This short sketch of the administrative structure shows that the Third Republic had established an *administration directe* from which the Algerians were excluded. It constituted an administrative apparatus working entirely in colon interests despite being manned in good part by Algerians. Some of the more able governors attempted to achieve at least a balancing of the interests of the two groups, but invariably encountered massive colon protests. As the colons controlled the Délégations Financières, the communes de plein exercices, the press, and the parliamentary delegations, they had far more leverage than the governors. Algerians were, and remained, the conquered. Their traditional structures of authority were deliberately destroyed and they were delivered over, willy-nilly, to processes of social disintegration. Officially the policy was gallicization, understood in liberal circles to be a melding of the two communities under the banner of French civilization, but in practice supporting colon hegemony. The colons thus, not surprisingly, showed no interest in Muslim education and consistently sabotaged such altruism as both the metropolis and individual officials occasionally revealed.[15] One need hardly accept the current thesis that before 1830 all Algerians could read and write because of the Koran schools. Still, the number of Algerian students rose very slowly, though this was doubtless in part due to a lack of Algerian enthusiasm for secular French education. The number of Algerians rose from 3,000 primary students in 1882 to 42,600 in 1914, and to 60,000 in 1929 (or 6 percent of all school-age children), and 100,000 in 1938.[16] The advanced secondary schools (*collèges*) of the Second Empire, which had provided instruction in both French and Arabic (the one in Constantine had 205 students in 1869, 116 of whom were Muslims), were closed in 1871. The new French collèges had only 150 Muslim students in 1914 and only 1,358 in 1940. Admittedly in the interwar period an increasing number of Algerians studied either in France or other Arab countries, but the academic elite was still extraordinarily narrow as late as 1954, the year of the Algerian revolt. It consisted of a few hundred lawyers, doctors, teachers, pharmacists—but only twenty-eight engineers.[17]

INDIRECT RULE, FRENCH VERSION: TUNISIA AND MOROCCO

Like Egypt, Tunisia was formally a part of the Ottoman Empire, but was in practice virtually independent. And like Egypt, as a result of increasing contacts with Europe, its rulers also attempted modernization from above—public works, army reforms, a constitution, representation of notables in 1861, and the Collège Sadiki in 1875. But with modernization came profligacy, and the bey was ruthlessly exploited by both the court camarilla and European creditors. Heavily in debt, his land wracked by famine, the bey had to submit in 1869 to an international finance commission. Under this *Protectorat à trois*, as the commission was known, British, French, and Italian companies vied for concessions, particularly for railways.[18] Rivalry commenced among the Powers, from which France, given a free hand by both London and Berlin at the Congress of Berlin in 1878, emerged the victor. With Gambetta's backing, Jules Ferry went into action in April 1881, landing 36,000 men in Tunisia. By 12 May 1881 the bey had been forced to sign the Treaty of Bardo, under which France assumed control of Tunisia's foreign affairs and guaranteed the security of the dynasty and internal peace and order. But the vague provisions of this treaty concealed France's will to assume full governmental powers. In the summer of 1881 unexpected tribal risings against the "intruders" occurred, forcing France to send additional troops to restore order. The bey was forced to sign a supplemental declaration on which the new Treaty of La Marsa was based. This treaty transformed Tunisia officially into a protectorate.[19] In Paris, a consensus had been worked out about the future system of rule. Although the press was talking about annexation, a protectorate had been determined upon from the beginning, for several reasons. First, the French desired to disturb the other Powers as little as possible. They also hoped that a protectorate might reduce burdens on the metropolitan budget and that such a form of rule might be more acceptable to the Tunisians, especially since they had promised to respect existing institutions. Although the Algerian rattachements dated from 1881, there was a strong desire to avoid a "new Algeria." The bourgeois liberal right in particular opposed an expensive bureaucratic regime and considered Tunisia ideally suited to French capital investment in large-scale farming, mining, and public works, but not for Algerian-style colon settlement.[20]

In international law, Tunisia remained in being as a state, represented by the bey, who, surrounded by splendor, ceremonial, and a royal guard, "ruled but did not govern."[21] Laws were issued in the bey's name, and the Tunisians, in contrast to the Algerians, were not granted French nationality. A Tunisian minister-president continued in office, as did two, and later three, Tunisian ministers. They were responsible for local administration, the administration of the *habous* (lands belonging to religious foundations), the religious courts, and Muslim education, in particular Zitouna University. But the protectorate power had complete de facto control. At the top was the resident general, sole representative of the Third Republic, to whom the entire administration and all military forces were subordinated. He also headed the ministerial council, and without his signature no *décret beylical* was legally valid. Along side the traditional administration, new ministries under French direction were created for finance, public works, education, economics, and the post office. Another key position was that of secretary-general for the Tunisian government, who was naturally a Frenchman.[22]

The traditional tribal administration remained in being externally. The caid was its central figure. He had administrative, financial, and judicial competences, and, though unsalaried, received 5 percent of the taxes he collected. At a lower level shaykhs ruled sections of tribes and villages. Thirteen French *contrôleurs* supervised the caids. Members of the old notable families continued to be appointed as caids. This was in keeping with the protectorate treaty, but it was also done out of awareness that protecting their prestige and concrete interests would help to secure French rule. They exploited their positions of power to their own advantage as they long had done, to enrich themselves, to usurp land, and to impose arbitrary justice. The contrôleurs removed or deposed them only when the abuses they committed became intolerably flagrant or when they stirred up trouble against the colonial power. In the main, however, the caids preferred to maintain good relations with the administration and the colons.[23] Their number was, moreover, reduced from eighty in 1883 to thirty-eight in 1900. The picture is the now familiar one of a traditional ruling elite being integrated into the colonial administration and receiving tasks for which it was unprepared. But it was also simultaneously corrupted, insofar as it was freed from the traditional sanctions protecting the ruled. It became in practice a message-bearer for the ruling power, while retaining its private powers and spheres of influence.[24] The old elite was able to survive in this system of putative indirect rule, but was unable in the following period to stem its decline in prestige or stave off the attacks of a national movement recruited from the urban, modern elite with rural mass support.

Representative institutions were restricted to a minimum. There was no community organization comparable to the commune de plein exercice. A "president" headed the Tunisian community (whose vice-president was a Frenchman). Although he and the village council were appointed, not only was their jurisdiction restricted but their decisions required administrative sanction. In accordance with the idea of a protectorate, this system made it possible to contain colon demands for autonomy and the right of independent decision, though the Tunisians themselves gained no rights to be heard. Much the same was true at a higher level. After 1896 a Conférence Consultative advised on the budget, and in 1907 a Tunisian section of sixteen appointed members was added to it.[25] Paris was forced to make additional concessions in 1922 in the form of a two-section Grand Conseil. The French section of the council consisted of commerce representatives and elected representatives from the French colony. The Tunisian section was indirectly elected in a way that assured the preponderance of reliable landed notables. The council received budgetary rights, though most "obligatory expenditures" were removed from its purview, and could advise on administrative and economic matters, though not on political ones.[26] If the two sections differed a rather complicated mediation procedure regulated matters. French and Tunisians could thus articulate their interests without impinging very much on effective executive powers which were well suited to hobbling those Frenchmen having notions of autonomy or seeking clear colon domination after the pattern of the Algerian Délégations Financières. They also served, however, to block Tunisian claims to participate in government.

The administration of Morocco was patterned in its essentials after that of Tunisia. Even the establishment of rule took a similar course. The sultan remained formally independent and continued to head the church, in contrast to the bey of Tunisia, but ruled over only a part of the country, the *bled makhzen*, or the coastal zone and the plateau between Marrakesh and Tangier. The *bled es-siba*, the mountainous east of the Berber tribes, acknowledged his sovereignty but grudgingly. Even in the bled makhzen, traditional Muslim administration was weak, restricting itself to the collection of taxes, which often had to be wrung from the recalcitrant tribes by military force. Although modernization efforts were modest, indebtedness to foreigners eventually led to the establishment of the Service de la Dette, which met amortization costs through customs duties. As in Egypt and Tunisia, capitulations guaranteed foreigners trial by consular courts. Revolts against the reigning sultan, Abdel-Aziz (1894-1907), aroused the appetites of the French. Algerian deputy Eugène Etienne's Parti Colonial was agitating for a gradual "penetration" of the east.[27] Under Foreign Minister Théophile Delcassé, Paris began to conclude a series of treaties establishing its claims, beginning with Italy and Spain in 1900 and concluding with the 1904 rapprochement with England. France encountered German resistance in 1905, but could not be prevented from bringing increasing direct and indirect pressure to bear on the sultan. This it did both from Algeria and by military actions along the coast.

After Germany had accepted a French protectorate in 1911, the sultan was also forced (on 30 March 1912) to acknowledge it, although not before hastily gobbling up huge estates by the most questionable means and extracting an immense sum as compensation for the new arrangements.[28] Only then did uncoordinated resistance develop, rather as had earlier occurred in Tunisia. In Fez, Moroccan troops mutinied against their unloved French instructors and temporarily took control of the city, and some of the surrounding tribes readied for battle. For a time the situation appeared very threatening for French troops. At this juncture, Paris perforce ended the existing administrative confusion by naming General Hubert Lyautey high commissioner and giving him extensive powers. The sultan had to abdicate in favor of his brother Youssef, and additional French troops were sent. Lyautey skillfully combined military action with attempts to win over the notables, in order to create some basis for mutual trust. Hardly was order somewhat restored in the Fez region, however, when a new danger arose in the south. With the support of the mountain population, the marabout El Hiba had himself proclaimed sultan on 3 May 1912 and occupied Marrakesh on 15 August, only to be defeated decisively early in September. Lyautey succeeded in winning over the "great caids" of the south—albeit by accepting their rule—but the military "pacification" continued for years (employing some 60,000 troops in 1913). Lyautey's policy of "showing force in order not to employ it" was clearly successful, especially as he combined it with protecting the traditional ruling class, using military units for civil matters such as road building and public health projects, and safeguarding the habous. He hence also succeeded in winning the trust of the population.

Institutionally, the protectorate in Morocco rather resembled that in Tunisia. The sultan continued formally as head of state and under him the *vezirs* (viziers) of the *makhzen* administered justice, the habous lands, the state domain. But the sultan was "advised" by a French *Conseilleur du gouvernement chérifien*. The French, moreover, ran the important "neo-shariffian" services, a resident general and secretary-general heading the protectorate administration.[29] Appointed pashas administered the cities, and caids the six-hundred-odd tribes, "supervised" by French contrôlleurs civils. Robin Bidwell has given us a revealing picture of this administrative system, which was based on the local notable class.[30] The caids, not officials as such, but "protectors of their flocks," enjoyed both administrative and judicial competences and drew 6 percent of the taxes they collected for pay. Their willingness to collaborate was magnanimously honored by outward attestations of honor. They proved able enough to exploit their opportunities to enrich themselves and were known to administer justice with palms outstretched.[31] In the interwar period, there was increasing criticism of this system, but the administration paid little attention to it. The south, moreover, remained under the sway of the great caids, the most notable of whom was

Thami Al-Glaoui, pasha of Marrakesh. Protected by the administration in return for guaranteeing the security of the south, he was able to establish a position of great power. It was based on his ability to act like a feudal potentate in matters of tax collection and in persecuting and ridding himself of opponents, while simultaneously cleverly exploiting modern economic possibilities; he had ties to mining interests and the Banque de Paris et de Pays-Bas.

Lyautey was without doubt the greatest of the French proconsuls. The protectorate he established and ran with such mastery was based on the upholding of local authorities, customs, and usages and the restriction of colonial power to supervision and direction.[32] The authority of the sultan, rather shaky by 1912, was maintained and emphasized for the benefit of the population, the makhzen and its political dignitaries reformed, and families of the notables built into the system as caids, who were largely protected from criticism. Yet what this amounted to was a sort of refeudalization, and one which not only stood in the way of modernization and democratization, but having lost its original functions threatened to degenerate into nepotism, arbitrariness, and self-enrichment.[33] Caids and pashas had indeed squeezed their subjects for goods and services since time immemorial, and one must concede that under the new administration this sort of pillage was not possible to the former degree. On the other hand, the traditional remedies of resistance (*siba*), protests to the sultan, and, in extreme cases, of assassination and rebellion were hardly employable in the colonial situation. The shaky precolonial equalibrium had thus been upset. The beneficiary of the new order was the traditional ruling class, so long as it was willing to bend its knee to the colonial power. This it proved more than willing to do, bound as it was by its interests to the colonial power. The saying circulated that "Morocco is a cow which the caids milk while the French hold its horns."[34] The dilemma inherent in any indirect administration also held good for Tunisia and Morocco: If supervision was too close and if officials interfered too much, the traditional authorities were reduced to lackeys who followed orders and were mere executive agents. If the colonial power held back, however, not only were all limits removed from abuses of power but such abuses received quasi-official sanction.

The foregoing must suffice to highlight the differences in administration. Algeria was declared an integral part of the national territory and ultimately received partial financial autonomy within the republic after decades of experimentation encompassing solutions as diverse as Napoleon III's "Arab" kingdom and the republic's rattachements of 1881. This was in keeping with the situation in a newly opened territory and the interests of the French settlers, who were both represented in Parlement and, in the form of communes de plein exercice, disposed of a most artful instrument of rule. The administration was direct, and little remained of the precolonial authority structure. The stated aim of the Algerian administration was the gradual assimilation of the Muslim population, meaning that they were to be transformed from subjects to French citizens. But this never got past its beginnings because the legal equality of Muslims and

French would have placed colon domination in question. It was therefore opposed by every means at hand. The results were very serious for the colonized. The great families of the traditional ruling class in good part disappeared. The Algerian peasants were exposed to a process of social disintegration and pauperization because the colons took the land, and a new, French-schooled bourgeoisie was able to form only very slowly.

The protectorates, in contrast, were based on the continuance of the traditional Muslim states and thus in form were fundamentally different from Algeria. "The idea was to leave existing structures in place and avail ourselves of them rather than replacing them with an entirely new colonial administration."[35] The forms were what counted here, insofar as rule was undertaken in the name of the sovereign, whose administration was reformed and modernized through the creation of new departments. In practice, however, it was not even necessary to create a parallel administration, but merely a hierarchical apparatus with the resident general at the top. The traditional ruling class of great families was not eliminated but integrated both at the local level and at the top. It was bound to the colonial power as much as possible by means of a "policy of little attentions (*égards*)."[36] At the same time, however, they were subordinated, to a much greater degree than in the Malay sultanates or Indian Princely States, to intensive administrative supervision. It was not so very different from *administration directe*—which Lyautey said was ingrained in the French character—as declarations to the contrary implied. It was also characteristic rather than otherwise that, despite Lyautey's most emphatic warnings against it, the protectorate was continually viewed as a transition stage on the way to later annexation and a definitive integration in a greater France,[37] and not as a form of rule that implied later independence. It was also characteristic that not only in the colonies and Algeria but also in the protectorates (especially Tunisia) Frenchmen occupied numerous posts in the lower administration, and in numbers, indeed, that reveal fundamental differences from British practice.

LAND ACQUISTION AND AGRICULTURE

Not only Algeria, but also Tunisia and Morocco seemed suited to French colonization. The legal and administrative situation in the protectorates, however, differed from that in Algeria. Because of unhappy Algerian experiences, there was less colonization in the latter and what there was took on a special character. But everywhere, the land question was dominant: how was the right to use the land to be provided to the settlers? The Maghreb was indeed thinly settled, though regional variations were considerable. Some of the tribes were nomadic or seminomadic, possessing fixed places of residence but grazing stock over a wide area. The nomads mainly inhabited the dry, mountainous regions of the hinterland. By right of conquest, the French took a portion of the lands unclaimed by the tribes or claimed only on the basis of custom. The tribes were given firm title to what remained to them. Aside from the fact that this cantonnement method of sequestration rested on force and restricted the tribal territories, sometimes to the point of actual crowding, it also failed to provide sufficient land for settlement. Frenchmen wanted firm individual titles, and a way had to be found to sell land governed by the provisions of Muslim law. This was particularly true of the *melk* lands, which under Muslim law were private property but held by families, or more accurately, a community of heirs, even if farmed by a single family. But the problem also existed with the *arch* land, which was collective tribal property, with firm and in some cases inheritable usufruct rights. The colons demanded mobilization and gallicization of the land, meaning that the traditional ordering of land relationships based on Muslim law and custom was to be shattered. At the same time the real property thus created was to be placed under the governance of French law.

> French policy faces the following dilemma. it can either posit measures which facilitate the mobilization of the land and permit Europeans to acquire native property without risk and thus create individual ownership where it had not existed; or, it can leave the natives on their lands, giving them full and entire ownership, and allowing the continuance of family ownership in the melks and community ownership in the archs.[38]

To the extent that this dilemma was recognized at all, massive colon pressure assured that it was resolved in their favor, especially in Algeria. The result was that in all three Maghreb territories a good part of the best land fell into colon hands, with the natives being reduced to tenants or rural laborers. This development had most serious consequences for a traditional society based on tribes and extended families.

In Algeria, one must distinguish between official and private colonization. We have already encountered the former from the period before 1870, and the Third Republic took it up again almost at once. It seemed the most suitable means to settle the largest possible number of French on the "new" lands. Entire villages of small peasants tilling their own land were created. The administration sold plots, or *lotissements*, or handed them out free and provided the necessary infrastructure. Between 1871 and 1890, 577,000 hectares were made available in this way, by 1920, 900,000, and by 1930, 1,648,000. Where did the land come from? First, from the land seized during the Kabyle rebellion; second, from existing state domain and other land which cantonnement had made available; and finally, from that acquired by purchase or expropriation "for creating or extending the perimeters of colonization." The results left much to be desired. Hundreds of villages, some with French names, were indeed founded. Although these marked the French implantation in a most emphatic fashion, official colonization was decidedly expensive. Many settlers were also badly prepared for the hard life in the new country on plots that were anyhow too small. Thus, the plots were often rented to tenants and the residence obligation evaded, or the land was resold. In order to limit sales to Algerians, which occurred in significant numbers during the two world wars, it was, for example, decreed in 1924 that a concessionaire could sell his piece of land to a non-European only after forty years.[39]

The private colonization was more important. The notorious Warnier Law of 1873 and its supplements provided the basis for "legal" purchase. Since what the law sought was to break up collective ownership in the melk lands, it was stipulated that individual plots were to be established and that these would become the private property of individuals under the provisions of French law. The idea was to gallicize all the land. If only a single collective holder desired it, the collective ownership of an entire holding could be nullified. The result was a veritable plundering of tribal properties, to the accompaniment of an increasing number of lawsuits, with legal costs to match. The natives began to sell their land, it sufficing in many cases that some interested party or creditor, covered by French mortgage law, demanded his share in order to force division and as a consequence the sale of other shares as well. The natives, unaccustomed to paper claims to ownership, often lost their titles, and since collective ownership did not necessarily mean that all holders actually farmed the land, the result was that those who actually did so were only granted a portion free and clear as owners. The seller received cash, mostly soon squandered, but lost his land.[40] Not only Frenchmen but also urban Algerians and Algerian notables thus acquired large holdings.[41] All this occasioned sharp criticism in the 1890s, but it had little effect. Why were the Algerians so ready to sell? Ageron holds that the common explanations of improvidence and sloth are incorrect, pointing out that the peasants mostly parted with bits and pieces of land very unwillingly, mainly in dry years. Seminomads were more apt to sell than the sedentary, particularly in more heavily settled areas. It was not uncommon, however, for land to be repurchased, often for a higher price than the colons had once paid.[42]

The administration was able to block "individualization" and sale of arch land, despite numerous colon attempts to bring it about. In 1926, however, the governor-general received the right under specified circumstances (among which was "when the interests of colonization required it") to divide into individual holdings the holdings of a *douar* ("a group of tents"; that is, a subtribal-sized social grouping).[43] The Third Republic's land legislation, in short, stood wholly in colon service and permitted the colons to acquire a goodly share of Algerian property by means of forced individualization of property rights.

French property ownership rose from approximately 800,000 hectares in 1870 to 1.6 million in 1890, 2.1 million in 1917, 2.5 million in 1934, and 2.7 in 1954. Assuming an arable area of six to eight million hectares, the European share was around 30 percent, though it should also be remembered that new land was also brought into cultivation through French colonization.[44] In 1930, 26,153 Europeans owned 2.3 million hectares, but 617,543 Algerians owned only 7.7 million. Table 8.1 shows the distribution of land ownership in that year.[45] As can be seen, the Europeans dominated the large operations, the Algerians the small.[46] Considering that an Algerian family required ten to twenty hectares to live "decently" the consequences of European land sequestration and rising population are not far to seek.

Table 8.1
Real Property Ownership in Algeria, 1930 (in hectares)

NATIONALITY	SIZE OF HOLDING	AVERAGE SIZE HELD	SIZE OF HOLDING	AVERAGE SIZE HELD
	up to 10		10-50	
Europeans	8,877		7,140	
Total area	42,534	4.7	21,678	29.2
Algerians	434,534		140,000	
Total area	1,738,000	4.0	2,635,275	18.8
	50-100		100 and over	
Europeans	4,725		5,411	
Total area	364,366	77.0	1,722,000	318.0
Algerians	35,962		7,035	
Total area	1,595,400	43.1	1,593,500	198.3

SOURCE: Cavelli, *Propriété Rurale*, 166f.

Other factors must also be considered. Although the "great European holding" arose everywhere alongside the "petty native holding," regional variations were still considerable. The European share of the fertile areas was significantly higher than of the less fertile, native families tended to be larger than European and their cultivation methods less intensive, and the contrast increased with time. Whereas small European farmers mostly raised truck crops in the areas around the cities, the actual colons—who in increasing measure were administrators employed by owners living in the cities—employed an Algerian work force, partly the so-called *khammés* (a traditional kind of sharecropper) and partly landless laborers. The colons employed modern plows and fertilizer and gradually shifted over to using tractors, which reduced their needs for labor. The Algerian peasant, in contrast, continued using his wood plow drawn by a span of oxen, having neither the land nor the capital to shift over to modern methods. Settler farms became larger with the employment of tractors and enclaves were bought out. The Algerians, on the other hand, divided their lands and then divided them again. Fallow and pasture were continually reduced, resulting in decreases in stock and fruit trees. Erosion worsened the situation.[47] The native area under grain remained about the same from 1877 to 1937 at 1.2 million hectares, but already low yields declined from 16 quintals per hectare before 1914 to 4.56 after World War II. Total grain yields accordingly fell from an average of 19.6 million quintals between 1901 and 1910, to 16 million for 1921 to 1930, to 14 million for 1941 to 1948. The number of sheep also fell from 8.9 million in 1910 to 5.3 million for 1921 to 1930 and 4.8 million for 1941 to 1948.[48] The colons naturally ascribed this to the flaws of Algerian character, if not specifically to sloth. It should be pointed out, however, that the administration hardly troubled itself about native agriculture. Communications and credit were oriented toward European needs. Although the Sociétiés Indigènes de Prévoyance had been created as early as 1893, they served more as window dressing than to meet urgent Muslim credit needs, for which they were wholly inadequate. After 1937 more energetic measures were at least begun. Adding to native difficulties was a complicated taxation system which burdened Algerians very severely. Ageron has shown how a boost in taxes between 1928 and 1932 coincided with a catastrophic fall in prices during the world economic crisis, hitting native Algerians especially hard.[49] Drought only made matters worse. A 1931 report stated:

> The native has reached the end of his tether. He has no more money or food. He is crippled by debt, his lands being mortgaged to the extreme limit. Sixty percent of his beasts are gone because of lack of pasturage, and he has been forced to sell the rest in order to meet the needs of his family and because he can no longer feed them. There is nothing but rock or bare ground anywhere.[50]

Problems also went beyond the fact that a great part of the best land had ended up in the hands of Europeans and a small class of Alger an large holders, and that the living standard of Muslim small holders, tenant farmers, and laborers, already close to the subsistence minimum, continued to sink. The individualization of real property and being placed under the *Statut immobilier du droit civil* called for a change in outlook for the Muslims and went far toward dissolving the traditional tribal, village, and family structures.[51] A process of pauperization commenced. It was characterized by under- and unemployment and the beginnings of migration to the already overcrowded casbahs of the cities and later to the *bidonvilles*, or shantytowns. In 1957 Germaine Tillon described this *clochardisation* (being reduced to vagabondage) in arresting terms.[52]

The wine industry constituted a special case.[53] While grain had long been farmed, the vineyards were the result of European colonization.Because Muslims drink no wine, grapes had been grown before 1830 only for immediate consumption. It was soon recognized that Algeria was suited for wine, but it was considered inappropriate to produce, or administratively subvene, on a large scale a colonial product that would compete with the agriculture of the metropolis.[54] Viticulture was suited to small holders and came naturally to immigrants from southern France, Spain and Italy, but required initial financial assistance that at first was unavailable. The profit per hectare, however, was several times that of grain, whose price was falling, and Algeria desperately needed a supplementary, high-yield, labor-intensive agricultural product. The catastrophic decimation of the French vineyards by phylloxera after 1875 was thus like a gift from heaven for the Algerians. Bank money suddenly started to flow in, and vineyards expanded rapidly, despite the phylloxera which hit Algeria in 1886 and required new plantings and despite looming marketing problems in the metropolis:

Table 8.2
Land Planted in Vineyards in Algeria, 1878-1938 (in hectares)

1878	1888	1908	1918	1928	1938
17,614	103,408	160,852	199,278	221,756	412,800

The main centers of cultivation lay in the plains around Bône, Philippeville, and Oran, and the hills of the Sahel region. According to Isnard, geographical factors were less important in determining location than the presence of European settlements and the state of communications.[55] Vineyard size continually increased. Initially, individual families picked the grapes, but paid labor was increasingly used, at first Europeans and then the cheaper natives. The colons became entrepreneurs and overseers. By 1908 there were already a thousand-odd estates of over twenty hectares, and twenty-four of these were over two hundred. In the Mitidja, corporations holding over a thousand hectares dominated things.

With increases in vineyard areas and with technical improvements, productivity and gross yields also rose, from 4.36 million hectolitres in 1908 to an average 9.2 million in the period 1919 to 1929, and 17.1 million from 1930 to 1932. Because it was part of the national territory, Algeria could export freely to France and succeeded in driving cheap Spanish and Italian wine from the home market. But the result was a campaign against Algerian wine in the metropolis, especially in the Midi. French growers asserted that the Algerians were ruthlessly expanding their acreage, enjoyed administrative support, and employed cheap labor, to which the Algerians responded that their transport and development costs were higher. After 1928 these disputes about acreage limitation, quotas, and compulsory distillation became particularly acute. Compromises which saved customs unity were achieved only with some difficulty.[56] Algerian viticulture constitutes a sort of classic example of colonial competition with the metropolis, standing in the most blatant contrast to the more usual sort of complementary relationships.

Viticulture was of first-rate importance to the Algerian economy, both because the prosperity of a great many European settlers depended upon it and because it supplied more than half of all Algerian exports. This fact became more significant in the 1930s when, in the face of a rising population, grain production stagnated. The traditional grain exports, varying sharply according to season, ceased, and Algeria had to resort to imports. But there was something paradoxical about all this, for a country the majority of whose people drank no wine had become one of the great wine producers. One can justly stigmatize this situation as being typically colonial because land for this production was acquired through dispossession or purchase from the natives and thus was withdrawn from food production. Still, while wine claimed a goodly portion of the arable, it yielded several times as much as grain and was roughly four times as labor intensive. Thus, despite the seasonal character and low pay of vineyard work, the result was much higher wage payments than grain would have permitted. According to

Ageron, when a Muslim grew grapes, which he seldom did, he enjoyed before 1914 roughly ten times the income that he would have had with grain.[57] Here again, we encounter the problem, or dilemma, resulting from the intensive cultivation of export products, mostly at the cost of foodstuffs, but yielding much higher profits per acre. It is thus hardly surprising that independent Algeria has continued viticulture after expelling the colons.

It has already been noted that Tunisia[58] appeared suited, not for small colonists like Algeria, but for *colonisation capitaliste*.[59] Even before the establishment of the protectorate, French financial organizations had acquired large estates, the best known being the Société Marseillaise de Crédit's purchase of Enfida, roughly 100,000 hectares in size and located north of Kairouan. The sellers were members of the Tunisian upper class, often of Turkish origin, who had received these latifundia as signs of favor from the bey but had never exploited them very intensively. The Land Law of 1885 made it possible to secure firm titles. Following the precedents of the Australian Torrens Act, the law provided that after formal statement of ownership claims, registration in the cadastres would follow, with a mixed tribunal settling disputed cases. In contrast to the Algerian legislation between 1873 and 1887, this law was not intended to break up traditional joint holdings, but it nonetheless introduced concepts of private ownership of real property.[60] Such concepts primarily served European colonists and some Tunisian "feudal" landholders who were transformed into bourgeois-capitalist latifundiasts. Although the Tunisian small holdings, the melk, in the more heavily settled regions were virtually closed to Europeans, a decree opened up the habous as early as 1886. The habous were foundations whose income initially went to the founder and his heirs but was later devoted to religious purposes. Habous were no longer to be periodically re-rented to the highest bidder, but could under specified conditions be rented on very long leases and even registered to one holder in the cadastres: Tunisian resistance to the dissolution of the private habous soon formed, however, and the administration was forced to proceed very cautiously. In 1926, despite massive pressure from the colons, who with some justice pointed out bad habous management, the administration moved to protect the claims of Tunisian peasants.[61] Not until Tunisia became independent were the habous dissolved, a deed often cited as an example of a progressive reform which became possible only after the end of colonial rule.

In the 1890s official colonization began, it clearly being the sole means of establishing an effective French-settler presence. The land corporation and large holders—116 French owners held over 400,000 hectares—had begun to sell off land, mainly to Italians or Tunisian tenants. Between 1892 and 1914, the administration distributed 140,000 hectares of good land to French settlers,[62] after placing *terres beylik* (former domain holdings) and in 1896 *terres mortes* (unused or seldom-used land) under control of the Service des Domains. The process was similar to Algeria but without sequestration. The individual parcels, a hundred hectares or more, were significantly larger than in Algeria, however, and no colonist villages were established. In 1898 a decree ordered the Djemaa, the central administration for the public habous, to turn 2,000 hectares a year over to the Direction d'Agriculture. The Tunisian peasants who had used this land to pasture stock were forced to use adjacent areas.

In the 1920s, spurred by the *péril italien* and the fact that Tunisians had begun to buy and repurchase French land, the administration pushed official colonization most energetically, in particular by organizing suitable credit. Between 1919 and 1929, the administration sold 1,357 plots totalling 273,000 hectares, the settlers being selected with more care than previously.[63] At the same time "resettlement" was restyled as a policy of "tying to the land," which is to say that Tunisian peasants living on colon or domainal land were also given *lotissements* (twenty hectares or less), in the expectation that this would create a group of small Tunisian peasants bound to the land. It has been shown, however, that the amounts given to Frenchmen were significantly larger and that they took the best land, with the result that in practice a great portion of the Tunisian peasants were expelled, with a minority eking out a miserable existence on the edges of European holdings.

> Instead of settling 13,000 families of small farmers (1920-1934), the result was the crowding together of nine-tenths of this population outside of their former holdings, and the de-racination and proletarization of thousands of peasants who were never able successfully to develop the plots they were supposed to get.[64]

Three and a half million hectares of Tunisia's 12.4 million hectares were unproductive, another 4.7 were low-yield pasture, 1.1 forests, 400,000 orchards, and only 2.8 million good arable land. In 1921, 641,000 hectares were in European hands,[65] and in 1937, 724,701.[66] In 1921 this meant that Europeans held roughly 5 percent of the total. When one considers, however, that European holdings were concentrated mainly in the fertile north (in the Tell) and the Sahel, the picture is entirely different, as table 8.3 shows. In the central and eastern Tell, Europeans held 20 to 27 percent, in the northern Tell, 10 to 16 percent, and in the Sahel 10 to 12 percent of the land.[67] There was a considerable increase in acreage after 1881. The colons also opened up new or poor land with modern plows and tractors in addition to farming relatively unused good land in the Tell. But there can be no doubt that European colonization of the Tell resulted in the displacement of thousands of Tunisian peasants onto less productive land in the south.[68] The number of European settlers, other than the French and the Italians, was astonishingly small, only 3,425 in 1921 and 4,649 in 1937.[69] It can also be seen in table 8.6 (note 69) that the French, even discounting corporations holding 10,000 hectares or more, held the bulk of the large holdings, whereas the Italians were concentrated on small holdings having an average of 29 hectares in 1937. Simplifying matters, one can say that the French raised grain and the Italians grapes and truck crops in the area around Tunis.

Table 8.3
Real Property Ownership in Tunisia, 1921 (in hectares)

NATIONALITY	NO. OF SETTLERS	SIZE OF HOLDING				TOTAL AREA	AREA IN THE TELL
		Up to 10	10-100	100-500	500		
French	1,708	365	401	744	198	554,000	305,000
Italians	1,565	1,040	425	79	21	61,000	44,000
Maltese and others	152	72	40	23	17	26,000	19,000
Europeans in toto	3,425	1,477	866	846	236	641,000	368,000

SOURCE: Goldstein, "Mise en Valeur," 61.

In the Tell in particular, one can fairly speak of grain monoculture. The French colons, often managers of the corporations, at first used the old *khammessat* form of tenantry,[70] but then changed over to wage labor, sometimes employing Europeans but mostly Tunisians. The workers were either hired for the entire year—they were often former khammés—or by the season, particularly in the case of workers from the areas of seasonal grazing. Modern equipment, such as wheeled and caterpillar tractors and gang plows, was employed very early on and enabled the colons to bring even the hill country under the plow. Large-scale treeless farms were created that required little labor, particularly in the dry farming area where half the land had to be left fallow every year. In the interwar period, silos were built for grain storage, and pickup balers and combines drastically reduced the need for seasonal labor. Mechanization also increased the incentive to round off holdings, meaning that very small Tunisian holdings were eliminated.[71] The yields per hectare were several times those of native holdings. This modern agriculture mainly produced wheat for export. Production rose from 300,000 quintals in 1917 to about two million in 1932.[72]

Although small numbers of Tunisians were able to participate in this modern large-scale grain production, most were forced off onto poor land and into the fringe areas. Acreage increased,[73] but so did population, and though holdings of two to fifteen hectares were much too small, parcellization continued. The fallow was reduced, but this meant less pasturage for stock. Hard wheat and some vegetables were grown for the table. Fertilizer was not much used, however, and yields stagnated. Although the Sociétés de Prévoyance helped the peasants survive the bad years, they were too weak to provide credit assistance. Day labor on colon estates might bring in a little income, parcels might be sold to colons and city notables, or the "surplus" family might migrate. Poncet and Bardin have provided us a graphic picture of this process of "involution."[74]

Something should also be said of the olive orchards of east and central Tunisia, in particular in the Sfax region. Companies and colons had purchased domainal land in this area very early. Heavy investments were unnecessary, because one could avail oneself of the old institution of the *magharsa*, meaning that a Tunisian peasant would plant and care for the olive trees until they matured (in fifteen to twenty years) and then receive half as his property. Since he had had to accept credit in the meantime, however, his debts were figured in when it came time to divvy up. The result frequently was that he received one-third or less, which in some cases he sold back to the property owner. In the interwar period, the Europeans, sometimes farming reduced areas, either went over to wage labor or settled nomads as workers. The Tunisians, both the peasants and the urban owners, had been able to hold their own with about four-fifths of both olive trees and oil production.[75] There was also something of a community of interest between Tunisians and Europeans vis-à-vis the administration. Both old and new urban bourgeoisie profited from olive processing and exporting.

The situation in the pasture areas, practically untouched by European colonization, can only be sketched here. What is important is that the development of the large European wheat farms and the expansion of the olive groves critically restricted the pasture available to the nomads and seminomads. This was particularly serious because the areas thus taken were in the climatically more favorable high elevations previously used by the nomads in winter (this seasonal movement is called "transhumance") or in periodic pasture changes during dry periods. The development, moreover, of a class of rural laborers and increasing mechanization reduced the nomads' opportunities for seasonal labor.

In Morocco, Lyautey had attempted to base French rule on the traditional social order and had opposed Algerianization.[76] But he was nevertheless convinced of the necessity to make it possible for colons to obtain land, because otherwise no economic development seemed possible. Even Lyautey had, indeed, been forced to retreat from his policy of accommodation under pressure from the homeland and the French in Morocco.[77] His successor, however, Théodore Steeg, the earlier radical-socialist governor of Algeria, most emphatically supported colonization: "We must assure the increase of the French people by a methodical development of colonization." Henceforth, as in Tunisia, small colonists were encouraged, who then in crisis years encountered difficulties from which the state had to rescue them. Land law and agricultural development thus had much in common with Tunisia.

Even before establishment of the protectorate, Europeans (in some cases, in the form of corporations) had acquired about 80,000 hectares, mainly in the Gharb region. Muslim-Moroccan land law did not provide secure titles and encouraged fraud on both sides, as was perhaps characteristic of initial contacts between natives and Europeans. Registration was thus introduced on 12 August 1913, through a *dahir*, or decree (the basic form of Moroccan legislation). Titles had thenceforth to be produced and entered in the *Livre Foncier Marocain*. Disputes over claims, among, say, joint owners, were decided by a French tribunal. Moroccans could use these courts but hesitated to do so because of the costs involved. Registration thus became primarily a means of purchasing melk lands, mainly family holdings, and securing clear individual title to them. Patiently, "sometimes with ruses, always with weapon of money,"[78] and also with administrative help, the colons acquired land.[79]

In the beginning, Lyautey showed little interest in official colonization, or the sale of land by the state. By 1918 only 8,000 hectares of domain land had been sold. Most of Morocco was the collective property of nomads or seminomads, used either as pasture or apportioned annually to the douars as arable by the *djemaa*, or tribal council. This collective land was protected from sale as early as 1 November 1912.[80] With the rise in land prices during the war and after, however, Lyautey provided new opportunities in the important dahir of 27 April 1919. Whether Lyautey was acting on his own or under colon pressure is unclear; probably he sought to reconcile the claims of colonization and collective ownership. The property rights of tribes, subtribes, and douars were acknowledged. The right to rent, sell, or divide collective land, however, was withdrawn from the djemaas and entrusted to a Conseil de Tutelle, headed by the director of native affairs, a Frenchman. This constituted a serious abridgement of democratic self-government within the tribes. At the same time, moreover, the state took unto itself the right of eminent domain "in cases of public need" and to create a "colonization perimeter." Since the administration could determine how much land the tribes "required," "surplus" land could be added to the state domain for modest compensation and resold to settlers. The criterion was supposedly 12 to 20 hectares "per tent" (per family), although 100 to 400 hectares was adjudged necessary for a colon holding.[81] Because the aim was compact agrarian settlements, if possible on the best land, resettlement was unavoidable. The same was true of *guich* lands, or tax-free lands which the sultan had given the tribes for military services. These were now purchased or condemned by the state and given to settlers. In the post-Lyautey period official colonization was pushed, especially from 1926 to 1932, when plot size was cut and the amounts of money and agricultural knowledge required of colons were also reduced. Table 8.4 presents French land sequestration in Morocco between 1913 and 1953.

Table 8.4
Acquisition by French Colonists of Land in Morocco, 1913-1953

	PRIVATE COLONIZATION		OFFICIAL COLONIZATION		TOTAL	
Year	Area in hectares	No. of farms	Area in Hectares	No. of farms	Area in hectares	No. of farms
1913	80,000	. . .	. . .	. . .	80,000	. . .
1921	175,000	. . .	46,963	. . .	220,000	490
1923	382,500	800	71,500	450	454,000	1,250
1926	. . .	. . .	. . .	. . .	643,990	2,103
1931	524,979	. . .	247,021	1,495	772,000	. . .
1935	569,000	2,068	271,000	1,754	840,000	3,822
1953	728,000	4,269	289,000	1,634	1,017,000	5,903

SOURCE: See note 82.

Assuming six to seven million hectares of arable, Europeans owned about 10 percent of it (making the additional assumption that two-thirds of their land was arable). That may seem none too much, especially when one considers that the colons brought new land into cultivation with their modern equipment. There can be no doubt, however, that colonists mainly took the better land in the plains, around the cities, and along the traffic routes.[83] Roughly one-third of European holdings were in the Gharb in the northwest and another third in the Casablanca region. These are the areas in which the expulsion of the Moroccans onto the poorer lands is easiest to see. Seven hundred Europeans owned half of the roughly 400,000 irrigated hectares in one district in the Gharb.[84] In the Meknès region, 65,000 hectares of the Beni-M'tir tribe's 115,000 hectares of guich land lay in the fertile plain. Between 1919 and 1927, they lost 16,000 hectares to official colonization. Because a quarter of the tribe had to be resettled, tribal property was divided among the individual families, with about 23.4 hectares going to each family. This land was, however, divided into ten parcels rather than being in contiguous blocks. Although herdsmen rather than farmers, these Berber tribesmen had become individual property owners. They proved all too ready to sell to the colons. By 1938, 40,000 hectares of the 49,000 that had remained to them in the plain were in European hands, meaning the tribe had been for all practical intents driven from the plain. "We sought to transform herdsmen into peasants; all we did was shatter their social structure."[85] Elsewhere, evidence shows that the traditional transhumance had been restricted, meaning that European land sequestration prevented the hill tribes from wintering their stock in the fertile plains. The partial shift to private ownership even on collective tribal lands had also led to social differentiation, because caids and notables, and Muslim front men as well, had purchased or in other ways acquired land.

The average size of European holdings declined somewhat, but still remained large in 1935, at 219 hectares (in the Gharb, 550 hectares). More than 80 percent of the land was devoted to wheat, mostly for export. Yields varied sharply according to rainfall and ranged from nine to twelve quintals a hectare. The administration assisted the colons in many ways. The colons had to pay an agricultural yield tax, the *tertib*, but received reductions for land brought under the plow. They were also the principal beneficiaries of the 50 percent tax reduction of 1923 on all land tilled by European methods. Premiums were also paid for mechanization, and fertilizer and agricultural equipment came in duty free. The colons received short and intermediate term credit from the Caisses Mutuelles de Crédit Agricole (which acquired the money through interest-free state loans). After 1924 the Caisse de Prêts Immobiliers du Maroc lent impecunious settlers up to two-thirds of the necessary mortgage credit.[86] Until 1929 soft wheat could be exported to France at considerably in excess of the world price. Then the depression set in, and prices fell. The metropolis developed its own wheat surplus. Justified by the argument that Morocco enjoyed the advantages of lower cost labor and reexported duty-free imported grain, quotas for Moroccan grain were set, despite the protests of the Moroccan agricultural boards. At the same time, colon indebtedness rose to 700 million-odd francs (1935-1938). The administration thus had to intervene both with moratoria and with massive support for the lending institutions. A conspicuous number of colons went bankrupt anyway, particularly the most recent arrivals.[87] And colons were favored in yet another way. The export quotas were divided between two state-supported cooperatives. The Moroccans, whose soft-wheat production now equalled that of the Europeans, received only 10 percent of the export contingent and were thus thrown back on the home market, where the price was 51 francs per quintal rather than the 94 francs paid in France.[88]

Native agriculture stagnated, but received little assistance.[89] Although the population increased steadily, it had lost a good portion of the best land. On the eight to ten hectares that a family might hold, one could hardly scrape together the minimum to exist in a dry farming area. Although European land sequestration was justified with the argument that the colon would be a modernizing influence because of his progressive farming methods, that did not really prove true. Even the small group of Moroccans who acquired large holdings mostly ran them on the traditional, exploitive, share-cropping basis. The mass of the Moroccan peasants plowed, sowed, and harvested as they had always done. They obtained small yields, which actually declined in the interwar period.[90] Thousands of families had less than five hectares and thus depended on day labor in European holdings or migrated to the cities. The beginning of the bidonvilles dated from the years before World War II.[91] The Moroccan peasant was, and remains, conservative, but he also lacked the means for a more intensive agriculture. Although every Moroccan paying the tertib had belonged to the Société Marocain de Prévoyance since 1917, the latter's assistance was largely confined to providing better seed and short-term credit. Long-term and mortgage credit was available to colons but hardly to Moroccan peasants. Agriculture had thus become grain monoculture, to the point that stock-raising declined, and with it, mutton and lamb exports. After 1929, indeed, imports of frozen meat increased. "The exports of former days have given way to massive imports, and one can only point out what an economic heresy this is for a country with a stock-raising heritage."[92] Some diversification began in the 1930s, mainly in the European sector. Viticulture increased from 9,500 hectares in 1929 to 24,500 in 1935, resulting very soon in overproduction. Citrus fruits and early vegetables were also introduced. Olive groves and almonds, however, remained in Moroccan hands.

COMMUNICATIONS, MINING AND INDUSTRY

For obvious reasons, the colonial power itself built railroads—4,375 kilometers in Algeria, 2,100 in Tunisia, and 1,600 in Morocco—harbor facilities and roads. It thus contributed to modernizing the Maghreb,[93] although critics point out today that some lines served military and political ends, the economically nonsensical line from southern Algeria to Fez being a prime example. Others tied concentrations of colonists to the coast. Automobile roads were said to reach every colon's farm, and then to degenerate into mere tracks.[94] There is no doubt that the communication network served mainly the modern market-oriented sector, and hence principally Europeans. Loans floated in Paris went mainly for the building and expansion of the transportation network. A Tunisian loan of 1902 for forty million francs went for railways, in 1907 another of seventy-five million was spent on streets and railways, and yet another of 1912 again went for railways.[95]

In mining, only phosphate achieved any real importance. Mining began in Tunisia in 1889 with the exploitation of deposits discovered in 1885, and the country soon became the world's most important producer. In 1930, 3.3 million tons were mined. Production began in Algeria in 1910, reaching 900,000 tons by 1925. Moroccan production rose rapidly from 8,000 tons in 1921, to 1.8 million tons in 1930 and 5 million tons in 1954. Most was exported, only a small part remaining at home to be manufactured into superphosphate fertilizer. During the depression exports fell drastically, while foreign competition, from Soviet Russia among others, increased. World cartel and Franco-North African arrangements were accordingly formulated for export quotas. Although phosphates constituted a considerable portion of exports, their relevance for Maghreb economic development was slight. In Morocco, however, Lyautey succeeded in transferring production and export to the state Office Chérifien des Phosphates, whose profits constituted a sizeable portion of state income until the depression. In 1930, profits amounted to 160 million francs out of a total state income of 802 million francs. Phosphates had, however, no complementary economic effects and were not labor intensive. Only 4,600 worked in the Moroccan phosphate industry in 1930, and the thousand-man technical cadre was French.[96]

The situation was similar in the other mining industries. The Maghreb exported iron ore, with Algeria shipping 3 million tons in 1938, Tunisia 981,000 tons in 1937, and Morocco 1.1 million tons in 1938. But there was little coal that was easy to mine. The Algerian deposits at Colob Bécher were, for example, very large, but the seams were narrow, the quality poor, and the distance from the coast, 550 kilometers, so great that coal-fired utilities had to use imported coal. Moroccan anthracite could not be used as coking coal. The necessary conditions for heavy industry were thus lacking in the Maghreb, the more so since hydroelectric power was not a serious alternative. Electricity cost more than in the home country. The colonial power can hence hardly be held responsible for the failure to develop heavy industry.

Matters were different in the capital and consumer goods industries. The industries which processed agricultural products achieved some importance, notably flour mills, olive oil factories, which in part displaced traditional native industries, pottery factories, and fish and vegetable canneries. There were also breweries—for Europeans—a cement industry, which profited from the construction boom in the European quarters but otherwise could not begin to meet local demand. Cork and esparto grass, however, were not worked up locally but purchased by European firms and exported. Beyond some repair facilities practically no iron-working industry ever developed, and until World War II there was no cotton-spinning or weaving industry in the Maghreb. Nor was there any leather industry, shoes being imported, and as late as 1940, "not a glass or casserole" was manufactured.

The reasons for this state of affairs are manifest. Given the insignificant buying power of the Muslim masses, the internal market was too small. Colonial customs policy provided no customs protection, and its provisions differed for each of the three territories. Algeria belonged to the national territory and was integrated into the French customs system. Tunisia retained a special status for trading with third parties, while Morocco was required by the treaties of 1906 and 1911 to treat all states equally and levied only very low duties. The French in North Africa, active in farming and trade, were disinclined to become industrial entrepreneurs. For their part, metropolitan industries had no wish to raise up competitors in the Maghreb and did, in fact, what they could to obstruct them, either through their influence with the banks or by dumping.[97] The local trades stagnated or declined, increasing both the dependence of the villages on farm income and unemployment and underemployment in the slums of the cities.[98] The industrialization of the Maghreb began only after World War II.[99]

The Maghreb thus became an important market for the metropolis, particularly Algeria with its large European population. Exports were dominated by the primary sector, agricultural and mining products.[100] The strongly unfavorable balance of trade was offset by French investment. French capital flowed into the Maghreb in large amounts, either through the network of banks, investment corporations, and industrial concerns, all having manifold links to one another, or as a result of administration loans placed in the metropolis. These investments went overwhelmingly into the modern sector, even if one accepts the building of railways, harbors, and roads as being in the national interest. The money went into colon agriculture, mining, and the construction of work places and homes for Europeans. Even electrical, gas, and water companies served mainly Europeans.[101]

The colonial economic structure was astonishingly similar in all three French Maghreb states. Not merely Algeria, but the protectorates as well, counted in the metropolis as settlement colonies. The ruling power's first and most urgent requirement was to create the legal basis for European land acquisition in areas inhabited in good part by nomads and seminomads. In Algeria the means selected was more or less open confiscation. In Tunisia and Morocco, confiscation was indirect. Although collective tribal property was recognized, allegedly unexploited land was claimed for official colonization. A kind of land law was introduced with registration, moreover, which made private land acquisition possible for Europeans. Although a policy of shattering the collective properties of tribe and clan was deliberately pursued only in Algeria, the new land law had a disintegrating effect on Muslim society everywhere. A significant portion of the good land, about 30 percent in Algeria and 10 percent in the protectorates, ended up in European hands. The number of colons was strikingly small, which is to say that the average European holding was several times larger than the average native holding. A specific form of colonial dualism resulted. On one side stood a minority of colon large holdings worked by natives, which went over to mechanized farming in the interwar period and produced largely for export. On the other side was a majority of native mini- and micro-farms, yielding little, their owners barely surviving.[102] On top of that, the administration provided the colon all sorts of support but did hardly anything for the Muslim peasant; indeed many of the latter's tax payments benefited the former.

Whether colonization, and specifically land sequestration, led to impoverishment in absolute terms, as is usually asserted, is certainly to be doubted. The arable increased considerably—in Algeria from 2.1 million hectares in 1870 to 3.4 million in 1940, in Morocco from 2 million hectares in 1919 to 4 million in 1944, and in Tunisia it also doubled. The per-hectare yield on colon farms increased as well. Even allowing for the fact that colons produced mostly for export, food production increased in the colonial period. Although per-capital yield fell,[103] the cause was mainly the population increase,[104] which was matched by no corresponding productivity increase in native agriculture. The food situation thus became especially critical in the mountainous regions of the Kabyle and the Atlas, where there were no colons. The logging off of the forests and consequent erosion, the decrease in fallow, and the fact that too little winter forage could be stored merely worsened the situation. The symbiotic relationship between cultivation and grazing was destroyed. The trend toward regional monoculture of products such as grapes, wheat, and olives became pronounced. Colonialism introduced some diversification, however, viticulture, citrus fruits, and early vegetables being examples. Colonial farming methods were also more intensive than traditional ones, and have been carried farther since independence.

A modern communications system, colon enterprises, new urban residential quarters and, not least, foreign trade, all revealed the *presence français* in the Maghreb. It was naturally amply celebrated by both the Maghreb and metropolitan French. But this "economic wonder" should not obscure how small the natives' part in it was, nor that they found themselves in the midst of a severe socioeconomic crisis. Jean Dresch exaggerated only slightly in his graphic 1952 characterization of the situation:

> Colonization has brought on a severe crisis in the traditional social structure and led to manifest economic and social segregation. Everywhere the old tribal associations, with their strong tradition of communal life, are breaking up. They live on in Morocco only because they are protected. . . . The compulsion to take up sedentary life, restriction of the tribal areas, the shift from collective to private ownership, the expansion of the arable as the result of progressive settlement and increasing population, and, finally, penetration of the money economy into regions heretofore living closed up unto themselves or bound together only through local trade relationships, have all favored the development of individualism and increasing social inequality. The rural population of peasants and villagers, tied as it is to an area carefully bounded by the Rif, the Atlas, and Anti-Atlas, the low mountains of Western Algeria and the Tunisian Sahel, lives hemmed in on its over-

populated territory. On the plains, tillers and shepherds share land become too scarce. Mostly petty tenants or landless laborers, they constitute a miserable rural proletariat. The wandering hill tribes, often despoiled of their pastures in the plains, must restrict their peregrinations. They thus have to farm their valleys. Finally, the nomads of the steppes have been driven out of the less arid regions; and they too have to farm land chronically threatened by drought or travel northward once more, but this time in search of jobs and security. Moreover, the competition of cheaper and better quality imported goods has signified ruin for the urban artisan, whose guilds are going under.[105]

NATIONALISM

The liberation movement in the Maghreb reveals very instructively how it was shaped both by the colonial context and transregional influences and relationships.[106] It also shows, however, that, even granted the particularities of the *présence française* in the Maghreb, and despite the divergent constitutional status of Algeria, Tunisia, and Morocco, the conflict between both traditional and modern elites and the colonial rulers followed a common pattern.

In Tunisia, the Collège Sadiki, founded in 1875 by the reform minister Khéréddine, formed the initial rallying point and provided the beginnings of a new, Western-educated elite.[107] This remarkable institution was intended to educate a Tunisian administrative cadre after the manner of European secondary schools. It combined education in Arabic and Muslim subjects, such as Koran studies, Arabic and Islamic law, with the modern natural sciences. Its most promising graduates were sent to Paris for additional education. Its students came mainly from the traditional ruling class which was in part of Turkish origin. Their fathers were landowners, religious dignitaries, and former beylical officials. From 1888 on the newspaper *El-Hadira*, which had some government support, was their mouthpiece. In it, they turned a critical eye on their own past, their present inactivity, and concrete aspects of the protectorate. In 1896 the Khaldounia, a cultural association, was established. It organized instruction in history, geography, and French, both as a sort of supplement to the orthodox instruction at the Great Mosque and as a deliberate attempt to educate a small modern elite. Former students from the Collège Sadiki founded another association, the Sadikia, in 1905 for the same purpose. Two years later, in 1907, the newspaper *Le Tunisien* began to appear under the editorship of the lawyer Ali Bach-Hamba, and in 1908 the *Jeunes Tunisiens*, or Young Tunisians, joined together in the Cercle Tunisien, which was really more of a club than a political party. Although the Young Tunisians most emphatically attested their loyalty to France, they demanded reforms at the same time, namely, school and tax reforms, a constitution, civil liberties, and most importantly, the provision of elections to a Conférence Consultative.

In November 1911, however, serious disputes arose about the Muslim cemetary of Djellaz (on the outskirts of Tunis), a place important in Muslim tradition. The upshot was bloody anti-Italian riots and the later boycott of Tunis streetcars in February 1912. These actions were not specifically anti-French, but they did reveal the gulf between the colonial power and the population. They also made the colons very nervous. The colons had suspected the Young Tunisians from the outset of being subversive and now accused them of being ringleaders in the disturbances. Although the charges could never be proved, the administration stepped in with repressive measures, banning four Young Tunisian leaders, among them Ali Bach-Hamba, and prohibiting the publication of *Le Tunisien*.[108]

The Young Tunisian movement, itself fashioned after the Young Turk movement and cultivating ties to Constantinople, served as the model for the Mouvement Jeune Algérien.[109] Since about 1900, the graduates of Franco-Muslim schools had maintained loose associations, publishing little magazines and offering what amounted to adult education courses. Those involved were primarily of bourgeois and urban origins, and as lawyers, doctors, teachers, and businessmen formed the core of the modern elite. No larger association was ever formed, nor anything like a political party. Nevertheless, when Paris was considering military conscription for Algerians, a delegation was scraped together and sent to Paris. It took with it a catalog of demands, the *Manifeste Jeune-Algérien*. The most important were abolition of the Indigénat, just taxation, representation in Algerian assemblies and in the metropolitan parlement, and simplified naturalization: "What they wanted was the right to enter the 'French city,' the right to be instructed in French schools. They demanded only a common law for all: equality before the courts and in taxation."[110] The assimilationist stance assumed by the young, bourgeois Algerian elite, who expressly rejected nationalist demands, reflected the strong attraction and formative influence of *la civilization française*. It also reflected, however, the peculiarities of the Algerian situation. France had ruled the country since 1830. It was an "integral part" of the republic, and its social structure had been so drastically deformed—Arabic was accounted a foreign language—that the Young Algerian liberation program was at first expressed as demands for individual civil liberties, most notably legal equality with the Algerian French. This espousal of assimilation and integration can still be interpreted as a sort of proto-nationalism, however, because legal equality for Muslims necessarily placed colon dominance in question and implied an Algerian takeover of the local administration. It is hence not surprising that while liberal metropolitan papers, particularly *Le Temps*, benevolently supported the Young Algerians, the colon press denigrated them.

The Maghreb remained quiet during World War I, the risings in Tunisia of 1915-1916 and in the Aurès Mountains occurring in the outlying areas under incomplete colonial control. The Maghreb provided, indeed, hundreds of thousands of soldiers and workers. Economic dependence on the Metropolis became all too visible in the form of transportation problems, sharply rising prices accompanied by wages hobbling along in ineffectual pursuit, and speculative coups, all of which heightened social tensions.[111] The Arab rising in the Middle East appealed strongly to Muslim leaders, and the new elite, for its part, was equally affected by the West's democratization propaganda and Wilsonian notions of self-determination.

In order to continue Algerian recruiting, Premier Georges Clémenceau felt constrained in 1917 to promise sweeping reforms, in particular naturalization with retention of personal status as a Muslim.[112] What was actually offered as a "magnanimous" reform in 1919, however, and only then after a parliamentary tug-of-war lasting months, was rather modest. Naturalization was made easier, insofar as certain "categories" of Muslims were allowed to claim French citizenship, but—and this was decisive—only if they abandoned their personal status. The number of Muslim representatives in the administrative bodies was increased, the franchise broadened, and participation in mayoral elections allowed. The Young Algerians were disappointed, but could not agree on any joint action. Their spokesman was initially Emir Khaled, a grandson of Abd el-Kader. After graduating from St. Cyr, he had fought with distinction and had been elected in 1920 to both the community council and the financial delegation. When President Alexandre Millerand visited Algeria in 1922, Khaled presented the demands of the *évolués*, as members of the new elite were styled. The most important was naturalization combined with personal status. In 1923, however, disheartened by the polemics against him, Khaled left the country.[113] Lyautey was outraged: "In conversations with my old Muslim friends during my stay in Algeria I was taken aback by the unexpected developments. . . . I have never seen such profound bitterness, discouragement, and ill-feeling. Our policy is truly criminal."[114] The évolués, estimated then at between ten and twenty thousand, acquired a new political forum in 1927 in the Fédération des Élus Indigènes under the leadership of Dr. Muhammed Saleh Bendjelloul and Ferhat Abbas. The latter, son of a caid and a druggist by profession, had as a representative of the French educated, urban bourgeoisie plumped for integrationist-assimilationist policies—in his 1931 book, *Le Jeune Algérien*, among other places—and as late as 1936 had denied the existence of an "Algerian nation" in an oft-cited article.[115] Still, he energetically pushed legal equality, parliamentary representation, abolition of the Indigénat, admission to the civil service, expansion of education, and other measures. But the metropolis was not ready. In 1927, indeed, the colons forced the resignation of the liberal governor, Maurice Violette. In 1933 both government and parlement refused to receive an Algerian delegation, which led 950 *élus indigènes* to resign from office. Finally, in 1935, Interior Minister Marcel Régnier instituted an antireform policy.

In addition to the évolués, other new forces began to appear. The Islamic reform movement had struck a certain resonance in Algeria even before 1914, but took concrete form only after World War I under the leadership of the striking personality, Abdelhamid Ben Badis.[116] The movement's main concern initially was religious and moral reform in the sense of a return to the "true" Islam, and Arabic journals and reform Islamic schools were accordingly established. Its adherents were mainly young people, some of whom had studied in Tunis. Their opponents were the marabouts and their brotherhoods. Reform became a political question almost immediately. The marabouts were accused of collaboration with the colonial power, "Francization" being declared anathema, and Algeria's Arab past was defended. In 1931 a nationalist history of Algeria appeared, with the motto: "Islam is our religion, Algeria is our fatherland, and Arabic is our language." In opposition to Ferhat Abbas it stated uncompromisingly:

> We have also studied our history and our present situation. We assert that an Algerian Muslim nation has taken shape and exists today, in the same manner as all other nations on this earth. . . . This Algerian Muslim nation is not France, can never be France, and does not wish to be France.[117]

In 1931, the Association des Ulémas Musulmans Algériens was formed. Politically rather restrained, it expected concessions from France. Because independence was stated as a goal, however, active hostilities with the colonial power were no longer to be avoided, particularly since the latter had, among other things, forbidden reformers the right to preach in the mosques in 1933.

Earlier, in 1926, Algerians working in Paris had organized the Etoile Nord-Africaine. They sought to appeal to the masses, and their leader after 1927 was Messali Hadj. Largely recruiting his following in the metropolis, he was himself unable to enter Algeria until 1936-1937. The sort of social protest they articulated was drawn from Communist, Socialist, and trade union sources. The latter, however, recruited mainly Frenchmen, with the exception of the Communist CGTU which had a not insignificant Algerian membership. The severe effects of the depression and the resulting migration to the cities and suburbs created a latent willingness to protest in any case, which was expressed after 1933 in numerous demonstrations.[118]

The electoral victory of the Popular Front in 1936 raised high expectations in Algeria. On 7 June 1936, the representatives of the élus, the ulema, and the Communists gathered in the first Muslim congress, and agreed on a "Charter of Restitution for the Algerian Muslim people." Reflecting the divergencies within the constituent groups, the demands themselves were rather a mixed bag: complete annexation to France, maintenance of personal status and separation of the Muslim cults from the state, and sweeping social reform. What was important, however, was that for the first time, thousands of Algerians had gathered together to promulgate their demands. At the end of the year the government offered the Blum-Violette reform package, which provided for naturalization combined with personal status, broadening of the franchise, a *collège unique*, and more parliamentary representation. This was less than the charter had called for, but nonetheless was greeted in Algeria by broad assent. The colons, however, raised such a storm of indignation that the package was never even brought before Parlement.[119] When General Charles De Gaulle took it up again in 1943/44 in hope of inaugurating a new Algeria policy it was far too late. Even a man like Ferhat Abbas was by then demanding a *République algérienne*.[120]

The Algerian liberation movement gained both in breadth and articulateness in the 1930s. One can thus speak of the beginnings of nationalism.[121] Still, the moderate évolués who yet sought assimilation and Muslim-national ulema reformers on the one side, and the social-revolutionary Etoile Nord-Africaine (which became the Parti du Peuple Algérien in 1937) and Communists on the other, followed divergent routes, and, with the exception of the congress of 1936, failed to combine in an all-Algeria movement or in a single political party. In Tunisia, in contrast, what characterized the interwar period was the shift from liberal associations of notables toward a tightly organized independence party with a mass basis.

The Young Tunisians had no scope for action at home after 1912. Such developments as occurred during World War II and after arose abroad. Ali Bach-Hamba, who died in 1918, had been at work in Constantinople and his brother had founded a Tunisian-Algerian Committee in Berlin. The latter then moved to Geneva and published—with Turkish and German financial support—the *Revue du Maghreb*. This journal at first took a rather moderate line, calling for a constitution, but not for independence. After President Wilson published his Fourteen Points, however, the *Revue* came out against French rule per se. In the fall of 1918, several Tunisians met in Paris and demanded a constitution, or *destour*. Their spokesman, Abdelaziz Taalbi, went to Paris where he established ties to leftist parties and in 1920 anonymously published the propaganda piece, *La Tunisie martyr, ses revendications*.[122] That same spring, apparently, the Parti Libéral Constitutional, usually called the Destour party, was formed. Its most important demands were a parliament elected by universal suffrage, separation of powers, individual civil liberties, free access to the civil service, and compulsory education. It did not demand independence though probably only for tactical reasons. Two delegations were sent to Paris, but neither was able to obtain concrete assent to any part of the program.[123] The only reform forthcoming was the replacement of the Conseil Consultative with the so-called Grand Conseil in 1922 (see p. 263 above), whose Tunisian representatives were thenceforth all elected. That naturally failed to satisfy the Destour party, particularly since the position of the landed notables was strengthened. The French, moreover, under the influence of the supposed *péril italien*, began encouraging "petty" colonization more actively, in order to tie Tunisia definitely to France.

The Destour party had a broader basis than the Young Tunisians. The representatives of the old families who had had Muslim or French educations were joined both by members of the new bourgeoisie and the "old turbans," or conservatives. The latter joined the party during the disputes over the habous in order to attain more influence. In the main, however, the Destour party was the vehicle of the urban leadership class, loosely organized as a party of notables and with important internal tensions. Although social and economic questions were discussed, they were clearly not the party's main concern. It did, however, attempt to establish ties to the Socialist party, assisted in the 1924 foundation of the Tunisian Trade Union (Conféderation Générale des Travailleurs Tunisiens, or CGTT) and participated in strikes and demonstrations against the high cost of living. On 25 February 1925, the Tunisian Cartel, consisting of representatives of the Destour, the moderate reformers, the native section of the Grand Conseil, and Tunisian SFIO members, sent a telegram to French Premier Edouard Herriot containing a list of political and administrative demands. No Tunisians had been appointed,[124] however, to the Commission for Tunisian Studies earlier convened by Herriot in 1924. The government, indeed, responded to the increasing political unrest with the two so-called villanous decrees, of 29 January 1926, which allowed for more active intervention against "political misdemeanors" and the Arab press. Discussions in the Grand Conseil, continued, but:

> Weakened by its political reverses, and gravely hampered by these decrees, the Destour decided to lie low and await better days. It was hardly visible between 1926 and 1931, and the country enjoyed relative calm. That signified only that the Destour abstained from action, and in place of carrying on a struggle in broad daylight from which nothing was for the moment to be gained, it prepared for the future by grouping Tunisians into associations of all kinds: cultural, theatrical, charitable, self-help, and even scouting. It also set to work quietly organizing rural political cells in order to interest the rural populace in Tunisian problems and win them over for the Destour. Sleep? No, retreat and reorganization, rather, against the day when the struggle would be resumed.[125]

After 1930 there occurred a "changing of the guard," either because of the depression, made worse in Tunisia by the bad harvests of 1931 and 1932, or events in the Arab world, or in answer to the Eucharistic Congress held in Carthage in 1930. The latter, like the centennial of French rule in Algeria, was celebrated with much pomp and circumstance. Like the *Dahir Berbère* in Morocco (on which, see below, p. 289), it was taken as a deliberate insult by the Arab-Muslim elite. Perhaps more important was the fact that since the war a new generation of Tunisians had grown up, educated in Tunisian-French schools and in Paris, but coming from poorer provincial classes rather than the mostly well-to-do established families in Tunis. They charged the Destour with lack of dynamism and were willing to take on the French as a colonial power, despite, or perhaps because of, their strong ties to *civilisation française*. Their spokesman was, besides Dr. Muhammad Materi, Habib Bourguiba. The latter, born in 1903 into a large petty-bourgeois Sahelian family, received his early education at the Collège Sadiki and the Lycée Carnot in Paris and later studied law and political science. He married a French woman and returned to Tunisia in 1927. A member of the Destour since 1922, he had first published the daily *La Voix du Tunisien* with party support, and then, after November 1932, the *Action Tunisienne*. But he encountered increasing difficulties within the Destour. When he called at the Party Day in May 1933 for a program aiming at "Tunisian independence, topped off with a treaty of friendship and union with the great French Republic," the administration stepped in and outlawed the party.

The splitting off and foundation of the Neo-Destour party followed in March 1934.[126] What was new was not the program, but the will to create a dynamic instrument with real striking power, tightly controlled but nonetheless capable of appealing to and organizing the masses. The Communist party, and in organizational terms the SFIO as well, served as the model, with a politburo at the top run by Bourguiba as general secretary and cells at the grass-roots level. Also important were numerous supplementary organizations such as Neo-Destourian Youth, the Scouts, and a variety of cultural organizations, some of which were already in existence but were now brought directly or indirectly under control of the party leadership. The associations in particular served to unify "the entire population under the flag of the Neo-Destour." "It is important," wrote Propaganda Chief Salah ben Youssef, in a circular of 17 September 1936, "that all organizations established in Tunis, and particularly in the interior, stay in contact with the party cells. It is necessary that all associations be progressively integrated into the party and that the latter gradually become the party of the entire nation and the expression of its desires and its will." Propaganda tours were undertaken to spread the message in the hinterland, signatures gathered on petitions, funerals exploited propagandistically, and boycotts of French businesses organized. Arrests of the leaders provided the occasion for demonstrations in which thousands from the neighboring villages participated. Space does not permit discussion of the polemical disputes with the old Destour, with Taalbi, who returned to Tunis in 1937, or within the Neo-Destour itself—Dr. Materi resigned in January 1938—or even of the relations with the protectorate power, which vacillated between tactics of repression and liberalization. Bourguiba, aiming at independence, at first hoped only for autonomy. He had placed considerable hope in the Popular Front government, and had talks with Leon Blum, its premier, and his special minister, Pierre Viénot. But little was achieved. The colons were arming for resistance, and a strike in the phosphate mines, beginning on 4 March 1937, in which the Neo-Destour was manifestly not involved, had raised tensions considerably. When bloody disturbances finally broke out on 9 April 1938 in Tunis, reaction followed swiftly. Bourguiba and several other party leaders were arrested, and the party was dissolved before having been able to react. The situation can be compared with that in India and Indonesia, in that the nationalist movements increased in breadth, being both able to mobilize the masses for demonstrative actions and to confront the colonial powers with demands for independence. In each case, however, the arrest of the leadership immediately shut the movements down. Although an organized mass party had been created in Tunisia, it remains questionable whether effective politicization had been achieved. It is also clear that, along with political and administrative demands, the social and economic aspects of the colonial situation were being called into question. Leaderships remained in the hands of the urban bourgeois elite, while the peasants still were largely inactive.

Morocco was at first more "backward" than the other two areas, but after 1930 rapidly caught up with them.[127] Administrative penetration into the farther reaches, beyond "useful" Morocco, occurred only after World War I, the post-primary resistance of Abd el-Krim being broken only in 1926 by massive employment of French troops. Lyautey's "policy of little attentions" supported the prestige of the sultan and the traditional ruling elite. The Muslim character of the country was largely undisturbed. Lyautey also sharply opposed "Algerianization" and recognized the necessity of allowing Moroccans to share in the administration of their country, particularly since he was well aware of the awakening of the Arab world and far-sightedly anticipated the end of French rule even in 1920.[128] But he wanted the modernization of Morocco to go forward under conservative auspices, supported by the old feudal as well as the city-notable classes and within a framework of rejuvenated Moroccan institutions and Arab-Muslim culture. It was in accord with his paternalistic notions that he took pains both to establish a school for the sons of notables and to assure that its graduates received administrative jobs. On the other hand Moroccan education as a whole was to proceed slowly, separated from schools for the French. Young Moroccans from good families were, if possible, to be deterred from studying in France.

Thus, it was natural that the liberation movement in Morocco, so strongly tied to Islam, took place within the framework of the Arab-Muslim reform movement, the *Salafiyya*. The beginnings were in Fez, the tradition-rich intellectual center of Morocco. The call for reforms centered on a return to the real Islam, and was taken up by the students of the mosque University of Quarawiyin in Fez. It was at first directed against the Muslim brotherhoods. To teach a modernized Islam, schools were founded in Fez and Rabat. Supported by the urban notables, these schools also taught the history of Morocco and propagated the idea that the pre-1912 sultanate was a modern state. Secret societies developed within these schools in 1925 and 1926, as well as discussion groups meeting in private houses. Books and newspapers from Algeria, Tunisia, and Egypt were studied and discussed, along with the Rif wars, the replacement of Lyautey by Steeg, Wafd party activity in Egypt, and the Destour in Tunisia. The members of these groups came from the upper-class clans in Fez and Rabat, one of them being the young Alal el-Fassi, who was also a Quarawiyin student. Close ties existed to small groups of évolués, who had combined in Paris in 1927 in the Association des Etudiants Musulmans Nord-Africains, one of whose founders was Muhammad Hassan el-Ouezzani, also the son of a notable. Before 1930, however, one can hardly speak of a nationalist movement as such, though the readiness for political activity was there. The *Dahir Berbère*, signed by the sultan on 16 May 1930, was what unleashed it.

The *dahir* inaugurated no new policy as such, merely continuing previous efforts to safeguard the particular legal institutions of the Berber tribes. It contemplated special "customary law courts" for civil cases and a French court for criminal cases, along with elimination of the Sharifian High Court that had appellate jurisdiction. This *politique berbère* rested on the thesis that the Berbers had long resisted Arabization and had opposed the authority of Koranic law (or *chrâa*).[129] It was further assumed they would be more accessible to French influences than other Moroccans. Special Franco-Berber schools were established to make the spread of Arabic more difficult. This policy of divide and rule reemphasized the old separation between the *bled el-makhzen* and the *bled es-siba* and also served to limit the influence of both sultan and ulema.

After some initial delay, resistance united under the slogan Islam in Danger. Appeals from the mosques—"Oh, Savior! Preserve us from the evil treatment of destiny and do not separate us from our Berber brethren"—were transformed into manifestations in which reformers, the orthodox ulema, and the évolués were all able to join. When one delegation sought to present its demands to the pasha of Fez, its spokesman, Muhammed Hassan el-Ouezzani, the recent recipient of a diploma from the Ecole de Sciences Politiques in France, was arrested and publicly whipped.[130] In August, further arrests followed, among them that of el-Fassi. The movement ebbed rapidly thereafter. The *Dahir Berbère*, which had unleashed a wave of indignation in the Arab world, remained in practice a dead letter. All the same, "the storm in Morocco" was the curtain raiser for the Moroccan nationalist movement, which was led by the younger, mostly French-educated, generation.[131]

Between 1930 and 1934 a complex organization, the Moroccan Action Committee, developed under the leadership of, among others, el-Fassi and el-Ouezzani. It had approximately 150 militants and roughly 200 to 300 sympathizers—though by March 1937 membership had reached 6,500. It issued newspapers, among them *L'Action du Peuple*, and placed both the associations of former Muslim college students and the scout leagues under its control. It can thus be compared with the Destour. The anniversary of the *Dahir Berbère*, Ramadan, and the day of Sidi Muhammad Ben Yussuf's ascent to the throne as the "sultan of the young" all provided occasions for demonstrations. It was thus possible to express both Muslim emotions as well as deeply rooted royalist loyalties. When such an occasion was "perverted" into a nationalist demonstration in May 1934, punctuated by cries of "Long live the sultan, long live Morocco, down with France!" the protectorate power stepped in and banned nationalist newspapers.

Nonetheless, on 1 December of the same year, 1934, a Plan for Moroccan Reform was presented to both Foreign Minister Pierre Laval and the sultan. It primarily reflected the demands of the Western-educated elite. Skillfully exploiting the protectorate treaty as the basis for its demands, the plan called for strict adherence to it, meaning that the French should confine themselves to an advisory role and Moroccan ministers should replace French. An elected national council was also proposed as a legislature. The plan further demanded that justice and education be reformed, with Moroccan certificates of completion and a university being provided, that freedom of speech and press be granted, that the mines, electric power plants, and the railways be nationalized, that official colonization be ended, that native agriculture be subvened, that taxes be reformed, and that mutual-aid societies be expanded.[132]

The French rejected this reform scheme, the "charter of the nationalist youth,"[133] out-of-hand in 1934. After the victory of the Popular Front it was presented once again. Viénot received a delegation led by el-Ouezzani with every manifestation of good will, and the resident general was changed for another, but no real change of direction was achieved. When another delegation returned empty handed from Paris in October 1936, the Moroccan Action Committee responded with public demonstrations of protest and the administration in its turn with arrests. The arrested were soon amnestied, however, and the committee tightened up its organization and began broadening its base of support. With the establishment of an annual congress, a national council, and a permanent executive, the committee had effectively become a political party. The number of sections rose from twelve in 1935 to thirty-five in 1937 and the number of members to about sixty-five hundred.[134] The leadership did not change much, however, el-Fassi remaining the driving force. Retailers and artisans, however, joined the existing membership of established bourgeois and intellectuals. Moroccan workers, who had participated in the strike movement of June 1936, also joined.[135] They were the more inclined to do so because, although the right to form unions had been granted on 24 December 1936, Muslim workers were expressly forbidden to join unions. The committee also made efforts to reach the rural population: "The nationalists invoked Salafiyya once again and permitted the peasants to regard them as the lay priests of a reformed religion."[136] The increasingly uneasy administration finally acted, outlawing the committee on 18 March 1937. The parallel with the events in Tunisia and Algeria is clear. The nationalists responded in April 1937 with the founding in secret of the National Party for the Realization of the Reforms, though without el-Ouezzani, who had fallen out with el-Fassi. Numerous, obviously coordinated disturbances, which met with some response even outside the cities, "forced" the government to "take action": the entire executive committee was arrested and el-Fassi deported to Libreville in Gabon.

This short sketch of the liberation movement in the French Maghreb should clarify the similarities and differences in the three areas under French rule. It is particularly clear in the Maghreb why one must proceed from the colonial context in order to understand the nationalist movement, and how this context influences the movement. Thus, the French-educated elite of Algeria stuck with integration and assimilation for an astonishing length of time, whereas in Tunisia and Morocco the institutional framework of the protectorate led naturally to demands for autonomy if not necessarily independence. As late as 1936, Ferhat Abbas and Bourguiba took opposite sides, although both rejected their status as "colonials" and demanded that the colonial power redeem the slogans it used to legitimize its rule. But these were slogans and promises that could not be kept if rule was to be maintained. Both integration and assimilation in the sense of full legal equality and full French citizenship for Muslim Algerians as well as a "return to the protectorate" and a takeover of domestic power were in practice incompatible with French rule. This was all the more true because the strong settler minority could only maintain its socioeconomic interests and its political strongholds within the framework of the colonial system of rule. It therefore vehemently opposed every attempt to liberalize the existing system. Seen in this light, the assimilationist attitudes of the Algerian évolués must be seen as a specific response to the French assertion that Algeria was an integral part of the French nation and understood as both a bill drawn against future liberation and as potential nationalism. The structures and the phases of the national movements also shared much in common. Except for the "old turbans," who viewed the Christian colonial power negatively or mistrustfully from the start, it was mainly the Tunisian and Algerian associations of young évolués who even before 1914 articulated their criticisms of the administration and then organized the first parties after World War I. External stimuli, particularly the Pan-Islamic movement, played no small role in all this. The metropolis demonstrated only tepid willingness to accept reforms and blocked access of the Western-educated elite to the administrative jobs and a share in political decisions. The "Franco-Muslim association" within a "greater France," propagated by the colonial power, and which potentially also included the protectorates, proved in the colonial context but a fiction, nullified as it was by the racism of the settler minority and the paranoid, defensive reflexes of the administration. The religious reform movement became effective in the postwar years, even where it was not organized in party terms—as for example, in Algeria where it was represented by the Ulema Assembly. In Morocco, it generated the strong support of the nationalist movement, and its secret brotherhoods can be regarded as a first step toward party formation.

With the foundation of the Neo-Destour and the Plan for Moroccan Reform, the year 1934 represents the transition to a heightened level of conflict with the colonial power. In place of the loosely organized associations of notables demanding reform within the system, active dynamic organizations reaching beyond a narrow circle of urban bourgeois intellectuals began to appeal to the masses and successfully mobilized them for demonstrative action. The leadership remained in the hands of the urban elite, but the base of support broadened somewhat— thanks in no small measure to trade-union collaboration—and gradually began to encompass the rural population. Aside from its small membership, it is fair to speak of the Neo-Destour as a modern mass party like those familiar to us from other colonial areas. Personal rivalries within the leaderships of the movements in all territories were frequent. Moderates and radicals might oppose each other, especially in Algeria, but so long as the disputes with the colonial power remained in the foreground, ideological and sociopolitical differences only appeared in incipient form.

The Popular Front government in France awakened great expectations in the Maghreb and encouraged attitudes of compromise among the nationalist leaders. All the greater was the disappointment when these hopes for a metropolitan policy of magnanimous reform were shattered and France turned again to a policy of repression in 1937 and 1938. It was certainly easy enough to cripple the nationalist organizations by arresting their leaderships, but the "law and order" thus established was only superficial. Open war between the colonial power and the nationalist movement could probably not have been very long avoided even without the coming of World War II.

NOTES

1. Charles Robert Ageron, *Histoire de l'Algérie Contemporaine (1930-1964)*, (2d ed., Paris: Presses Universitaires de France, 1964). For the period before 1871: Charles André

Julien, *Histoire de l'Algérie Contemporaine: La Conquête et les Débuts de la Colonisation (1827-1871)*, (Paris: Presses Universitaires de France, 1964). For the period 1871-1919: Charles Robert Ageron, *Les Algériens Musulmans et la France* (2 vols., Paris: Presses Universitaires de France, 1968). For the period 1919-1939: Wolfgang Ohneck, *Die französische Algerienpolitik von 1919-1939* (Cologne, Opladen: Westdeutscher Verlag, 1967).

2. The majority of liberal economists, for example, opposed the expedition; Julien, *Histoire*, 45f. On Marseille, see ibid., 119, and P. Guiral, "L'Opinion Marseillaise et les Débuts de l'Enterprise Algérienne," *RH*, 214 (July-September 1955).

3. On Abd el-Kader as an extraordinary figure and leader of the national resistance, see Julien, *Histoire*, 180ff. and René Gallissot, "Abd el-Kader et la Nationalité Algérienne: Interprétation de la Chute de Régence d'Alger et les Premières Résistances à la Conquête Française," *RH*, 233 (April-June 1965).

4. Charles Robert Ageron, "Premières Négociations Franco-Algériens," in his *Politiques Coloniales au Maghreb* (Paris: Presses Universitaires de France, 1973).

5. Xavier Yacono, *Les Bureaux Arabes et l'Evolution des Genres de Vie Indigènes dans l'Ouest du Tell Algérois (Dahra, Chélif, Ouarsenis, Sersou)*, (Paris: Larose, 1953). Rather critical are Julien, *Histoire*, 330-341; Ageron, *Histoire*, 29.

6. Julien, *Histoire*, 240f.; Ageron, *Histoire*, 23.

7. An example: "Lapasset, returning to Orléansville after an absence of a dozen years, found the greatest tribe of all 'diminished by half and completely ruined' after 'the colons had taken what was without exception the most fertile land.' He noted with bitterness, 'the moral disarray, the social and agrarian revolution, or, to sum up inadequately, the anarchic chaos' "; quoted in Julien, *Histoire*, 405.

8. In addition to Julien, *Histoire*, 423f., see Charles Robert Ageron, "L'Evolution Politique de l'Algérie sous la Second Empire," in his *Politiques Coloniales*.

9. On the revolt, see, in detail, Julien, *Histoire*, 473ff., and also Ageron, *Algériens Musulmans*, I, 1ff.; idem, *Politiques Coloniales*, 219f.

10. "The insurgents should be despoiled of their lands, stock, and all other goods..., what we seek is a cantonment and resettlement"; *L'Algérie Française*, 21 May 1871, as quoted in Ageron, *Politiques Coloniales*, 228.

11. Ageron, *Histoire*, 44.

12. An uncommonly graphic impression is left by Henri Pensa (ed.), *L'Algérie: Organisation Politique et Administrative—Justice—Sécurité—Instruction Publique—Travaux Publics—Voyage de la Délégation de la Commission Sénatoriale d'Etudes des Questions Algériennes, présidée par Jules Ferry* (Paris: J. Rothschild, 1894). For details, see Ageron, *Algériens Musulmans*, I, 447f. Jules Ferry commented: "We have seen these pitiable tribes which colonization has pushed aside, which sequestration has obliterated and which the forestry service has hounded out and impoverished....We think that something has transpired that is unworthy of France"; ibid, 451. On Ferry, see also Ageron, "Jules Ferry et la Question Algérienne en 1892," *Revue d'Histoire Moderne et Contemporaine*, 10 (April-June 1963).

13. Ageron, *Algériens Musulmans*, I, 452; II, 622f.

14. On their position, reimbursement, recruitment, and performance, see ibid., II, 630f. The tendency toward "bureaucraticizing" them is clear.

15. On the opposition to Cambon and his school program, see ibid., I, 534.

16. Gabriel Esquier, *Histoire de l'Algérie (1830-1957)*, (2d ed., Paris: Presses Universitaires de France, 1957).

17. Ageron, *Histoire*, 86.

18. Jean Ganiage, *L'Expansion Coloniale de la France sous la Troisième République, 1871-1914*, with Daniel Hémery (Paris: Payot, 1968), 66. The foregoing summarizes Ganiage's magisterial *Les Origins du Protectorat Français en Tunisie, 1861-1881* (Paris: Presses Universitaires de France, 1959). Brief, but making the necessary distinctions about the financial interests is Alexander Schölch, "Wirtschaftliche Durchdringung und politische Kontrolle durch die europäischen Mächte im Osmanischen Reich (Konstantinopel, Kairo, Tunis)," *Geschichte und Gesellschaft*, 1: no. 4 (1975), 415. On Gambetta's attitude, see Charles Robert Ageron, "Gambetta

et la Réprise de l'Expansion Coloniale," *RFHOM*, 59: no. 215 (1972).

19. "In order to facilitate the French government's fulfillment of its Protectorate, His Majesty the Bey of Tunis engages himself to carry out the administrative, judicial, and financial reforms that the French government may judge beneficial"; (Article 1).

20. On this see Pierre Bardin, "Les Débuts Difficiles de Protectorat Tunisien (Mai 1881-Avril 1882)," *Revue d'Histoire Diplomatique*, 85 (January-March 1971), and above all, Jürgen Rosenbaum, *Frankreich in Tunesien: Die Anfänge des Protektorates 1881-1886* (Zurich: Atlantis, 1971). Both authors demonstrate the decisive influence of the first resident general, Paul Cambon.

21. "His presence, his submission, and his signature, are cheap at the price of fr. 900,000 a year. We save much more than that in garrisons, functionaries, the repression of rebellions, and the prevention of disturbances"; Paul Leroy-Beaulieu, *L'Algérie et la Tunisie* (Paris: Guillaumin et Cie., 1887), 377. "We govern Tunisia at all levels in the name of the bey"; Paul Cambon, *Correspondance 1870-1924*, ed. Henri Cambon (3 vols., Paris: B. Grasset, 1940-46), I, 156.

22. The administration is outlined in the accounts of Paul Sebag, *La Tunisie: Essai de Monographie* (Paris: Editions Sociales, 1951); Henri Cambon, *Histoire de la Régence de Tunis* (Paris: Berger-Levrault, 1948). See also Daniel Goldstein, "Mise en Valeur et Mise en Marche Nationale: Les Répercussions de la Première Guerre Mondiale sur la Tunisie" (Dissertation, Zurich University, 1973). Published as *Libération ou Annexion aux Chemins Croisés de l'Histoire Tunisienne 1914-1922* (Tunis: Maison Tunisienne de l'Edition, 1978). Citations are from the dissertation.

23. Goldstein, "Mise en Valeur," 17, 157f.

24. "Indeed, the task of the shaykh becomes more difficult every day. Nearly always illiterate, this agent is supposed to keep accurate financial records. In the colonized regions, the difficulties are insuperable. Some colons treat the shaykhs like domestics while simultaneously complaining to them about the natives, failing to understand that after having destroyed their authority by exposing them to public derision, it then is ridiculous to appeal to their authority and unreasonable to consider it somehow amiss when their authority proves ineffective. The shaykh also hesitates to enforce his will on those beneath him. If he acts with vigor, grievances pile up against him, but if he lets things ride, the disorder becomes such that he has to be replaced. Considering that remuneration is nearly always minimal, it is hardly surprising that the shaykhs are guilty of frequent abuses and that the majority of the well-off landowners refuse to accept the position"; Congrès Colonial, *Compte Rendu*, 506.

25. For how they were selected, see Goldstein, "Mise en Valeur," 23.

26. "The discussion of any demands of a constitutional or political nature is forbidden"; (Article 12). On the Grand Conseil, see Robert Bloch, "Die französischen Colons im Protectorat Tunesien, 1923-1929" (Dissertation, University of Zurich, 1975), 41f.

27. On Etienne's Morocco policy, see Herward Sieberg, *Eugène Etienne und die Französischen Kolonialpolitik, 1887-1904* (Cologne, Oplanden: Westdeutscher Verlag, 1968), 117f.

28. For this and the following I follow E. Trautweiler's dissertation, now in progress, on the beginnings of the protectorate.

29. For the details about the administration, see Alan Scham, *Lyautey in Morocco: Protectorate Administration, 1912-1925* (Berkeley: University of California Press, 1970).

30. Robin Leonard Bidwell, *Morocco under Colonial Rule: French Administration of Tribal Areas, 1912-1956* (London: Cass, 1973).

31. "Among the tribes, justice is rendered with a venality so hair-raising as to be scarcely imaginable," noted a judicial expert in 1933; quoted in ibid., 82.

32. This is covered in detail in my *Decolonization*, 347f.

33. Jacques Berque, *Le Maghreb entre les deux Guerres* (Paris: Editions du Seuil, 1962), 42.

34. Bidwell, *Morocco*, 81.

35. Goldstein, "Mise en Valeur," 4.

36. It was summed up as "Making the old local elite collaborators in colonization by transforming it into a parasitic class"; Abdallah Laroui, *L'Histoire du Maghreb: un Essai de Synthèse* (Paris: F. Maspero 1970), 316.

37. For evidence, see Albertini, *Decolonization*, 356. As early as 1887 Leroy-Beaulieu, who vigorously defended the protectorate from "Algerianization," commented at the end of his

important book: "We want to maintain the Protectorate as long as possible. The day may come, however, forty or fifty years from now, when it will be difficult to uphold the nominal authority of the bey and we will be constrained to annex Tunisia to France"; Leroy-Beaulieu, *L'Algérie*, 450.

38. Victor Demontès, *L'algérie Agricole, suivie de quelques Renseignements sur les Produits de la Steppe at des Forêts* (Paris: Larose, 1930), 94.

39. Ageron, *Histoire*, 50; and idem, *Algériens Musulmans*, II, 766; Ohneck, *Algerienpolitik*, 119. Also critical is Victor Piquet, *L'Algérie Française: Un Siècle de Colonisation, 1830-1930* (Paris: A. Colin, 1930), 80ff. For the period 1921-1933, Calvelli writes of a "winding down and cessation of creation of any new villages. . . and the saving of others about to go under by an extension of their holdings and the consolidation of colon debts"; Marcel André Emile Calvelli, *Etat de la Propriété Rurale en Algérie* (Algiers: Ancienne Imprimerie V. Heintz, 1935), 38.

40. An official in the Oran region wrote in 1887 to the governor-general: "As soon as the titles are handed over to the tribe, the natives are dispossessed and dispoiled by dishonorable speculators using written claims often going back for years. Some douros lent at fifty percent interest for three months, a niggardly bit of merchandise delivered for an exaggerated price, add up in a very short time to a large amount of money. Signed notes, judgments, and registered mortgages, such are the methods used. The day the titles are handed over, the process servers set out for the country to seize the land. . ."; quoted in Ageron, *Algériens Musulmans*, I, 99. For the details of the agrarian legislation and its consequences up to 1919, see the appropriate chapters in ibid., and also Calvelli, *Propriété Rurale*, 35f.

41. A striking example is noted in Djiali Sari, "Le Demantèlement de la Propriété Foncière," *RH*, 249 (January-March 1973).

42. Ageron, *Algériens Musulmans*, II, 760; Piquet, *L'Algérie Française*, 102.

43. Ohneck, *Algerienpolitik*, 119. "The essential aim is suppress *arch* land as rapidly as possible in the interest of colonization and of individual Europeans and natives. . . . The complete gallicization of Algerian land is the ultimate degree of assimilation to be sought. However, an overhasty sequestration should be avoided. . . . The improvidence of the Arab will lead to the ruin of the better part of the fellahin in the *arch* lands if each of them is given an individual French title to his land"; Calvelli, *Propriété Rurale*, 42.

44. Demontès, *L'Algérie Agricole*, 140, gives the available arable at 6.5 million hectares in 1928. On p. 104, he states that Europeans held 2.4 million hectares, 2.1 million of which was unwooded, and that Algerians held 12 to 13 million hectares, as if the land was equally valuable in both cases. Other figures are given in René Gendarme, *L'Economie de l'Algérie: Sous-développement et Politique de Croissance* (Paris: A. Colin, 1959), 80. Of 6.9 million hectares of "cultivatable land," in 1954, 4.75 million hectares, or 69 percent, was in Muslim hands; ibid., 165.

45. Calvelli, *Propriété Rurale*, 166f.

46. Hildebert Isnard, "Agriculture Européenne et Agriculture Indigène en Algérie (Etude Comparée de leur Structure Régionale)," *Les Cahiers d'Outre-Mer*, 12 (April-June 1959).

Table 8.5
Ownership of Cultivated Land in Algeria (in percentages)

Region	Europeans	Algerians
Sahel	85.0	15.0
South	12.3	87.7

47. For a striking picture, see Robert Tinthoin, "Les Trara: Etude d'une Région Musulmane d'Algérie," *Bulletin de la Société de Géographie*, 73 (1961).

48. Ageron, *Histoire*, 81-82. Cattle and goats also declined; Gendarme, *L'Economie*, 33.

49. Charles Robert Ageron, "Les Paysans Algériens du Constantinois devant la Fiscalité Française et la Crise Economique (1920-1935)," in idem, *Politiques Coloniales*.

50. Quoted in André Nouschi, *La Naissance du Nationalisme Algérien 1914-1954* (Paris: Editions de Minuit, 1952, 1979), 48.

51. "It is necessary to integrate them into the colonial legal structure. That means not only acquiring certain ideas, certain new reflexes, but in part revamping their mental structures"; Jean-Paul Charney, *La vie Musulmane en Algérie, d'après la Jurisprudence de la Première Moitié du XXe Siècle* (Paris: Presses Universitaires de France, 1965), 140.

52. Germaine Tillon, *L'Algérie en 1957* (Paris: Editions de Minuit, 1957).

53. On this, see the mammoth work, Hildebert Isnàrd, *La Vigne en Algérie: Etude Géographique* (2 vols., Gap: Ophrys, 1951, 1954).

54. From a commission report of 1833: "The grape will succeed, but one should not consider it in the French interest to cultivate it in Algeria. . . . Viticulture ought not to be among those things encouraged by the government. For this reason, it would be prudent if grapes, of all the things already encumbering French agriculture, were to remain uncultivated in Algeria, either for production of raisins or for local consumption as fruit. The government probably cannot block it outright, but it ought not to encourage it"; Isnard, *La Vigne*, II, 27f.

55. Ibid., II, 133.

56. Ohneck, *Algerienpolitik*, 112f.

57. Ageron, *Algériens Musulmans*, II, 842.

58. Basic reading is Jean Poncet, *La Colonisation et l'Agriculture Européenne en Tunisie dépuis 1881: Etude de Géographie Historique et Economique* (Paris: Mouton, 1962). See also, idem, *Paysages et Problèmes Ruraux en Tunisie* (Paris: Presses Universitaires de France, 1963).

59. For French attitudes in the 1880s, Leroy-Beaulieu, *L'Algérie*, is good. For example: "As for using in Tunisia the savage methods of expropriating the Arabs sometimes employed in Algeria. . . no one considers it. . . . Land is still available in Tunisia, however"; p. 338.

60. "This procedure purges the land of all mystical ties and frees it irrevocably from third party claims"; quoted from *Afrique Française*, 2 (1892), 5.

61. Goldstein, "Mise en Valeur," 165f.

62. Poncet, *Colonisation*, 198.

63. Bloch, "Colons," 101f.

64. Poncet, *Colonisation*, 289; Bloch, "Colons," 198f.

65. Statistics for 1921 are in Goldstein, "Mise en Valeur," 60.

66. The figures for 1937 are in Sebag, *La Tunisie*, 43.

67. See the map in Poncet, *Colonisation*, 319.

68. "In Tunisia it must be frankly admitted that the native countryman has been treated as a *quantité negligeable*. Although the establishment of colons on thousands of acres has been encouraged, no one troubles themselves much about what has become of the natives, the original holders of the land. We have, it is true, transformed an arid and desolate plain into a smiling and fertile countryside but who can say what has become of the natives, the fellahin, who cultivated, or, at any rate occupied, the land before us? At every step we discover traces of their passage. There, where the harvest flourishes so, was a native hut; here some piled up stones indicate a cemetery; but where have the inhabitants of the huts gone, and where are the descendents of the dead? In their struggle for existence, our colons are not much concerned to answer such questions. They care little for their predecessors, or where those who sold to them now pitch their tents. But it is true nonetheless that generations of natives were born there and lived there, and that, moreover, they have disappeared without anyone even being able to say where they went. Is this the work of civilization and social progress that France promised to accomplish in this country?"; Congrès Colonial, *Compte rendu*, 468.

69. Goldstein, "Mise en Valeur," 61, basing his account on Rodd Balek in *Afrique Française* (1921), 373.

Table 8.6
Real Property Ownership in Tunisia, 1937

	Frenchmen	Italians	Others	Total Europeans
Hectares	627,700	70,120	26,881	724,701
Farms	2,185	2,380	84	4,649
Average in hectares	286	29	320	155

SOURCE: Sebag, *Tunisie*, 43.

70. M. Péret, president of the Comité Agricole, wanted to tempt the money interests: "Cereals are obtained through the labor of the khammès. The khammès is a man who one attaches to oneself through indebtedness. He is furnished with a plow and harness at fr. 15 and a draft animal at fr. 90"; *Afrique Française*, 1 (1891) 12.

71. A description of a 1,500 hectare-holding some 200 kilometers west of Tunis is in the *Quinzaine Coloniale*, 25 November 1929. Poncet, *Paysages*, 145 speaks of a "depopulated countryside."

72. Poncet, *Colonisation*, 256.

73. Table 8.7 gives further data.

Table 8.7
Acreage and Yields in Tunisia, 1921-1935

	hectares	quintals	q/ha.
1921-25	480,000	1,398,000	2.9
1931-35	642,000	1,776,000	2.7

SOURCE: Ibid.

74. Poncet, *Paysages*, 48. Pierre Bardin, *La Vie d'un Douar: Essai sur la Vie Rurale dans les Grandes Plaines de la Haute Medjerda, Tunisie* (Paris: Mouton, 1965).

75. Poncet, *Colonisation*, 288; Sebag, *La Tunisie*, 75; Bloch, "Colons," 154f.

76. In addition to Albert Ayache, *Le Maroc: Bilan d'une Colonisation* (Paris: Editions Sociales, 1956), see especially Charles F. Stewart, *The Economy of Morocco, 1912-1962* (Cambridge: Harvard University Press, 1964). I also base my account on a 1969 seminar paper by Willi Loepfe on European land sequestration in Morocco before 1932.

77. In a speech to the Lyons Chamber of Commerce on 29 February 1916, Lyautey stated it was said of him that "he did not like colons, pure and simple"; Louis Hubert Gonsalve Lyautey, *Paroles d'Action: Madagascar—Sud-Oranais—Oran—Maroc (1900-1926)*, (Paris: A. Colin, 1927), 397. As late as 1923, deputy Gabriel Abbo inveighed in parlement on 14 March 1923 against Lyautey: "There are no colons in Morocco. . . . There is no wish to admit colons. . . . Although the Protectorate ought, indeed, to have a colonization program, it has up till now refused to institute a serious and practical one"; quoted in *Afrique Française*, 33 (1923), 201f.

78. *Afrique Française*, 48 (1938), 177.

79. See the 1928 instructions to the contrôleurs civils quoted in Ayache, *Le Maroc*, 151.

80. "Quasi-Draconian protection," quoted in Pierre Courageot, *Les Communautés Agraires du Maroc et le Protectorat Français* (Toul: Imprimerie Toulois, 1934), 89 as quoted by Loepfe (see n. 76 above). In the literature, the law of 7 July 1914 is usually the earliest law mentioned.

81. Stewart, *Economy*, 73; *La Quinzaine Coloniale*, 10 December 1929, 562.

82. Distilled from various sources by Loepfe. The figures for 1953 I owe to the courtesy of Charles Robert Ageron.

83. This is clearly shown on the map in *Histoire du Maroc*, by Jean Brignon et al. (Paris: Hatier, 1967), 359.

84. Stewart, *Economy*, 80.

85. Loepfe, usually using mainly the *Afrique Française*, 1938, 124f.

86. Between 1925 and 1930 there were 1,273 loans totaling fr. 140 million; René Hoffherr, *L'Economie Marocaine* (Paris: Librairie de Recueil Sirey, 1932), 134.

87. On the regional and social origins of the settlers, and the failures of some during the depression, see Jacques Gadille, "L'Agriculture Européenne au Maroc: Etudes Humaines et Economiques," *Annales de Géographie*, 66 (March-April 1957).

88. Stewart, *Economy*, 90.

89. "Native agriculture hardly evolves at all, partly because of the habits of the farmers, but also because Protectorate services have few ways of reaching them, as is not true for European farming"; Marcel Amphoux, "L'Evolution de l'Agriculture Européenne au Maroc, "*Annales de Géographie*, 42 (March 1933) 175.

90. Table 8.8 compares grain yields as follows:

Table 8.8
Grain Yields in Morocco, 1921-1940 (in quintals per hectare)

	Hard wheat	Soft wheat	Barley
1921-1925	6.36	8.58	7.58
1926-1930	6.07	5.70	7.10
1931-1935	5.86	6.04	7.64
1936-1940	4.72	5.51	7.79

SOURCE: Abdel Aziz Belal, *L'Investissement au Maroc (1912-1964) et ses Enseignements en Matière de Développement Economique* (Paris, La Haye: Mouton, 1968), 97.

91. Robert Montagne, "Naissance et Développement du Prolétariat Marocain," in *Industrialisation de l'Afrique du Nord*, exposé de Ch. Celier et al. (Paris: A. Colin, 1952).

92. Hoffherr, *L'Economie*, 149.

93. For figures, see Gendarme, Sebag, Ayache, and Stewart, and also Jean Dresch's piece in *Industrialisation*.

94. Stewart, *Economy*, 154.

95. Sebag, *La Tunisie*, 46.

96. René Gallissot, *Le Patronat Européen au Maroc: Action Sociale, Action Politique, 1931-1942* (Rabat: Editions Techniques Nord Africaines, 1964), 230. For 1952, Ayache gives employment at 11,071, of whom about 1,000 were Europeans. One billion francs went to Moroccans in salaries and 574 million to Europeans, giving an average monthly wage of fr. 40-50,000 for Europeans and fr. 8,330 for Moroccans; Ayache, *Le Maroc*, 167.

97. For Algeria, see the examples in Gendarme, *L'Economie*, 170. See, along the same lines, Georges Spillmann, *L'Afrique du Nord et la France* (Paris: Editions Boursiac, 1947), 188.

98. Complaints were already being made at the Congrès Colonial de Marseille of 1906: "Gentlemen, Tunisian industries which foreign competition or changes in consumer preferences have seriously compromised are legion"; Congrès Colonial, *Compte Rendu*, 484. "In the towns the few native industries yet remaining are at death's door, the trades which support numerous corporations are gradually disappearing in the face of the perfection of modern machine industry"; ibid. 495. "One can say without exaggeration that with colonization native pauperization has come to Tunisia; formerly one never saw, as one does today, the swarms of beggars of every age and both sexes which invade the streets and cafe terraces at certain times in the towns of the Regence"; ibid.

99. According to Amin, total industrial production (including mining, electricity, manufacturing industries, and construction) was as follows:

Table 8.9
Total Industrial Production in the Maghreb, 1880-1955 (in billions of francs)

	1880	1910	1920	1930	1955
Algeria	17	30	44	60	170
Tunisia	. . .	10	19	25	45
Morocco	. . .	. . .	25	42	182

SOURCE: Samir Amin, *L'Economie du Maghreb* (2 vols., Paris: Editions de Minuit, 1966), I, 66.

100. See, for example, the Tunisian export figures for 1938, which clearly reveal the dominance of the primary sector:

	Million francs
Grain	192.5
Olive Oil	308.1
Wine	176.5
Esparto Grass	50.0
Phosphates	132.6
Iron Ore	107.1
Zinc and Tin	58.9

Total Exports 1353.0 (Primary sector 75.8 percent)
From the *Revue d'Economie Politique*, 64 (1954), 201.

101. For Morocco see, in detail, Belal, *Investissement*, 18f.

102. For Algeria: "One notes (in 1950-52) 434,500 Muslim holdings of less than ten hectares: Although a certain proportion of these are devoted to high-value products such as wine, tobacco, and garden truck and can thus be considered adequate, they are a minority. Indeed, an appreciable portion of Muslim holdings between ten and fifty hectares, situated in the drier areas, are also submarginal. It is probably not excessive to consider around seventy percent of North African Muslim holdings too small to be viable under normal conditions. Such are the inevitable consequences of universal rural overpopulation"; René Dumont's comments in *Industrialisation*, 49.

103. able 8.10 gives farm yield data:

Table 8.10
Farm yield per Capita, Algeria and Morocco, 1911-1950 (in quintals)

Algeria	1911	4.1
	1936	2.8
Morocco	1931	3.7
	1950	2.5

SOURCE: Ibid, 50; See also Gendarme, *L'Economie*, 33; Amin, *L'Economie*, 37.

104. The population grew as follows:

Table 8.11
Population Growth in the Maghreb, 1876-1956 (in millions)

	Algeria			Tunisia			Morocco	
	Muslim	Non-Muslim		Muslim	Non-Muslim		Muslim	Non-Muslim
1876	2.5	345,000	1881	ca. 1.5	18,000			
1911	4.7	752,000	1910	1.7	120,000	1921	4.2	81,000
1931	5.6	882,000	1936	2.4	213,000	1931	5.0	172,000
1954	8.4	984,000	1956	3.6	255,000	1952	7.4	363,000

SOURCE: For Algeria and Tunisia, Amin, *L'Economie*, 21, 33; for Morocco, Stewart, *Economy*, 60.

105. Jean Dresch, "La Situation Economique et Sociale de l'Afrique du Nord," in *Industrialisation*, 228f.

106. Charles André Julien, *L'Afrique du Nord en Marche: Nationalismes Musulmans et Souveraineté Française* (Paris: R. Julliard, 1952); Roger Le Tourneau, *Evolution Politique de l'Afrique du Nord Musulmane, 1920-1961* (Paris: A. Colin, 1962).

107. In addition to Nicola A. Ziadeh, *Origins of Nationalism in Tunisia* (Beirut: American University of Beirut, Faculty of Arts & Sciences, 1962), see in particular Peter Sidler, "Die

'Jeunes Tunisiens': Ihre Bewegung, das 'Mouvement Jeune-Tunisien' und ihre Rolle bei den Unruhen in Tunis von 1911/12" (Dissertation, University of Zurich, 1974). See also Charles André Julien, "Colons Françaises et Jeunes Tunisiens (1882-1912)," *RFHOM*, 54: nos. 194-197 (1967).

108. Sidler, "Jeunes Tunisiens," has provided the first account of these events based on the documents.

109. Charles Robert Ageron, "Le Mouvement 'Jeune Algérien' de 1900 à 1923," in *Etudes Maghrébines: Mélanges Charles André Julien* (Paris: Presses Universitaires de France, 1964).

110. Ibid., 230.

111. Made explicit through the use of a local example by G. Meynier, "Aspects de l'Economie de l'Est Algérien pendant la Guerre de 1914-1918," *RH*, 247 (January-March 1972). Goldstein, "Mise en Valeur," covers Tunisia in detail.

112. For a detailed account see Ohneck, *Algerienpolitik*. For the interwar period see in addition Nouschi, *La Naissance du Nationalisme Algèrien*; and Mahfoud Kaddache, *La Vie Politique à Alger de 1919 à 1939* (Algiers: SNED, 1970).

113. Charles Robert Ageron, "L'Emir Khalêd, Petit-fils d'Abd el-Kader, fut-il le Premier Nationaliste Algérien?" in idem, *Politiques Coloniales*; Kaddache, *Vie Politique*, 65ff., emphasizes Khalêd's nationalist aspects.

114. From a private letter quoted by Ageron, "L'Émir Khalêd," 277.

115. Cited by among others, Ohneck, *Algerienpolitik*, 149. The attitude of the *élus* is clearly shown in R. Zenati, *Le Problème Algérien vu par un Indigène* (1938). Zenati, a Kabyle, was a French citizen and a high official in the school administration. Among other things, he criticized the land policy very sharply, the result being "pauperism, caused by fraudulent use of documents," p. 115. But politically he still favored integration: "Algeria should live in peace and tranquility under the aegis of France"; p. 122. He also warned, however, that without reforms "there will be no French Algeria"; p. 180.

116. Ali Merad, *Le Réformisme Musulman en Algérie de 1925 à 1940: Essai d'Histoire Religieuse et Sociale* (The Hague: Mouton & Co., 1969).

117. Le Tourneau, *Evolution*, 319; Merad, *Réformisme Musulman*, 398.

118. André Nouschi, "Le Sens de Certains Chiffres: Croissance Urbaine et Vie Politique en Algérie (1926-1937)," in *Etudes Maghrébines*; Kaddache, *Vie Politique*, 203f.

119. Covered in detail in Ohneck, *Algerienpolitik*, 129f., and Kaddache, *Vie Politique*, 296f.

120. Albertini, *Decolonization*, 373f.

121. Ageron, *Histoire*, 88, has it beginning in 1931; Le Tourneau, *Evolution*, 319, in 1936.

122. For details, see Goldstein, "Mise en Valeur."

123. Resident General Lucien Saint warned his officials against sympathizing with Tunisian nationalists: "I note with regret that certain officials, French and Tunisian, of the Regency administration adhere to the disruptive doctrines of certain groups whose aims are manifestly hostile to France.... The Protectorate government will not permit an official ... to be a member of a party which has as its program the ruination of French authority in Tunisia"; quoted in *Afrique Française*, 32 (1922), 461.

124. Covered adequately for the first time in Bloch, "Colons," 181ff.

125. Le Tourneau, *Evolution*, 69.

126. Based on unpublished materials and numerous interviews is Yvonne Bogorad, "Tunesischer Nationalismus, 1934-1938: Die Neo-Destour-Partei in ihrer Frühphase" (Lizenz Thesis, University of Zurich, 1971). See also Ridha Abdallah, "Le Néo-Destour," *Revue Juridique et Politique d'Outre-Mer*, 5 (July-September 1963).

127. In addition to Julien and Le Tourneau, see, in detail, John P. Halstead, *Rebirth of a Nation: The Origins and Rise of Moroccan Nationalism, 1912-1944* (Cambridge, Mass.: Harvard University Press, 1967); idem, "The Changing Character of Moroccan Reformism, 1921-1934," *JAH*, 5 (July 1964).

128. Albertini, *Decolonization*, 353.

129. Charles Robert Ageron, "La Politique Berbère du Protectorat Marocain de 1913 à 1934," in Ageron, *Politiques Coloniales.*

130. Ibid., 138. Halstead does not mention this whipping.

131. The title of a newspaper article by Daniel Guérin; Ageron, "Politique Berbère," 138.

132. On the origins, foreign models, and content of the plan, see, in detail, Halstead, *Rebirth*, 210f. The plan was largely based on articles in *Maghreb* and *L'Action du Peuple*.

133. Robert Montagne, "La Crise Nationaliste au Maroc," *Politique Etrangère*, 2 (December 1937), 542.

134. Halstead, *Rebirth*, 241.

135. Albert Ayache, "Les Grèves de Juin 1936 au Maroc," *Annales: Economies, Sociétés, Civilizations*, 12 (July-September 1957).

136. Halstead, *Rebirth*, 241.

PART III

SUB-SAHARAN AFRICA[1]

9

BRITISH WEST AFRICA: NIGERIA AND THE GOLD COAST

In 1865 a parliamentary committee recommended that the government abandon ideas of further expansion and prepare the "natives" for assuming control of all existing holdings, "with a view to our ultimate withdrawal from all, except, probably, Sierra-Leone."[2] The members of the committee were entirely serious about this matter. The failure of the Niger Expedition of 1841 and the hostilities with the Ashanti in 1863 had had a sobering effect. The 1860s were also the day of Little England, and British traders, backed by the fleet, dominated the African coast.[3] The humanitarian impulses behind the antislavery movement, moreover, had largely ebbed. Nonetheless, expansion continued and patently could no longer be stemmed. London did not deliberately seek expansion for, though it was willing to support trade, it hesitated to commit itself to military operations on the mainland and showed little interest in increasing its administrative obligations. "We want of course free access to the interior but we cannot undertake the task of controlling all the powerful coastal tribes; and if we succeeded in getting them under our control, we should immediately come into collision with tribes beyond, and so on till we come to Timbuctoo."[4] That was in fact the difficulty. Free access to the hinterland seemed essential, particularly to the Niger and Benue River territories. Liverpool firms whose trade depended on good relations with the African coastal states such as Brass and Old Calabar opposed expansion. The question really was whether expansion could stop once one had become ensnarled in internal African conflicts.

The shift from informal empire to effective colonial control was so gradual it was hardly perceived.[5] The initiative came not from London but from the men on the spot, the consuls and governors in West Africa. The latter, not always very gladly, had to take stands when friction between British traders and the coastal states arose or when inland trade routes were blocked. But they were not above pursuing a "forward policy" and presenting London with faits accomplis, later condemned, perhaps, but never undone. Other expansionist influences were the trading firms, which sought direct access to the interior and thus stirred up military confrontations, and the missionaries, both European and native, who called for British protection and support. Foreign policy considerations also played no small role in West Africa. The worry, whether justified or not, that a European Great Power, particularly France, might establish itself in the British sphere of interest and trade led a passively inclined British government to respond on a number of occasions. London rather feared that France, once established, would favor its countrymen in customs matters.[6]

More and more British commercial vessels entered the Niger delta in the 1870s. Stations were established, and conflicts with African intermediaries, whose palm oil transportation business was being ruined, were frequent. When the Africans defended themselves, or went over to the attack to assert their old positions as middlemen, warships came and bombarded African cities and commercial centers.[7] In 1879, moreover, George Goldie Taubman succeeded in uniting rival Niger trading firms as the National African Company, thus forming a "monopoly by agreement." Although the French began to horn in only after 1880, the Compagnie Française de l'Afrique Equatoriale rapidly established a series of posts on the Niger and Benue. The company's agent, Antoine Mattei, concluded treaties with African chiefs and in 1883 Navy Minister Jean Jauréguiberry ordered him to concentrate on concluding additional treaties on the left bank of the Niger, in order to gain control of the trade of the Chad and Bornu regions. As early as 1885, however, price-cutting by the National African Company had forced the Compagnie Française to throw in the towel and sell its encampments.[8] London was able to gain acknowledgment of British hegemony in the lower Niger valley at the Congo Conference of 1884-1885, but nevertheless felt obliged thenceforth to pursue a more active policy. In 1885, the Oil River Protectorate was established and the British consul instructed to conclude treaties with the African city-states in which the latter promised to accept free trade and not to conclude agreements with other powers. This initially hazy claim to intervention rights soon led to numerous actions in defense of British trade. It also led to conflict with Jaja, ruler of Opobo. Jaja was an Ibo slave who had come to power in 1869 and had successfully entered the palm oil trade. He had taken pains to maintain good relations with the English, even supplying them a contingent of troops for the Ashanti war of 1874. A modern ruler, he had sent his son to school in Glasgow but had also refused entry to missionaries, which earned their hostility.[9] His attempts to monopolize trade within his territory had also excited the hostility of Liverpool merchants, particularly since he demanded fees from British traders and sought to export directly to England.[10] British consul Harry Johnston first put pressure on him and then, after Jaja had come to parley in 1887 under guarantee of safe conduct, Johnston took him prisoner and exiled him. Foreign Secretary Lord Salisbury condemned the act, noting that "in other places it would be called kidnapping," but otherwise did nothing. Further intervention followed, at first mainly in the coastal states. Consuls were inclined to interpret their powers rather broadly, forcing both great and petty chiefs to renounce collecting trading fees and to disband their military forces. The next step was usually to create a local system of duties and a small militia. In most cases these changes were effected without violence, but in the case of Benin, hostilities developed and it was overrun and plundered in 1897. In the Ibo territory, which lay to one side of the trading states in the delta hinterland, no states of any size with kings or chieftains existed, merely a great many independent towns and villages which had little contact with Europeans. It took military expeditions and the work of several years before the Ibo territory could be regarded as within the British administrative system. The British imposed the administrative models of the coastal zone on this hinterland, establishing native courts with chiefs in order to avoid direct administration. But, in fact, the old order had been disrupted and the new was perceived as foreign.[11]

The British encountered relatively slight resistance in the west among the Yorubas, whose states warred continuously with each other and had on occasion called upon the British governor in Lagos, under British rule since 1861, as arbiter. London long delayed intervention, despite the demands of missionaries, active in the area since the 1840s, that it step in to support one or another of the Yoruba states. As late as 1886, the governor had entrusted an African, Reverend Samuel Johnson, with a mission of conciliation. The sharp drop in palm oil prices, however, and the resulting acute economic difficulties in Lagos led traders and English chambers of commerce to exert the utmost pressure on the government. They demanded that the trade routes into the interior be placed under British control and that African middlemen be shut out. France's attempts to establish a connection from Porto Novo to Abeokuta for the purpose of gaining control of the exports going out through Lagos led to African defensive boycott measures. When the French responded with a thrust toward Abomey, the British intervened militarily.[12] The Yoruba country was soon brought under control, since the war-weary population was quite willing to accept British rule. As early as 1895, a railway was begun toward Ibadan, a measure which Western-educated Africans in Lagos also greeted as a sign of progress. The line was intended to proceed from Lagos into the backcountry and eventually reach the Muslim north.[13] The Yoruba states, having lost the right to levy transit duties, worried about losing their autonomy as well. The governor, however, was able to bring them around by means of patient negotiation, and new sources of income, controlled by the colonial power, were created for them. In 1906 the colony of Lagos and the protectorate of Southern Nigeria were merged administratively.

In the north, the Niger Company, which had received the charter Taubman had foreseen for it in 1886 as a result of the Congo conference, was entrusted with maintaining British interests. The company established a modest administrative apparatus and concluded protectorate treaties. As a monopoly company, it was naturally much disliked by the African coastal states, who lost their economic roles as middlemen. "Punishment expeditions" were dispatched against villages and African traders who opposed the company's monopoly claims within its concession area. When Brass warriors attacked the harbor of Akassa, the company seat, protectorate troops had to be sent to defend it. Further expansion occurred only when the French pushed northward after conquering Abomey with the intent of obtaining access to the navigable portion of the middle Niger and thus mastery over the Fulani kingdom. On behest of the Niger Company, Captain Frederick Lugard forestalled the French by occupying Nikki in 1894, and Ilorin and the Nupe emirates in 1897. London also felt constrained to act. Colonial Secretary Joseph Chamberlain had no wish to leave "Nigeria with its thirty millions of Hausa and its civilizations and wants"[14] to the French. He instructed Lugard to create an army, nullified the charter in 1899 and appointed Lugard High Commissioner of Northern Nigeria on 1 January 1900.[15] "A colonial governor can seldom have been appointed to a territory so much of which had never been viewed by himself or any other European."[16] The conquest began a year later and by 1903 the emirates of Kontagora, Borgu, Kano, and Sokoto had been conquered. The Muslim rulers fought against the unbelievers, but had no real notion of how to exploit their military opportunities. Lugard, indeed, was accompanied by only two whites and about eighty African soldiers. The emirs sent cavalry against machine-guns and allowed themselves to be dispatched in detail. Lugard's assumption that Sokoto's vassal emirates and the subject Hausa population would rebel against their masters proved correct only in part, however. Some emirs refused to fight, but others swore their fealty, and 25,000 loyalists accompanied the son of the fallen sultan of Sokoto on his flight into the Sudan. The mass of the Hausas did not resist very energetically and reacted rather passively to the defeat of their Fulani rulers, a fact that considerably simplified the establishment of British rule.[17]

Despite the recommendation of the parliamentary committee of 1865, expansion into the hinterland also occurred on the Gold Coast. In 1872 the English took over the Dutch forts, Elmina among them, that would have allowed the Ashanti access to the coast. Negotiations broke down, and the Ashanti attacked in 1874,only to be defeated. "The name of England will now be respected on the Coast—the superiority of her soldiers acknowledged; and I do not think we shall be troubled during the present generation with more Ashanti invasions of the Protectorate."[18] The Fanti of the south, banded together in a loose federation since 1868, had even supported the British troops. In July 1874 the British proclaimed the Gold Coast a protectorate and, in so doing, their intent to maintain political control in the interests of trade. At first, however, London withstood the pressure from the men on the spot to move against the weakened Ashanti. In 1891 the king of the Ashanti refused the suggestion of the governor that he voluntarily accept British "protection" with the words: "I am happy to say that we have arrived at this conclusion, that my kingdom of Ashanti will never commit itself to any such policy; Ashanti must remain independent as of old, at the same time to be friendly with all white men." But Joseph Chamberlain finally gave the green light. In 1895 the governor at the head of three thousand men marched into the Ashanti capital of Kumasi and occupied it without resistance. Since the king was unable to come up with the unreasonable sum in gold the British demanded as indemnity, he was summarily seized and deported. When the British prohibited not only slavery but also forced labor for public works, and on top of that imposed taxes and demanded, in 1900, the delivery of the Golden Stool, symbol of the Ashanti nation, the Ashanti rose in revolt. It took months to suppress the rebellion. In 1902 the Ashanti territory was annexed and declared a Crown Colony. The conflict in values involved here was typical of imperialist expansion. While the Ashanti defended their independence and manner of living, in which slavery and human sacrifice formed a part, the British considered themselves downright obliged to end these "atrocities" and to eliminate this "savage and barbarous power."[19] One can summarize by noting that the initial impetus for expansion into the north came from the traders on the coast. For economic reasons, they demanded access secured by the colonial power to the Ashanti kingdom. But political considerations also played an important role. First, it was considered important to meet traditional obligations to the coastal tribes. Second, the British wanted to secure their frontiers against European competitors, most notably France. Finally, the differences in the systems of values provided the moral justification for the brutal actions finally undertaken.

INDIRECT RULE

In the interwar period, the British took pride in their practice of Indirect Rule, first employed in Nigeria and associated most importantly with it, but later employed elsewhere in West and East Africa. It also provided the colonial civil service with a unifying doctrine. The system met the need to rule broad areas with millions of subjects of diverse races and levels of development with the least possible outlay and a minimum of British personnel. Even more, it accorded with the values, attitudes, and life-styles of a corps of colonial officials a good percentage of whom had been educated at public schools and elite universities, took naturally to hierarchy, were trained to leadership, and kept their distance socially. It was also a corps, moreover, which claimed to act from pragmatic rather than doctrinaire motives and, while not inclined to oppose social transformations seen as necessary, was also disinclined to accelerate them. Frederick Lugard (later Baron Lugard), whose name is inseparable from Indirect Rule, was able, moreover, in his "Political Memorandum" of 1918 and his great book, *Dual Mandate in Tropical Africa*, of 1922, both to systematize a system of rule and to state the necessary guidelines and doctrine for rule in suitably liberal phraseology.[20]

Lugard obviously did not really "invent" Indirect Rule. The British had long ago decided not to administer parts of India and Malaya directly. They had recognized existing territories and structures of rule and contented themselves with residents, who personified British authority and saw to the reforms necessary for British economic penetration. In Uganda, whose conquest Lugard had participated in, the well-organized Buganda were not displaced but rather built into the system of colonial rule (see p. 445 below). In Nigeria, the thrust into

Yoruba country was followed up rather haltingly, with very little interference in political and social relationships at first, and Goldie Taubman also recommended relying on native rulers and chiefs in his area. Northern Nigeria was well suited to such a policy, because the Fulani emirates administratively controlled a huge area and had a developed taxation and judicial system. As Lugard had only a small staff and limited means at his disposal, it clearly made sense not to break up the defeated emirates but to make do with British residents, after having brought in new rulers. The residents controlled certain matters, such as police, taxation law, and the disposal of land, while the administration was otherwise carried on in the name of the emir in the traditional manner. One of the residents characterized this system aptly as early as 1904:

> What is the attitude of the British Administration toward these states? Briefly it is construction, not destruction. Our aim is to rule through existing chiefs, to raise them in the administrative scale, to enlist them on our side in the work of progress and good government. We cannot do without them. To rule directly would require an army of British magistrates which both the general unhealthiness of the country and the present poverty forbid. My hope is that we may make of these born rulers a high type of British official, working for the good of their subjects in according with the ideals of British Empire, but carrying on all that is best in the constitution they evolved for themselves, the one understood by, and therefore best suited to the people.[21]

The significance of Lugard and his writings lay particularly in his clearly working out the elements of this method of rule and in his having emphasized that it was not merely an opportunistic employment of existing structures of rule, with the idea of going over to direct rule when sufficient money and personnel were available. It was, rather, a unified, self-contained system resting on specific principles and was intended to provide a pattern for British rule over "backward peoples" in the future as well. The existing society and its various institutions, authorities, and customs were to be modernized from the inside out, and brought into accord with the dictates of modern civilization. Emirs and chiefs were not merely to be executive agencies but were actually to rule, though it was also emphasized that "there are not two sets of rulers—British and native—but a single government."[22] In that regard, the rulers were agents of the governments, and the chain of command from the governor to the residents and district commissioners and the African authorities was clear. The latter were not merely intended to carry out orders from above, however, but were supposed to make decisions and issue instructions in their own names to their subjects. The British confirmed the emirs and chiefs and deposed those who were manifestly incompetent or incurably recalcitrant. They did not name chiefs arbitrarily, however, but whenever possible followed the traditional modes of succession and election.

Two areas of competence in particular were what gave Indirect Rule its characteristic stamp. First, the chiefs were to have their own funds. Lugard's successor in Northern Nigeria introduced native treasuries in 1907, which were fed by direct taxes. Half the tax went to the British administration, but the other remained available for local expenditure, on salaries for the chief and his officials, for road building, prisons, festivities, or whatever. The administration maintained a close watch, to be sure, but left the chief rather broad powers of decision. Second, the chiefs retained certain jurisdictional competences, and administered justice in the native courts. Death sentences had to be confirmed by the governor. All the same, even in Northern Nigeria the British interfered considerably from the beginning. The autocratic power of the emirs had been broken, and in practice rule had devolved in good measure upon the residents.[23]

Indirect Rule was developed in Northern Nigeria by Lugard in the beginning, then by his successors and collaborators. The tendency was to interfere as little as possible, to give the emirs and chiefs plenty of elbow room, and to overlook as much as one decently could. But effective control was difficult and the British expected to stay a long time. In a huge area with some ten million inhabitants, there were altogether 250 British officials (administrative officers) in the interwar period. Residents and district commissioners sometimes remained in Northern Nigeria for decades, identified themselves with "their" Muslim rulers and sufficed themselves with loose supervision and advice, made effective through close personal relationships with the emirs.[24] The emirates were treated as quasi-independent states, somewhat analogous to the Indian Princely States. This was particularly true in Sir Charles L. Temple's day. Temple, governor from 1914 to 1917, idealized the Muslim feudal structures and sought insofar as possible to prevent their contact with the modern world.[25] The residents insisted on freedom from interference from the governor, and he, in turn, defended the special position of the north against the governor-general in Lagos and the Colonial Office. In the 1920s tensions arose among the officials in the technical departments, who considered their work hindered by the desire of the residents to turn all administrative activity over to the Native Authorities and to eliminate the influence of Lagos to the greatest extent possible.[26] In order to avoid friction with the emirs, the missions were hindered in establishing schools. The result was that the north, which had in the nineteenth century led the south with its substantial Muslim educational system, gradually fell behind. That was one reason why before and after World War II Ibos from the south came to fill internal administrative posts in the north, thus conjuring up the communal conflict that was one of the causes of the civil war of 1966.

Indirect Rule in Northern Nigeria undoubtedly had positive effects. Raiding parties disappeared and warfare ceased. Slavery and the slave trade were gradually eliminated and certain limits set on the feudal Fulani administration. British rule was not burdensome, and the alienation syndrome so often a part of colonial dependence was hardly apparent, particularly in the great mass of the population. On the other hand, the tendency of Indirect Rule was undoubtedly conservative and had indeed some reactionary effects, to the extent that a feudal social order was shielded from modernizing, if disintegrating, influences. It has been pointed out that this had not been Lugard's intention, as Lugard always saw Indirect Rule as a dynamic thing, a mode of rule not intended to block social change and the impact of Western civilization. Donald Cameron in particular, who was governor-general from 1931 to 1934, always emphatically opposed the conservative interpretation of Indirect Rule. In a much-noted speech of 6 March 1933 to the legislative council, in his *Principles of Native Administration* of 1934, and in his correspondence with the Colonial Office, he insisted that Indirect Rule ought not be made a dogma nor was the north "likely to become a separate self-contained political and economic unity."[27] He also rejected comparisons with the Indian Princely States. Indirect Rule was not meant, he stated, to establish a feudal and corrupt rule or shield the Islamic north from the outer world, but had the task of facilitating the smoothest transition to modernity. The northern administration was nonetheless largely able to stave off this "interference" from Lagos.

In 1912 Lugard had been named governor-general of Nigeria and given the task of "amalgamating" the northern and southern administrations. The north was running in the red and was requiring subsidies both from London and the south, railroad building called for coordination, and the hinterland was to be tied to the coast. His solution went into effect in 1914. It retained the two large units, the north and south, with Lagos as the capital. It is sometimes asserted by today's critics that if Lugard had accepted proposals to divide the state into four or more provinces Nigeria might have been able to develop into a unit more easily.[28] Lugard also centralized only the most important departments, the military, the railway, the post office, and the high court. He left the two lieutenant governors very extensive powers of decision, in good part, it would seem, because he did not intend to stay in Nigeria indefinitely himself.

Lugard also attempted at the same time to introduce, or more accurately, to employ more consistently, Indirect Rule in the south. The main measure was, in practice, introduction of direct taxation, since without it no effective native authority seemed possible. The south, however, differed from the north, where the Hausa population had already paid taxes to their Fulani rulers in precolonial times. In the south, however, the rulers and chiefs had never levied regular taxes, nor, indeed, was their status equivalent to that of the emirs. Even the Obas of the southwest did not rule autocratically, but rather through local notables as *primi inter pares*. In Benin, the introduction of taxes and the establishment of native authority went smoothly enough, because the state, conquered in 1897, had until then been ruled directly, and installation of a new Oba in 1914—he was the son of one earlier deposed—was welcomed. In practice, it did not change things very much.[29] In Oyo in 1916,[30] however, and especially in Abeokuta, which had been largely autonomous before 1914, the population rebelled in 1918. In the violence which followed, more than five hundred of the rebels were killed. An investigating commission, one of the members of which was a Nigerian jurist, openly criticized Lugard's attempt to force a novel form of government on the population.

Indirect Rule proved an even more questionable innovation in the southeast, particularly in the Ibo region. Ibo social structure was based on the village and the clan. There were no units of rule of any size.[31] The British had, as already mentioned, grouped several villages together in a native court and appointed a "warrant chief." They evidently did this because they assumed that there had to be some sort of chief here as elsewhere and out of a desire to base their rule on fair-sized administrative units. But the warrant chiefs they appointed were unpopular, and they and their courts frequently had no legitimacy as natural leaders. Their appointment undermined the democratic system of the villages, with its elders, influential secret societies, and age groupings. The chiefs were supposed to adjudicate disputes according to customary law, but British legal practices were also introduced, such as imprisonment for theft rather than draconian traditional punishments. They were also required to supply porters and laborers. As they were inclined to exploit their positions to their own advantage, they came to be seen as a group of corrupt, particularly hateful, half-educated subaltern officials. After long hesitation, the administration decided in 1927 to introduce direct taxes, the revenues of the warrant chiefs having heretofore consisted of legal fees and fines. But these taxes were considered to be incompatible with the dignity of a free man and to require formal recognition of British rule. The well-organized market women of Aba, who mistakenly assumed they would also have to pay these taxes and were unhappy about the poor prices they received, began a protest movement in 1929 which finally spread over a good part of the Eastern Province. Native courts were destroyed and warrant chiefs and their officials attacked, some being killed. But the rebellion was, in fact, against the colonial power. It was essentially conservative, insofar as it opposed the social changes brought about by the whites and attempted to throw off the foreign yoke. It never, however, attempted to establish ties to the urban, educated classes and the sort of nationalism they represented.

The report of the commission investigating these happenings did not mince words. It demonstrated that the much praised Indirect Rule was a cover-up for direct administration in the southeast—the warrant chiefs and native courts constituting an artificial administrative creation rather than a native administration in the true sense of the word. Here too Cameron attempted reforms. Comprehensive ethnological studies were to provide the basis for an administrative reorganization. Councils of elders were reactivated, numerous new native courts were created, and steps were taken to assure that "educated elements" would be drawn into the administrations of the native authorities. Although Nigerian historians pay tribute to these British reform efforts, they also note that the attempt to mold the local administration to the existing ethnic situation in the spirit of Indirect Rule unintentionally strengthened tribal consciousness. Tensions were thus created that were later to complicate the process of national integration.[32]

In the Gold Coast, Sir Gordon Guggisberg, probably the most progressive West African governor during the interwar period, attempted to integrate the chiefs more fully into the system of rule. The chiefs had enjoyed rather extensive internal autonomy since 1874, both in judicial matters and in expenditure of their revenues. A decree of 1904, which established governmental confirmation of their elections, further strengthened their positions. Western education and economic development, however, increased the discontent of the younger generation, and the chiefs were increasingly deposed, or "de-stooled," to use the local phrase. "Everywhere is to be found a spirit of impatience and intolerance among the younger men. The latter, with a mere smattering of education, resent and impede the authority of the Chiefs and elder men, few of whom can either read or write."[33] Governor Guggisberg promised the chiefs government support, but in so doing heightened the tension between the old authorities and the younger, educated Africans. The painstakingly worked-out Native Administration Ordinance of 1927 regulated anew the election and de-stoolment of chiefs, but also placed their judicial powers under strict control. Provincial and district commissioners received the right to interfere in trials or to bring them under their direct supervision. The critical question of taxation and the financial resources for the native authorities remained unclarified, however. Administrators criticized a system without treasuries, which ran counter to Indirect Rule as understood in Northern Nigeria and left the chiefs with too much unsupervised authority.[34] Not until 1939 was a law passed allowing for the formation of native treasuries, fed by direct taxes and bound up with the obligation to keep well-ordered books.

After the war of 1900 British rule in the Ashanti region was largely direct. But they also sought to break the resistance of the "Nation" with a policy of divide and rule. After World War I, however, Guggisberg shifted to Indirect Rule. In 1921 an ethnological bureau was established under Robert S. Rattray. It uncovered "democratic" elements in the Ashanti system of rule and pointed out the preeminent significance of the Golden Stool. When the latter unexpectedly turned up again, its importance was emphasized as never before. The exiled King Prempeh was allowed to return to Kumasi in 1924 as a "private citizen." In 1935 Prempeh's successor was recognized as Asantehene and the Confederacy Council as the supreme executive, legislative, and judicial body. Crowder's comment on all this was: "The British, quite unlike the French, actually bothered to put together a state they had once destroyed."[35]

The situation was not without irony, because while the colonial administration was attempting with some success to carry out Indirect Rule in areas outside the north, the concept itself was coming in for increasing criticism both inside and outside the administration.[36] Critics pointed out the danger that it not only preserved but actually strengthened feudal structures, because the traditional sanctions of de-stoolment, assassination, or flight of the populace were no longer available, the rulers being able to call on British support. Far too much corruption and injustice was tolerated, either because the administrator did not wish to intervene or feared to do so because overriding a chief would be booked against him. Or, alternatively, if an administrator did intervene, giving orders and taking over the administration, he made Indirect Rule little more than a fiction. What, indeed, was the real difference between "advice" and "orders"? Whether rule was direct or indirect, chiefs or councils of elders were the executive organs of the colonial administration, autocratic in their dealings with the population, but themselves dependent on the trust of British officials. However much one might seek to maintain their status and prestige, in the last analysis their power depended on the very fact of their appointment, which the British controlled, and their acts were supervised. The supposedly democratic character of the native councils, which in fact were mostly new institutions with functions differing from those of the traditional councils, was in most cases a myth. In the colonial situation, critics argued, there was no getting around the fact "that there was a difference between governing Africans through African institutions but according to European principles and governing Africans according to African principles. Not even in the Muslim emirates was the latter the case."[37] The native authorities were seen as the local government, in which the African population could actively participate, and which could take up modernization efforts, rather than merely being the object of, or the passive executive agents for, a foreign administration. But were the chiefs and councils of elders, who often could neither read nor write, up to these technical and civilizing obligations? This dilemma was fully recognized only during World War II, when the modernization and democratization of local government was finally taken in hand.

There was yet another dilemma that became apparent only rather gradually, namely, could one support the traditional authorities and base one's administration upon them without simultaneously offending the new and growing class of Western-educated Africans, forcing them to take an antigovernment, anticolonial stance? Tensions between the old and new elites, which mostly did not come from the old ruling class, were anyhow of long standing and tended to worsen with time. The young, innovative Africans, who often grew cash crops for the market, had attended mission schools, and regarded their chiefs with a critical eye, had no place in the native authorities. Guggisberg and Cameron both made some effort to provide educated Africans more access to the native councils. Advocates of Indirect Rule also pointed out that educated persons were needed in the courts and in the administration. Governor Sir Bernard Bourdillon claimed in 1939 that the native authorities were "almost always anxious to obtain the advice and assistance of the highly educated and more widely experienced members of the community," and that in many councils "educated persons" had been admitted.[38] But power and the right of decision remained, in fact, with the traditional elite. The educated classes not surprisingly attacked Indirect Rule as an example of the colonial power's way "of putting the clock fifty years back" in order to block the road to self-government along Western lines.[39]

In practice, Indirect Rule was conservative in function. Its positive aspects ought not, however, to go unrecognized. The British did not treat the traditional social structures, religious ties, and customs with the disregard, or scorn, typical of many missionaries and also usual within the French administrative corps. They also tried to prevent the rapid disintegration of African society. At the time, it seemed reasonable to believe that a way had been found within the system of colonial rule which, first, would allow the mass of the population to continue their way of life and yet gradually adapt to the demands of modern existence, and which, second, did not damn them to passivity but permitted them a certain amount of local self-government. It also accorded with the ideological justification employed by the colonial powers, especially the English, who held that they had been summoned to "educate" the "primitive" peoples for self-government. Finally, it was consonant with the notion of a trusteeship embodied in the mandatory framework of the League of Nations. The actual state of development of Africa must ever be kept in mind, and it seems historically unjustified to make light of the intensive efforts to build up or expand native administration or to assume it was merely a maneuver to stabilize British rule. In the interwar period, British policy appeared liberal and more likely to serve the future than the much more problematic direct administration. Judgments are more critical today, of course, because of, first, an emphasis on the discrepancies between theory and practice, to the extent that the native authorities and their chiefs merely veiled the colonial structures of authority; and second, because Indirect Rule proved a very suitable instrument for finding the needed "collaborators" when trials of strength with the liberation movements commenced. In the beginning, the establishment of colonial rule had been a great blow to the emirs and chiefs, but they had come to terms with it, and became supporters of colonial rule when opposition arose from the masses. Neither the traditional rulers nor British colonial officials were interested in rapid social change during the interwar period, and they were united in the mistrust, indeed open distaste, with which they encountered the African educated class. Lugard strongly shared such feelings. He would have gladly moved the capital of Nigeria from Lagos to Kaduna in the north to escape the unsympathetic atmosphere of the port city and its African bourgeoisie. Even Guggisberg felt this way, and these feelings seem to have been if anything stronger on the part of the governors, residents, and district commissioners, who because of birth and upbringing got on much better with the emirs, chiefs, and notables than with members of the new elite. The claims of the latter to be the spokesmen for the African population were rejected with unconcealed scorn. The new men were alleged by reason of their professions and life-style to have lost contact with the masses and to represent the interests of only a tiny urban upper class. The more clearly the liberation movement took shape, the more the colonial power was criticized in the legislative council or the press, and the more the colonial system itself was called into question, the greater the importance of Indirect Rule as a stabilizing ideology. As such its function was to neutralize the intelligentsia and the closely allied African bourgeoisie, small though the latter might be, and to isolate it in the cities, while simultaneously maintaining and building up the traditional authorities, who themselves had to defend their positions against the Western-educated elite and were thus willy-nilly forced to collaborate with the colonial power.

It thus comes as no surprise to find that efforts to open up or simplify access for educated Africans to leading positions in the administration did not amount to very much.[40] Things had been different in the mid-nineteenth century, when numerous Africans held responsible positions and even served as district commissioners and colonial secretaries. Such men were usually West Indians, mixed bloods, returnees from Brazil or Cuba, or Sierra Leonians. The latter were often freed slaves who, having acquired an education in Sierra Leone, had then come to Nigeria and the Gold Coast as businessmen, missionaries, doctors, and officials. Some of the latter often held important posts. One such official, Henry Carr, had attended Forah Bay College in Sierra Leone at the age of nineteen, had received his Durham B.A. (see p. 328 below) in mathematics, had become head of the secretariat in Lagos in 1889, school inspector in 1892, assistant colonial secretary in 1900, and finally deputy director for education. It can thus hardly be argued that the colonial power would have had to build up the necessary educational institutions before Africanization was possible. In fact, during the nineteenth century Africans were rather calculatedly shut out. With the discovery that mosquitoes carried malaria and yellow fever, it became possible substantially to improve living conditions for whites. The expansion into the hinterland and the intensive administrative penetration that began under Colonial Secretary Joseph Chamberlain was accompanied by stricter procedures for administrative appointments. Irregularities on the part of African officials compromised their appointments, but it was mainly racism and the feeling of being called upon to rule that led to open and legal discrimination. The chief of the Africa division in the Colonial Office thus baldly asserted in 1886 that "the educated native is the curse of the West Coast," and that "all natives are incorrigible liars." In 1898 the governor of Sierra Leone decreed that both the head and the deputy head of all departments had to be European. In 1902 the two African officers in the West African frontier force were pensioned, while at the same time it was enacted that in the future, European training or no, African doctors could no longer be members of the medical service. Whereas in 1883 nine of 43 higher administrative posts were filled by Africans, in 1908 the number had fallen to 5 out of 274.

One of the watchwords of Indirect Rule was the proposition that no African could be taken into the administrative service, supposedly because the British district commissioners were serving only on a temporary basis and as of a certain time would no longer be needed, the native authorities being sufficient unto themselves and no longer needing "advice." To appoint Africans would thus run counter to Indirect Rule, because it would create vested interests that would be difficult to push aside when the native authorities took over. Margery Perham, one of Lugard's colleagues and a resolute defender of Indirect Rule, expressively emphasized such considerations as late as 1937. Educated Africans, she noted, had tasks within the native authorities, but not as administrators.[41] The administration was questioned by an elected representative from Lagos in the legislative council about why more Africans were not allowed into the administrative service, and why only 4 of 365 slots were filled by Africans, these all being in the central secretariat.[42] The administration's answer emphasized Perham's considerations, and while it had a certain inner logic, it revealed that Indirect Rule was being asked to bear too heavy a doctrinal load. One thing, however, was clear enough. Since British rule was supposed to continue for several more decades, bringing Africans into the inner sanctums of the colonial civil service would not only endanger standards and internal cohesiveness but appear as a loosening up of the structure of rule, something at all costs to be avoided. Only in 1942 were the first two Africans—Busia was one of them—appointed assistant district commissioners.

Few Africans served in responsible positions even in the technical departments. Guggisberg had considered it one of his responsibilities to open up the civil service to Africans. In 1921 he received permission from London "to afford a definite path of promotion from the lowest to the highest service and to carry out the Government policy for the steady replacement of Europeans by Africans."[43] He was motivated both by a genuine will toward modernization and fiscal considerations. Africans cost less than Europeans, who had to be paid supplements, given home leave, and so on. Fiscal considerations were all the more important because the development policy he intended to follow would require an increase in the technical cadre. Guggisberg went a step farther, developing a twenty-year plan in 1925 in which the ratio of Europeans to Africans in senior posts was to shift from 481 to 28 in 1925-1926 to 319 to 229 in 1945-1946. This program looks modest enough today, but at the time it marked a new beginning and was badly received within the administration.[44] Under Guggisberg's successors, African appointments fell far below his targets. In 1942 Africans held only 46 and in 1946 only 89 senior posts. Nigeria was no different, with only 23 senior posts being in African hands in 1939. In the lower ranks, the junior posts, Africanization had naturally proceeded much farther, but still with clear hierarchical limits reminiscent of the English class structure; limits which, in the colonial situation, were perceived as racist separatism.[45]

Guggisberg himself discovered that the number of educated and qualified Africans was inadequate for his needs. There were, indeed, jurists with English university educations, but they preferred the better-paid legal work to sitting in courts, where they had little prospect for advancement. Only a very few of the Africans who could pay the high costs of European study went into the technical disciplines. But university certificates were a prerequisite for the senior posts. Educational possibilities in West Africa, on the other hand, were until World War II rather limited. England had left education largely to the missionaries and did not begin to provide supervision and support until 1925. In 1939 education still only got 4.3 percent of the Nigerian budget, and in the Gold Coast in 1938 £213,000 out of a total of £3.6 million was spent on education.[46] Advanced secondary schools such as Forah Bay College in Sierra Leone, founded in 1827, or Kings College in Nigeria were open to Africans, but, as boarding schools, had room for relatively few students.[47] Yaba Higher College, which was opened in 1934 near Lagos, educated doctors, teachers, veterinarians, and agronomists, but its diplomas were valid only in Nigeria and qualified their holders only for junior posts. The Technical School in Accra provided fourteen to sixteen graduates a year. Achimota College, a creation of Guggisberg's, is justly accounted an institution with excellent teaching. It was a public school designed to meet African needs and provided some opportunity for university correspondence degrees (for example, a B.S. in engineering from the University of London). A good part of the Ghanaian ruling class attended this school. Although Guggisberg considered higher education a necessary presupposition for Africanization, West Africa remained until World War II without its own university.[48]

All the same, Africanization could probably have been pushed more energetically had the administration been more convinced of its utility or necessity. Guggisberg's views made him an isolated phenomenon and he had no worthy successor. Haste seemed neither appropriate nor desirable. When questions were asked in the legislative councils about Africanization, the laconic answer was always the same: suitable candidates were being sought and Europeans would be replaced by Africans in due course.[49] As late as 1940, a conference called by the governor of West Africa still spoke against employing Africans in the leading civil service positions.[50]

COCOA, PALM OIL, AND PEANUTS

In the early nineteenth century, the rapidly growing trade in palm oil gradually replaced the slave trade as the basis for economic relations between Europe and West Africa. The form of the palm oil trade changed very slowly. Palm oil was either purchased at the coast or obtained through barter of the traditional trade goods of textiles, liquor, or guns. Although palm oil prices dropped sharply in the 1880s, European demand increased. It now included a market for the meat as well as for the oil because in 1870 the process for making margarine from it had been discovered. The effort to break the monopoly position of the coastal trading states—in part the result of the fall in prices—and achieve direct access to the interior tribes played no small role in the expansionist movement (see p. 301 above) as did the desire to open and secure trade routes periodically endangered or blocked by internal African wars and tensions or rivalries among the Great Powers on the coast. With the conquest and gradual establishment of colonial rule before 1900 and after, new opportunities developed, primarily for Europeans but also, as should not be overlooked, for Africans. The beginnings of incorporation into the world economy had already occurred, and interest in European consumer goods already existed.[51] Pacification removed earlier obstacles and provided a considerable impetus to both inner African trade between north and south and coastal trade. The colonial power unified the currency and immediately began building railways, in order to open up the hinterland. In Nigeria, the long stretch from Lagos to Kano was opened up between 1896 and 1912, and between 1913 and 1926 the line from Port Harcourt via Enugu to Kaduna. In the the Gold Coast, lines from Takoradi and Accra to Kumasi were begun in 1898. In 1939 Nigeria had a rail network of 1,500 miles, the Gold Coast, 510. The administration financed them with the help of British loans.

It should be stated at the outset that government did not have to use compulsion to secure the desired increase in production and delivery of cash crops. Some forced labor was required to build the railways, but never the amount used in the French or Belgian colonial empires. The use of taxes to force the local population to grow export products or to work as wage labor was of some importance in northern Nigeria, though not in the south, where direct taxes were introduced very late, and in the Gold Coast not until 1940. There was never any need to force the cultivation of specific products as was done in the Belgian Congo. The climate was unsuitable for European settlers. Plantations were certainly a possibility—they existed on the Ivory Coast, the German Cameroons, and the Congo—but the British government turned down land concession requests from Lord Leverhulme both before and after World War I, and was proud that the "economic revolution" in British West Africa was based on "native farming" rather than forced cultivation or plantations. The reasons for this probably had less to do with the notion of trusteeship that the British paraded at every opportunity than with the opposition of Manchester and Liverpool traders and probable African protests.[52]

The expansion of cocoa in the Gold Coast after 1900 was very spectacular and only a little less so in southwest Nigeria, as shown in table 9.1.

Table 9.1
Export Tonnage of Cocoa in the Gold Coast and Nigeria (by five-year averages)

	GOLD COAST	NIGERIA
1892-1896	12	32
1897-1901	329	144
1902-1906	4,711	462
1907-1911	20,934	2,375
1912-1916	58,306	6,002
1917-1921	118,290	17,294
1922-1926	205,858	37,017
1927-1931	225,732	49,749
1932-1936	256,033	75,690

SOURCE: "Report of the Commission on the Marketing of West African Cocoa," 16.[53]

Missionaries from Basel brought cocoa plants to the Gold Coast and encouraged their cultivation as early as 1857. An equally important impulse, however, had come from an African worker who had returned in 1879 from a plantation on Fernando Po. The British administration evidenced its interest by giving out a million seedlings between 1904 and 1906. But the main initiative was African, coming in good part from immigrants who sought a substitute for the products of "legitimate trade."[54] There was already talk of the "enterprise and industry of the indigenous population" by 1908.[55] The Gold Coast became the greatest cocoa producer in the world, with a share of 40 percent of the world's total. Cocoa was farmed first on the coast, but then spread inland, developing in Ashanti as soon as the line to Kumasi was completed. Calabar was the starting point in Nigeria, but the center of production soon shifted to the southwest. The Nigerian share of world production was 14 percent in 1937.

Cocoa production expanded so rapidly because it fit nicely into the traditional economic and social structure. Plentiful land "belonged" to the tribes, villages, and clans, but the produce from it went to the individual farming family. Immigrant families "rented" land, cleared the jungle, and planted both foodstuffs and cocoa seedlings, which bore after four to six years. After thirty or forty years, yields began to fall, and the old plants had to be replaced. In 1936 the number of African cocoa holdings was estimated at around 300,000, each averaging four to five acres. These holdings produced low yields compared to the plantations, because care of the plants was no better than fair and no fertilizer was available. It was extensive rather than intensive farming and was well suited to the natural conditions. But the results seen elsewhere, erosion and retreat of the forest, also appeared here, though the administration attempted to oppose them with protective measures in the 1930s. In the chief cocoa areas food production declined and there was a corresponding rise in imports from neighboring regions or from overseas, such as Norwegian salt cod. It also sometimes happened that despite, or because of, a shift to cash crops, there was too little to eat.[56]

A social transformation began. There was not only a rapid shift from a subsistence to a money and market economy, but also individualization and social differentiation. Enterprising Africans established large holdings, sometimes purchasing those of Europeans, in one or several locales. The chiefs also engaged in trade or became planters. Labor had to be brought in, and thousands of seasonal laborers came during the following period from the north or from French territories in the cocoa region. Polly Hill has described this new class of rural capitalists, who in contrast to the mass of the peasants calculatingly produced for the market and invested their profits in land.[57]

The land was also subjected to this individualization process. In the strict legal sense private property in land was not possible, but nevertheless forms were developed for the acquisition of land that closely approached individual ownership. This phenomenon was more pronounced in the Gold Coast than in Nigeria. Anyone planting seedlings that would bear only after some years wanted a secure title. The administration helped, but found itself on the horns of a dilemma, because it both wished to maintain collective ownership and yet considered making the land individually owned and private property the prerequisite for economic and social progress. Sale of land was thus in practice possible. Still, difficulties occurred with such transfers because of a lack of fixed titles and cadastres. During the interwar period experts critically noted the increase in litigation about land questions, the origin of which was often farmer indebtedness.[58] Indebtedness was, in fact, becoming a serious problem. Cocoa producers accepted cash advances against the harvest or mortgaged their lands, the money then being spent for anything from more land, to consumer goods, to festivities and funerals. Interest rates reached 50 percent and more, and repayment was difficult or impossible. In 1934 a study revealed that three-quarters of all farmers had pledged some portion of their harvests.[59] Trade was arranged accordingly and "interest slavery" institutionalized. European commercial firms, led by the United Africa Company, a Unilever subsidiary,[60] established a network of purchasing offices and depots, but left the actual buying to a horde of African middlemen,[61] who either as employees or independents trafficked with the African farmers. The buyers then offered both advances and loans to assure themselves the delivery of the next harvest. The richer farmers and chiefs were also often buyers and lenders, which additionally strengthened their economic positions.

Dependent on the world market, cocoa prices fluctuated violently. Between 1900 and 1920, the price level was nominally very high, despite a quadrupling of the cocoa supply. Price fell in 1920-1921, recovered until 1924, rose sharply between 1925 and 1927, only to fall yet again, reaching unheard-of depths during the first half of the 1930s. The recovery of 1936-1937 turned out to be short-lived. The African producers naturally attributed these fluctuations to the machinations of the big firms, especially after the firms had combined in buying pools. Producers could either combine themselves and protest against the pools and low prices, or they could create their own marketing organizations to bypass the European firms by shipping direct, or they could store—or "hold up" —the harvest to await better prices. The idea was to force the firms to alter their pricing and purchasing policies. The farmers' own marketing organizations generally failed almost at once, by reason of their lack of capital, bad management, opposition of the established firms, lack of connections with buyers, or the mistrust of the farmers themselves. That meant that the only effective form of resistance was to "hold up" harvests.

Such boycott movements occurred during the harvest seasons of 1921-1922, again in 1930-1931,[62] and most importantly in 1937-1938.[63] In the face of sharply falling prices, a pool of twelve firms led by the United Africa Company concluded a buying agreement in September 1937. When this agreement became known, the farmers quickly organized for resistance. A central committee representing local farmer groups supervised and coordinated resistance in the various parts of the colony. Most of the chiefs at first stood aside, but then under massive pressure from the boycotting farmers wheeled into line, supporting the movement and punishing strikebreakers. Both the trading firms and the government interpreted the boycott as an intolerable interference with freedom of trade; the chiefs themselves preferred the risks of "illegal" action to de-stoolment. In Ashanti the Farmer's Union organized the holdup, but the decisive factor in maintaining the resistance was the attitude of the Asantehene, the paramount chief of the Ashanti, who spoke in favor of the boycott in January 1938.

The government attempted to get both sides, the farmers and the pool firms, to compromise, but to no avail. For six months most of the 300,000 farmers on the Gold Coast held up their cocoa, simultaneously boycotting European stores, blocking streets, and in some areas burning cocoa. In this situation London perforce set an investigating commission to work. In the course of the most wearisome negotiations the commission succeeded in April 1938 in getting the pool firms and the farmers' representatives to come to terms. The firms agreed to dissolve the pool agreement for the coming harvest season if the farmers would agree to a normal sale of the harvest. The radical reorganization of the trade which the commission called for was, however, rejected by both the firms and the colonial administration as impracticable. Only after World War II was the marketing system, which set buying and selling prices, developed. Although the holdup can hardly be described as a nationalist, anticolonial action, it nonetheless laid bare the rural unrest and the mistrust, amounting to hatred, of the monopolistic trading firms. It thus played an important role in the development of Ghanaian consciousness and national integration.

The cocoa boom made the Gold Coast the most prosperous colony in West Africa during the period before and after World War I, at least by contemporary lights. The rapidly increasing production brought the African cocoa farmer considerable income and a certain prosperity, even though the financial yield from the average holding of but a few acres was not very high. Farmers paid for streets and roads themselves and even supported schools. The colony as a whole also profited. Ninety-eight percent of agricultural exports and 63 percent of total exports consisted of cocoa in 1936.[64] Export fees and, more importantly, customs duties on the imports the sale of cocoa made possible, constituted 76.8 percent of the state revenues. They made it possible for Guggisberg to propose a development plan for 1919-1929 which foresaw expansion of the rail and road networks and harbors and called for establishment of a cash reserve and provision of funds for education and health. The economic crisis set limits on this effort at planned development, to be sure, particularly since the necessary loans became a heavy budgetary burden when terms of trade became unfavorable and cocoa prices fell.[65]

In Nigeria, cocoa did not play such a dominant role, the export of palm oil and palm kernels remaining more important even in the south (see table 9.2.).

Table 9.2
Production and Export of Palm Products in Nigeria, 1900-1939 (in tons)

	PALM OIL PRODUCTION	PALM OIL EXPORTS	PALM KERNELS
1900-1904	117,358	53,729	120,778
1910-1914	154,876	77,771	171,236
1920-1924	180,463	90,352	203,021
1930-1934	244,070	122,302	274,584
1935-1939	296,889	139,000	334,000

SOURCE: R. O. Ekundare, *An Economic History of Nigeria, 1860-1960* (London: Methuen, 1973), 166.

The oil palm's being a native plant made it easier for the slave-trading coastal states to switch over to "legitimate trade," though for a time the chiefs' own interest in palm oil increased their personal stake in slavery. The production of palm oil fit well into the traditional rotation schemes and permitted the simultaneous cultivation of both foodstuffs and a cash crop within an agrarian structure based on the family. The tendencies toward private property and social differentiation were weaker than with cocoa cultivation, and outside labor was seldom required. The problems of erosion and deforestation also developed in the oil palm regions, but here population increases were the main cause, and led to measures such as the shortening of the fallow periods. In a densely populated province such as Owerri, with more than six hundred persons per square kilometer, a genuine crisis had developed as early as the 1930s.

I believe that the frequent unrest is a natural outcome of the intense overcrowding of the people and the consequent shortage of land. Such intense crowding on an intrinsically poor soil and with an extensive rather than an intensive system of farming (except on compound land) must lead to a hard struggle for existence. In bad times when the price of produce is low it is probable that in the worst areas the people is underfed in quantity and undernourished in quality of food.[66]

Prices fell, however, during the depression, and the competition from the plantations of Malaya, Sumatra, and the Belgian Congo not only had negative effects but rather suggested the plantation system was the solution for Nigeria. The fact that extensive methods of native farming went with native oil production methods, which produced neither the amount nor the quality of oil of modern presses reinforced the case for plantations.[67] The administration established experimental stations, laid out gardens for the better varieties of seedlings, and recommended the building of a simpler kind of press, but even a much larger agricultural service would hardly have been able to raise very considerably the yield per farm and with it the income of the African producer. His income remained low and, when prices were low, hardly met his modest needs for consumer goods.

In Northern Nigeria, peanut farming expanded rapidly (see Table 9.3) after the railway reached Kano in 1911 and made it possible to ship produce to the coast. The initiative for this did not come from the administration, which was at first, like the French, more interested in cotton. Cotton growing was also supported by the British Cotton Growing Association, founded in 1902, but never amounted to much. "Farmers near Kano had already taken up groundnut farming for export. . . . They found that groundnuts gave a better return than cotton, which required more labour, took more out of the soil, and, in the last resort, could not be eaten."[68] The Hausa traders especially encouraged the peasants to farm peanuts, in some cases advancing money and buying the crop, in order to resell it to European firms. In the thinly settled north land was available, and peanuts could be farmed along with foodstuffs, with one acre of a four- or five-acre family holding going for peanuts. When trucks became available for transport after World War I, acreage was expanded sharply, the increase between 1911 and 1937 amounting to a million acres.[69] Along with cocoa, the peanut is an excellent example of the readiness of the African farmer to shift to new products when these seemed compatible with the natural conditions, required little capital investment, and appeared profitable. Modernization of cultivation methods did not, however, occur, fertilizer, for example, coming only slowly into use after World War II. Still, productivity was very high, twice as high as in India.[70] Given the low value of peanuts, particularly in comparison to cocoa, the cash profit per family necessarily remained low, and social structure and life styles did not change much.

Table 9.3
Peanut Exports from Nørth Nigeria, 1900-1939 (in tons)

YEAR	AMOUNT	YEAR	AMOUNT
1900-1904	475	1920-1924	49,278
1905-1909	1,531	1925-1929	109,065
1910-1914	8,195	1930-1934	188,744
1915-1919	41,300	1935-1939	249,600

SOURCE: Ekundare, *Economic History*, 172.

In both the Gold Coast and Nigeria, in contrast to French West Africa, some mining developed. Gold had been exported from Ashanti since the time of the Portuguese. The British expeditions of 1874 and 1900 set off minor gold rushes and, after the railways were completed, gold mining machinery could be brought in. Because the land was recognized as tribal property, the chiefs were the ones who gave out concessions. Because the chiefs granted concessions in such a disorderly manner, the administration attempted between 1894 and 1897 to tax their grants with a Lands Control Bill and to monopolize the grant of mining rights. The chiefs protested vehemently.[71] Certain supervisory rights were the best the administration could obtain, but it was still possible for the Ashanti Gold Fields Corporation to obtain a very extensive concession. Production rose from 71,000 ounces in 1903 to 462,000 in 1915, fell to 221,000 in 1921, and was 557,000 in 1937. In the latter year, the Gold Coast was also the world's third largest producer of diamonds and manganese. Mining earned £5.5 million, but only about a million was paid to African personnel, plus some in addition to the chiefs. A 5 percent royalty on profits and a very low export duty provided the colonial administration with little income, and corporate income taxes, dividends, and a good part of the costs for European personnel flowed back to England.[72] It is the familiar picture of a colonial enclave economy. The Nigerian tin industry, located on the Hos plateau, developed in a similar manner. By 1910 fifty companies had secured mining rights, and by 1914, 6,000 tons a year were being exported. Fifteen to twenty thousand Africans, recruited more or less by force, hauled the tin over two hundred miles to the Benue River.The railroads reached the mines only in 1914.[73] In 1926 the mines employed 22,000 African workers, a considerable number of whom were from French territories. In the 1930s, wages fell by two-thirds.[74]

No factory industry developed before 1940, with the exception of the usual mills, sawmills, railroad repair facilities, breweries, and small operations making cigarettes and soap. Whether the prerequisites for industrial development existed or not is questionable. The trading companies were neither prepared for nor interested in such activities. They were also involved in the import of consumer goods, and were better situated to secure monopoly profits from such imports than from the export of cash crops.[75] England wanted to keep the market for cotton goods—the leading import—for itself. In 1934 import quotas were set for Japanese imports into West Africa, which burdened the African consumer and led to protests in the legislative councils. The question of whether native trades were displaced by European imports is still disputed. A. G. Hopkins argues against the opinion generally held today, namely, that they were displaced. He points out that the cost relationship between handmade and factory-made goods tilted sharply toward the latter in the last half of the nineteenth century, but that handwork production may still have increased in absolute terms because improved transportation permitted such a large total market increase. Investigations have also shown production of regional artisan specialties increased. There is also no question that the hand weaving of the finer stuffs, which varied in color and design according to locale, was able to hold its own, or that older trades were able to adapt by employing new techniques, as, for example, the tailors by using sewing machines.[76]

In answering the question to what degree African traders were displaced or eliminated one must make a number of distinctions.[77] There is no doubt that by 1850 a new trading class had risen alongside the old, whose members mostly came from the ruling clans. This new class, whose members were commonly Sierra Leonians with mission schooling and European names, enterprisingly worked its way into the goods trade and played a large part in both the export and import trades. The recession of the 1880s, however, created difficulties for small and one-man operations, both African and European, and they gave way to larger enterprises organized as corporations. After the price fall in 1920 and the ensuing economic crisis, European, mainly British, firms completely dominated trade. These firms had combined as oligopolistic units, as they alone could dispose of adequate reserves to bridge price fluctuations, could claim special rates from the shipping companies, and had access to bank credit.[78] But it should not be assumed that the African middleman was eliminated from the expanding export trade. On the contrary. European trade firms indeed owned a great number of inland purchasing agencies, but plenty of room for thousands of brokers remained, many of whom did a considerable business. New opportunities also opened up in transport and trade, as for example, in trucking cash crops. The new merchant princes, whose stories are now being told,[79] constitute exceptions, particularly the Levantines, who were able to establish themselves as retailers and moneylenders between the British wholesalers and African consumers in West Africa, as elsewhere.[80]

The economic development of British West Africa between 1880 and 1940 is thus a classic example for externally induced growth based on the enormous expansion of three main cash crops, palm products, cocoa, and peanuts, with rubber and cotton being of secondary importance. The impulse came from outside in the form of rapidly rising European demand. At the same time England as colonial power established its much praised pax Brittanica and also removed the existing obstacles to cultivation and transport through the construction of railways, currency regulation, and reduction of maritime shipping costs. The country had already been opened up to outside influences by trade in slaves and other products in the nineteenth century. The Africans participated very energetically and fully exploited the opportunities colonialism made available to them. The cultivation of cocoa, oil palms, and peanuts was not forced upon the African peasant. The more recent research, in particular, shows that the initiative was largely theirs and that they very quickly reoriented themselves toward cash-crop production. Not only the coastal zone, but also wide expanses of the hinterland shifted to a cash economy, and in so doing became dependent upon the fluctuations of the world economy. If the total economic picture is considered, the development and modernization effects of the foregoing are difficult to deny, the more so since a budget supported by customs duties and British loans financed the necessary infrastructure for further development as well as such things as schools and health services.

The expansion of cash crops was largely possible because of increases in the area under cultivation and higher labor inputs, and there was little intensification or modernization of traditional cultivation methods. With the exception of a few densely settled areas, land was, and still is, there in ample quantity, and labor also. Foodstuff production was generally able to keep step with population increases, though productivity rose but little and remained low. The economic development of West Africa thus fits nicely into Mynt's model. The cash income of the African peasant remained, with the exception of the cocoa planter, modest, particularly since the terms of trade were favorable only until 1915 and thereafter until 1945 either worsened or stagnated. Income trends, or price multiplied by production, improved, indeed, even in the 1930s, because low prices encouraged higher inputs of land and labor and more was produced and exported. But this improvement was one taken for the community as a whole rather than for individual producers. Only in the years between 1946 and 1956 was there a real price boom and a consequent sharp increase in per capita income.[81] What the African peasant bought with his income from cash crops differed little from what he previously acquired at the local market during the days when he was supposedly engaged in subsistence farming, namely, cotton goods and simple household articles. The modernization and multiplier effects of such production were doubtless higher than those associated with plantation agriculture but were not high in relation to the high production and export figures.

One can speak of a dual economy on the west coast of Africa only to a limited extent because "native farming," in contrast to enclave plantation farming, integrated cash-crop production into the traditional system of production. Still, the export and import trades, banks, shipping companies, and mines were in European hands. New opportunities for African middlemen opened up in the rapidly expanding domestic trade, but Africans were completely forced out of the trade with Europe. Social differentiation occurred in the areas where export crops were cultivated. Especially in the cocoa areas, a planter bourgeoisie began to develop. At the same time, the number of Africans with little or no land also rose. When graphed, export and import totals are roughly parallel, meaning that African farmers spent their incomes immediately.[82] African capital formation remained low, and the commercial class correspondingly small. No industrialization occurred and was in fact impossible so long as imports flowed in unhindered from the industrialized states and so long as industrial economic development was mainly thought of in terms of the development of foreign trade. The administration was, moreover, conservative in the interwar period, and saw its task principally as one of "holding the ring" or, put another way, setting limits to the social and economic transformation of African society. The educational system, particularly secondary and preuniversity education, was not oriented toward economic development, and even less toward agriculture.[83] The economic crisis also struck West Africa very hard, driving down the income of individuals as producers, and forcing the administration to scale down its objectives. Wage earners, both workers and salaried employees, lost real income. In short, even in the case of British West Africa, one can speak of lopsided economic growth.

SELF-GOVERNMENT: WHEN AND HOW?

To grasp the objectives of the new African elite in their confrontation with European civilization it is necessary to begin rather early, around the middle of the nineteenth century and thus before colonialism actually began.[84] This elite, as has already been mentioned, at first came mainly from Sierra Leone or the West Indies rather than from Nigeria or the Gold Coast. Even those who had formerly been Yoruba slaves had been Christianized and educated in Sierra Leone. Many of them were themselves missionaries who, stamped with a Victorian piety, morality, and life-style, returned to their homelands and saw their duty as one of leading their African brethren to both salvation and civilization. They felt they owed to England both their emancipation and their education, considered themselves loyal subjects of the Crown, and built their missionary efforts on British assistance. They not only approved of English activities on the coast but on occasion also encouraged London's forays into the interior. They did this not only during the early phases, as during the takeover of Lagos between 1851 and 1861, but as late as the turn of the century. A British protectorate or British rule seemed the prerequisite for any sort of civilizing and modernizing of Africa which might eventually qualify the Africans themselves to conduct their own affairs once again. Rejuvenated through the acquisition of Western civilization they might then be accepted as partners by their white masters.[85] No state or nation in the Gold Coast or Nigeria was yet visible, it then being merely a matter of the African race regaining its sense of dignity. Intellectually, a fine thread connects these protonationalists with the Pan-Africanism established and propagated by the West Indians and American blacks.

The relationship of the black missionaries to traditional African societies was ambivalent. As Africans marked by Christianity and European influences, they were critical of their peoples and to some extent alienated from them. But they also considered themselves irrevocably bound to their people. They thus considered it their duty to enlighten both Africans and Europeans about their peoples' histories, in order to establish proof of both African ability and their right to existence. Some significant work resulted from these efforts, for example, the Reverend Samuel Johnson's *History of the Yorubas* of 1897, Joseph Ephraim Casely Hayford's *Gold Coast Institutions* of 1903 and John Mensah Sarbah's *Fantis National Constitution* of 1906.[86] The most notable of such men, however, was that singular personality, Edward W. Blyden (1823-1912). Born in the West Indies, Blyden emigrated to Liberia in 1851 and represented his adopted country as ambassador in London in 1877. He also enjoyed a lively career in Sierra Leone, and for a time in Lagos, as journalist and teacher. As late as the 1880s he encouraged British expansion into the backcountry and welcomed the French thrust into the western Sudan. He dreamed of a West African state, which at first would be under British rule and would later become a dominion. He was one of the early advocates of a West African university. He levied sharp attacks at the missions and their disintegrating influence on African society, however, and himself turned to Islam, which he considered especially suited to the renewal of the black race. Blyden was one of the intellectual fathers of the West African Congress, and even a man like Nnamdi Azikiwe paid him the tribute of his admiration.[87]

England established a protectorate in the hinterland but never made any effort to carry out the withdrawal suggested by the 1865 parliamentary committee, a failure to which both the missionaries and Blyden called attention. The colonial system was only then being established and taking root, Africans being after 1890 gradually excluded from the administration. After 1880 discrimination found its way even into the mission churches. Bishop Samuel Crowther, named by the Church Missionary as bishop of Nigeria, resigned in 1891 as a protest against such discrimination.[88] About this same time a separatist church was established, encouraged in no small part by a sensational speech Blyden had made in Lagos. But this church never came to much. Illusionary hopes, indeed, were shattered. Open protests were hardly to be considered, and educated Africans could do little more than adapt to the new situation. They lived in the coastal cities, notably in Accra and Lagos. Here also was the government, as were the headquarters of the trading firms and the African businessmen themselves. The latter felt increasingly hemmed in by the European firms, but made money all the same from the growing trade. The doctors and journalists were also there, nineteen papers being published in Accra alone in 1900. This new elite, part Sierra Leonian, part West Indian, part mulatto, was mission educated, had often concluded its studies in England, and lived and dressed like Europeans. They had scarcely any direct ties to the population in the hinterland, though some ties to the traditional ruling class remained.[89]

In any event, the defense of African institutions offered a suitable means for linking the defense of one's own identity with protests against individual measures of the British administration. Caseley Hayford (b. 1866), a Cape Coast attorney and the most important representative of its educated elite, accordingly pointed out the discrepancy between the colonial reality and European pretensions, and opposed European materialism with specifically African notions of value. He also contrasted the allegedly representative and democratic nature of African rule with the authoritarian structures of the colonial system of rule. The legislative council, he asserted, with its majority of British officials and scattering of African members—and these few appointed—did not represent the will of the African people and guaranteed the governor more power than the king of England.[90] In actuality, it was precisely the legislative council which made it possible to express criticism and posit demands, the more so because the British allowed the African papers considerable latitude for expression. The governor retained freedom of decision, but on occasion preferred to withdraw or alter bills in order to avoid unrest and the need for repressive measures. The disputes over the land law, which stood in the foreground in both Nigeria and the Gold Coast in 1914, have already been mentioned. The administration saw itself forced to intervene to prevent the uncontrolled grant of concessions to the mining companies. Misunderstanding traditional land law, the administration declared all "waste land" to be Crown land. A storm of protest arose against this encroachment on the part of the British, which ran counter to the protectorate treaties and constituted an attempt to seize African land in order to give it to the plantation and mining interests, or so it was alleged.[91] The chiefs and the educated urban elite joined forces in this protest, and the administration backed off. The first political associations were founded, the Aborigines Rights Protection Society of 1897 on the Gold Coast, which sent a petition to the colonial secretary in the year of its founding, and the less effective People's Union in Nigeria. A politicization process thus began in West Africa which forced London to shift to a course of reform, albeit a very cautious one.

The expansion of the legislative council through the addition of African representatives and the introduction of elections, understood as the first step down the road to self-government, were the main demands articulated by the restricted educated elite before World War I and after. Hugh Clifford gave in to the pressure somewhat as governor of the Gold Coast in 1916 and responded on 2 November 1918 to the reproach of Caseley Hayford that England yet refused the franchise with the noteworthy statement that "I fully agree that in the fullness of time it is possible that every part of the British Empire will be as completely self-governing as the Dominions are today."[92] This little-known declaration parallels the India Declaration of 20 August 1917 (see p. 80 above) as well as the citizenship law for the Four Communes in Senegal (see p. 365

below), which were similarly issued as a result of the war. Clifford's statement also constituted a statement of British intentions about what they thought the future should be. But what did "in the fullness of time" actually mean?

The National Congress of British West Africa demanded self-government in the not very distant future, when it met in March 1920 in Accra in fulfillment of planning dating back to 1914.[93] The meeting was a significant one. Delegates from the Gold Coast, Nigeria, Sierra Leone, and Gambia joined for the first time in a common determination to form an organization with nationalist aims, although the concept "nation" was then applied to West Africa as a whole and not to the individual colonies. The urban elite under Casely Hayford's leadership was the group behind the congress and its principal supporter. The congress's demands primarily reflected its interests: half the seats in the legislative council for elected Africans, expansion of the school system, a West African university, and Africanization of the administration. The congress also demanded that Leventines, whose competition was increasing, be repatriated. The lawyers also loosed some shots against the colonial judicial system, as African lawyers were forbidden to practice in certain courts. The congress sent a delegation to London, but the colonial secretary refused to hear it after the important and influential Fanti chief, Ofori Atta I, sharply rejected the claims of the congress to speak for the people in the legislative council. This act also permitted the governors of Accra and Lagos to take a clear negative stance toward the congress. Clifford spoke with open scorn about a "self-selected and self-appointed congregation of educated African gentlemen," mocked talk of a West African nation, and commended them to their "Natural Rulers," to whom the populace owed obedience.[94] This was an example of the tendency mentioned above to employ Indirect Rule to strengthen the traditional authorities and build them firmly into the apparatus of rule, in order to neutralize the influence of the new elite and restrict it to the cities.

All the same, Clifford was still disposed to accept some of the demands of this elite and give it more voice in the legislative council, in marked contrast to Lugard, whom he had replaced as governor-general of Nigeria in 1919. In 1918 Lugard had restricted the competence of the legislative council in Lagos, which had in 1906 been expanded to all of Southern Nigeria, to the port city itself. He had also established a Nigerian council, which had an official majority and three appointed representatives for north and south, but no legislative power. In practice, all it did was receive an annual address from Lugard, which the chiefs, whose English was generally poor, probably did not even understand. Lugard did not conceal his scorn for the "arrogant" educated elite of Lagos and had no intention of exposing his authoritarian administration to the criticisms of journalists and lawyers. The papers, not unnaturally, attacked him most sharply. Clifford attempted to make a new political and administrative beginning.[95] Elections for the Lagos town council were introduced in 1920, and Lugard's council replaced by a new legislative council in 1922, which consisted of forty-six members, of whom twenty-seven were officials. Three of the nineteen unofficial

African members were to be elected from Lagos and one from Calabar. The remainder represented economic groups and, as appointees, the rest of Southern Nigeria. The north was at first not included because suitable candidates were allegedly not available, but in reality because few ties and little in common existed between north and south. Clifford was manifestly interested in providing the urban elite with a forum. In 1924 elections were introduced in Sierra Leone, and in 1925 in the Gold Coast. Three of the fourteen unofficials in the Gold Coast legislative council were elected, from Accra, Cape Coast, and Sekundi, another six from the newly created provincial councils, in which the most important chiefs sat. Guggisberg thus had made an interesting attempt, and one that pointed the way to the future, to combine the election of representatives with Indirect Rule in order to tie the coast and the hinterland more firmly together. Since he also attempted to provide a counterweight to the educated class in the form of the chiefs, his reform led to sharp though passing protests from urban nationalists.

These constitutional arrangements were not altered again during the interwar period. Further steps in the direction of self-government which might be compared with the reforms in India and Ceylon never took place. This conservative attitude was in no small measure conditioned by the prospects of the future which emerged from the rapidly petrifying doctrines of Indirect Rule. Although there was talk of self-government and even nationhood, these stages were not to be reached through the usual expansion of the legislature councils by measures such as increasing the number of elected representatives, including the northern provinces or Ashanti, and eventually allowing an unofficial majority. The method was rather to build up the native authorities into independent entities on an ethnic basis. These could then be combined regionally and remain territorial units under British leadership, at least for the foreseeable future.[96] The opposition to a representative system along British lines eased somewhat with time, but until World War II the British thought they could avoid the decisive step, accepting an unofficial majority. From experience they knew that this would either lead to open conflict between the legislature and the executive, and a consequent stalemating of the latter, or necessarily to dominion status. The dilemma created by offering prospects of reform short of an unofficial majority and without endangering one's own rule emerges very clearly in Governor Bernard Bourdillon's important *Memorandum on the Future Political Development of Nigeria* of 1939.[97]

The introduction of elections between 1922 and 1925 encouraged politicization, though it was restricted to a few cities. Elections called for parties, even when the number of electors was limited. Under the leadership of Herbert Macaulay, a grandson of Bishop Crowther, the National Democratic party was organized to contest the election of 1923. It promptly won three seats and in the following years became the spokesman for the bourgeois elite. In the Gold Coast, the Aborigines Rights Protection Society at first attempted to boycott the elections foreseen under the new constitution. But upon more considered reflection, it put up its secretary, Casely Hayford, for election in 1927 and thereafter went over to a policy of loyal collaboration within the new order.[98] The modus operandi of the legislative councils of the 1920s and 1930s, the style and manner in which African representatives agitated within parliament, and the stance of the administration in response to criticism and demands, have as yet not been much studied. We do know that the councils were not mere acclamatory bodies, but on the contrary played a considerable role, permitting the spokesmen of the nationalist movement to function as a parliamentary opposition and follow a path toward national liberation along constitutional lines within the British empire. Their demands remained largely those of the West African Congress, namely, more seats for elected Africans, the appointment of one or two Africans to the executive council, Africanization, and, above all, the removal of discriminatory civil provisions. In the critical dialogues about Indirect Rule, a democratization of the native authorities by means of strengthening the councils and adding educated Africans was proposed. In the Gold Coast, there was discussion of the possibility of the provincial council substituting a representative of the new elite for a chief as its representative in the legislative council. Economic questions became more important with time, yet without dominating things. Efforts to stabilize cocoa prices, the provision of agricultural credit as a means of combatting indebtedness, better agricultural schools, and some efforts toward industrialization were all requested of the administration.[99] These demands and the way they were put in the councils, as well as the rather loose forms of political organization, bespeak an already established bourgeoisie. In the interwar period, this class broadened considerably. Finding discrimination within the colonial situation an aggravation, it supported efforts at national liberation and equality at a considerable sacrifice, but followed a reformist course and hardly questioned the colonial system as such.

A new phase in the national movement began in West Africa in 1934. The crisis years were followed by a period of economic recovery, and the governors attempted to reduce tensions. A new leadership generation arose, however, which took a considerably more radical line and attempted to create a broader basis for nationalist agitation. One very important phenomenon was the trend toward the amalgamation of associations. Since the 1920s, numerous associations based on origin or tribes had been formed, such as the Onitsha and Owerri Unions, the Calabar National Institute, the Ibio Union, and in 1935, the Ibo Union, the result of the merger of Lagos Ibo organizations. These groups formed first in cities where members of the same ethnic group came together, and then were organized at the provincial level. Although the initiative came mostly from the educated elite, illiterate Africans and notables were not excluded. The groups pursued a variety of self-help, educational, and democratization aims, within the native administrations as well as outside them. They were not in themselves political, but they supported attempts being made to use political movements and political actions to create mass support. This "ethnic nationalism" thus served as a sort of bridge between precolonial and postcolonial Africa. The number of professional organizations continued to grow, however, a clear indication that professional and social differentiation was becoming more important. A broader class of Africans outside the traditional social order also began to organize and to attempt articulation of their needs and desires. Obafemi Awolowo, for example, first appears politically as the secretary of the Ibadan branch of the Nigerian Produce Traders Union, which in 1937-1938 had 9,348 members.[100]

The disputes about Yaba College, centering on the fact that its examination certificates were good only for Nigeria, were what led to the foundation of the Lagos Youth Movement, which restyled itself the Nigerian Youth Movement in 1936. Only in 1937 with the arrival of Nnamdi Azikiwe and his new paper, *West African Pilot*, in Lagos, however, did it become a genuine nationalist party. Azikiwe was not from the older elite, but was the son of an Ibo employee working for an Ibo regiment in the north. In other words, he grew up within a class of petty employees and officials living away from its tribal homeland. He also had eked his way through an American black college and then had studied at Columbia. From 1935 on, he had published a newspaper in Accra.[101] The *Pilot* struck a rather hostile and provocative tone and lit into the colonial administration rather more sharply than had till then been usual. It also did not refrain from attacking the reform course usually propagated by African spokesmen. It pursued a quasi-Marxist interpretation of the colonial economy, which it said rested on structural dependence on the metropolis and blocked the way to modern development.[102] The Youth Movement took part in the dispute with the pool firms with mass meetings, slogans of protest, and propaganda tours. In 1938 it challenged Macaulay's heretofore uncontested domination of Nigerian elections, achieved by putting up his own candidates. The movement succeeded in winning the elections to the Lagos town council and the African seats in the legislative council. It also published the Nigeria Youth Charter, which demanded "complete autonomy within the British Empire...and complete independence in the local management of affairs," which was rather throwing down the gauntlet. More important still was the successful attempt to break out of the confines of Lagos and create an organization to bridge the gap between city and country. It did this by creating numerous sections, in so doing becoming at least incipiently a mass party, with ten thousand members in 1938.[103]

The Gold Coast Youth Conference never achieved a like significance. Organized by the lawyer, Joseph Boakye Danquah, one of Afori Atta's half-brothers, it was not a party so much as a coordinating agency for several associations and clubs. But some chiefs also joined, and thus proved that existing tensions could be bridged, as occurred in no small measure as a result of the cocoa holdup. The conference also signified that the national movement had, before World War II, entered a new phase. The concept "nation" still meant a variety of things, from a Pan-African movement oriented around race, to a vague, African-oriented movement, or some sort of regional-tribal movement. Azikiwe himself plumped for West Africa: "So long as we think in terms of Nigeria, Gold Coast, Sierra

Leone, Gambia, and not as one United West Africa we must be content with a colonial dictatorship." The Nigerian Youth Movement might want to achieve "better understanding and cooperating and a creation of common ideals among the tribes of Nigeria," but one of its leaders could still simultaneously assert, "We are either Calabarians or Nothing."[104] The ties to the Islamic north, and to Ashanti as well, were still loose, and the Gold Coast and Nigeria appeared within their colonial limits to be rather insubstantial bases for nations, but communications within the colonial administrative units integrated things administratively and economically. The political liberation movement was thus no longer restricted to a narrowly limited elite group in a few towns, but was able to appeal beyond them to those thousands of Africans who had had at least rudimentary educations. Azikiwe and Danquah were the two new political leaders who after World War II were to force the British to withdraw, the one employing the party formations of the National Council of Nigeria and the Cameroons and the other the United Gold Coast Convention. Kwame Nkrumah's Convention People's Party split from the latter in 1949, and as a party for mass agitation completed the breakthrough to independence in 1957.

NOTES

1. From the more recent literature on Sub-Saharan Africa, see William Malcolm Hailey, Baron Hailey, *An African Survey* (rev. ed., London, New York: Oxford University Press, 1957); Roland Anthony Oliver and John D. Fage, *A Short History of Africa* (Harmondsworth: Penguin Books, 1964); Henri Brunschwig, *L'Avènement de l'Afrique Noire du XIXe Siècle à nos Jours* (Paris: A. Colin, 1963); Robert I. Rotberg, *A Political History of Tropical Africa* (New York: Harcourt, Brace & World, 1965); Jean Ganiage, Hubert Deschamps, and Odette Guitard, with Andre Martel, *L'Afrique au XXe Siècle* (Paris: Sirey, 1966); Lewis H. Gann and Peter Duignan (eds.), *Colonialism in Africa, 1870-1960* (5 vols., London: Cambridge University Press, 1969-1975); Hubert Deschamps (ed.), *Histoire Générale de l'Afrique Noire, de Madagascar, et des Archipels: Vol. II, De 1800 à nos Jours* (2 vols., Paris: Presses Universitaires de France, 1970-1971); *Britain and Germany in Africa: Imperial Rivalry and Colonial Rule*, ed. Prosser Gifford and William Roger Louis, with Alison Smith (New Haven: Yale University Press, 1967); *France and Britain in Africa: Imperial Rivalry and Colonial Rule*, ed. Prosser Gifford and William Roger Louis (New Haven: Yale University Press, 1971); Catherine Coquery-Vidrovitch and Henry Moniot, *L'Afrique Noire de 1800 à nos Jours* (Paris: Presses Universitaires de France, 1974); Joseph Ki-Zerbo, *Histoire de l'Afrique Noir, d'hier à demain* (Paris: Hatier, 1972); Robert Cornevin, with Marianne Cornevin, *L'Afrique Noire de 1919 à nos Jours* (Paris: Presses Universitaires de France, 1973); Robert I. Rotberg and Ali A. Mazrui (eds.), *Protest and Power in Black Africa* (New York: Oxford University Press, 1970); Henri Brunschwig, "De la Résistance Africaine à l'Imperialisme Européen," *JAH*, 15 (January 1974).

2. "Report of the Select Committee of the House of Commons on the British Establishments in West Africa, 26th June 1865," as excerpted in Colin W. Newbury (comp.), *British Policy Towards West Africa, Select Documents, 1786-1914* (2 vols. Oxford: Clarendon Press, 1965,1971), I, 529.

3. Crowder, *West Africa*; J.F. Ade Ajayi and Michael Crowder (eds.), *History of West Africa* (2 vols., London: Longman, 1971); Michael Crowder (ed.), *West African Resistance: The Military Response to Colonial Occupation* (London: Hutchinson, 1971); Newbury, *British Policy*. On Nigeria, see James Smoot Coleman, *Nigeria, Background to Nationalism* (Berkeley: University of California Press, 1958); Michael Crowder, *The Story of Nigeria* (London: Faber,

1966). On the Gold Coast, see F.M. Bourret, *Ghana, the Road to Independence, 1919-1957* (London: Oxford University Press, 1960); David Kimble, *A Political History of Ghana: The Rise of Gold Coast Nationalism, 1850-1928* (Oxford: Clarendon Press, 1963).

4. Lord Kimberley in November 1872, as quoted in Jean Herskovits Kopytoff, *A Preface to Modern Nigeria: The "Sierra Leonians" in Yoruba, 1830-1890* (Madison: University of Wisconsin Press, 1965), 157.

5. John D. Hargreaves, *Prelude to the Partition of West Africa* (London: Macmillan, 1963). A good summary is John E. Flint, "Nigeria, The Colonial Experience," in Gann and Duignan, *Colonialism*, I. See also, among others, Tekena N. Tamuno, "Some Aspects of Nigerian Reaction to the Imposition of British Rule," *Journal of the Historical Society of Nigeria*, 3 (December 1965).

6. Brilliantly demonstrated by Colin W. Newbury, "The Tariff Factor in Anglo-French Partition," in *France and Britain in Africa*.

7. Kenneth Onwuka Dike, *Trade and Politics in the Niger Delta, 1830-1885: An Introduction to the Economic and Political History of Nigeria* (Oxford: Clarendon Press, 1956), 203f.

8. Colin W. Newbury, "The Development of French Policy on the Lower and Upper Niger, 1880-1898," *JMH*, 37 (March 1959). On the Royal Niger Company, see John E. Flint, *Sir George Goldie and the Making of Nigeria* (London: Oxford University Press, 1960).

9. Dike, *Trade and Politics*, 182ff.; Crowder, *West Africa*, 119; Emmanuel Ayankanmi Ayandele, *The Missionary Impact on Modern Nigeria, 1842-1914: A Political and Social Analysis* (London: Longman, 1966), 93f. Obaro Ikime, "Colonial Conquest and Resistance in Southern Nigeria," *JHSN*, 6 (December 1972), emphasizes the divergent interests of the African states.

10. Cherry Gertzel, "Relations between African and European Traders in the Niger Delta, 1880-1896," *JAH*, 3 (April 1962), emphasizes the role of Liverpool traders in Jaja's deposition.

11. Joseph C. Anene, *Southern Nigeria in Transition, 1885-1906: Theory and Practice in a Colonial Protectorate* (Cambridge: Cambridge University Press, 1966).

12. See the very suggestive essay, A. G. Hopkins, "Economic Imperialism in West Africa: Lagos, 1880-1892," *EcHR*, 21 (December 1968).

13. Flint, *Nigeria*, 240.

14. Quoted in Ajayi and Crowder, *History*, II, 419.

15. Lord Salisbury summarized some of the grounds in a letter of 15 June 1899; Crowder, *Nigeria*, 210.

16. Margery Freda Perham, *Lugard* (2 vols., London: Collins, 1956, 1960), II, 27.

17. For an older account, see Charles William James Orr, *The Making of Northern Nigeria* (London: Macmillan and Co., 1911). See also Perham, *Lugard*, II; Crowder, *Nigeria*, ch. 13; Tamuno, "Nigerian Reaction," 288f.

18. Crowder, *West Africa*, 146. See in addition, Kimble, *Ghana*, ch. 7; Edward Reynolds, "Economic Imperialism: The Case of the Gold Coast," *JEH*, 35 (March 1975).

19. B. Wassermann, "The Ashanti War of 1900: A Study of Cultural Conflict," *Africa*, 31 (April 1961).

20. The following are noted from the extensive recent literature: Anthony Hamilton Millard Kirk-Greene (ed.), *The Principles of Native Administration in Nigeria: Selected Documents, 1900-1947* (London: Oxford University Press, 1965); Robert Heussler, *The British in Northern Nigeria* (New York: Oxford University Press, 1968). Critical of Lugard is I. F. Nicolson, *The Administration of Nigeria, 1900-1960: Men, Methods and Myths* (Oxford: Clarendon Press, 1969). See also Prosser Gifford, "Indirect Rule: Touchstone or Tombstone for Colonial Policy?" in *Britain and Germany in Africa*; Crowder, *West Africa*, 217ff.; Albertini, *Decolonization*, 124f.; *West African Chiefs: Their Changing Status under Colonial Rule and Independence*, ed. Michael Crowder and Obaro Ikime, with translations from the French by Brenda Packman (New York: Africana Publ. Corp., 1970).

21. Quoted in Crowder, *Nigeria*, 212.

22. Frederick John Dealtry Lugard, Baron, *The Dual Mandate in British Tropical Africa* (Edinburgh and London: W. Blackwood and Sons, 1922).

23. African historians particularly emphasize this; see for example, A.E. Afigbo's essay in Ajayi and Crowder, *History*, II, 454f. For details, see J. N. Paden, "Aspects of Emirship in Kano," in *West African Chiefs*.

24. In this, Heussler, *The British*, is revealing.

25. M. Bull, "Indirect Rule in Northern Nigeria, 1906-1911," in Kenneth Robinson and Frederich Madden, eds., *Essays in Imperial Government: Presented to Margery Perham by Kenneth Robinson and Frederich Madden* (Oxford: B. Blackwell, 1963).

26. See, for example, "Notes of a Meeting called by H.E. the Governor between Administrative Officers and Heads of Central Departments (Confidential), 26 September 1929," Rhodes House, Oxford.

27. Albertini, *Decolonization*,136; Heussler, *The British*, 66f. See also Cameron to Colonial Secretary Sir Philip Cunliffe-Lister, 10 December 1931 and 17 March 1932. Lethem, however, wrote Lugard on 23 December 1932 that the jurisdiction and authority of the emirs ought not be restricted by direct controls, as Cameron had proposed; Rhodes House, Oxford, "Lethem Papers", MSS. British Empire, 276.

28. Crowder, *Nigeria*, 242.

29. P. A. Igbafe, "British Rule in Benin, 1897-1920: Direct or Indirect Rule?" *JHSN*, 3 (June 1967).

30. J. A. Atanda, "The Iseyin-Okeiho Rising of 1916: An Example of Socio-Political Conflict in Colonial Nigeria," *JHSN*, 4 (December 1969). According to Atanda, the resistance was not so much against taxes as against a tendency toward administrative centralization and the new native courts which, among other things, made divorce easier for women.

31. Nigeria, Commission of Inquiry Appointed to Inquire into the Disturbances in the Calabar and Owerri Provinces, *Memorandum*... (Lagos: Gov't. Printer, 1930). Excellent are A. E. Afigbo, "Revolution and Reaction in Eastern Nigeria, 1900-1929 (The Background to the Women's Riot of 1929)," *JHSN*, 3 (December 1966); idem, "The Native Treasury Question under the Warrant Chief System in Eastern Nigeria, 1899-1935," *Odu: A Journal of West African Studies*, 4 (July 1967); idem, "The Warrant Chief System in Eastern Nigeria: Direct or Indirect Rule?" *JHSN*, 3 (June 1967).

32. Afigbo, "Revolution," 571f.

33. Quoted in Kimble, *Ghana*, 472.

34. See, for example, the comprehensive memorandum of 13 July 1936 on the native administration by the Commissioner of the Western Province, Duncan-Johnstone (hereafter cited as Duncan-Johnstone, "Memorandum"), in Rhodes House, Oxford, MSS. Africa, S. 593, Box 5 File 5. The 1931 attempt to introduce an income tax in accord with the dictates of Indirect Rule encountered such spirited opposition from traders and the urban intelligentsia that the administration abandoned it; Stanley Shaloff, "The Income Tax, Indirect Rule and the Depression: The Gold Coast Riots of 1931," *Cahiers d'Etudes Africaines*, 14: cahier 54 (1974).

35. Crowder, *West Africa*, 233. See also William Tordoff, *Ashanti under the Prempehs, 1888-1935* (London: Oxford University Press, 1965).

36. Albertini, *Decolonization*, 130. A good example is Robert Sutherland Rattray, "Present Tendencies of African Colonial Government," *Journal of the Royal African Society* (1933/34).

37. Mary Henrietta Kingsley, *West African Studies* (London, New York: Macmillan, 1899), as quoted in Ajayi and Crowder, *History*, II, 465.

38. Nigeria, Governor-General, 1935-1943 ([Sir Bernard] Bourdillon), *Memorandum on the Future Political Development of Nigeria* (Lagos: Gov't. Printer, 1939), 7. Hereafter cited as Bourdillon, *Memorandum*.

39. Duncan-Johnstone, "Memorandum," 13.

40. For the following, see Symonds, *The British*, 119f.

41. Margery Freda Perham, *Native Administration in Nigeria* (London, New York: Oxford University Press, 1937), 301.

42. "It. . .is not desirable for two reasons. . . .Public Opinion would at present be strongly opposed to such appointments. . . .In the second place, even if the feelings which make such appointments impossible at present were to disappear, there remains the objection that they would be opposed to the whole policy of Native Administration as at present conceived and applied. It is the essence of that policy that the British Administrative Services should gradually be reduced, its functions being taken over the the Native Administrations themselves. It is therefore in the Executive service of Native Administration that educated Africans should seek employment of a purely administrative nature. The Government is fully aware that at the present moment there are few if any posts of this nature which offer either prospects or emoluments equal to those open to Africans in the technical services of the Government, but as the Native Administrations increase in efficiency and the scope of their functions is extended such posts are bound to emerge.

"The answer must not be taken to imply any promise of an early reduction of the number of British Administrative Officers. The moment when such a reduction can begin is not yet in sight, but in the meantime a gradual growth in the number of executive Native Administration posts for which the qualification of heredity or local connection are not necessary may be confidently expected"; Nigeria, Legislative Council, *Debates*, 11 July 1938, pp.4-5.

43. Ronald E. Wraith, *Guggisberg* (London: Oxford University Press, 1967), 215f.

44. "No provision for the training of African candidates was made and a hope that the right type of man would emerge in profusion from the shortly-to-be-opened Achimota [college], formed the only foundation of what was intended to be a noble and somewhat ambitious structure"; Great Britain, Colonial Office, West Africa, "Report of an Investigation on the Scope for the Africanisation of the Senior Posts of the various Gov. Departments" (1942), 309.

45. Coleman, *Nigeria*, 154f.

46. Crowder, *West Africa*, 377.

For Nigeria, students were distributed as follows:

Table 9.4
Student Enrollment in Nigeria, 1913-1959

	1913	1919	1929	1938	1959
Primary	36,640	78,418	146,598	314,051	2,775,938
Secondary	. . .	. . .	1,140	5,425	146,134
(of which technical and vocational)	. . .	. . .	n.a.	n.a.	4,065
Higher (includes Yaba College)	. . .	. . .	. . .	61	2,112

SOURCE: Gerald K. Helleiner, *Peasant Agriculture, Government, and Economic Growth in Nigeria* (Homewood, Ill.: R. D. Irwin, 1966), 433.

47. On the latter point, there were 500 applicants for the entrance examination but only 20 were allowed to take it because places were lacking for more; Nigeria, Education Department, *Annual Report* (Lagos: Gov't. Printer, 1936), 43.

48. Frederick Gordon Guggisberg, "Annual Address to the Legislative Council (1925)," as cited in G.B. Kay (ed.,), *The Political Economy of Colonialism in Ghana: A Collection of Documents and Statistics 1900-1960* (Cambridge: University Press, 1972), 289.

49. The response of the African representative from Secondi was: "I am convinced in my own mind, that such talk is merely to throw dust into one's eyes"; Gold Coast (Colony), Legislative Council, *Debates*, 14 March 1939, 160.

50. Ade Fajana, "Colonial Control and Education: The Development of Higher Education in Nigeria, 1900-1950," *JHSN*, 6 (December 1972), 334.

51. The basic book today is Anthony G. Hopkins, *An Economic History of West Africa*

(London: Longman, 1973), which does not, however, treat some important topics and problems. Older works are Sir Alan William Pim, *The Financial and Economic History of the African Tropical Territories* (Oxford: Clarendon Press, 1940); A. Baron Holmes, "The Gold Coast and Nigeria," in Lewis, *Tropical Development*. For Nigeria, see Cyrill Daryll Forde and Richenda Scott, *The Native Economies of Nigeria* (London: Faber and Faber, 1946); Penelope A. Bower, *Mining, Commerce, and Finance in Nigeria* (London: Faber and Faber, 1948); Helleiner, *Peasant Agriculture*; R. Olufemi Ekundare, *An Economic History of Nigeria, 1860-1960* (London: Methuen, 1973).

52. See Hopkins, *Economic History*, 210f.

53. In *Sessional Papers*, 1937-38, Cmd. 5845, IX, 191, p. 16. Hereafter cited as "Report on Cocoa." On cocoa farming see, in addition to Forde and Scott, *Native Economies*, Cecil Yaxley Shephard, *Report on the Economics of Peasant Agriculture in the Gold Coast* (Accra: Gov't. Printer, 1936). Basic is Polly Hill, *The Gold Coast Cocoa Farmer: A Preliminary Survey* (London: Oxford University Press, 1956).

54. Hopkins, *Economic History*, 217, based on Polly Hill's works.

55. From an Agricultural Department report, as quoted in Hill, *Cocoa Farmer*, 104.

56. "An appreciable number of the people are receiving an inadequate diet. . . . There is no reason why West Africa should have to rely on imported supplies"; Great Britain, Colonial Office, *Report by the Hon. W. G. A. Ormsby Gore, M.P. (Parliamentary Under-Secretary of State for the Colonies) on His Visit to West Africa during the Year 1926* (Cmd. 2747),(London: HMSO, 1926), 77. Hereafter cited as Ormsby Gore, *Visit to West Africa*.

57. Polly Hill, *Studies in Rural Capitalism in West Africa* (Cambridge: Cambridge University Press, 1970), 22f.

58. Ormsby Gore, *Visit to West Africa*, 117; Shephard, *Report*, 40.

59. Shephard, *Report*, 41f. Pim, *Financial and Economic History*, 53, noted "the extent of the economic servitude to which, judging from experience in India and elsewhere, a large portion of the farmers must have been reduced and which is always a fruitful source of trouble."

60. William H. Lever, Lord Leverhulme and head of the Unilever combine, had purchased the Niger Company in 1920. In 1929 it was merged with the African and Eastern Trading Company to form the United Africa Company, whose share in Gold Coast cocoa exports was around 40 percent.

61. Their number was estimated in 1938 at 1,500 brokers and 37,000 sub-brokers; "Report on Cocoa," 29.

62. S. Rhodie, "The Gold Coast Cocoa Hold-up of 1930-31," *Transactions of the Historical Society of Ghana*, 9 (1968).

63. "Report on Cocoa." One-sidedly anticolonial is Ajayi and Crowder, *History*, II, 584. I base my account on Franz Ehrler, *Handelskonflikte zwischen europäischen Firmen und einheimischen Produzenten in Britisch-Westafrika: Die "Cocoa-Hold-Ups" in der Zwischenkriegszeit* (Zurich: Atlantis Verlag, 1977).

64. "Report on Cocoa," 17.

65. D. K. Greenstreet, "The Guggisberg Ten-Year Development Plan," *Economic Bulletin of Ghana*, 8 (1964).

66. From a report quoted in D. H. Urquhart, "Land Usage and Utilization in Southern Nigeria," *The Nigeria Forester (Farm and Forest)*, 1 (1940), 52. See also R. K. Udo, "The Migrant Tenant Farmer of Eastern Nigeria," *Africa*, 34 (October 1964). Because of declining yields due to lack of fallowing and fertilization in the heavily settled areas, people migrated into thinly settled areas to rent land. How cultivation was adapted to changing land quality is shown in A. L. Mabognje and M. B. Gleave, "Changing Agricultural Landscape in Southern Nigeria; The Example of Egba Division, 1850-1950," *Nigerian Geographical Journal*, 7 (1964).

67. To a question about whether European firms had received land for palm plantations, the administration replied that very little had been handed out, namely, 13,596 acres. A recent request had been refused. It then noted: "The interests of the Nigerian producer of palm products can only be protected fully in face of the growing competition from other countries

and from other sources if he himself is prepared to take the necessary steps to improve the quality and increase the quantity of the Nigerian product. The Government and its advisers are convinced that in the present conditions of the world markets the most economic and effective method of production is the cultivation of oil palms in plantations— whether individually or communally owned—and the extraction of the oil by some sort of mechanical press. The plantation system rests on cultivation of the most productive strains of palm and the elimination of those less satisfactory, while the use of presses for extracting the oil reduces waste and increases production"; Nigeria, Legislative Council, "Minutes," 28 November 1938.

68. Hopkins, *Economic History*, 219.

69. Helleiner, *Peasant Agriculture*, 111.

70. Ibid., 112.

71. Kimble, *Ghana*, 334; Bourret, *Ghana*, 125f.

72. Bourret, *Ghana*, 127f.

73. Allan McPhee, *The Economic Revolution in British West Africa* (London: G. Routledge & Sons, 1926), 56f.

74. Bower, *Mining, Commerce, and Finance*, 24. In 1926, African workers were paid £446,000, but only £98,000 in 1933, although profits amounted to £238,000 in the latter year; ibid., tables 18-19. The analysis of "extraterritorial enterprise" is excellent.

75. On the trading firms' lack of interest in manufacturing and industrialization, see ibid., 68, 116.

76. Hopkins, *Economic History* 250f.; Helleiner, *Peasant Agriculture*, 322.

77. Hopkins, *Economic History*, 202f., 240f., 256.

78. Bower, *Mining, Commerce, and Finance*, 22.

79. See, for example, Felicia Ekejuniba, "Omu Kwei, the Merchant Queen of Ossomari: A Short Sketch," *JHSN*, 3 (June 1967).

80. "The native of this country...will soon find himself ground to powder between the stones of European and Asiatic economic aggression....What has the government done to improve conditions of the native traders with a thousand and one European branch shops at our door, and with all the primary produce market monopolized by European firms and the Syrian seizing the little that could have remained for us?" *African Messenger*, 29 May 1925, as quoted in Ajayi and Crowder, *History*, II, 584. According to Bower, *Mining, Commerce, and Finance*, 99, in 1939, 230 Levantines lived in Kano alone.

81. Helleiner, *Peasant Agriculture*, 5, 20; Hopkins, *Economic History*, 180, following Helleiner. See also the series for the terms of trade and "external buying power in real terms" for the Gold Coast in Sieber, *Realen Austauschverhältnisse*, 152f.

82. Helleiner, *Peasant Agriculture*, 22.

83. See the brilliant analysis by Cyril Ehrlich, "Building and Caretaking: Economic Policy in British Tropical Africa," *EcHR*, 26 (November 1973).

84. J. F. Ade Ajayi, "Nineteenth Century Origins of Nigerian Nationalism," *JHSN*, 2 (June 1961), in German in Albertini, *Moderne Kolonialgeschichte*. See also Robert William July, *The Origins of Modern African Thought: Its Development in West Africa during the Nineteenth and Twentieth Centuries* (London: Faber, 1968); Immanuel Geiss, *Panafrikanismus: Zur Geschichte der Dekolonisation* (Frankfurt a. M.: Europäische Verlagsanstalt, 1968), in English as *The Pan-African Movement: A History of Pan-Africanism in America, Europe, and Africa*, trans. Ann Keep (New York: Africana Publ. Co., 1974). Citations are from the German edition. See also idem, "Das Entstehen der modernen Eliten in Afrika seit der Mitte des 19. Jahrhunderts," in International Congress of Historical Sciences, 13th, Moscow, 1970, [*Reprinted Papers*], (3 vols., Moscow: Nauka, 1970).

85. "In plain words we must go straight to Kumasi and occupy or annex it declaring Ashantee a British protectorate"; *Gold Coast Chronicle*, 30 November 1894, as quoted in Kimble, *Ghana*, 285.

86. Samuel Johnson, *History of the Yorubas from the Earliest Times to the Beginnings of the British Protectorate* (London: G. Routledge & Sons, 1921); Joseph Ephraim Casely Hayford,

Gold Coast Native Institutions: With Thoughts upon a Healthy Imperial Policy for the Gold Coast and Ashanti (London: Sweet and Maxwell, 1903); John Mensah Sarbah, *Fantis National Constitution: A Short Treatise on the Constitution and Government of the Fanti, Asanti, and Other Akan Tribes of West Africa, etc., etc.* (London: W. Clowes and Sons, 1906).

87. Hollis R. Lynch, "Edward W. Blyden, Pioneer West African Nationalist," *JAH*, 6 (July 1965).

88. On this, see J. F. Ade Ajayi, *Christian Missions in Nigeria, 1841-1891: The Making of a New Elite* (Evanston: Northwestern University Press, 1965); Ayandele, *Missionary Impact.* About this time, the Niger Company forced the African traders out of the Niger area; Emmanuel Ayankanmi Ayandele, "Background of the 'Duel' between Crowther and Goldie on the Lower Niger, 1857-1885," *JHSN*, 4 (January 1967); idem, *Holy Johnson, Pioneer of African Nationalism, 1836-1917* (London: Cass, 1970).

89. See the helpful figures in Martin L. Kilson, "Social Forces in West African Political Development," in Peter J. M. McEwan (comp.), *Twentieth Century Africa* (London, Ibadan: Oxford University Press, 1968). The latter also provides a quotation from Mary Henrietta Kingsley, *Travels in West Africa: Congo Français, Corisco and Cameroons* (2nd ed., London, New York: Macmillan, 1897): "You will find, notably in Lagos, excellent pure-blooded Negroes in European clothes, and with European culture. The best men among these are lawyers, doctors, and merchants."

90. July, *Origins*, 433f.

91. Joseph Ephraim Casely Hayford, *The Truth about the West African Land Question* (New York: Negro Universities Press, 1913, 1969).

92. George Edgar Metcalfe (ed.), *Great Britain and Ghana: Documents of Ghana History, 1807-1957* (London: T. Nelson, 1964), 560.

93. Treated in detail by Geiss, *Panafrikanismus*, 220f., among others.

94. Excerpts are given in Coleman, *Nigeria*, 192f.

95. Tekena N. Tamuno, "Governor Clifford and Representative Government," *JHSN*, 4 (January, 1967). In a dispatch of 26 March 1921, Clifford put the following arguments to Colonial Secretary Winston S. Churchill: "None the less, there is growing up among the more educated classes a feeling that the machinery in existence for the discussion of local affairs is wholly inadequate and that the Government occupies a position of untrammelled autocracy which is without a counterpart in the other West African Colonies. That this is, in fact, the case cannot be gainsaid.... Sooner or later the position must be recognised as intolerable by the more advanced sections of the indigenous population, and I suggest that it is preferable that the initiative in the matter of reform should be taken by the Government....The privilege of electing their own representatives is much sought after by politically minded persons in West Africa"; ibid., 122. Clifford is also judged positively by Jide Osuntkun, "Post-First World War Economic and Administrative Problems in Nigeria and the Response of the Clifford Administration," *JHSN*, 7 (January 1973).

96. Albertini, *Decolonization*, 138f. See also Duncan-Johnstone, "Memorandum."

97. "I hold it to be a serious mistake to regard an unofficial majority as a normal step on the road to responsible government...." The legislative council, Bourdillon continued, had indeed been useful, but should now be replaced with regional councils for the north, west, and east, "with a central Council in Lagos"; Bourdillon, *Memorandum*, 9.

98. Kimble, *Ghana*, 451f.

99. These demands emerge very clearly in a petition submitted to the Colonial Office in 1924. The petition demanded, among other things, abandonment of the waterworks ordinance, which was most unpopular; Great Britain, Colonial Office, *Papers Relating to the Petition of the Delegation from the Gold Coast Colony and Ashanti* (*Gold Coast*, No. XI) (Accra: Government Printer, 1934). See also Bourret, *Ghana*, 129, and Anthony G. Hopkins, "Economic Aspects of Political Movements in Nigeria and the Gold Coast, 1918-1939," *JAH*, 7 (January 1966).

100. I follow here Th. Lanz-Schärer's dissertation, presently under way, on the politicization of Nigeria before World War II.

101. Nnamdi Azikiwe, *My Odyssey: An Autobiogrpahy* (London: C. Hurst, 1970).

102. Hopkins, "Economic Aspects," 150.

103. Coleman, *Nigeria*, 220f., gives the figure of 10,000.

104. Ajayi and Crowder, *History*, II, 592f.

10

FRENCH WEST AND EQUATORIAL AFRICA: FROM SENEGAL TO THE CONGO

France's main thrust from the coast inland proceeded from Senegal and was aimed at the upper Niger region of the western Sudan.[1] No belt of primeval jungle blocked the way. Since the end of the eighteenth century a series of exploratory expeditions had crisscrossed the enormous territory and had suggested the best approaches. St. Louis had been the most important French station in West Africa since the seventeenth century, trade relations with the interior being of long standing. Around 1850, Marseille and Bordeaux trading houses began to press for expansion, and the governor and military later joined them.[2] General Louis Faidherbe (1854-1865) had outlined France's aim, control from Bamako to Timbuktu on the Niger, which was to create a French territory in Africa equal to British India.[3] As late as the 1880s, there was talk of millions and millions of Africans in the western Sudan.[4] These Africans were tempting enough both as producers and potential consumers of French goods to make the risks of a thrust toward the Sudan seem acceptable, even to a mother country disinclined to undertake military expeditions and additional financial burdens. But military force was clearly going to be necessary because the Tukulor empire centered on Ségou blocked the way to the Niger. Although a loosely organized state, it was itself expansive in policy. Its leaders were experienced and talented soldiers, El-Hajj Umar in Faidherbe's day, and later Umar's son Ahmadou. They soon divined French aims and were prepared for war. Roughly contemporary with this new French effort, the brilliant Samory was building up an empire farther to the south in Fouta Djallon. Although he employed force, he also enjoyed both the charisma of a Muslim ruler and the ability to tie the tribes and villages he had conquered to him administratively. He armed his troups, moreover, with European weapons.[5]

The energetic governor of Senegal, Louis A. E. G. Brière de l'Isle (1876-1881), decided to act. What was at stake was buttressing French claims vis-à-vis the British and anticipating supposed British aspirations to the upper Niger. A railway was to be built from St. Louis to Bamako as the first section of a later trans-Sahara line. Skillful propaganda in Paris played upon the strong contemporary interest in great railway projects to secure parliamentary agreement to the first credits in 1879.[6] But exaggerated expectations were soon disappointed, and Parlement thereafter rather dragged its feet. The soldiers, however, Gustave Borgnis-Desbordes, Joseph Galliéni, and Louis Archinard, were provided the chance to push ahead smartly with their own operations. "By 1882 the military factor in Sudanese policy was supreme."[7] Bamako was occupied in 1883, Galliéni thereafter expanding the position thus secured. His successor Archinard struck out against Ahmadou in 1888, and Ségou fell in 1890. It took another six years (1891-1898), however, to overcome Samory.

Recent scholarship has thrown considerable light upon the complicated political context within which the French thrust into the western Sudan occurred. Both French and Africans combined military operations with elaborate diplomatic moves. Treaties were concluded, evaded, and broken all around. The expanding, conquering colonial power collided with two polities which tenaciously defended their independence and freedom of action. But these African states were politically unstable, enabling the French to exploit the fear of Ahmadou and Samory by promising their subject tribes protection and support. Thus, Galliéni sought to win over the Bambaras at the very time he sought a treaty with Ahmadou. A treaty was, in fact, concluded in 1879, in which Ahmadou, sizing up French aims correctly, conceded the French the Niger trade but not the right to build a fort. The Africans in Bamako allowed French entry as a riposte to Ahmadou. And because Samory was warring against the ruler of Sissoko, the latter allied with the French and allowed them to occupy Ségou, although later joining Samory to fight against the French. Samory himself finally sought a rapprochement with the Tukulor in order to offer joint resistance to the French, but by then it was too late.

It is particularly difficult in western Sudan to answer the question of whether Africans uniformly resisted the French or whether, indeed, African collaboration simplified the establishment of colonial rule. Collaboration certainly played a considerable role, because every kingdom and tribe acted in isolation to maintain its most immediate interests. They were therefore agreeable to loose protectorate treaties when such treaties did not seem to endanger their interests. But there was also widely based resistance which was only broken by military force. Thus it was that the Damel of Cayor, who had allied with the French in 1875 against the Tukulor, rose in revolt in 1882 when the French began to build a railway from St. Louis to Dakar. The Damel feared that such intensive economic and political penetration of Cayor territory would destroy his previous relationship of loose dependency, and that loss of independence and destruction of Cayor's social institutions was only too likely.[8] The French suffered some embarrassing military rebuffs before restoring order. Despite the usual sort of negative judgments of Africans as a primative, blood-thirsty, and devious lot, which were intended to legitimize their subjugation and the French *mission civilisatrice*, even contemporaries acknowledged Samory's military genius, and not simply to make French successes appear the greater. Africans today like to see Samory as a great precolonial ruler and proto-nationalist. A more critical historiography considers Ahmadou and Samory to be important representatives of primary resistance. Both men built their feudal-military states shortly before, and in part as a response to, European pentration. They recognized the European threat and bitterly resisted it, though futilely, given the enormous expansive force of a late nineteenth-century European Great Power.

The Ivory Coast had long proved rather unattractive. In 1843 some forts and trading stations were established, but in 1870 the navy ministry determined to close them because they cost too much. In 1878, A. Verdier, a trader from La Rochelle, was chosen official resident, in order to sustain French claims. In 1885 a customs system was introduced to create some income. It took the Congo acts and the related attempt to tie the western Sudan to the Guinea coast, which would simultaneously block English access to the Sudan, to get expansion moving. The immediate aim was to bring the trade center, Kong, and the strong Mossi kingdom under French control. In 1889 Louis Gustave Binger, who had travelled east 4,000 kilometers from Bamako, met Marcel Treich-Laplène, who had marched north from the Ivory Coast, in Kong.[9] The ruler of the Mossi considered these white expeditions a threat to his independence. He therefore, with initial success, tried to play the Germans, English, and French off against one another, but in 1897 after a short struggle perforce accepted a protectorate treaty.[10] On the coast, in the meantime, some of the old stations had been reoccupied, and chiefs who had rebelled against the administration and customs duties demoted. Numerous missions penetrated the primeval rain forests, concluded treaties, and established strong points, through French rule was still not very firmly established.[11] There were numerous rebellions, mainly because of the obligation to provide porterage. They were put down by "punishment expeditions." Economic exploitation went nowhere. Only in 1908 did Governor Gabriel Louis Angoulvant, determined to get things cleared up, undertake methodic pacification by systematic application of military force. He counted an area as pacified when the following conditions had been met: "Absolute respect, payment in full of taxes, genuine cooperation in the construction of roads and paths, acceptance of paid porterage duty, adherence to our advice about the need to work, and recourse to our courts."[12] Complete disarmament was intended to assure the colonial power a monopoly of force, to forestall possible resistance or rebellion, and to force the population to shift from hunting to agriculture. Tribes and villages that attempted to escape French pressure or failed to pay the taxes required of them as a sign of submission had to anticipate repressive action such as the burning of villages and harvests. At the same time, the scattered settlements were to be regrouped into larger units.[13] It took years before pacification was in some measure complete, which explains why thousands evaded tax payments, forced labor, and forced recruitment during World War I by fleeing to the Gold Coast.

The Ivory Coast natives were grouped into countless small village and tribal units, difficult to reach through the dense jungle. Lacking any common overall political organization, however, they also lacked the military strength to evade the embraces of the colonial power. In the area between Lagos and Accra, on the other hand, the kingdom of Abomey opposed the French. Its rulers had grown rich from the slave trade in the eighteenth century and created a military state of some importance, which then pushed east into Nigerian Abeokuta and south toward the coast. As a response to the British occupation of Lagos in 1863, the French had established a protectorate over the coastal kingdom of Porto Novo, which they renewed in 1883 at the request of King Toffa. Abomey interpreted their treaty of 1868 with France concerning Cotonou merely as conferring trading privileges, but the French considered that it separated Cotonou from Abomey. Still, the French hesitated to go to war with Abomey, waiting until 1890-1892 to strike. Their excuse for action then was that they wanted to put an end both to Abomey's provocations and its custom of human sacrifices. Actually, they wanted to suppress the independent native kingdom, which had followed their thrust in from the coast with considerable mistrust, and open the way into the hinterland.[14]

Roughly contemporaneous with the French thrust into the western Sudan was the thrust into the Congo. Although the navy ministry had once said it wished to evacuate Gabon on 1 January 1874, between 1875 and 1878 the explorer Pierre Savorgnan de Brazza, a naturalized Frenchman of Italian origin, followed the Ogowe River and reached the Congo River upstream of the great rapids. He had done this without official backing, and his reward was to become famous overnight, the toast of Paris. Nevertheless it was not the French government but the French committee in King Leopold II's International Africa Society which backed de Brazza's next venture. On 10 September 1880, he concluded a treaty with the ruler, or *Makoko*, of the Bateke, claiming the territory to the west of the Congo River. After an intensive campaign on the part of French colonial circles, Parlement, which regarded the British occupation of Alexandria of 1882 as a diplomatic setback and a blow to French prestige, ratified the treaty in November 1882.[15] After the Congo conference, French expeditions marched their way to the north, finally linking up in 1900 with troops from the Sudan at Chad. Here too, pacification went on for several years before it could be regarded as complete.[16]

ADMINISTRATION: CENTRAL AND DIRECT

Starting from a series of tiny and insignificant coastal settlements, France had in a few years conquered an enormous colonial empire, which reached in a mighty arch from Dakar over Lake Chad to the mouth of the Congo. This was also the time when Tunisia, Indochina, and Madagascar were acquired. The government had pushed this expansion, partly covertly and partly in the open. Parlement and public opinion, however, with the exception of the economic interests organized in the Parti Colonial and the deputies from the port cities, had always been lukewarm at best and at worst openly opposed to expansion, an attitude that was not to change much in the future. No one, indeed, demanded that the colonies be given up, and some little emphasis was given development (*mise en valeur*) but most Frenchmen bothered about the overseas possessions only now and again, most notably when national prestige seemed at stake. Thus, as in England, financial demands upon the metropolis had to be as small as possible.

But the empire which the soldiers had conquered had to be administered. The old factories on the coast had been subordinate to the navy ministry, and military expansion had taken place under its aegis. Tension between the soldiers and economic interests, plus the desire for administrative independence in order to be better able to voice colonial interests in Paris, led in 1887 to the creation of the office of undersecretary of state for the colonies. It was located first in the navy ministry, then in the trade ministry, and finally was transformed into an independent colonial ministry in 1894. Félix Faure of Le Havre, Maurice Rouvier of Marseille, and above all, Eugène Etienne pushed through this solution in the face of military resistance.[17] Etienne was an Algerian Frenchman who for years was the unchallenged leader of metropolitan colonial interests within the Chambre and beyond it, and was also undersecretary of state during the crucial years from 1887 to 1892. That did not signify, however, that the colonial ministry enjoyed much regard in the cabinet or that politicians counted it a great plum. Although some striking personalities from the right and the center filled the office, it was seen mainly as a way station to better things. Its incumbents but seldom had a genuine interest in colonial happenings. There too, France was not much different from England.

The expansion into the hinterland and the delimitation of French territory as a result of border settlements with rival powers called for the creation of an administrative structure. Dahomey became an independent colony as early as 1889, with Guinea following in 1891, the Ivory Coast in 1893, and the Sudan in 1899. A fuller degree of coordination seemed called for, however, both to eliminate personal rivalries and in the interest of political and economic coordination, and led to the French West African Federation in 1895. The governor-general was relieved of responsibility for Senegal in 1902 and shifted his administrative seat from St. Louis to Dakar. In 1903 additional powers devolved upon the federation, which in 1904 received its own budget. In 1910 a similar French Equatorial African Federation was created. The individual colonial governors were directly subordinate to Dakar or Brazzaville and were forbidden direct communication with Paris. Although the individual governors received considerable power, their financial dependence on Dakar or Brazzaville tended to strengthen the position of the two governor-generals over time (as only the latter, for example, could float loans). It also created some unhappiness in the richer coastal colonies which had to help finance the poorer ones inland, and thus to a degree foreshadowed the gradual dissolution of the federations after 1946.[18]

The creation of these huge administrative units differed from British practice, in which British colonies, be they ever so small, were directly subordinate to the

Colonial Office. The difference documented the strongly centralist character of French administration, as did the fact that French colonies, in contrast to British, had no legislative powers. Only Paris could make laws for the colonies. In practice, indeed, Paris "ruled" by decree, which by law the president of the republic had to sign, but which had originated in the colonial ministry in close consultation with the governor-generals. But the tendency was still to make the most important decisions in Paris. That was quite in keeping with the centralized French bureaucratic structure, which also allowed the départements very little financial and administrative independence. England, on the other hand, stood fast upon its tradition of local self-government and created a decentralized imperial structure. In practice, however, the differences were not so great as theory would suggest.

The internal administration of the colonies shows similar divergences and similarities. As in India, Indo-China, and British West Africa, the task in French West and Equatorial Africa was to create, without using much money or very many people, an apparatus of rule capable of governing a vast area with millions of subjects. There was a clear division between the central administration, which included the governor with his secretariat and departments, especially the technical ones, and the administrator off in the bush. There was no great difference between a "resident" and a "district commissioner" or a *commandant du cercle*, who despite his martial title was a civilian. Far from the central administration, dependent on their own resources and without much staff support, they discharged their obligation to rule, some with initiative and enthusiasm about their roles and with the interests of their subjects at heart, others in the spirit of routine, neglect, and authoritarianism.[19]

In the early years, it was necessary to recruit most of the cadre locally, meaning that its quality was dubious. As late as 1907 only 70 of 489 officials in French black Africa had come from Ecole Coloniale in Paris, which had been founded in 1888.[20] By the interwar period, however, that institution provided the better part of the cadre. The school had no parallel in England. It was in keeping with French centralist notions that graduates were employed in all parts of the empire without receiving any regionally oriented education, either in language instruction or in the foreign civilizations they would encounter. Transfers from Indochina to Africa and vice versa were a source of frequent complaint. Even in the colonies, the maxim prevailed that shifts from *cercle* to *cercle* made for more efficient and less corrupt administration. Those returning to Dakar after home leave often did not know until they arrived where they would be assigned. It is thus not surprising that few took the trouble—in contrast to the British—to learn the local languages, particularly since the spread of French was accounted a considerable portion of the *mission civilisatrice* and French also served as an instrument of rule.

Much has been written in recent years about the differences, real or apparent, between the French practices and doctrine of *administration directe* and British doctrines of Indirect Rule. Whereas the British recognized the precolonial authority structures, and limited themselves to supervision and advice to the emirs, chiefs, and notables, the French shattered and largely eliminated the traditional African ruling classes in order to create a centralized, hierarchical administrative apparatus that reached from the top down to the very village chiefs that the French themselves installed. The British understood the native authorities to be the local government, who were to be given gradually increasing autonomy, and the protagonists of Indirect Rule prided themselves on making "good Africans." The French, on the other hand, pursued the aim of Frenchifying the colonies and making their subjects into "good Frenchmen." But it has also been, and still is, held that, although Indirect Rule as doctrine contrasted sharply with the concepts of integration and assimilation embodied in the slogan, The France of a Hundred Million, the actual exercise of rule in both French and British territories worked within the concrete facts of the situation, tending to obliterate the doctrinal differences between the two systems.[21]

French military expansion encountered resistance particularly from the greater and more mighty African rulers. In the end, they all had to sign protectorate treaties that in practice bound them over to the colonial power. These treaties were often concluded with rulers who had come to power only a short time before or at the moment of capitulation, and who thus had not solidified their rule and were dependent on their conquerers. Their rule generally represented a transitory French effort to leave ruling structures and territories as they had been. Most were deposed shortly after conclusion of the protectorate treaties or forced into a position of overt dependency. The kingdom of Abomey was thus divided, the king exiled, and the royal palace transformed into a museum, although members of the royal family continued to serve as *chefs de canton*. In the remote, mostly thinly settled and economically unimportant hinterland, the Sudan and Chad, the French ruled through existing rulers and notables. The Naba accordingly continued to rule the Mossi of present-day Upper Volta, though his position was weakened because of French support for his vassals. The refusal of the Mossi to pay taxes in 1910 also met with repression; but the administration still required few Europeans, one Frenchman sufficing for 60,000 Mossi.[22]

In 1913 Governor-General William Ponty issued a memorandum about native policy calling for an action of liberation, in which slavery was to be abolished and captives freed.[23] He also called for the administration "to aim at suppressing native feudalism and to establish on a firm and rational basis our political policy toward that mass of humanity whom we seek to liberate from the yoke." Ponty thus sought to undermine both the structures making for the loyalty of the followers and the authority of their leaders, in order to retain better control over the mass of French subjects. A part of this effort was the "policy of races." It comprised the elimination of existing sovereign relationships imposed by one tribe upon another, the exploitation of intertribal tensions to destroy the larger polities, the elimination of existing ruling groups, and, finally, the maintenance within each cercle of an ordering into the smallest of ethnic groups in a clear and direct command relationship with the commandant himself. In contrast to the protectorate system of the English, Ponty wrote, the French system of rule rested upon "a policy of races and direct administration."

Another specifically French innovation was the *chef de canton* imposed between French officials and the *chef de village*. This was a sort of artificial chiefdom without any traditional standing, to which even members of strange tribes might be appointed, if they had some knowledge of French and any rudiments of administrative experience. The usefulness of the chef de canton as a conveyer belt for administrative orders depended in no small measure, however, on his character and personal presence, as Robert Delavignette, sometime governor, strikingly stated. "On the one hand, it is clearly essential to let the chef de canton retain his native personality and to exploit through him those feudal sympathies which still persist. On the other hand, we are led by the ineluctable force of colonialism itself to mold him to our own administrative mentality."[24] In 1937 the fifteen million living in French West Africa were divided into 118 cercles, 2,200 cantons, and 48,000 villages. At the level of the chefs de village the French retained more of the traditional order, though often dispensing with any sort of election. The French were also much more ready than the British to legitimize alternative candidates, and often appointed former soldiers and scribes as chefs de village.

Governor-General Martial Merlin outlined their functions to the Conseil de Gouvernement in 1923 with disarming candor:

> Is it not to this collaboration on the part of the chiefs that we owe the perfect submission of natives to our various obligations? Whether it be a question of collecting taxes, or providing corvée, or assembling recruits, or helping line things up for police investigations, whether it is a question of participating in our works of relief and assistance, in every aspect of administrative activity we find him always at our side, the faithful executer of our orders.[25]

It was no accident that tax collection received first mention. We have already noted that even during the expansion and pacification phases taxes were collected in kind or in cash. Because African resistance was directed against taxes and because taxes caused countless rebellions, regular payment of taxes was accounted by the administration definitive proof of submission; or, in the euphemism of the rulers, the loyalty of the subjects. It was with corresponding pride that the administration reported the rapid rise in tax collections. For the Africans, however, the payments were more than symbolic and constituted a severe burden which bore the most heavily on those producing but little for the market, who were only gradually exposed to the cash economy. To pay taxes in money was tantamount to compulsion to bring goods to market or, if this was impossible, to work for wages away from home. The Mossi were thus forced by their heavy tax obligations to work as seasonal laborers in the south.[26] But the administration considered taxes to be vital not only because along with customs duties they provided most of its revenue (and to a far greater degree than in British West Africa).[27] The administration also believed the economic development that it desired to be impossible without wage labor:

> The head tax is above all a very effective agent of civilization. . . . As soon as possible, cash is demanded, and as a result the use of money expands. To acquire money for taxes, the native is obliged to do more work, and in particular to organize his work. He is no longer contented, and comes to see how things are, and the labor market gradually comes into being.[28]

The author of the above text also pointed out what were doubtless frequent abuses. Inhabitants in the vicinity of administrative seats were taxed more heavily than those farther off, and higher population figures were sometimes given than really existed, the tax screw being tightened accordingly. Whole villages sought to escape taxes by migrating or, "In one cercle I crossed, when a village could not or would not pay its taxes in full, the custom was to seize a child and place him in a village named Liberty, until the tax was paid."[29] The village chief was not only obligated to come up with the taxes and punished or deposed when he failed to do so, he was also exposed to the temptation to enrich himself, favor his intimates, and sock it to his enemies. The commandant usually preferred to overlook such things if the money came in.

Forced labor grew out of the colonial situation itself. The colonial power needed workers, particularly porters during the period of expansion when sovereignty was being established, and then for the construction and maintenance of the new communications system. But free labor either did not exist or was insufficiently available, because, while the African peasant in the bush had work to do in his own society, particularly land clearing, working for wages was a notion largely foreign to him. He considered it unworthy of a free man, something that made him rather like a slave. He thus had no occasion to work for compensation outside his home area. The colonial power needed a work force that was concentrated both in terms of time and place, however, whether for porterage for expeditions, or the construction of railways and paths. The British also introduced forced labor, as for example in the building of the railways from Lagos to Kano. But they later gave it up. The French felt they could not do so, however, and tenaciously evaded pressure from the International Labor Organization during the 1930s to give up all forms of unfree labor. Forced labor was abolished only in 1946.

Every native was obligated to work up to twelve days a year for the administration, not without pay, to be sure, and if possible in the immediate area at times other than the harvest season.[30] In practice, however, these stipulations were often evaded, with the result that this corvée—*prestations* was the new word—became a severe and hated burden, particularly in the Congo.[31] More dubious still was the recruitment of labor for the private sector, the railway companies, plantations, and lumbering operations. Prestations were supposed to be used for public works, especially for construction and maintenance of roads. Actually, however, the administration intervened in the interests of the private sector. It forced the chiefs to provide labor which was then employed far from home under extremely severe working conditions. As late as the period 1925-1932, the construction of the railroad from the coast to Brazzaville cost the lives of thousands of natives, many of whom had been rounded up in the north.[32] When the Popular Front government prohibited the administration from assisting in the provision of workers in 1936 both businesses and the colons protested vigorously, particularly on the Ivory Coast. During World War II, open or covert forced labor was widely employed for forced production.

It was the duty of the chiefs to provide the workers. If some immediate benefit to the village was apparent, such obligatory work could be regarded as a continuation of earlier communal obligations. Mostly, however, pressure or force was required, and severe punishments were threatened when a village attempted to evade its obligations.[33] Here too, the chief was exposed to temptation not to furnish the strong and healthy needed to farm at home, but rather the weak, the old, and the sick. That in no small measure was the cause of the high worker mortality. The agents of the colonial firms also did not hesitate to bribe the chiefs to secure urgently needed labor.

It is obvious that tax collection and provision of workers decisively affected the position of the chief and thus the social order as a whole. As executive agent of the colonial power, it was the lot of the chief to fulfill precisely those obligations which the individual African found most hateful. The latter might well understand that the chief was himself acting under pressure, but it must have been difficult for him to acknowledge the chief as mainstay and the center of his social order. And the more hatred and alienation the chief encountered, the more support he had to seek from the administrateur.

In the interwar period, several governor-generals issued instructions to show the chiefs more regard, in part because of the impression made by the British administration, apparently so successful. But they were also alarmed by the disintegration of African society. "We have made the error of completely shattering every native social cadre, instead of improving them for our own use," noted Merlin in 1920.[34] More efforts seemed to have been made to recognize the legitimate chiefs and to strengthen their positions, insofar as this could be done by decree. But the chief still had the look of a bureaucrat, which his being paid a fixed salary only emphasized. The decisive difference from the British native authorities lay in the fact that the French chiefs lacked both their own treasuries and judicial powers. These were the things that under Indirect Rule provided the chiefs with a certain independence of decision and thus fostered their prestige. The French chief was much more the administrateur's errand boy and executive agent; they have been compared to noncommissioned officers. The French system was also more authoritarian than the British in largely eliminating the precolonial elements of feudal or democratic joint decisions within the village and tribe. The French, indeed, saw the great mass of Africans as supervised subjects, within the framework of administrative units to which the latter felt no loyalty.

The relative lack of friction accompanying the elimination of the chiefs after independence is often taken as evidence today that they were hated or at the very least had lost their roots. It should be noted, however, that their loss of prestige and functions varied according to the area. They clearly retained more of their old stature in the less closely administered and more thinly settled areas, where the African population seldom saw a white administrator face to face and in daily life the traditional chief exercised his leadership sanctioned by custom and religion, as of old. In the areas where export goods were produced and in the cities an individualization process was under way which willy-nilly undermined the position of the traditional elite and called for new forms of local administration. That was also true in the British colonies. It is hard to say whether Indirect Rule or *administration directe*—to the degree that one holds to this distinction—was by current lights a more efficient means of modernization and acculturation. The command structure with commandant at the top and village chief at the bottom doubtless made for passive resistance and reluctant compliance, quite aside from the matters of forced labor and forced cultivation, and threatened to undermine the stated aim of developing individual initiative and pushing ahead with social change. On the other hand, the employment of évolués as chiefs may have reduced the tensions between old and new elites and simplified adaption to modern life.

ECONOMIC DEVELOPMENT

"I am one of those who believe that we ought to devote our efforts to the commercial development of our colonies," averred the governor-general of French West Africa, Jean Baptiste Chaudié, in 1896. On another occasion he was more specific: "The wealth and vitality of a colony depends entirely on the value and abundance of the products it exports."[35] The governor-general's programmatic utterance perhaps lacked novelty, but it stated clearly enough that the administration considered its primary task to be the encouragement of exports as the basis for an expanding trade between the metropolis and the colonies. But French West and French Equatorial Africa belonged in terms of geography, climate, and economy to different areas. British West Africa and French West Africa constituted a unit, and the same could be said of the Belgian Congo and French Equatorial Africa.[36]

Colonial expansion led only gradually to changes in the economic structure of French West Africa. Trade followed the flag. French trade houses, in St. Louis and elsewhere, and local mulatto traders were able gradually to widen the area from which they drew trade goods and to build up a network of agents and stations. But the old pattern of trade continued, with Africans supplying the products Europeans bought and themselves buying European consumer goods. West Africa was not considered a settlement area like north Africa, and the trade houses successfully blocked the sort of monopoly concessions awarded in the Congo. As had happened in the Gold Coast, however, a tendency toward concentration was apparent even as the French were establishing their rule, with countless firms going under or being sucked up by others. By 1914 some rather large firms had become established, the Compagnie Française d'Afrique Occidentale in 1887 and the Société de l'Ouest Africain in 1906. Thereafter, these firms largely controlled the French West African trade. Concentration was accompanied by the elimination of the older trading classes of Africans and mulattoes in St. Louis and Gorée who had played an important role as late as the 1880s and in some cases had exported directly to France.[37] The shift of the federation administration to Dakar and its expansion as a port and hence as the center of the colonial economy contributed to the decline of the Africans. The financially weaker Senegalese traders were not up to the competition with the large firms which developed around 1900, and their numbers declined. The pressure rather increased, indeed, when the administration began to support the immigration of Syrian and Lebanese traders, whose numbers increased from around 100 in 1900, to 500 in 1914, to 2,000 in 1930, and to 4,000 in 1939.[38] Yet other local traders went under during the depression.[39] Not only was the development of a Senegalese-African commercial bourgeoisie largely blocked, but the precolonial beginnings of this class were largely displaced.

Once Europeans began to push into the hinterland, the intra-African trade began to decline in importance. The Sudan was not only administratively but also economically oriented toward the coast. It lost its role as a way station to the Sahara and ultimately became a labor reservoir for the expanding production of cash crops in the coastal areas. The administration contributed to this development by building railways and roads. The loan of 1903 paid for the most important lines, the St. Louis-Dakar-Niger line and the branch lines inland from Guinea, Dahomey and the Ivory Coast. Governor-General Ernest Roume, a "promoter," summed it up thus: "The old land routes, proceeding by day stages, create vacuums around them, whereas railways and riverine navigation attract people and the economic activity that goes with them."[40] The rail lines, built with forced labor, were of dubious quality, but they served to open up the country economically by making it possible to ship goods to the ports.

In Senegal there was a spectacular increase in peanut farming.[41] Of South American origin, the peanut was probably brought to Africa by slavers. It had long been grown in the Senegambia area as food. The first shipment of seventy tons of peanuts to Rouen occurred as early as 1841. The rising demand for fat for soap-making and margarine was the great spur to production, as was also true of palm products. The loose soil and the climate of Cayor proved especially suitable, and cultivation fit easily into the traditional crop rotation. Peanut, millet, and fallow fields adjoined one another or produce was cropped successively in the same field. Land was cleared and rid of brush, the ashes from burning the brush providing a modest degree of fertilization. Cultivation with the traditional hackhoes followed. Continuing care and harvesting were simple, requiring but little agricultural skill or exactitude. Since the peanut is an annual, there were no land-law problems. Though the village "owned" the land, the cultivating family had usufruct rights. The French in analogy to the metropolis attempted to establish individual small holdings and introduced registration in cadastres. That made the land private property which could be alienated, but little use was made of the opportunity thus created, which blocked the decline of the peasants into tenantry.[42] Cultivation expanded rapidly along the railroads, first in Cayor between St. Louis and Dakar and then from Dakar toward the Niger, and finally into Casamance in the period before and after World War II. Cultivation centered in the area of Sine-Saloum and the city of Kaolack, which was developed as a harbor. The export figures are shown in table 10.1. This expansion attracted tens of thousands of seasonal workers, the *navétanes*, from the Sudan and upper Guinea. Working under contract, they performed most of the field work for wages and were also allowed to have some extra land on their own account. Their profits went for taxes and some goods and they then returned home to the villages.

Table 10.1
Export of Agricultural Products from French West Africa, 1845-1939 (in tons)

YEAR	AMOUNT
1845	187
1854	5,000
ca. 1900	120,000
1913	242,000
1938-39	580,000

SOURCE: Derived from various sources.

It soon turned out, however, that the land was being overused, and yields declined.[43] The rather sparse tree cover was uprooted, which upset run-off patterns. Fallow time was reduced and, as population increased, the practice of shifting areas of cultivation, which was extensive but allowed the land to regenerate itself, declined. The land received no manure, because the Africans, with the exception of the Sérères, kept no stock, the herding of which was left to the nomadic Peulhs. The growth of foodstuffs was also neglected, either because the administration pushed export crops or because the Africans had become oriented toward growing peanuts for cash. Food had increasingly to be imported, notably rice from Indochina. It should be noted that before World War II rice prices were low, whereas peanuts enjoyed a somewhat protected French market. A kilo of peanuts thus sold for more than the cost of a kilo of shelled rice. Only after World War II did the ratio worsen to the point that three or four kilos of peanuts were required to purchase a kilo of rice.[44] The colonial administration did not pay much attention to agriculture until the interwar period, after agrarian experts like Senator Henri Cosnier sharply criticized the existing situation in 1921: "The technical and scientific personnel of the agricultural service, very much reduced, badly paid, bullied about, have deserted the cadres and have created a most unflattering and amply merited reputation for the colonial administration."[45] Better seed was handed out, and more adequate tools were introduced, but otherwise traditional cultivation methods did not change much. No experiments with artificial fertilizer, for example, were made before 1945. The peanut provided 430 million francs out of total Senegalese exports of 503 million francs in 1936. Little was invested in peanuts per se, however, and they contributed little to the social mobilization of the people, a good part of the scant income from them being extracted as taxes. Savings were hence hardly possible. An interesting exception, however, were the Mourides, an Islamic brotherhood founded in 1886. Their marabouts propagandized peanuts early on, and stated that hard physical labor was the key to salvation. They thus accumulated considerable wealth.[46]

In 1910 a rather interesting attempt was made to group African producers in a cooperative organization, the Sociétés Indigènes de Prévoyance.[47] Its main purpose was to assure sufficient seed for the next planting and to meet modest credit needs. Since a suitable management cadre was wanting, however, after some initial hesitation the French administrator assumed its presidency. Membership became obligatory, with annual dues. It doubtless provided worthwhile assistance, but fell too much into administration hands. The dues came to be seen as another tax, and the function of the cooperative, which was to train members to stand on their own feet, was not fulfilled.[48]

Trade took the forms familiar to us from other colonies. The African peasants brought their bags of peanuts to trading posts and sold them to the agents of European firms or to Levantines, who also sold them the trade goods they wanted and thus profited on both ends of the deal. The Lebanese and Syrians adapted very quickly to African conditions and successfully worked their way into both the purchasing trade and the wholesale and retail trades. As has been mentioned, the Africans were largely displaced from trade, continuing to function only as petty traders and delivery agents, and later as transporters, but otherwise solely as producers.[49] Given the low value of peanuts, the yield from a single family's plot was low, with the result that, except for the Mourides, a class of prosperous African peasants which might have become the supporters of social and political liberation never formed.

The price of peanuts rose over time, but continued to reflect sharp world-market price fluctuations and collapsed completely during the depression.[50] The peasants were deceived of the hopes which the administration had raised within them and went back to farming millet and manioc (cassava). That led the administration to push peanuts more vigorously then ever, both for the sake of the budget and for exports.[51] It also began in 1932 to regulate trade, until then free. The dates of the beginning of the harvest and its sale were set by decree, in order to prevent the harvest of unripe crops and to limit price fluctuations. The number of trading stations was restricted, in order to force the traders to compete with each other, and prices were publicized more fully than formerly. The

Sociétés de Prévoyance received the right to market the products of their members, which infuriated the trading firms.[52] The shift to a quasi state-purchasing monopoly, however, followed, as in British West Africa, only after World War II.

Compared with the Senegal peanut boom, the export figures for other products remained modest. The temporarily high prices for rubber after 1900 led to a rubber "rush" particularly in Guinea, but it petered out after a few years because the traditional West African methods could not compete with East Asian plantation rubber.[53] Palm oil and palm kernels were harvested in the Ivory Coast and Dahomey, and tropical hardwoods had long been exported. The administration had taken great interest in cotton and attempts to grow it in Senegal valley dated from the early nineteenth century. France hoped to become independent of imports from the United States and thought it had suitable land and an appropriate climate in the thinly settled area between the Niger and Lake Chad. The means used was forced cultivation. The chiefs were compelled to have cotton planted under the watchful eye of the administrateur. After 1931 the Office du Niger received massive capital sums for an irrigation system for large-scale cotton and rice production. Instead of the million hectares foreseen, however, in 1953 only 25,000 hectares were irrigated and only 2,000 tons of cotton were delivered in 1940.[54] But cotton was at least introduced into the Sahel, providing the present-day independent states of Niger and Chad limited but vitally necessary foreign exchange.

While Senegalese land and climate were ideally suited to peanuts, the tropical jungle of the Ivory Coast was equally suited to coffee and cocoa. The latter enjoyed a boom like that on the Gold Coast, but a generation later.[55] Verdier, the leading French merchant and resident, had smuggled in coffee seedlings from Liberia about 1880. Settlers had experimented with cocoa, but the Ivory Coast produced only two tons as late as 1908, very little in comparison with the Gold Coast's 20,000 tons. Governor Angoulvant resorted to forced cultivation, obligating each village to plant seedlings. Many Africans, however, destroyed the seedlings as soon as the administration's back was turned.[56] But by 1916, the reports were reading, "the adoption of cocoa trees by the natives is general. . . . Indeed, it has become something of a craze. Everyone is starting nurseries, everyone is planting."[57] All the same, the breakthrough occurred only in 1925 for cocoa and in 1935 for coffee. The export of cocoa rose from 6,000 tons in 1925 to 60,000 in 1939 and that of coffee to 18,000 tons. In the 1920s, colons also planted cocoa and coffee, some at their own cost and some financed by corporations. They formed a tiny but influential settler class, dependent on African labor. For that reason, the question of recruitment and worker contracts became a most serious matter for the administration. A decree of 1925, which provided for administrative assistance in recruitment, was largely the result of colon pressure. The result was a veiled form of forced labor. Nevertheless the African share in production steadily increased.[58]

Although the peanut was an annual, the cocoa plant required several years to bear. The social effects of this have already been outlined above (p.321). While cultivation of peanuts and foodstuffs such as millet and manioc and even the gathering of palm and cola nuts were compatible with the traditional division of land by village chiefs and heads of families, cocoa and coffee cultivation called into question older customs of land use. A young African who had decided on coffee or cocoa wanted security, some sort of contract with the village, and began to think of the land he had cleared and planted as private property, his own land. Since the new crops required the continuing presence of the planter, moreover, the plants themselves bearing only for some twenty-odd years and then having to be abandoned, and since cultivation had become widespread, the planter families necessarily often settled quite far from the villages. This also encouraged individualization and the loosening of close links to the old, closed society. "Instead of all the huts of family members being concentrated around the hut of the patriarch, they are breaking free and setting up independent households, with the links to the chief weakening in direct proportion to their distance from him." The same official noted in 1948 that "the planter, now an emancipated worker, the sole master of his family and enriched by the sale of his products, is today establishing an individual landed property, an isolated holding farmed by a nuclear family. He is unconsciously working a great economic and social revolution."[59] Köbban has also pointed out an additional dislocation factor at work in one traditional society without individual property rights. Among the Agni, who were particularly active in cocoa production, rights of inheritance went to brothers and nephews rather than sons. One can appreciate however, that a prosperous cocoa planter, whose own family had cultivated the land, would want to pass his holding to his sons rather than, say, a nephew. But this led to intrigues, law suits, mutual accusations of poisoning, all typical signs of the crisis resulting from the collision of the closed production and resident community of traditional society with cash crop production based on individual performance and the social differentiation that necessarily accompanied it.[60]

Coffee and cocoa plantations are climate bound and were thus concentrated in the coastal strip, particularly on the southeastern Ivory Coast. They required additional labor which they sucked in from the north and the hinterland. Like the *navétanes* in Senegal, the Mossi on the Ivory Coast were mostly seasonal laborers, working for a share of the harvest. They were thus participants in the production of export goods. There was nevertheless an acute lack of manpower, which resulted in tension between the colons and the administration and the colons and African planters; the Mossi themselves by preference avoided corvée, forced cotton cultivation, military drafts, and high taxes by mass flight to the Gold Coast where better working conditions prevailed.[61]

The relatively high cash income from the sale of coffee and cocoa and the open or covert shift to private property in land enabled individual Africans, as in the Gold Coast, to accumulate several smaller holdings or a single larger holding and to work such holdings with outside laborers, sometimes over a hundred in number. An African planter class thus arose which with its cash-crop wealth became an element of the class structure of traditional society. Living sometimes at peace but more usually at odds with the traditional authorities, it gradually established itself as a new leading class. It was the successful and well-off planters, indeed, who were best able to utilize the opportunities to provide their sons with Western educations. When the administration discriminated in favor of the colons during World War II by providing them scarce labor and allowing them higher support prices than the Africans received, the latter joined in 1944 into an association which at first pursued mainly economic aims. It soon, however, got into difficulties with the colonial power, becoming the basis for the Rassemblement Démocratique Africain.[62] Its leader was Félix Houphouet-Boigny, who, as Baoulé chief, graduate of the Ecole William Ponty, and planter, personified both the old and the new elites.

In contrast to West Africa, the French considered that the Congo could only be opened up economically by granting corporations monopoly concessions.[63] In 1886 a "Congo Colony" had been created, with Brazza as high commissioner, and by 1900 expeditions had pushed north to Chad, but one could still hardly speak of real administrative penetration of this inaccessible, thinly settled area, which had, moreover, a miserable climate. No one even knew the true population, the number surmised being strikingly wide of the mark. Economic prospects were not exactly rosy, with modest quantities of rubber and ivory coming out through Libreville in Gabon being the sole exports. Since free trade had to be permitted in the Congo basin, little customs income stood in the offing. Nor were parlement or the colonial ministry ready to assume administrative or development costs. Because Great Britain and Belgium had both apparently had good initial experiences with the grant of concessions to well-capitalized corporations, France followed their example. Although Eugène Etienne's initial plan to turn the administration over to the companies was rejected, in 1899 forty concession contracts were granted. They provided thirty-year concessions to exploit a specified territory without much let or hindrance, so long as financial and investment obligations were met. Anyone thinking that this was the way to start development and provide the budget with vitally needed revenues soon learned better. Brazza had been among them, though he had no ties with Parisian financial circles and for humanitarian reasons was later to become a critic of the system. Concessions were granted for regions as yet unexplored, capitalization was typically too low, obligations were imprecisely formulated and hence evaded, and the administration had neither the personnel nor the will to perform its mandated supervisory duties.[64] The administration had, indeed, only been able to push its expeditions northward by the ruthless impressment of porters, whose resistance or, really, rebellion, it suppressed with bloodshed. In the concession areas, the rule was slash and burn and terrorism. Every means was employed to force the natives to deliver rubber. First a tax, payable in rubber, was used, in order to force the allegedly lazy blacks to accustom themselves to the civilizing effects of labor. Initially, the concession companies were charged with collecting this tax because they had the personnel to do so. In an oft-quoted decree of

1903, the governor, hard pressed financially, warned his subordinates that their careers depended on the zeal with which they collected taxes.[65] One of them, in his turn, characerized the forced rubber production system in 1907:

> Too often that the black has been transformed into a serf, forced to collect rubber and compelled to transport it to the factories, where he receives payment, if at all, at the pleasure of the master. Murder, rape, robbery, torture by starvation, and beatings with truncheons are the means employed by both whites and black agents.[66]

In 1905 the French public learned of conditions in the Congo. France, like Germany, had its colonial scandal.[67] The government found itself obliged to dispatch an investigating commission under Brazza's leadership, but then both the administration and the companies did what they could to sabotage the commission's efforts. Brazza's report was never published, but the abuses leaked out and could not be whitewashed. Some reforms were undertaken after 1909. The Congo was divided into three autonomous colonies, Gabon, Moyen Congo, and Oubangui-Chari, with federative ties intended to strengthen the administration's hand. Better supervision of the companies to assure they met their obligations, suspension of their power to collect taxes, and, perhaps most important of all, two loans between 1909 and 1914 to provide the necessary infrastructure, were additional reforms.[68] More important than the actual reforms, however, was that rubber-gathering had proved unprofitable. The companies, a few of which had made high profits but more of which had gone under, thus gave up their concessions and were reorganized as the more usual sort of trading companies. Still, as late as 1927, André Gide in his *Voyage au Congo* was able to report on the rapacious economic methods used by the Compagnie Forestière Sangha-Oubangui.[69]

French Equatorial Africa remained the Cinderella of the French colonial empire into the interwar period. Financially, it barely kept its head above water, because, as Governor-General Antonetti noted in 1928, "our trade still largely depends on the gathering and sale of wild products."[70] After 1923 the export of okoumé wood from Gabon increased sharply,[71] but raised anew the question of labor. Cutting and transport were labor intensive and occurred within geographically limited areas. But European firms no longer depended merely upon timber cut by the Africans with great difficulty and dragged to a watercourse as they had before the war. They went over to large-scale cutting, though the use of machinery remained modest. Both the need for labor and its attrition rate were high, wages being low and sanitary conditions precarious. The areas hit by recruiting and migration lacked the manpower to cultivate foodstuffs, the birthrate fell, and entire villages went under.[72] A certain social stabilization and rise in individual African living standards came only with the cultivation of coffee and cocoa.[73] Gabon was the richest colony in the federation, but never got past the beginnings of development before World War II, and its stock of schools and hospitals was accordingly modest.[74]

As can be seen, the structural differences between British West Africa and the French African colonies were not all that great with the exception of the Congo, which initially closely resembled the Belgian Congo. With expansion into the hinterland and the establishment of an efficient administration, the "treaty economy" in which a few European traders exchanged European consumer goods for products the Africans collected, came to an end. African traders and middlemen had played a considerable role in this system, but not in the colonial economy which followed. The latter was characterized by encouragement of farming of specific export crops suited to the region of their growth. The result was a rapid rise in both exports and imports. The administration used loans to finance the infrastructure, meaning mainly railways and harbors and, later, roads. Cash crops were mainly the product of "native farming" rather than forced cultivation, which was a geographically limited phenomenon. Cultivation methods remained about the same. The African's cash income remained low, although he was not confronted with a cash economy and affected by the price fluctuations of the world market; the effects on the African social structure have been noted. At the same time Africans were forced out of commerce, their places being taken by European trading firms and Levantines. The interwar period saw considerable European private investment, but mainly in trade—and in a few plantations and lumbering firms.[75] Industrialization was neither encouraged nor did it occur. Even so trivial and obvious an exploitation of colonial raw materials as the shelling of peanuts and the production of peanut oil encountered resistance from metropolitan interests. After 1920 some oil mills were established in the port cities but they were constantly under fire from the Marseille and Bordeaux mills, which in 1939 succeeded in getting a quota on refined oil imported into France.[76] The Conférence Impériale of 1934 expressly rejected industrialization.[77] The French customs system differed greatly from the British by deliberately orienting trade toward metropolitan France by imposing high duties on outsiders. In practice the difference may not have been so great, because British West Africa trade was primarily with England.[78]

EVOLUÉS, ASSIMILATION, AND INTEGRATION

Although French West Africa was structurally very similar to British West Africa, development began later and was less intensive. This must always be kept in mind when considering the évolués and the inconsiderable degree to which demands for national liberation had been raised before 1939. The differences between administrative structures and political aims also count for a good deal. England early on opened the channels for the formulation of the political will, whereas France, working within its centralizing and bureaucratic tradition, was not ready to loosen its authoritarian rule and sought to prevent a politicization of its African colonies. England spoke of the coming of self-government, at any rate in "due time," but France followed a policy of administrative integration and cultural and political assimilation, the implications of which in the interwar period could be evaded by a vague ideology of "association."

Some schools were naturally founded in the trading towns of the nineteenth century. Faidherbe had made an interesting attempt with his "Ecole des Fils des Chefs" to reach beyond Europeans and mulattoes into the hinterland and to render the school a serviceable instrument of administrative penetration. Basically, however, the colonial educational system dates from the period after expansion, having been founded in 1903 and expanded in 1924.[79] The assimilatory aim of the school system was always emphasized. Whereas the English proceeded from the civilization that they found, teaching in the native languages and attempting to educate the coming leadership class of an autonomous if not necessarily independent state, the French, convinced of the superiority and universal applicability of French civilization, sought to make "Frenchmen" out of Africans, which would also have had the happy effect of tying the overseas area to the metropolis forever.[80] "What we want is for every child born under our flag, though remaining very much a man of his time and place, to be true Frenchman in language, spirit, and vocation."[81] Instruction in the French language, even in schools in the bush, thus assumed a primary importance, for, "when the natives express themselves in French, it will be easier for them to think in French." An anticlerical and republican France also forced the missions out and, in contrast to England, built a state school system early on. In the interwar period the economic value of the schools was emphasized, particularly in Sarraut's well-known circular of 1920.[82] On the other hand, serious efforts were made, despite the current impression, to adapt instructional materials at the primary level to local African conditions.[83] Governor-General Brévié attempted after 1931 to create an education for the "masses" directed to their agricultural needs which would serve to integrate the village schools into the modernization process. Unfortunately this effort, farsighted in itself, largely failed, having all too often achieved ends quite opposite of those sought.[84]

Educationally, one progressed from the *école du village* to the *école regionale* to the *école primaire supérieure* and from there either to the Ecole de Médicine in Dakar or the Ecole de Médicine Vétérinaire in Bamako to be educated as a medical auxiliary. Alternatively, one might attend the important Ecole William Ponty, founded in 1913, which trained teachers and administrative personnel. The school was somewhat comparable to the Achimota College in the Gold Coast. It proved especially important because a significant number of political leaders of the post-1945 period and the first premiers all attended it—Houphouet-Boigny, Modibo Keita, and Mamadou Dia, among others. Circles of friends reaching beyond territorial boundaries were formed there, and by 1940 some 1,550 Africans had graduated from it. University preparatory education remained restricted, however, the two lycées in St. Louis and Dakar being intended mainly for the French. Africans could attend, but the transition from African schools was difficult. In 1926 only two of the sixty students in the Dakar lycée were black,[85] and outside the Four Communes of Senegal there were no such schools. Attendance at French universities was not encouraged, and the African bourgeoisie, in contrast to that of British West Africa, was too poor to send its sons for an expensive education in the metropolis.[86] Léopold Sédar Senghor, after going to a missionary school in back country Siné, attended a seminary and then the lycée in Dakar. He won a scholarship in 1928 for the renowned Lycée Louis-le-Grand in Paris. In 1933, he became the first African agrégé and as such a lycée teacher. Amadou Lamine Gueye from St. Louis became in 1922 the first African to become a J.D.[87] Both could be regarded as the products of a successful policy of assimilation, although Senghor was already pondering his African origins in the 1930s and developing his conception of "Négritude." Later he sought to express his membership in two cultures with the aphorism, "assimilate, but do not be assimilated."[88]

Governor-General Jules G. Carde ordered, "teach the masses and separate out the elite"; and the administration continually emphasized how much importance it placed on education. What was achieved by 1940, however, was modest enough as table 10.2 indicates. The administration said finances and the difficulty of recruiting teachers were the grounds for this backwardness. The proceeds from both the budget and loans were used as elsewhere, however, for the infrastructure needed for export production, leaving only limited sums for education. The French were also much more logical than the English about the need for administrative cadres. They had no wish to create a group of déclassés, and accordingly no more candidates were accepted by the Ecole Primaire Supérieure et Professionelle than there were administrative slots available.[89] The number of students thus decreased during the depression, and no less a man than Henri Labouret noted in 1936 the "wise reduction in effectives."[90] In the interests of stabilizing its rule, the colonial power successfully contained the liberating effects of the schools by taking most of the évolués into the administration.

Table 10.2
Education in French West and Equatorial Africa, 1938

Area	Population (in thousands)	Students	Percentage of eligibles attend.	Schools		teachers in publ. inst.	
				pub.	pri.	cadre metro.	cadre local
West Af.	15,200	71,200	2.4	104	530	373	1,026
Equat. Af.	3,490	21,050	3	91	141	...	...
Cameroun	2,390	107,100	22	87	...	36	174
Togo	755	10,860	7	53	53	10	104

SOURCE: Autra, "Historique," 75.

A deliberate Africanization of the cadre did not, however, occur. There unfortunately are no detailed investigations of what happened, but one can probably assume that in comparison with British West Africa the amount of Africanization was slight. The number of Frenchmen living in the colonies was relatively large, and even in Africa Frenchmen filled lower-level administrative posts. Only French citizens could "exercise authority," and, until 1946, only they could attend the Ecole Coloniale in Paris. One could petition for citizenship rights, but only at the cost of giving up "personal status" and meeting numerous other conditions that were difficult for a young African to fulfil. Some West Indians, among them the legendary Félix Eboué, who in 1940 was to make possible the joining of French Equatorial Africa with General De Gaulle's Free France,[91] filled important offices in the interwar period and served as proof that the French did not engage in racial discrimination. Though that might startle a Briton, it ought not to conceal the fact that the rise of a native African was almost out of the question. Blaise Diagne's appointment as high commissioner for recruiting in black Africa during World War I was the exception that proves the rule. Educated Africans naturally obtained positions as secretaries, subaltern officials, teachers, teachers' aides, medical assistants, and agricultural advisors. As late as 1954 in French Equatorial Africa there were 88 Africans in a cadre of 1,327 middle-level officials, and in the economically less developed portions of the Sudan, the percentage was even smaller.[92] There was talk of liberalizing Africanization at the time of the Popular Front,[93] but serious efforts began only in the 1950s.

In Senegal alone was there the sort of political life which made it possible for Africans to express their criticisms of the colonial system, state their demands, and have some sort of voice in the administration. Even in Senegal this sort of political life existed only in a few towns and in the Four Communes. Integrated into the national territory in 1794 and again in 1848, the cities of St. Louis, Gorée, Dakar, and Rufisque enjoyed the status of *communes de plein exercice*, electing their own mayors, having a general council like the metropolitan départements, and after 1879 electing their own deputy to the parlement in Paris. Everyone born there was a French citizen and could therefore vote and without loss of personal status. The rather brisk political disputations were at first mostly between the fully assimilated Creole businessmen and the representatives of French trade houses, and between the latter and the governor.[94] In 1914, however, Blaise Diagne from Gorée, who had earlier worked in the customs administration abroad, succeeded in exploiting the tensions within the Creole oligarchy, organizing the évolués, and gaining the support of both the Lebou notables and the Mourides to become the first elected African deputy.[95] He successfully opposed efforts to restrict the rights of African citizens and in the discussion of military service obligations of 1915-1916 managed to nail such rights down for good.[96] After the war, however, he soon came to terms with both the traders from Bordeaux and the colonial administration. In 1931-1932 he became undersecretary of state for the colonies in the administration of Pierre Laval. Diagne not only often proclaimed his adherence to the ideal of assimilation, but as late as 1930 as representative of the French government sought in Geneva to justify forced labor.[97] Although much battered in the political wars and considered a traitor by the younger generation of Africans, he managed to retain his seat in parlement until his death in 1934. His successor was Galandou Diouf, who had first been one of his followers, then his opponent. In June 1935 Lamine Gueye organized the Parti Socialiste Sénégalais. It made a series of socio-political demands, criticised the existing press law, demanded that citizenship rights be extended to "subjects," and openly proclaimed its adherence to social and political assimilation.[98] In 1938 the still small party amalgamated with the Senegalese section of the SFIO.[99]

The Four Communes thus remained "equalitarian islands in an authoritarian sea."[100] The millions of Africans in the rest of French black Africa were and remained "subjects," subject in particular to the indigénat. Although the évolués attacked the indigénat as the classic symbol of colonial discrimination, its terms were loosened but little until after World War II.[101] Only a fortunate minority ever succeeded in obtaining French citizenship rights, and the administration did nothing to make them easier to get. In all of French West Africa only 2,000 subjects had become naturalized citizens by 1936. The provisions were recast at the time of the Popular Front, but remained so convoluted that they signified no effective liberalization. They certainly did not express the alleged will of the metropolis to push ahead with a citizenship policy in accord with the notion of a "*plus grande France*." The oft-used word "association" was ideally suited for sidestepping both an expansion of citizenship and of local representative bodies. It signified administrative petrification and depoliticization.[102]

Before World War I, the conseil général did make it possible to engage in political discussions and thus to challenge the authoritarian political position of the governor-general. Still, it was in no small measure the rise of Diagne that provided the impulse for replacing the conseil général with a conseil colonial. This change emphasized the unhappy separation of the Four Communes from the rest of Senegal but at the same time neutralized the citizen-elected representatives by bringing in appointed chiefs. The new council never achieved any significance. It met only a few days a year, received the governor's address, and discussed budget questions,[103] but was not permitted to discuss other political questions. The situation was worse in the other colonies in West and Equatorial Africa. In 1925, the subjects of Guinea, Dahomey, the Ivory Coast, and the Sudan received the right to elect representatives to the conseil d'administration, but the property qualification to vote was high and the representatives had no effective powers. These councils can in no way be compared with the legislative councils of British West Africa. Press control was also much more strictly exercised than in British colonies, with the result that virtually no opposition voices were to be heard outside Senegal. There was not even any opportunity for political activity at the local level, for even a city the size of Abidjan received commune de plein exercice status only in 1945. The formation of trade unions was not permitted until 1937, when the Popular Front government granted it to those of its subjects with a command of French.[104]

It is hardly surprising that the governors could speak of the complete calm which prevailed in French Africa. Today, however, we can no longer remain blind to acts of protest, even if they were in many cases more concerned with local grievances than with nationalist political aims. Recruiting in World War I led to disturbances and mass flight to neighboring British territories, and in 1923 there was a genuine revolt in Dahomey which had to be put down by force of arms.[105] Its cause was quarrels within the ruling house and tax increases just at the time that the postwar recession began to make itself felt.[106] In 1938 railway workers on the Dakar-Niger line struck. The penetration of Islam into West Africa (and notably to the Mourides, whose founder, Bamba, remained exiled) and the striking success of syncretist religious movements in the Ivory Coast and West Africa must be understood as a form of protest and a search for identity occasioned by the colonial situation. As soon as any tendency toward political action became visible, the administration moved to suppress it.[107] The évolués in Senegal and the other colonies gathered in countless friendly associations (*amicales*). There were associations of graduates of certain schools, sports clubs, reading groups, and mutual aid associations, some organized on a tribal basis. The administration tolerated them, even supported some, but also kept a close watch on them.[108] Their political attitudes are still rather hazy and were never clearly spelled out. Most were probably assimilationist in sentiment. The young évolués, drawn by the powerful attraction of French civilization, still heartily believed in their liberation within a greater association of French states. They wanted better education with study in France, liberalization of naturalization, more and better jobs in the administration, elimination of social discrimination, and expansion of local representative bodies. Except for Senegal things never reached the point of political party formation. The administration successfully blocked this with their policy of depoliticization, nor indeed was there either incentive or need to form parties so long as there were no elections and the road to political participation was blocked in both the colonies themselves and in parlement in Paris. When France finally cleared the way in 1945, the évolués who had grown up during the 1930s were also to form the now necessary parties overnight and to begin the mobilization of the rural masses. Still, it took the disappointment with the Fourth Republic's institutions after 1946 and the grant of self-government to the Gold Coast to move the évolués to demand national independence.

NOTES

1. In addition to the works cited above, see also Jean Suret-Canale, *Afrique Noire* (2 vols., Paris: Editions Sociales, 1964); John D. Hargreaves, *West Africa: The Former French States* Englewood Cliffs, N.J.: Prentice-Hall, 1967). See also the following from the more recent literature: Henri Brunschwig, in addition to *L'Avènement*, "French Exploration and Conquest in Tropical Africa from 1865 to 1898," in Gann and Duignan, *Colonialism*, I; John D. Hargreaves, in addition to *Prelude*, "West African States and the European Conquest," in Gann and Duignan, *Colonialism*, I; Alexander Sydney Kanya-Forstner, *The Conquest of the Western Sudan: A Study in French Military Imperialism* (London: Cambridge University Press): Colin W. Newbury and Alexander S. Kanya-Forstner, "French Policy and the Origins of the Scramble for West Africa," *JAH*, 10 (April 1969); B. Olatunji Oloruntimehin, "The West African Sudan and the Coming of the French," in Ajayi and Crowder, *History*, II.

See also the essays in *France and Britain in Africa*, in Crowder, *West African Resistance*, and in idem, *West Africa*, 69ff.

2. It has recently been shown how the owners of a Bordeaux firm began to develop, post-1851, a program of expansion in the direction of the Senegal River. They also had a part in the appointment of Faidherbe; Leland Conley Barrows, "The Merchants and General Faidherbe: Aspects of French Expansion in Senegal in the 1850s," *RFHOM*, 61: no. 223 (1974).

3. Newbury and Kanya-Forstner, "French Policy," 256.

4. See, for example, *La France dans l'Afrique Occidentale, 1879-1883: Sénégal et Niger: Texte* (Paris: Challemel aîné, 1884), 374, which speaks of thirty million living in the "arch" of the Niger alone.

5. Yves Person, "Samori and the Resistance to the French," in Rotberg and Mazrui, *Protest*; idem, *Samori, une Révolution Dyula* (2 vols., Dakar: I.F.A.N., 1968-70), an exhaustive account of its subject.

6. Brunschwig, "French Exploration," 137f.

7. Newbury and Kanya-Forstner, "French Policy," 266.

8. Vincent Monteil, "Lat Dior, Damel du Cayor, et l'Islamisation des Wolofs," *Archives de Sociologie des Réligions*, 16 (1963); Germaine Ganier, "Lat Dyor et le Chemin de Fer d'Arachide, 1876-1886," *Bulletin de l'IFAN*, 27 (1965).

9. Paul Atger, *La France en Côte d'Ivoire de 1843 à 1893: Cinquente Ans d'Hesitations Politiques et Commerciales* (Dakar: no pub., 1962).

10. Elliot Percival Skinner, *The Mossi of the Upper Volta: The Political Development of a Sudanese People* (Stanford: Stanford University Press, 1964), 142f.

11. Christolphe Wondji, "La Côte d'Ivoire Occidentale: Période de Pénétration Pacifique (1890-1908)," *RFHOM*, 50 (1963); Gabriel Louis Angoulvant, *La Pacification de la Côte d'Ivoire, 1908-1915: Methods et Résultats* (Paris: E. Larose, 1916); Werner Plüss, "Friedliche Durchringung oder militarische Unterwerfung? Die Etablierung der französischen Herrschaft in der Elfenbeinkuste bis 1914" (Dissertation, University of Zurich, 1975); and the case study of a specific region, Claude Meillassoux, *Anthropologie Economique des Gouro de Côte d'Ivoire: De l'Economie de Subsistance à l'Agriculture Commerciale* (Paris: Mouton, 1964), 48, 101, 292ff.

12. Angoulvant, *Pacification*, 57

13. Plüss, "Friedliche Durchdringung," 57. In an order to the governor of Senegal of 17 November 1917, Governor-General Joost van Vollenhoven instructed the former to seize the base of Casamance. He recommended procedures successfully employed on the Ivory Coast. Troops were to be stationed in the area in question, to assure regular payment of taxes and the building of roads by the natives. The latter thus had to be disarmed, and to do this it was necessary to "occasion the natives to evacuate their small isolated encampments and gather in villages, where they will henceforth reside." Should they refuse to move, their "encampments were to be systematically destroyed." Particular "hotbeds of revolt" were to be suppressed, the leaders were to be arrested and, though their followers were to be treated more leniently, "contributions in money or in kind" were to be exacted. Villages and crops were to be destroyed only in the most extreme circumstances, and even then tree crops were to be spared. "It is necessary that, security and order once assured, the populations which have been given unto us be set immediately to work developing the natural riches of the country"; ANSOM, Sénégal et Dépendences, VII, 78.

14. Robert Cornevin, *Histoire du Dahomey* (Paris: Berger-Levrault, 1962); idem, "Les Divers Episodes de la Lutte contre le Royaume d'Abomey (1887-1914)," *RFHOM*, 47 (1961). See also the section in Crowder, *West African Resistance*.

15. The most detailed account is in Brunschwig, *L'Evènement*, 133f.

16. In the language of the day: "As soon as we affirm our authority, or even secure its acknowledgement, we run up against the hostility of the inhabitants; some of the more powerful enter into open rebellion, while others oppose our acts with a weighty passive resistance and an ill-will that is difficult to overcome"; quoted from the report on the 1910 colonial budget in France, *Journel Officiel: Documents Parlementaires*, no. 2762 (1909).

17. Sieberg, *Eugène Etienne*, 38f.

18. Colin W. Newbury, "The Formation of the Government General of French West Africa," *JAH*, 1 (January 1960).

19. Robert Louis Delavignette in his revealing book, *Les Vrais Chefs de l'Empire* (Paris: Gallimard, 1939), emphasized their dash, initiative, and achievements, whereas the Marxist, Suret-Canale, *Afrique Noire*, II, 401ff. emphasized their brutal and tyrannical side.

20. Catherine Coquery-Vidrovitch, "French Colonization in Africa to 1920: Administration and Economic Development," in Gann and Duignan, *Colonialism*, I, 69. On the social origins of the French administrative cadre and the Ecole Coloniale, see William B. Cohen, *Rulers of Empire: The French Colonial Service in Africa* (Stanford: Hoover Institution Press, 1971). The number of officials was in fact significantly higher. Henri Brunschwig comes up with a total for West Africa of 1,085 officials, plus another 1,090 in the technical services (public works, post, and education) and for Equatorial Africa, 358 and 175 respectively; personal information from Brunschwig.

21. Hubert Deschamps, "Und nun, Lord Lugard?" and the rejoinder by Michael Crowder, "Indirekte Herrschaft—französisch und britisch," both in Albertini, *Moderne Kolonialgeschichte*. See also Crowder, *West Africa*, 174f.

22. Treated in detail in Skinner, *The Mossi*, 154ff.

23. ANSOM, AOF I/19, p. 14f.

24. Robert Louis Delavignette, *Service Africain* (3d ed., Paris: Gallimard, 1946), as quoted in Cornevin, *L'Afrique Noire*, 70. See also "Le Problème des Chefferies en Afrique Noire Française," *Notes et Etudes Documentaires*, 2508 (1959); translation in *West African Chiefs*.

25. *Afrique Française*, "Renseignements Coloniaux," 33 (1923), 431.

26. An administrator described the situation as follows: "This tax, light at first, has grown rapidly over the last few years. In 1906 it was 311,000 francs for the territory of Quagadougou, which had a population of 861,000 inhabitants. In 1907, the tax was raised to 360,000 francs; in 1909 to 555,000 francs; and in 1910 to 656,000 francs. Furthermore, from 1908 onward this tax was exacted with such rigor and on such short notice that it was exactly as though the amount had been tripled. Under the circumstances, the Mossi were compelled to resort to trade in order to obtain the French money they did not have, since the local currency is the cowry and the French administration does not wish to receive it.... To meet this difficult situation the Mossi now organize small caravans in the villages, and send the young men to Wanke to sell cattle, sheep, goats, asses, horses, and bolts of cotton. They bring back with them either French money or kola nuts"; Skinner, *The Mossi*, 157.

27. In 1933, for example, 28.7 percent of the budget of French West Africa came from direct taxes, against 18.5 percent in Nigeria and only 7 percent in the Gold Coast; Ajayi and Crowder, *History*, II, 522.

28. Georges Déherme, *L'Afrique Occidentale Française: Action Politique, Action Economique, Action Sociale* (Paris: Bloud et cie, 1908), 56.

29. Ibid., 57-58. For a specific example see Meillassoux, *Anthropologie Economique*, 295f.

30. See, for example the governor-general's circular in *Afrique Française*, 9 (1899), 299. See also, among others, Henri Labouret, "Main d'Oeuvre dans l'Ouest Africain," *Afrique Française* 40 (1930).

31. Robert Delavignette noted in *Service Africain*; "There rules are violated by abusive prolongation of service beyond ten days, by the employment of women and children, and by inclusion of work places which are not five kilometers but five days' march distance and where the workers are not fed"; quoted in Cornevin, *L'Afrique Noire*, 88.

32. Gilles Sautter, "Notes sur la Construction du Chemin de Fer Congo-Océan (1921-1934)," *Cahiers d'Etudes Africains*, 7 no. 26, (1967). See also the journalistic account, Albert Londres, *Terre d'Ebène (la Traite des Noirs)*, (Paris: A. Michel, 1929). For the Ivory Coast, see Meillassoux, *Anthropologie Economique*, 301f.

33. For example: At the end of 1916 and again early in 1917, the inhabitants of the east coast of the Ivory Coast complained to the governor that they had had to work for three months on

the road from Bassam to Azuretti, and during the peak of the fishing season. The native police had beaten the less industrious workers "with their weighted canes," dragged people off, thrown chiefs in jail and "forced them to engage in humiliating work in the streets of Bassam." Yet *préstations* were not to be exacted during the harvest season, were not to exceed twelve days, and were, moreover, to be used only to maintain existing roads, not to build new ones. Finally, "we have no school in our village and none of our children knows how to read." Because the colored deputy from the West Indies, Candace, intervened, an inspector was instructed to investigate the matter. The latter confirmed that road construction had indeed gone on for three months, but that not everyone had been engaged in it. It was anyhow a "track" rather than a "road," and it served the natives' needs. It was the chief's fault that old persons had been supplied, because he was the one who designated those who had to serve. Beatings had been administered and the chiefs had in fact been jailed, but only because they had refused to furnish *préstation* labor. The argument about the schools, moreover, did not hold water, because the inhabitants (who were Fantis) sent their children to the Gold Coast to learn English: ANSOM, Côte d'Ivoire, "Affaires Politiques," Carton 566, 2.

34. Quoted in Cornevin, *L'Afrique Noire*, 70. On French discussions of the matter, see also Albertini, *Decolonization*, 338f.

35. Governor-General Jean Baptiste Chaudié, speaking before the St. Louis Chamber of Commerce on 13 January 1896; *Afrique Française*, 6 (1896), 84; and again, at the opening of the Senegal Conseil Général, ibid., 8 (1898), 55.

36. There is no economic history of French Africa. Important is Hopkins, *Economic History*; Heiko Körner, *Kolonialpolitik und Wirtschaftsentwicklung: Das Beispiel Franzosisch Westafrikas* (Stuttgart: G. Fischer, 1965); Samir Amin, *L'Afrique de l'Ouest Bloquée: L'Economie Politique de la Colonisation, 1880-1970* (Paris: Editions de Minuit, 1970), which last, however, has but little on the period before 1945; Suret-Canale, *Afrique Noire*, I; Jean Jacques Poquin, *Les Rélations Economiques Exterieures des Pays d'Afrique Noire de l'Union Française, 1925-1955* (Paris: A. Colin, 1957).

37. Colin W. Newbury, "Trade and Authority in West Africa from 1850 to 1880," in Gann and Duignan, *Colonialism*, I, 82.

38. On the Levantines, see Crowder, *West Africa*, 293f.; R.B. Winder, "The Lebanese in West Africa," *CSSH*, 4 (July 1961-62); Rita Cruise O'Brien, "Lebanese Entrepreneurs in Senegal: Economic Integration and the Politics of Protection," *Cahiers d'Etudes Africains*, 15: no. 57 (1975).

39. Samir Amin, "La Politique Française à l'Egard de la Bourgeoise Commerçante Sénégalaise (1882-1960)," in *The Development of Indigenous Trade and Markets in West Africa: Studies Presented and Discussed at the Tenth International African Seminar at Fourah Bay College, Freetown, December 1969*, ed. Claude Meillassoux (London: Oxford University Press, 1971), 366; idem, *Le Monde des Affaires Sénégalaise* (Paris: Ed. de Minuit, 1969), 11f.

40. Déherme, *L'Afrique Occidentale*, 155.

41. See Paul Pelissier's great work, *Les Paysans du Sénégal: Les Civisations Agraires du Cayor à la Casamance* (Saint Yrieix, Haute Vienne: Impr. Fabrègue, 1966); idem, "L'Arachide au Sénégal," *COM*, 5 (July-September 1951). See also Joseph Fouquet, "La Traite des Arachides," *Etudes Sénégalaises*, 10:no. 8 (1958); Yves Pehaut, "L'Arachide au Sénégal," ibid., 13 (1961); Jean Suret-Canale, "Quelques Aspects de la Géographie Agraire au Sénégal," *COM*, 1 (October-December 1948); Robert Louis Delavignette, *Les Paysans Noirs: Récit Soudanaise en Douze Mois* (Ed. nouv., Paris: Stock, 1946).

42. A circular of 5 March 1913 from the governor-general stated: "If you want to obtain more work from the cultivator and new and better crops, some of which pay off only in the long term, it is necessary to guarantee him his rights to the land he works and to fix them in a clear and unequivocal fashion; it is necessary to assure him long-term security and the certitude that he will not be dispossessed of his land and that he can plant, cultivate, and harvest it in absolute tranquility; and that he and his family will profit from the fruits of his labor," quoted in Fouquet, "La Traite," 201.

43. *Quinzaine Colonial*, 25 May 1914, 367, was already speaking of a "disquieting retrogression."

44. Dumont, *Paysanneries aux Abois*, 187. In 1950, approximately 1.2 million hectares, or an eighth of the arable, was in peanuts, Poquin, *Rélations Economiques*, 44.

45. Henri Cosnier, *L'Ouest Africain Français: Ses Ressources Agricoles, son Organisation Economique* (Paris: E. Larose, 1921), xx. In 1928, only 2 percent of the budget was devoted to agriculture; Körner, *Kolonialpolitik*, 62.

46. Hopkins, *Economic History*, 221. Vincent Monteil, "Une Confrérie Musulmane: Les Mourides du Sénégal," in *Esquisses Sénégalaises* (Dakar: I.F.A.N., 1966).

47. On their origins in Sine-Saloum, see Martin A. Klein, *Islam and Imperialism in Senegal: Sine-Saloum, 1847-1914* (Stanford: Stanford University Press, 1968), 181. From the period: Georges Péter, *L'Effort Française au Sénégal* (Paris: E. de Boccard, 1933), 95. Critical is Suret-Canale, *Afrique Noire*, II, 299f.

48. "It is necessary to associate the natives in the administration of their society. In this respect this country is very backward, as even the chiefs often are afraid to say anything"; Report, 28 February 1939, p. 41, from the administrator, Louveau, on the situation in the upper Ivory Coast, in ANSOM.

49. Poquin, *Rélations Economiques*, 102, 104, gives a breakdown in percentages of the export price for peanuts in 1954 to 1956:

Producer	64.0
Taxes	15.5
Transport	3.2 (for Kaolack; for Kayes 12 Percent)
Services	6.2
Spoilage	.4
Profits and financing costs	10.6

50. Prices for peanuts in West Africa, with 1938 = 100.

1925	107
1927	144
1929	129
1930	188
1931	84
1933	46
1935	75
1937	76

Source: ibid., 261.

51. Revealing is Henri Labouret, "La Grande Détresse de l'Arachide," *Afrique Française*,42 (December 1932), 731f. "In my view all administrators and officials ought to make the rounds of the villages before the distribution of the seed, checking over the sowings and offering words of encouragement to those willing to venture the effort"; Governor of Senegal, 27 May 1933, at the opening of the Conseil Générale, ibid., 8.

52. *Quinzaine Coloniale*, 25 January 1934, and again on 10 July 1935: In the Union Colonial, a ministerial decree was read which stated: "Because of the persistence of obsolete methods in the peanut trade, the payment of a host of middlemen weighs heavily on the product." This decree was absurd; "the eyes of the public authorities ought to be opened to the dangers in store for the natives and in the operations of the cooperatives"; ibid., 413.

53. On Guinea, see Jean Suret-Canale, "La Guinée dans le Système Colonial," *Présence Africaine* (1959-1960). Georges Déherme quotes from a report stating that: "When one talks to the Sousous about all the crops which they could cultivate without any trouble. . . they answer

that they are off to hunt rubber in the Upper Guinea to sell in Conacry; they have no time for crops"; *L'Afrique Occidentale*, 144.

54. Suret-Canale, "La Guinée," 354f.

55. Excellent is A. Köbben, "Le Planteur Noir," *Etudes Eburnéennes*, 5 (1956). In addition, see Hubert Tréchou, "Les Plantations Europeénnes en Côte d'Ivoire," *COM*, 8 (1955). On the Ivory Coast in general see F. J. Amon d'Aby, *La Côte d'Ivoire dans la Cité Africaine* (Paris: Larose, 1951).

56. *Revue Indigène*, 9 (February 1914), 117.

57. Quoted in Köbben, "Le Planteur Noir," 18.

58. In 1939 colons farmed only 8,000 out of 180,000 hectares in cocoa. Africans planted about 55,000 hectares in coffee, the 218 European planters some 19,000; Suret-Canale, *Afrique Noir*, II, 283f.

59. Raymond Lefèvre, "Cacao et Café, Cultures 'Révolutionnaires'," *La Revue de Géographie Humaine at d'Ethnologie*, 1 (October 1948-October 1949), 55. See also Bohumil Holas, *Changement Sociaux en Côte d'Ivoire* (Paris: Presses Universitaires de France, 1961).

60. A. Köbben, "L'Héritage chez les Agni: L'Influence de l'Economie de Profit," *Africa*, 24 (October 1954).

61. A report from the Inspection du Travail gives the number of 80,000 for 1938 and attributes it to the reasons named; see material cited n. 48 above.

62. Among others, Ruth Schachter Morgenthau, *Political Parties in French-Speaking West Africa* (Oxford: Clarendon Press, 1964), 170; Amon d'Aby, *Côte d'Ivoire*, 112f.

63. Catherine Coquery-Vidrovitch, *Le Congo au Temps des Grandes Compagnies Concessionnaires, 1898-1930* (Paris: Mouton, 1972); Samir Amin and Catherine Coquery-Vidrovitch, *Histoire Economique du Congo, 1880-1968: Du Congo Français a l'Union Douanière et Economique d'Afrique Centrale* (Dakar: IFAN, 1969); Catherine Coquery-Vidrovitch, "L'Echec d'une Tentative Economique: L'Impôt de Capitation au Service des Compagnies Concessionnaires du Congo Français (1900-1909)," *Cahiers d'Etudes Africains*, 8, Cahier 29 (1968).

64. In 1905 there were only a hundred officials in the Middle Congo, and fifty-four of these were in Brazzaville.

65. Coquery-Vidrovitch, *Le Congo*, 125. This decree was published in *Humanité* on 27 September 1903.

66. Quoted in *Revue d'Histoire des Colonies*, 40 (1953), 424. See also *Revue Indigène*, 3 (February 1908).

67. Jules François Santoyant, *L'Affaire du Congo 1905* (Paris: Epi, 1905, 1960); Félicien Challaye, "Le Congo Français," *Cahiers de la Quinzaine* (1906).

68. As late as 1911 Maurice Violette wrote in the "Rapport" on the colonial budget for 1912: "No one pays any attention any more to irregularities in the assessment and collection of native taxes. Arbitrariness prevails." In Gabon the chiefs never got the 5 percent taxes due them. King Denis's son, to whom the French had given Gabon, fled with his family when the Europeans were announced. The companies still counted on the help of the administration to force the natives to deliver rubber; *Journel Officièl, Documents Parlementaires*, 1911, Annex 1251, sp. 1732f.

69. On this, see Coquery-Vidrovitch, *Le Congo*, 184f.

70. Quoted in *Quinzaine Coloniale*, 10 January 1929, p. 6. In 1925 in Chad, there were only two veterinarians for an estimated million cattle; Jacques Boisson, *L'Histoire du Chad et de Fort Archambault: Documents, Renseignements, Commentaires Pris, Vécus et Conçus de 1940 à 1966* (Paris: Editions du Scorpion, 1966), 169.

71. The tonnage of exports from 1898 to 1937 was as follows:

1898	700
1913	134,200
1930	381,800
1937	407,000

72. A typical demand from a lumber company in the Union Coloniale was: "Could not the governor general be asked to intervene to assure that the number of workers placed at the enterprises' disposal correspond as closely as possible to their needs?" *Quinzaine Coloniale*, 10 January 1931, p. 25.

73. Gilles Sautter, "Les Paysans Noirs du Gabon Septentrional," *COM*, 4 (April-June 1951). Up to 1930 the population had declined and around 1925 roughly one third of the adults were engaged in lumbering; idem, *De l'Atlantique au Fleuve Congo: Une Géographie du Sous-peuplement: Republique du Congo, République Gabonaise* (2 vols., Paris, The Hague: Mouton, 1966) II, 853f.

74. Raymond Susset, *La Vérité sur le Cameroun et l' Afrique Equatoriale Française* (Paris: Editions de la Nouvelle Revue Critique, 1936), 161f.

75. A 1943 inquest revealed that of frs. 1,891 million, 737 million went for trade, 344 for plantations, and 237 for forests; Jean Dresch, "Recherches sur les Investissements dans l'Union Française Outre-mer," *Bulletin de l'Association Géographique Française*, 231-232 (January 1953); Poquin, *Rélations Economiques*, 189.

76. Jean Suret-Canale, "L'Industrie des Oléagineux en AOF," *COM*, 3 (1950); Poquin, *Rélations Economiques*, 45; Körner, *Kolonialpolitik*, 59.

77. Körner, *Kolonialpolitik*, 59.

78. In 1930 the metropolitan share of French West Africa's foreign trade was roughly 50 percent, whereas British West Africa drew about 75 percent of its imports from England. The latter took about half of West African exports; Hopkins, *Economic History*, 174; Poquin, *Rélations Economiques*, 163. After 1932 the metropolitan share increased in both areas.

79. Among others, Ray Autra, "Historique de l'Enseignement en AOF," *Présence Africaine* (February-March, 1956). From the period: Péter, *L'Effort Français*. The important thesis, Denise Bouche, "L'Enseignement dans les Territoires Française de l'Afrique Occidentale: Mission Civilisatrice ou Formation d'une Elite?" (2 vols., Dissertation, University of Lille, 1975), was not available to me.

80. See also the evidence in Albertini, *Decolonization*, 344f.

81. Quoted in Denise Bouche, "Autrefois, notre Pays s'Appelait la Gaule...Remarques sur l'Adaptation de l'Enseignement au Sénégal de 1817 à 1960," *Cahiers d'Etudes Africains*, 8, "Cahiers" (1968), 111.

82. "The fundamental duty to teach our subjects and native protégés agrees moreover, with our most basic economic, administrative, military, and political interests. The first effect of instruction is to increase considerably the value of colonial production, by multiplying in the throng of colonial workers the qualities of intelligence and the number of capacities"; *Afrique Française*; "Renseignements Coloniaux," 1920/12, 235.

83. Bouche, "Autrefois," 111.

84. *Afrique Française*, 1926/1, 20.

85. Autra, "Historique," 72.

86. In the report for the colonial budget of 1927 it was possible to assert: "We have not hesitated to permit our natives to obtain the same degrees as the French. We have established, wherever it was possible to do so, higher education. One can take a law degree at Dakar"; *Journal Officiel, Documents Parliamentaires*, 1926, sp. 1659.

87. Lamine Gueye, *Itineraire Africain* (Paris: Présence Africain, 1966).

88. Jacques Louis Hymans, *Léopold Sédar Senghor: An Intellectual Biography* (Edinburgh: Edinburgh University Press, 1971).

89. "It is, however, necessary to note the present mood among the youth being instructed in our schools. Believing themselves called upon to play a great role with the masses, they have made themselves into propagandists and acidulous critics of the administration. Although this movement is for the moment a limited one, one ought have no doubt that a few faithless intellectuals, if sufficiently stirred up, can subvert the sound bulk of the population"; "Rapport Annuel," Dakar, in Archives Nationales, Micro 1757/3, p. 2. Hereafter cited AN/Micro. (I have

taken some manuscript references from W. J. Jurt's 1972 Lizenz thesis about political life in Senegal from 1930 to 1940.)

90. *Afrique Française*, 26 (February 1936), 156, with statistics.

91. Brian Weinstein, *Eboué* (New York: Oxford University Press, 1972).

92. Virginia M. Thompson and Richard Adloff, *The Emerging States: French Equatorial Africa* (Stanford: Stanford University Press, 1960), 68.

93. From a speech of Governor General Jules de Coppet before the Conseil de Gouvernement: "We ought to take decisive steps to conciliate native university graduates and thus make them supporters of our administration. How many times, gentlemen, has the voice of alarm not been raised about this native intellectual proletariat, which arises through the lack of adequate opportunities, making it discontented, and, also, our worst enemy..."; *Afrique Française*, 28 (February 1938), 22.

94. Francine N'Diaye, "La Colonie du Sénégal au Temps de Brière de l'Isle, (1879-1881)," *Bulletin IFAN*, B/2 (1968), and H.O. Idowu, "Assimilation in 19th Century Senegal," ibid.

95. G. Wesley Johnson, "The Ascendency of Blaise Diagne and the Beginning of African Politics in Senegal," *Africa*, 36 (July 1936); idem, *The Emergence of Black Politics in Senegal: The Struggle for Power in the Four Communes, 1900-1920* (Stanford: Stanford University Press, 1971); and his essay in Ajayi and Crowder, *History*, II.

96. "The natives of the four communes de plein exercise of Sénégal and their descendants are and remain French citizens, subject to the military obligations foreseen in the law of 19 October 1915"; Law promulgated in September 1916.

97. Albertini, *Decolonization*, 288.

98. "1. We have no foreign policy. Our lot is tied to that of France; its foreign policy is our own.... That having been stated, we can see that our political activity ought to be confined to domestic matters. We participate in a great association, the French Empire. In this association, our charter is enscribed: a Senegal which votes has the rights of a metropolitan department"; *L'AOF*, no. 1895, 26 June 1935.

99. Ibid., no. 2,000, June 1938. On the parties, see also Morgenthau, *Political Parties*, 130f.

100. Quoted in Ansprenger, *Politik*, 45.

101. In the Cercle Bas-Sénégal, in the year 1935 alone, some 928 punishments were imposed, most for tax derelictions; AN Micro 1766/10, Bas-Sénégal, "Rapport Annuel" (1935), 8. In the 1935 report it was stated: "Despite the generally favorable mood of the population, the *Indigènat* remains nonetheless an indispensible institution"; ibid., 1755/5.

102. For example: "Our aim is not to make the native a metropolitan Frenchman but rather a French colonial and we ought to enable him, not to participate in the government of France, but to collaborate in the administration of his own country"; *Journal Officiel, Documents Parlementaires*, 1926, sp. 1,660.

103. G. Wesley Johnson, in Ajayi and Crowder, *History*, II, 550, is of another opinion.

104. Crowder has for the first time exploited archival material Ajayi and Crowder, *History*, ch. 13.

105. Virginia M. Thompson and Richard Adloff, *French West Africa* (Stanford: Stanford University Press, 1957), 557.

106. J. A. Ballard, "Les Incidents de 1923 à Porto Novo: La Politique à L'Epoque Coloniale," *Etudes Dahoméennes*, 5 (1966).

107. Georges Balandier, "Messianisme et Nationalisme en Afrique Noire," *Cahiers Internationaux de Sociologie*, 14 (1953). Thompson and Adloff, *French Equatorial Africa*, 308f.; Bohumil Holas, *Le Séparatisme Religieux en Afrique Noire: L'Example de la Côte d'Ivoire* (Paris: Presses Universitaires de France, 1965).

108. Immanuel Maurice Wallerstein, *The Road to Independence: Ghana and the Ivory Coast* (Paris: Mouton, 1964); James Smoot Coleman and Carl Gustav Rosberg (eds.), *Political Parties and National Integration in Tropical Africa* (Berkeley: University of California Press, 1964); Morgenthau, *Political Parties*, 17.

11

THE BELGIAN CONGO

In the scramble for Africa, a lion's share went to a country that had become an independent state only in 1830, had not participated in ancien régime colonialism, and had established in neither Asia nor Africa the sort of coastal factories that tempt men to move inland. The country was Belgium, though not so much Belgium as a state, but as an individual Belgian, King Leopold II.[1] Leopold was one of a very few European statesmen who, having dreamed of empire from the days of his youth, had consistently ordered his political activities toward acquiring an overseas empire.[2] Leopold is perhaps best compared with Cecil Rhodes. His aim was fixed even as crown prince: Belgium was to become a colonial power; overseas territories were to be won as sources of raw materials for his densely populated European state and as a market for its goods; and they were to be a direct source of wealth, such as Indonesia was for the Netherlands in the mid-nineteenth century. Initially, his interest was in Asia—Sarawak, the Philippines, China—and shifted to Africa only after 1875. A year later, 1876, Leopold founded the International Africa Society in Brussels, nominally as a philanthropic and scholarly institution, but one which he well understood how to bend to his aims. In 1878 he got in touch with Henry Morton Stanley, who a few months earlier had with his sensational expedition established that the east African lakes fed the Congo and had hacked his way to the mouth of the Congo. A Committee for Upper Congo Studies was created as the financial underpinning for a great colonial trading company for the Congo territory. At the behest of Leopold, in 1879 Stanley concluded a multitude of treaties with the African chiefs living below the Stanley pools—the great Congo rapids—and established trade stations. The idea was not to establish territorial rule but a trade monopoly, which was to follow the construction of a railway to open up the interior. Stanley was also ordered to "purchase all the ivory that can be found in the Congo."

Jean Stengers has shown that Brazza's thrust into the Congo and the ratification of the Makoko treaty by the French parlement in 1881 were what led Leopold to abandon his original, purely commercial aims in favor of territorial aims and the attributes of sovereignty that went with them. His new policy was, in other words, a counterthrust against the French.[3] The first talk of a new state surfaced in January 1884. To win over England, who had responded to the Makoko treaty with negotiations with Portugal (over the latter's claims to the mouth of the Congo River), Leopold gave up his claims to monopoly and promised free trade without customs and other charges. Navigating skillfully on the seas of high policy, he succeeded in first mollifying the French and then in bringing Bismarck around. The result was that during the Berlin Congo Conference of 1884-1885 the Great Powers recognized the state whose frontiers Leopold had outlined so generously on the map.

Thus was a structure created which was unique and at the same time characteristic of the imperialist phase of European political development. A territory eighty times the size of Belgium was marked out on the map and recognized as an independent state, without even protectorate treaties with the African rulers to give it any sort of formal basis. The sovereign remained, nominally, the International Africa Society, but everyone knew that only the king counted. He claimed all legislative and executive power unto himself and, on top of that, was also the "owner" of the Congo. He accordingly set about exploiting his "estate" economically. Belgium qua state was not involved. Parlement had merely given its assent to Leopold acting as ruler of the Congo state. But the Congo's administrative seat was Brussels and the administration, the army, and even the missions recruited mainly Belgians. The patriotic king's profits thus accrued to Belgium.

In the beginning, of course, profits were hardly to be expected. Nothing was known of the potential wealth of the Congo. At the mouth of the Congo, a few traders bartered a modest amount of goods. The Upper Congo trade was in the hands of Arab traders, with the most famous being the uniquely fascinating Tippo Tip, who had accompanied and assisted Stanley in 1877 and then attempted to use Leopold for his own purposes. The Arabs transported ivory and slaves to the east coast. The king had to invest his private fortune and might well have gone bankrupt, had his gambler's luck not saved him: the Congo supplied rubber, and European demand for rubber rose rapidly. Rubber-gathering became the basis for Leopold's highly personal system of colonial exploitation. In outline it was very similar to that of French Equatorial Africa, but it was employed with singular relentlessness.

The system by which the land question was regulated was also unique. As in other colonies, all supposedly uninhabited land was declared state property in 1885. After 1892 state land was again divided into private (meaning royal) domain and into land to be apportioned to concessionaire corporations. The king managed the private domain directly—something else for which there was then no precedent—and excluded all private traders. Income from the rubber and ivory trades went directly into the Congo treasury or the king's. But the natives had to be forced to deliver, as the money economy was not yet established and the prices paid were not much of an inducement. Compulsion was at first open but then became covert with its transformation into a tax of forty hours of work a month. Encouraged to deliver as much rubber as possible and involved financially themselves, officials were given a free hand to make exorbitant demands. Rubber was often located several days' march distant, and "sentinels" were stationed in the villages to assure that the rubber came in. The most brutal sort of compulsion was used. Hostages were taken, natives were beaten with clubs, and in hard cases the motley Congo army (later Force Publique) was called in. It did not stick at murder and brought back masses of severed appendages—ears and the like—to prove it had done its duty. When whites or rubber collectors were announced in the villages, the population fled into the bush. That was usually the signal for truly drastic punishment, the memory of which is said to be green even today.[4]

Conditions in the concession company areas were even worse. In addition to rights of exploitation the companies also had the right to collect taxes and to exact forced labor. The Congo Free State participated in the work and collected dividends accordingly.[5] Even the official investigating commission of 1905 had to concede: "It is hardly disputed that in the various posts of the ABIR [Anglo-Belgian Rubber Company] [that] we have visited female hostages are imprisoned, chiefs are subjected to servile work and humiliations are inflicted upon them, rebels are clubbed into submission, and brutalities by blacks placed in charge of detainees are the general rule."[6] The Belgian historian Stengers speaks of a "veritable hell on earth."[7] The entire area along the rivers not surprisingly became depopulated.

Forced labor was used for so-called public purposes and made legal, as was to be expected since other colonial powers had also been unable to make do without it. Porterage was the main occasion for it. To traverse the enormous distances through the Congo jungles to inaccessible areas required thousands of porters, who provided the heartening picture of undernourished columns collapsing from the weight of their burdens. Forced labor was also made available for railway construction. The lines were urgently needed to span the rapids separating the navigable upper Congo from the lower, as Stanley had early foreseen. Here Leopold had to draw upon private capital for fiscal reasons. A Belgian syndicate established the Compagnie du Chemin de Fer du Congo, which built the 388 kilometers from Matadi to Léopoldville between 1890 and 1898. Labor had to be recruited from as far away as Senegal and the Gold Coast. Since the required capital was enormous and the expected profits small, land concessions along the railway were given either to the railway itself or to other companies owned by the syndicate financiers. The intent was for these uncapitalized enterprises to raise money by selling off land to smaller corporations, plantation companies, and planters. Several million hectares were handed out in this way.

The same was true of mining in Katanga. Gold finds were announced in the eastern provinces, whose borders had not even been firmly established at the Berlin Congo Conference. About 1890 not only Belgian, but also British-South

African expeditions coming from the east, pushed into the general area. The Belgian Compagnie du Katanga, which in 1891 had received a third of the king's private domain plus mining rights, was able to establish itself in the territory of King Msiri, whom one of the company's officers murdered. Shortly thereafter, gold deposits were announced in South Katanga and in 1892 copper as well. In order to assure his influence, the king constituted the Special Katanga Committee (two-thirds of whose members represented the state and one-third the Compagnie du Katanga), which was granted mining rights for, and the political administration of, the entire Katanga province. The British were squared with a compromise which granted the Tanganyika Concessions Company a prospecting area of some fifteen million hectares, though the king himself was compensated by receiving forty thousand shares in the company. Finally, in 1906, the Union Minière du Haut-Katanga was founded, with the state participating in the guise of the special committee with a majority of shares. Otherwise the Union's finances were controlled by the Société Générale, which also named the directors. At the same time, the Compagnie du Chemin de Fer du Bas-Congo au Katanga (or BCK) and the Forminière were founded to exploit the diamond reserves of the provinces of Kasai. The Forminière was backed by the state, the Foundation de la Couronne, American copper firms, and Belgian finance syndicates, but both it and the railway were controlled by the Société Générale.

The financial situation of the Congo, as has been said, was shaky in the early years. Belgium had to step in with loans in 1890 and 1895 to stave off bankruptcy. The export of rubber, however, rose from a few hundred tons in 1890 to 1,300 tons in 1896 and 6,000 tons in 1901. In the latter year, the private domain provided incomes of eighteen million francs and thus a revenue surplus, which was not reinvested, nor used to expand the administration, nor employed in the service of the natives, but flowed instead into the Fondation de la Couronne, which built parks, swimming pools, and similar amenities in Belgium. When dissolved in 1908, the foundation transferred sixty million francs to the treasury.[8] It was a particularly blatant example of colonial exploitation for the benefit of the mother country.

Critics of the Congo Free State and native mistreatment in the collection of rubber appeared early on. As Stengers has shown, they initially disturbed the king, who for a time began to doubt the value of his work.[9] Later, however, he reacted defensively, believing himself unjustifiably attacked, particularly since the English were his most persistent critics. The Aborigines' Rights Protection Society stepped in, the matter was debated in the commons, and, in 1903, the British government asked its consul in the Congo, Roger Casement, to report. His report, when publicized, led to the foundation of the Congo Reform Association, which under the leadership of Edward Morel unleashed a regular campaign against the Congo Free State and the king.[10] It could with some justification be alleged that the England of the Boer atrocities was hypocritical in acting as the protector of Africans, and that English firms supported the campaign because Leopold's monopoly practices ran counter to their interests. An international investigating commission of 1904-1905, however, largely confirmed Casement's report. It contributed importantly to the Belgian parlement's agreeing, 90 to 48, after protracted debates, to the *Charte Coloniale* and the takeover of Leopold's Congo by the Belgian state.

Belgium took over the Congo without enthusiasm. The *Charte Coloniale* made it possible to place it under parliamentary control and to provide the administrative autonomy also required. Executive power remained formally in the king's hands, but his acts now had to be countersigned by a minister, and in fact the colonial minister now ran things. The Congo was declared to be national territory, but subject to legislation by decree. The governor-general could issue ordinances, but these had to be confirmed by decree within six months. The budget had to be presented to parlement, as did state-guaranteed colonial loans. The more important decrees had to go before a colonial council. These arrangements rather resembled France's and were centralist in character, though without later integration and assimilation being anticipated. The Belgian style was strictly pragmatic, and they thought it possible to avoid a discussion of future prospects even after World War II.[11] No representative body was ever established in the Congo, and the Congo sent no representatives to the Belgian parlement. Africans and Belgians were equal in having no political rights, a sort of depoliticization that naturally failed to prevent the companies in particular from bringing influence effectively to bear in both Léopoldville and Brussels. They had in any event largely escaped administrative control.

The native administration was modelled rather along English lines.[12] The size of the area and the lack of a trained administrative cadre made it seem logical to depend on the chiefs and formally establish indirect rule. There were few African kingdoms of any stability and size, however. Some were eliminated during the expansion phase, and the exploitive machinery of the Congo Free State had transformed the chiefs into followers of orders, with those who were difficult being arbitrarily replaced. In 1906 a decree confirmed the intent to acknowledge traditional authorities, counting in particular on the chiefs, who were given salaries and judicial powers. In practice a multiplicity of chiefships and underchiefships of a somewhat artificial character developed, which only revealed the disintegration of traditional society. In 1917 there were some 6,095 chiefdoms in a population of about six million. Some comprised only a few hundred natives. Clans were recognized at the cost of larger tribal units, and all too often straw men were appointed as chiefs. After World War I an attempt was made to subdue this anarchy by combining the smaller chiefships into *secteurs*, with several chiefs forming a council presided over by the sector chief.[13] Inaugurated by Colonial Minister Louis Franck, this policy was enshrined in 1926 in the Native Tribunal Decree (*Décret des Tribunaux indigènes*) and in 1933 was amplified by another creating native districts (*circonscriptions indigènes*). In 1938 there were thirty sectors and 1,212 chiefships. These efforts can be compared with British efforts to introduce Indirect Rule into southeastern Nigeria, and the results were equally ambiguous. Like the native councils with their warrant chiefs, the sectors were largely artificial structures and their chiefs lacked any traditional roots, often being évolués who served the administration as executive agents. The chiefs received their own revenues, mainly court fees, and functioned as the local administration. The councils never acquired any importance, and the abuses of the sector chiefs both undermined their subordinates, the genuine chiefs, and compromised the Belgian administration.[14] The latter was more tightly knit than the British and had a heavier hand. Forced labor, forced cultivation, and the forced supply of workers for the mines made Belgian indirect rule appear a highly dubious sort of a doctrine in any case, as Governor Pierre Ryckmans so strikingly revealed in his *La Politique Coloniale* in 1934:

> A mediocre chief is better than no chief at all. The native chiefs are such delicate instruments to manage, and they are so fickle and so devious. But they are irreplaceable nonetheless. To act upon the masss, we have to go through them. Despite all our strength, they are still stronger. They have the authority of tradition, all the weight of legitimacy. But often their submission to the invader has compromised their prestige, and the sort of dramatic actions needed to reestablish it we condemn as barbaric. We require them to respect the rights of those they administer, but in redressing the injustices they create, we sap their power. And it is these very chiefs whom we have weakened that we ask to provide more and more active support—their people regard their complicity as more and more criminal—for collecting the head tax, for recruiting workers and soldiers, for introducing suspicious novelties, and for laying waste ancient customs. Their role is an ungrateful one, rendered the more so because the whites forget that the more docile they are, the less they are obeyed, that they are not solely transmission belts for orders to the masses but also the spokesmen for the masses, indeed that they transmit not only orders from above, but word of grievances from below. "Discuss things with blacks?" some administrators ask, themselves smitten with their own authority; a *chef* who permits discussion of his orders is lost. . . .[15]

In practice the local situation and the nature of colonial economic exploitation decided the question of whether rule was more direct or indirect. Nor was Belgian indirect rule directed toward eventual self-government as British was, but was an integral part of an essentially paternalist system of rule. This system sought to master social disintegration and to draw the native as a functioning being into the colonial economic polity, which itself rested on mining, plantations, and European settlers rather than native farming.

When Belgium took over the Congo, Leopold's domainal system ceased, meaning that the state abandoned its monopoly right to purchase directly products such as rubber and to regard the profits of their sale as state revenue. The way was thus open for private trade. It was accordingly possible to end the worst abuses in a relatively short time, the civil service being confined to genuinely administrative functions. In 1914 a tax was introduced or, more accurately, made general for the entire Congo, though its incidence varied by region. It was to be paid in cash, and the chiefs were to be integrated into the collection process. The intent was, first, to provide the budget with needed revenues; and second, to mobilize the natives for migration for work outside their own narrow homelands, a matter of vital importance for the Congo.

New regulations were issued for land concessions.[16] The corporations had to give up most of their original areas of exploitation, but in return could regard their new, smaller holdings as private property. The Forminière, for example, traded 1.1 million hectares for 150,000 in forty blocks. The CSK (Compagnie du Sud Katanga) remained in possession of forty-five million hectares, however, while being relieved of administrative responsibilities, an arrangement rightly described as "a mammoth present for the company."[17] In 1928 the Kivu National Committee was constituted after the Katangan model. A sort of government-corporation combine, it was given twelve million hectares. The area was reduced to 400,000 between 1933 and 1935, an area still large enough so that land could with profit be transferred to smaller companies. It was natural that the concession companies would take pains to secure the most valuable land possible in the wearisome negotiations which determined actual property rights. Since 1906 the administration had stipulated that only vacant land could be dispersed, and that the natives had to be allowed an area three times that actually cultivated. In practice it proved impossible to prevent both larger and small tribal units from being displaced or reduced to tenantry. In some areas, moreover, the native reserves hardly sufficed for peripatetic cultivation. Still, the land question never had the looming importance that it attained in the British settlement colonies in East Africa.

European agriculture was based on plantations rather than settlers. The administration encouraged colonization through credit grants, travel grants, and start-up help, if the settler had a basic capital stake. In 1930, however, there were only 420 settler farms, mainly in Katanga and Kivu. Mine settlements seemed to have hindered rather than helped small-scale settlement, because the mines' need for labor conflicted with the settlers.'[18] The settler element assumed a certain importance only after 1945 and was then able to organize to secure its demands.[19] In general, though, the assumption from the outset was that profitable modern agriculture was only possible on plantations. The administration assisted by hanging on to state land in specified areas, in order to assure the plantations a labor supply. Usually only a portion of the land was cultivated.[20] The mines were interested in stock raising, done on enormous ranches, to provide meat for the miners. Unilever was the most important of the plantation companies. Lord Leverhulme's efforts to secure on the west coast of Africa the necessary raw materials for the fat and soap trust he was creating had collapsed against the resistance of the British administration (*see* p. 320 above). The Belgian government, however, sought foreign capital. It thus gave Leverhulme by way of the Société des Huileries du Congo Belge the rights to 750,000 hectares of palm trees. This was supposedly domain land without native owners, but the company actually took the most favorably situated land without much regard for the Congolese. Palm plantations were not laid out until 1924, and they yielded considerably less than those in Southeast Asia. Having its own oil mills and fleet, Unilever controlled Congo palm oil production, which rose from 6,000 tons during World War I to 58,00 tons in 1936, making the Congo the world's third largest producer, after the Netherlands Indies and Nigeria.[21] There were also rubber and cocoa plantations, and a colonial trading company for the import of consumer goods. Finally, Forminière controlled plantation companies farming about 100,000 hectares.

Whereas in West African native farming the most important export products were peanuts, cocoa, and palm products, in the Congo these products came from European plantations. The Africans were not farmers but rural laborers. Native agriculture was reduced to the growing of foodstuffs, primarily for subsistence, and received little administrative support.[22] Efforts to bring the Africans more fully into cash-crop production came only with the depression. The impulse came from no less a person than the crown prince, who after a tour of the Congo made a sensational speech in the senate attacking Belgian methods that left economic development almost entirely to corporations and regarded the native as nothing more than an "instrument of production." The most immediate result in practice was an expansion and intensification of forced cultivation. It had been legalized in 1917 in order to ensure rice production for the East Africa expeditionary corps. Later, it was intended partly to encourage the growth of foodstuffs but mainly to speed up the cultivation of cash crops not grown on plantations, such as cotton and peanuts. On occasion, even the planting of palms was declared obligatory. The administration provided seed and supervised the cultivation, mainly by enlisting the chiefs and giving them cash incentives for delivery. Minimum prices were set, but the companies were also provided with specified purchasing areas, which tended to turn the minimum price into the maximum price. In 1938 two hundred thousand families, or about one million natives altogether, were said to be involved in forced cultivation. "The system... has given the Congo a physiognomy unique among African colonies. No other colony, indeed, has known agricultural constraint on such a scale or for such duration.... The entire economic edifice was built on constraint, constraint which one scarcely dared to disturb."[23] Among the reasons turned up by the senate in 1947 for the exodus from the cities, besides the numerous corvées, was imposed cultivation.[24] Stengers points to the forced cultivation system that in the year 1952 alone resulted in twenty thousand fines and prison terms, to explain the "revolutionary explosion in the Congo."[25]

The real economic importance of the Congo, however, was as a mining colony. The complicated Leopoldian system of layered concession companies—which along with mines included electricity works, railways, plantations, and other enterprises—remained in being under the management of finance capital and with the state as a shareholder. Among the four finance groups that controlled the Congo economically the most important was the Société Générale, which as a holding company was a virtual monopoly. "If you leave out the Société Générale group, the Congo in economic terms can hardly be said to exist."[26] It controlled about 70 percent of the £143 million of estimated 1936 investment and Katanga almost totally. Production and exports rose rapidly after the railway reached Elizabethville in 1912 and after other mining centers had been hooked into the communications network in the following period. Copper production rose from 2,494 tons in 1912 to 26,000 tons in 1917, to 56,221 tons in 1923, and 138,949 tons in 1930. Katanga was and remains the world's third-largest copper producer, and the situation was similar for gold, diamonds (319,000 carats in 1920, and 8.3 million carats in 1939), cobalt, and, later, uranium. Capital returns in the development phase were rather modest. The state had to advance money until 1925 and provide a guaranteed return on capital as well. It also received, however, a guarantee of return on capital, which, as it was a stockholder, was a sort of compensation for the grant of land and subsurface rights. A significant portion of the budget came from taxes, but the companies are alleged to have succeeded in partially evading them through financial manipulations.[27]

The very rapid expansion of mining made the labor problem an acute one. It was analogous to that of the settlement colonies, but concerned the needs of the mines and plantations. It is no exaggeration to say that it determined the resolution of a broad complex of native policy issues, and that native policy itself in good part simply reflected the need for labor, even though the government felt constrained to undertake some protective measures. The recruiting methods are already familiar, especially those of the expansion phase. Black and white agents, often a ruffianly lot of adventurers, moved into the villages to woo the workers, which they did with presents and promises, or open or barely concealed force. The recruits were then conducted over often considerable distances and with heavy losses to the mines, railways, and plantations. Chiefs were bribed with presents; and expropriation of land freed labor. Semiofficial recruiting occurred first in the immediate neighborhood of the mines and other economic centers and often involved entire populations. It came gradually to encompass more and more remote regions. In 1920 there were 125,000 wage laborers and by 1927, 427,000. During the depression the number fell, but had reached 530,000 by 1939.[28] The social consequences are well known. A great part of the younger males were absent from the villages for months and farming was left to women. The birth rate fell, native society became truly demoralized. These effects were so serious that an investigating commission was appointed in 1924. It discovered that only 5 percent of the male population could be absent any considerable time from the villages without socially harmful effects, though the absence of another 20 percent was still tolerable. Although this finding was enshrined as a rule, it was not adhered to in many districts. Instances are known where as many as half of the men were absent.[29] But the administration also adopted other measures. Certain regions were placed entirely off limits for recruiting or could at most be used for agricultural recruiting. Areas were reserved for specific companies, and in yet other areas no new mining concessions were issued.[30] In the annual report for 1929 both the "inadmissible wastage" and the "abuses" in employment of miners were noted,[31] yet the governor was simultaneously issuing instructions to "encourage the natives to work by every possible means,"[32] which was the equivalent of offering administrative assistance.

The chronic lack of workers, which at times prevented increases in production, led the Union Minière to shift over to a calculated policy of tying the worker to the mines. African miners serving under short-term contracts showed low productivity, and in thinly settled Katanga the labor question was particularly acute. The company hence concluded renewable three-year contracts, enabled men to bring their wives, and began building workers' cities, which provided the workers with decent accommodations, medical care, and schools for the children. Success was almost immediate. More and more workers renewed their contracts. The number of new recruits needed every year declined, productivity increased, and both frequency of accidents and mortality, previously high even for those in their twenties, fell.[33] Other companies followed this example. In following this stabilization policy, the Congo differed from South Africa and neighboring Rhodesia (*see* p. 473 below), where analogous efforts did not come until after World War II. An additional difference was that the Belgian Congo undertook Africanization of the lower-level cadres in mining and the railways rather early. That meant that a class of skilled workers developed that could replace more expensive European labor. As late as 1955 at least one observer was struck by a black engineer's taking over the train when it crossed the Rhodesian border into the Congo.[34] It is clear that financial considerations supported the greatest possible substitution of Africans for Europeans. The leading positions remained reserved for Europeans, which was characteristic of the de facto—though not de jure—color bar that characterized relations between black and white in the Congo.[35]

Education was as much influenced by the expanding economy as the system of rule itself. Like England, Belgium left education largely to Catholic missionaries, and instruction was in the local languages. Whereas the French and British systems were oriented toward producing an educated elite, the Belgians were mainly interested in the masses. Herein the interests of the missionaries coincided with the colonial power's interest in "civilized" workers and officials.[36] The number of students was accordingly much higher than even in West Africa, despite the latter's much longer standing ties to Europe. In 1938 there were one million students in a population of ten million.[37]

The road to higher education, however, was largely blocked. There were no Congo university graduates before World War II: neither jurists, nor doctors, nor agronomists, nor engineers. The first Congo student matriculated at Louvain only in 1952. Although it was reiterated with monotonous regularity that education had to start at the bottom and that the Congolese were not yet ripe for secondary and higher education, the striking fact was that 249 Congolese were serving as Catholic priests in 1954. They were manifestly able to cope with theological training lasting several years but evidently not that required to become agronomists. The Congo administration's attempts to prevent the rise of a Congolese elite were indeed rather blatant, and such an elite would undoubtedly have sooner or later forced the Belgians to concede reforms. But Belgium intended to stay in the Congo, and Africanization was unnecessary because there were enough Belgians. Ex-governor Ryckmans was able to write as late as 1955: "There can be no doubt that such a policy would not have been justified in an independent country such as Libya or in one which had been promised independence in the near future, like Somaliland. In such countries native cadres must be educated. The reason we have no black doctors, veterinarians, or engineers is that we can send white doctors, veterinarians, and engineers."[38]

It was thus possible for the évolué class to be quite large and still to count for nothing politically so long as none of them had had anything more than a primary school education and could not constitute a leadership class. Even the beginnings of a Congolese bourgeoisie were modest and perforce would remain so, because the corporations and, in the agrarian sector, the plantations ruled the economy and thus left few chances to rise economically. Retail trade, transport, and similar activities which increased as the economy expanded naturally provided some opportunities, but even here the Europeans were dominant. The Tschombe family, a Katangan business dynasty, was an exception.

Still more important was the deliberate depoliticization in the Belgian colonial system, which did not even allow the modest amount of political collaboration which the French permitted in certain representative bodies in their African colonies. There were no elections of any kind. The first elections came only in 1957, at the communal level. But since the Belgians had no councils of any kind either, there was less occasion to ask for African representatives than as happened in, say, Kenya or Rhodesia. Without councils and without elections, there was also no need for political parties, quite aside from the fact that the administration forbade them anyhow. The same was true for the press. The first African journals appeared only in 1957, only to be immediately suppressed. Even in comparison with a settlement colony like Kenya, the repressive pressure exerted against organizations with the merest political tinge is striking. In this climate trade-union gatherings were naturally also forbidden. During the 1920s and 1930s, if the administration noticed that a miner was speaking in "arrogant tones," or that, in another instance, the unemployed seamen of Matadi were striking "arrogant attitudes," the report usually followed that "they were immediately taken under close surveillance."[39] Even voluntary associations were few in number before 1940.

All this explains in good part why syncretist and messianic movements struck such a strong resonance in the Congo, especially among the Bakongo in the lower Congo. Although their kingdom stemmed from antiquity, not only had it been exposed to intensive missionary activity but it suffered severely under the Congo Free State. It supplied most of the porterage from Matadi around the rapids before the railway and then supplied labor for the railway and the later roads. On top of all that, the tribe was also decimated by sleeping sickness.[40]

In 1921 Simon Kimbangu, having received a revelation and, some believed, the healing touch, unleashed a genuine mass movement. Workers laid their tools down and streamed to the New Jerusalem. Although Kimbangu worked solely as a Christian, calling on the Bible as his authority, and was at worst potentially anti-European, the administration stepped in immediately, having him condemned to death on the flimsiest of evidence. He was pardoned by the king, but nevertheless disappeared into prison, not to emerge until his death in 1951. But his movement continued to burgeon, spreading to the Bakongo in French Equatorial Africa. When the Salvation Army became established in the lower Congo, its arrival was connected with the coming return of the messiah, the "S" in "Salvation," having been taken to signify the "S" in "Simon." And at about the same time, the Jehovah's Witnesses (*see* p. 478 below) became established in Katanga.

I have noted repeatedly that the messianic religious movements must today be considered as representing more than emotional demands insufficiently fulfilled by the missions and more, indeed, than attempts to reconcile Christian and traditional systems of values. They were, perhaps most important of all, reactions to the social dislocation, frustration, and repression of the colonial situation. In the paternalistically governed Congo, where every form of political activity was forbidden and a large portion of the population was at the same time reduced to nothing more than manpower in a system of intensive economic exploitation, religious and eschatological hopes and expectations were bound to appear to be the sole possibility for articulating resistance against the colonial pressure and inferior status in which one was held by main force.

NOTES

1. Roger Anstey, *King Leopold's Legacy: The Congo under Belgian Rule, 1908-1960* (London: Oxford University Press, 1966); Michel Merlier, *Le Congo, de la Colonisation Belge à l'Indépendence* (Paris: F. Maspero, 1962); René Lemarchand, *Political Awakening in the Belgian Congo* (Berkeley: University of California Press, 1964); Robert Cornevin, *Histoire du Congo* (Paris: Berger-Levrault, 1963). See also Jean Stengers' incisive chapter, "La Belgique et le Congo: Politique Coloniale et Décolonisaton," in *Histoire de la Belgique Contemporaine: 1914-1970* (Brussels: La Renaissance du Livre, 1975).

2. Auguste Roeykens, *Léopold II et l'Afrique, 1855-1880: Essai de Synthèse et de Mise au Point* (Brussels: Académie Royale des Sciences Coloniales, 1958); Jean Stengers, "La Place de Léopold II dans l'Histoire de la Colonisation," *La Nouvelle Clio* 2 (1950); idem, *Belgique et Congo: L'Elaboration de la Charte Coloniale* (Brussels: La Renaissance du Livre, 1963); idem, "The Congo Free State and the Belgian Congo before 1914," in Gann and Duignan, *Colonialism*, I; idem, "Léopold II et la Rivalté Franco-Anglaise 1882-1884," *Revue Belge de Philologie et d'Histoire*, 47: no. 2 (1969).

3. See particularly Stengers' "Léopold II et la Rivalté." On Brazza's role, see Jean Stengers, "L'Imperialisme Colonial de la Fin du XIXe Siécle: Myth ou Réalité?" *JAH*, 3 (July 1962). Henri Brunschwig noted his agreement in his *L'Avènement*, 167ff.

4. In 1899 an official commented to a British consular agent: "His method of procedure was

to arrive in canoes at a village, the inhabitants of which invariably bolted on their arrival; the soldiers were then landed, and commenced looting, taking all the chickens, grain, etc., out of the houses; after this they attacked the natives until able to seize their women; these women were kept as hostages until the Chief of the District brought in the required number of kilograms of rubber. . . "; quoted in Anstey, *King Leopold's Legacy*, 6.

5. The ABIR was capitalized at 232,000 Belgian francs but in 1906 showed a profit of six million; Stengers, "Belgique et Congo," 47.

6. Merlier, *Le Congo*, 32.

7. Stengers, "Congo Free State," 270.

8. Ibid., 272ff.

9. "These horrors must end or I will retire from the Congo. I will not allow myself to be spattered with blood or mud; it is necessary that these villanies cease" (or so the king noted on 18 January 1900; quoted in ibid., 28.

10. William Roger Louis, "Roger Casement and the Congo," *JAH*, 5 (January 1964). For an older account, see Alphonse Jules Wauters, *Histoire Politique du Congo Belge* (Brussels: P. van Fleteven, 1911).

11. See the discussion of Belgium in Albertini, *Decolonization*, 507f.

12. Anstey, *King Leopold's Legacy*, 33, 46f., 62f.; G.E.J.B. Brausch, "Le Paternalism: Une Doctrine Belge de Politique Indigène (1908-1933)," *Revue de l'Institut de Sociologie*, 30: no. 2 (1957); Hailey, *African Survey*, 550f.

13. "If we don't watch out, the day will come when there won't be any more native authorities. . . .It is obviously necessary to sustain the structure of native society and to ready organizations to support it in areas where it has become weakened."; Colonial Minister Louis Franck, 1920, as quoted in *Congo: Revue Générale de la Colonie Belge* (1921) 42. See also Franck's "Quelques aspects de notre Politique Indegène au Congo," in idem (ed.), *Etudes de Colonisation Comparée*, (2 vols. Brussels: Goemaere, 1924), I.

14. Jean de Hemptinne, *préfet apostolique* of Katanga, gives an example of the extravagent punishments handed out by a *chef du secteur*, who alleged that customary law justified them; *Congo* (1929), 189. The author was responsible for initiating an acrimonious discussion of native policy in 1928.

15. *La Politique Coloniale* (1934), 42. See also Pierre Ryckmans, *Dominer pour Servir* (Brussels: A. Dewitt, 1931).

16. Merlier, *Le Congo*, 58f.

17. Stengers, *Belgique et Congo*, 212.

18. Merlier, *Le Congo*, 74.

19. Lemarchand, *Political Awakening*, 76f.

20. Chalux [pseud.], *Un An au Congo Belge* (Brussels: A. Dewitt, 1925). Originally a newspaper series for the daily, *Nation Belge*, it provides a lively account of such plantations, where, for example, it took 350 blacks and three white overseers to operate a palm, banana, and cocoa plantation of 500 hectares; p. 38. Others were from five to ten thousand hectares in size and required the labor of hundreds of Africans.

21. Sally Herbert Frankel, *Capital Investment in Africa: Its Course and Effects* (New York: H. Fertig, 1938, 1969), 299.

22. "It is absolutely essential to encourage fish-growing. Agriculture hardly exists in the Congo. The entire colony is insufficiently fed" (the governor-general, as quoted in Chalux, *Un An*, 176).

23. Stengers, "La Belgique et le Congo," 407.

24. Belgium, Parlement, Sénat, *Rapport de la Mission Sénatoriale du Congo et dans les Territoires sous Tutelle Belge* (Brussels: n. p., 1947), 13.

25. Stengers, "La Belgique et le Congo," 407.

26. Quoted in Frankel, *Capital Investment*, 295. Frankel also provides the following more precise information: in 1932 there were approximately two hundred companies with a capital of nine billion francs, seventy-one of which were controlled by four finance groups,

forty-one by the Société Générale, five by the Empain Group, nine by the Cominiére, and sixteen by the Bank of Brussels. The forty-nine Société Générale companies were engaged as follows: railways, three; "general activities," three; banks, two; mines, twelve; plantations, six; financing companies, three; industry and trade, eleven; furniture, one. The Société Générale controlled practically the entire production of copper, diamonds, radium, and cement, and part of the gold production; ibid., 292f.

27. Anstey, *King Leopold's Legacy*, 112.

28. Merlier, *Le Congo*, 133.

29. Anstey, *King Leopold's Legacy*, 91.

30. In 1929 the Société Générale complained about the "draconian application of the offical ordinances regarding the employment of native labor"; *Congo* (1930), 292.

31. *Annuaire de Documentation Coloniale Comparéé* (Brussels, 1929), 19. Ryckmans spoke in 1936 of massive attrition. Porterage was still being exacted, the number of low-paid workers in agriculture was increasing, rather than machinery, tractors, and plows being utilized, as was being done in the Sudan or Zanzibar; ibid., (1936), I, 15.

32. Governor Tilken's circular, quoted in *Quinzaine Coloniale* (1928), 233, which also reported that the Commission de la Main d'Oeuvre au Congo was considering whether corporal punishment might not be substituted for imprisonment, ibid., 424.

33. Anstey, *King Leopold's Legacy*, 118. Whereas the Union Minière had to recruit about ten thousand workers a year between 1921 and 1929, the number had fallen to 1,800 for the period 1935-1942. Mortality fell from 117.8 per thousand in 1914 to 39.1 per thousand in 1925-1929 and 7.1 per thousand in 1935-1939; ibid., 120. Colonial Minister Henri Jaspar spoke in parlement in February 1929 of the "catastrophic mortality" among black workers; *Annuaire de Documentation Coloniale Comparée* (1929), I, 43.

34. Albertini, *Decolonization*, 502.

35. An example: "Is it not shocking to think that a certain black Catholic abbé, traveling by boat on one of our large lakes, was not allowed access to the European's deck? That is particularly shocking because a priest was involved. But one can well believe that lay évolués are likely to be equally sensitive to such matters"; *Rapport de la Mission Sénatoriale*, 19.

36. "For the elite, this education is completed in our schools; and especially in the professional schools, which prepare the auxiliaries destined for the European and native administrations; clerks, skilled workers, medical assistants, veterinary assistants, and agricultural instructors"; Governor Alfred Moeller, "La Politique Indigène de la Belgique au Congo," *Journal of the Royal African Society* (July 1936), 237. On the school system see, among others, Lemarchand, *Political Awakening*, 133f.; Stengers, "La Belgique et le Congo," 398f.

37. Anstey, *King Leopold's Legacy*, 90.

38. Unpublished manuscript quoted in Lemarchand, *Political Awakening*, 133. The first two Congo universities were established in 1954 and 1956. In 1960, the year of independence, the Congo had a total of sixteen university graduates.

39. The annual report for 1928: "The calm prevailing in our territories is characterized by the absence of repressive military interventions: neither military operations, nor police operations have been required anywhere in the colony"; *Annuaire de Documentation Coloniale Comparée* (1929), I, 6, and ibid., (1933), I, 14.

40. Treated in detail in Anstey, *King Leopold's Legacy*, ch. 7; Crawford Young, *Politics in the Congo: Decolonization and Independence* (Princeton: Princeton University Press, 1965), 284ff.; Lemarchand, *Political Awakening*, 168ff.

Albert Wirz 12

THE GERMAN COLONIES IN AFRICA

African historians nowadays are inclined to see European rule of African peoples as a mere episode in the great continuum of African history. Such a characterization is particularly apt for German colonial rule.[1] With its defeat in World War I, Germany lost its colonies, acquired a scant thirty years earlier. Remaining was the dream of an empire which also included overseas territories, and agitation for the return of the colonies was a part of the struggle against the Versailles "*Diktat.*" All the same, the colonies were irrevocably torn from Germany's grasp in 1920 and made League of Nations mandates. The victors believed that Germany "had brought intolerable burdens and injustices on the helpless people of some of the colonies, which it annexed to itself; that its interest was rather their extermination than their development; that the desire was to possess their land for European purposes, and not to enjoy their confidence in order that mankind might be lifted in those places to the next higher level"—or such was the verdict of Woodrow Wilson, president of the United States.[2]

Along with Belgium and Italy, Germany was one of those countries that had become colonial powers only in the "new imperialism" era, and had no older colonial tradition to guide it. In fact, Germany's move into Africa was of especial importance for the colonial division of black Africa. Germany did not initiate the scramble for Africa, but it dynamized the process and, by calling the Berlin Conference of 1884, helped to regularize and stabilize the process in terms of international law. The fight over the division of Africa had begun before 1884—Germany was a late comer—and the German colonial empire was a correspondingly motley one. On account of its economic and political power, however, Germany was universally viewed with fear or at least suspicion, and its aspirations and acts profoundly affected the attitudes of the other Powers.

The German colonial empire can be considered to have been born on 27 April 1884, the day Bismarck wired the German consul in Capetown to declare "officially" that the Southwest African holdings of the Bremen merchant, Franz A. E. Lüderitz, lying north of the Orange River were under protection of the Reich. In July of the same year, the German flag was hoisted on the Togo coast and in the Cameroons. Both were areas where Hanseatic merchants had erected major trade stations. Finally, in February 1885, Carl Peters's East African possessions were taken under imperial protection. "Exploring expeditions" and military columns pushed inland during the following years, in order to establish German claims to sovereignty in the interior and to assure the coast settlements the largest possible hinterland. The settlement of the frontiers followed, mostly in the form of bilateral negotiations with individual European rivals. They were concluded by 1900. Only a single territorial alteration occurred thereafter, and that was when the French ceded the New Cameroons to Germany in 1911 in the course of the settlement of the second Morocco crisis.

But what, indeed, were the grounds for Germany's acquisition of a colonial empire in 1884? In 1880 the Reichstag had refused to intervene in Samoa, and Bismarck had never concealed his distaste of any sort of formal territorial rule. He had always consistently turned down requests for intervention from missionaries, traders, and colonial propagandists, repeatedly declaring colonies to be a luxury that Germany could not afford.[3] The shift has been explained in various ways. Orthodox diplomatic historians had seen the state intervention overseas as one of Bismarck's foreign policy moves on the chess board of Anglo- and Franco-German relations.[4] Other historians have emphasized domestic considerations and election tactics, noting his regard for the Liberals and public opinion, which in 1884 was suffused with a virulent colonial chauvinism—the German Colonial Association, founded in 1882 to represent and propagandize colonial interests, already had 15,000 members by 1885.[5] Yet others have seen the grab for overseas territory as a corollary of the neo-mercantilist economic policy symbolized by the tariff of 1879.[6] Finally, Hans Ulrich Wehler states that Bismarck's shift toward imperialism was intended on the one hand as a countercyclical measure to combat the "Great Depression" of the years after 1873 and on the other as a measure to stabilize the existing social order by deflecting social conflict outward, away from the fatherland.[7] Although Wehler's social-imperialism thesis is probably the most convincing, it ought not be forgotten that Bismarck did not contemplate the state's acquisition of an actual colonial empire even in 1884. Only subsequent developments revealed that hoisting the flag, intended to be a merely symbolic act, had in fact ushered in a period of German colonial rule in Africa. Bismarck, indeed, stuck to the assertion that he acted merely to protect German merchants located in overseas territories as yet unoccupied by other European powers. In keeping with this fiction, the German acquisitions were not designated "colonies" but "protectorates," over which the Reich claimed unrestricted sovereignty but where it did not wish to employ state power to its full extent. "My aim is a government of merchant companies, upon which the supervision and protection of the Reich and the Emperor is imposed," Bismarck explained to the Reichstag, after he had explicitly referred to chartered companies such as the British East India Company as possible models.[8]

But his program shattered on the realities. The Hanseatic traders, who had worked to secure the intervention of the metropolis to safeguard their own economic interests in the Slave Coast (Togo) and the Cameroons, were unwilling from the outset to assume administrative obligations.[9] The same was true of the German Colonial Corporation for Southwest Africa (*Deutsche Kolonialgesellschaft für Südwest Afrika*, or DKGSWA). Founded in 1885 as the legal successor to Luderitz's interests, it possessed Angra Pequena and broad expanses of desert supposedly rich in minerals along the southwest African coast. It did not want letters patent, for its strength was unequal to making good claims of sovereignty or even of exploiting its rights of economic monopoly. The company was bankrupt by 1889, the hoped-for profits never having appeared, and it had to sell some of its mining rights. In 1888, moreover, the Herero tribes in the hinterland had rejected German "protection" because the latter had not, as hoped, assisted them in wars with their neighbors, the Nama, and ties to Great Britain had hence come to seem more advantageous. If Germany did not wish to lose Southwest Africa to Great Britain, it was going to have to take on the administration itself, because the DKGSWA was itself unable to act. In Berlin, the initial hope was to get by with sending a twenty-man troop disguised as a scientific expedition. But this move had more profound consequences, as it led ineluctably to the establishment of a governmental colonial administration.[10]

The course of events was about the same in East Africa, despite the sort of arrangements Bismarck had foreseen already being in existence. Here, the twenty-eight-year-old historian Carl Peters'[11] Corporation for German Colonization (Gesellschaft für deutsche Kolonisation) had on its own behest and in open competition with similar British enterprises concluded treaties with African chiefs in the Dar es Salaam hinterland. The intent was to create an agricultural and trading colony for Germany. Bismarck initially opposed these efforts, East Africa commonly being accounted a British "preserve." The company was granted imperial letters patent in 1885, however, according to which it was to exercise sovereignty in the territories it had acquired. The company was reorganized in the same year as the German East-African Company (Deutsch-Ostafrikanische Gesellschaft). It set about fulfilling its grandiose plans with energy and ruthlessness, errecting a whole series of stations inland and pushing ahead toward the sources of the Nile, which directly threatened British interests. Despite its inability to pay dividends—it was losing money—the company appeared to be operating very successfully. In 1888, it concluded a treaty with the sultan of Zanzibar, who ruled the coast from Cape Delgado to Kipini. This treaty was meant to transfer the administration of the coast from the sultan to the company, which was also to collect customs duties in the sultan's name in return for an annual payment of tribute. If the treaty had gone into effect, it would have provided the company an important source of income and assured it the effective control of the East African coast, because the important export harbors and thus the export trade would have fallen under its control. But the Arab-Swahili upper class living in the coastal towns rose against the treaty, because they considered their own hegemony threatened and feared for the loss of their main source of income, the East African caravan trade.

The company was powerless against the armed resistance which flared up in the coastal towns as soon as it attempted to exercise its new treaty rights, especially since the Yao and other local African peoples had joined the resistance along with most of the sultan's askari troops.[12] The rebels overran all of the company's stations except Bagamojo and Dar es Salaam. The company had to ask for help from the metropolis. The Reichstag immediately voted two million marks for reconquest. But it was characteristic of the time that this military intervention was justified by those responsible as a contribution in the struggle against the slave trade rather than as making good German claims to rule in the face of local resistance and to establish effective colonial occupation. After a year's fighting the rebellion had largely been put down. East Africa had also received direct Reich administration, however, matters being regularized by the so-called settling-up treaty of November 1890 between the government and the company. The company lost its sovereign rights, which it had proved unable to make good, but its quasi-monopoly privileges in regard to mining, the ownership of unoccupied land, and the right to establish a bank of issue, were confirmed. It also received a ten million mark "loan," which was to be amortized by the state. The latter proviso was but another sign of the degree to which contemporaries felt the state had to sue for the favor of private capitalists.[13]

Thus Bismarck's program for a "colonial empire with limited liability," fell apart in less than six years, at least as regards Africa.[14] In New Guinea the rule of private corporations lasted until 1899 and in the Marshalls until 1906. At the same time, of course, the colonial enthusiasm had proved entirely unjustified. Colonies, instead of bringing profits, required appreciable state investment. The general public thereafter viewed colonial affairs without much interest. General Leo von Caprivi, Bismarck's successor, also added his voice to the chorus of disappointment. But whenever he personally considered withdrawal or sale, as a politician he was forced to recognize that "the way things are today, we cannot retreat without loss of honor, and also money; our only course, therefore, is to get on with it."[15]

This statement of intent was by itself hardly enough to satisfy those circles interested in colonial matters, particularly since the Anglo-German colonial treaty of July 1890, the Helgoland-Zanzibar treaty, had also been a disappointment. The treaty settled a variety of frontier questions in east, west, and southwest Africa, transferred the North Sea island Helgoland to Germany, and provided German Southwest Africa access to the Zambesi River in the form of the Caprivi Strip. The British also promised to support the establishment of German rule over that portion of the east African coast nominally under the sway of the sultan of Zanzibar. But Germany also had to renounce aspirations to establish a protectorate over Zanzibar itself and to give up Uganda, and hence the sources of the Nile, to Great Britain. Carl Peters complained, "we have exchanged three kingdoms for a bathtub." The banker and Progressive party deputy, Ludwig Bamberger, undoubtedly spoke for the majority of his countrymen, however, when he said, "the less Africa, the better."[16]

The Reich administration faced a number of tasks as a result of taking over the African territories. It had to create a central office for colonial matters, it had to regulate finances, and it had to establish an orderly administration in the individual colonies themselves. In part to conciliate colonial enthusiasts still smarting from the Helgoland-Zanzibar treaty, the Colonial Division was established within the Foreign Office in 1890. Its head (*Kolonialdirigent* and after 1894 *Kolonialdirektor*) was directly subordinate to the Reichskanzler, although his competence was restricted by the Foreign Office and by the fact that colonial troops were controlled by the Navy Ministry until 1896.[17] Only in 1907 was the Reich Colonial Office with its own secretary created. A colonial council, comprising representatives of the various colonial interests, was also established to provide the Colonial Division with expert opinion. It became the spokesman for economic interests, the missions, and the colonial interests represented in the German Colonial Society. It had only consultative functions, however, and tended to lose importance as Reichstag interest in colonial matters increased. It was finally dissolved in 1908.

One of the peculiarities of German colonial policy was that the Reichstag was able to exert a very important influence on the development of the colonies.[18] First, the Reichstag had to consent to Reich subsidies. These were of great significance to the colonies as long as they failed to produce revenues anywhere nearly matching their outlays. From their beginnings until 1914, the German African colonies received 451.5 million marks in subsidies, of which 278 million went to Southwest Africa, 122 million to East Africa, 48 million to the Cameroons, and 23.5 million to Togo.[19] Second, a law of March 1892 provided that the budgets of the individual colonies were subject to Reichstag budgetary controls. The Reichstag interpreted this right as providing it with supervisory authority and used it as an instrument to expand its initially very limited legislative competence. The result was that the German colonial administration became extremely centralized and that colonial development was very dependent on the metropolitan political constellations of the moment. For their part, the colonists could submit petitions to the Reichstag.

Because the parliament took its supervisory functions very seriously, discussions of all aspects of colonial policy were more or less continual, as was true nowhere else. Before 1907, however, aside from the National Liberals and Free Conservatives, the parties regarded the colonies with scepticism, lack of agreement (the left Liberals, Center Party), or, in the case of the Socialists, downright abnegation. The Reichstag majority showed little sympathy for state intervention in the overseas possessions, and given the deficits in the Reich budget itself could indeed hardly be expected to. Thus an adequate financial basis for a constructive colonial policy was long wanting, which resulted in the colonial administration becoming dangerously dependent on private economic interests. It also led the administration to seek every means, including those which time was to show were self-destructive, to increase its income as rapidly as possible. The result was often pressure on the Africans that exceeded any tolerable measure. An improvement came only in 1907, when Bernhard Dernburg, a banker who specialized in restoring ailing corporations to health, reformed colonial finances along Anglo-French lines, and gave the financial autonomy of each colony the force of doctrine. Henceforth, the Reich was to pay only military outlays, all other expenses having to be met by the colonies themselves. He also put the borrowing of money on a new footing, with the Reich providing guarantees. That made it possible to finance the infrastructure necessary to open up the colonies, railways in particular.[20]

Prussian administrative practice guided local colonial administration. There were no basic differences between German practices and those in use elsewhere, except that Germany, unlike France or Portugal, never pursued the goal of assimilation and integration into the homeland.[21] In 1890 governors representing the German Empire replaced the imperial commissars. Supported by a continually expanding bureaucracy, the governors possessed rather broad powers. They not only headed the central civilian administration, they were also, even if civilians, commanders-in-chief of each colony's military forces. That did not prevent colonial soldiers' frequently acting in contravention of the governor's will and presenting him with faits accomplis, particularly during the period of conquest. The conquest and occupation of the North Cameroons in 1901, indeed, occurred despite the declared opposition of both the governor and Foreign Office to it.[22] After 1903 the governors were advised by government councils whose official members joined with appointed representatives of the white colonial population to discuss budget questions and whose opinions were sought before important administrative decrees were issued. Because of his decree-issuing powers, however, the governor could largely set down the law as he saw fit. Finance, in contrast, was closely controlled from Berlin. That had inhibiting effects and encouraged tendencies toward overbureaucratization and nit-picking. These tendencies were reversed only with Dernburg's administrative reforms.

The traders wanted to expand their stagnating trade, which by the end of the century was at least offering better prospects for profit. What they wanted was direct contact with the producers of export goods, from whom the Africans living on the coast had successfully isolated them. They envisaged extensive inner African markets and accordingly agitated for opening up the trade routes and expansion of the area truly under control of the colonial administration. Entrepreneurs who hoped for speculative gains from the founding of plantations also sought military intervention. And those who had been talking for decades about the need for settlement colonies hoped the military would open up the climatically more salubrious highlands of the interior. The officers of the colonial troops pushed for making good the claims to sovereignty which reflected strategic considerations, but which had been agreed to at the international negotiating tables without much knowledge of the local situations. Such officers were only too ready to give way to the pressures of the economic interests and colonial chauvinists. The logic of the situation led to intervention, and the colonists' marked awareness that colonial rule mainly rested on the right of the stronger both prepared the way for war, and by assuming the military resistance of the Africans, made it a sort of self-fulfilling prophecy.[23]

Rebellions, disturbances, and military clashes thus largely characterized the first two decades of German colonial rule in Africa. It would nevertheless be mistaken to interpret all African military actions as resistance to the Europeans. Indeed, in many cases, Africans themselves sought to gain access to Europeans after having been blocked off by other groups who had settled in the neighborhood of traders and officials. Every group tried to bring the Europeans under its influence insofar as possible, which in addition to conflicts with the Europeans themselves also led to difficulties with neighboring groups. That, in turn, provided the colonial rulers with grounds to intervene militarily. And the Germans could in many cases count on support from African rulers, at least in the beginning. The protectorate treaties, which formed the legal basis for the proclamation of colonial rule, were in some cases more the result of trickery than negotiation but not uncommonly were sought by the African rulers themselves. The intervention of a European power seemed to promise considerable advantages, both by way of securing their social and political standing in their own societies and as protection and aid against third parties. The treaties appeared all the more unsuspicious because Germany promised not to interfere in existing internal relationships.[24]

The treaties were broken, all the same, as soon as the colonial rulers felt strong enough to do so. If the Africans violated some treaty provision or sought to nullify it altogether, a "punishment" expedition was dispatched which ended in the military subjugation of the Africans. Contractual regulation of relations between Germans and Africans was as a rule sought only until such time as German claims to rule could be sanctioned under international law. Thereafter, the colonial rulers assumed that all Africans living within the colonial frontiers had to subordinate themselves unconditionally to the Germans and their laws. The Africans were asked to refrain from settling conflicts with one another by warlike means; they were not to disturb the "king's peace." They were also to cease all customs and usages that ran counter to contemporary European usages, such as trading slaves and imprisonment for debt, and they were to carry out with goodwill all demands their colonial masters made of them. These ranged from sale of food to touring Europeans, to the provision of porters and workers, to the building and maintenance of paths and roads, and the payment of tribute. These demands were later regularized in the form of tax payments. In addition, they included provision of export goods for European trade, the cultivation of products of value for the colonial economy, and the grant of land to colonists and colonial enterprises. It need hardly be said that these demands stemmed from the needs of the colonial rulers and were made without much regard for whether the Africans could meet them. As a rule, neither the number of inhabitants nor the structure of African society was known. But colonial rule was considered a priori good, because it brought order into African "chaos." That colonial rule had, in fact, rather the opposite effects no one had any way of recognizing. Societies which offended against the new order, for whatever reason, or refused to bend to it, were simply overrun.

Major Theodor Leutwein, however, who was chief administrator (*Landeshauptmann*) and governor of Southwest Africa from 1894 to 1905, sought to follow Caprivi's injunctions for peaceful conquest, "without bloodshed."[25] But Leutwein was very conscious that colonial rule meant that Africans had to submit themselves to the German state, meaning they had to give up such rights to self-determination as they possessed. He also believed that this would have no negative consequences for the individual African and that if the administration proceeded with caution, the African would become wholly reconciled to the new political situation. Leutwein knew that the colonial economic aim of a settlement colony with large European stock farms was incompatible with the precolonial African economic order, and particularly that of the seminomadic Herero. The latter neither wished to sell land to Europeans nor would they themselves exploit their herds in what Europeans considered a rational manner. Instead of bringing cattle to market, they accumulated as many as possible. Thinking in terms of European economic assumptions, Leutwin believed that the Herero had more land and cattle than they could use. He hence believed that their tribal territories and cattle stock could be reduced for the benefit of Europeans without any real loss to the Herero themselves. He never recognized the close relationship between wealth in cattle, social prestige, and political power in Herero society.

Leutwein's policy was based on local compromises and alliances with individual African chiefs, pursued with diplomacy as well as by military force. Roughly, he followed the policy of divide and rule that he had learned from the study of English colonial history. However reasonable this policy may sound, it was stoutly resisted by settlers, the colonial corporations, and colonial military officers, all of whom pressed for a more radical policy of conquest. Leutwein nevertheless concluded his first treaty with Hendrik Witbooi, the leader of the Nama people, despite public opinion favoring exemplary punishment of the Nama, who had been engaged in guerrilla warfare with the Germans since 1891. Leutwein sought collaboration, not submission, and success seemed to justify his policy, because the Nama obligated themselves to provide the Germans with military service. In 1894, Samuel Maherero, whose rivals challenged his position as paramount chief of the Hereros, turned to Leutwein with a request for assistance. Leutwein accepted, because it allowed him to intervene as arbiter in Herero political disputes, and in addition stationed a garrison in Okahandja. Samuel Maherero made yet additional sacrifices. For a yearly payment, he agreed to a treaty fixing the southern and northern boundaries of Hereroland. The new borders isolated the Herero (from the Ovambo people, for example) and penned them in, forcing them to give up large amounts of territory. Those most directly concerned, the Mbanderu, or East Hereros, were unwilling to accept this. They recognized neither Samuel Maherero's authority nor the newly drawn boundaries. When they set out to defend their claims by force, however, they found themselves without allies and hence unequal to the Germans, who could count on the alliances with Hendrik Witbooi and Samuel Maherero. Leutwein's policy had thus destroyed the unity of the Herero and unleashed rivalries benefiting the Germans.

In the end Leutwein still failed. In 1904, his ally of long years, Samuel Maherero, called upon his people for war against the Germans and a restoration of the old ways. Leutwein's prudent policy of trimming had been unable to prevent Herero society from reaching a state of crisis in its confrontation with German colonization. The Hereros responded by rising in desperate rebellion. The Germans were completely surprised by the rising—Leutwein called it a riddle—the more because, for them, the colonial economy was for the first time truly beginning to prosper.

For the Herero, however, it was a time of the severest privation.[26] In 1897 rinderpest had annihilated a good two-thirds of their stock. The result was that the Herero fell into dependence on the Europeans and had perforce come to see land as an object of trade. Yet the social-psychological consequences of this natural catastrophe were more serious, perhaps, than the economic. Bley speaks of a cultural crisis in Herero society following the rinderpest. Europeans indeed profited from the misery of the Africans. The completion of the Swakopmund-Windhoek railway had improved communications and, encouraged by government financial support, Europeans streamed in. Between 1897 and 1903, their number almost doubled, from 2,828 to 4,682. Among them were colonial officials, farmers, businessmen, craftsmen, and missionaries.[27] The newcomers did not stick to the ground rules of the various local compromises, which was bound to have serious effects. They assumed, in fact, the airs of masters. They took no account of African values and customary arrangements and were on the contrary convinced that the Africans were, like all primitive peoples, destined to go under. And they let the Africans sense these opinions. The whites committed countless offenses, and the administration usually backed them up. Both in missionary circles and in the administration there was talk of creating land reserves, in order to protect the Hereros from the land hunger of the whites, but the Africans themselves interpreted this talk as the beginning of a general dispossession. The Hereros were also forced to give up large amounts of land without compensation for the construction of the Otavi railway, which was to cross their homeland. Although there was certainly no acute shortage of land in 1903, the seminomad Hereros were bound to feel increasingly hemmed in, accustomed as they were to wide-open spaces. An ordinance issued by the governor in 1903 put them in still greater jeopardy. It stated African debts more than a year old were no longer valid. The traders hence set about collecting outstanding debts by every possible means, including the unilateral seizure of cattle as security. In the eyes of the Herero that was theft and equivalent to a declaration of war. The herds of the Herero, once estimated in the hundreds of thousands, had within a few years shrunk to around fifty thousand,[28] much pasturage had been lost to Europeans, and lack of legal security and social discrimination confronted the individual African with German pretensions to power. When German troops were pulled out of Hereroland in January 1904 for employment elsewhere, the Hereros went into action. They were led by Samuel Maherero who, after the deaths of his rivals, had been able to create a new power base using income from land sales. Ten months later, Hendrik Witbooi also led the Nama against the Germans. They had initially fought beside the Germans, but the colonial rulers, in their war hysteria, had repeatedly threatened that all Africans would suffer the fate of the Hereros.[29]

The Leutwein system had collapsed. Their security threatened—the Hereros having massacred 123 colonists in the first days of the rising—the colonial rulers reverted to the policy of the sword. General Lothar von Trotha was made commander-in-chief of German troops in Southwest Africa. He erected a military dictatorship and waged war against the Africans using a strategy of annihilation, the horrors of which the proclamation of the "Great General of the Mighty Kaiser" to the Hereros reveals: "All Hereros must leave the country. If they do not do so, I will force them to do so with a great gun. Inside the German border, every Herero, with or without rifle, or with or without cattle, will be shot. I will take in no more women and children, but will drive them back to their people or have them shot."[30] And he meant what he said. About two-thirds of all Hereros died in the rebellion, many perishing in the barren Kalahari Desert where they had been driven by German troops. Others died in prison camps. The Nama also suffered great losses, estimated at half the tribe. "The first war of Wilhelmine Germany" cost the colonial rulers around 585 million marks, over 2,000 dead, and lasted from 1904 to 1907. The money had to be raised by loans.[31]

But the German troops were meanwhile creating an even greater bloodbath in East Africa, where after 1905 the entire country south of the Dar es Salaam-Kilosa-Lake Nyasa line was in open rebellion.[32] The area in question was thinly settled, being inhabited by segmented Bantu societies each occupying a rather limited area. German colonization had initially affected them only marginally. The uprising had begun in July 1905 with an attack on the house of an *akida* (an Arab or Swahili subofficial) in the Mtumbi Hills near Kilwa and then had spread like wildfire throughout the entire south. The Ngoni assumed an especially important role in the rebellion, although they had not offered any particular opposition to the German occupation. The Hehe, by contrast, who had fought the Germans as late as 1898, now remained loyal to their colonial masters. The rebels directed their acts against their white masters, including missionaries, their colored collaborators, and Indian, Arab, and African traders and money-lenders as well. The direct occasion for the rebellion was the ruthless collection of the head and hut taxes by the colonial administration's local auxiliaries. Those who could not come up with the money were pressed into public service or put to work on private plantations. Another cause of the rebellion was the compulsion with which the colonial officials under Governor Adolf von Götzen sought to encourage cotton production for export. In 1902 the administration had begun erecting communal shambas (houses) in suitable villages and had demanded of the people that they—men and women, free and slave—cultivate cotton in common on specified plots. They were paid for only a small portion of this work. The administration had introduced this system, which endangered subsistence agriculture, in more and more localities. It was not a matter of chance, then, that the uprising began in a region that the authorities themselves recognized had suffered greatly under forced cultivation, nor that it coincided with the time set by the state for the cotton harvest. The rebellion was not directed solely at the various abuses of colonial rule, however, but had broader aims. A letter from a Ngoni chief to the Yao Mataka reveals some of them.

> We received an order from God to the effect that all White Men had to quit the country. . . . This war ordered by God must come first. Send 100 men with guns. Help me in taking the boma. . . . Once we have taken the boma of Songea we shall move against the stations of Lake Nyasa, you and I together. Let us now forget our former quarrels. This bottle containing medicine was sent by Kinyala himself, the leader of the war.[33]

The common aim of war against the colonial ruler and for restoration of the status quo ante united tribes which had earlier been in conflict. The leadership, however, was new, resting not so much with the traditional tribal chiefs, as had still been the case with the resistance to the occupation, but rather with prophets. Through manipulation of the symbols of the traditional cults, the latter successfully mobilized the masses and were able to create a cohesion that extended beyond the tribal boundries. The rebels believed that through consecration with holy water (*maji*) they became invulnerable; whence the name of the uprising, the Maji-Maji rebellion.[34]

The maji-maji cult, which assured the rebellion its early successes, soon proved to be its nemesis, as against modern weapons and well-organized and well-led European troops, it could do little. After faith had been shredded by rifle fire, the rebels splintered into tribal groups, who were delivered over almost helpless to the ruthless repression that followed. According to official estimates, some 75,000 died in the fighting and during the famine and epidemics which followed.[35]

The situation was not much better in the Cameroons, where a colonial policy of laissez-faire in economic matters ended with disturbances in the southeast.

The close connection between the colonial administration and the economy has already been alluded to. Economically, the colonies never achieved much importance in Germany. Their share in the total German foreign trade amounted to 0.5 percent in 1913. Private and state investment rose from a few million marks in 1885 to around 290 million marks in 1906 and 940 million in 1914. Total German foreign loans on the eve of World War I, however, were estimated at at least twenty billion marks, and in 1913 there were barely 20,000 Germans living in all the colonies.[36] In short, the projections of the colonial enthusiasts during the 1870s and 1880s remained chimeras. Nevertheless, all those pushing an active colonial policy were convinced that they served primarily the interests of the home economy. They sought to open up new markets for industry and to assure its supply of tropical raw materials, or, put another way, to integrate additional human and material resources into the Western market economic system.

The colonial government saw itself in explicit terms as the servant of the economy. The dependency of the colonial government on the colonial economy was also a very tangible one, because the colonial administration once in place depended on customs duties to cover its expenses. This was particularly true because the watchword in Berlin as in other metropolitan capitals was, "the colonies must not cost anything," and it supported the colonial fisc to the minimum degree necessary to make good the claims of sovereignty. The state did not consider itself responsible for expenditures on the economy, and the bureaucrats believed it could be left to its own devices. Only in proportion to its success in creating new sources of income through taxing the Africans was the colonial government able to loosen its bonds to the economy and assume its new role of mediator between the Africans and colonial economic interests.

First, however, the businessmen had to be interested in the colonies. Outside the Southwest Africa Company, the East African Company, and a number of Hanseatic trade houses—Woerman, Jantzen und Thormählen, Gaiser, and O'Swald, among others—hardly anyone had invested any money in the newly acquired overseas territories by 1890. Because of the high risks there seemed, indeed, few who were inclined to exploit the economic possibilities of the colonies. High finance, in particular, was extremely cautious,[37] though the Diskonto-Gesellschaft, the Dresdner Bank, and the Deutsche Bank had taken shares in both the Southwest and East Africa companies. Although the latter companies had not fulfilled their administrative obligations and could boast no economic success, Berlin persisted in granting additional monopoly rights to other entrepreneurs. Two heads of the Colonial Division, Paul Kayser (1890-1896) and Georg von Buchka (1898-1900), especially, saw the foundation of concession companies as a suitable means for opening up the colonies without burdening the state treasury.

Accordingly, in the 1890s five new concession companies were founded in Southwest Africa, where the discovery of rich ore deposits was anticipated and it was hoped colonists would settle. The concession area of all of the companies together comprised no less than two-thirds of the entire area of the colony, or 287,000 square kilometers altogether.[38] A potential source of conflict, however, stemmed from their disinclination to sell land—except at rather elevated prices—and their preference to rent it or even to leave it fallow in the hope of later mineral discoveries. The expansive drive of the settlers thus spilled over into the areas still not usurped, notably Hereroland, where the best pasturage was. The companies hindered rather than helped the opening up of the colonies. They sent out exploratory expeditions and prospectors, but neglected construction of an infrastructure. Such, indeed, were the conclusions of a Reich commission which investigated the activities of the concession companies in 1905. The outcome of its study was that the companies concerned lost prospecting and mining monopoly rights within their concessions and had to turn over most of their land to the treasury for resale.[39]

Very large concessions were also granted initially in the Cameroons.[40] The South Cameroons Company (Gesellschaft Süd-Kamerun), founded in 1898 with German and Belgian capital, received a concession of over 80,000 square kilometers in the southeast Cameroons. The company was able to take possession of all the so-called Crown Lands in this wholly unexplored area, and no obligations were imposed upon it. The state reserved only enough land for the construction of public buildings and rights to 10 percent of the profits. Rising rubber prices and reports of abundant rubber in the forests of the southeast assured the founders millions in stock flotation profits and led others to petition the bureaucracy for the grant of a land concession in the northwest. In the meanwhile, however, lively criticism of the colonial director's generosity had arisen, and this second concession carried with it specific obligations in regard to opening up the country economically. The new company, the Northwest Cameroons Company (Gesellschaft Nordwest-Kamerun), undertook to respect freedom of trade within the 90,000-plus square kilometers of its concession and to invest at least three million marks within ten years. The concession was limited to fifty years. In contrast to the South Cameroons Company, the Northwest Cameroons Company was not a success, and because it failed to fulfill its obligations regarding the construction of roads and paths, its concession was withdrawn in 1910.

In this same period, the Cameroons was ravaged with a veritable fever of plantation building. Governor Jesco von Puttkamer (1895-1907), also staking everything on the money interests, pursued the plan of creating a plantation economy on the volcanic and very fertile soil of the Cameroon hills. His model was the Portuguese possession, São Tomé.[41] He blindly supported anyone who wished to invest capital in plantations. And not without success. By the end of 1901, no less than thirteen companies with paid-in capital of several million marks had been formed. Thanks to the government's land policy, the companies were able to amass an immense territory in the Victoria district virtually for nothing: by 1904 it exceeded 50,000 hectares. The West African Victoria Plantation Company (West-Afrikanische Pflanzungsgessellschaft Viktoria), founded in 1897, was the foremost and became one of the leading plantation operations of its day, holding some 18,000 hectares, mainly in cocoa, and employing some twenty Europeans and two thousand Africans. A similar development occurred in East Africa, where the East Usambara highlands, close to the coast, encouraged the establishment of coffee plantations and later the cultivation of sisal and rubber.[42]

Even as early as 1894-1895, the Cameroons colonial administration had occupied the Cameroons mountain area by force of arms, because of its potential for the establishment of plantations. The local population, the Bakweri, had been forced to sign a peace treaty, which denied them their existing area of settlement and obligated them to provide workers. The legal basis for the grant of land to plantations and concession companies was then created by means of the Crown

Land Ordinance of 1896 (or 1895 for East Africa). It specified that all land not subject to well-founded third-party claims—the so-called ownerless land—was Crown land and thus state property which the governor was empowered to sell or rent.[43] The rights of the Africans to the land they occupied or cultivated were not infringed upon, but in practice this respect for the rights of the Africans amounted more to recognition of the right to sufficient land than a recognition of specific holdings. The Germans knew full well that ownerless land did not exist according to customary law and that the colonial government would have been able to retain no land whatsoever for plantation companies if the claims of the local population were recognized in their fullest extent. According to the ordinance, the alienation of Crown land was to be the task of a special land commission. But the first land commission was formed only in 1902, after the outraged protests of the Basler mission and interested trade circles enlightened a wider metropolitan public about the excesses of disorderly land expropriation. The colonial administration had also come under fire in the Reichstag. The plantation companies themselves had not hesitated to crowd the local population into insufficient reservations, mostly on the worst land. They also had the administration's connivance for policies which aimed at forcing the Bakweri "through hunger" to work on the plantations, by means of reducing their land holdings to the greatest possible extent.[44] Although pressure from the metropolis led to a reexamination and revision of land policy in the Cameroons, it was still years before enough land could be sliced out of the plantations to meet in some measure the real needs of the Bakweri. It was not so much that the local population was reduced to a proletariat as that the hopeful beginnings of African cocoa production already existing in the region were ruthlessly destroyed.[45]

The first flowering of the colonial economy around 1900, and more specifically the establishment of plantations, raised the question of how Africans living in a subsistence economy could be won for wage labor in service of the economy and administration. Because it became continually more acute, the labor question came to be seen by contemporaries as the chief problem of colonial policy.[46] It was not that Africans could never be interested in wage labor. The possibilities for earning enough for prestige goods, such as were necessary for marriage, in the colonial economy was an inducement not to be underestimated. There were always enough hands for adequately remunerated skilled labor, as shown by the example of the migratory workers on the West African coast and later by the graduates of local mission and government schools. The problem was unskilled labor, the demand for which skyrocketed around 1900. In the beginning, recruiting was undertaken in the neighboring colonies, but the costs in the long run seemed too high. In any case, the governmental agreements which provided the legal underpinnings for recruitment were not renewed after 1900. The employment of Asian coolies was considered but rejected on the grounds of cost. All that remained was local recruitment, and the economy counted on active administrative support.

As a result, the colonial administration made it a custom to demand of defeated tribes the provision of workers as punishment. They were then used as needed for such public services as road and path building, the provision of modern harbor facilities, and the construction of railways, or were turned over to individual plantations. One gets the impression, indeed, that many a so-called punitive expedition was principally aimed at securing cheap labor for the administration and economy. The colonial administration also concluded treaties with individual, influential African chiefs to provide a regular delivery of workers. In 1899 the colonial administration in the Cameroons appointed a labor commissar, whose principal duty was not so much the inspection of plantations as the recruitment of contract laborers. Paralleling his efforts were those of private recruiters, crisscrossing the hinterland. After they had been provided official identification in 1902, they could claim the support of the colonial administration for their activities.

Despite all these efforts, the gap between supply and demand for labor grew wider. This was hardly astonishing because of recruiting methods, which not uncommonly recalled those of the slavers, and because of the frequently dreadful conditions on the plantations, on which mortality reached 75 percent.[47] The planters stood in united opposition to official efforts at legal regulation of, and improvement of, working conditions and argued in the best liberal manner that the state had no right to meddle. But they also argued continually that the government should create a legally based system of forced labor. Direct taxation of Africans thus came to be seen as a means of forcing them to undertake wage labor, or, in the euphemism of the day, "educating the African for work." Although the hut tax was levied in East Africa as early as 1897, the Cameroon's administration considered itself in a position to levy taxes in "pacified" areas only in 1907. Earlier attempts in Duala and the surrounding areas had collapsed in the face of the resistance of the potential taxpayers.

Although the trade firms used force to recruit porters if they could round them up in no other way, they opposed any other sort of institutionalization of forced labor and any sort of state intervention in labor matters. The heads of some trade houses actively joined with the missionaries in favor of effective worker-protection measures. The Bremen merchant J. K. Vietor earned particular laurels in the reform of the "native policy."[48] The attitude of the traders is in part to be accounted for by the fact that Africans preferred working as porters to the drudgery of the plantations. Absences from home were shorter and fit better into the traditional cultivation cycle. Porters could also do a little trading on their own. Second, the traders had no interest in the rise of a plantation economy, and indeed feared for their business. They depended on the products the Africans delivered, but could make little money from plantation workers, particularly since the latter were often paid in goods.

The traders had influence. Despite the rise of modern plantations, it should not be overlooked that the colonial economies in the Cameroons, East Africa, South Africa, Southwest Africa, until the dispossession of the Herero and the

Nama, and most of all Togo, with its fourteen agricultural enterprises holding a scant 1,343 hectares as late as 1913, were all classic "trade economies."[49] These economies were based on the exchange of the raw materials produced by traditional African gathering and agriculture economies for European imports. Palm oil and palm kernels were the main product exported from Togo. From East Africa, the main export was ivory (though it was falling rapidly) and rubber; from Southwest Africa, cattle (to South Africa), hides and fells; and from the Cameroons, palm products and rubber. The rising demand for rubber, indeed, led to a mammoth increase in trade in the south Cameroons.[50] Once the intermediary trade monopoly of the African coastal societies had been broken by military force, European traders and their African employees pushed from Kribi ever deeper into the interior. No adequate infrastructure was created, however, and the colonial government had in fact not even made good its claims to rule. The fact that the South Cameroons Company claimed huge territories in the southeast— 1.5 million hectares was handed over to it in 1905—stoked the fires of expansion. What occurred was plunder pure and simple, and of a ruthlessness that gave even a roughneck like Captain Dominik pause:

> I know. . . what it looks like after this struggle for the gold of the primeval jungle has raged. Blind desire to get rich quick and fear of rivals drives out all regard for anything else, and even local people are caught up in the frenzy. They slaughter everything, they don't plant and they don't harvest, but only make rubber, rubber, rubber. A place is lucky when the crest of the wave rolls past, when the rubber is gone; but then come the. . . columns of porters and there is not enough to eat, and people turn nasty and violent.[51]

Many villagers attempted to escape the pressure by easing off into remote forested regions, but this merely increased the misery of those remaining. If the Africans sought to defend themselves by force, the colonials took this as an indication of the expected general resistance to colonial rule, as a frivolous disregard for their cultural efforts, and finally, as an attack on German national honor itself. Concerned about its prestige among Africans, prestige that according to the ideology of rule could only be established *ex definitionem* through the exercise of power, and at pains to defend themselves against charges of the militant colonialists in the metropolis that it could not defend trade and was failing its duty, the colonial government considered any recalcitrance from the local population as a provocation and went into action with its entire machinery of repression. It was particularly serious that such undertakings, because of their notorious ginger, were often counterproductive. Things planned as limited actions widened because they encouraged resistance, becoming full-scale war, as happened with the South Cameroons disturbances of 1904-1906.

German ruling practices were oriented one-sidedly in the interests of the colonial economy and aimed at an unconditional subjugation of the ruled. Little regard was paid to the dislocation of traditional social and political structures that the confrontation with colonialism had led to. In many areas, however, this disruption provoked African resistance and ended in slaughter. The war in Southwest Africa, the Maji-Maji rebellion, the disturbances in the southeast Cameroons, which led the Duala to complain about the local colonial administration—"an out and out scandal for the most meritorious German Reich" [52]—were signs that German colonial policy had reached a dead end and led to a very serious political crisis in the metropolis. In September 1906, Reichskanzler Bernard von Bülow appointed the banker Bernhard Dernburg as head of the colonial division in order to parry Reichstag attacks from the Center, the Socialist, and the left Liberal parties.[53] When the Socialists and the Center rejected a supplemental appropriation for Southwest Africa in December 1906, Bülow seized the opportunity to dissolve a Reichstag become hostile to him. The election which followed in January 1907, the so-called Hottentot election, fought with colonial slogans, brought victory to the Conservatives, National Liberals, and Progressives. Both Bülow and the colonial bureaucracy could thus count on a friendly Reichstag for the immediate future. What was of particular significance was that the elections also implied electoral support for a reformed colonial policy, the bases of which Dernburg had set forth in a whole series of election campaign speeches. German colonial policy had thus reached a turning point. What was paradoxical and bore within it the seeds of conflict, however, was the government's desire to follow the colonial policy of the opposition.

Dernburg accepted the charges critics had leveled against prior colonial policies, taking up reformist efforts of the previous years, and developing a program of "rational" or "scientific" colonial policy. Instead of working with "destructive means" the new policies were to employ "conserving methods," by which he meant that colonialism implied the planned exploitation of colonial resources for the benefit of the colonists.[54] What was new was his repudiation of the laissez-faire policies of his predecessors, and his talk of state encouragement of economic development. By that he meant mainly the improvement of the infrastructure through railway construction. But he also contemplated scientific exploration and abetting the cultivation of farm products useful to the colonial economy through the construction and expansion of state agricultural services. Dernburg laid especial emphasis on the encouragement of cotton farming in the German colonies as he hoped to overcome the German "cotton famine," or, in other words, to free the German textile industry from the American cotton "monopoly." As in other questions of economic development and exploitation of the colonies, he largely accepted the views of the Colonial Economic Committee of the German Colonial Society. What was especially novel was his belief that the "natives" constituted the "largest asset" on the colonial balance sheet. They thus had to be protected and assisted, both for reasons of optimal exploitation and for ethical reasons.

The organizational bases for realizing the new program were created through the erection of a Reich Colonial Office and through decentralization of financial administration, including a revamping of borrowing arrangements. In the individual colonies, too, a transmission was made from the "heroic" era to an "orderly, bourgeois, commercial period," as Dernburg himself characterized the change.[55] It was accompanied by administrative reorganization. First, new governors were appointed. General von Trotha had been recalled from Southwest Africa as early as 1905, to be succeeded by Friedrich von Lindequist. In 1907 Governor von Puttkamer, compromised by many abuses, departed the Cameroons. His replacement, Theodor von Seitz, was a man after Dernburg's own heart. In East Africa, Baron von Rechenberg replaced von Götzen. There were no changes, however, in Togo, a circumstance which strikingly emphasized the special position of Germany's smallest colony. A pressing task was the unification of the administration, most notably by replacing soldiers with civilians at the local level. Henceforth, rule was to be assured by peaceful means. Individual localities, particularly on the coast, had already been transferred to civilian control. This transfer policy was followed with some degree of consistency only after 1906 and was not complete by the outbreak of World War I.

Heading the local administrative units or districts (*Bezirke, Distrikte*) were district commissioners (*Bezirksamtmänner*) and station heads (*Stationsleiter*), whose positions corresponded to those of the British district commissioners and the French cercle commandants. Like the latter, they exercised executive, legislative, and judicial control over the Africans and thus possessed a plentitude of power and extremely broad jurisdiction. They also had to see to a multitude of tasks. These ranged from keeping law and order, which they had the police forces to do, to collecting taxes and rendering justice, to the building of roads and maintenance of experimental farms. But tax collection became the most important task of administration.[56] Direct taxation was regarded as "peaceful conquest," or so Governor Seitz said. The colonial administration was much exercised with securing the penetration of the cash economy at long last, as the colonial enterprises themselves had done nothing in this direction. Closely related was the hope of using taxes to pry the African out of his alleged self-sufficiency and move him to take up production of export goods or wage labor. In addition, the issuing of tax ordinances was a regulatory measure setting binding norms for native tax payments. In the Cameroons, for example, six marks was due or, alternatively, thirty days labor on station farms, or building stations and roads, with the worker meeting his own costs. The administration itself was primarily concerned with creating new sources of income or increasing the yield from old ones in order to become independent of both the metropolis, meaning the Reichstag, and economic interests. Another important consideration was being able to pay off the loans used to finance the measures finally being systematically undertaken to open up the country. The costs thus incurred were considerable, interest payments sopping up some 32 percent of East African state income in 1914.[57]

Like other colonial rulers, the Germans had to reach a modus vivendi with the leaders of African societies, because both men and money were lacking for direct administration from top to bottom. The Germans were madly pragmatic, the solutions adopted varying according to time and locale, and bore the strong personal stamp of whichever officer or official happened to be in charge at the time. There was neither any unified German policy nor any unity within individual colonies. Particularly in those areas where Germans far in the field encountered well organized "feudal states" with their own administrations they usually settled for the Anglo-Dutch model of appointing a resident who was merely meant to guide the local ruler with advice without interfering with administration or justice. Such residents nonetheless retained the power to undertake police measures and could also manipulate the native succession to power. Residencies were established in the Hima states (Ruanda, Burundi, and Bukoba[58]); in the Lake Chad region (Mora); among the Fulbe-Lamidats in the Cameroons, which in precolonial days had belonged to the emirate of Adamawa, itself a vassal state of the caliphate of Sokoto (Garua, Ngaundere); and in Bamum, bordering Adamawa on the southwest. Bamum's ruler, Njoya, astonished the Germans with his facility for invention, developing, among other things, a system of writing for his people's language. Finally, the residency system was used in the Caprivi Strip in Southwest Africa. Because all of these regions could be only loosely integrated into the colonial economic system, colonial rule was largely limited to an assertion of sovereignty and maintenance of the status quo. Aside from economic grounds, open admiration for the African savannah kingdoms played an important part in the choice to employ indirect rule. Here the kind of order already seemed to exist that the Germans were finding so difficult to create in the forest country, with its geographically restricted societies, the bases of which were kinship structures. This policy encouraged a sort of "subimperialism," such as that of the Islamic Fulbe of the Cameroons, who by exploiting the "peace of God" that the Germans had created, were able to bring within their sway previously independent, segmented non-Islamic societies. This "unconditional subjugation of the fetish worshipping blacks, cannibals, and other wildmen"[59] was not seen as a disadvantage, but was considered a prerequisite for opening up the land for trade. The Germans were thus willing to tolerate it, if not actually to support it.

Along the East African coast and in certain interior districts, the Germans continued the administrative system that the Arabs had established in precolonial days. Outsiders of Arab and Swahili origin served as salaried supervisors (*akidas*) over groups of villages and their chiefs (*jumbes*).[60] In most localities, however, the Germans attempted to make the traditional repositories of authority, the chiefs, into the executive agents of the administration, in a sort of institutionalization designed to secure German rule. Their authority was recognized through the symbolic conferring of flags, scepters, chief's books, and red kepis. If necessary, the colonial administration supported them against their fellows and subjects. On the other hand, they had to transmit German orders and in return for a 5 to 10 percent share of tax revenues were responsible for the fulfillment of the numerous demands of the colonial power and for keeping law and order. Although the colonial rulers also usurped power over high justice and transferred it to the heads of the administrative districts, it was found impossible not to leave jurisdiction in petty civil and criminal matters in the hands of the chiefs. In Duala and its environs, the government even went a step further, creating "native arbitration courts" in the 1890s. These institutions, reminiscent of British "Native Courts," remained an experiment, not employed elsewhere.[61]

In the early years the bureaucrats paid hardly any regard to African customs, institutions, and ideas of law, unless absolutely constrained to do so by the strength of individual African societies. Except in Southwest Africa, however, after 1906 the assumption was that the traditional order ought not be thoughtlessly destroyed but ought to be fostered and used. Colonialism had nonetheless created an entirely new situation. A three-cornered power structure of colonial government-chiefs-subjects, replaced the bipolar structure of precolonial days. "It was a situation fraught with possibilities of chicanery and deception, and rich in tests and new interpretations of loyalty," as anthropologist Otto Friedrich Raum put it.[62] The new system would not work without a certain amount of arbitrariness. The problems began with attempts to identify the chiefs, particularly in areas where the legitimate representatives of African societies had led the primary resistance against the military conquest. Such leaders did everything to conceal their identities from their colonial masters. The problem also arose, however, in the "acephalous" societies, which had no institutions comparable to chiefdoms, but merely leaders of smaller social units such as clans, lineages, or families.

The crisis of 1906-1907 thus inaugurated a new and unquestionably successful phase of German colonial rule, characterized by administrative reform and a real effort on the part of the colonial authorities to avoid warfare between the colonizers and the colonized. The economic upswing in every colony was also unmistakable during this period, and there were, in fact, no more great risings. The increasing conflict between the colonial authorities and the representatives of the economic interests clearly reveal that officials took their protective functions seriously and made good in practice their rights of intervention. A great many regulatory ordinances (on the payment of natives in cash, on porters, and on working conditions, for example) were issued to protect the Africans from the shortsightedness of the economic interests. Great efforts were made to fight endemic diseases and the missions enlarged and expanded their schools.

As in other colonies, the missions provided most of the education available in German Africa. Their work concentrated on the village and elementary schools. If German was taught and the curriculum otherwise met with official approval, the authorities subsidized mission efforts. In German East Africa, the German colonial schools taught Swahili, the lingua franca of the entire region, before beginning instruction in German, an enormous service that greatly facilitated later national integration. In 1911 there were 1,836 elementary schools with 113,356 students in the German African colonies; 58 higher schools for the education of auxiliary personnel for the administration, missions, and economy, with 3,244 students; and 37 vocational schools (for the trades, agriculture, and, for girls, domestic service) with 837 students.[63] Finally, in both settlement colonies, Southwest and East Africa, there were special schools for the children of the non-African population.

"Rational colonization" did not necessarily imply, however, any attempt to meet the needs of the colonized or a reduction of their burdens, as the brief allusions to the taxation problem illustrate. The needs of the colonizers remained decisive. Dernburg himself was too much the politician not to bend to pressure and avoid major obstacles in his path.

The weight of established interests manifested itself most notably in East Africa, where the settlers undercut attempted reforms. The governor, Baron von Rechenberg, was a diplomat who preferred trafficking with the urbane Muslim shaykhs and Asiatic merchants of Dar es Salaam to the boorish settlers in the bush. The Maji-Maji rebellion had convinced him a radical change of course was unavoidable if the Africans were to be reconciled to colonial rule.[64] His program called for an end to policies favoring European settlers and plantations and the encouragement of traditional African agriculture. Instead of a settlement and plantation colony, Rechenberg sought to make East Africa a trading colony along the lines of Togo. Togo had had no great rebellions and budgets had been balanced since 1906, earning it the reputation of a model colony. Rechenberg believed that any large-scale European settlement would necessarily lead to conflict with the Africans, a conflict "to be resolved only by the shedding of blood."[65] He understood that plantations were dependent on African labor and that compulsion was necessary to recruit such labor.But he was outraged by the way this labor was treated. He was also convinced that the capital-intensive plantations would not be competitive when markets were bad. The rubber boom of 1910 brought the plantations an amazing prosperity, but the rubber depression shortly before World War I did, in fact, force many into bankruptcy. Rechenberg contrasted East Africa with the neighboring English colonies, where the opening of the Uganda railway led to a noteworthy increase in African cash-crop production and integrated previously isolated areas into the market economy. These developments also redounded to the benefit of colonial treasuries, whose incomes rose considerably, and without the risks of conflict latent in the plantation economy. Rechenberg thus set his hopes on the extension of the trunk line from Dar es Salaam to the Lake Victoria region. He also succeeded in convincing Dernburg, who made a ten-week inspection tour of East Africa in 1907, of the correctness of his economic and political ideas. The central trunk line project thus was incorporated in the great colonial railway bill of 1908, which resulted in five lines totalling 1,460 kilometers and bore witness to new state policies subventing economic development.

Rechenberg could count on the trading class and, to some extent at least, the German East Africa Company to support his plans. The settlers, in contrast, felt he threatened their existence. Despite there being only 315 settlers in East Africa in 1907, this small, by no means unified, group was able to influence government policy and make East Africa a settlement colony. The reason they succeeded was that they counted as allies the right-wing parties in the Reichstag. They were, to be sure, unable to prevent Rechenberg from engaging in 1909 in a sort of administrative clean sweep in which he disbanded all communal associations founded in 1901 except the city councils of Tanga and Dar es Salaam. Through these bodies, Europeans had been able, as far up as the district level, to determine the use made of 50 percent of the hut tax and 20 percent of the business tax.[66] They succeeded, however, in forcing Dernburg to shift gears in 1910, winning him over to the extension of the northern railway for the opening up of the area around Mount Kilimanjaro for settlement. They had long sought this measure, but the government had in the past always turned it down. In opposition to Rechenberg's will, Dernburg also agreed to an unofficial majority in the government council, thus supporting colonists' demands for a greater voice in political affairs. Although Rechenberg succeeded in pushing through a reordering of worker legislation, the jurisdiction of these ordinances was so limited that the historian Rainer Tetzlaff sourly commented that "the official native policy became a reductio ad absurdum because of the deadweight of settler interests."[67]

If Dernburg had already begun to veer around to the settlers' side during his term of office, under his successor Friedrich von Lindequist they had things entirely their own way. Lindequist (1910-1911) was a convinced adherent of settlement and had earlier been governor of Southwest Africa. He hardly troubled to conceal his opposition to Rechenberg. Even as under secretary of the Reich Colonial Office, he had led an expert commission for the study of settlement possibilities in East Africa and had determined that 12,000 square kilometers was available for settlement in the northern part of the colony and that it offered settlers the most hopeful sort of opportunities.[68] Rechenberg's successor, a career official from the Colonial Office named Heinrich Schnee, made additional concessions. He restricted the immigration of Indians, who were monopolizing the retail trade and acting as moneylenders. He lengthened the time period of worker contracts, and made it easier to buy state land by reducing prices and simplifying conditions for assuming ownership. Finally, he granted the Europeans in the government council a great majority and larger governmental powers. Compared with neighboring Kenya, the German settlers of East Africa had far more influence and more authority in 1914.[69]

German East Africa had not become a "black country under the German flag," as critics feared it would, but "white man's country." The number of settlers rose from 180 in 1905 to 882 in 1913, and their proportion of the white male population from 13.3 percent to 25 percent. The area in plantations rose from 8,235 hectares in 1902 to 106,292 in 1913, and the total settler area to 542,124 hectares, the period of most rapid increase being, ironically enough, under Rechenberg. Plantations employed 91,892 in 1913.[70] The plantations or, in other words, the European agricultural sector, were the locus of economic growth. They were also principal beneficiaries of the expansion of the excellent agriculture services—research and teaching institutes, and agricultural credit facilities.[71]

Still, African export production had reached a value of 15.2 million marks by 1913, or 46 percent of total exports, thus in principle justifying the expectations of reformers.[72] The rise in production was the result of the progressive opening up of the country by modern communications. The efforts of the administration to introduce and propagandize modern production techniques, accomplished through specially trained travelling instructors, also deserves mention, however. In addition, the taxation of the Africans forced them to cultivate cash crops to pay the hut tax, for which, to give an example, thirty pounds of unginned cotton was necessary. Increased African buying power, as demonstrated by the rise in consumer goods consumption, clearly developed, but at the cost of greater dependence on the market, as increased food imports showed. The rise in African production should also not be allowed to conceal the fact that cultivable land had become scarce in many areas as a result of the expansion of the plantations, the areas most affected being the northern Tanga districts, Wilhelmsthal, Moschi, and Arusha. In several areas the several years' fallowing which traditional African agriculture required was no longer possible, and prospective African innovations were at the very least made more difficult. The Chagga would, for example, have liked to farm coffee, but they lacked the necessary additional land, whereas the Europeans had more land than they could farm.[73]

The administration in the Cameroons faced equally perplexing problems. Although the plundering of rubber resources continued in the southeast, the administration was through intervention and ordinance able to prevent the worst excesses. Plantations continued to expand, but remained considerably less extensive than in East Africa, because the climate made the Cameroons unsuitable for settlers.[74] Like Governor Rechenberg, the Cameroons administration staked its policy after Puttkamer's dismissal on encouraging and modernizing the African production sector.[75] African entrepreneurial initiatives were no longer fought as unwanted competition for European colonial companies, as had been true in the beginning, when African cocoa planters in the Victoria district had been dispossessed and the African trading chiefs forced out of the export trade. With both surprise, because it contradicted current notions about "lazy niggers," and satisfaction, because it fit in with administration aims, it was noted that former Duala traders had gone over to cash-crop production. It has also been recognized that expansion of colonial trade and the European sector of the colonial economy would lead to disaster if food production could not be simultaneously pushed above the subsistence level. But the latter would be hard to do if colonial development increasingly siphoned off the productive forces of the African economy. The problem became particularly acute when, under the watchword of "rational colonization," a really serious effort was made to build a modern infrastructure.

First, to build roads and railways, hundreds of thousands of workers had to be employed, the majority recruited through administrative compulsion and their provisioning secured through the market. Second, if at all possible, the profitability of the railroad had to be assured. It was understood that viability could only be achieved through raising the African production of such things as rubber and mass production of corn, cocoa, palm oil and palm kernels. Merely expanding the traditional gathering economy, as typified by existing rubber collection methods, would not suffice. The administration accordingly set out to create an elaborate agricultural service like those in Togo and East Africa. That demonstrates once more that the colonial administration was quite capable of learning from its errors. Nonetheless, the means devoted to encouragement of African agriculture stood in grotesque disproportion to the job at hand. As late as 1912, there were only forty-two agricultural officials in the Cameroons, and the means at their disposal amounted to only 3 percent of the entire budget. The entire program was, moreover, threatened after 1905 by the sharply rising demand for labor, the private sector pressing ever more urgently for official assistance in recruiting it. Still, small though the successes in the agrarian sector may have been before 1914, the heirs of German colonial rule were filled with admiration for what their predecessors had created.

Southwest Africa also enjoyed a considerable economic efflorescence after 1906. In March 1908 rich diamond fields were discovered in portions of the Namibian desert within the concession area of the German Southwest Africa Company. Dernburg turned over the exploitation and marketing of these diamonds to private monopolies, in which the Southwest African Company and the great metropolitan banks played a leading role.[76] Dernburg had thus reverted to the concessions policy of his predecessors, which he had once so vigorously protested; indeed, only in April 1908, the mining administration had reverted from the mining companies back to the Reich. His action was severely criticised, and particularly by the settlers of Southwest Africa themselves, who considered that the colonial administration had shut them out of the lucrative diamond business. The government got its cut in the form of an excise tax on diamond exports and a mining tax, which in 1913 was changed into a tax on net profits. These new incomes rose as diamond production rose. In 1908 production was 38,275 carats and by 1913 1.5 million, and treasury receipts rose from 6,334,000 marks in 1908 to 23,299,000 marks in 1914.[77] This money was available for other development projects. In order to secure control of this income and assure that it profited European agriculture, the settlers beat the autonomy drum with increasing vigor.

The thirst for political autonomy had long since become a bitter one indeed, and Governor Schuckmann (1907-1910) in particular pushed for an expansion of self-government. In 1907 he requested the lord mayor of Bückeburg, Wilhelm Külz, to work out a system of self-government for the colony. Külz presented his proposal in 1908. It placed communal administration in the hands of an elected community council. It contemplated a Landesrat ("council of state") half of whose members were to be elected by district associations and half appointed by the governor.[78] Officials and unofficials were to be equally represented, though the Landesrat, like the older government council, was to be purely consultative in competence. Dernburg himself had postulated the collaboration of the white population in the administration and, after some initial hesitation, called for support for the proposal. The new system was widely supported in the Reichstag and went into effect in 1909. It pleased neither the governor nor the settlers, however, the settlers wanting more power. In 1913 the Landesrat was given control of a portion of the budget and control of a series of local matters. It thus had become in a restricted sense a legislative body. Africans were, of course, not represented, for Southwest Africa was a settlement colony, in which the administration and settlers alone determined and pursued what they themselves entitled a "policy of domination." In 1913 roughly one-sixth of the entire territory was private farmland.

Every reform attempt by Dernburg and others in the metropolis foundered on the rock of the settlers, who had been radicalized by the war and whose will to rule remained unbroken.[79] The very question of how the Africans were to be treated revealed with especial clarity the gap between the aspirations and realities of Dernburg's reform policy. The policy of annihilation was, indeed, abandoned and the Africans were conceded the right to exist. But the desire to hold the Africans in total dependence remained as strong as ever, as was the intent to strip them of every sort of independence. As Paul Rohrbach, Commissioner for Settlement from 1903 to 1906, put it: "Our job is to strip the Herero of his heritage and national characteristics and gradually to submerge him, along with the other natives, into a single colored working class."[80] And Dernburg, whose platform had called for a new, "humane native policy," could in his 1908 tour of Southwest Africa speak of an improvement of native conditions only to the degree that they "were to be preserved as a labor force in the present and as progenitors of a healthy younger generation for the future."[81] Can this be called progress?

As a result of the uprisings between 1904 and 1907, the surviving Herero and Nama, scattered by both accident and plan over the entire colony, lost their entire tribal property. The Germans did not hesitate to seize all their stock and land. Thenceforth, Africans needed the governor's consent to own large or riding animals or even land, which was tantamount to prohibition. Having remained loyal during the rebellion, the so-called Bastards of Rehoboth were exempt from this proviso, as were the Ovambo, whose settlement area in the north remained closed to all Europeans. On top of all that, the colonial masters created a very refined, compulsory labor system in 1908. Every African more than eight years old had to carry a passbook at all times. Should he desire to leave the district where he lived, he needed a travel pass. Anyone not under labor contract could be arrested as a vagrant (rather like Portuguese practice). Only the great lack of labor in the steadily growing colonial economy—in 1913, the Ovambo were even taken on for the first time as contract migratory laborers in the diamond fields—and the simple impossibility of imposing effective police controls over such a vast area mitigated somewhat the harshness of the system.

Many Hereros secretly fled from their homeland to British Bechuanaland or South Africa. But anyone seized in flight had to reckon with capital punishment. The refusal of the settlers to allow the Africans any sort of legal security made things worse. Not only were the various ordinances protecting Africans conceded no validity, but the settlers claimed the right to punish Africans themselves. When Colonial Secretary Wilhelm Solf visited the colonies in 1912, he noted in his diary: "Most whites, especially the farmers, consider the native an animal." And: "the natives hate the whites, and the whites scorn the natives. No position between these extremes seems to exist. Friendliness is accounted weakness, and curses and blows are the natural language of discourse."[82] An investigation in the central Herero territory revealed a majority of employers followed a policy of "systematic and in part deliberate undernourishment."[83] A series of trials occasioned because of mistreatment with fatal consequences and even murders of Africans were held between 1911 and 1913. Causing a great stir, they also revealed the horrors of the colonial reality.

The trials at least signalled a change in the attitudes of officials themselves. The colonial government was the plaintiff against the settlers and the defender of the Africans. The striking drop in African birthrates had alarmed the more farsighted of the colonial masters. It also did not escape them that the Africans never acknowledged their dispossession and that an underground unification was taking place among the Hereros. Mass conversations in 1909 were the overt sign of this movement.[84] Yet despite the easing of the prohibition against owning large animals after 1912, the employment of commissars to supervise native working conditions, and the attempt to regenerate the health of the Hereros on government farms, both the will and the strength to bring about a basic change of course was absent. Woodrow Wilson's judgment of German colonial rule thus, on account of what happened in Southwest Africa, hardly surprises one, even if it was unjustifiably sweeping.

NOTES

1. Henri Brunschwig, *L'Expansion Allemande Outre-Mer du XVe siècle à nos Jours* (Paris: Presses Universitaires de France, 1957); Robert Cornevin, "The Germans in Africa before 1918," in Gann and Duignan, *Colonialism*, I; *Britain and Germany in Africa*, with extensive bibliography and important essays on particular problems by, among others, William Roger Louis, Henry Ashby Turner, Arthur J. Knoll, Jean Stengers, Colin W. Newbury, Elizabeth M. Chilver, Helmut Bley, and John Iliffe.

2. Quoted by Jean Stengers, "British and German Imperial Rivalry: A Conclusion," in *Britain and Germany in Africa*, 346.

3. In 1871, he stated that colonies for Germany would be "rather comparable to silken ermines for Polish noblemen lacking shirts"; quoted in Wehler, *Bismarck*, 192.

4. For an argument along such lines see Alan John Percivale Taylor, *Germany's First Bid for Colonies, 1884-1885: A Move in Bismarck's European Policy* (London: Macmillan 1938).

5. William Osgood Aydelotte, *Bismarck and British Colonial Policy: The Problem of South West Africa, 1883-1885* (Philadelphia: University of Pennsylvania Press, 1937); but see also Erich Eyck, *Bismarck* (3 vols., Erlenbach-Zurich: E. Rentsch, 1941-44), III.

6. William Otto Henderson, *Studies in German Colonial History* (London: F. Cass, 1962).

7. Wehler provides an extensive criticism of the older interpretations; *Bismarck*, 412-23. Klaus J. Bade, *Friedrich Fabri und der Imperialismus der Bismarckzeit: Revolution, Depression, Expansion* (Freiburg i. Br., Zurich: Atlantis, 1975), provides rich material supporting Wehler's thesis.

8. Germany, Reichstag, *Stenographische Berichte über die Verhandlungen des Reichstags*, VI. Legislatur-Periode, II. Session, 1885-86, 117; V. Leg., IV Sess., 1884, II, 1062. Hereafter cited as *Verhandlungen*.

9. See H. P. Jaeck, "Die deutsche Annexion," in Helmuth Stoecker (ed.), *Kamerun unter deutscher Kolonialherrschaft: Studien* (2 vols., Berlin: Rütten & Loening, 1960, 1968), I, 81ff.; Helmut Washausen, *Hamburg und die Kolonialpolitik des Deutschen Reiches 1880 bis 1890* (Hamburg: H. Christians, 1968); Wehler, *Bismarck*, 320ff.

10. Horst Drechsler, *Südwestafrika unter deutscher Kolonialherrschaft: Der Kampf der Herero und Nama gegen den deutschen Imperialismus (1884-1915)*, (Berlin: Akademie-Verlag, 1966), ch. 1; Wehler, *Bismarck*, 284-90.

11. "Penniless, gifted, energetic, without scruple; wily, self-satisfied, and utterly lacking in tact; in short an adventurer and compleat con-man"; Fritz Ferdinand Müller, *Deutschland—Zanzibar—Ost-afrika: Geschichte einer deutschen Kolonialeroberung 1884-1890* (Berlin: Rütten & Loening, 1959), 98; Wehler, *Bismarck*, 333-72.

12. Müller, *Deutschland*, 370f., 376-91. But see also the contemporary account of Rochus Schmidt, *Geschichte des Araberaufstandes in Ostafrika: Seine Entstehung, seine Niederwerfung und seine Folgen* (Frankfurt a.d. Oder: Verlag der Königlichen Hofdruckerei, Trowitzsch, 1892).

13. Müller, *Deutschland*, 509f.

14. Fieldhouse, *Kolonialreiche*, 323.

15. *Verhandlungen*, VII. Leg., I. Sess. 1890-91, I, 39.

16. Müller, *Deutschland*, 496.

17. On the development of the central administration and the various interest groups, see Harry Rudolph Rudin, *Germans in the Cameroons, 1884-1914: A Case Study in Modern Imperialism* (New Haven: Yale University Press, 1938), ch. 4, a classic work in modern colonial history; see also Karin Hausen, *Deutsche Kolonialherrschaft in Afrika: Wirtschaftsinteressen und Kolonialverwaltung in Kamerun vor 1914* (Freiburg i. Br., Zurich: Atlantis, 1970), ch. 1.

18. Hans Spellmeyer, *Deutsche Kolonialpolitik im Reichstag* (Stuttgart: W. Kohlhammer, 1931). See also Hans-Christoph Schröder, *Sozialismus und Imperialismus: Die Auseinandersetzung der deutschen Sozialdemokratie mit dem Imperialismusproblem und der "Weltpolitik" vor 1914* (Bonn-Bad Godesberg: Verlag Neue Gesellschaft, 1975).

19. "Reichszuschüsse," in *Deutsches Kolonial-Lexikon*, ed. Heinrich Schnee (3 vols., Leipzig: Quelle & Meyer, 1920), III.

20. Werner Schiefel, *Bernhard Dernburg 1865-1937: Kolonialpolitiker und Bankier im wilhelminischen Deutschland* (Freiburg i. Br., Zurich: Atlantis Verlag, 1974), 89f., 92ff.

21. Rudin, *Germans*, ch. 5.

22. See Albert Wirz, *Vom Sklavenhandel zum kolonialen Handel: Wirtschaftsräume und Wirschaftsformen in Kamerun vor 1914* (Zurich: Atlantis Verlag, 1972), 175f.

23. "Let's at least be honest with ourselves and drop this beautiful fairy story that we are going to Africa to do good works for the Negroes. Talk of 'Civilizing missions'. . . and all the rest of that malarky is nothing more than a fig-leaf for the plain and simple employment of the brutal natural law of the stronger. . . . We need not be ashamed of this naked truth, namely, that we are engaged in Realpolitik"; Franz Karl Hutter, "Kamerun," in *Das überseeische Deutschland: die deutschen Kolonien in Wort und Bild, nach den neuesten Stand der Kenntnis* (2 vols., Stuttgart: Union Deutsche Verlagsgesellschaft, 1911), I, 160f.

24. Cf. the protectorate treaty with the Duala in Stoecker, *Kamerun*, II, 259f., and the interpretations of Jaeck, ibid., I, 84f., and Wirz, *Sklavenhandel*, 54.

25. *Verhandlungen*, VIII. Leg., II. Sess., 1892-93, II, 1350. The following is based mainly

on Helmut Bley, *Kolonialherrschaft und Sozialstruktur in Deutsch-Südwestafrika 1894-1914* (Hamburg: Leibnitz-Verlag, 1968), pts. 1 and 2.

26. Drechsler, *Südwestafrika*, ch. 2.
27. Bley, *Kolonialherrschaft*, 172.
28. Drechsler, *Südwestafrika*, 149.
29. On the course of the Herero and Nama rebellions, see ibid., ch. 3.
30. Ibid., 184.
31. Bley, *Kolonialherrschaft*, 193.
32. See John Iliffe, *Tanganyika under German Rule, 1905-1912* (London: Cambridge University Press, 1969), ch. 2.
33. Quoted by Rainer Tetzlaff, *Koloniale Entwicklung und Ausbeutung: Wirtschafts-und Sozialgeschichte Deutsch-Ostafrikas 1885-1914* (Berlin: Duncker und Humblot, 1970), 218.
34. John Iliffe, "The Organization of the Maji Maji Rebellion," *JAH*, 9 (July 1967)), 495-512, and Robert I. Rotberg, "Resistance and Rebellion in British Nyasaland and German East Africa, 1888-1915," in *Britain and Germany in Africa*, 689. The parallels with the Congo rebellion of 1964-1965 are striking.
35. Tetzlaff, *Koloniale Entwicklung*, 220.
36. Brunschwig, *L'Expansion Allemande*, 176; "Kapitalanlagen und Bevölkerung der Schutzgebiete," in *Kolonial-Lexikon*, II; Hausen, *Deutsche Kolonialherrschaft*, 15.
37. Manfred Nussbaum, *Vom "Kolonialenthusiasmus" zur Kolonialpolitik der Monopole: zur deutschen Kolonialpolitik unter Bismarck, Caprivi, Hohenlohe* (Berlin: Akademie Verlag, 1962), 54ff., 130ff.
38. Drechsler, *Südwestafrika*, 141.
39. Herbert Jäckel, *Die Landgesellschaften in den deutschen Schutzgebieten: Denkschrift zur kolonialen Landfrage* (Jena: G. Fischer, 1909).
40. J. Ballhaus, "Die Landkonzessionsgesellschaften," in Stoecker, *Kamerun*, II, 99-179.
41. Hausen, *Deutsche Kolonialherrschaft*, 216-24; A. Rüger, "Die Entstehung und Lage der Arbeiterklasse unter dem deutschen Kolonialregime in Kamerun," in Stoecker, *Kamerun*, I, 162-67; M. Michel, "Les Plantations Allemandes du Mont Cameroun, 1885-1914," *RFHOM*, 57: no. 207 (1969), 183-213.
42. Tetzlaff, *Koloniale Entwicklung*, ch. 4.
43. On land policy, see Rüger, "Entstehung," 182-91, and Heinrich Krauss, *Die moderne Bodengesetzgebung in Kamerun, 1884-1964* (Berlin, New York; Springer-Verlag, 1966).
44. Quoted from a 1905 report about the activities of the Land Commission of the Buea district in Rüger, "Entstehung," 189.
45. Wirz, *Vom Sklavenhandel*, 203-7.
46. Rüger, "Enstehung," and Hella Winkler, "Das Kameruner Proletariat, 1906-1914," in Stoecker, *Kamerun*, I, 243-86; Hausen, *Deutsche Kolonialherrschaft*, 274-90; Patrice Mandeng, *Auswirkungen der deutschen Kolonialherrschaft in Kamerun: Die Arbeiterbeschaffung in den Südbezirken während der deutschen Kolonialherrschaft 1884-1914* (Hamburg: Buske, 1973), ch. 4; Tetzlaff, *Koloniale Entwicklung*, 193ff., 233-51.
47. Rüger, "Entstehung," 231; Winkler, "Kameruner Proletariat," 275.
48. O. Diehn, "Kaufmannschaft und deutsche Eingeborenenpolitik von der Jahrhundertwende bis zum Ausbruch des Weltkrieges" (Dissertation, University of Hamburg, 1956); Erik Halldèn, *The Culture Policy of the Basel Mission in the Cameroons, 1886-1905* (Lund: Berlingska Boktryckeriet, 1968), 121ff.
49. "Pflanzungen," in *Kolonial-Lexikon*, III. On Togo in general, see Arthur J. Knoll, *Togo under Imperial Germany, 1884-1914: A Case Study in Colonial Rule* (Stanford: Hoover Institution Press, 1978); M. B. K. Darkoah, "Togoland under the Germans: Thirty Years of Economic Development (1884-1914)," *Nigerian Geographical Journal*, 10: no. 2 (1967), 107-22; ibid., 11: no. 2 (1968), 153-68; and Robert Cornevin, *Histoire du Togo* (Paris: Berger-Levrault, 1959).
50. Hausen, *Deutsche Kolonialherrschaft*, 261ff.; R. Kaeselitz, "Kolonialeroberung und Widerstandskampf in Südkamerun," in Stoecker, *Kamerun*, II, 11-55; Wirz, *Sklavenhandel*, 107-47.

51. Quoted in Wirz, *Sklavenhandel*, 137.

52. Germany, Reichstag, *Stenographische Berichte über den Verhandlungen des Reichstags: Anlagen zu den Berichten*, 4. Anlageband 1905-06, Dok. 294, Anlage 1, p. 339f.; A. Rüger, "Die Duala und die Kolonialmacht, 1884-1914: Eine Studie über die historischen Ursprünge des afrikanischen Antikolonialismus," in Stoecker, *Kamerun*, II, 201-14.

53. Schiefel, *Dernburg*, 35ff. Dernburg was of Jewish origin on his father's side.

54. Dernburg's colonial program is discussed in detail in ibid., 55-66, but see also Dernburg's own *Koloniale Erziehung* (Munich: Münchener Neueste Nachrichten, 1907), and *Zielpunkte des deutschen Kolonialwesens: Zwei Vorträge* (Berlin: E. S. Mittler, 1907).

55. *Verhandlungen*, vol. 236, 7192.

56. Iliffe, *Tanganyika*, 76, notes that under Rechenberg, "the local administration became a vast tax-collecting bureaucracy." See also Hausen, *Deutsch Kolonialherrschaft*, 96ff.

57. Charlotte Leubuscher, *Tanganyika Territory: A Study of Economic Policy under Mandate* (London, New York: Oxford University Press, 1944), 154, as cited by Iliffe, *Tanganyika*, 76.

58. William Roger Louis, *Ruanda-Urundi, 1884-1919* (Oxford: Clarendon Press, 1963); Ralph A. Austen, *Northwest Tanzania under German and British Rule: Colonial Policy and Tribal Politics, 1889-1939* (New Haven: Yale University Press, 1968).

59. Jesco von Puttkamer in an 1889 report to Bismarck, as quoted in Wirz, *Sklavenhandel*, 170.

60. O. F. Raum, "Changes in African Life under German Administration, 1892-1914," in *History of East Africa*, II, 174ff.

61. Rudin, *Germans*, 198-206.

62. Raum, "Changes," 179.

63. Martin Schlunk, *Die Schulen für Eingeborene in den deutschen Schutzgbieten am 1. Juli 1911: Auf Grund einer statistischen Erhebung der Zentralstelle des Hamburgischen Kolonialinstituts* (Hamburg: L. Friedrichsen & Co., 1914), 143, 360-63; Johanna Eggert, *Missionsschule und sozialer Wandel in Ostafrika: Der Beitrag der deutschen evangelischen Missions-gesellschaften zur Entwicklung des Schulwesens in Tanganyika, 1891-1939* (Bielefeld: Bertelsmann Universitätsverlag, 1970).

64. On the following see Iliffe, *Tanganyika*, ch. 4., and Schiefel, *Dernburg*, 67-73.

65. As quoted by Tetzlaff, *Koloniale Entwicklung*, 107.

66. On Rechenberg's administrative reforms, see in addition to Iliffe and Tetzlaff, Detlef Bald, *Deutsch-Ostafrika 1900-1914: Eine Studie über Verwaltung, Interessengruppen und wirtschaftliche Erschliessung* (Munich: Weltforum Verlag, 1970), pt. 2.

67. Tetzlaff, *Koloniale Entwicklung*, 232.

68. Since the report ran counter to Dernburg's plans, it was published only in 1912: Friedrich von Lindequist, *Deutsch-Ostafrika als Siedlungsgebiet für Europäer unter Berücksichtigung Britisch Ostafrikas und Nyassaland: Bericht der 1908 unter Führung des damaligen Unterstaatsekretärs Dr. von Lindequist nach Ostafrika entsandten Kommission* (Munich, Leipzig: Duncker & Humblot, 1912).

69. Iliffe, *Tanganyika*, 205.

70. Figures are from Tetzlaff, *Koloniale Entwicklung*, 62, 115, 188, 194.

71. Bald, *Deutsch-Ostafrika*, 161-71. Raum, "Changes," 190: "If the African economy had enjoyed comparable government support, African native agriculture might have been much more effectively developed, and might have earned praise for having 'opened up' the country."

72. Tetzlaff, *Koloniale Entwicklung*, 177.

73. Ibid., 134.

74. Hausen, *Deutsche Kolonialherrschaft*, 220.

75. On the following see Wirz, *Sklavenhandel*, 209-22.

76. Schiefel, *Dernburg*, 101-8.

77. "Diamanten und Finanzen," in *Kolonial Lexikon*, I.

78. Wilhelm Külz, *Die Selbstverwaltung für Deutsch-Südwestafrika* (Berlin: W. Süsserott, 1909); Bley, *Kolonialherrschaft*, 223-34.

79. I follow here Bley, *Kolonialherrschaft*, pt. 3.

80. Paul Rohrbach, *Deutsche Kolonialwirtschaft* (Berlin-Schöneberg: Buchverlag der "Hilfe," 1907), 285.

81. From a speech to the administrative officials of the Windhoek government, on 12 August 1908, quoted in Bley, *Kolonialherrschaft*, 266.

82. Quoted in ibid., 306.

83. Johannes Gad, *Die Betriebsverhältnisse der Farmen des mittleren Hererolandes (Deutsch-Südwestafrika)*, (Hamburg: L. Friedrichsen & Co., 1915); the formulation is from Bley, *Kolonialherrschaft*, 288.

84. See O. Köhler, "The State of Acculturation in Southwest Africa," *Soziologus*, N. F., 6 (1956), 81ff.

Albert Wirz **13**

PORTUGAL IN AFRICA

Portuguese mariners were the first Europeans to explore the African coasts. At the very beginning of the modern era, they set up forts and trading stations in Africa, both to secure the sea routes to India and to exploit local riches. Until the nineteenth century, effective political control was restricted to a few islands off the coast (the Cape Verdes, São Tomé, Principé, and the island Moçambique), some ports (Luanda, Benguela), and their immediate surroundings. Still, it is worthy of note that Portugal was sending military expeditions inland as early as the sixteenth century in order to exert direct influence on the hinterland. They also concluded alliances with African rulers and built inland trading posts and fortified strong points along the most important trade routes. They hung on to them through the succeeding centuries—Tete and Sena on the Zambesi are examples. Such is the basis for Portugal's claim to have been the oldest African colonial power.[1]

Portugal's ties to the Bakongo kingdom date back to the fifteenth century and constitute a phenomenon unique in the history of European-African relations. They do so because neither military conquest nor economic exploitation was involved, Portugal's principal aim being the peaceful propagation of Christian culture. The relations between Portugal and the Congo kingdom rested on a basis of complete equality between the two states.[2] In the course of the sixteenth century, however, the Portuguese came to see the Congo kingdom mainly as a vast source of slaves. The result was the development of unbridgeable conflicts of interest, and the alliance ended amid scenes of horror. Commerce subdued civilizing ideals, and thenceforth determined the course of events. What remained was the mythical ideal that a special relationship existed between Portuguese and Africans and that Portugal had an historical African mission.

With the beginning of the transatlantic slave trade, Portuguese interest came to center on São Tomé, where a profitable plantation economy and one of the most important entrepôts for the trade with black Africa developed. The second important area was the Mbundu territory south of the Congo, whose ruler, Ngola, gave the colony its eventual name, Angola. Angola acquired an unhappy notoriety as the foremost supplier of slaves for Brazilian plantations, until Sá de Bandeira formally abolished slavery in Portuguese territories in 1836. Benguela, founded in 1617, and more importantly, Luanda, founded in 1575, developed into flourishing cities thanks to the slave trade, at the cost to the interior of three centuries of war, famine, and depopulation. The total number of Angolans dragged in chains to the New World remains unknown, but there is evidence that the Portuguese alone shipped some 1.4 million slaves out of Angolan ports during the eighteenth century.[3] The end of the slave trade brought a severe economic crisis to Angola (and also to Guinea, another favored slave-loading area) which was not really overcome until the twentieth century. Grandiose plans for colonization, intended to make Angola a "second Brazil," achieved very modest results: a few coffee planters settled in the central highland (the Huila plateau). Thus, while the dominance of the trading class continued, a small settler class with its own political goals arose alongside it. In wild rubber, moreover, the Portuguese had a new, easily collectible, potential export product. But the transition from a labor-exporting economy to one which utilized local natural resources seems to have been beyond Portuguese strength.

The gold and silver of the Monomotapa kingdom, whose former greatness the ruined city of Zimbabwe still reveals today, also lured the Portuguese to the east coast. Here, the Portuguese competed with Arab traders. This area, too, came to supply the ruinous transatlantic slave trade. It was less extensive than in Angola but therefore all the harder to suppress. In the sixteenth and seventeenth centuries, Portuguese and Indians from Portuguese Goa had conquered immense latifundia from the Africans which were then acknowledged by the Portuguese Crown as *prazos*. Their holders, the *prazeiros*, ruled like medieval aristocrats, waging war as often against Portuguese garrisons as against the African tribes of the area.[4] Only toward the end of the nineteenth century was the state able to bring the prazeiros, who had intermarried with Africans and by then formed a sort of mulatto aristocracy, under effective state control. This was a part of a general assertion of Portuguese colonial sovereignty, and it cost the prazeiros their latifundia. The hereditary rental system itself, however, was continued under the great Moçambique land-concession companies.

Early Portuguese colonization in Africa was more a series of spectacular and occasionally suicidal individual actions than the result of any consistent state policy. The African colonies were also subservient to the needs of the more important Asian and South American possessions. Moçambique was actually administered from Goa until the middle of the eighteenth century. In the nineteenth century that changed, both because Brazil became independent in 1822 and perhaps more importantly because of the unwelcome competition with other European powers in Africa itself. The competition with France was for the Casamance area and with Britain for the island of Bolama; it also arose out of the long struggle over Delagoa Bay, one of the best harbors on the east coast of Africa; and finally, it arose out of the disputes over the rights of sovereignty over the mouth of the Congo which culminated in the Berlin Conference of

1884-1885. Earlier, the journeys of the Scottish missionary David Livingston in the Zambesi and Rovuma regions, along Lake Nyasa, and through Benguela had brought the Portuguese African possessions to the attention of a wider European public. Livingston sharply criticized the Portuguese African presence: "The Portuguese pretense to dominion is the curse of the Negro race on the East Coast of Africa."[5] Such criticism was picked up by a variety of philanthropists, chauvinists, and colonial propagandists and largely determined judgments of Portugal's existing colonial efforts.

The Portuguese themselves did not dispute that, after three centuries, Portuguese colonization in Africa still constituted more of an assertion than a reality. Ferreira d'Almeida, navy minister in 1887 and again in 1895, was far from the only one raising doubts about Portugal's competence to rule an empire that had, to be sure, shrunk over the course of the centuries, but was still extensive enough. To reduce Portugal's burdens, he brought in a bill in parliament to sell Guinea, Moçambique, Goa, Macao, and Timor, and to concentrate on Angola. But his bill failed. Those who saw imperial expansion as cure for Portugal's domestic political difficulties and as, indeed, a guarantee for Portugal's continued independence and existence as a viable national state, proved to be too influential.

Portuguese illusions were soon shattered in the scramble for Africa. Historical claims turned out to matter less in the imperial struggle for colonies than the real strength of the metropolis. However, Portugal, riven by domestic political crises and economically backward, was unable to play an independent role in the European concert of powers. Portugal ultimately emerged from the scrimmage with one of the largest empires, but it owed it less to its own strength than to the conflicts among the other European powers. Although Portugal sought support first from England and then from France and Germany,[6] it had to abandon its claims to the Congo basin and the lower Congo River. It was, however, able to retain the Angola coast as far as the mouth of the Congo and the Cabinda enclave to the north of it. But the newfangled project of a transcontinental colonial empire shattered on British resistance. In 1890 Lord Salisbury issued an ultimatum ordering the withdrawal of A. A. du Rocha Serpa Pinto's expeditionary force from Nyassaland. Because Britain threatened the breech of diplomatic relations, Portugal had to give in. The Portuguese public responded with cries of injured national pride to this "humiliation" by "perfidious Albion." Although the government fell, the dream of a rose-colored map was dead forever.

Even after conclusion of treaties with France, Great Britain, Belgium, and Germany which delimited frontiers, Portugal could hardly rest easy in possession of its colonies. Germany in particular still cherished hopes of acquiring Portuguese territory in southern Angola and Moçambique, because the bankrupt Portuguese could not pay their foreign debts. Germany claimed these territories in a secret treaty of 1898 with England. Portugal, however, took pains to avoid giving Germany an excuse to intervene by pledging its colonial customs revenues to the payment of its debt. The British, for their part, renewed in 1899 their long-standing guarantees of Portugal's colonial empire in return for Portugal's neutrality in the Boer War. New dangers threatened only when the second Morocco crisis led British Foreign Secretary Sir Edward Grey to revive the 1898 treaty proposal as a means of reaching a modus vivendi with Germany. World War I broke out, however, before the treaty could be ratified. In the war itself, German troops from Southwest Africa invaded southern Angola, and General Paul Emil von Lettow-Vorbeck led his troops into Moçambique to gather strength in 1917-1918. But the German defeat in Europe and the Versailles treaties finally ended the danger of a new partition of the Portuguese colonies.

The onset of modern Portuguese colonization in Africa was thus doubly threatened by inner crises and external dangers. The government had not only to mollify opponents of the colonial empire within its own ranks and overcome local African opposition but at the same time fight off European claimants and critics. These factors made imperative a rapid transition from the heretofore purely nominal or at best indirect rule to effective political control. But how could this be accomplished except through the establishment of military rule? At least in the eyes of those responsible, military occupation of the territories claimed seemed the only way out, especially since they were determined to make good Portuguese claims to sovereignty. Without regard for the high costs incurred, they began to establish a network of fortified posts. Wherever the Portuguese encountered resistance to their claims to rule, they launched systematic military campaigns, with trade routes and potential settlement areas being the primary targets of the soldiers. Within two decades, a handful of self-confident officers, who often pushed on against the wishes of a metropolis constrained to pay some attention to costs, had succeeded in breaking African primary resistance. Superior technology and the inability of contemporary African leaders to join forces assisted them.

The principal military actions in Angola were concentrated first in the Dembos region north of Luanda. This area had been in revolt since 1872 and was only subdued finally in 1907. Second, there was fighting along the southern border, where in 1904 the Cuanhama inflicted a severe defeat on invading Portuguese troops. This area was not accounted "pacified" until World War I. Third, the Bailundo campaign of 1902 subdued the Ovimbundo region.[7] In Moçambique, military efforts were mainly directed against Gungunhama, ruler of Gaza, which lay in the area bordering the Transvaal. Gungunhama, who attempted to play the Portuguese and the British South Africa Company off against each other, was taken prisoner in 1895, led in triumph through the streets of Lisbon, banished to the Azores, and baptized a Christian.[8] Additional campaigns reduced the Barue territories and the Yao on the eastern shore of Lake Nyasa (1898-1912). A series of minor campaigns waged between 1906 and 1910 subdued the recalcitrant chiefs along the coast opposite the island of Moçambique. Finally, between 1890 and 1914, Guinea was also the scene of a variety of campaigns, in which the Fula of the savannah assisted in overcoming the coastal peoples.

These military actions swallowed up the better part of the colonial budget before World War I and necessitated large subsidies from the Portuguese treasury. Between 1895 and 1912, Angola alone required 5,022 million escudos to cover its budget deficits.[9] These subsidies, however, also facilitated the strengthening of local executive agencies and experimentation with new administrative structures. The latter were better suited to local needs than the liberal centralism of the nineteenth century, which had encouraged the administrative petrification.

A series of ad-hoc administrative measures was taken around the turn of the century during the course of the expansion. They were sanctioned in 1907 by Ayres de Ornelas's colonial reform law, which established model administrative structures for the Portuguese colonies. The law was reconfirmed by the colonial reform acts of 1930, which were valid until very recently.[10] Given the lack of money and personnel, however, this system could be introduced in the colonies only by stages. In Moçambique the state left the assertion of sovereignty for almost half the territory to private land concession companies. The Companhia do Nyassa administered the region north of the Lurio River until 1929. The Companhia de Moçambique administered the Manica and Sofala districts from 1891 to 1942. The latter company was truly a state within a state, which had its own governor in Beira and was on the whole very successful. Even mistrustful officials from the state administration in Moçambique had to concede that the company's administration was a model of its kind.[11]

Like France, Portugal followed the principle of direct rule, and the parallels between the two systems are unmistakable. Heading each colony as the supreme representative of the Portuguese state was the governor-general, who had district governors serving under him. Wherever there was a white colonial population of any size, it was organized as a council (*concelho*), having representative organs and some administrative autonomy. As soon as they could be accounted pacified, the rural areas inhabited mainly by Africans were divided into circumscriptions (*circunscriçãos*) under a government-appointed administrator (*administrador*). To the Africans he represented the colonial power, and there were very few limitations on his authority.

There was no division of powers. The administrador embodied military, administrative, and judicial authority, all three. He saw to law and order, the execution of the law, and the completion of public works. He supervised tax collection, administered the census, and watched over and advised local chiefs. He also served as the lowest level of the judicial system, since, in contrast to British practice, there were no native courts. Finally, it was the administrador's duty to see to it, as the law quaintly stated, that "the natives gave up their habits of indolence" and became peasants and agricultural laborers. The administrador was thus a sort of white paramount chief, a "real chief of the empire," as Delavignette characterized his French opposite number, the commandant de cercle.[12] Directly subordinate to the administrador were administrative officials, chefes do posto, who represented him in the outlying areas and were principally responsible for timely tax collection. The Africans themselves were grouped into regencies (*regedoria*) that corresponded somewhat with traditional divisions. They were under the authority of an African regent (*regedor*) appointed by the administrador or an African chief (*régulo*) acknowledged by the colonial power. The law stated that the régulo be chosen according to local rules of succession, meaning that he had to come from the traditional ruling class. His position, however, was no longer that of the traditional chief. He was an agent of the colonial power, legitimized by it, and in its pay. In addition to a monthly salary, the régulo received an annual bonus, the size of which was determined by the size of tax revenues. Former soldiers and other colonial auxiliaries were not uncommonly appointed régulos.

Like other colonizing powers, the Portuguese also acted on the maxim of divide and rule, destroying the larger African polities in order to integrate the smaller divisions into the colonial state. That radically altered the political landscape and also ushered in fundamental social and economic transformations. The latter did not always signify progress for the Africans but because they lay outside the ken of colonial officials went unconsidered by them. Pössinger, an agricultural expert, pointed out the consequences for the Cuanhama of their kings' loss of political power: the central allocation of grass and water rights, which was in the interest of all tribes, ceased. Good pasture was overgrazed and some good water holes completely destroyed.[13]

The régulos' duties were to see to law and order, collect taxes, provide workers for the colonists, and to supervise the forced native cultivation of those crops, such as cotton, where the colonial power sought increasing production for export. The régulos had no official judicial functions, though they might advise colonial officials about sentencing. There was also no thought of building or developing the African institutions encountered at the beginning of colonization into future organs of self-government. The ultimate aim, nonetheless, was assimilation.

The Portuguese thus succeeded in incorporating the traditional elite into a hierarchical system of colonial administration. They also used this elite to exercise and maintain Portuguese rule. The power of this elite no longer flowed smoothly from legitimization within traditional society, but rested on a diametrically opposed Portuguese conception of legality.[14] The elite were no longer leaders of an African community, but representatives of a hierarchical colonial authority. Through collaboration, the chiefs generally gained in power, but they largely lost their earlier authority over their fellow men. They were also faced with conflicting loyalties of the sort familiar from other colonial areas. These conflicts persisted into the postcolonial period with decisive effects on politics at the local level.

The creation of a unified territorial administration was one of the aims sought by reformers around the turn of the century. Another no less important aim was securing more autonomy for the individual colonies. These demands, coming from leading colonial officials, coincided with wishes which local communities of white settlers and businessmen had been expressing for years through pamphlets and petitions from organizations like Associação Commercial de Loanda of 1863.[15] Among the soldiers, settlers, and merchants of Benguela were also to be found adherents of secession, some of whom had called in 1822 for confederation with Brazil. Although the settlers and merchants assumed autonomy would bring greater political influence, the reformers meant by autonomy more power for the local bureaucracy and a more clearly drawn line between colonial administration and politics. The reformers wanted more legislative and executive power for themselves, in order to be able to determine the course of events in the colonies independently and without continually consulting Lisbon. In reaction to the crippling centralism of contemporary colonialism, they pushed for decentralization.

They were also repudiating the idealistic colonial policy of nineteenth-century Portuguese liberalism. Proceeding from the assumption of equality, the latter understood motherland and colonies, strikingly enough called overseas provinces after 1834, as an integral unity. Metropolis and overseas possessions were subject to the same laws and, accordingly, all free men living under Portuguese sovereignty, without distinction of race or religion, were recognized as Portuguese with equal rights before the law (in the constitution of 1822). Although this egalitarian doctrine of leveling assimilation remained without great significance in the colonial reality, the strict centralization and concentration of legislative power in the metropolitan parliament that went with it was of most serious consequence. It meant that not only did Lisbon, frequently without much precise knowledge of actual local conditions, determine the colonial budgets, but it meant that individual divisions of the navy ministry, to which the overseas provinces were subordinate until 1911, had officials in every colony over whom the governor had no control.

This unitary bureaucracy was so muscle-bound that any active policy was impossible. But by the end of the nineteenth century the soldiers were calling for active policies. In order to achieve effective occupation, royal commissars with special authority were appointed in the 1890s. The latter, however, wanted no such ad hoc special regulations, which could always be nullified by the navy minister, but fundamental changes. They demanded that the metropolis be limited in function to serving as the court of last resort for disputed decisions and to supervisory and regulatory functions after the British model. Initially, the reformers, António Enes, E. da Costa, and Mouzinho de Albuquerque went unheard, and when Mouzinho was forced to give up his commissar powers in 1898, he resigned in fury from the colonial service altogether.[16] After the collapse of the Braganza monarchy, however, the new republic largely met these demands for more autonomy. The republican constitution applied the reform principals inaugurated in Moçambique in 1907 to all the colonies and recognized decentralization as the basis for colonial administration. In 1914 the African colonies were conceded autonomy and administrative responsibility under general metropolitan oversight and financial control. Although World War I delayed the realization of the new provisions, after the war reform was pushed a step further, with Angola and Moçambique receiving financial autonomy in 1920. The results were not, however, all that satisfactory. The reason may have been that only the governor and the high commissioners actually received more power, as critics noted, and not the colonies as a whole. Frequent personnel changes at the top levels of the colonial administration also hampered any sort of coherent policy. Between 1910 and 1926, Moçambique had no less than twenty-three new governors, and Angola had its twenty-three between 1907 and 1921. These changes reflected metropolitan political difficulties in which one government succeeded another in rapid succession.[17]

Angola, in particular, had an unhappy experience with the new arrangements. José de Norton de Matos, who had determined the fate of the colony from 1912 to 1915, returned in 1920 as high commissioner determined to use his mandate to open up the colony economically with all possible speed. Even so late, a modern infrastructure was lacking and administrative penetration of the colony was incomplete. The Portuguese state, weakened by the war, lacked the means to do the job. Norton de Matos therefore attempted to place loans on the international financing market. The issuing institute was the Banco Ultramarino, which flooded Angola with paper money for which there was insufficient metallic backing. The result was speculation which brought on a severe economic crisis, with galloping inflation and an indebtedness that consumed 13.71 percent of the budget for 1926 in interest charges.[18] The fact that the administration had ballooned in size only made things worse. Personnel costs consumed 58.9 percent of the ordinary budget, or an amount roughly equal to the deficit.[19] Norton de Matos, to be sure, did build harbors, and hundreds of kilometers of roads and railways. His enemies compared him to Caligula, the despotic Roman emperor, and despite the Cortes expressing its confidence in him in 1924, he had to resign that very year.[20]

Lisbon was itself in the midst of a profound economic crisis, which raised new doubts in diplomatic circles about Portugal's viability in general and competence for colonial rule in particular. When Portugal made soundings at the League of Nations about the possibility of a loan, voices were raised anew calling for division of the Portuguese colonial empire or its transformation into League mandates. Once again, however, external peril led the Portuguese to pull themselves together.

Given the Angolan disaster and the newly awakened greed of putative heirs, it is not surprising that the soldiers, who had seized power by a coup in 1926, and Antonio de Oliveira Salazar, who followed them, called once more for centralization. The pendulum swung back from colonial autonomy toward more complete integration of the colonies into the political and economic systems of the metropolis. The New State (*Estado Novo*), Salazar's corporative state, desired to breathe life into the Portuguese imperial tradition. The Pan-Lusitanian community foreseen in the official ideology rested on the political and legal unity and economic solidarity of the metropolis and the colonies. The colonies did not, indeed, lose all their autonomy, but the Portuguese reverted to more complete centralization and, with it, more complete metropolitan control over the colonies. The colonial minister ruled by decree through a tightly organized bureaucracy, in which corps of inspectors played an especially important role. The executive did not lose its preponderance, which was rather in accord with the authoritarianism of the Salazar regime. Indeed, the beginnings of representative and democratic institutions, which were able to develop in some colonies despite the dictatorial airs assumed by some governors, were forbidden. In place of the newly minted legislative councils, the purely governmental councils of the pre-World War I days were revived once again. These bodies, however, had only consultative and deliberative functions. Not until 1955 were legislative councils hazarded once again. The basis of this new-old order was set down in the colonial acts of 1930 which, supplemented on individual points, were incorporated into the constitution in 1951. The latter once again designated colonies as overseas provinces and declared them an "integral part of the Portuguese state."[21]

The economic links between the colonies and the metropolis were also strengthened. Preferential tariffs protected shipping and trade between the colonies and Lisbon and discriminated against foreign flag trade. Exports and imports from the Cape Verdes, São Tomé, and Principé could, in fact, proceed only through Lisbon. The Salazar government also sought to restrict the influence of foreign capital in the Portuguese colonies insofar as possible, by nationalizing the colonial economy and placing it under Portuguese control.[22] The watchword for the future was "balanced budgets" above all else. This drastic medicine did end the chronic budget deficits in a very short time. The result, however, was insufficient funds to develop the country. Salazar's conservative finance policies and the close ties between the colonies and the weak Portuguese economy were thus responsible for the economic stagnation of the Portuguese African colonies until World War II. One should note, however, that at the same time that Portugal began to integrate colonies and metropolis once again, legal distinctions between colonized and colonizers were being established which made integration a utopian prospect.

The new doctrines of identity differed fundamentally from the liberal doctrines of the nineteenth century. "Leveling assimilation" was condemned as foolish and unrealistic and "spiritual assimilation," or selective cultural assimilation, was substituted for it.[23] The aim of Portuguese colonialism remained the integration of the colonized into the Portuguese nation, but the assumption was now that, because the Africans lived in a primitive society, it was neither possible nor desirable to place them under the same laws as the Portuguese. It hence followed that they could not be given the same rights. Proceeding from the undeniable differences in civilization between colonizers and colonized, a special statute was created for the latter in 1926: the Political, Civil, and Criminal Statute for the Natives of Guinea, Angola, and Moçambique. Only the Cape Verdes were accounted assimilated and were thus not subjected to this law. The roots of this racial policy reached back into the "heroic" period of Portuguese colonization at the end of the nineteenth century. The modern governing of natives was based on the thinking of men like António Enes, Mouzinho de Albuquerque, and Eustacio da Costa, whose attitude toward Africans was indistinguishable from the prevailing social-Darwinist racism of the day.

As natives, or *não-civilizados*, the colonized had no civil rights and no representation in colonial or metropolitan legislative bodies such as municipal or legislative councils or national assemblies. They were also, as has been mentioned, subject to the virtually unrestricted powers of the administradores. The natives were also subject to separate judicial procedures, which were supposed to take traditional African legal custom into account but which were administered by whites. The natives had to pay a hut and head tax and were subject to a special labor code, the import of which was that they were legally obligated to work. The state could thus impose an extremely varied group of tasks upon them, from public works to raising export crops such as cotton. Until 1935 a native could own no land as private property and could not serve in the administration, except as a policeman or régulo. He had, in addition, to carry an identity card at all times, which opened the way for all sorts of abuses. Finally, for travel outside his own district, the native needed the consent of the local officials.

As the child grows up to become a full-fledged member of the adult world, the African, in colonial parlance often compared to a naughty child, could also win equality with the colonizers, the *civilizados* or "non-natives." He did this by striving for assimilation, which was defined rather precisely by law in 1921. The prerequisite, however, was that he break completely with traditional society and give up tribal practices such as polygamy. He had to convert to Christianity, demonstrate mastery of Portuguese, and assume a European life-style. Last, but not least, he had to show that he had property or wages sufficient to support a family. Later, he had to have a good service record.

There was as such no discrimination in Portuguese colonies based on racist criteria, a fact of which Portuguese authors are justifiably proud. The Portuguese also had liberal views about miscegenation and freely recognized legitimate mixed bloods, or mestizos, as Portuguese citizens. This mixing of the races was by no means deliberate state policy, as the Brazilian sociologist Gilberto Freyre asserts, but at best tolerance of behavior common to the colonizers in all colonial areas. Such behavior did not prevent social discrimination against Africans.[24] Instead of racial there was cultural discrimination, which was no less humiliating to those on the receiving end. African nationalists expressed bitter scorn for the Portuguese assertion that there was no racism in their territories. Amilcar Cabral rightly emphasized that assimilation doctrines were based on racist notions about the lack of ability and dignity of Africans and in general implied that African culture and civilization had no value whatever.[25]

The state tirelessly reiterated that assimilation was the aim of Portugal's colonial activity, indeed, its historical mission. It is all the more surprising, then, how modest their success was before World War II. The census of 1940, however, makes the situation plain enough, as table 13.1 demonstrates. The modest success revealed here is explained, first, by gradualism—or ought one say immobilism?—being counted a virtue, it being argued that the natives should not be wrenched out of their familiar world. Second, the desolate condition of the educational infrastructure assured that only Africans living in cities or close to missions, to whom education of the natives was entrusted in 1926, had the chance to acquire the knowledge needed for assimilation.[26] Strict upper-age limits for entry into state schools and the size of private school fees in practice discriminated against the African. But there were many illiterates in Portugal itself. Many colonial officials, moreover, viewed the education of Africans as a luxury and praised the educational virtues of wage labor for Europeans. Nevertheless, great efforts were made during the 1920s to expand the school system. At the lowest levels, schools were separated into those for the civilizados and those for the natives. The latter went to the "rudimentary elementary school," which lasted three years and in 1939 was attended by some 56,306 Africans in Moçambique. Instruction, mainly by Africans, concentrated on Portuguese and the propagation of Portuguese cultural values. It was oriented toward producing manual laborers. Very few passed on to the next stage, the state four-year elementary school which Africans, mixed bloods, and Europeans all attended together. In the year 1939 in Moçambique there were 2,118 Africans, 1,960 mixed bloods, and 2,957 whites in the four-year elementary schools. In the same year, 1,620 Africans attended vocational schools. In the lycée founded in 1918, however, there was only one African among the 471 pupils.[27]

Table 13.1
Civilizados in Portuguese Africa, Native and Non-native, 1940

	Whites	Mestizos	Asiatics	Blacks	Total Black Population
Angola	44,083	23,244	63	24,221	3,665,829
Guinea	1,226	1,719	...	3,064	423,064
Moçambique	27,438	15,641	10,596	1,776	5,027,591

Source: Portuguese and Angolan records.[28]

The so-called native policy did, of course, embody some elements of trusteeship insofar as it provided the African state protection against shortsighted European economic interests. Examples of such protection are the safeguarding of African land rights and the attempts to supervise and regulate working conditions. Still, the impression is inescapable that native policy served mainly to uphold the economic and political status quo. The mass of Africans was never shown any way to escape the role of cheap, dependent labor in service of the colonial economy. Because of its extreme selectivity assimilation served at best as a safety valve, but otherwise set African against African.

Neither the weight of elegant juristic treatises on colonial problems in the Portuguese literature, nor the resonance which the heroic deeds of bold men struck in a public not otherwise much interested in colonies, nor yet the insistence on Portugal's so-called civilizing mission could conceal what was at the heart of Portuguese colonialism. In the end, economic activity was what mattered. The Portuguese always emphasized the civilizing aspects of their work, and the military expansion around the turn of the century certainly cannot be explained on purely economic grounds. Indeed, it made no sense economically, given its disregard for Portugal's real needs or potential. Portugal's African imperialism has thus been described as uneconomic imperialism.[29] Still, Portugal had to bear the economic consequences of its imperial strivings. These weighed all the more heavily because Portugal itself was an economically backward and deeply indebted country. It had no internal market of any size, nor any industry hungering for expansion. Portuguese African possessions promised no easy riches like those of the Rand in South Africa or those of the central African copper belt. European rivals stood in the wings, moreover, in case Portugal proved incapable of meeting its obligations. The latter consisted of "pacification," imposition of effective administration, and economic exploitation. Enes formulated the imperatives of the day in unmistakable terms when he stated in 1899: "Portugal must bring prosperity to its African inheritance and must do so unconditionally and without delay. The solution to this problem is perhaps the solution to the national crisis itself."[30] The measure of the so-called prosperity was the rapidly rising foreign trade and rising revenues, which made near-term financial self-sufficiency for the colonies seem likely. There were no illusions about the fact that everything depended on the labor of Africans. But how could the colonized be brought into service and mobilized as workers?

Until the 1870s the colonial economy had rested on slavery. An enlightened state had, however, since then pushed through the abolition of slavery against the resistance of conservative colonists and colonial officers. New ways thus had to be found, especially since hopes that abolition of slavery would automatically create a free labor market had been disappointed. Contemporaries saw administrative compulsion as a solution to the problem, the labor required for the colonial economy being pictured as an essential contribution toward the "civilizing" of the Africans: "an education which will change brutes into men," or so the argument ran.[31] Article 1 of the *Regulamento* which went into force in 1899 stated:

> All natives of the Portuguese overseas provinces have the moral and legal obligation to try to obtain those means through work which they need for their sustenance and the improvement of their social situation. They have complete freedom to select the manner in which they will fulfill these obligations, but should they fail to fulfill them, the public authorities can compel them to do so.[32]

The colonial state itself took in hand the recruitment of African workers for the economy. An entrepreneur wanting workers could apply to the colonial officials, and they would in turn demand that the African chiefs provide the number of workers called for. The worker was under contract, the breech of which was severely punished. By stipulating an obligation to work and legalizing administrative compulsion, the door was left wide open to arbitrary abuses, because the administration was too weak to enforce protective contract provisions on the employers.

An insight into the horrifying realities of Portuguese labor policy came after 1900 in the form of the cocoa scandal. In 1903 an English journalist named Henry W. Nevinson journeyed to São Tomé and Angola, "the jewel of Lusitanian colonies," in response to information from the British Aborigines' Rights Protection Society. Nevinson's investigations confirmed the worst of the rumors, for he ascertained that the workers on the cocoa plantations, who were mainly from Angola, had by no means accepted labor contracts voluntarily, and that, altogether, the recruiting methods did not differ all that much from those of the days of slavery. Even worse, it was doubtful whether the estimated seventy to a hundred thousand contract laborers who had been dragged off to work the cocoa plantations between 1878 and 1908 had even been able to return home at the end of their five-year contract period. Nevinson's reports about Portugal's "modern slavery," as he called it, unleashed a storm of indignation in the European public, shaken already by the Congo atrocities.[33] Outrage was so great that the British chocolate industry boycotted cocoa from São Tomé and Principé. The leading chocolate manufacturer, the Quaker William Cadbury, had in 1908 been able to convince himself of the justice of Nevinson's accusations.

Portugal officially denied the accusations. Officials pointed to efforts already undertaken to improve the situation, and the Portuguese were in any case exasperated that the British philanthropists always criticized little Portugal while being blind to events in French and German colonies. Still, the international pressure was economically dangerous. The government thus had to give way to those internal forces that were also pushing for labor reform, forces whose previous initiatives had collapsed against the resistance of colonial entrepreneurs interested in the cheapest possible labor. As late as 1912, the governor-general of Angola, Colonel Manuel Coelho, had resigned, considering his struggle against forced labor in vain. In 1913 a rebellion broke out in the Congo district as a result of the ruthless deportation of laborers to São Tomé, another warning sign. The young republic immediately sent an investigating commission to Angola, and the government between 1911 and 1914 altered some provisions of the Labor Law of 1899 in favor of the Africans. It left unchanged the basic obligation of the natives to work, and this proviso continued to be a mainstay of Portuguese policy. Africans who did not accept this obligation willingly could be pressed into public works or handed off to private employers. Anyone unable to pay his taxes in money also had to work for the state—for *one hundred* days. Although the governors of Moçambique and Angola (Norton de Matos) signed decrees against forced labor, in practice very little changed, as new reports of horrors from foreign journalists and scholars revealed. They were discussed in the League of Nations even during the 1920s.[34]

The new government of 1926 had come to power by means of a military putsch and was thus concerned about international recognition. It hoped to still international criticism, which once again had become very sharp, with a new labor law, the Labor Code for the Natives of the Portuguese Colonies of Africa, of 1928. The code held fast to the moral obligation to work, but provided no legal sanctions to do so. It borrowed from the French system of corvée by imposing limited forced labor for projects in the public interest. Tax evaders and convicted offenders could, however, still be forced to work, and officials continued to contract for labor in behalf of private enterprises. Despite these improvements, Portugal's labor legislation was still backward in comparison to that of other colonies and stood in contravention of international conventions against forced labor. Portugal did not sign such a convention until the 1950s, after additional reforms.

There are indeed few areas where a legal text and legal reality were as far apart as in Portuguese colonial labor legislation. Henrique de Paiva Couceiro, governor-general of Angola from 1907 to 1909, and a participant in drafting the legislation, called it an example of the "the paper-addicted, ultra-mandarin, super-sophistical character of our official practice."[35] The detailed reports which Colonial Inspector Henrique Galvão laid before the national assembly in Lisbon in 1947 highlight the fact that at the end of World War II Portugal still faced the same problems it had in 1900.[36] Galvão himself could look back on years of experience as an official in Angola. In his report, he stated that there were hardly any free laborers in Angola or Moçambique, and that workers were in general recruited by force as they had always been, with the colonial power depending on the despotism of local African chiefs. According to Galvão, working conditions were catastrophic; he said mortality reached 40 percent. Workers were also often employed far from their homes, and no one took any account of possible evil effects on health of climatic differences. Traders swindled workers out of their miserable salaries, and one still encountered among whites the "spirit of extermination," which had been the characteristic way of approaching the black around the turn of the century. Huge population decreases were the result. A great portion of the population in the border areas had simply emigrated to where working conditions were better and wages higher. At least two million had thus eased out of Angola and Moçambique—and the total population was less than four million—and each year another hundred thousand departed. Poor rural sanitation resulted in extremely high child mortality, up to 60 percent, and other gaps in the administrative infrastructure worsened the depopulation for which the prevailing labor system was primarily responsible. The underpopulation of Angola, one of its foremost problems, had become a veritable catastrophe. Galvão concluded with doubts about whether existing production levels could even be maintained.

There is no reason to doubt the justice of Galvão's charges. The government withheld Galvão's incriminating report, because it too directly contradicted the claims of the Salazar government to be following a model colonial policy and seemed, moreover, to place the economic basis of the colonial economy in the balance. And it should be noted that the treasury was also actively interested in labor exports, particularly in Moçambique.

As early as the 1860s, or before Portuguese colonization, young Thonga tribesmen from southern Moçambique were going off to Natal and the Transvaal for a few months of labor.[37] After the completion (January 1895) of the Lourenço Marques-Johannesburg railway, built with British capital and forced labor, this emigration swelled to a flood. Mouzinho de Albuquerque hence felt constrained, in 1897, to conclude an agreement with the Transvaal government placing this emigration under state control; a complete prohibition would have been impossible. Henceforth, recruiting agents required licenses from the Portuguese colonial government, which for its part set up a trusteeship in Johannesburg to safeguard the interests of the emigrants. In the Moçambique Convention of 1909, as a quid pro quo for the mine workers, Transvaal agreed to transship 50 to 55 percent of its exports and imports through the port of Lourenço Marques. In further negotiations in 1928, the maximum yearly recruitment figure was set at 100,000, only to be reduced to 80,000 in 1934, with a minimum figure of 65,000. The actual recruitment, after 1903, was handled by the Witwatersrand Native Labour Association, which worked in the closest collaboration with local Portuguese officials. In the beginning at least, when the long duration of the contracts—two and three years—and poor working conditions frightened people off, it employed rather dubious methods. But the mines paid much better than Portuguese colonial companies, by as much as double on occasion. Force soon became unnecessary. A similar agreement with Southern Rhodesia, concluded in 1928 and revised in 1934, also permitted that adjoining country to recruit 15,000 mine workers a year in Moçambique.

Emigrant fees accounted for no small portion of Moçambique revenues, amounting in 1898-1899 to 1.6 percent, in 1908-1909 to 6.7 percent, and in 1929-1930 to as much as 11.3 percent.[38] In addition, all but an insignificant portion of the workers' wages was paid in Moçambique, which provided the fisc with desperately needed foreign exchange and permitted the administration to levy considerably higher taxes in the main recruiting areas, Lourenço Marques and Inhambane, than were tolerable elsewhere.

This state-controlled and abetted export of labor was a clear sign of the weakness of the colonial economy of Moçambique and of its great dependence on the economies of neighboring territories. This dependence becomes yet more visible when one compares the colony's own foreign trade with the transit trade to and from South Africa, Rhodesia, and Nyasaland (see table 13.2). Although the income from labor exports and the transit trade helped the colony balance its budget, the colonial government could hardly gainsay that it was following the path of least resistance, thinking as it did only of railways and harbors and neglecting the rest of the colony. The state emigration, to which has to be added the uncontrolled flight noted by Galvão, harmed the colony more than it helped it, because it cost the colony the labor necessary for growth. Despite the continuing reiteration of these criticisms, this economic dependency on the neighboring states did not change before World War II. It was the cheapest policy, and the mother country either could not or would not assume the task of long-term economic development. Private capital, on the other hand, was only available for such projects, such as the construction of transit facilities, which promised a quick, sure payoff. The British were the heaviest investors in Moçambique, and it was they who made possible the building of the railways and modern ports.[39] The railroads served, however, the mining industries of the neighboring interior states and only secondarily the economic development of Moçambique.

Table 13.2
Moçambique's Foreign Trade, 1910-1940
(in thousands of gold escudos)

	SPECIAL TRADE		GENERAL TRADE	
	Import	Export	Reexport	Transit
1910	8,779	4,196	8,314	34,519
1920	13,614	7,802	29,831	42,124
1930	21,692	9,732	12,292	99,005
1940	17,053	6,592	11,690	114,782

SOURCE: Moçambique, *Annuário Estatístico*: 1940, 136f.

The British were also behind the three great concession companies, the Companhia de Moçambique, chartered in 1891, the Companhia do Nyassa, also dating from 1891, and the Companhia da Zambézia of 1842. In 1900 these companies controlled more than two-thirds of the entire area of Moçambique.[40] As early as the sixteenth and seventeenth centuries, Indian colonization had been the work of monopoly concession companies. Toward the end of the nineteenth century, this system enjoyed a general renaissance. Great Britain, France, and Germany all saw the grant of monopoly rights as a suitable means to hasten the imposition of effective control over African colonial territories and to mobilize the capital to open up the colonies economically. The concession company system was doubly attractive to a poor and weak state like Portugal, which after 1892 could not even meet its debts. It permitted the state, in fact, to disburden itself of both administrative and economic obligations.

As competitor to Cecil Rhodes's aggressive and successful British South Africa Company, the Companhia de Moçambique received privileges in the Manica and Sofala districts: fifty-year trade, mining, and fishery monopolies (the latter for coastal waters), the right to build transportation routes, banking monopolies, and, finally, the right to grant subconcessions and alienate land to third parties. In return, the fisc demanded 10 percent of the capital shares and 7.5 percent of the net profits. The state also turned over to the company the task of upholding Portuguese sovereignty and hence the administration of the concession territories. The state retained supreme authority which it exercised through a resident in Beira, a difference from early modern times, when the concession companies had been totally sovereign. The right to raise taxes gave the company an efficient means of creating a labor force and for encouraging the production of cash crops, but, taken altogether, the administrative obligations proved a heavy burden. Still, the Moçambique Company had the good fortune to profit from the mining activity in adjoining colonies. The Beira railway, built by the British South Africa Company as subconcessionaire, carried an enormous amount of transit business to and from Rhodesia and Nyasaland.

The situation of the Companhia do Nyassa, also quasi-sovereign, was quite different. Its concession reached from Lurio to the northern borders of Moçambique. Its railroad plans came to nothing, no minerals were found, and altogether the company was unable to raise enough capital to exploit its huge concession area. The administrative obligations exceeded its strength. Its concession was accordingly withdrawn in 1929 as a part of Salazar's efforts to block off foreign influences from Portuguese colonies and to nationalize their economies. Economically, the most successful was the Companhia da Zambézia, which in contrast to the other two companies had no administrative obligations and established plantations for sisal, copra, and tea in the rich prazo areas of Quelimane and Tete. It also made frequent and very successful use of its power to grant subconcessions.

Nevertheless, as in French Equatorial Africa, the Moçambique concessions must share the blame for the relative stagnation of the economy as a whole. In general, all that developed were mere enclaves of commercial activity in an otherwise undeveloped country.[41] The colonies thus revealed the picture characteristic of colonial development. What was unusual about Moçambique, however, was that development was induced, not as a result of the mother country's needs, but because of those of the mining industry of a bordering inland country. Private capital, indeed, was available above all for the mining industry and its expansion. But institutional structures were created in this manner which even today control the country's economy and prejudice further development. Although it contravenes its political program, the government of the new state of Moçambique still has to export labor to hostile South Africa, because the jobs simply are lacking at home.

Angola was accounted the richest and most Portuguese of the African colonies. The full extent of Angola's mineral wealth was discovered only after World War II, but even before that Angola was tied into the great southern African mining complex in a multitude of ways. First, Angola was an important labor reservoir for the mining industries of neighboring colonies. Like Moçambique, Angola concluded an agreement in 1934 with Southern Rhodesia for the recruitment of 15,000 workers a year. The great and uncontrolled African emigration into neighboring mining districts has already been mentioned. Second, in the interwar period, an important mining industry arose in Angola itself. Two prospectors found diamonds in 1912 in the Luanda district, in the extreme northeast near the Kasai border. This led in 1917 to the founding of the Companhia de Diamantes de Angola (Diamang), behind which were the financial circles supporting the Belgian Forminière.[42] Portuguese colonial officials granted Diamang a prospecting monopoly for the period 1921-1951 for the better part of the territory of Angola and an exploitation monopoly for their actual finds that was good forever. The company seat for tax purposes was not Luanda but Lisbon. The company's imports of mining equipment and other capital goods were duty free, as were its exports of diamonds. Even so, the Diamang developed into one of the mainstays of the colonial budget, because the state held 5 percent (and after 1955, 11 percent) of the company's stock and had rights to 40 percent of the annual net profits. Altogether, between 1921 and 1940, the treasury collected £1,299,417 as its share of profits and £93,750 in dividends. In addition, the company lent the colonial government more than a £million between 1921 and 1939.[43] Production rose rapidly, from 93,529 carats in 1920 to 329,824 carats in 1930, and 784,271 carats in 1940. Diamond exports constituted 30 percent of total Angolan exports, and 5 percent of total world diamond exports.[44] The Diamang was the greatest employer in the colony, though like all colonial companies of its day, it used cheap contract labor, whose wages were in the greatest contrast to the high profits of its investors. The company maintained its own plantations to provide its work force with food, ran both its own schools and a model health service which cared for the entire Luanda district. The company pointed with especial pride in its annual reports to its own museum and the scholarly researches it had supported. The Diamang thus constituted a typical enclave, Galvão and Selvagem speaking ironically of it as the "ninth province of the empire."[45]

The most important railway in Angola, the 1,347 kilometer-long Benguela line, was also built to serve the mining industry. Begun in 1904 and completed in 1929, its specific purpose was to bring copper from the Katanga mines. It was another enclave enterprise, built with foreign, in this case British, capital.[46]

In contrast to Moçambique, which because of climate long seemed unsuited for European settlement, Angola was seen early as a home for the surplus population of the mother country. Since the middle of the nineteenth century, the colonial administration pursued a policy of settlement with a varying but generally increasing degree of zeal.[47] The idea underlying this policy was to turn the traditional emigration to Brazil toward the colonies instead, in order better to secure the colonial possessions. But Angola had too bad a reputation for Portuguese peasants simply to go there on their own. The state's having sent *degradados* (common criminals) and political prisoners there as banishment hardly made it very inviting. As early as the mid-nineteenth century, the state attempted to plan and encourage peasants to settle there. The bureaucracy provided the colonists with land in the Huila highlands and provided start-up assistance for the first five years. At the end of this period, however, many settlers preferred to become traders or move into the coastal cities. Even subordinate positions in the government or business seemed preferable to them to the hard and difficult life of a settler. Mostly coming from the poor and poorest classes of Portuguese society, they had neither the necessary technical knowledge nor the capital to undertake successful agricultural operations in a country that until well into the twentieth century lacked any modern infrastructure.

In the cities, the refugees from the country competed for jobs with culturally assimilated Africans and mestizos. The assimilados had won influential positions during the nineteenth century and risen to become a genuine bourgeoisie. When increasing numbers of Europeans began to arrive with the onset of modern colonization, however, the position of the assimilados greatly worsened, because the colonial government extended a protective hand over the new immigrants and tightened the conditions for African entry into administrative service. In 1921 the service was reserved entirely for Europeans and a separate branch, to which Africans could belong, established. But assimilados were only employed in subaltern positions and were paid on a differential salary scale.[48]

In the interwar period, the Portuguese made great efforts to settle Europeans in the rural areas. A colonization project passed in 1928 envisaged the emigration of entire villages, and the authorities were to provide seed, livestock, and other assistance. The project was generally a failure, however, because the depression prevented the state from raising the necessary capital. The Benguela Railway Company was not much more successful in its efforts to settle Europeans along the right-of-way. Every settler was supposed to get a grub stake, house, and twenty-five morgens of already planted land (a morgen equals 2.116 acres), and mortgage payments were to start only after the end of the eleventh year. Only nineteen families accepted the railway's offer, however, and by 1949 all but nine families had either returned home or found spots elsewhere in the colony.

From 1900 until the outbreak of World War II, over a million Portuguese emigrated to the classic American settlement countries, the United States, Brazil, and Argentina. Only 35,000, however, went to Angola, and in 1950 less than 10 percent of these were active in agriculture.[49] The majority of agricultural enterprises were concentrated in the Huila Plateau south of the Cuanza River, where immigrants from Brazil were already coming in the 1850s, and great coffee plantations were dominant. The post-World War II coffee boom encouraged a wave of immigration, however, further abetted by Portugal's making white settlement in the colonies a central feature of its overseas policy.

From the beginning, European plantation production received administrative support in the form of assistance in the recruitment of labor, the construction of a suitable infrastructure, and the grant of as much credit as possible. The colonial officials, however, hindered rather than assisted African agriculture, although the latter furnished the better part of the export products. As early as 1913, Norton de Matos declared that the aim of colonial economic policy should be the creation of a "new native," who would work not as a laborer in the pay of European businessmen or planters but would earn his living as an independent peasant or artisan. The state's job was to protect, educate, and advise him.[50] At first, these ideas had no practical consequences whatever. When the European cotton plantations ran into financial difficulties in the 1920s, however, the colonial rulers began to pay more attention to African agriculture, which they came to see as a less risky, because less capital-intensive, means of providing the home textile industry with raw cotton.[51]

Africans were thus to farm cotton as a cash crop, under the guidance and control of European trading companies. In 1926 the latter were given concession areas where they had a cotton-purchasing monopoly. The rule was that in areas suited to cotton every healthy man had to plant 2.5 morgens in cotton, and single women and old men, 1.5 morgens. The fields were divided up arbitrarily. The prices the company paid, however, were kept so low they provided the Africans no incentive. That led the officials to take cotton in hand themselves at the end of the 1930s. Prices remained very low, but the administration used pressure to carry out its program. The result was that cotton became the most important export from Moçambique, its share in total exports reaching no less than 46.57 percent in 1942. Cotton production in Angola rose from 432 tons in 1928 to 5,265 tons in 1939.[52] The boost in export production came at the cost of food production, which in many areas declined so sharply that famine threatened.[53]

The economies of the Portuguese colonies were rather more notable for stagnation than change, and development within the Portuguese colonies in the interwar period limped along far behind that of other African colonies. One should not forget, however, how fundamentally the individual African societies within Portuguese territories were altered over time. The degree of change naturally varied according to the cultural predisposition of the African society involved and its distance from the centers of colonial rule. What is striking is the degree to which the colonizers projected their own inertia onto the colonized and thus failed to recognize the manifold expressions of change, if they were not directly opposed to their own aims.

The Ovimbundu, who lived in the central Angolan highlands and were the numerically most important population group, thus went through an entire cycle of development during the nineteenth century and after.[54] At first hunters and warriors, their society was based on village communities organized by kinship, which in turn were grouped into various kingdoms. In the course of the nineteenth century, they developed an intense trading activity. Their great caravans, often a thousand strong, pushed north to the Congo River, to the great African lakes, and into the Kalahari desert in search of slaves, ivory, and beeswax. They exchanged these products at Portuguese trading settlements along the coast for cloth, Brazilian rum, and European weapons. They not only blocked other Africans from contact with the Portuguese, but forced the Portuguese *Sertanejos* out of this profitable trade. After the official abolition of the slave trade, wild rubber became their most important trade goods, but the rubber trade ended about 1911 when slavery was finally suppressed.

Once in contact with the market economy, the Ovimbundu social order changed. The capital accumulated in commerce by the most important trading chiefs served not only the expansion of their economic activities but also to solidify their social and political positions in their own societies. The political system thus came to be increasingly centralized and hierarchical. More and more people gathered in very large villages under the authority of individual trading chiefs. The power of some of these great chiefs, which was based on trade, was in fact what lead the Portuguese to intervene and to impose effective control over the highlands militarily. First, the Portuguese wanted to break the Ovimbundu trading monopoly. Second, they wanted to open up the highlands as a settlement area for Portuguese immigrants. Finally, they sought to clear the way for the construction of the Benguela railway. These Portuguese colonial efforts coincided with the collapse of the rubber trade. After the turn of the century wild rubber competed with masses of ever cheaper plantation rubber, which between 1911 and 1914 led to a crisis from which there was to prove no recovery. After 1900 the Ovimbundu hence lost both their political independence as well as the basis for their previous economic success. Being an innovative people, the Ovimbundu adapted rapidly to their new situation, taking up production of cash crops such as corn, beans, and wheat, and, in the 1930s, coffee. And they did this despite the fact that farming had traditionally been women's work.

The transition to market crops did not have disruptive effects on Ovimbundu society, as the cultivation of cash crops simply took the place of trade. In the long run, it nevertheless had far-reaching consequences. Landownership came to assume an entirely new significance. Searching for fertile ground, individual clans emigrated from the old villages, scattered over an ever wider area, and shook loose from the traditional hierarchy. The Portuguese administration did its bit, also weakening the political power of the old chiefs by integrating the leaders of smaller units into the expanding administration as régulos. The latter were then subordinated to the administrador and their ties to the kings dissolved.

The cultivation of cash crops, and perennial crops in particular, soon led to the Ovimbundu regarding their land as private property. The fallow was no longer returned to the clan but held as family property. Although at first inheritance followed the old laws of matrilineal succession, a tendency soon developed for inheritance to proceed from parents to children. The result of this development was independent families without close clan ties, which after the weakening of the old paramount chiefs also led to the weakening of the clan chiefs. The missions encouraged this individualization and found in the Ovimbundu eager students. The more cash-crop production increased, the more noticeable grew the shortage of land, made more serious because the fertility of the land decreased with one-crop farming and insufficient fallowing and because European planters and plantation companies were also pushing into the highlands at the same time. The tendency to expand one's holdings and cultivate more land led to further damage to the already shaken village structure. It also led to villages with widely separated family holdings. The individual family gradually became the fundamental economic and social unit. Whoever lacked land to farm market crops, however, was forced to work for wages for European enterprises.

The stance taken by the assimilados and the mestizos was characterized by a similar adaption to the colonial situation and exploitation of it to their own advantage. It was they who started the modern liberation movement in Portuguese Africa. It was in no small measure the increasing discrimination toward the end of the nineteenth century which encouraged the process of political fermentation among the assimilados and mestizos. Their protests were at first unorganized. They had in the numerous weekly and daily papers in Luanda and Benguela, however, the means to state their grievances, and they made skillful use of their opportunities.[55] In common with the numerous Portuguese who had been exiled to Angola, they propagated republican ideals and hoped that greater autonomy would permit the attainment of their ideals of Portuguese colonization, with which they themselves identified. Today, these assimilado protests can be considered the precursers of Angolan nationalism, because for the first time a community of interests consisting of all those born in Angola, the "sons of Angola," was postulated and announced its aims in "modern form."[56] Yet it should be noted that the colonial elite of the late nineteenth century remained loyal to Portugal. Its representatives demanded an intensification of colonial activity rather than its end, and they were in no way desirous of entering into any struggle against the whites like those embodied in the traditional rural resistance movements of the day or the messianic movements which flared up in the 1930s like Kimbangism in the Belgian Congo.[57]

The assimilados fought corruption, social injustice, and the export of workers in newspaper articles. They also fought for economic reforms and, above all, for better schools. They represented primarily the group interests of the urban colonial elite, who worried about their jobs in the administration and sought greater participation in the exercise of power. The most important and most radical exponent of this critical journalism was the lawyer and civil servant, José de Fontes Pereira.[58] His commentaries and articles reveal both assimilado radicalization and the total ineffectuality of their protests. His growing disillusionment led him to declare during the political crisis of 1890, which the Salisbury ultimatum had caused that it would be better if England took Portugal's place. A further indication of the hardening of the fronts was the collection of newspaper articles published in Lisbon in 1901 (*Voz d'Angola clamando no deserto*), in which the disappointed Angolans complained that 400 years of Portuguese presence in Angola had brought Africans no progress but only stagnation, exploitation, and misery and that under the sign of the new racism every kind of social progress had come to a halt. Here, too, they also called for more and better schools.

The colonial elite's protest movement entered a new phase after the fall of the Braganza monarchy, which the assimilados greeted with high enthusiasm. A short period of very intense political activity and organization commenced both in the metropolis and in the colonies. The assimilado administrative cadre created its own political organizations after the models of the European republican parties then developing. These assimilado organizations were based on social associations and clubs, some of long standing.[59] This was how the Liga Angolana came to be founded in 1913. It pursued reformist ends and worked in close collaboration with the colonial government, its members considering themselves loyal republicans. Its demands were maintenance of Angolan interests, better schools for Africans, protection of the rights of the colonial elite and, of all things, instruction in gymnastics. This group ought thus to be considered less a nationalist party than a lobby representing the interests of the colonial elite, working within the boundaries of the existing colonial system. Nevertheless, the Liga was a thorn in the flesh of conservative settlers, who considered the assimilados to be the wire-pullers behind traditional resistance movements which had appeared everywhere in the interior during the war years. The Congo district, and the Cuanhama, Dembos, Amboin, and Seles regions were those particularly affected. Although accusations of assimilado manipulation were repeatedly made, neither the administration nor the settlers were ever able to prove them.

During the republican period, Africans also formed political associations in Lisbon, namely the Liga Africana in 1919 and its competitor, the Partido Nacional Africano in 1921, which brought together assimilados from the various Portuguese colonies. They also pursued reformist ends and sought greater local autonomy. They talked about democracy, constitutionalism, and freedom, opposed every form of discrimination, and demanded a better economic shake for Africans, all of which they considered prerequisites for elite political conquest of the representative bodies. They also maintained ties to the League of Nations and to the Pan-Africanist movements of W. E. B. Du Bois and Marcus Garvey. In December 1923 the Liga Africana was actually host for Du Bois' Pan-African Congress in Lisbon.

The days of political freedom did not last long, not long enough, indeed, for African political parties of greater effectiveness to develop. In February 1922 Norton de Matos dissolved the Liga Africana and suspended its publications, after having previously subjected its newspapers to state censorship.[60] Anyone not bending to the state's will found himself at a lonely post off in the bush or actually deported. The Salazar dictatorship tolerated no African political parties whatever, except the semiofficial Liga Nacional Africana. Like the metropolis, the situation of colonies was characterized by depoliticization. Behind the population's enforced silence, however, the resistance was building up that led at the beginning of the 1960s to open warfare against Portuguese colonialism.

NOTES

1. Every account of Portuguese colonial history suffers from the fact that, as David Birmingham puts it, "there is virtually no such thing as modern history writing in Portugal itself, let alone in its 'Ultramar'." See his essay, "Themes and Resources of Angolan History," *African Affairs*, 73 (April 1974), 199. The best survey remains James Duffy, *Portuguese Africa* (Cambridge, Mass.: Harvard University Press, 1959).

2. W. G. L. Randles, *L'Ancièn Royaume du Congo des Origins à la Fin du XIXe Siècle* (Paris, The Hague: Mouton, 1969).

3. Philip D. Curtin, *The Atlantic Slave Trade: A Census* (Madison: University of Wisconsin Press, 1969), 211, and H. S. Klein, "The Portuguese Slave Trade from Angola in the 18th Century," *JEH*, 32 (December 1972), which confirms Curtin's findings. Gladwyn Murray Childs, *Umbundu Kinship and Character: Being a Description of Social Structure and Individual Development of the Ovimbundu of Angola, with Observations Concerning the Bearing on the Enterprise of Christian Missions of Certain Phases of the Life and Culture Described* (London, New York: Oxford University Press, 1949), 193, hazards an estimate of a total of three million slaves all told.

4. Allen F. Isaacman, *Moçambique: The Africanization of a European Institution, the Zambese Prazos, 1750-1902* (Madison: University of Wisconsin Press, 1972); M. D. D. Newitt, "The Portuguese on the Zambesi from the 17th to the 19th Century," *Race*, 9: no. 4 (1968), 477-98.

5. David and Charles Livingston, *Narrative of an Expedition to the Zambesi and its Tributaries: And of the Discovery of the Lakes of the Shirwa and Nyasa, 1858-1864* (New York: Harper & Brothers, 1866), x.

6. There is no lack of good diplomatic studies: Richard James Hammond, *Portugal and Africa (1815-1910): A Study in Uneconomic Imperialism* (Stanford: Stanford University Press, 1966); Françoise Latour da Veiga Pinto, *Le Portugal et le Congo au XIXe Siècle: Etude d'Histoire des Relations Internationales* (Paris: Presses Universitaires de France, 1972); Philip R. Warhurst, *Anglo-Portuguese Relations in South-Central Africa, 1890-1900* (London: Longmans, 1962).

7. René Pelissier, "Campagnes Militaires en Sud-Angola 1885-1915," *Cahiers d'Etudes Africaines*, 9: no. 1 (1968), 4-73.

8. Douglas L. Wheeler, "Gungunyane the Negotiator: A Study in African Diplomacy," *JAH*, 9 (October 1968), 585-602.

9. José Mendes Ribiero Norton de Matos, *Memórias e Trabalhos da minha vida: Factos, Acontecimentos e Episodios que a minha Memoria Guardou, Conferências, Discoursos e Artigos e suas Raizes no Passado* (4 vols., Lisbon: Editoria Marítimo Colonial, lda., 1944-45), III, 83f.

10. On the administrative development of the Portuguese colonies, see Alfredo Hector Wilensky, *Tendências de la Legislación Ultramarina Portuguesa em Africa: Contribución para su Estudio en los Países de Habla Hispana* (Braga: Editoria Pax, 1968); and the older accounts, Michel Frochot, *L'Empire Colonial Portugais: Organisation Constitutionelle, Politique et Administrative* (Lisbon: Editions SPN, 1942), and Hailey, *African Survey*.

11. Henrique Galvão and Carlos Selvagem [pseud.], *Império Ultramarino Português: Monografia do Império* (4 vols., Lisbon: Empresa Nacional de Publicidade, 1950-1953), IV, 181.

12. Delavignette, *Service Africain*.

13. Hermann Pössinger, *Landwirtschaftliche Entwicklung in Angola und Moçambique* (Munich: Weltforum Verlag, 1968), 124 ff.

14. Eduardo Mondlane, *Kampf um Mozambique* (Frankfurt a. M.: März-Verlag, 1970), 40. Translated in English as *The Struggle for Mozambique* (Baltimore: Penguin, 1969).

15. Douglas L. Wheeler and René Pelissier, *Angola* (London: Pall Mall, 1971), 65.

16. Joaquim Augusto Mousinho de Albuquerque, *Moçambique, 1896-1898* (Lisbon: M. Gomes, 1899), is filled with biting criticism of official colonial policy.

17. José Nicolau Nunes de Oliveira, *Moçambique* (Lisbon. 1943), 15, and Renato Antunes Mascarenhas, "Norton de Matos" (Dissertation, ISCSPU, Lisbon, 1970), 123. The eventful post-World War I years, so important for the later development of the colonies, have regretably been very little studied.

18. Vincente Ferreira, *A Situação de Angola: Cucular-Cousulta envida ás Associaçãos comercials, industrais e agrícas de Província de Angola* (Luanda: Imprensa nacional, 1926), 9. See in addition the works of Norton de Matos himself: *Memórias*, and *A Nação uma; Organização politica e administratia dos Territoriós do Ultramar Português* (Lisbon P. Ferreira, Filhos, 1953).

19. Ferreira, *A Situação*, 8.

20. See the attacks of Francisco Pinta da Cunha Leal, *Caligula em Angola* (Lisbon: n.p., 1924).

21. Wilensky, *Tendências.*

22. Alan K. Smith, "Antonio Salazar and the Reversal of Portuguese Colonial Policy," *JAH*, 15 (October 1974), 653-67.

23. On the following see Duffy, *Portuguese Africa.*

24. For a criticism of Freyre, see Roger Bastide, "Lusitropology, Race and Nationalism," and idem, "Class Protest and Development in Brazil and Portuguese Africa," in Ronald H. Chilcote (comp.), *Protest and Resistance in Angola and Brazil: Comparative Studies* (Berkeley: University of California Press, 1972), 225-40.

25. Amílcar Lopes Cabral, *Unité et Lutte* (2 vols., Paris: F. Maspero, 1975), I, 77. A somewhat abridged version was recently published in English as *Unity and Struggle: Speeches and Writings* (New York: Monthly Review Press, 1979).

26. Michael Anthony Samuels, *Education in Angola, 1878-1914: A History of Culture Transfer and Administration* (New York: Columbia Teachers College Press, 1970); Martins dos Santos, *História do Ensino em Angola* (Luanda: Edição dos Servicos de Educação, 1970); Manuel Dias Belchior, "Evolução Politica do Ensino em Moçambique," in Lisbon, Universidade Tecnica, Instituto Superior de Ciêcias Sociais e Politica Ultramarina, *Moçambique: Curso de Extensão Universitária: Ano Lectivo de 1964-1965* (Lisbon: n.p. 1965), 637-45.

27. Mozambique, Reportição technica de Estatística, *Anuário Estatístico: 1940* (Lourenço Marques: Imprensa Nacional de Mozambique, 1941), 82-85.

28. Portugal, Instituto Nacional de Estatística, *Anuário Estatístico, ano de 1940* (Lisbon: Imprensa Nacional, 1942), ch. 14, "Apêndice," 3, 32, 110; Angola, Repartição de Estatística Geral, *Anuário Estatístico de Angola: Anos de 1940 a 1943* (Luanda: Imprensa Nacional, 1944), 43f.

29. This is Hammond's thesis; see his essay, "Uneconomic Imperialism: Portugal in Africa before 1910," in Gann and Duignan, *Colonialism*, I, as well as his larger work, cited n.6 above.

30. "Relatório da Commissão de 1898," in *Antologia Colonial Portuguesa* (Lisbon: Divisão de Publicaçãos e Biblioteca, Agência Geral das Colónias, 1946), I, 153.

31. António Ennes, *Moçambique: Relatório Apresentado ao Govérno de sua Magestade* (Lisbon: Divisão de Publicaçãos e Biblioteca, Agência Geral das Colónias, 1893, 1946), 75.

32. For a semiofficial account of Portuguese labor policy, see Joaquim Moreira da Silva Cunha, *O Trabhalho Indígena: Estudo de Direito Colonial* (Lisbon: Agência Geral do Ultramar, Divisão de Publicaçãos e Biblioteca, 1959), who is criticized by James Duffy, *A Question of Slavery* (Oxford: Clarendon Press, 1967).

33. Henry Woodd Nevinson, *A Modern Slavery* (London, New York: Harper, 1908).

34. Edward Alsworth Ross, *Report on the Employment of Native Labour in Portuguese Africa* (New York: Abbott Press, 1925).

35. Henrique de Paiva Couceiro, *Angola: Dois Anos de Governo; Junho 1907-Junho 1909: História e Comentários* (Lisbon: Ediçãos Gama, 1948), 228.

36. A summary of this report was published in Henrique Galvão, *Santa Maria: My Crusade for Portugal*, trans. William Longfellow (Cleveland: World Publishing Co., 1961), 55ff. See also his earlier work, *Angola (para uma nova Política)*, (Lisbon: Livraria Popular de F. Franco, 1937), in which he offered persuasive criticisms of overbureaucratization and excessive centralization in Angola.

37. Antonio Rita Ferreira, *O Movimento Migratório de Trabalhadores entre Moçambique e a Africa do Sul* (Lisbon: Junta de Investigaçãos do Ultramar, 1963), and Marvin Harris, "Labour Emigration among the Moçambique Thonga: Cultural and Political Factors," *Africa*, 29 (January 1959), 50-66 and the resulting exchange with Rita Ferreira, ibid., 30 (April, July 1960), 141-52, 243-45; ibid., 31 (January 1961), 75-77.

38. José Cardozo, "Finances et Crédit," in Portugal, Colonie de Moçambique, *Exposition Coloniale Internationale, Paris 1931* (Lourenço Marques, Imprimerie Nationale, 1931), x, 29.

39. Frankel, *Capital Investment*, 169.

40. On the concession companies, see Hammond, *Portugal and Africa*, 147-50.
41. Frankel, *Capital Investment*, 24, 213.
42. Companhia de Diamantes de Angola, *A Short Report on its Work in Angola* (Lisbon: n.p., 1963).
43. Ibid., 93f.
44. *Anuário estatístico de Angola, anos de 1940 a 1943*, 305.
45. Galvão and Selvagem, *Império*, III, 56.
46. S. E. Katzenellenbogen, *Railways and the Copper Mines of Katanga* (Oxford: Clarendon Press, 1973).
47. On settlement policy, see Ilídio de Amaral, *Aspecto do Povoamento Branco de Angola* (Lisbon: Junta de Investigiçãos do Ultramar, 1960), and Gerald J. Bender, "Planned Rural Settlement in Angola, 1900-1968," in Franz-Wilhelm Heimer (ed.), *Social Change in Angola* (Munich: Weltforum Verlag, 1973), 235-41.
48. Wheeler and Pelissier, *Angola*, 96-98, 124.
49. Bender, "Rural Settlements." Although Galvão, *Angola*, I, 223f., also characterized official colonization as a failure, he nonetheless spoke of the "triumph of free colonization." And, in fact, along with Rhodesia, Angola had the greatest density of whites of any country in black Africa.
50. Norton de Matos, *Memórias*, II, 306.
51. Nunes de Oliveira, *Moçambique*, 34; and see also Ernesto de Queiroz Ribeiro, *O Algodão em Moçambique* (Beira: n.p., 1939).
52. José Pereira Neto, "Comércio externo de Moçambique," in *Moçambique: Curso de extensão*, 302, and João Maria Cerqueira d'Azevedo, *Sidsídios para o Estudo da Economia de Angola nos Ultimos cem Anos* (Lisbon: Impr. Nacional, 1945), 47.
53. C. F. Spence, *The Portuguese Colony of Moçambique: An Economic Survey* (Cape Town: A. A. Balkema, 1951), 54. Mondlane, *Kampf*, offers some severe criticisms of forced cultivation.
54. I follow here Hermann Pössinger, "Interrelations between Economic and Social Change in Rural Africa: The Case of the Ovimbundu in Angola," in Heimer, *Social Change*, 31-52. See also Childs, *Umbundu Kinship*, and Adrian C. Edwards, *The Ovimbundu under Two Sovereignties: A Study of Social Control and Social Change among a People of Angola* (London: Oxford University Press, 1962).
55. Julio de Castro Lopo, *Jornalismo de Angola: Subsídios para a sua História* (Luanda: Centro de Informação e Turismo de Angola, 1964), 75-83.
56. Wheeler has done the pioneer work here; see his chapters in Wheeler and Pelissier, *Angola*.
57. Alfredo Margarido, "Movimenti Profetici e Messianici Angolese," *Rivista Storica Italiana*, 80: no. 3 (1968), 538-92.
58. Douglas L. Wheeler, "An Early Angolan Protest: The Radical Journalism of José de Fontes Pereira (1823-1891)," in Rotberg and Mazrui, *Protest*; idem, "Origins of African Nationalism in Angola: Assimilado Protest Writings," in Chilcote, *Protest and Resistance*, 67-87.
59. Wheeler and Pelissier, *Angola*, 115-28.
60. Cunha Leal, *Caligula*, 133ff.; José Mendes Ribiero Norton de Matos, *Província de Angola* (Porto: Edição de Maranus, 1926), decree no. 99.

14

BRITISH SETTLERS IN CENTRAL AND EAST AFRICA

West Africa's contacts with foreign culture and its relations with the outer world were the result of the slave trade. Its people, particularly those living on the coast, thus became participants in a trading system reaching far beyond Africa. East Africa, on the other hand, was drawn into an Arabic trading empire that reached from Oman on the Persian Gulf to the island of Zanzibar and reached inland in Kenya and Tanzania to the great lakes.[1] This "empire" only began to assume a very tangible form in the early nineteeth century, however, when the important ruler, Imam Seyyid Said, moved his residence to Zanzibar and made the island the entrepôt for East Africa.[2] Arab plantation owners began to raise cloves for export, using slaves from the interior as their work force. Indians were already at work as moneylenders. Arabs had long lived on the coast and had intermarried with Africans. These "Arabized" Muslim Swahili recognized the sultan of Zanzibar as their ruler. They constituted a rather prosperous and highly differentiated community, and the sultan in fact contented himself with taking a small cut of import duties. Every year a great number of caravans set out from these stations for the hinterland, trading cloth and weapons for slaves and ivory. Zanzibar did not attempt direct rule. Some several stations served the caravans as strong points, and Arab traders took up residence inland and formed their own settlements. Trade treaties with African rulers were concluded, and it was the latter, as earlier in West Africa, who delivered the human trade goods. Under Said, Zanzibar's foreign trade increased rapidly. American and German ships, as well as British and French, stopped at the island. Trade treaties were concluded, consuls named, in 1839 by France, and soon thereafter by Great Britain. The British consuls, particularly Sir John Kirk, who was an active member of the antislavery movement, gained increasing influence. In 1873 Sultan Bargash was forced under threat of naval blockade to accept a treaty outlawing the slave trade and closing the slave markets. Although the slave trade had been increasing, particularly from the port of Kilwa, the economic changeover proved relatively simple. Rubber took the place of slaves, with cloves coming second. Customs revenues increased from £65,000 in 1869 to £100,000 in 1876.

In the interior, however, the manhunts apparently peaked in the decade 1880-1890, in part because the Arabs were pushing deeper into the interior and exploiting slaves ruthlessly as porters and in part because firearms intensified tribal warfare.

Although the mid-century European exploration expeditions following Arab caravan routes had described the people and the country around the lakes, Europe began to show a real interest in East Africa only in the 1870s. Following Livingston, missionary efforts proceeded outward from Lake Nyasa, reaching Buganda in 1877. The latter was a firmly knit polity that later became a key point for British rule. The land provided ample food, thus forming the basis for a kingdom, whose ruler, the kabaka, disposed of a highly differentiated bureaucracy, collected taxes, claimed personal service, and surrounded himself with a court. He also armed his soldiers with rifles which they employed on plundering expeditions to seize the goods—slaves and ivory—needed for trade with the Arabs. The kabaka, nominally a Muslim, accepted the missionaries because he was interested in schools. But he never trusted them, and his mistrust increased when the White Fathers appeared in 1879. About this same time, Stanley had established the link from the east coast via the lakes to the Congo. General Charles Gordon, governor of the Egyptian Sudan province of Equatoria, even pushed through to Buganda from the north and "annexed" the region around Lakes Victoria and Albert, thus cutting across Zanzibar's claims. These notions of expansion had, indeed, already been abandoned by 1880, though they moved the sultan of Zanzibar to establish closer ties to England.

German activity was what eventually moved the British to fuller commitment. The British had not opposed the German protectorate treaties in the area inland from Zanzibar on the coast and in the case of the German treaty with Witu had actually pressured the sultan to give in. The efforts of Kirk and William Mackinnon, the philanthropic owner of an Indian Ocean shipping line, to found a concession company for the area between Mombassa and the lakes were, however, favorably received in London. In 1886 the first Anglo-German border treaty was concluded. It divided East Africa into a British and a German sphere of influence. The sovereignty of the sultan was recognized and Witu remained for the time in German hands. In 1887 Mackinnon's British East African Association received a concession from the sultan, and in 1888 Lord Salisbury gave in and granted it a charter.[3] The company was principally intended to secure the sources of the Nile against foreign seizure. Since the long-contemplated retreat from Egypt was proving impossible, the sources of the Nile had assumed a crucial importance for London. A race between British and German colonial companies for control of Uganda did in fact now commence. Carl Peters concluded a treaty in February 1890 with the kabaka, but the Anglo-German negotiations had already begun which led to the Zanzibar-Helgoland Agreement of May 1890. Germany conceded Uganda and Witu to England and accepted a British protectorate over Zanzibar.[4]

At the behest of the East Africa Company, Lugard (then a captain) signed a sovereignty treaty with Buganda in December 1890. In the following months he eliminated both the Catholic French party and the Muslim exiles. He also expanded the area under British rule. Uganda's old rival, the kingdom of Bunyoro was first isolated and then defeated militarily in 1894, the kingdom of Buganda being enlarged at Bunyoro's expense. In the meanwhile, however, the company's finances had become desperate and it had decided to withdraw from Uganda. Lord Rosebury, who as a "Liberal imperialist" was, like Salisbury, unwilling to abandon control of the sources of the Nile, and Lugard's press campaign were, with the help of the churches, missions, and antislavery movement, eventually able to move Parliament to erect a protectorate over Uganda in 1894, and to create the East Africa Protectorate in 1895.

As one can see, the British were interested almost exclusively in Buganda. The later Kenya did not enter their field of vision, and even the Foreign Office considered it a sterile region. No prospective exports seemed available, the distance from the coast was enormous, and porter transport was very expensive. The company set up some stations in Kikuyu territory because the fertile land facilitated the provisioning of caravans. Agents went on plundering expeditions in the surrounding areas; "by refusing to pay for things, by raiding, looting, swashbuckling and shooting natives, the Company has turned the whole country against the white man."[5] The warlike Masai, as herders eternally on the hunt for pasture land and accustomed to pillaging their neighbors' cattle, had been weakened since the 1880s by rinderpest, smallpox epidemics, famine, and internal tensions. Although that facilitated settler acquisition of land and the establishment of colonial rule, it really took the building of the railway evidently needed to link Uganda with the coast to start the process of settlement.

Farther south, between the Limpopo River and Lake Tanganyika, the thrust inland did not proceed from the coast, nor was it England as a European power which expanded its imperial position for strategic or political reasons. It was, rather, South African settlers who pushed north in continuation of a process that had begun in the eighteenth century. The rivalry between the Boers and the British effectively accelerated developments, however. Consistent with his dream of a mighty British Empire organized into dominions, Cecil Rhodes raced ahead with expansion in order to contain the Boer Republic of Transvaal in the north and west and to cut it off from German Southwest Africa. In 1885 southern Bechuanaland was annexed and a line established between the Boers and the Kalahari desert along the Missionary Road, and farther to the north a British protectorate was established. But only a year later, the gold rush began in the Transvaal and interest shifted to the area north of the Limpopo. It also raised the issue of how to deal with Lobengula, king of the Matabele (or, more properly, Ndebele), who had earlier, in 1837, been forced out of the Transvaal and had resettled in the southwest portion of Mashonaland. The Matabele were militarily organized cattle herders and did little farming. They also sent plundering expeditions into neighboring regions and had subdued a portion of the Mashona, though not all of Mashonaland.[6] When Khama, the ruler of Bechuanaland, had sought British protection to escape pressure from both the Boers and Lobengula, the latter had proved quite ready to fight for his independence. Sly, mistrustful, and, in the opinion of whites, underhanded, he made some concessions but otherwise attempted to play off against each other the whites who were now beseiging him for concessions.

In 1887 he concluded a friendship treaty with the Transvaal. Considering this a direct provocation, Rhodes managed to bring about the signing of a treaty on 11 February 1888 between Lobengula and a representative of the Cape Colony government which obligated the former to undertake no negotiations with foreign powers without the consent of the high commissioner. At the same time, Lobengula was recognized as the ruler of all Mashonaland. In September 1888 Lobengula granted Charles Rudd, one of Rhodes' agents, an exclusive gold mining concession in return for an annual payment and the delivery of 1,000 modern rifles a year. No more than ten whites, moreover, were to enter Mashonaland at any one time. Lobengula manifestly believed "that in signing the concession he had reconciled the irreconcilable and dealt satisfactorily with the external threat without at the same time unduly heightening that from within."[7] But, he reined in his young warriors, knowing full well that they would be no match for the whites if serious warfare broke out.

Using the Rudd concession as a starting point, Rhodes, or rather his British South Africa Company, received its charter as a colonial corporation with the right to administer land acquired in the future. Lobengula's attempts to repudiate the concession and to call on Queen Victoria as arbitrator came too late. Rhodes began the occupation of Mashonaland. In 1890 a column of 200 picked men crossed the border and, avoiding Matebeleland in order to prevent a clash with Lobengula, hoisted the Union Jack in the middle of Mashonaland at what was to become Salisbury. Every pioneer received the promised prospecting rights and about 3000 acres of land, in clear violation of the treaty of 1888. Lobengula and Rhodes both wanted to avoid hostilities, however, even after Matabele warriors on a raiding expedition had killed Mashonas working for the whites and under their protection. Leander Starr Jameson, the administrator of Mashonaland, considered the time was ripe, however, and calling for volunteers, he struck. The Matabele warriors proved no match for machine guns. Lobengula fled, dying early in 1894 of smallpox.

The Matabeleland Order in Council of July 1894 regulated the position of the company in what was to become Southern Rhodesia. The company, with London's agreement, was to appoint and pay administrators. They received legislative authority, the right to collect taxes, and a four-man council to advise them. A three-man land commission, one of whom the colonial secretary appointed, was to supervise the division of land and to assure the Matabele sufficient land "for their occupation...and suitable for their agricultural and pastoral requirements, including in all cases a fair and equitable proportion of springs and permanent water." Knowing from experience that a free hand for the settlers would lead to new conflicts, London had attempted to set definite limits on land expropriation. Two great reservations were immediately established but soon proved unusable because the land was so poor. The volunteers of 1893, moreover, had been promised land, and soon had seized the fertile Matabeleland. The Matabele thus found themselves forced to pay rent in kind or work on farms if they did not want to lose their land altogether. The great herds of cattle, formerly Lobengula's property, were confiscated and divided up. In the end, the Matabele got only 41,000 of 250,000 animals. When rinderpest broke out in February 1896, moreover, many sound animals were killed along with the diseased. And with the search for gold came forced labor. Native police, the majority former Matabele slaves, dragged people from the villages, and working conditions matched recruiting methods.[8] The idea was to shatter Matabele society: the monarchy was to disappear, the system of military organization was to be destroyed, and the Matabele aristocracy was to be humiliated. The entire effort seemed to have succeeded and the police were pulled out. The Matabele rebellion of March 1896 thus came as a complete surprise to the whites.

The Mashona also rebelled, despite having remained quiet in 1893 and, if not exactly welcoming the whites, having at least tolerated them, in part as protection against the Matabele. But the land seizures had created tensions, and the whites were beginning to punish Mashonas. They were ignoring the chiefs and carrying on as the rulers of the country: "Why did God send the white man to kill and outrage the native peoples?" The introduction of the hut tax in 1894 forced the issue of recognizing white rule and encountered covert and occasionally open resistance. The recruitment of workers was another grievance. In short, the Mashona chiefs also felt their existence was at stake. Within a few days, the Africans had overrun white outposts and slaughtered settlers on isolated farms, but a few strong points held fast and the white counterattack soon began. The settlers demanded unconditional surrender. No less a person than Rhodes himself, however—in "his finest hour"—negotiated a treaty of surrender with the Matabele which promised the rebels freedom from punishment and provided the chiefs a way to act as spokesmen for their peoples within the native administration. "Resistance, far from preventing future political activity, helped the Ndebele to move into a new political era."[9]

The settlers' land seizures, forced recruitment of workers, and taxation were the causes of this desperate attempt of the Matabele and Mashona to rebel against the whites and win back their independence. The attempt failed, and was bound to fail. Control over land, labor, and taxation remained the goals of the settlers, and gave the systems of rule in Rhodesia, and Kenya as well, their characteristic stamp.

LAND AND LABOR

Kenya. In 1895 the British government dissolved the East Africa Company but its interest, too, at first centered on Uganda. It therefore established its rule over the area that was to become Kenya only gradually, one reason, indeed, there was never any great rebellion such as occurred in German East Africa. The British consul in Zanzibar at first served as high commissioner, the administration being moved to Nairobi, an important staging point for railway construction, only in 1907. The great danger seemed initially to be the warlike Masai. Although the railway passed along the edge of their grazing area, it did not vitally threaten them. The British also took pains to secure good relations with the Laiban, their high priest, as the Masai were not ruled by a single chief. Although these efforts were successful with the Masai, the British had to use force against the other tribes. Over the years, numerous punitive expeditions scoured the area around Nairobi and east of Lake Victoria. The men on the spot often proceeded so ruthlessly that London felt constrained to admonish them sharply.[10] The British also exploited traditional rivalries. They supported the Masai against the Kikuyu, and the Luo against the Nandi. It is thus inaccurate to contrast German brutality and employment of military force with "peaceful" British penetration. In contrast to Buganda, the tribes of Kenya were not organized as kingdoms. That naturally made the work of the British easier, though in the following period it complicated the consolidation of power and of the administrative structure. Upon whom, indeed, should the British base their rule, when neither large African polities nor paramount chiefs could be acknowledged in the localities as native authorities? The African societies in the area were also not well known, and the Nigerian experience was naturally as yet unavailable. The administration thus appointed men who appeared suitable as headmen or chiefs and legalized their positions in the Village Headmen Ordinance of 1902. Practice soon revealed, however, that these chiefs had no real authority. Often men had been chosen who had simply offered their services, or, in other words, collaborators, or caravan leaders, or others who had had some contact with Europeans, or who knew Swahili, or had done good service when the railway was being built. But these men did not enjoy popular regard and proved all too ready to abuse their positions. The colonial power also imposed new duties upon them, such as tax collection, provision of workers, clearing of paths, and the like. After 1910 the British attempted with but partial success to anchor the native authorities more securely in native society by establishing councils of elders, whose primary functions were judicial but who were also to maintain a watching brief over the chiefs. The chiefs in Kenya remained artificial creations of the colonial power, and were the appointed rather than the truly legitimate leaders and spokesmen of their peoples. Further reform efforts came in the 1920s. Native councils with some elected members were created which could issue "by-laws," had some revenues of their own, and could, though with British officials in the chair, discuss local issues. The councils fulfilled the function of a local government within the reservations. The mission-educated young people were to be integrated in this manner and enabled to undertake modernizing activities—and any potentially subversive attitudes they might have were nullified.[11] There were, however, no efforts corresponding to those in the Gold Coast or Nigeria to combine these councils at the regional level. The native administration in the

Kenya reserves borrowed some features of Indirect Rule, but did not consider them preparation for future self-administration. In the last analysis Indirect Rule proved incompatible with a settler-dominated system.

The East Africa Company began construction of a railway from Mombasa to Lake Victoria in 1896. The line was considered necessary to open up Uganda. But the costs, assumed by the British government, proved higher than expected. Large amounts of traffic could hardly be anticipated early on, and amortization and operating expenses would clearly place undue strain on the modest budget of the protectorate. London, however, looked with hostility toward supporting such deficits for years on end. Thus it was that interest shifted to the Kenya highlands, whose climate, unlike that of the coast or West Africa, appeared suitable for European settlers.[12] Large stretches of the country were uninhabited. Although the first settlers came with the railway, London kept up the pressure and various schemes were considered, from bringing in Indians to providing the Zionists a national home. The new high commissioner, Sir Charles Eliot, considered that East Africa had the prerequisites for a prosperous settler community and was disinclined to pay much regard to African land claims.[13] In 1903 he sent an agent to South Africa to lure settlers away. In the same year, 100,000 acres of grazing land were given to Lord Delamere, who had in 1898 crossed the country on a hunting safari.[14] The southern Rift Valley, which offered fertile land on the rail line, seemed to have the most potential, but the Masai used it as grazing land. The British concluded a treaty with them in 1904, however, which provided them with two reservations for "so long as the Masai race shall exist." The British had handled the Masai very circumspectly during the preceeding years, allowing them to take part in punitive expeditions and letting them keep a portion of confiscated cattle. That behavior plus decimation through disease and internal tribal tensions probably explain their readiness to leave their old pastures and homelands. In 1911 the British had to apply considerably more pressure to get the Masai to agree to give up one reservation in return for enlargement of the other, south of the railway. They were subsequently left largely to themselves, not being forced to provide laborers, and thus caused the administration few difficulties. Their reservations, moreover, were large enough to prevent acute land shortages even when herds increased.[15]

Matters were different with the Kikuyu. The common assertion that they were driven out of the highlands reserved for the whites, however, requires considerable qualification. During the course of the nineteenth century, the Kikuyu were pushed from the north into the south, mainly into the area south of Mount Kenya. Nairobi lay on the southern edge of Kikuyuland. In the early years, a few settlers put down roots there and "bought" land which was then added to the territory reserved for whites. Toward the end of the century lands were added to these reserves if they were uninhabited and appeared ownerless, the Kikuyus being much diminished by smallpox and their stock decimated by cattle diseases. As the land commission was to ascertain in 1932, the tribe lost "only" 109.5 square miles of land out of an entire tribal property of some 1,800 square miles, though this was fertile land suitable for coffee. But what really mattered were Kikuyu notions of the law, and for them, there was no ownerless land. Tribal and clan land claims remained valid even when the land was not being used and, indeed, even when according to European notions the land had legally changed hands. The feeling of unity between clan and land, characteristic of nearly all African peoples, was especially marked with the Kikuyu. Land was the embodiment of the vitality and existence of tribal society. When the Kikuyu began to recover their numbers, however, and return to the areas they had abandoned, they found white settlers occupying their lands. They were at best able to stay on as squatters on the land they claimed. Although a great part of the highland had been in fact effectively ownerless and Kikuyu losses were relatively slight, the white assumption of land seemed to the Kikuyu like robbery and a threat to their tribal existence. Such feelings created both frustration and latent antiwhite attitudes, which were further encouraged by the establishment of property boundary lines. These kept the whites out of Kikuyu land, but they also confined the latter to reservations and limited their potential for growth, though there was for the moment no question of population pressure.[16]

The question of land for white settlers was bound up inextricably with the question of labor. It was not yet clear what crops Kenyan land and climate were best suited for. Settlers from South Africa and moneyed English gentlemen at first thought to live in the tradition of English gentry. That meant, to them, sheep grazing and grain farming. The difficulties were great, however, and expectations were disappointed. By 1910 the colony was on the verge of bankruptcy.[17] Capital began to flow in the following years, however, corn proving not only a suitable crop but one that brought good and rising prices. Coffee also began to be intensively farmed on plantations. It should be emphasized that the individual African tribes quickly adapted to the new situation and largely took over corn growing. The Luo, who lived in the densely settled Nyanza district east of Lake Victoria, proved especially adept. They had not had to give up any land to settlers and their administrator was the highly regarded John Ainsworth.[18] In 1913, 70 percent of Kenyan exports came from African producers, and the Nyanza farmers were the railway's best customers. Settlers need workers, however, especially as Kenya was not suited for small farms. Africans were available on the reservations being gradually marked out. The only problem was getting them to work for wages, impossible without state assistance. Taxes were the most obvious recourse, and they followed hard on the establishment of rule and the beginnings of settlement. First came a hut tax, essentially a tax on entire families, and then a poll tax on individuals. They were meant to encourage young people in particular to earn away from the reservations the necessary money to pay them. Taxes did not suffice to end the labor shortage, which came to seem the most important obstacle to opening up the colony economically. Both direct and indirect administrative compulsion and recruiting agents proved necessary. Such measures had the usual effects on the position of the chiefs, who were enlisted in the service of a native policy oriented toward the needs of the settlers. The chiefs were forced, and sometimes bribed, to assist in providing workers and were able to maintain their positions, which were neither strong nor uncontested, only with administration support.

The settlers exerted pressure on the administration from the beginning, demanding it provide sufficient workers and take additional measures to force the "lazy Africans" to leave the reservations. Thus in 1906 a Masters and Servants Ordinance patterned after that of Transvaal was considered. It would have punished breach of contract with imprisonment. In 1907, however, the newly appointed secretary for native affairs established that abuses in the treatment of natives had occurred[19] and prohibited an ordinance which would have forced the chiefs to provide workers. Africans were to work on white farms only of their own free will. That was in concert with the ideas of the Liberal government in London, which strove to end the yet remaining forms of forced labor. These "extraordinary labour rules" were bitterly attacked and in 1908 led to an open clash between the settlers and the governor. The settlers continued to reiterate their demands in the years to come. They were: higher taxes for Africans; no further expansion and ideally, contraction, of reservations; introduction of pass laws with the aim of ascertaining the potential labor force and tying it down as completely as possible; and administrative assistance in recruiting labor on the reservations. The Colonial Office and the local administration had no little difficulty in withstanding this pressure and had to make concessions to it.

Yet another question, the position of Indians in the protectorate, aroused the settlers against the administration and strengthened their demands for direct participation in administration. As already mentioned, London had initially weighed the idea of bringing in Indian peasants as well as white settlers to exploit the large uninhabited areas. By 1902, however, twenty-two white settlers had already caucused, electing a representative committee, and were pestering Sir Charles Eliot, the high commissioner, to reserve the highlands for whites. Despite warnings from London that to do so would prejudice the policy of segregation, Eliot gave the settlers every encouragement. In 1905 East Africa was placed under the colonial secretary and received a legislative and an executive council. A land board under clear settlers' control was also created. In 1906-1908 Secretary Lord Elgin conceded, though in veiled form, that "grants in the upland area should not be made to Indians."[20] As colonial undersecretary, however, Winston Churchill thought it reasonable to name an Indian to the legislative council.[21] The Kenya Indians were not, as is often alleged, coolies left over from building the railway, but had either been merchants active for generations in Zanzibar or inland or were newly immigrated Gujeratis, who soon monopolized the artisan and retail trades and in some cases assembled considerable wealth. They formed their own organizations to fight discrimination and settler attempts to legalize land segregation in the cities and in the highlands.[22]

The war and the period immediately thereafter led the settlers to pose their demands with renewed vigor and with success. Kenya was not a war theatre, but did provide African soldiers who fought in Africa and abroad. It also supplied porters for the Tanganyika campaign.[23] Losses were high, less because of the hostilities themselves than because of sickness. The porters were poorly provided for, and recruiting was impossible without compulsion. Influenza had annihilating effects. Among the Kikuyu alone, 120,000 died. The settlers were either utilized for military purposes or volunteered for European duty. Economic difficulties stemming from the war made matters worse.

The Natives Registration Ordinance had already strengthened the position of the European employers in 1915. The measure was superseded in 1920 by an ordinance that required all male Africans aged sixteen or older to register. A workbook then provided information about present contractual obligations and past employment. The measure resembled pass laws long in effect in South Africa. The required fingerprint and the obligation to show the pass at the request of any white did not make this measure of humiliating discrimination the less hated. In 1919, moreover, Governor Sir Edward Northey notified district officials "to induce an augmentation of the supply of labor for farms and plantations in the protectorate." This was tantamount to calling for compulsion rather than persuasion and put the squeeze on the chiefs. This was a long-sought settler aim and meant, de facto, forced labor. The war, however, had encouraged a more active sense of obligation to the natives, and protests from East African missionaries were taken up by humanitarian circles in London. Churchill, Milner's successor as colonial secretary, was thus forced to disavow Northey and reiterate the instructions of 1908, "to take no part in recruiting labour for private employment." Although the district officials themselves had expressed doubts about Northey's policy,[24] even the new instructions did not relieve them in practice of the duty to encourage young Africans to leave the reservations temporarily to work.

The settlers had more luck in the squatter question. Since settlement, seasonal laborers from the reservations had furnished only a part of the vitally needed work force. Blacks, mainly Kikuyus, were thus permitted to settle with their families and cattle as "resident labour." They built huts, and planted crops and in return paid a sort of rent. Some Europeans criticized this system of "Kaffir farming" as a veiled enlargement of the reservations and a danger to the labor supply. In 1918 the Resident Natives Ordinance therefore stipulated that in the future no Africans could settle on European land without being liable for 180 days of labor service a year. That effectively blocked any possible African acquisition of land outside the reservations and transformed the squatter into a serf-like rural laborer.

The legislative council also moved to meet settler demands to exclude Indians from the upland reservations. In 1910 the Convention of Associations had been formed to coordinate the attainment of settler demands. Lord Delamere was its speaker. In 1913 the convention had come out for elections, under the slogan No Taxation without Representation. The convention did not concede the applicability of such claims to Indians and Africans, because in the long run that would have been tantamount to self-government. London initially turned them down,[25] but in 1916 gave in, though delaying implementation to the end of the war. The Indians, however, had in the meantime formed the East African Indian National Congress. Inspired by postwar nationalist agitation in India itself, the Indians determined to ask for the vote for themselves. There ensued a wearisome three-cornered discussion between London, the settlers, and the Indians in which the participants wrestled over the questions of the highland reservations, segregation in the cities, and the so-called common roll or common electoral-voter lists, as opposed to representation by race. At the bottom what was at issue was whether London would concede Kenya to be "white man's country" and would in due time open the way to responsible government. Both London and the local British administration proved receptive, but an odd combination of forces, the churches and missions and the British Indian government, opposed it. The latter wished to avoid stirring up the Indian national movement unduly. London's escape from this situation was to proclaim rather abruptly the "paramountcy of native interests." It thus brought the interests of the black population into the discussion.[26] The highland reservations and the common roll remained, but London again underlined its role as trustee and thus refused the settler minority responsible government for the foreseeable future. When one considers that in the same year, 1923, the settlers of Southern Rhodesia had received quasi-dominion status which effectively deprived London of control over internal matters, the far-ranging significance of the Devonshire formula—after Lord Devonshire, the colonial secretary—becomes apparent. Kenya remained a colony, and the British government retained its powers of final decision. It and not the settlers would decide on matters of future status. The question flared up again between 1926 and 1930 in the form of the "closer union" controversy (over the eventual amalgamation of Kenya, Uganda, and Tanganyika). Colonial Secretary L. S. Amery and Governor Sir Edward S. Grigg, both "pupils" of Milner's, favored a future white dominion.[27] Although the paramountcy of native interests was watered down through application of the dual policy formula, which implied primarily the encouragement of African farm production inside the reservations, the decision had fallen against the white man's country and concept of settler self-government. In 1960 London was thus able to trim with "the winds of change" and open the way to Kenya's becoming independent as an African state.

In the interwar period, economic tensions between the settlers and natives increased in spite of the dual policy. The attempt to settle war veterans as farmers proved a mistake. Large enterprises soon took over their land, farming corn over broad areas of the uplands. The production of corn increased from 339,000 bags (of 200 pounds each) in 1922 to more than a million bags in 1928. Import duties favoring the settlers also made possible profitable grain growing and an expansion of milk production. Agricultural methods were modernized, machinery being employed. Yields per acre remained rather modest. Even in the reserved highlands, wide areas were short of water and permitted only extensive farming.[28] The white Highlands, in which only Europeans could acquire land (on 999-year leases) comprised some 7.5 million acres in the 1930s or about 20 percent of the usable land. In 1928, however, only about one-eighth of the occupiable land was actually farmed.[29] The number of European farms had increased a little, to about two thousand, meaning that a tiny minority had reserved the relatively fertile highlands for itself. Besides corn, wheat, and dairy products, coffee and sisal, both plantation products, increased in importance and provided about half the exports. In contrast to the prewar period, the great portion of the exports now came from European farms. That provided an additional argument for the settlers and their defenders, who claimed the settlers were the mainstays of Kenyan economic development and prosperity, especially since it could also be pointed out that the highlands were only a fraction of the size of the reservations.

The land question nonetheless remained the most important point of friction. Propaganda in favor of white settlement and veterans' settlement necessarily appeared to the Africans as threats to their reservations and land rights, especially in view of demands for a white man's country and self-government. And with some reason: when gold was discovered on the heavily settled Kavirondo reservation in the Nyanza district, prospecting rights were high-handedly placed under special regulation in utter disregard for tribal claims to royalties.[30] The Kikuyu Land Commission of 1929 and the Kenya Land Commission of 1932 (which issued the Carter Report of 1934) both examined land claims and land sequestration with some objectivity. Both also explicated African ideas regarding real property and regarded some sort of compensation and expansion of the reservations as necessary. The Native Lands Trust Ordinance of 1938 declared the reservations to be tribal property—until then it had been Crown land. But this only marked more sharply than ever the separation between European and African territory.

The African population on the reservations increased, mainly because of declining child mortality and better disease prevention. Some districts, especially those of the Kikuyu, were already heavily settled, and the result of decreased mortality was increasing population pressure. This was mitigated somewhat through seasonal work on European farms and migration to nearby Nairobi. But the new problems of unemployment and a landless proletariat were beginning to be visible. And that was not all. Population pressure and increases in the cattle herds were leading to land erosion, since the fallow time was shortened, the forests logged off, and the pasture land overgrazed. Despite some improvement in techniques, such as the replacement of hack-hoes with plows, and increasing production of grain and corn on the reservations, cultivation methods remained basically the same. The fact that in 1929 up to one-quarter of the men between 16 and 40 worked elsewhere for months at a time hardly encouraged African production. The agriculture department concentrated its activities almost exclusively on the European sector until the 1930s, and the means dedicated to the reservations remained small.[31] The taxes on individual Africans increased during the depression, though both farm profits and wages fell.[32] Whites, however, were hardly taxed at all and until 1937 were able to stave off the income tax long regarded by the administration as necessary.[33] A 1932 commission indeed noted that no such amounts as were collected from Africans in taxes were spent on the reservations. Of the 544 miles of railway built after 1920, 397 miles went through white lands and only 147 through African territory. The same was true for roads.[34]

The settlers also managed to prevent the Africans from growing coffee, which they were doing successfully in Uganda and particularly in Tanganyika. The settlers argued that diseases might pass from the less carefully maintained African plantations to European ones. In practice of course, they were mainly interested in keeping down potential competition and not endangering their own labor supply, coffee being labor-intensive. But Kikuyuland was well suited to Arabica coffees, which would have provided these densely settled areas with valuable income.[35] The younger generation of Africans justly interpreted this frustration of native economic development as a particularly shameful kind of discrimination, and one which stood, moreover, in the greatest contradiction to the administration's much advertized dual policy. Nor is it hard to see why administration measures against erosion, which were clearly necessary, and its efforts to reduce over-large herds, or "de-stocking" as it was called, were seen as underhanded and encountered both open and covert resistance.

The squatter's lot was also worsening. Counting families, the total squatter population had risen to between 100,000 and 130,000. Housing, food, and educational opportunities were deficient.[36] Squatter herds were increasing, overgrazing the land—in 1930, about a million acres—and with the expansion of European pasture land, they were beginning to impinge on the arable. The result was new white efforts to prune back squatter rights still more.

Kenya was the classic settlement colony in the British Empire, particularly in the interwar period after Southern Rhodesia had achieved quasi-dominion status. Railway construction toward Uganda had made it seem proper to reserve the supposedly "empty" and climatically suitable highlands for Europeans. The implications of this policy became clear almost at once. The African tribes were forced into reservations and excluded from the thinly settled highlands in order to create the prerequisites for gentlemen farming. The latter, dependent on cash crops, required railways, roads, and services of all kinds. But what they needed most of all was workers, and these could be obtained only by measures of taxation and compulsion. Native farming and the capitalist settler economy proved antagonistic, because a deliberate encouragement of production on the reservations would have dammed up the stream of cheap labor. The prohibition of coffee farming is the most striking proof of this, though it also served to prevent the rise of an enterprising African peasant class with cash in its hands. Indeed, young workers were siphoned out of native farming, and taxes collected from Africans, at least until the 1930s, mostly profited the highlands. In both Kenya and England men like W. McGregor Ross and Dr. Norman Leys stepped forward to oppose the powerful settler community and the white-man's-country imperialists in the metropolis. They came from the missions, the Labour party, and even from the reservation bureaucracies, and they prevented Kenya from going the way of Southern Rhodesia. But the thesis of the paramountcy of native interest and the dual policy remained only words, veiling what in practice was a racist system of rule, in which a minority of roughly 17,000 whites stood alongside 40,000 Indians against more than three million Africans, whose economic and social order was subverted to the needs of the dominant minority.

Uganda. The Kingdom of Buganda attracted European attention around the middle of the nineteenth century. It became a goal for both missionary and political aggrandizement. It remained in the center of British political and economic interest even after the establishment of a protectorate over Uganda in 1894 and the Uganda Order in Council of 1902. The latter divided the new territory into provinces and districts and gave the new administration a legal basis. For the general public, indeed, Uganda and Buganda were identical, as was understandable, since the African kingdom appeared to be not only a well-ordered state, but one revealing an especial ability to absorb Western culture. It converted to Christianity and took up cotton farming. In the following period, it thus appeared an exemplar of Indirect Rule, with the possibility of economic development through native farming, and a territory that England was extraordinarily proud of.[37]

The treaties of 1892 and 1893 did not stabilize British rule definitively. In 1897 King Mwanga rebelled against British rule and the restrictions on his internal position but was supported neither by his Christian ministers nor his chiefs. The latter had gained in power and influence under the British, as was regularized in the Agreement of 1900. Buganda was declared a province of the protectorate of Uganda, but received considerable additions to its territory. The kabaka was to be addressed henceforth as "Your Highness," but his autocratic power was diminished to the extent that he had to share executive power with three ministers, the katikiros. The lukiko, a sort of parliament with legislative and judicial power, replaced the earlier, more informal, consultative council of chiefs. More important was the revolutionary solution taken to the land question. Half of the kingdom was declared Crown land, but the other half was given to the kabaka, his family, the ministers, and the greater and lesser chiefs as freehold property, which they could rent in return for fees. The smaller, mostly heathen, clan chiefs got nothing. England thus took over the Buganda system of government, but at the same time created an oligarchy from the existing ruling class of Christian chiefs appointed by the kabaka. Through its gifts of land, however, the British strengthened this oligarchy vis-à-vis the kabaka, and in the lukiko provided it a forum where it could defend its special interests, if necessary, even against the British. But this class owed its new position and its economic advantages to the colonial power and was thus bound to it. England was in fact largely able to restrict its role to advice and supervision, the more so as the ruling class acquired Western educations and demonstrated administrative competence; Sir Apolo Kagwa was prime minister for thirty-seven years. This ruling class soon did little more than defend its privileges and played only in a restricted sense its expected role of a "modernizing gentry." In comparison to Nigeria, where Indirect Rule led to making the sultans and chiefs into greater autocrats, it was the subchiefs who were strengthened at the expense of the ruler. These subchiefs were recognized as native authorities and the British administration trafficked directly with them and the ministers. The kabaka was forced into a largely ceremonial position.

The Buganda system was imposed on other Uganda kingdoms, the British going so far as to use Bugandan chiefs and officials elsewhere, a system some called subimperialism.[38] Bunyoro, in particular, was treated as conquered territory and was ruled on into the 1920s by Bugandan chiefs. Its autonomy was returned only in 1933. Toro, on the other hand, was guaranteed its independence from Bunyoro in a series of special agreements between 1900 and 1906. Only a few of its chiefs, however, received freeholds. The British brought the other districts of Uganda only gradually under control.

In the early years, the protectorate stood on rather shaky footing economically.[39] The traditional exports of ivory dropped sharply, and as late as 1903, 84 percent of the administrative budget consisted of British subsidies in the form of grants-in-aid. The railway reached Uganda in 1902, but suitable exports and markets were yet to be developed. Direct taxes, introduced in 1900, could initially be paid either in cash or in kind. Whereas in Kenya land granted to settlers was to assure the profitability of the railway, in Uganda cotton was intended to foster economic development and make the colony self-sufficient. Cotton had long been grown in Uganda but not for the market. In 1903 a Danish missionary had brought in cottonseed, and a mission trading company, the Uganda Company, provided an important impetus. The administration experimentally handed out a ton-and-a-half of seed in 1904, with the support of the British Cotton Growing Association. By 1907-1908, 4,000 bales valued at £51,000 were being produced, or about 35 percent of Uganda's exports. By 1914-1915, the latter had reached £369,000 and allowed stopping the grants-in-aid. The administration beat the drum for cotton, giving out seed and instruction, and pressured the chiefs to produce. In contrast to cocoa farming in West Africa, the rapid expansion of which was mainly due to individual African initiatives, the shift to cotton occurred with the help of the chiefs. At first merely obeying administration orders, they quickly saw the financial advantages of cash-crop production. In all this the administration faced the dilemma of how to awaken the interest of the peasants in cotton without making the farming of it appear merely an additional burden, and without at the same time alienating the chiefs. Indeed, despite the noteworthy success of cotton, it was still an open question in 1914 whether the economic future of Uganda ought to rest on native farming, on settlers, or on plantations. In 1914 there were around 130 plantations, mainly for coffee and rubber, but they were not particularly successful and their share in exports remained modest.

The war gave these economic discussions new life and purpose. A development commission spoke against native farming in 1920 and raised the issue of labor. The governor proved receptive to its arguments, but not the chief of the agriculture department. Falling prices for coffee and rubber (whereas cotton prices remained high until 1925), the as yet inadequate internal transportation network, and the abolition of forced labor in 1923 finally led to a decision in favor of native farming. What had counted was thus neither a clear early decision nor a clear vision of the future, but simply the concrete economic and social possibilities of the situation. Additional grounds were British pragmatism and the fact settlers had not been recruited as in Kenya after 1900. Their number thus remained low. Despite similar organization and aims, the settlers were hence unable to exert pressure in Uganda and on the British government comparable to that in Kenya. Finally, cotton production continued to rise and made the African peasant sector economically dominant. Besides Buganda, cotton growing expanded in the eastern provinces in particular. The development of the rail and road nets played a decisive role. In 1936, 1,487,000 acres were planted, as opposed to 120,000 before the war. An interesting sidelight was that the steel plow's replacing the hack-hoe and wooden plow simplified adding to the cultivated area but did not increase yields.[40]

The expansion of the money economy and the communication network provided a personal incentive to grow cotton, as did rising interest in imported consumer goods. Direct compulsion on the part of the chiefs, however, also played no small role during the interwar period. Ugandan native farming ought not be idealized. The privileges granted the aristocracy bore heavily on the peasants. The chiefs drew considerable income from their right to rent the land given them for cash or a month's labor. By the 1920s, the administration was already trying to protect the African tenants, by limiting rent and other traditional obligations, by creating the possibility of dissolving the work obligations, and through encouragement of individual private landownership. A class of African peasants thus did arise that was able to escape direct dependence on the chiefs. Although property titles could be registered, this also opened the possibility of parcelization and mortgage indebtedness to Indian moneylenders.[41]

The administration also tried to restrict the ability of the chiefs to overburden their peoples and to enrich themselves unduly. This was done by substituting a salary for the percentage of tax collections the chiefs had hitherto received. The demands of the clan leaders, who had come away with nothing in 1900, also caused trouble. They wanted freeholds, or, as in Toro, usufruct rights, changed into direct ownership. The administration was well aware that "there has been a total absence on the part of the beneficiaries of any attempt to develop these estates, and they have been content to draw rents without consideration of their obligations as large land-owners."[42] It thus mostly rejected such claims, but sought compromise because in the last analysis its rule depended on collaboration with oligarchic ruling class. It dared not place their loyalty in the balance. It is tempting, indeed, to compare England's ambivalent attitude in this matter with its stance regarding the zamindars in India.

In Uganda, or more precisely, Buganda and other kingdoms, discussion centered on the land question. At stake was not so much a confrontation between settlers and Africans, but the African ruling class's attempt to defend and expand its privileges in the face of administration opposition. The latter sought to protect the mass of the peasants and to encourage the process of individualization, either out of trusteeship obligations it took seriously or to assure the African peasant a sufficient share of the cotton profits. The question of labor, on the other hand, never counted for much. The sharply rising demand for labor due to the expansion of acreage was met through great seasonal laborer migration from the neighboring territories of Tanganyika, the Nyanza district of Kenya, the Belgian Congo, and the mandate territory of Burundi.[43] There developed a tendency to regard the districts less favored by climate and communications as worker reservoirs and hence to put off their economic development.[44]

Another matter much discussed was the regulation of cotton buying and the closely connected question of ginning. In the beginning, the administration had stood aside, simply encouraging hand ginning. But by 1908 they had discovered that hand-ginned cotton was poor and uneven in quality. Criticisms of it endangered the export trade just getting under way. Reform was quick and drastic. Only one variety was allowed, and hand gins were confiscated and destroyed—"ruthless reforms," indeed. Without assistance from the chiefs, meaning without compulsion, the reforms would have been impossible.[45] In the following period, the ginners' most potent argument in their campaign to get the administration to bring marketing under control was the need for quality control. The other aim was to assure the African producer a fair price and to protect him insofar as possible from being swindled by buyers. These measures redounded mainly against African and Indian traders and middlemen. The number of gins rose from nineteen in the year 1916 to 155 in 1925, and more than 100 were in Indian hands. The result was an overcapacity that meant higher prices for the farmers. British firms, however, having higher salaries and thus higher operating costs than Indian firms, were naturally hard pressed. They joined together to reduce the already price-depressing effects of overcompetition. Additional new licenses were periodically withheld, zones were established within which cotton had to be sold and ginned, minimum prices were set, the number of marketplaces limited, and trade was in general subjected to strict controls. The administration, in other words, accepted a control system that protected established, mainly British, interests and that was intended to prevent competition from newcomers. In practice, where ginning agreements cut off competition, African producers were paid lower and not higher prices. In addition, the economic and social rise of Africans as buyers was largely undercut. In 1935 there remained only forty-four independent African buyers in the cotton trade. The regulation of markets resulted in a "rigid system which the petty African entrepreneur found it virtually impossible to work his way into."[46] The Africans protested in vain against these agreements, zones, and market controls, and demanded free competition. The protestors included not only the African producers' organizations but also the chiefs and the Young Busag Association, the spokesman of the younger generation. The outrage over the marketing system was to be one of the important causes for the unrest after 1945 and led to the formation of the Uganda National Congress.

Cyril Ehrlich has elegantly demonstrated the consequences of this paternalistic system. It was designed to protect the Africans against abuses and exploitation. But this system, justified on the grounds of African inexperience with money and the operations of the market economy, actually made the African's adaptation to the modern money and market economies more difficult, if not downright impossible. An African entrepreneurial class, the absence of which critics noted before World War II and after, was in fact hardly allowed to arise. The presence of Indians perhaps contributed to this but cannot be made solely responsible for it. Uganda, again meaning mainly Buganda, which had shown itself assured and adaptable in the nineteenth century, had become a largely static society by 1939. The administration, though starting out as an active initiator of economic development "had been transformed into an administration that valued stability above economic progress." The chiefs, so innovative in the beginning, had for their part become a rentier class and a group of gentry concerned to defend their positions. The pioneering Indian merchants had attained a monopoly position in both ginning and retail trade, "operating within a rigidly controlled framework of commerce," while the Africans were tied down firmly as producers.[47]

The same dead-end paternalism characterized policies of government which claimed to follow Indirect Rule, and in a satisfactorily undoctrinaire fashion, but which thought solely in terms of individual tribes, kingdoms, and clans. Uganda was an administrative unity, but not the framework for a future self-governing colony. African aspirations themselves centered on traditional units and their future autonomy: "The Buganda Agreement is the very life blood to us as a nation. . . . Our desire is to be left alone to carry on in the same way as we have been doing since the solemn promise which marked the signing of the agreement."[48] The other tribes mainly sought to maintain themselves against the Buganda and win internal control within their own territories. Africans were not represented until 1935 in the legislative councils, which were created in 1921 to provide the whites a forum. Within the council discussions analogous to those in Kenya took place concerning the number of Indian representatives and other such matters. There was a general lack of bitterness, however, because the number of Europeans remained small, being only 2,000 in 1931, and the possibility of Uganda's becoming a white man's country with responsible government was never at issue. The administration, moreover, made a certain effort to ease African entry into the administration. That occurred at the cost of the Indians, who were viewed with hardly concealed mistrust. Because of the early entry of missionaries and conversion to Christianity, the number of students was relatively high. The education department, however, warned against rapid expansion of the schools and limited entry into Makerere College to the number of positions open in the administration. Governor Sir Philip Mitchell was in

1934 the first to make any great effort in regard to higher education, initiating the expansion of Makerere College into a university as a commission report had earlier recommended.[49]

England can justly claim to have established in Uganda a system of rule that was accepted by both the precolonial ruling class and the mass of the population after a short transitional phase. The administrative apparatus remained small, and the natives were able to decide a good many matters themselves. They were not dispossessed, forced labor was abolished, and an agricultural system based on native farming brought the native relative prosperity.[50] But the contradictions within this bureaucratic paternalism have already been outlined. The possibility for Africans to shift over from cash-crop production to trade—or in other words, into the secondary sector—was largely blocked. The protection of established British interests was in this matter inextricably bound up with a deep-rooted distaste within colonial officialdom for retail trade and their feeling they should not be overhasty in exposing the African to the disintegrative effects of the modern monetary and industrial economy:

> Should they have done this they would equally inevitably have moved out of the control of traditional authority and hence of the indirect rule system on which so much depended. This would have exposed the basic contradictions implicit in that system—if Africans moved out in sufficient numbers, if they were able to accumulate capital and establish an independent economic base, then the structure of assumptions which sustained the whole colonial system would be brought into question.[51]

Tanganyika. Tanganyika was the former German East Africa,[52] which had been given to Britain in 1920 as a League of Nations mandate. The administration had to report annually to the League, and the Mandate Commission examined its report in detail. The commission, made up of distinguished representatives of the colonial powers, among them Lord Lugard, could also require supplementary information and make criticisms, but could not itself visit the mandate territory. How much influence either the mandate principle or the commission itself actually exercised on the colonialism of the interwar period is difficult to say. London was at any rate convinced that its notion of trusteeship was synonymous with the mandatory principle, at least insofar as it politically implied "developing" and "civilizing" peoples not yet adjudged able to rule themselves. Indirect Rule was readily legitimized by the mandatory principle. Perhaps more important was that Governor Sir Donald Cameron was able to use Tanganyika's special status to escape the clutches of those in London and Kenya behind the Closer-Union movement and by pointing to mandatory status to extract his colony from the grasp of the settlers. Although German East Africa was taking on the characteristic stamp of a white man's country before 1914, Tanganyika was in structure closer to Uganda than Kenya in the interwar period.

Tanganyika had suffered grievously from the war: there were human and material losses, torn-up communications, uprooted tribes, critical finances, and, to top it off, devastating polio and smallpox epidemics and, in 1919, famine. The rulers also changed, though this was not accompanied by much disruption. Still, conflicts in loyalties occurred and much mental gear-shifting was required. In some places, German-appointed chiefs were deposed out of hand by their subjects, and educated African auxiliary personnel followed the Germans on their retreat. England took over the bulk of the German administrative structure, at first even the akidas. The weak early governors mainly concerned themselves with rebuilding and left the district officials considerable freedom of action. As Ralph Austen has shown for the Lake Victoria region, British officials were more authoritarian than the Germans and intervened more energetically than their predecessors. Senior chiefs were installed in office and visits from mission schools were sought, manifestly with the aim of creating a leading class like that in Buganda. Bukoba, to the west of Lake Victoria, received institutions entirely modelled on those of Uganda.

It was Sir Donald Cameron, however, who, as governor from 1925 to 1931, took these beginnings of Indirect Rule, developed them with some consistency, and stamped Tanganyika with the impress of his strong personality. As former chief secretary of Nigeria, his orientation was West African, but as he was not doctrinaire he was able to do justice to the specific situation in East Africa. "Being convinced that it is neither just nor possible to deny permanently to the natives of the territory any part in the government of the country,"[53] he nevertheless did not believe that Western institutions could be simply plugged in and the natives Europeanized without further ado. He considered it his task to make the native a "good African" and to give him a part in the administration immediately. If the chiefs were merely used as "our mouthpieces," as order-carriers for the administration, and native institutions not strengthened, then they would collapse as they had in neighboring territories. But the accent was conservative all the same, as he wished to pull the rug out from under the "class of politically minded natives." "We are not only giving the natives a share in the administration of the country but we are at the same time building up a bulwark against political agitators."[54]

Directly before Cameron's arrival the first decisive step had already been taken. The traditional fees and labor obligations due the chiefs had come to be abused with development of a cash economy and farming of commercial products. The chiefs were therefore put on state salaries. With the Native Authority Ordinance of 1926, Cameron went a step farther, providing native treasuries along Nigerian lines. These treasuries numbered 166 by 1929 and provided for the salaries of chiefs, subchiefs, and officials and money for additional tasks as well. Houses, roads, and some schools were built, emergency aid-stations readied, and measures undertaken against the tsetse fly and erosion. Although the system was rather successful, some of the weaknesses and limitations of a native administration primarily dependent on the chiefs began to appear in the later 1930s. Administrative units were too small and had to be amalgamated. Ethnological studies having become fashionable, the "real" chiefs were sought out.

That, however, did not always prevent the man so chosen from being perceived as illegitimate. But it showed most of all that despite all efforts to prevent it, the traditional ruling class had been weakened in the colonial situation. Backed by the administration, it had become more authoritarian, while simultaneously proving unable or unwilling to assume specific modern requirements, starting with that of keeping accurate books for the native treasuries. The administration attempted to intensify its controls, to end abuses, and to unload additional novel tasks on the native authorities. The result was a distinct tendency toward bureaucratization. The administration thus faced the dilemma of legitimacy versus efficiency. Was the legitimacy of the chiefs to come first, as Indirect Rule prescribed, or was the efficiency with which the native authorities carried out their local government tasks to be the dominant consideration?[55] Schools, missions, cash-crop production, and migratory labor all naturally encouraged individualization, in Tanganyika as elsewhere, and created tensions between the chiefs and the younger generation. The chiefs rather opposed the young men's associations and in so doing failed to fulfill their role as foreseen both by Cameron and under Indirect Rule as the active supporters of social and economic development.

As in other matters, the British acted pragmatically in the land question. The plantations and farms seized during the war were not in fact returned, but only German properties on the upper slopes of Mount Meru and Mount Kilimanjaro were transferred directly from Germans to Africans. In the latter case the British had during the auctions exercised their rights in favor of the tribes, in order to reduce somewhat the pressure on the land. The great part of German property, however, merely changed hands, ending up with Greeks, among others, as owners. The administration made it clear from the beginning that Tanganyika was not considered a settlement colony and that it favored native farming. The governor accordingly resisted attempts to settle veterans there, which earned him the epithet "Negrophile" in the settler press. In agreement with article six of the mandate treaties, the important Land Ordinance of 1923 documented the British will to tax land transfers and otherwise restrict them. Existing property rights were conceded, but in the future title was granted only in the form of long-term leases. Grants of any size required the assent of the Colonial Office. Around 1930 further grants to whites were restricted in several districts. No reservations were ever created in Tanganyika.

Indirect Rule notwithstanding, Cameron was not in principle opposed to plantations and European farms, because they brought capital into the country and provided financially needed export products. He thus noted on one occasion: "This land in the Iringa District has been alienated in spite of the fact that Tanganyika is a country in which the interests of the natives are dominant and should remain dominant. We are proceeding on the basis that the European is the experimental factor and not the native."[56] But he thought primarily in terms of African land needs and could see that land was already becoming short in some districts. He took seriously the policy of the paramountcy of native interests and was thus able to say in 1928, "...if I left Tanganyika tomorrow and my successor endeavored to alienate land to non-native use which political officials considered should not be alienated, there would be sufficient strength in the Administrative Service to prevent a Governor from transgressing in this manner."[57] In contrast to Kenya, the agronomists were employed in the native sector, and the sisal plantations got hardly any administrative support.

In 1903 only 3,125 square miles of 340,500 of the largely uninhabited and, indeed, largely uninhabitable, territory were in non-African hands. These portions were concentrated as in German times in the province of Tanga and in the Kilimanjaro region, or in other words, on fertile land usually near rail lines. In the Tanga coastal zone, Arabs and Indians owned coconut and sugar plantations, while the sisal plantations, which required much capital and considerable technical skill, were exclusively in European or Indian hands. The production of sisal rose from 20,834 tons in 1913 to 45,828 tons in 1929 and provided roughly half of the country's exports. Labor was an acute problem, because the forty to fifty plantations employed as many as 50,000 Africans, who were mainly seasonal laborers from the hinterland or from other provinces. Forced labor for public purposes was abolished only in 1930. In 1923, however, a combined tax had been introduced for the localities, though it was not meant to aid in recruiting workers. In 1926 Granville St. John Orde Browne was appointed special labor commissioner for Tanganyika. He became in the years following a recognized expert on the labor problems of East and Central Africa. It was largely his service to have alerted London to the need to impose state controls on working conditions, especially worker recruiting. It is nonetheless characteristic of the colonial administration, however, that his important post was abolished in 1931 as a depression cost-cutting measure, although the catastrophic collapse of sisal prices had led to greatly worsened conditions for African sisal workers. Sisal prices fell from £32 per ton in 1929 to £21 by the end of 1930, to £12/10 in 1932. They rose again to £20 per ton in 1933 and £29 in 1935. Wages fell about half. The Baker Report of 1933 pointed out that seasonal workers hardly cleared enough to take any savings home and that wages were too low to provide adequate diet and housing.[58] Desertion was therefore very high, despite deserters' being liable to criminal sanctions. Although the plantations were the source of vitally needed foreign exports, they provided their workers with bare subsistence and did nothing to raise general living conditions.[59]

Native farming of coffee, by contrast, was quite successful. The plantings which the enterprising and adaptable Chagga in the Mossi district of Kilimanjaro had made during the German period had gone under during the war because markets had been cut off. British district commissioner Charles Dundas, however, casting about for an "economic crop," revived the native farms again. The number of planters and production rose rapidly and brought the Chagga a certain prosperity, increased by their farming of the more valuable Arabica varieties. As in Kenya, the European coffee planters of the Kilimanjaro area attempted to forbid African coffee growing or at least limit it to the Rubosta varieties, but without success. In 1924 the Chagga planters formed the Kilimanjaro Native Planters Association, which a few years later specified that its members had to sell all coffee through it. That led to friction and, in the face of a new fall in prices, in 1937 to disturbances. It was an example of the sort of problems created when a state-sanctioned cooperative organization runs afoul of the process of individualization.[60]

The depression led the administration to launch a great "grow-more-crops" campaign that was of some success and reduced necessary food imports. The administration also shifted away from laissez-faire in other areas, notably in the campaigns against the tsetse fly, and in favor of "mixed farming," and in measures against land erosion. But it lacked both the means and the time to lead the way in modernizing traditional farming methods in so large and thinly settled an area as Tanganyika. And some measures were paternalistic in character, as for example, the Restriction of Credit to the Native Ordinance which sought to reduce African personal and mortgaged indebtedness to Arabs and Indians.

In 1926 Governor Cameron established a legislative council, in order to provide a forum for Europeans and to give them a greater part in determining the fate of the mandate territory. The official majority constituted five appointed Europeans and two appointed Indians, with native interests allegedly being adequately represented by the government itself. The main thing, however, was that Cameron turned down settler demands for real power, which necessarily would have come at African expense.[61] The council did show some activity, without, however, heightening racial tensions as happened in Kenya. Cameron had blocked the way to a white man's country, though it is not clear what his own vision of the future was. In his memoirs, *My Tanganyika Service and Some Nigeria* of 1939, he wrote of regional councils of chiefs, which could eventually combine as a native council. Its delegates could in turn join at the appropriate time with those of a "Non-Native Council" to assume the functions of a legislative council.[62] After World War II, constitutional reforms took place along these lines, ultimately debouching into the familiar progression toward responsible government and independence.

In retrospect, the situation in Tanganyika revealed all the salient characteristics of British colonial policy in the interwar period: First, the efforts to achieve effective native administration rested on the chiefs, whose positions were constitutionally regularized and whose native treasuries provided the means to do the new jobs given them. Second, an experienced administrative cadre avoided the use of force wherever possible and for that very reason toward the end was confronted with the beginnings of the younger generation's liberation movements. Third, it accepted of an economic structure based on native farming, which did not exclude a narrow but important plantation sector; and, finally, it took a somewhat paternalist approach, which was mitigated by lack of both the will and the means to carry out a policy of planned development. The 6 million Africans remained bound to their old social structures, and the population's manner of living and production remained tied to a subsistence economy that changed very little. Trade remained in the hands of Europeans or Arab and Indian minorities. Cameron did a good deal for education, but the educated African class, mostly teachers and petty officials, remained small. The first African doctor entered state service only in 1940. The administration provided no impetus toward integration of the colony, though it would seem to have been a necessary prerequisite for a colonial policy aimed at future self-government.

Rhodesia (excluding Nyasaland, the present-day Malawi).[63] After the rebellion, the rights of the conqueror to gold and land for settlement could be made good in Matabele- and Mashonaland. Expansion had proceeded from south to north. In it, Rhodes was the dominant personality, though the British high commissioner backed him. Whites from the south, both Britons and Boers, had followed the call from Rhodes and his company and ventured the hazardous trek into Mashonaland. As pioneers they had survived the bloody conflict with the Africans. What wonder then that this enormous land, much of it uninhabited and with a climate so suited to European settlers, seemed naturally to belong to the south and early on was accounted potential white man's country? It did not seem destined to be ruled from London as a Crown Colony but, like the Cape Colony and the Boer republics, was meant to receive self-government after the initial shakedown and consolidation phases. It might then be joined federatively with the older states to form a mighty British Dominion of South Africa. Such indeed was the aim of both Cecil Rhodes and Alfred Milner and also such exponents of British expansion in Africa as Harry Johnston. The latter, founder of the Nyasaland Protectorate, could thus write in 1893, "Africa south of the Zambezi must be settled by the white and whitish races and that Africa which is well within the tropics must be ruled by whites, developed by Indians, and worked by blacks."[64]

Southern Rhodesia, meaning the portions of Matabele and Mashonaland south of the Zambezi, received new constitutions in 1898. Prime responsibility went to the British South Africa Company, which appointed an administrator, while London was represented in the colonial capital of Salisbury only by a resident subordinate to the high commissioner in the Cape Colony. The 13,000-odd whites (including women and children), were immediately provided a legislative council with five appointed and four elected members. There was thus still an official majority, but the electoral principle, which Kenya was conceded only during the war, had already been accepted. It was, in fact, "the first step in the direction of self-government," as Rhodes correctly noted. Tension between the company and London surfaced almost immediately, over land, taxes, and workers.

The country had first to be opened up. It took weeks to travel by ox cart from Capetown through Bechuanaland to Salisbury. For both agriculture and mining, railroads were a necessity. Between 1892 and 1898 the link had been established to Portuguese Beira despite great obstacles. In 1897 a line had been pushed as far as Bulawayo from the Cape. At Bulawayo the line split, one branch proceeding to Salisbury and the other proceeding north via the Victoria Falls—which became an immediate tourist attraction. In 1909 the line connected with the Congo railway. The lines were financed by the British South African Company rather than by London, as had been the case with the West African and Ugandan lines. Although Rhodes had pushed north and Lobengula had been pursued by the hordes of concession hunters in the hope of finding a second Witwatersrand, all were to be disappointed. The gold was there, but it was scattered and difficult to come by. It nonetheless became the mainstay of the economy and provided the vitally needed initial income. Even before 1914, however, coal, asbestos, and chromium mining had begun. In order to be more independent of imports, agriculture was encouraged. In 1908 an agriculture department was established along with a land bank. Settlers were also encouraged to immigrate by grants of financial support. There are, indeed, many points of analogy with what happened in the case of the Kenya railway.

Land seemed to be richly available. "Vast spaces of a smiling country are waiting, waiting for someone to come and plow and develop them. . . . It is ripe for cultivation but there is no population."[65] Promises of land wooed the first settlers and, in turn, the war with Lobengula. The company, which had all unalienated land at its disposal, granted land generously to both companies and settlers. Only in exceptional cases were Africans dispossessed. Native commissioners were instructed to set aside sufficient land for present and future use, not in order to push Africans off into segregated areas, but to assure their possession of land not for sale to whites. At the same time, areas for potential land sales were demarcated. Early British land policy in Central and East Africa in fact embodied conflicting aims characteristic of British rule in these areas. The intent was to protect African rights, while simultaneously holding open possibilities of development for white settlers. The policy was also ambiguous in its assumptions that only a part of the Africans would live on the reservations while others would wish to work as laborers on white farms or would make their livings as tenants. The reservations, moreover, were thought sufficiently large to absorb an increasing population, assuming agricultural methods were improved. In 1920 the following situation existed: 23 percent of the land was in reservations, 32 percent belonged to the settlers, and 45 percent was still undivided, open to both blacks and whites. The African population was estimated at 732,000 in 1915, of whom 405,000 lived on the reservations. The European population was 34,000. The discrepancy becomes even more glaring when one notes that four-fifths of European land, but only one-third of reservation land fell within a twenty-five mile radius of the railway.

More serious in the early years, from both black and white points of view, was the labor question. Not only railway construction and porter transport, but also the mines and the settlers depended on African labor. The situation was now the familiar one. Africans showed no interest in wage labor. They had been warriors, like the Matebele, or peasants like the Mashona. They had hunted, watched over herds, or cleared land. Field work had been left in part to women and slaves. Still having little contact with the money economy, their needs for European goods were slight. Wages and working conditions in the mines and on the farms were indeed hardly such as to tempt Africans to work for Europeans. The latter, however, saw the natives as lazy savages who had to be forced to work. Given English domestic opinion on such matters, however, forced labor was out of the question, and the Indian government had forbidden the importation of coolies. After the recruiting offices of the mines had failed, the only thing left was parental persuasion, as Mason called it, the parents being officials and chiefs. The chiefs were supposed to "enjoin" their people to work for Europeans. As in Kenya and elsewhere the settlers demanded in their newspapers and in the legislative council that the administration exert massive pressure. Although London ostensibly refused to exert it, it followed in practice all the same. How, indeed, was a chief or headman to distinguish between the nuances of invitation and compulsion? Meanings distinct within the hypocrisies of Victorian society became blurred among settlers newly established and fighting for their very existence. And the "other" means, taxes, was also used; as set at one pound per capita, it roughly equalled a month's wages. As early as 1903, the settlers were demanding that it be raised to £2. They got nowhere, because the resident intervened as watchdog.[66] All the same, by 1905, 25,000 Africans were already working outside the reservations, and by 1910, 38,000 Africans were working in the mines alone. As many as 50 percent of the men between fifteen and forty left their villages for months at a time. This was an enormous percentage, when one considers that in the Congo during the 1920s 5 percent was regarded as the maximum that could be taken without severe social consequences and neglect of the cultivation of foodstuffs. The above strictures also quite neglect the question of how hard the work in the mines actually was. Death rates were high—the miner's heirs got £5—the journey to the work places was difficult, and once there, the worker faced corporal punishment and, on the farms, insufficient food, as even a legislative council investigating commission was constrained to note in 1911.[67]

But it was not enough that the mines and the settlers needed and exploited their cheap labor. The structure of rule, which gradually assumed a class character, was bolstered and solidified by legalized discrimination and segregation. In 1903 the death penalty was introduced for rape of white women—by Africans. A white found guilty of trafficking with blacks would be condemned to two years at hard labor. On the other hand, a white man's raping a black woman was not punishable, nor was sexual intimacy or concubinage. South African-Boer influences are apparent here, as well as a deep-seated fear of a new native rebellion, which was expressed in hatred and degradation of the black as a human being. The conquered had to be kept in his place, and had indeed to be prevented from approaching the white in status or from bridging, whether in the short or the long run, the gap between himself and the ruling minority.[68] All-white juries and the forcing of the natives into black ghettos were another reflection of this feeling.[69] The reaction of the Africans, who had to accept all these aspects of the new rule passively, was stated plainly enough by an old Matabele chief: "There will never be peace between the black man and the white man until you give our women the protection you demand for your own."[70]

As early as 1903, the settlers received as many seats in the legislative council as the administration. In 1907 they received a majority. At that point, the British South African Company, which until then had conciliated settlers in order to lure more Europeans to South Africa, no longer had any real way to escape white pressure. It had to reconcile itself to eventual self-government and decided with the election of 1914 that the moment had come when the European population was strong enough and Rhodesia sound enough financially to bear the burdens of administration. In 1915 the Colonial Office consented to the changes, an action consistent with policies accepted in 1898 which foresaw Southern Rhodesia becoming white-man's country and an eventual member of the Union of South Africa. Some years of tedious negotiations were yet required between the three interested groups, the settlers, the government, and the company, before the terms for the financial dissolution of the company could be settled. (The company had never paid a single dividend in the entire previous thirty-three years.) As colonial secretary, Churchill met his friend Jan Christian Smuts of South Africa halfway and offered the settlers a referendum in which they were allowed to choose between joining the Union of South Africa and quasi independence. On 22 October 1922, 8,774 voted for independence and 5,989 against it. The Africans were naturally not consulted. The constitution, which went into effect on 1 October 1923, established Southern Rhodesia as a quasi dominion having a parliament with thirty members and a responsible government. London remained responsible for foreign affairs, and laws "whereby the natives may be subjected to disabilities to which persons of European descent are not also subject" required the colonial secretary's consent. With this reservation, England thought to make good its claim to act as trustee for the Africans and to escape the reproach that it was delivering up the Africans to the white minority. Yet experience in Canada and New Zealand and, most of all, with the adjoining Boer republics had shown all too clearly that such caveats were worthless and that London had to refrain from interfering in domestic matters. It retained responsibility without the power to make it good.

Southern Rhodesia as a dominion has no place in this account, and the way the settlers used their power to consolidate their rule can only be outlined. The electoral law was, as in the Cape Colony, color-blind, thus meeting British demands and also taking account of Rhodes' principle of "equality for every civilized man." Property qualifications sufficed to keep the Africans away from the ballot boxes, and could be raised as necessary; indeed, by 1912 the original qualification had already been doubled.[71] In 1938 there were only thirty-nine African voters out of a total of 24,626. The land question was settled with the Land Apportionment Act of 1931. By 1926 Africans had exploited the provisions to acquire land outside the reservations by taking 45,000 acres, a mere nothing compared to the 31 million acres Europeans had acquired. Yet apparently even this morsel was considered too much by the whites and represented a danger for the future. Of the 96.2 million acres in the entire territory, 49.1 million were reserved for whites, 21 million for reservations, and another 7.5 million for individual African purchasers. This land, however, was far removed from the communications network and was in part waterless, with the result that by 1939 only 839 Africans, among them policemen, teachers, and pastors, had acquired any of it.[72] More important was the prohibition against squatting, or to use the Rhodesian term, "Kaffir farming." That meant that on land reserved for whites no African tenants were permitted, only rural laborers, if possible only "permanent servants in the employment of the estate." In practice this amounted to a new form of slavery, as no less a person than the prime minister personally expressed it.[73]

The Industrial Conciliation Act of 1934 legalized the color bar in industry. It recognized white unions but no combinations among Africans. It sanctioned, in veiled form, job reservation, which protected whites from incipient black competition and bound the latter firmly to the bottom step of the social ladder. It was also explicitly stated that the term "employee" could not be used to refer to blacks. Blacks could also live in cities only if they already had secure employment. The Native Registration Act of 1936 and the Native Passes Act of 1937, both modelled after South African practice, further tightened controls on Africans outside the reservations. A system was thus created which reserved for a tiny minority of the population roughly one-twentieth of the total, approximately half the total land, and either confined Africans to reservations at some remove from the communications network or legally transformed them into a sort of black proletariat. The reservations, indeed, proved impossible to develop very fully. The white minority, moreover, proved determined to defend the position of sovereignty created for it by the constitution of 1923 with every means at hand against both internal liberation movements and onslaughts from outside. The constitution of 1923 led, indeed, though by way of the abortive Central African Federation of 1953, to the unilateral declaration of independence of 1965.

Northern Rhodesia. The present-day Zambia, Northern Rhodesia, chose another way, though one determined more by circumstance than the result of any deliberate plan from London. Johnston and Milner had earlier grouped the area north of the Zambesi with East Africa rather than placing it within the South African sphere of influence, and Milner had characterized it as a potential "black dependency." It was also characteristic that when the two existing regional administrations were unified in 1911, British law became valid and not, as in Southern Rhodesia, the law of the Cape Colony. Policemen were also recruited from among blacks rather than whites. No legislative council was at first established, and a resident commissioner was appointed only in 1911. Economically, the territory seemed to have little to offer after hopes for gold had proved groundless. The British South Africa Company regarded Northern Rhodesia mainly as sort of an annex to the more important Southern Rhodesia. Southern

Rhodesian coal was exported to Katanga, which in turn sent out copper through Beira. Land along the railway was given to settlers. It proved fertile and especially suited to corn, which was, however, only consumed locally. Because of high transportation costs, it never proved as important as tobacco from the south. In this thinly settled area, containing, in 1914 about a million blacks and 1,500 whites, there was little friction. Barotseland had in any case a special position of autonomy.

During and after World War I, the company pushed for annexation to Southern Rhodesia. The settlers of both Northern and Southern Rhodesia opposed this, however, though for different reasons. In 1924 the Colonial Office took over Northern Rhodesia and the settlers, whose numbers had risen to 3,500 by 1931, received a legislative council. Five members were elected, under provisions that excluded Africans from voting. The separation from Southern Rhodesia thus was sharply drawn, insofar as Northern Rhodesia was directly under London's control. The latter fulfilled its duties as trustee with a minimum of energy, preferring to come to terms with the settlers but setting some limits on the settler rule and legal racial segregation. London also held open the question of future status.

For the future, what was to prove decisive was the economic and social copper-mining "revolution." Copper had long been manufactured and traded in Africa. Geologists had at the beginning of the century managed to pinpoint deposits in the future copper belt, which formed a geological unity with the Katanga deposits. In contrast to the latter, however, the ore was poor, and the deeper-lying deposits of higher quality demanded capital investments that before the war seemed unreasonable. With the auto and electrical industries' rapidly rising demand for copper during the 1920s, however, interest began to grow. The South African Ernest Oppenheimer's Anglo-American Corporation and the Rhodesia Selection Trust, which had American capital behind it, began the construction of mines and the railways to support them in 1928. In 1930-1931 production and exporting began, at the very onset of the depression. Copper prices fell from £72 per ton to £27. Not until 1933-1935 did exploitation begin to go smoothly. Production had already reached 210,000 tons by 1937, which amounted to 13 percent of the world's production. Northern Rhodesian exports rose from £215,000 in 1918 to £6,000,000 in 1936, and 95 percent came from mining. The latter furnished 45 percent of the budget in 1937 and 70 percent in 1939, a great amount compared to the modest budget, though not much in relation to corporate profits. The companies' royalties (£300,000 in 1937) did not go to the colony but to the British South African Company as the concession granter. Since the companies' seats of business were in London, they were subject to British taxes, which amounted to 25 percent of the profits. The British took half and left the other half to the colony (or, in 1936-1937, £500,000). In short, a great portion of the companies' payments flowed toward England and did not benefit the colony. In 1943 it was calculated that between 1930 and 1940 England had collected £24 million from the copper belt.[74] Dividends to stockholders are not counted in any of these calculations. As early as 1938 it was being argued that the colony should get a greater share of the profits.[75]

With the expansion of mining, the need for labor increased.[76] Some white technicians and skilled workers came from South Africa, often for only a few years. They had to be lured north—as earlier had been true of the Southern Rhodesian gold mines—with salaries far above English levels. By 1931 there were 4,000 whites in the copper belt alone. In 1924 there were only 1,300 Africans but by 1930, 22,000 were employed, many in construction. The number fell by one-third during the crisis years but was up to 30,000 again by 1937. They came for a few months or a few years, lived in huts and barracks belonging to the mining companies, and were adequately provided with food and medical care. Otherwise, they were totally unprepared for their new lives and lacked the supports and controls of traditional society. Temporary housekeeping with black women was one sign of this. Some brought their wives and children, but neither adequate educational opportunities or housing existed for families. As late as 1941 the minimum wage was sh.22/6 a month underground, and sh.12/6 above, plus food and housing. This wage stood in enormous contrast not only to white wages but also to the needs created by the mines themselves, such as for suitable industrial clothing, only purchasable at excessive prices from company stores. In contrast to Katanga, the mine managements and government seem to have troubled themselves very little about stabilizing the African work force. The reasons may have been a desire to save the cost of the necessary settlements and keep wages low so that, in case of another economic crisis, workers could be sent home again. Or there may have been fears that such a stabilized work force might eventually protest against the humiliating living and working conditions they suffered. The administration seems to have been influenced by Indirect Rule, which had been introduced into rural Northern Rhodesia in the 1930s, native treasuries and all. A stabilized work force was thus seen as one that had been "detribalized," and was thus to be prevented from developing if at all possible. Such views did not take sufficient account of the damage which seasonal work was already doing to the villages, or of the fact that an increasing number of workers were putting down roots in the copper belt and were unwilling to return to the villages. The British officials, moreover, were accustomed to dealing with the chiefs and with other blacks living within the traditional society. They were not equipped to deal with the situation, problems, and needs of Africans living in the mines compounds or in the suburbs. In 1938 Orde Browne's *Report on Labour Conditions in Northern Rhodesia* appeared. But in 1940 there was still no labor officer in the copper belt. Until the coming of the Labour government in 1945 African unionization received no support.

In 1935 six Africans were killed in the first of the mine strikes. An investigation of the strike revealed that contact between management and workers had all but ceased. It also pointed out the amount of open discontent and the beginnings of a new, nontribal consciousness directed particularly against the color bar and racial discrimination.[77] The latter was not so pronounced as in Southern Rhodesia, since the scarcity of whites made necessary the employment of black artisans, truck drivers, secretaries, petty officials, and other such personnel. Construction was almost entirely in African hands. A class of skilled workers was also beginning to form in the mines who could take over from whites even underground, and from management's point of view had the great advantage of being much cheaper. The Africans were aware of this themselves. They suggested to a commission that had come to investigate a strike in 1940 that a team of whites and blacks should be matched against each other and their performances compared.[78] Blacks never rose any higher than foreman. White workers nevertheless felt their existence and status were threatened and formed a union in 1937, characteristically on the initiative of a South African trade-union secretary. Although the percentage of whites below ground declined, the extreme disproportion between white and black salaries, 28 to 1 in 1937, actually climbed to 34 to 1 by 1940.[79] The color bar was never legalized as in Southern Rhodesia, depending instead on a gentlemen's agreement between the union and management.[80]

The land question was less acute in Northern Rhodesia than in Southern. Perhaps it would be more accurate to say it took another form. In 1928-1929, reservations amounting to 34 million acres were created in three regions (not including Barotseland's 37 million), and 8.8 million acres were set aside for Europeans. Ninety-four million acres remained undivided and were declared a native trust in 1947. The white share was thus much smaller than in Southern Rhodesia. The fertile land lay along the railway, however, where some 5,000 white farmers with very large holdings mainly grew corn for the internal market and for export. In the 1920s Africans also began to grow corn along the railway, using modern plows to do so. By 1927 their sales reached 30,000 bags and by 1935, 100,000. Compared with cocoa and cotton farming, this corn growing is not well known, but was nevertheless another example of African readiness to adapt to the market, even without administrative assistance. On the contrary, under the pressure from white settlers, in the course of forming reservations in 1928, Europeans got the choice land along the railways and in 1936 the newly formed Maize Control Board set the African share of the buying pool at 25 percent, in order to protect white farmers from the competition of lower-cost African producers.[81]

Only about 7 percent of the reservations and native trust land were suitable for agriculture. Individual districts were already drastically overpopulated. Given the needs of the cattle herds for pasture and shifting-field farming methods, 6.4 persons per square mile was considered the land's upper limit. In the Fort Jameson District, however, population density was four times that, being 25.1 and in spots as much as 100 per square mile. That resulted in overexploitation, which eroded the soil and threatened to narrow very gravely the bases of black existence.[82] Modern cultivation methods and land improvements such as mixed farming could only help over the long term, especially since in Northern Rhodesia as elsewhere agriculture services could claim few men and little money. The poorer the land and the denser the population, the more men migrated: to the mines, to

European farms, or to the towns of Northern Rhodesia. But they also went to Katanga, the Tanganyikan sisal plantations, Southern Rhodesia, or even the Union of South Africa. Up to half the men were gone for months or years at a time, with the now familiar effects of neglected crops, huts, paths, and wells, and even declines in the birthrate. In 1939 an investigation revealed widespread undernourishment, a shocking result for a colonial administration that prided itself on being a trustee and one, moreover, which had taken on the obligation to maintain and foster traditional African society.[83]

Northern Rhodesia showed, and still shows, very clear hallmarks of a dual economy, with its juxtaposition of a still widespread subsistence agrarian economy and a mining enclave which drew its capital goods and the bulk of the provisions and consumer goods for its European personnel from abroad, in part from Southern Rhodesia and South Africa, and whose profits were either reinvested or repatriated. No subsidiary industries developed. Mining itself was concentrated in a minute portion of a huge territory. It was, in addition, capital rather than labor intensive and remained an island in a colony still living primarily from agriculture. With the exception of the construction of railways and electricity-generating plants, it contributed little to Rhodesian economic development. As it was, the puny budget went mainly to the modern sector to support, for example, the European quarters of the towns. Africans, under the constraints of taxation or population pressure, did find work in the mines and in the towns, but for wages that hardly reached the existence minimum and permitted no savings. The disgraceful disproportion between white and black wages and the de facto color bar which the structure of colonial rule made possible made it difficult for Africans to rise socially. The dual economy was the foundation of this structure and combined with the other factors to assure that Africans drew precious little profit from the mining boom.

It was understandable that the settlers wanted to maintain their dominance and thus protested violently in 1930 against the Passfield Memorandum. The memorandum confirmed the paramountcy of native interests as the Devonshire Declaration had done in 1923 for Kenya. It thus seemed definitely to block the road to Northern Rhodesia's becoming a self-governing white-man's country like Southern Rhodesia.[84] London did water down the concept of paramountcy immediately, the administration going very far in the following years toward meeting settler demands, but the future had been settled. The settlers therefore asked in 1936 that the colony be joined to Southern Rhodesia. A study commission under Lord Bledisloe (1938) could not get around the fact, however, that most Africans viewed the proposed link with the settler government in the south with pronounced distaste. As one African put it: "They do not look upon the black man as a person, they just treat them as dogs. The only time they look after them is when they want money from them. . . . I am a person, not a dog."[85] Confronted with white demands and black anxieties, the commission dodged the issue, but held that joining the two states would at the moment be untimely. After World War II, Northern Rhodesia was incorporated into the Rhodesian

Federation against the will of the blacks. It did retain, however, its status as a Crown Colony, which permitted London to begin the transfer of power to Africans in 1960. The Zambesi in the end had marked the limit of the settler governments from the south, as Lord Milner had foreseen.

PROTEST MOVEMENTS AND PROTO-NATIONALISM

No one denies the existence of West African nationalism in the interwar period, even though its representatives and adherents were recruited from a still limited urban intelligentsia and the African bourgeoisie so closely allied with it. Their parties were hardly more than loose groupings of notables and the colonial territory was only just coming to be seen as the basis for a future nation and state. One can trace the proto-nationalism of these groups back into the nineteenth century, insofar as particular Africans postulated a renewal and modernization of their social and intellectual tradition and were themselves oriented toward future self-government in the sense of a representative system borrowed from England. Analogous East and Central African movements did not develop until after World War II, but then came on very rapidly indeed. The implications of the war itself do not suffice to explain this change. The more recent research, particularly that of Terence O. Ranger and Robert I. Rotberg, has been much concerned with this question. Such research has emphasized the very divergent forms in which the Africans expressed their specific grievances and both their open or covert rejection of colonial rule. We are thus provided with a fascinating picture of the protest movement which led after 1945 into the Congress movement and thence into the struggle for independence. Whether one characterizes such efforts as nationalist or proto-nationalist depends on how such concepts are formulated and appears of secondary importance compared with the essential perception that the African reaction to loss of inner and outward independence, to the colonial economic system, and to the loss of confidence in traditional values could be expressed not only by the new, Western-educated elites, political parties, and publications but also in forms better suited to the traditional society.[86]

West Africans had contacts with Europe long before the colonial expansion. I have already pointed out the specific forms which the coastal and intermediary trade took and that the "educated Africans" class played a considerable role itself as a future ruling class during the phase when colonial rule was being established. It found in both the legislative councils and in the press means to express its grievances and declare its will toward liberation. In East and Central Africa, however, contact with European civilization, a few missions excepted, came largely as a result of the military establishment of colonial administration. Earlier contacts with the outside world had been through Arab rather than European traders, and a Western-educated native class did not exist. Perhaps more important still, European settlers streamed in almost immediately, seized land, and demanded workers. An economic and social system was established that hardly permitted collaboration and straightaway reduced the African in status to the level of a persecuted "minority." They were forced to pay taxes and confronted with the implications of a money economy, but economic development was not based on native farming, the coffee planters of Tanganyika and Ugandan cotton growers being exceptions. It was based, rather, on white settlers dependent on wage labor. The mass of Africans remained bound to the subsistence economy of the reservations or was forced into a proletarian existence on European farms, plantations, and mines.

Educational opportunities also lagged far behind those of West Africa, particularly since the settlers were able to use their influence to assure that only minimal amounts were spent on native education. In 1942 there were only 3,000 students in their fifth year of school in Northern Rhodesia and only thirty-five students in secondary schools.[87] There were hardly any university graduates, jobs in industry and the administration being either reserved for whites or monopolized by Indians. In 1940 not a single African sat on any legislative council. One hunts in vain for instruments of African public opinion comparable to the West African press. The administration, at least indirectly dependent on the settlers, kept a much closer eye on political activity and acted much more swiftly to repress it than the British administration in Nigeria or the Gold Coast. Although the colonial system of Central and East Africa burdened the mass of the population much more severely than that of West Africa, there were no legal channels for expressing the resulting frustration and discontent, to say nothing of aspirations for the future. All this explains both the significance and the forms of East and Central African protest movements.

The numerous separatist churches represented an important manifestation of protest. They had splintered off from mission and other regular churches in order to escape white control and to be able to appoint African pastors from their own ranks. The ordination of black clergy had followed the equivocal course characteristic of the churches' other efforts to adapt to African societies and milieus.[88] Separation amounted to a claim for independence and responsibility as well as an Africanization of the service, with African songs and dances, changes in baptismal ceremonies, and acceptance of polygamy. Northern Nyasaland with its intensive missionary activity based in Livingstonia became a center for this separatist activity, with manifold connections reaching the Ethiopian Church of South Africa and American black churches. The discrepancy between the Christian message and the behavior of the whites, combined with the missionaries' paternalism, led the blacks to criticize foreign rule and to reject the discrimination they suffered.

> There is too much failure among all Europeans in Nyasaland. . . . The three combined bodies, Missionaries, Government and Companies, or gainers of money, do form the same rule to look upon the native with mockery eyes [sic]. . . . If we had power enough to communicate ourselves to Europe we would advise them not to call themselves "Christendom" but "Europeandom."[89]

A revivalist movement within the Anglican church spread from Ruanda to Uganda and Kenya and led in Nyanza to the unification of several groups into the African Orthodox Church.[90]

More worthy of note, perhaps, was that singular figure, John Chilembwe. After visiting the Blantyre mission in Nyasaland, he spent the years 1897 to 1900 in America, being ordained a pastor in the National Baptist Convention. Upon his return, he founded his own Providence Industrial Mission with some American black support. He also established schools and encouraged his followers to take up better farming methods, to keep their villages clean, and to wear European clothing, among other things. He profoundly resented both the way blacks were being held back and white arrogance. When the outbreak of World War I dashed his hopes for reform and white withdrawal, the recruitment of porters led him in January 1915 to call for rebellion. Some especially hated planters were cut down, though their wives and children were not harmed. The mystifying personality of Chilembwe himself and his rebellion, the only one between the post-primary resistance and the Mau Mau movement, has been much studied. It is still an open question, however, whether he hoped to unleash a general rebellion to drive out the whites, or whether, knowing in advance he would fail, he courted a martyr's death for himself and his followers to draw the attention of England and whites in general to the lot of Africans.[91]

The transition from separatist church to sect was not precisely marked, chiliasm often being closely tied up with antiwhite protest. Some sects were offshoots of existing European or American sects, loosely organized, emotional, and often employing "magic." They were led by men calling themselves prophets and often apocalyptically proclaiming the imminent coming of the millenium. It was to be a new Jerusalem without whites, which would bring prosperity and joy to the blacks. The most important sect was undoubtedly the Watchtower movement, or Jehovah's Witnesses,[92] which also got started in Nyasaland. Its leader was Elliot Kamwana, who had been schooled in the Livingstonia mission. After his return from South Africa, he gathered more than 10,000 followers in only a few months. He protested school fees and taxes, and announced that British rule would end in 1914. "We shall build our own ships, make our own powder, and make or import our own guns." The British deported him in 1909 but his movement did not fade away. Indeed, after the war it spread to other territories. In Northern Rhodesia, 138 of its adherents were arrested in 1919, but the sect continued to surface sporadically on into the 1950s. One of its Ndola District members prophesied in 1929: "The white people has now no power and they will come to be the last people; and the black people will be first; these white people who are here now came to our country and did not deliver the things they were told to deliver to us."[93] Some indeed, thought the Witnesses were behind the copper belt strike of 1935.

In the southern part of Nyanza province, the Mumbo cult flourished during and after World War I. It had some points of contact with Christianity, but was fanatically antimissionary and anti-European: "The Christian religion is rotten, all Europeans are your enemies," it stated, while promising a coming golden age.[94] Kenya also had its own Watu-wa Mungu, or People of God, sect. Its indigent preachers wore lion and leopard skins and carried a shield and spear as symbols of their struggle against evil spirits—and also whites and missions. They prayed facing Mount Kenya. In 1934 and 1947 they had bloody clashes with the police, and some have connected them with the Mau Mau and Jomo Kenyatta.[95]

So long as no new leaders and political parties arose to give expression to anticolonial protest, the sects and cults met deeply felt needs of both the semieducated and the masses in their time of social and intellectual crisis. They expressed their secret hopes of an imminent end to white rule; better still, they mostly posited a future rule of blacks over whites. But they also opposed the rule of their own chiefs because they were dependent on the colonial power and no longer embodied the unity of the tribe. They tended to establish ties beyond their own areas and encouraged feelings of a shared super-tribality, though one having little in common with nationalism or the sense of belonging to a common polity. Ranger has pointed out the importance of religious and chiliastic factors in the post-primary resistance movements such as the Matabele-Mashona rebellion of 1896 and the Maji-Maji rebellion of 1905. He has also noted the links to the phase of mass nationalism, which was in no small measure based on foundations prepared by the awakening and protest movements. The struggle against the colonial power and the winning of independence was usually pictured in such movements as the coming earthly Elysium.[96]

In the interwar period, an association movement developed in all the territories under discussion and often had personal links to the separatist churches. Many of these associations were based on tribes—Bataka Association, the Luo Union, and the North Nyanza Native Association, for example—and were locally based, whether in the towns or in the mine compounds.[97] Others were professional associations such as the African Association of petty officials in Tanganyika or the African Civil Servants Association in Northern Rhodesia. Their founders and leaders tended to be pastors, teachers, and lower officials with a modest amount of mission schooling. They were concerned above all with economic and social questions, such as the struggle against further land sequestrations and tax hikes, or for better schooling and health care. "They learned to deal with the white man on his own terms; they agitated, drove shady bargains, talked, and wrote. In the tribal and atribal associations these younger men amassed valuable experience in administration, negotiation, and in the manipulation and propagation of protest."[98] The administration's stance varied from providing some support, to accepting passively, or to viewing association activities with suspicion. The associations stood openly or covertly outside the native administrations, or assumed immediate political relevance and were then suspected of subversion. The best known of the associations organized on a tribal basis was the Kikuyu Association, founded in 1920 by Harry Thuku, a mission student and later a telegrapher, in Nairobi. After his arrest in 1922, it became the Kikuyu Central Association, and from 1928 on, its secretary was Jomo Kenyatta.[99] The land question was its main concern. It first sought definitive determination of reservation boundaries, and then the creation of private property rights within the reservations and the prohibition of coffee-growing outside them. When the missions intensified their campaigns against female circumcision in 1929, without allowing for its central importance in the complex Kikuyu society, Kenyatta and the Central Association took up the struggle for this rite of initiation as the very symbol of Kikuyu identity. Local sections were founded, meetings were organized, and petitions presented to the administration.[100]

In Nyanza a simultaneous rise in taxes, cut in salaries, and introduction of the pass system led to the foundation of the Young Kavirondo Association in 1921. It brought up specific grievances and occasioned the governor to justify his policy.[101] In Southern Rhodesia, the Matabele movement, led by one of Lobengula's sons, gained some importance after the war. It sought a restoration of the Matabele kingdom as a protectorate and can be seen as a manifestation of Matabele nationalism. It appealed to veterans, teachers, and pastors and had connections with the South African Congress. In 1923 the Rhodesian Bantu Voters Association was founded. It was a super-tribal association of voters oriented toward modern political decision-making bodies. Its leader was a woman, Martha Ngano, and along with the franchise question, it also took up the land question and acted as spokesman for African opinion before the Carter Commission of 1925, though quite without effect.[102]

The separatist churches, cults, and associations all demanded expansion of education and its separation from the missions.[103] In the early colonial phase, interest in European education was by no means universal. Buganda had opened itself to missions in 1877, "to be taught to read and to write." The Barotse, the Tonga in Nyasaland, and the Luo in the later Kenya acted similarly. Other tribes stood altogether aloof or at least hesitated, the Masai, for example, showing little interest, then or later, in European education. In the interwar period, schools were sought most energetically, manifestly in the consciousness that education was the most important requisite for winning a new social status within the system of colonial rule. Even before the war, however, criticism of the mission school system had begun, whether because of the fees, or because missionary influences were felt to endanger the forms and values of tribal life. That was in part why secondary schools and instruction in English were sought. Instruction in native languages could be interpreted as a deliberate attempt on the part of the missions and the administration to cut the blacks off from the modern world and to affix them forever in their inferior status. Ranger has called our attention to the efforts of the independent schools, and not only those of the Ganda, but those founded and supported by the separatist churches and the numerous welfare associations. The Kikuyu were particularly active in such efforts, the Independent School Association founding an increasing number of schools and in 1939 even their own teachers' seminary.[104] Given the lack of trained personnel, money, and supervision, however, the standard of these schools was necessarily low.

As important as the associations were, their elite character should not be overlooked. Founded and supported in Central and East Africa by a narrow class with rudimentary educations, they were concentrated in a few of the urban centers. They had scant means of establishing contact with the rural population. In the settler-dominated territories, a real leadership class could form only very slowly. Still, the way led directly from them to the congress movements during and after World War II—the Kenya African Union, the Uganda National Congress, the Northern Rhodesia Congress, and the Nyasaland African Congress—at least to the extent that the congresses served as umbrella organizations for the associations and thus formed bridges to political parties with a mass basis. It was these parties, under the charismatic leadership of men like Kenyatta, Julius Nyerere, Dr. Hastings Banda, and Kenneth Kuanda, that took up the struggle for liberation and forced England to grant its Central and East African colonies independence after 1960.

NOTES

1. In addition to the works cited p. 335 above, see the following general accounts: *History of East Africa*; Kenneth Ingham, *A History of East Africa* (London: Longmans, 1962); Alfred John Wills, *An Introduction to the History of Central Africa* (London: Oxford University Press, 1964); Alexander John Hanna, *The Story of the Rhodesias and Nyasaland* (London: Faber and Faber, 1960); Philip Mason, *The Birth of a Dilemma: The Conquest and Settlement of Rhodesia* (London, New York: Oxford University Press, 1958, 1968); Eric Stokes and Richard Brown (eds.), *The Zambesian Past: Studies in Central African History* (Manchester: Manchester University Press, 1966); *Aspects of Central African History*, ed. Terence O. Ranger (London: Heinemann, 1968); John G. Pike, *Malawi: A Political and Economic History* (London: Pall Mall Press, 1968); Lewis H. Gann, *A History of Northern Rhodesia, Early Days to 1953* (London: Chatto & Windus, 1964); E. A. Brett, *Colonialism and Underdevelopment in East Africa: The Politics of Economic Change, 1919-1939* (London: Heinemann, 1973).

2. See in particular the contributions in the *History of East Africa*, I.

3. John S. Galbraith, *Mackinnon and East Africa, 1878-1895: A Study in the "New Imperialism"* (Cambridge: Cambridge University Press, 1972).

4. The literature on Anglo-German rivalries is extensive; but see Müller, *Deutschland*; Robinson and Gallagher, *Africa and the Victorians*; John Gray, "Anglo-German Relations in Uganda, 1890-1892," *JAH*, 1 (April 1960); G. N. Sanderson, "The Anglo-German Agreement of 1890 and the Upper Nile," *English Historical Review*, 78 (January 1963).

5. Roger Portal, who had been sent to report on the situation in Uganda and who had declared a protectorate, in a letter to his wife, 3 February 1893, as quoted in *History of East Africa*, I, 417. The author of the essay from which this quotation is taken alleged that the limited financial strength of the company was the reason for these plunderings, the stations having been ordered to support themselves.

6. Excellent is Terence O. Ranger, "The Nineteenth Century in Southern Rhodesia," in *Aspects of Central African History*, and Richard Brown, "Aspects of the Scramble for Matabeleland," in Stokes and Brown, *Zambesian Past*.

7. Ranger, "Nineteenth Century," 134.

8. A missionary who had welcomed the fall of Lobengula noted with disillusionment in 1896: "A proud and hitherto unconquered Matabele cannot be turned in a month, or a year, into a useful servant by kicks, sjambok and blows. You cannot civilize him by quarreling with him a few days before his pay is due, by stoning or unjustly beating him, by cursing him for not understanding an order given in English"; quoted in ibid., 151.

9. Terence O. Ranger, "African Reactions to the Imposition of Colonial Rule in East and Central Africa," in Gann and Duignan, *Colonialism*, I, 307. On the rebellion, see also Terence O. Ranger, *Revolt in Southern Rhodesia, 1896-97: A Study in African Resistance* (Evanston: Northwestern University Press, 1967); idem, "The Role of the Ndebele and Shona Religious Authorities in the Rebellions of 1896 and 1897," in Stokes and Brown, *Zambesian Past*.

10. In addition to the *History of East Africa*, see Gordon Hudson Mungeam, *British Rule in Kenya, 1895-1912: The Establishment of Administration in the East African Protectorate* (Oxford; Clarendon Press, 1966).

11. "To get some sort of assembly which will attract the younger and more vigorous brains among the natives and lead them to take an active part in their own administration, and thus to ensure that they are for the Government and not against it"; quoted by J. M. Lonsdale, "Some Origins of Nationalism in East Africa," *JAH*, 9 (January 1968), 128.

12. "Here we have a territory (now that the Uganda railway is built) admirably suited for a white man's country, and I can say this with no thought of injustice to any native race, for the country in question is either utterly uninhabited for miles and miles, or at most its inhabitants are wandering hunters who have no settled home or whose fixed habitation is in the lands outside the healthy area"; from a report of 1901, as quoted in Mungeam, *British Rule*, 102.

13. "No doubt on platforms and in reports we declare we have no intention of depriving natives of their lands but this has never prevented us from taking whatever land we want for Government purposes or from settling Europeans on land not actually occupied by natives. . . . There can be no doubt that the Masai and many other tribes must go under. It is a prospect that I view with equanimity and a clear conscience. I wish to protect individual Masais . . . but I have no desire to protect Masaidom. It is a beastly, bloody system, founded on raiding and immorality, disastrous both to the Masai and their neighbours. The sooner it disappears and is unknown, except in books of anthropology, the better"; Eliot to Landsdowne, 9 April 1901, as quoted in ibid., 113.

14. Elspeth Joscelin Grant Huxley, *White Man's Country: Lord Delamere and the Making of Kenya* (2 vols., London: Macmillan, 1935).

15. Gordon H. Mungeam, "Masai and Kikuyu Responses to the Establishment of British Administration in the East African Protectorate," *JAH*, 11 (January 1970), 127-43.

16. Louis Seymour Bazett Leakey, having grown up among the Kikuyu as a missionary's son, discussed this in detail as early as 1937: *White African* (London: Hodder and Stoughton, 1937), and reprinted several times since.

17. I follow here principally the *History of East Africa*, I, ch. 5.

18. On this, see Bethwell A. Ogot, "British Administration in the Central Nyanza District of Kenya, 1900-1960," *JAH*, 4 (April 1963).

19. "One might almost say that there is no atrocity in the Congo—except mutilation—which cannot be matched in our protectorate"; Memorandum of 1908, quoted in Mungeam, *British Rule*, 195.

20. Ibid., 200f.

21. "There can be no reason for excluding this large and meritorious class"; quoted in *History of East Africa*, I, 280.

22. J. S. Mangat, *A History of Asians in East Africa, 1880 to 1945* (Oxford: Clarendon Press, 1969); Robert G. Gregory, *India and East Africa: A History of Race Relations within the British Empire, 1890-1939* (Oxford: Clarendon Press, 1971).

23. Donald Savage and J. Forbes Munro, "Carrier Corps Recruitment in the British East African Protectorate, 1914-1918," *JAH*, 7 (April 1966); Ogot, "British Administration," 259.

24. Writing to the chief secretary, a provincial commissioner alluded to the comments in the bishops' memorandum on forced labor and noted: "in our efforts to force labour out of the Reserve by administrative pressure unbacked by force of Law we are compelled to follow the line of least resistance which results in the same male adults going out time after time owing to their being too poor or too friendless to escape the Headman's levy. The rich native or the Headman's relative or favourite gets off free each time"; "Huxley Papers," MSS. Afr. 782, Box

1/3, Rhodes House, Oxford. On these discussions see also Brett, *Colonialism and Underdevelopment*, 188.

25. Mungeam provides documentation for the rejection of settler demands before 1914. Churchill, for example, commented in 1907: "We must not let these first few ruffians steal our beautiful and promising protectorate away from us after all we have spent on it—under some shabby pretext of being a 'responsibly governed colony.' The H. of C. will never allow us to abdicate our duties towards the natives as peaceful industrious law-abiding folk as can be found anywhere"; *British Rule*, 186.

26. "Primarily Kenya is an African territory, and HM's Government think it necessary definitely to record their considered opinion that the interests of the African natives must be paramount, and that if, and when, those interests and the interests of the immigrant races should conflict the former should prevail. . . . HMG cannot but regard the grant of responsible Self-Government as out of the question within any period of time which need now be taken into consideration. . ."; quoted from "Memorandum Relating to Indians in Kenya," in *Sessional Papers*, 1923, Cmd. 1922, XVII, 141, p. 10f. The question is also discussed in Albertini, *Decolonization*, 146ff.; Robert G. Gregory, *Sidney Webb and East Africa: Labour's Experiment with the Doctrine of Native Paramountcy* (Berkeley: University of California Press, 1962); *History of East Africa*, I, ch. 6.

27. Grigg commented at a governor's conference in 1930: "The security of the Empire in East Africa was not inseparable from the success of white settlement. White settlement had gone so far that a really serious setback which endangered confidence in its future would endanger at the same time our whole civilization in East Africa"; quoted in Brett, "Colonialism and Underdevelopment," 94.

28. Geoffrey Bussell Masefield, sometime agricultural official in Uganda and later lecturer in colonial land economics at Oxford, noted critically that "with many individual exceptions the standard of farmers in Kenya has always been disappointingly low." He also noted that while on the great farms there was always money for comfortable houses, too little was set aside for drought and the inroads of locusts; *A Short History of Agriculture in the British Colonies* (Oxford: Clarendon Press, 1950), 101.

29. Brett, "Colonialism and Underdevelopment," 172.

30. Hugh Fearn, *An African Economy: A Study of the Economic Development of the Nyanza Province of Kenya, 1903-1953* (London, New York: Oxford University Press, 1961), 133f.

31. Until 1923 reservations were visited only occasionally. In 1924 there were eight agronomists available and in 1937, seventeen: "It is to be recognized that while a few years ago natives were indifferent to the services for development given by this Department, to-day the urge for further services is coming from the natives themselves. . . . Government should realize that the development of the Native Reserves which it has so greatly desired is likely to lead to economic and sociological deterioration in the absence of a trained supervisory staff to induce sound methods"; quoted from "Memorandum on Native Agricultural Development in the Native Reserves, July 1937," in Kenya, Department of Agriculture Library (typescript). "Up to recently the works of the agricultural and veterinary departments was mainly concentrated on the European areas"; Pim, *Financial and Economic History*, 120.

32. Cattle hides, for example, fell from sh. 36 in 1928 to sh.4 in 1932. "The fall in prices and the increased burden of real taxation had destroyed the natives' purchasing power. . ."; "Report by the Financial Commissioner, Lord Moyne, on certain questions in Kenya," in *Sessional Papers*, 1931-32, Cmd. 4093, VI, 545, p. 10f. Hereafter cited as "Moyne Report."

33. The Moyne commission recommended the introduction of an "income tax on non-natives"; ibid., 59.

34. Brett, "Colonialism and Underdevelopment," 202; "Moyne Report," 26, "From my experience of ten years. . . the very large bulk of the expenditure of the taxation has been poured into that 6,000,000 acres of European land to the detriment of the remainder"; the chief native commissioner before the Joint Select Committee of Commons in 1930, as quoted in Brett, "Colonialism and Underdevelopment," 197.

35. See the discussion in ibid., 208f.

36. Colin Maher, of the department of agriculture, "African Labour on the Farm in Kenya Colony," *East African Agricultural Journal* (April 1942), 228f.

37. See in particular *History of East Africa*, I. In addition, see, among others, A. S. Baxendole and Douglas Johnson, "Uganda and Great Britain," *Historical Journal*, 8 (1961); C. C. Wrigley, "The Christian Revolution in Buganda," CSSH, 2 (October 1959-60), 33-48.

38. A. D. Roberts, "The Sub-Imperialism of the Buganda," *JAH*, 3 (July 1962).

39. In addition to Ehrlich's essay in the *History of East Africa*, 1, and Brett, "Colonialism and Underdevelopment," see C. C. Wrigley, "Buganda: An Outline of Economic History," *EcHR*, 10 (April 1957).

40. Table 14.1 describes agricultural production in Uganda, 1923-1935.

Table 14.1
Agricultural Production in Uganda, 1923-1935

Years	No. of plows	Lbs. of cotton/acre
1923/24	282	307
1928/29	3,400	218
1934/35	11,615	119

SOURCE: John Douglas Tothill (ed.), *Agriculture in Uganda* (London: Oxford University Press, H. Milford, 1940), 56.

41. Vincent Liversage, *Land Tenure in the Colonies* (Cambridge: Cambridge University Press, 1945), 56.

42. Uganda, Committee of Enquiry into the Grievances of the Mukama and the People of Toro, *Report* (Entebbe: Government Printer, 1926), 6.

43. In 1937, 91,000 unskilled laborers a month on the average and in the course of the entire year some 100,000 left Burundi; Uganda, Protectorate, Committee of Enquiry into the Labour Situation in Uganda, *Report* (Entebbe: Government Printer, 1938), 17.

44. An order was issued "to refrain from actively stimulating the production of cotton or other economic crops in outlying districts on which it is dependent for a supply of labour for the carrying out of essential services in the central or producing districts," quoted in *History of East Africa*, II, 428.

45. For the details, and also on what follows, see *History of East Africa*, II, 405; Brett, "Colonialism and Underdevelopment," 237f.

46. Cyril Ehrlich, "Some Social and Economic Implications of Paternalism in Uganda," *JAH*, 4 (April 1963).

47. See Ehrlich's essay in *History of East Africa*, I, 469.

48. Quoted in *History of East Africa*, I, 521.

49. Great Britain, Colonial Office, Col. 142, Commission on Higher Education in East Africa, *Report* (London: HMSO, 1937).

50. G. S. K. Ibingira, *The Forging of an African Nation: The Political and Constitutional Evolution of Uganda from Colonial Rule to Independence, 1894-1962* (New York: Viking Press, 1973), 68.

51. Brett, "Colonialism and Underdevelopment," 261.

52. See in particular the essays in the *History of East Africa*, I, and Brett, "Colonialism and Underdevelopment." Also excellent is Austen, *Northwest Tanzania*.

53. Tanganyika, Colonial Government, *Native Administration* (Dar es Salaam: Government Printer, 1927), Cameron's "Foreword," 7. See also Margery Perham, "The System of Native Administration in Tanganyika," *Africa*, 4 (July 1931).

54. Cameron in the legislative council, as quoted in Perham, "Native Administration," 20.

55. Austen, *Northwest Tanzania*, 192.

56. Quoted in James Clagett Taylor, *The Political Development of Tanganyika* (Stanford: Stanford University Press, 1963), 60.

57. Quoted in Brett, "Colonialism and Underdevelopment," 229.

58. Tanganyika, Colonial Government, *A Report by Mr. E. C. Baker on the Social and Economic Conditions in the Tanga Province* (Dar es Salaam: Government Printer, 1933), 56ff.

59. Orde Browne commented bitingly in a letter of 10 October 1937 about recruiting policies since his departure: "Again they have over a hundred recruiters. I got the number gradually down to something under twenty, but aimed at eight or ten. . . . Now of course all the scum and riffraff that I weeded out are back again. . . . Native hospitals are understaffed, and are overfull with cases due chiefly to neglect of labour conditions. . . ." He also noted that polio was spreading because recruiting had been allowed in infected areas; "Orde Brown Papers," MSS. Afr. 118, Box 2/5, Rhodes House, Oxford.

60. Tanganyika, Legislative Council, *Sessional Papers*, S.P. no. 1, 1937, "A Memorandum on the Recent Disturbance in the Moshi District of the Northern Province, Tanganyika Territory."

61. Cameron told the settlers: "You. . . press insistently for the development of the political side so far as it affects not the natives but the Europeans. You want that side strengthened as soon as possible so that you may go from strength to strength and become so securely entrenched that there will be no place left for the native in the political structure unless you please to give it to him. You desire to create here an ultimate complete dominance for the white man based on what you call 'responsible government' "; quoted in Brett, "Colonialism and Underdevelopment," 49.

62. Ibid., 115-16.

63. See the literature cited n. 1 above, and in addition, Richard Gray, *The Two Nations: Aspects of the Development of Race Relations in the Rhodesias and Nyasaland* (Westport: Greenwood Press, 1974, 1960).

64. Mason, *Dilemma*, 214.

65. Lord Winchester in London in 1907, quoted in Wills, *Introduction*, 197.

66. Hanna, *The Rhodesias*, 180.

67. Rhodesia, Southern, Native Affairs Committee of Enquiry, 1910-1911, *Report* (Salisbury: Government Printer, 1911), 28ff. Hereafter cited as Native Affairs Committee, *Report*, 1911.

68. See Mason, *Dilemma*, 238f. The Native Affairs Committee recommended prohibiting whites to marry blacks or keep them as concubines, since the Africans considered their inability to do likewise as discrimination; *Report*, 1911, 7.

69. In 1908 a jury acquitted four whites accused of beating to death two blacks suspected of theft; Hanna, *The Rhodesias*, 177.

70. Quoted in Mason, *Dilemma*, 242.

71. Characteristically, the Native Affairs Committee recommended abolition of the native franchise; *Report*, 1911, 25.

72. *Aspects of Central African History*, 277.

73. Quoted in Hanna, *The Rhodesias*, 186.

74. *Aspects of Central African History*, 165.

75. "If Northern Rhodesia gets an unduly small share of the proceeds of its only important asset, which is moreover a wasting asset, the reason does not lie so much in an inadequate total taxation as in the relatively small share of the profits of the industry which accrues to the revenue of the country"; Great Britain, Colonial Office, Col. no. 145, Commission Appointed to Enquire into the Financial and Economic Position of Northern Rhodesia, *Report* (London: HMSO, 1938), 136; the so-called Pim *Report* and hereafter cited as such.

76. International Missionary Council, Department of Social and Economic Research and Counsel, *Modern Industry and the African: An Enquiry into the Effect of the Copper Mines of Central Africa upon Native Society and the Work of the Christian Missions*, by J. Merle Davis (2d ed., London: Cass 1967, 1932); Great Britain, Colonial Office, Col. no. 150, *Labour Conditions in Northern Rhodesia, Report by Major G. St. J. Orde Brown* (London: HMSO,

1938); Robert E. Baldwin, *Economic Development and Export Growth: A Study of Northern Rhodesia, 1920-1960* (Los Angeles: University of California Press, 1966); Ian Henderson, "The Limits of Colonial Power: Race and Labour Problems in Colonial Zambia, 1900-1953," *Journal of Imperial and Commonwealth History*, 2 (January 1974); Elena L. Berger, *Labour, Race, and Colonial Rule: The Copperbelt from 1924 to Independence* (Oxford: Clarendon Press, 1974).

77. Robert I. Rotberg, *The Rise of Nationalism in Central Africa: The Making of Malawi and Zambia, 1873-1964* (Cambridge, Mass.: Harvard University Press, 1971), 159ff., provides telling evidence.

78. Rhodesia, Northern, Commission Appointed to Enquire into the Disturbances in the Copperbelt, *Report*, July 1940 (Lusaka: Government Printer, 1941).

79. Baldwin, *Economic Development*, 89.

80. The slogan "equal pay to equal work" and the closed shop were proved methods for favoring white workers; Berger, *Labour*, 50. The administration opposed such favoritism but sought to avoid provoking trouble with the whites.

81. Baldwin, *Economic Development*, 147f.

82. Gray, *Two Nations*, 86.

83. Audrey Isabel Richards, *Land, Labour and Diet in Northern Rhodesia: An Economic Study of the Bemba Tribe* (London, New York: Oxford University Press, 1939).

84. "British Colonists do not regard native policy and administration in East Africa as 'one of the most important matters, if not the most important, dealt with in the Report.' They hold that the British Empire is primarily concerned with the furtherance of the interests of British subjects of British race and only thereafter with other British subjects, protected races. . . . Faced with the declared determination of the Imperial Government to prefer the interests of alien and barbarous races to those of their own, they may seek and find sympathy and aid from neighbouring colonies enjoying freer institutions and more equitable opportunities"; from a telegram from the elected members of the legislative council to the colonial secretary, 27 June 1930, "Correspondence with Regard to Native Policy in Northern Rhodesia," in *Sessional Papers*, 1930-32, Cmd. 3731, XXIII, 119, p. 3f.

85. Testimony before the Bledisloe Commission in 1939, quoted in Gray, *Two Nations*, 192.

86. Terence O. Ranger, "Connections between 'Primary Resistance' Movements and Modern Mass Nationalism in East and Central Africa," *JAH*, 9 (July, October 1968); idem, "African Reactions," and his essays in *Aspects of Central African History*, 166f., 190ff.; Robert I. Rotberg, "The Rise of African Nationalism: The Case of East and Central Africa," *World Politics*, 15 (October 1962); idem, *Rise of Nationalism*; Lonsdale, "Some Origins."

87. *Aspects of Central African History*, 166. The first secondary school was opened only in 1940, Kenneth Kuanda being among the first thirty students; Kenneth David Kuanda, *Zambia Shall Be Free: An Autobiography* (London: Heinemann, 1962), 13. In 1937 a mere £28,305 was available for native education; Gann, *Northern Rhodesia*, 313.

88. *Aspects of Central African History*, 194. The first Livingstonia pastor was ordained in 1914 but had completed his studies as early as 1902.

89. From a pamphlet of 1911, quoted in ibid., 145.

90. *History of East Africa*, II, 380.

91. Among others, Robert I. Rotberg, "Psychological Stress and the Question of Identity: Chilembwe's Revolt Reconsidered," in Rotberg and Mazrui, *Protest*.

92. Rotberg, *Rise of Nationalism*, 136f.

93. Ibid., 140.

94. Audrey Wipper, "Gusii," in Rotberg and Mazrui, *Protest*.

95. *History of East Africa*, II, 373; W. E. Mühlmann, "Die Mau Mau Bewegung in Kenya," *Politische Vierteljahreschrift*, 2 (March 1961).

96. Ranger, "Connections."

97. Rotberg, "Rise of African Nationalism," 80.

98. The Broken Hill Welfare Association of Northern Rhodesia stated its aims as follows in 1930: "Cooperation and brotherly feeling, to interpret to the Government native opinion on matters of importance, to encourage the spread of civilization, and to protect any further native interests in general"; quoted in ibid., 78.

99. *History of East Africa*, II, 356ff; Carl Gustav Rosberg and John Cato Nottingham, *The Myth of the "Mau Mau": Nationalism in Kenya* (New York: Praeger, 1966), chs. 3-5.

100. A petition to the Colonial Secretary, Lord Cunliffe-Lister, on the occasion of his 1934 visit to Kenya contained the following points:

1. An expression of regret that the Secretary had refused to receive a delegation
2. A representation in the Legislative Council
3. Election of a paramount chief by a council of approximately a hundred members
4. Secondary education for Africans, scholarships for university study in England, and instruction in English
5. Complaints that additional land had been sequestered because of the new gold rush
6. Abolition of the hut tax, which particularly burdened widows
7. Raising chiefs' salaries
8. Permission to grow coffee, as could be done in Uganda and Tanganyika
9. Opposition to settler self-government

"McGregor Ross Papers," MSS. Afr. S1178(4), Rhodes House, Oxford.

101. Ogot, "British Administration," 223f.

102. *Aspects of Central African History*, 223f.

103. Terence O. Ranger, "African Attempts to Control Education in East and Central Africa, 1909-1939," *Past and Present*, 32 (December 1965).

104. Its role was stated to be: "To further the interests of the Kikuyus and its members and safeguard the homogeneity of such interests in matters relating to their spiritual, economic, social and educational upliftment"; quoted in Rosberg and Nottingham, *Myth*, 127.

15

A SUMMING UP: SOME REFLECTIONS ON COLONIALISM

This book has considered the fate of a great variety of territories under colonial rule with the intent of establishing the facts about what actually happened. It is no simple task to point out common features and general aspects of development without immediately rising to a level of generalization so abstract that it blurs beyond all usefulness distinctions between geographical situations, levels of civilization of the colonized, duration of colonial rule, the socioeconomic situation, the character of the administrative structure, and, finally, the aims of the colonial powers. Still, some useful things can be said.

Our starting point must be the colonial situation, which existed only after establishment of effective foreign rule. I have thus largely ignored the structures of informal empire, either of the older kind that preceeded effective colonial rule, or the more recent sorts, some of which still exist today. It is hence appropriate to consider the colonial administration yet again. However it may have been legitimized in ideological terms, it was by definition foreign rule. Its primary task was to make this rule effective, to assure its long duration, to end or neutralize opposition, and to make possible European activity in the colony. This activity primarily meant exploiting the country economically and was intended mainly for the advantage of the metropolis. A minority of Europeans—officers, officials, businessmen, or settlers—thus ruled a population of a different race or civilization which, however willing it may have been to collaborate and to concede the technical and cultural superiority of the ruling power, in the last analysis bore this rule grudgingly and hoped eventually to shake it off. In contrast to earlier conquerors, who very often mixed with the conquered peoples and thus came to appear as one's "own" rulers, under European colonial rule a clear line separated rulers and ruled. Although Europe might believe its rule secure for the foreseeable future, those actually responsible for running things understood very well that they were strangers in a strange land and would remain so. This awareness helped create a racist syndrome of rule in which consciousness of one's superiority was closely bound up with anxiety and insecurity in the face of a foreign world. Social distance was a natural concomitant of these feelings, as was a close sense of corporate identity, which in turn fostered authoritarian or paternalistic attitudes. Colonial rule was more than mere repression, however. Repressive measures, were, in fact, rather seldom used once rule was established. But both rulers and ruled knew how things were. The former could not give up its monopoly of force and dared not allow the *fonction d'authorité* to be seized from its hands. The ruled, for their part, had to make their peace with the colonial situation as best they could, seeing themselves, in extremis, delivered over to a process of alienation and repudiation of their innermost selves, which ended only when the Transfer of Power was a settled matter.

I sketched the creation of the formal administrative structures only briefly. The final power of decision, of course, always remained in the metropolis, with the colonial ministries and parliaments. The latter always reserved certain questions for itself, but never concerned itself very intensively with colonial questions. It is also noteworthy that the specialists in colonial affairs within the political parties were invariably outsiders. That does not mean there was no colonial lobby. On the contrary. Precisely because an atmosphere of indifference surrounded parliamentary discussions of colonial policy, except when public disturbances ignited a momentary flicker of interest, pressure groups were able to lobby effectively both in parliament and in the rather more important colonial ministries. In the latter, all the threads came together, decisions were made, directives issued, and the course set. Still, the governors on the spot were left a rather large field for independent decision. France tended to centralize, England to decentralize, but the differences ought not be exaggerated. The telegraph had conquered distance, which in the early days had meant that questions and answers spent months coming and going. Still, only the governor could see things firsthand, and only in the interwar period did a few colonial ministers make orientation visits to the colonies. It is the historian's task to elucidate the relationships between governors and ministries in individual cases. Because of an especially favorable constellation of sources, we know, for example a fair amount about relations between the viceroy of India and the colonial secretary. These relations varied considerably according to the personalities involved. It can in general be stated the governors not only made known the specific problems of their colonies, but also, in some senses identifying with their territories, articulated their own aims regarding metropolitan interests, or in some cases, special interests, in particular in the economic arena.

Within the colonies there was a clear division between central and local administration. The governor, his top officials, and their special departments sat in some key city. In numbers this apparat was not large, but it implied a new order to the colonized. It was not only the tangible embodiment of foreign rule, but even where a precolonial central administration had existed, it differed sharply from it. It was rational, its work was divided by function, and it impersonally set its business down on paper, whereas the ruling structures of traditional society depended on a welter of personal relationships, themselves determined by caste and class. The primary task of administration was summed up by the phrase, "maintenance of law and order," and in practice that meant that rule had to be made good throughout an entire territory. In the beginning, centers of resistance had to be eliminated, and the local ruling class had to make formal obeisance to the new rulers. A communications network consisting of post and telegraph facilities had to be established, along with a police force and central courts. An expansion of the taxation system was hardly of less importance, because the colonies needed their own incomes and had to free themselves from metropolitan subsidies as soon as possible. Economic matters were distinctly secondary and were important in proportion to the need to create the infrastructure for economic development.

In the localities, rule had a much more personal touch. The foreign administration might indeed penetrate the territory much more effectively than its predecessors, but control was still relatively loose. Scattered over huge areas, residents, district officers, and commandants worked in the field with tiny staffs. Largely left to their own devices, they were truly jacks-of-all-trades, being responsible for police, tax collection, provision of porters and other workers, building roads, fighting pestilence, and everything else. They were on the road much of the time and were in personal contact with tribal and village leaders, whether commanding or mediating, authoritarian or paternal.

At the very outset, the question arose everywhere of what stance the colonial power ought to take in regard to the natives, who lived within their own systems of authority and society, and, in particular, what ought one do with the traditional bearers of this authority, the princes, feudal rulers, chiefs, and other notables? Should the social forms of the particular society be left as much as possible intact, or should they somehow or other be built into the structure of rule? Should the old rulers be incorporated as well into such structures, or should they be cast out, to be replaced either by European officials or by new local cadres? One is accustomed to speaking of the differences between direct and indirect rule, and to account France as following the former and England the latter. I too have used these concepts, but I have also attempted to make clear that in practice the boundaries between the two were fluid. They are most important as indications of divergent aims. At various times and places all colonial powers employed both systems. Kings and feudal rulers who resisted were expelled, while others, especially those in the back country, retained their offices. England ruled British India directly, while sufficing itself with residents in the Princely States after the Mutiny. It did the same, *mutatis mutandis*, in Malaya. In Vietnam one can characterize French administration as direct, whereas in Cambodia and Laos it was indirect. In North Africa France operated behind the fiction of protectorates. In black Africa England practiced Indirect Rule, raising it to the level of dogma during the interwar period. France, in contrast, worried less about traditional authorities, but in the thinly settled Sahel found itself unable to do without them. Dutch administration in Java was direct despite employment of the old aristocracy, but was indirect in the Outer Islands. I do not intend to discuss here once again the basic difficulties of colonial rule at the lowest clan and village levels. No rule, no matter how direct, could dispense with the native chiefs or village elders, yet even under indirect rule such authorities became in practice executive agents for the administration. One way or the other, their social positions changed decisively, because their authority no longer rested on traditional canons of legitimacy but on their appointment or recognition by the colonial power. Whereas their positions were strengthened to the extent that older control mechanisms such as de-stoolment and councils of elders fell into disuse, their prestige suffered from their having to accept such unwelcome tasks as tax collection, road building, and vaccination. At the same time, an individualization process began which, though it differed greatly at different times and places, loosened the traditional obligations of obedience and loyalty. Toward the end of our period, as the new communications network, the market economy, and the new market relationships assumed a stronger hold, this individualization process led to open or covert conflicts between the traditional rulers and the Western-educated younger generation. As the colonial power found itself increasingly confronted with the disintegration of traditional society, which it had itself begun, it tried to slow it down in the interests of maintaining or stabilizing its rule. At the same time, however, it was demanding ever more from the traditional authorities in the interests of economic development. As these two policies were incompatible, the position of such authorities became increasingly difficult. In the outlying areas, which had only nominally been brought under administrative control and were on the very fringes of the market economy, the traditional rulers might indeed continue in their roles as leaders of the people. They lost their functions of representation and leadership, however, wherever colonial penetration was at all pervasive or wherever the social disintegration caused by the latter was pronounced. In such places they often stayed on as a privileged and largely parasitic upper class, whether with or without administrative functions, bound to the colonial power to a degree which increased as a new elite arose to challenge them. Or they became, especially at the lowest level, quasi bureaucrats without any real roots in their own societies, and also without the training that would have been necessary for them to make a good job of their local administrative duties. In the interwar period, Indirect Rule and its variants appeared to be a liberal and progressive policy because it did not tear down the old social structures, but by giving them new tasks sought to prepare them from within for the coming new day. Today, however, we are more apt to emphasize the retardant side of Indirect Rule and to regard it as an instrument which preserved "feudal" structures and, lacking its own policy of modernization, limited itself to "holding the ring," as Margery Perham, Lugard's biographer, put it.

Eisenstadt had pointed out the discrepancies between administrative modernization at the central as opposed to the local level. The most important alterations occurred within the central institutions. They were the result of introduction of unified administrative systems, general taxation, the establishment of a modern court system, and, later, the development of representative bodies. The same was true for the economic sector and modern education. Nevertheless, the colonial powers saw their tasks as bringing about these changes only within the framework of existing institutions:

At the local level, the colonial powers attempted to contain most changes within the confines of traditional groups or even to limit, as much as possible, the extent of any change. Although much change did materialize within local communities, as the literature on detribalization of the family indicates, most of the administrative efforts of the rulers were aimed at strengthening existing organizations and relations, at maintaining peace and order, and at reorganizing local systems of taxation. Thus, while the colonial regime attempted to introduce innovations, it tried to accomplish this within a relatively unchanging social setting, with the implicit goal of confining its efforts to technical matters. Consequently, a basic contradiction tended to develop: On the one hand, attempts were made to establish broad, modern, administrative, political, and economic settings; on the other hand, these efforts were to be limited and based on relatively unchanged subgroups and on the maintenance of traditional attitudes and loyalties.[1]

In fact, central administrations tended to become somewhat muscle-bound, which hampered the transmission of impulses toward modernization to the local levels and increased the tendency toward bureaucratization of the capitals. After its Western-educated elites took over the administration, this tendency became stronger, and in the face of new development tasks the central administration ballooned out. The rural areas, on the other hand, remained underdeveloped administratively. Only the beginnings existed of a modern local administration capable of meeting the demands of a modernization imposed from above, which required enlisting the active participation of the population. "Since the colonial powers and native rulers both emphasized having politically loyal subjects, they tended to encourage relatively passive forms of obedience and political identification. If it was in any way possible to do so, they sought to exploit existing bonds of loyalty or to carry them over into the new system without modifying the social and cultural fundaments very basically."[2] What Tignor says about British policy in Egypt and Lord Cromer's attitude applies nearly everywhere. Given their lack of technical, military, and financial means, the British could not bring about a social revolution by instituting the necessary measures of fundamental reform. The colonial masters might think of themselves as reformers,

but none were willing to push the process of modernization to the point where societies would lose their internal cohesiveness. Therefore they adopted the expedient of attempting to raise standards of living without changing class structures. They attempted to make their authority felt without undermining the position of the traditional ruling classes. They governed behind these ruling classes.[3]

In reality, despite their will toward modernization and all the compulsion they applied to bring it off, the colonial powers were at bottom conservative socially and thus took care to support existing social structures. That ought not to be taken to mean that without colonial rule social revolution would have occurred. Feudal orders proved extraordinarily stable in precisely those countries that never became colonies, such as Ethiopia, Persia, and Afghanistan.

The administrative dualism so characteristic of colonialism should also be noted. The central administrative cadres and the technical branches were primarily European and to an extent floated above the traditional society. The natives shared administrative duties only in very subaltern positions, acting more as order followers than as active participants in the apparatus of rule. This apparatus did indeed fulfill a modernizing function, but also because of its discrimination underlined the separation between the modern and traditional sectors of society. When eleventh-hour localization efforts came to be made during the decolonization phase and the tiny, Western-educated, largely urban, elite took over the modern apparatus, the discrepencies between the central and local administrations lingered on to hamper the efforts of the new local power elite to integrate the masses of their peoples into the process of modernization. The new elites took over the jobs in the colonial administration, assuming the privileges that went with them, most notably salaries that stood far above the income levels of the masses of the people. Such conduct threatened to widen the abyss between center and periphery so much that bridging it became ever more difficult if not downright impossible.

Yet another aspect of colonial administration must be noted here. It is usual to refer to the colonies, which in some cases were altogether artificial creations, as if they were territorial unities. Such designations are particularly inapt when applied to black Africa, though much less so to North Africa and Asia. But even in the latter areas—such as British India, Vietnam, Burma, Ceylon, Egypt, and Morocco— where one can hardly speak of artificial creations, the colonial powers created large-scale administrative frameworks. These replaced precolonial structures that no longer existed or that merely represented claims which could not be made good. Since the administration was in European hands, however, inner unity remained precarious, though not particularly because the colonial powers followed a policy of divide-and-rule, which I believe anticolonial nationalists overemphasize. It was rather because, while foreign administrations created states that the representatives of today's independent peoples have no wish to give up, they turned rather late to the tasks of integration and nation-building in the sense of political participation. The greater the degree to which rule was indirect and depended on existing authorities and loyalties, the greater the discrepancy between the efficient modern central administrations and the socially conservative local administration. This discrepancy necessarily meant that old and new internal rivalries and tensions, which in the colonial situation remained latent or could be held in check, burst forth after independence and threatened to shatter the bounds of the polities which the colonial powers had created.

Although noneconomic interests, motives, and pressures may have played a role in establishing a given colonial rule, the latter was the prerequisite for full-fledged economic exploitation. But economic exploitation was also urgent, because of the need to make the colony financially independent as soon as possible. That this exploitation occurred primarily in the interest of the colonial power hardly needs to be reemphasized. Colonies were there to deliver tropical foodstuffs and raw materials, to absorb immigrants, and to provide markets for home industry. It ought to be noted, if only parenthetically, that the desire to be independent of imports from one or another country played a very considerable role. Under mercantilism, one sought to hang on to cash. England encouraged cotton growing in India in the mid-nineteenth century, in order to escape complete dependence on the United States. After World Wars I and II, the colonies were looked to to help make up dollar shortages.

Trade between Europe and the tropics was of long standing. Over the centuries it had been conducted between independent and equal partners. European traders on the coast bought tropical products in an *économie de traite* against payment in money or in exchange for textiles, weapons, or liquor; and to that degree the later colonies became part of the worldwide trade system. With the establishment of rule came various forms of direct or indirect compulsion or, in other words, open exploitation. Forced cultivation and monopolistic price-setting were the forms it took in the Spice Islands and Java, as in late eighteenth-century Bengal and the later Congo. These well-known examples of plunder economics, that are repeatedly trotted out as examples, were by no means characteristic of colonial economies—nor do even the apologists for colonialism seriously deny them.

Attempts to legitimize colonial rule in economic terms usually began with development, meaning the colonial power's opening up of the country economically, which secured for both the colonial powers and the colonial peoples short-and long-term advantages such as direct profits, state revenues, higher living standards, and new forms of production. It is argued further that the European powers went over to free trade in the nineteenth century and gave up monopolistic trade practices. Through the erection of an efficient administration, creation of trade routes into the interior, the building of railways, harbors, and roads, investment in plantations and mines, the colonies were integrated into the world economic system. Although Europe dominated this system, it provided the impulse for development and modernization of the colonies in the form of import needs, capital exports, and technical skill according to the classical-liberal model of comparative advantage in international trade.[4] For the very reason that an industrializing Europe had a rapidly increasing need for tropical foods and raw materials, the overseas countries were vouchsafed opportunities to exploit their natural resources, or so continues the argument, and develop themselves economically. As a result, rising foreign trade, particularly exports, came to be seen as an indicator of growing colonial prosperity and as proof of economic development.

In recent years, a lively discussion has gone on about a number of problems important for the development of economic theory. Why, for example, have the former colonies, some of which had very high exports, remained underdeveloped? Why, in the colonies in particular, did industries never become established, and why did the expansion in exports, often very striking, not prove the prerequisite for self-sustaining growth? The adherents of the dependency theories and structural imperialism have actually stood the older thesis on its head, claiming that integration of the peripheral countries in the world economy induced, not development, but underdevelopment. The phrase in which the foregoing is summed up is "growth without development," meaning that growth took place as measured by production figures and the extent of foreign trade, but not in terms of the ability to overcome poverty and technological backwardness through use of local resources. The possibility for development, indeed, was blocked by economic orientation toward the metropolis.

I noted in the Preface that this explanation seemed to me too limited to be acceptable, even if it is qualified by distinguishing between "un" and "under" development (see p. xxi above). It is my firm conviction that although the world economy based on free trade did primarily suit British interests—and by extension those of all industrial states—because it opened things up for a superior British industry, it also profited Britain's trading partners. It did so because it in fact allowed them to develop their own productive forces and to accumulate capital which could be employed in the process of modernizing their own countries. That was true for the countries of Europe, which began their own industrializations rather early and perhaps still more for the new countries such as the United States, Australia, and Canada. The latter countries owed their rapid economic rise to export booms in a single or very few agricultural products. Such exports would not have been possible had not demand been increasing very rapidly in Europe or if freight costs had not been declining rapidly and investment capital coming in. Japan could also be used as an example, because its industrialization was due in no small measure to the rapidly expanding production and export of raw silk.[5] Even in colonies with a large expansion in exports, per capita income increased, and most of all where native farming shifted over to cash crops. Increases in food production roughly kept pace with the increase in population, while exports permitted the purchase of imported consumer goods. They also provided through taxes, customs, and export duties the budgetary resources needed to create a modern infrastructure and modern health and educational services. The extraordinarily small increase in the social product in India is thus, seen in these lights, not the consequence of growing dependence on foreign trade, but a reflection of how little exports contributed to national income and how slowly exports were increasing before 1914.[6] Even making every possible allowance for unequal distribution of income and the flow of profits back to the metropolis, it seems mistaken to me to interpret such economic development and its socio-cultural implications narrowly as development or underdevelopment, and to hold integration into the world economy responsible for specialization in a particular export product needed in the metropolis. Without the latter, the colonies would have remained largely undeveloped.

Export-induced growth was the prerequisite for "genuine" development and modernization, even though we may today emphasize in retrospect the one-sidedness and distortions of the colonial economy. To put it another way, expanding foreign trade was a necessary but not a sufficient condition for diversified autonomous economic development. But none of the foregoing considerations really answers the question of why the colonial context was unique.

The effects of the terms of trade are also in dispute. Around 1950 Raul Prebisch and H. W. Singer in particular stated that over the long term the relationship between raw material and industrial prices worsened. In industrial countries production declined during depressions but monopoly practices kept prices high. In boom periods, however, because of trade union pressures, among other reasons, wages and hence prices rose, whereas the prices of products from the colonies and developing countries were exposed to the cold blasts of competition.[7] The raw materials producers thus received ever fewer factory goods for a given amount of exports. That was a form of indirect exploitation. It decisively delayed their development and continues to hamper it still. Despite all kinds of studies intended either to verify or refute the Prebisch Thesis, what actually happened is still not entirely clear. There are disagreements about the statistics, and the differences according to country and product are great.[8] Taken in the large, this apparently is what happened. Between 1880 and 1913 the terms of trade remained largely constant despite temporary fluctuations. During the war and immediately after, terms sharply worsened for the Third World countries, to improve again toward the end of the 1920s. The terms worsened disastrously during the depression, only to improve again after 1933, and to rise sharply during World War II. This trend lasted until 1952 and reversed thereafter. One can thus hardly speak of a secular trend in the worsening of the terms of trade in Prebisch's sense, though the results are unambiguous enough for the period 1913-1940.[9] Income terms, or price times production (or export value) rose for many products, however.[10] The world trade in raw materials and tropical foodstuffs increased, though less rapidly than before World War I. Colonial incomes from exports may therefore, except during the depression, not have decreased and may in many cases have actually increased. But there is also little question that there was a pronounced decline in opportunities to earn the necessary capital through food and the industrial raw-material export taxes for either increased consumption or for expansion of the infrastructure or industrial investment.[11] Export-oriented growth certainly heightened the dualistic character of the economy, since efforts at diversification and industrialization came only with the Depression (see p. 505 below). The level of mass consumption remained low and hardly permitted the formation of savings. Whether that justifies concluding that the colonial standard of living generally stagnated during the interwar period or even fell seems questionable, even if one takes no account of the possibility that the urban middle class may have bettered its situation at the expense of the peasant masses. One must distinguish between regions where expansion of cultivation was possible, such as, say, West Africa, or where the expansion of the plantations and mines occurred and those areas, such as Tonkin, India, lower Burma, or Egypt, where no additional reserves of land were available and population was beginning to increase sharply. The latter situation was the one in which Nurkse's notorious "vicious circle of poverty" ruled, being characterized by low-productivity-induced poverty preventing savings and capital formation, which in turn prevented raising productivity, and so on.

The foregoing represent boundaries limiting or making more difficult the economic development of the colonies and developing countries during the interwar period. An additional question to be answered is whether the specific relationship of dependency implied in the concept of colonialism constituted a factor hindering development or leading to its one-sidedness. Was it true, indeed, that export-induced growth "did not lead to the transition to a more complex economy based on a wide variety of activities including factory industry"?[12] The colonials were, willy-nilly, forced to confront the modern world, particularly in the form of the money economy, and the specific policies of the colonial powers also destroyed, or at least severely disturbed, the socioeconomic equilibrium of the subsistence economy. The question is, to what extent did these factors at the same time inaugurate a comprehensive economic modernization which had latent within it the possibility of self-sustained growth? To put the matter more plainly still, why were no non-European societies except Japan able to follow the Western road to industrialization? Was colonial dependency at fault?

This is the place to discuss the variously stated complex of ideas bound up in the "drain of wealth" thesis. Developed in India, a summary statement of the thesis is that a great part of the colonial surplus was transferred to Europe and was thereby drawn out of the colonial economy. It is not relevant in discussing this matter to drag in yet again the early plunder economies, the monopolistic gains of the mercantile system, or the open transfer of colonial profits to the metropolitan budgets, as occurred under Bosch's culture system in Java and later in Leopold II's Congo Free State. In the latter cases a drain of wealth unmistakably occurred. Otherwise, despite the assumptions often made, it must be shown that no transfer from budget to budget in the sense of tribute payments occurred. The drain thesis refers to the moneys that flowed out of the country in the form of interest and repayment of loans, as officials' salaries not spent in the colonies, or as pensions and repatriated profits of private corporations. I have given some figures for India and Java, and have also discussed some of the arguments which nationalist historians have presented. I do not think interest and amortization charges can simply be declared a drain. In the cases of the United States and the white dominions, whose economic and industrial development, particularly railway building, was financed with British loans, hardly anyone speaks of a drain in favor of London. On the contrary, development would have been significantly slower without foreign capital. Even in Japan, in 1913, 60 percent of the state debt was in foreign hands, and debt service swallowed up one-quarter of export income.[13] Interest on state guaranteed colonial loans was not higher but rather much lower than loans to independent countries. One ought thus to speak of a drain only when one can prove that instead of domestic capital foreign capital was brought in or that the latter was not employed productively, or both. Such may occasionally have happened, but can scarcely be asserted to have been general. I think it also inconsistent to point to India's unfavorable balance of payments with England and then to contrast it unfavorably with the favorable dominion balance with England; what this proved, in fact, was that England invested too little in India, not too much.[14] As for salaries and pensions, a drain really occurred only to the extent that it can be proved that natives could have run the administrative and technical services as well as the Europeans did. High salaries for foreign experts were the consequence, not the cause, of underdevelopment. But one can probably count as a drain the moneys expended on military forces garrisoned in a given colony. In the matter of profits, the character of a given investment and the amount of risk assumed must be considered in judging whether profits were excessive or not. Some firms certainly earned such profits, but countless other firms went bankrupt. In short, a drain of wealth doubtless occurred, but as a tool for analyzing the colonial economy and the consequences of dependency it seems to me not to offer very much.

The concept "dual economy" seems more useful.[15] Impressed by the fact that the lot of the Javan masses had not improved or had even gotten worse despite intensive Dutch economic penetration and activity, about 1910 the Dutch economist J. H. Boeke worked out the fundamental difference between European and Asian approaches to economic activity. Whereas the European was at bottom an economic man, Boeke argued, with a limitless need to consume and a corresponding readiness to work, the Asian had another scale of values and did not behave according to capitalist economic norms. If, for example, the price for coconuts went up, he picked fewer and if his wages on the plantation were higher than the norm, he worked less. The Oriental certainly was able to appreciate speculative profits but was disinclined to organize and invest for the long term. Thus, Boeke thought Western economic theories and policies were not well employed in a tropical setting. The capitalist system that had been introduced had indeed led to the disintegration of traditional society but had not itself been assimilated. Instead, a virtually unbridgeable gap had developed between two basically divergent systems which coexisted within the colony. On one side was the subsistence economy, relatively static and uninnovative, not market oriented, in which the mass of the population continued to live. On the other side was a modern, capital-intensive, market-oriented, dynamic sector that was mainly in foreign hands and in practice contributed little to development. Boeke was himself pessimistic about the possibilities of a development policy based on Western models and favored a patient encouragement of agriculture within a village framework.[16]

Boeke's dual-economy concept encountered lively criticism and was generally rejected in the 1950s. It was certainly possible to prove that both African and Asian peasants were ready to accept innovation and adapt to new products, along with reacting "rationally" to price fluctuations and gladly developing into consumers. It was accordingly argued that the thesis of a fundamental irreconcilability between Western and non-Western behavior was mistaken.[17] Still, when one looks at the regional differences within the Western-capitalist industrial countries themselves, and particularly at the tensions between north and south in Italy, the criticisms of Boeke seem overly harsh. The Mezzogiorno problem has, in fact, many analogies with the problems of the colonies and developing countries. In the course of national unification, the feudal, agrarian, and conservative society of the south was delivered over to the domination of the bourgeois capitalism of the industrially more developed north. The result was that the development gap increased rather than decreased, and to put it bluntly, the south was exploited and depressed to the level of a labor reservoir for the north. The important point is that the two socioeconomic sectors exist alongside one another and despite contact remain un- or insufficiently integrated.

More recently there has been a tendency to reject the concept as such because the very presence of two largely unconnected sectors is said to conceal the symbiotic links between the subsistence and capitalist economies, at least insofar as the latter was not only superimposed on the former but transformed it structurally so much that one can hardly speak any longer of an undisturbed traditional society.[18] This objection is certainly justified, but I still believe that the heuristic value of the concept is considerable. The concept "dual economy" is not in and of itself tied to colonialism, though it took on a characteristic stamp within the colonial situation. The modern sector, as was not true in, say, Japan, had no organic ties to the traditional sector, but was bestowed from without by the colonial power and remained at the disposal of the latter.

I have already mentioned some aspects of this dualism. In my account, which was ordered by regions to start with, the administration can be characterized as dualistic. The modern administration not only followed European bureaucratic models but was manned by Europeans. They thus appeared as ruling orders superimposed on traditional society. Because the natives played a small part in them, they became separated to some degree from the societies they ruled and perpetuated the disequilibrium between the central and local administrations that Eisenstadt has analyzed. As I have also shown, the law and court systems were also examples of this dualism. Western law, particularly land law, property ownership law, and legal procedures were not so much taken over as introduced, with consequences not altogether anticipated for traditional society, among them dissolution of the communal order and loss of a feeling of legal security.

But the economic area is more important. Still open for discussion, certainly, is the question of whether a dualism can be said to exist in the matter of native farming. The peasants who had shifted to production of export crops became a part of the market sector, dependent as producers on the world market and directly in contact with European traders. They also became consumers of imported goods.[19] The principal examples are the cotton growers in India, Egypt, and Uganda, the rice peasants of Vietnam and Burma, and the cocoa, peanut, and coffee planters of Africa. I would argue that such producers lifted themselves out of the subsistence economy to the degree that they produced for the market, but that their farming methods and hence the agrarian structure as such did not change very much. Cultivation was by traditional family methods, though seasonal workers were also used somewhat, using hack-hoes, oxen, and simple plows, without manuring. Expansion occurred because labor and areas increased, but productivity remained low. One can in fact apply the term "involution" which Geertz developed for Java to other areas as well, in situations where labor inputs increased with rising population, but holdings themselves became more fragmented and the land was overcropped because of lack of manuring.

I do not myself think the often mentioned neglect of foodstuffs in favor of cash crops, or the so-called negative effects of monoculture, was as important as it is now usually considered to be. The total area under cultivation increased during the colonial era, in some areas by very considerable amounts. Only in a very few restricted areas did cash-crop production completely displace growing foodstuffs. Specialization in one product was generally dictated by climate and soil and can be defended in economic terms, because the yield-per-acre for cash crops was worth more than that of food, and populations in the cash-crop regions increased. Such crops were, in other words, relatively labor-intensive.[20] The area devoted to cash crops was in any case a smaller portion of the cultivated area taken as a whole than is generally believed, excepting Egypt and the sugar-growing islands. During the interwar period, when population began to increase rapidly—though at nothing like today's rates—foodstuffs production barely met demand and had to be supplemented with imports. I attribute this, however, less to a one-sided drive for export production than to the extremely low land-per-capita ratio and low productivity. In the latter respect, indeed, peasants producing for the market remained all too firmly ensconced in the traditional sector.

The question arises of why production rose in colonial agriculture but not productivity, particularly in food production. The contrast with Japan is especially striking. Despite fragmented holdings, debt, and miserable existences as tenants, Japanese peasants were able to double their productivity between 1880 and World War I.[21] Even if one sets a very high estimate on the specific sociocultural predisposition of the Japanese for modernization, one is still thrown back on explaining things in terms of the colonial context. Specific features of importance were the questionable assumption of individualist European concepts of property ownership, the basing of one's governance on a traditional ruling class that had been forced to become rentiers, high taxation combined with trivial expenditures on native agriculture, the exception here being the irrigation expenditures which permitted increases in the cultivated area, and a one-sided encouragement of cash crops. But a definite answer to the productivity question is hard to give. It is all too easy to overemphasize the positive or negative effects of colonial dependence, particularly when one fails to compare colonial areas with those African and Asian states that remained independent or when one attributes the difficulties the developing countries are presently having in raising output to the alleged exploitative or other colonial features that inhibited development.

I also consider the native cash-crop farming dualistic in that purchasing, warehousing, and transport were and still are largely in the hands of European trade firms. The same was true of shipping lines and merchant banks. Asian and African wholesalers, active in their own countries on into the nineteenth century were, as has been mentioned, largely displaced under colonialism. Concentration occurred first in the European economic sectors. This led to oligopolistic control of trade by a few large firms, which also engaged in importing.[22] It is true that a new class of middlemen, native transporters, and the like, developed, but they remained dependent on the modern sector and were hardly in a position to develop as a native bourgeoisie, the less so because the colonial powers either permitted or actually encouraged the immigration of foreign minorities: Chinese, Indians, and Levantines. The latter filled the interstices between the two sectors, monopolizing the retail trades, the artisan trades and retail credit, and generally contributing to the creation and maintenance of a plural society. In such a society, the role of the locals was to serve as producers and laborers, whose income and ability to consume remained low. Trade and banking, indeed the entire service sector, remained in the hands of Europeans and foreign minorities, who kept to themselves in their own ghettos, favoring their own and repatriating most of their earnings.

The existence of a dual economy is unmistakable in the presence of plantations and mines. Capital, skills, and management personnel came from outside, their products were exported, and profits reinvested or repatriated. Natives were often recruited by force, badly paid, and served only in unskilled capacities. No real learning took place. One speaks of enclaves, which were fundamentally nothing more than the advanced outposts of the metropolitan economy and had but tenuous connections with the rest of the colonial economy.[23] Their forward-and-backward linkages and multiplier effects were minimal, since machinery and equipment was imported and the raw products were seldom manufactured in the colonies themselves. Even the salaries of European personnel, many times those of the workers, only benefited local trades and consumer-goods industries in a very marginal way, because exacting European tastes could only be satisfied through imports. Mines and plantations were lightly taxed, customs alone providing significant income. The enclaves, however, were represented by very formidable pressure groups, which saw to it that duties remained low. The procurement of foreign exchange, which today appears one of the primary tasks of plantations and extractive industries in developing countries, was significant only to a degree, because colonial currencies were tied to those of the mother countries and the dollars or pounds earned by exporting could be, and were, used to support metropolitan balances of payments. Although in colonial times the rising production and export figures attributable to the mines and plantations served as proof of colonial economic development, today what one must emphasize is their limited impact on development. They were indeed the modern sector, but their connections with the remainder of the traditional economy and society were so tenuous that they enhanced the possibilities for development very little.

In the case of the settlement colonies—Algeria, Rhodesia, Kenya, and even Tunisia and Morocco—it is even possible to speak of a specific kind of dualism, because a modern sector with white leadership arose within a traditional economy and society. When the settlers streamed in, the natives willy-nilly lost their habitation and pasture rights, either as a result of war, or confiscation, or land legislation that simplified the dissolution of collective ownership and permitted a sort of expropriation barely consonent with the proprieties. At the same time, taxation served as the needed instrument to force the natives to work on white farms. Although the economic successes of these enterprises were real enough—exports rose and modern centers developed—nothing could conceal the exploitative and racist character of this system, rigged as it was entirely in favor of the whites. Native agriculture received little support, investment mainly profited the modern economic sector, and political rule, which largely escaped metropolitan control, remained firmly in settler hands.

When the formula "growth without development" is used to characterize the dualistic structure of the colonial economy, those doing so use it with the failure to industrialize in mind. Industrialization is taken as proof of modernization and hence of "real" economic development. Whether this is a reasonable way of looking at things certainly needs discussion today. The central question in any case remains how much the lack of or one-sided industrialization was a consequence of colonial dependence. An answer to this question was suggested in the chapter on India. It calls for fuller discussion here, however, though space only permits discussion of certain aspects of it.

I consider that, while one's starting point must be the worldwide process of industrialization, the colonies are to be regarded as latecomers or late starters, with all that that implies, both in terms of handicaps and advantages. These are matters, indeed, which economic historians have only recently taken under scrutiny. Comparisons with England are clearly inadmissible. Instead, comparisons must be with countries which had to carry off their industrial revolutions in the face of existing English advantages and competition, though also with the assistance of English entrepreneurs and technicians.[24] Such was the case with western and central Europe, to which Scandanavia, Russia, and Italy were to be added between 1890 and 1914. With the exception of Bohemia, the rest of eastern and southern Europe remained, however, outside the privileged area and today is still not wholly an integral part of it. The new countries, the United States, and the British dominions, can be regarded as special cases, though Canada, Australia, and most of all, New Zealand, based their rise on single-product exports. The industrialization of Japan falls in the same period, and constitutes its sole non-Western example. Although latecomers such as Germany, the United States, Japan, and the Soviet Union at times had higher rates of growth than England, it seems justified to conclude that, to use Rostow's terms, the start and take-off to self-sustaining growth became more difficult as the nineteenth and twentieth centuries progressed. This seems true even leaving out of account specific sorts of sociocultural predispositions toward industrialization, or even climatic or geographic conditions: the industrial countries all lie in the temperate zone.

The colonial powers opened the areas they ruled to their own imports. In so doing, they exposed the traditional artisan trades, some of which employed highly qualified and highly specialized workers, to the competition of cheaper, machine-made industrial products. Most notorious is the case of India (see p. 48 above), which as late as the eighteenth century exported fine woven stuffs to England and Europe. In the early nineteenth century, however, it was swamped with Lancashire cotton goods, first on the coast and later, with the construction of railways, in the interior. Similar cases exist in all colonies. In this area, indeed, the consequences of dependence on the metropolis are the most readily discernable, even though specialists may quarrel over whether one ought to speak of an actual destruction and displacement of native handicrafts. At a minimum, there was a stagnation in such trades that carried the most serious social implications in its train. Internal social specialization, as reflected in artisan castes, the relationship between town and country, and the role of crafts in agriculturally inert societies, was disrupted and a reruralization was encouraged. That intensified the process of involution within the villages and encouraged dualistic structuralization, in which trade in imported goods came into foreign hands.

But in Europe, too, industrialization had led to crises within the traditional trades and cottage industries, and many had disappeared. The difference was that—leaving possible state intervention out of the picture—European industrialization not only absorbed the labor that it had displaced but sucked up the surplus agrarian population. The latter, in contravention to Malthusian theories, gradually achieved a higher income, which in turn fostered further industrialization. It was with these things in mind that Marx worked out his interpretation of India's situation. England, had, indeed, destroyed the Indian textile industry and created a railway net to gain access to raw materials, but this opening of the Indian market and the introduction of machinery in transport would inevitably lead to Indian industrialization (see p. 48). But Marx was wrong. Cotton and jute industries did arise in India, to be sure, but it is impossible to speak of a genuine industrialization in the British period. The case was even worse for Indonesia, Vietnam, Egypt, or North Africa, if one leaves out of account grain, oil, and rice mills, and some breweries, sugar refineries, and cement works. But why was this so?

Was it a lack of raw materials, particularly the coal and iron on which the first industrial revolution was based? Japan shows that their presence was not a sine qua non, but it should still be noted that the larger and more densely populated colonies and developing counties are poorly provided with them. Coal was mined in India, Tonkin, and Algeria, but iron ore was uncommon, and more important, coal and iron were usually not present together as was true in the industrial heartland of the West. India was an exception, and a steel industry in fact developed there before 1914. Start-up conditions were, in short, unfavorable.

Bairoch has emphasized the rapid drop in transportation costs after the mid-nineteenth century, meaning that when latecomers on the periphery started to industrialize distance provided them no protection.[26] Although, for example, railway construction created a decisive impulse for industrialization in Europe and the United States, it did far less for India, because rails and rolling stock could be imported without prohibitive transport costs. It is not mere chance that in businesses where transport costs were an appreciable factor local production started. Breweries, furniture factories, and cement works are examples of such industries. On the other hand, low transport costs meant, and still mean, that raw materials could be shipped great distances to the metropolises, which was how enclaves originated.

Bairoch has also pointed out that in contrast with early industrialization more and more capital came to be required. At the beginning of the nineteenth century it was still possible with relatively little capital and technical knowledge to build machines and factories. Later, and in the twentieth century in particular, much heavier commitments were required and several times as much capital per worker. Despite being able to borrow technology, it was thus increasingly difficult to industrialize competitively and to absorb surplus labor,[27] especially since population was already rising more rapidly than had happened with the early starters.[28]

That raises the question of capital formation. More recent scholarship accounts as very important an "agrarian revolution," or a massive increase in production and productivity. First, such a revolution assures the food supplies of the growing nonagricultural population. Second, it increases buying power and facilitates the formation of savings, which banks or the fisc can transfer to industry. Japanese industrialization was in good part financed by rents and taxes squeezed from the peasantry.[29] In the colonies, the production of cash crops rose rapidly, but not productivity. The incomes of the peasant masses remained depressed, and in addition acreage per family was low and got lower. Insufficient buying power undoubtedly placed narrow constraints on industrialization. Plants working at half steam and hence unprofitably despite existing need for their production are an all-too-common phenomenon in today's developing countries. Foreigners' high incomes went for luxury imports and did not significantly broaden the internal market, and the same can be said for the narrow class of rich natives, who tended to ape the consumption habits of the foreigners.[30] Still, particularly in the populous colonies, there was probably a market for numerous articles, from cloth to simple machines, despite low per capita income.

Local capital generally existed, either in the hands of the old feudal class or the new bourgeoisie of landowners and businessmen. Socio-cultural considerations doubtless come into play here, insofar as there was, and is, an especially strong tendency to invest capital in land or at most in trade. Even in Japan, prodding from above and even veiled compulsion was needed to get the landowner class to finance industry. The peculiarities of the colonial capital markets and banking systems must also be considered. Whereas the moneylender provided the peasant with advances and credit, the European banks specialized in short-term commercial credit and were either ill-equipped for industrial financing or had little interest in it. Natives were considered dubious credit risks and themselves complained about money shortages. If one follows Alexander Gerschenkron and emphasizes the special role of the banks as instruments for mobilizing capital for the industrialization of the later-comers, then it is clear that the colonial banking system if anything hindered rather than helped industrialization.[31] And a comparison with Japan confirms this.[32]

Did entrepreneurial talent exist in the non-Western societies? That is Max Weber's old blockbuster of a question, and an unbiased answer is difficult to provide. It is too easy simply to say native entrepreneurialism did not exist, as it necessarily appeared to those with a colonialist-enthnocentric viewpoint, or alternatively that it obviously did, as those of a nationalist or Marxist viewpoint are likely to hold. Bert Hoselitz has emphasized the need to consider the sociocultural context.[33] Organizational rationalism, the mind set needed for saving and risk-taking, and a technological cast of mind developed in Western bourgeois civilization and differed fundamentally from the values, codes, and behavioral norms of the trader. There have been wholesale merchants in every civilization, but not factory builders and directors. The stronger the feudal agrarian tradition was and the weaker the urban and bourgeois, the more of a hindrance the sociocultural tradition has proved in the transition to industrialization.[34] One can counter this with arguments like "opportunity makes not only thieves but also entrepreneurs" (Siegenthaler). It was also true in the colonies that natives (as in India) or foreign minorities could have been supporters of industrialization as well as Europeans. In some cases they were, as Owen's examples of Greeks, Jews, and Italians in Egypt show (see p. 244). As long, however, as the export of cash crops and the import of European industrial products occurred within the context of the world economic system and produced the expected profits, there was little occasion for diversification. The coalition of interest between native and large foreign producers (large landowners, and plantation and mining companies) and largely foreign owned trade firms had no trouble bringing its influence to bear on the colonial administration. Local capital also went into the export sector, which means that native businessmen necessarily saw no particular advantages to import substitution. An awareness of the foregoing underlies Johan Galtung's concept of "bridgeheads" and his other researches into the possibilities and limits of "peripheral capitalism."[35]

Although we still need more research on the matter, it is striking that during the depression, when export prices collapsed, industrialization efforts either commenced or were pushed ahead more resolutely, in both colonial and noncolonial Third World countries. Additional investment in land and mining may not have appealed, and native capital thus turned to industrial investment. Or the governments, constrained to act by the manifest social crisis, may have paid more attention to diversification and shifted over to a policy of customs protection and industrial subvention. This shift was made easier because industrialization was directed against Japan, which neutralized metropolitan resistance to it. I have already mentioned India and Java, and in Latin America, Brazil is a good example. In the latter country, the collapse of the coffee boom created a strong impulse toward industrialization.[36] These developments also point out the limitations of a colonial economic policy based on the foreign trade theories of classical economics. Export-oriented growth hindered or blocked altogether the development of complementary industries and thus created the picture of a lopsided economic development.

It is also clear that the colonial powers had no interest in industrialization. The colonies were economic complements to the metropolises. Their development was based on metropolitan needs and was not intended to constitute a competitive capacity. We have seen that even where settlers—as, say, in the French Maghreb—constituted a powerful lobby well able to make their weight felt, metropolitan interests proved stronger still and compromises resulted. One obviously cannot simply speak of "the economy" which hobbled colonial industrialization, because, to take one example, metropolitan machine-tool industries were certainly interested in delivering the requisite capital goods. Nevertheless, one can accept ex hypothesi that the metropolis looked to the colonies as markets for its own industry and was therefore disinclined to encourage industrialization on the periphery. Industrialization was not actually forbidden as under ancien régime mercantilism, but the colonies were exposed to the icy winds of competition, either in the form of the English and Dutch versions of free trade or in the form of the French imperial tariff which set high duties against outsiders and let metropolitan goods in free. Customs protection was not granted the colonies, although even in classical economics "development" duties were regarded as theoretically admissible. Indian nationalists also justly pointed out that late starters like Germany, the United States, the dominions, and Japan had either introduced or assisted industrialization by customs manipulations. Although historians may argue about the significance of this customs protection in individual cases, London, at least, accepted the protectionist measures of the dominions very grudgingly. It had to accept them, however, and rather early on, to prevent dissolution of the empire. France, indeed, had a protectionist tradition. There are those who refuse to consider tariffs any sort of panacea for industrialization and point out the dangers of keeping industries alive artificially. Even they must concede, however, that deliberate customs protection provided important early assistance for numerous industries, even during the period when investment per worker was not very large and the snowball effect was less pronounced. It is characteristic that during World War I, when deliveries from Europe ceased, all sorts of enterprises were established, most of which went under during the 1920s.

But customs protection alone would hardly have sufficed. Flanking measures were both necessary and possible. These ranged from state orders and acceptance commitments to subventions, favorable tax treatment, and moral support. No less a man than Gerschenkron has emphasized the special role the latecomers' states must play. "The historical experience of European countries seems to warrant the generalization that in cases of very considerable backwardness the policies of the state tended to play a very important positive role during the years of the big upsurge of industrial development."[37] Japan is the prime example. As an independent state, it inaugurated forced industrialization from above, employing state assistance and successfully mobilizing national energies for the task. Japan may perhaps be a special case, but the fact remains that the colonies as a dependent periphery lacked autonomy and failed to receive the necessary support from the political authorities. They were thus delivered over defenseless to the international economy. But this system offered limitless possibilities for exporting as the sine qua non for economic development, and also, according to Myrdal, had a tendency, whatever the doctrine of comparative international advantage might imply, to concentrate the "spread effects," in the sense of complementary industrialization, upward shifts in the technological learning curve, and enhanced income, in the already developed metropolises.[38]

In concluding, one can state that colonial economies cannot be understood through concepts such as plunder economics and exploitation. Economic development did occur, although it was export-oriented growth primarily profiting the metropolises and was one-sided in character. The colonial administrations assisted development most importantly by building communications systems—post, telegraph, roads, railways, and harbors—the value of which should not be underestimated even though they were primarily intended to open up the hinterland and thus to serve foreign trade.[39] Development policy in the modern sense, however, implying a careful orientation to the specific needs of a given area and having as first priority the raising of agricultural productivity, was only in its beginnings. The necessity of such measures came to be seen only gradually during the 1930s. Until World War II, the metropolises were hence unwilling to budget moneys for development. The colonies could indeed borrow, but the costs burdened their own budgets, which meant the poorest territories had to be the most cautious. We have seen how Sarraut's great program for development was nibbled to death by parlement in 1921, and the British Colonial Development Fund of 1929 was mainly intended to reduce English unemployment.[40] But though the question of colonial industries was increasingly discussed during the 1930s, the basic assumption that colonial industries could not compete with those of the metropolis was never abandoned.[41] The economic development of the colonies until World War II and after thus remained subordinated to metropolitan interests, which were one-sidedly committed to exports and dualistic in structure. That was to complicate extraordinarily the transition to self-sustaining growth after independence, especially given the very rapid population increases since the 1920s.[42] This foreshadowed the alarming and all-too-familiar situation of today, in which very considerable increases in agricultural and industrial production are simply overwhelmed by the population explosion, with the result being little or no improvement in per capita income.

How did Africans and Asians respond to the colonial situation? It is usual today to emphasize the very different forms resistance took. That is in accord with an anticolonial and nationalistic historiography and is an interpretation especially sympathetic to national and revolutionary liberation movements. I only scratched the surface of the expansion and conquest phases of colonialism, but I assume still made clear enough that in the moment when Europeans no longer limited themselves to treaty relationships, trade, the grants of credit, and the informal influence or dependence that grew out of these things, and for whatever reason shifted over to establishing their rule, they encountered a much fiercer degree of military resistance in both Asia and Africa than traditional colonial historiography has been inclined to acknowledge. Force was necessary not only during the process of penetration and the establishment of rule, the phase of colonial wars so glorified by contemporaries, but afterwards as well. It generally took years, if not decades, until the colony-to-be was pacified, meaning that open resistance had finally collapsed. This resistance was not really nationalist, for whatever importance that may be, but generally amounted to self-assertion and defense of independence based on some narrower polity, whether the tribe, the clan, or some other such unity under the leadership of traditional authorities.

To be precise, we must distinguish between primary and post-primary resistance. European expansion and conquest in many cases occurred without encountering great difficulties. Sometimes a local ruler, threatened by neighbors or enmeshed in struggles over the succession, sought to employ the Europeans to his own ends and himself asked for a protectorate treaty. Such rulers misunderstood the import of such treaties, or, alternatively, they gave in after a short military resistance or the mere European threat of hostilities. But the displacement of the ruling class which followed, the limitations on inward freedom of action, the confiscation of land, the increases in taxes, forced labor, and, in general, the interference in the everyday lives and religious worlds of the defeated then created situations of open conflict. These expanded into genuine colonial wars, because by now the greater part of the population was involved, and resistance was transformed into a holy war against the invader. The Javan wars between 1825 and 1830, Abd el Kader's Algerian war, the Ashanti wars, the Matabele war, the Herero and Maji-Maji rebellions, and the Indian Mutiny of 1857 were all wars of that kind.[43]

The most recent researchers have also emphasized more than earlier historians the countless rebellions or, indeed, full-scale revolutions, during the actual colonial period. The administration played these down as disturbances, and they left few traces behind. They did not seriously shake existing rule and often were not even aimed at the colonial power. But in retrospect, even the latter movements show that beneath the law and order that in large part legitimized colonial rule, the old spirit of resistance lived on, foreign rule was accepted only within limits, and new frustrations were fermenting, which now and again burst into the open as sporadic acts of violence.

Still, however much one may emphasize, and rightly, the open and concealed resistance from the colonized, one ought not overlook the role collaboration played both during the establishment of rule and in institutionally securing it. Robinson has recently begun to work out a more highly differentiated theory of imperialism. This theory does not start from specific European economic and political constellations as both Marxist and non-Marxist theories have until now done. Rather, he also brings in the prerequisites on the periphery for colonial expansion and rule. "The theory of the future will have to explain how a handful of European proconsuls managed to manipulate the polymorphic societies of Africa and Asia, and how, eventually comparatively small, nationalist elites persuaded them to leave."[44] On the one hand, the lack of collaborators or their refusal to, in fact, collaborate was during economic penetration invariably the occasion for direct military action. And even ruling apparatuses of very impressive outward appearance usually rested on local collaborators: "Colonial rule represented reconstruction of collaboration," by means of patronage, grants of honors, and economic privileges. While the ruling power concentrated on the center and on economic activity, it left collaborators wide freedom of action at the regional and local levels. The result was a kind of gentlemen's agreement to mutual noninterference. If one group of collaborators grew too strong, patronage was shifted to another. What was important was to prevent any group of collaborators from uniting urban elites and peasant masses. When unity actually occurred in the nationalist movements, and "the colonial rulers had run out of indigenous collaborators, they either chose to leave or were compelled to go."

Donald A. Low raised the same question, namely, why was European rule so long accepted?[45] He emphasized, first, the military subjugation and the monopoly of force which the colonial power had disposal of. But he also noted the importance of collaboration. There were examples of the Europeans simply taking the place of another ruling power, with little change at first for those at the bottom; the losers might simply concede Europeans the rights of conquest they had once claimed for themselves. The traditional order remained in good part intact, the colonial power basing its rule on rajahs, zamindars, village headmen, and chiefs. Certain groups in the local population had a vested interest in maintaining colonial rule. Low also called attention to the psychologist Dominique O. Mannoni's finding that the population of Madagascar had a dependency complex, meaning the traditional society's acceptance of hierarchic rule as a guarantee for individual security was simply displaced onto the colonial power.[46]

Since World War II, resistance has stood at a premium, whereas collaboration has a negative ring. "There are, however, many ways of collaborating. There are those who seek the master's favor, and those who seek to acquire his science, in order to beat him on his own ground."[47] That may serve as the theme for the liberation movement. One may glorify both the active and passive resistance of the colonized and note with a new interest the various forms the societies in question used in an attempt to maintain their identities in the colonial situation. One can also, with T. O. Ranger, attempt to lay bare the connections between the primary resistance and the later nationalist movements.[48] The fact remains, however, that it was the new, Western-educated elites that finally forced the colonial powers to withdraw, after having long agitated—which is to say, collaborated—within the framework of colonial rule. The traditional ruling class was the mainstay of primary and post-primary resistance. They were then either displaced or allowed themselves to be incorporated into the structure of rule. In certain areas they became an upper class devoid of political functions. Usually large landowners, they thus found themselves forced in the following period to seek the support of the colonial power. They might retain significance as representatives of the old order with the "objective" function of self-assertion in a colonial situation where their own civilization was in the process of disintegrating. But they played no real part in the modernization process itself. That does not necessarily mean that one does not encounter individual representatives of this class in the reform movements and in later political associations and parties. They started going to Western schools early on, had money, leisure, and a great deal of social prestige, all of which provided them with a certain independence, particularly in regard to the colonial powers, which undertook repressive measures against members of the old elite most unwillingly. The challenge to the colonial powers, however, came not from the old but from the new elites, particularly from those living in the towns and cities. The latter constituted a Western-educated intelligentsia of officials, journalists, teachers, and professionals who, choosing from what Western civilization had to offer, acquired the ability to assert themselves within the colonial system of rule and to articulate their claims for participation in government and self-determination with growing self-confidence.

Does the above scenario apply to all colonies? There is still little research on elite and mass attitudes in the period directly after the establishment of rule and the end of resistance. Collaborationists placed themselves at the disposal of the new masters, and the powerlessness of the old masters forced the mass of the population into passive acceptance of the new structure of rule. Individual members of the old ruling class, foreign minorities, and such persons as had already come into contact with Western civilization—because, say, they had been to mission schools—were inclined to acknowledge the success of the conquerers as a sign of superiority. Having done so, they then assumed Western life-styles and settled into the *situation coloniale*, either to exploit as individuals the new opportunities, or in the hope of having the colonial power accept them as partners because of their willingness to assimilate. But this adaptation soon encountered the limits that the system of rule established, and the result was frustration and the compulsion to reconsider one's own racial origin, religion, and systems of values. It is thus characteristic that the numerous reform movements in the Hindu, Islamic, Buddhist, and even African areas all insisted on strict observance, on going back to the sources, and glorified the past. Yet at the same time, they also undertook intensive efforts to renew their own cultural inheritances and societies through criticism, rejection of ossified standards, thought patterns, and behavioral norms. The aim was to meet the challenge of a Western civilization based on modern science and individual attainment. The representatives of these movements and the members of the associations that supported them came partly from the old elite, partly from the new urban bourgeoisie, and most were sharply at odds with orthodox forces.

Such organizations at first took the form of voluntary associations, or, in other words, informal groupings, circles, and clubs and were mainly located in the coastal cities. The preeminent importance of the associations in the formation of public opinion and onset of politicization has only become clear in recent years.[49] Their statements of ostensible purpose varied. Some were culturally oriented, others were essentially mutual aid societies. Some were associations of the graduates of certain schools. Common geographic, tribal, or caste origin were rallying points. What mattered, however, was that these societies stood outside of, or at most on the edges of, traditional societies and thus allowed the young intelligentsia to make its voice heard. Political demands either took second place or were moderate and reformist, aiming mainly at individual civil liberties. The emphasis was on extension of education, representative bodies, and access to the administration, or, in other words, demands that corresponded to the specific socioeconomic interests of bourgeois urban elites. Colonial rule was hardly questioned. Indeed, emphatic declarations of loyalty were really more than tactical measures intended to avert repression. They revealed that, despite all the criticism of specific measures and conditions, membership in the British empire or avowal of *civilisation française* appeared compatible with attempts to define a racial-cultural identity and with claims for equality within a colonial situation characterized by discrimination and a tendency to make distinctions based on externals.

These associations formed the bases for the first political parties, the situation being analogous to that of early European liberalism. The parties were parties of notables, loosely organized without many members, who went into action with the first elections. Since property qualifications restricted the franchise to a tiny minority, there was no reason to appeal to wider circles. One may reasonably speak of national movements and parties in this context, although initially local, regional, religious, caste, or class orientations tended to be dominant. The units which the colonial power had created were only occasionally posited as the polity within which political self-determination was to occur.

I have outlined for the individual regions how the transition from parties of notables to mass movements came about. In the beginning, the largely urban groups, "the half-educated," the retailers, teachers, petty officials, and employees were the groups appealed to and organized. "Sections" developed in the provincial cities, often patterned after socialist or communist party models.

Auxiliary organizations, such as young persons' or women's associations, and professional and union organizations as well, provided a potential mass base. Political discussions became more heated. Reforms were no longer sufficient, and independence or at least the greatest possible degree of autonomy was demanded. Demonstrations, boycotts, and strikes commenced, and the administration responded with repression. Un- and underemployment, rootlessness, life at the thin edge of existence, the catastrophic effects of the depression, the dualism in the economic structure, combined with racist social discrimination, the abyss separating European and local life-styles, all these things made colonial rule appear to be a system of capitalist exploitation which only revolution could end. More important, indeed, than Communist propaganda was the colonial situation itself, which positively demanded political and social liberation. Susceptibility to Marxist appeals was all the greater, however, because they offered the colonial intelligentsia and the new members of the elite from the upper classes an all-encompassing world view that could be harmonized with their own cultural and religious past. Appeals to national history and culture, and the glorification of former polities and the resistance to the colonial power played a role in Asian and African nationalist movements similar to that in nineteenth-century Europe. They encouraged a sense of community, awakened sleeping energies, and served to create a sense of individual identity. They were also agitationally effective, because they mobilized the hatred of the oppressor and made it possible to proclaim that independence would usher in a golden age.[50]

How much the peasant masses were actually caught up in all this is an open question. The new political leaders such as Gandhi, Sukarno, and Bourguiba were indeed welcomed with enthusiasm when they travelled about their countries spreading the word. Although rural notables and prosperous peasants became firm party supporters, effective politicization often proved very ephemeral, if the ease with which such movements could be shut down by the arrest of the leaders is any indication.

Perhaps more important than parties when considering the attitudes of African and Asian peasants in the *situation coloniale* were the religious movements with their sects, secret societies, and separatist churches. These movements helped transmit traditional values and awakened chiliastic expectations. The most recent scholarship has devoted particular attention to them, interpreting them as an answer to the "orientation vacuum" (Dahm) resulting from social changes under colonial rule, which robbed the masses of their traditional leaders, loosened the old communal ties, and exposed each one to the individualization and differentiation processes bound up with the cash economy. The agrarian revolts in Southeast Asia between 1926 and 1930 revealed a crisis that was social as well as intellectual and can be seen as the first stages of the socio-revolutionary liberation movement coming to fruition during and after World War II.

The colonial powers met the nationalist challenge of the interwar period in part with repression and in part with reforms. It has been noted that Great Britain and France sought opposite ends. The former was oriented toward future colonial self-government, the latter in the direction of a "greater France," understood as administrative integration with parliamentary representation and the grant of citizenship to "subjects." But haste seemed in no way called for. In its Asian territories, however, England at least showed a notable flexibility. Attempting to satisfy the demands of the collaborationist moderate wing of the national movements at least temporarily, England built up representative assemblies and even conceded executive powers. The other colonial powers demonstrated little willingness to make concessions, preferring to oppose the liberation movements with repression. But even in the case of Britain, one can hardly speak of a deliberate decolonization policy.[51]

Finally, one must ask how Europe's rule over a major portion of the globe fits into the context of world history. It is my firm view that the colonial expansion of the modern period fits into a larger framework of migrations, conquests, colonization, and empire building such as are familiar to us from the histories of other cultures and peoples. What gave European imperialism its singular stamp was the Industrial Revolution. The latter provided this "appendage of the Asian Continent" (Paul Valéry) with not only the technical and military superiority for conquest and rule, but also unleashed an economic and intellectual dynamism that shrank distances, allowing everything outside Europe to become the industrial countries' periphery, and thrust fundamental transformations upon the societies of Africa and Asia. This last was dignified ideologically as "civilizing" the peoples of other races, who for their part experienced it as a loss of inner independence, economic exploitation, and cultural alienation. But I consider it mistaken simply to interpret colonialism as exploitation, which—as is often asserted today—actually was responsible for the Industrial Revolution and the prosperity of the West and whose corollary was the underdevelopment of the colonized. The Industrial Revolution was a very complex affair, which must be explained largely in terms of the specific economic, social, and intellectual prerequisites possessed by Western Europe, most notably England. The capital accumulated under old-style colonialism played at best a very secondary role. For the high capitalism of the outgoing nineteenth and early twentieth centuries tropical raw materials were naturally a sine qua non, and the dynamic effects of the expanding world trade that was based on such raw materials ought not be denied. Still, the ability of the colonials to absorb industrial products and investment capital was modest, compared to the expanding markets of the United States, the dominions, and Latin America—which explains the special place the latter has in contemporary imperialism research. India was doubtless important to Great Britain, but in the larger economic picture important only to Lancashire for cotton exports.[52] In short, while the colonial territories obviously served the functions of both contributing to expansion and stabilizing economic fluctuations, these ought not be overemphasized.

I consider equally mistaken the thesis that Asian and African peoples could have brought off modernization *à la japonaise* and without colonialism would today be developed countries. Despite the risk of appearing an imperialist and colonialist lackey, I remain committed to the view that the colonial period was a period of modernization for the colonized. The imposition of peace, meaning putting an end to tribal warfare—for the Pax Britannica was in wide areas no empty slogan—the creation of larger territorial units, establishment of modern administrations and communications systems, and economic development were a part of this modernization, as were expansion of education and health services. The conserving of old ruling structures notwithstanding, foreign rule in the end was destabilizing and launched social changes that characterized the Western way to modernization as the ideal way. There were other ways, certainly, and it is not impossible that in the foreseeable future past decades of European rule will appear as a sort of entr'acte, after which the underlying continuity with the precolonial times will assert itself and provide the peoples of Asia and Africa with new identities.

NOTES

1. S. N. Eisenstadt, "Social Change and Modernization in African Societies South of the Sahara," in *French-Speaking Africa: The Search for Identity*, ed. William H. Lewis (New York: Walker, 1965), 223; idem, "Soziologische Aspekte der politischen Entwicklung in den Entwicklungsländern," in Albertini, *Moderne Kolonialgeschichte*.

2. Eisenstadt, "Soziologische Aspekte," 443.

3. Tignor, *Modernization*, 105.

4. On this, see the famous essay by Hla Mynt, "The 'Classical Theory of International Trade' and the Underdeveloped Countries," *Economic Journal*, 68 (June 1958), reprinted in his *Economic Theory and the Underdeveloped Countries* (New York: Oxford University Press 1971). Mynt argues that "classic theory" was one-sidedly tied to Ricardo's doctrine of comparative costs and had overlooked Adam Smith's emphasis on the fact that wider markets encouraged better exploitation of productive forces. In the colonies, such exploitation took the form of the use of untilled land and the employment of labor forces which had lain fallow in the subsistence economy with its minimal market incentives.

5. "During the early period of Japan's modernization a key position had been occupied by the raw silk industry which provided a very high proportion of her exports, for without the foreign earnings so obtained the country could hardly have imported the capital equipment and raw materials required for her new industries"; Allen, "The Industrialization of the Far East," 883.

6. Table 15.1 gives further data:

Table 15.1
Index of export values, 1913
(1883 = 100)

Ceylon	523	India	235
Indochina	426	West Africa	548
Indonesia	311	Egypt	277

SOURCE: "Foreword," in Lewis, *Tropical Development*, 15.

7. Raul Prebisch, *The Economic Development of Latin America and Its Principal Problems* (Lake Success: United Nations, Dept. of Economic Affairs, 1950); idem, "Die Rohstoffexporte und die Verschechterung der Terms of Trade," in Bonnet, *Nord-Süd Problem*; H. W. Singer, "The Distribution of Gains between Investing and Borrowing Countries," *AER*, 40, *Papers &*

Proc. (May 1950), 477f. Prebisch took the English net barter terms of trade as his starting point, which according to his exposition fell steadily from an index figure of 100 in 1876-1880 to 64.1 in 1936-1938.

8. Sieber, *Realen Austauschverhältnisse*.

9. See the series from 1871 to 1965 in Sir William Arthur Lewis, *Aspects of Tropical Trade, 1883-1965* (Stockholm: Almqvist & Wiksell, 1969), 49-50. Graphed, these figures reveal the following:

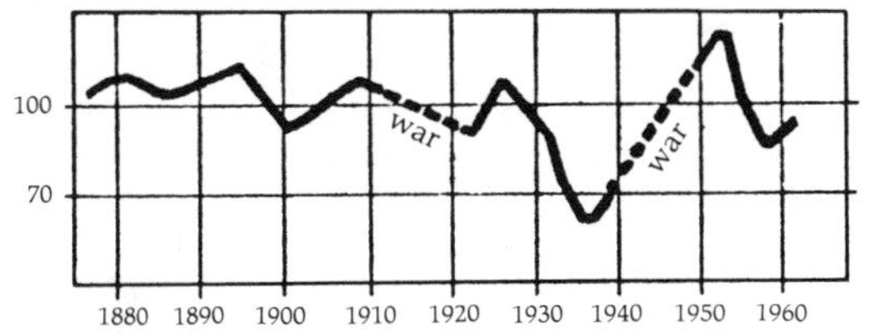

Source: ibid., 25. Sieber does not employ overall indices, but his case studies confirm Lewis's findings. As evidence for the rather insecure character of available figures and their interpretation, one can cite Paul Bairoch, *Révolution Industrielle et Sous-Développement* (Paris: Société d'Edition d'Enseignement Superieur, 1964), 188, who posited a worsening of the terms of trade between 1873 and 1938. Taking up the question anew in 1967, however, he corrected his figures and stated that for the period 1876-1880 to 1926-1929 an improvement in the terms of trade of 20 to 40 percent had occurred. Unfortunately excluding the depression years from consideration, he concluded that from 1924-1928 to 1950-1952 a further improvement of about 24 percent occurred; *Diagnostique de l'Evolution Economique du Tiers-Monde, 1900-1966* (Paris: Gauthier-Villars, 1967), 155f.

10. Lewis, *Aspects*, 48; Sieber, *Realen Austauschverhältnisse*, 148f.

11. "If the modern sectors had continued to grow at the same rate, without the interruptions of the First World War, the great depression of the 1930s, and the Second World War, the leading tropical countries would now be unrecognizable"; Lewis, *Tropical Development*, 44.

12. Owen, *Cotton*, 355. See in particular the summarizing concluding chapter.

13. Kenneth Berrill, "Auslandskapital und Take-Off," in *Industrielle Revolution: Wirtschaftliche Aspekte*, ed. Rudolf Braun et al. (Cologne: Kiepenheuer & Witsch, 1972), 260.

14. Bagchi, *Private Investment*, 421.

15. On the concept "dual economies," see *Entwicklungspolitik: Handbuch und Lexikon*, ed. Hans Besters and Ernst E. Boesch (Stuttgart: Kreuz-Verlag, 1966), 1079-82.

16. In addition to Julius Herman Boeke, *Economies and Economic Policy of Dual Societies as Exemplified by Indonesia* (Haarlem: H. D. Tienk Willink & Zoon n.v., 1953), see Koninklijk Institut voor de Tropen, *Indonesian Economics: The Concept of Dualism in Theory and Policy* (The Hague: W. von Hoeve, 1966).

17. Important for this discussion is Benjamin Higgins, "The 'Dualistic Theory' of Underdeveloped Areas," *Economic Development and Cultural Change*, 4 (January 1956). The criticisms of Boeke are valid, but Higgins's alternative nonetheless is typical of Western thought in the 1950s. What was called for was a "shock treatment" in the form of "large amounts of capital investment" to break the circle of poverty; ibid., 113-14. Today Boeke's remedy of village development would receive a more kindly hearing.

18. A neo-Marxist criticism from Alberto Martinelli, "Dualismus und Abhängigkeit: Zur Kritik herrschender Theorien," in Senghaas, *Imperialismus*, 22, 24. For a detailed consideration of "the dualistic economic structure as a basic problem of development," see Hans-Balz Peter, *Sozioökonomische Grundprobleme der Entwicklungsländer* (Zurich: Theologischer Verlag, 1972), 64ff. Peter does not, however, consider the neo-Marxist critique.

19. Holding against this view is, among others, Körner, *Kolonialpolitik*, 86. For a more restrained statement, see Owen, *Cotton*, 367.

20. For example, Pierre Gourou, *Les Pays Tropicaux: Principes d'une Géographie Humaine*

et Economique (Paris: Presses Universitaires de France, 1966), 217. Bairoch's judgment takes in too little, considering only production figures and not acreage; *Révolution Industrielle*, 184. He speaks, moreover, only of plantations and does not distinguish between plantations and native farming.

21. *Cambridge Economic History*, VI: 1, 42.

22. Mynt, *Economic Theory*, 80, emphasizes that the result was that the peasant was hit with unfair prices coming and going and that a portion of the profits left the country to boot. Owen, *Cotton*, 368, accepts this thesis for Egypt only in part.

23. John Stuart Mill had already seen this. The West Indian colonies, he stated, "are hardly to be looked upon as countries carrying on an exchange of commodities with other countries, but more properly as outlying agricultural or manufacturing establishments belonging to a larger community"; quoted in Baldwin, *Economic Development*, 2. But see Singer, "Distribution of Gains," 475.

24. William Otto Henderson, *Britain and Industrial Europe, 1750-1870: Studies in British Influence on the Industrial Revolution in Western Europe* (Liverpool: University Press, 1954, 1965).

25. Phyllis Deane, "The Long Term Trends in World Economic Growth," *Malayan Economic Review*, 6 (October 1961), 24.

26. Bairoch, *Révolution Industrielle*, 176f.

27. Ibid., 166. "It is probably about seventy times as expensive to put one man to work in a technically conventional industry in an underdeveloped country as it was in France at the moment of its industrial revolution"; ibid., 153. H. W. Singer, "Obstacles to Economic Development," *Social Research*, 20 (Spring 1953), 26, argues along similar lines.

28. The annual population increase in Britain, France, Germany, Belgium, Switzerland, and Italy was between .4 and .8 percent during the take-off period; Bairoch, *Révolution Industrielle*, 145. In contrast, non-European countries had percentage figures like these (ibid., 142):

Japan (1870-1910)	.9
India	1.5
Algeria	2.3
Egypt (1880-1920)	2.2

29. G. Ranis, "Die Finanzierung der wirtschaftlichen Entwicklung Japans," in *Industrielle Revolution*, 239f.

30. "The concentration of a large share of export industry income in the hands of foreign factors and a small group of luxury imports resulted in no domestic mass market for anything above the subsistence level"; Jonathan V. Levin, *The Export Economies: Their Pattern of Development in Historical Perspective* (Cambridge, Mass.: Harvard University Press, 1960), 9.

31. Alexander Gerschenkron, *Economic Backwardness in Historical Perspective* (Cambridge: Harvard University Press, 1952, 1962), 15. For Italy, Sellin has pointed this out; *Organisierter Kapitalismus: Voraussetzungen und Anfänge*, ed. Heinrich August Winkler (Gottingen: Vandenhoeck und Rupprecht, 1974), 94.

32. Yasuzo Horie, "Capital Formation in the Early Stages of Industrialization in Japan," in International Conference of Economic History, 2d, Aix-en-Provence, 1962, [*Proceedings*] (Paris: Mouton, 1965), 685-700.

33. In, among other places, "Ein Soziologischer Ansatz zur Theorie der wirtschaftlichen Entwicklung," in Berthold Frank Hoselitz, *Wirtschaftliches Wachstum und sozialer Wandel* (Berlin: Duncker & Humblot, 1969).

34. For the period before 1933, Lewis, *Tropical Development*, 43, concludes: "When one has been through all the other factors, one is left with lack of domestic entrepreneurship as most powerful explanation of failure to make significant progress in manufacturing, since almost any Latin American or Asian country could have supported enough manufacturing to employ, say 6

to 8 percent of its population in factories in 1913, with moderate tariffs. One should not be surprised at the lack of domestic industrial entrepreneurship; it takes more than thirty years for such a class to evolve. Germany, for example, was still relatively untouched by the Industrial Revolution in 1830, when both Britain and France had been modernizing rapidly for at least thirty to forty years."

35. Galtung, "Strukturelle Theorie." Also worthy of note is F. H. Cardoso, "Brasilien—Die Widersprüche der assoziierten Entwicklung," in *Lateinamerika, Faschismus oder Revolution*, ed. and trans. by Heinz Rudolf Sonntag (Berlin: Rotbuch-Verlag, 1974).

36. Frank, *Capitalism and Underdevelopment*, 176.

37. Gerschenkron, *Economic Backwardness*, 79, and, supplementing Gerschenkron, Borchardt, *Europas Wirtschaftsgeschichte*, 29. For Germany, see, among others, Wolfram Fischer, "Das Verhältnis von Staat und Wirtschaft in Deutschland am Beginn der Industrialisierung," in *Industrielle Revolution*, 290f.

38. Gunnar Myrdal, *Economic Theory and Under-Developed Regions* (London: Duckworth, 1957). In German translation as *Ökonomische Theorie und interentwickelte Regionen* (1974). Citations are from the German edition. His concept, "circular and cumulative causation" is particularly valid for colonies. Singer, "Distribution of Gains," 477f., argues along similar lines. Besters, among others, in *Entwicklungspolitik*, 243ff., has challenged these arguments. Mynt, indeed, on theoretical grounds refuses to accept that increased demand for industrial goods created more demand for capital goods and thus was an accelerator in the industrial countries, pointing to the rigid structures in the developing countries. But he also emphasizes that the growing demand for primary products only leads to expansion in acreage, the "educative effect" on local agriculture being very slight; "The Gains from International Trade of the Backward Countries," in Mynt, *Economic Theory*, 112f.

39. See, for example, Brett, *Colonialism and Underdevelopment*, 280, who argues from the dependency theory, and Myrdal, *Ökonomische Theorie*, 63.

40. Albertini, *Decolonization*, 104. For France, see Körner, *Kolonialpolitik*, 53; for Britain, Brett, *Colonialism and Underdevelopment*, 116f. Even the Labour party proved to be against colonial industrialization; see George C. Abbott, "A Re-Examination of the Colonial Development Act," *EcHR*, 24 (February 1971).

41. For this insight, I should like to thank Dr. Herward Sieberg, who is working on a study researching the early history of development assistance.

42. Bairoch, *Diagnostique*, 18, provides the following percentage figures for the growth rate of the developing countries:

1900-1920	0.3
1920-1930	1.4
1930-1940	1.2
1960-1963	2.1

43. Brilliantly analyzed by Stokes, "Traditional Resistance Movements." The factor of fantasy and disillusionment during the primary resistance phase is emphasized by Brunschwig, "De la Résistance."

44. Ronald Robinson, "Non-European Foundations of European Imperialism; Sketch for a Theory of Collaboration," in *Studies in the Theory of Imperialism*, ed. Edward Roger John Owen and Bob Sutcliffe (London: Longman, 1972).

45. Donald A. Low, "Empire and Authority," in Low, *Lion Rampant*.

46. Dominique O. Mannoni, *Psychologie de la Colonisation* (Paris: Ed. de Seuil, 1950); titled in English as *Prospero and Caliban: The Psychology of Colonization*, trans. Pamela Powesland (New York: Praeger, 1956).

47. Brunschwig, "De la Résistance," 59.

48. Ranger, "Connections."
49. Above all, see Wallerstein, *Road to Independence* and *Political Parties.*
50. I borrow here a passage from the introduction to *Moderne Kolonialgeschichte*, 32.
51. Treated in detail in Albertini, *Decolonization.*
52. In the interwar period England drew but 5 percent of its imports from India, which took only 10 percent of English exports; Ian M. Drummond, *Imperial Economic Policy, 1917-1939: Studies in Expansion and Protection* (London: Allen & Unwin, 1974), 428. For pre-World War I France, Jean Bouvier, "Les Traits Majeurs de l'Impérialisme Français avant 1914," *Le Mouvement Social*, 86 (January-March 1974), comes to the same conclusion.

MAPS

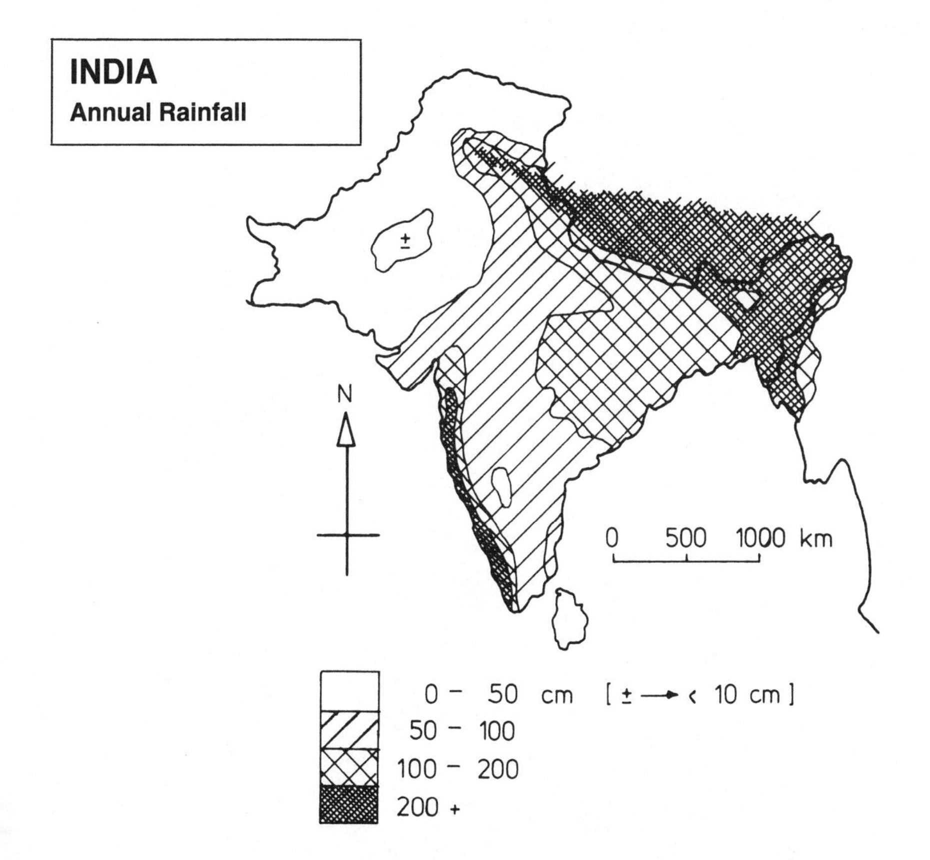

INDIA
Annual Rainfall
N
0 500 1000 km
0 - 50 cm [± → < 10 cm]
50 - 100
100 - 200
200 +

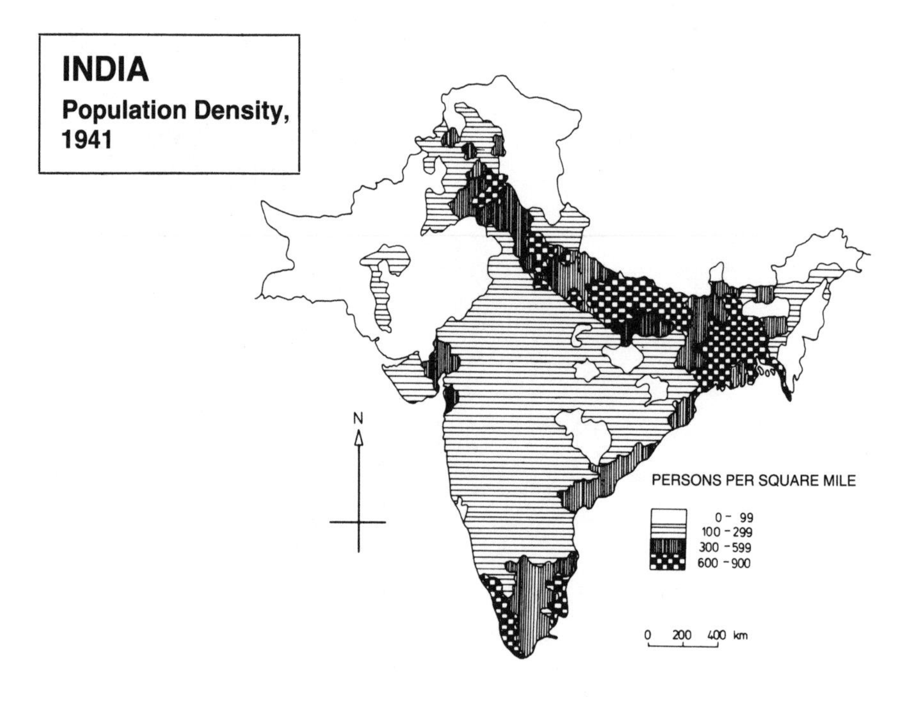
INDIA
Population Density, 1941
N
PERSONS PER SQUARE MILE
0 - 99
100 - 299
300 - 599
600 - 900
0 200 400 km

INDIA
Princely States and British Provinces, 1941
JAMMU & KASHMIR
AMRITSAR
PUNJAB
BALUCHISTAN
LUCKNOW
RAJPUTANA
UNITED PROVINCES
ASSAM
SIND
HYDERABAD
WEST. STATES
INDIA
BIHAR
BENGAL
EASTERN STATES
CENTRAL PROVINCES
JAMSHEDPUR
N
BOMBAY
ORISSA
POONA
HYDERABAD
MADRAS
Princely States
British Provinces
MYSORE
PONDICHERRY
BANGALORE
MADRAS STATES
0 200 400 km

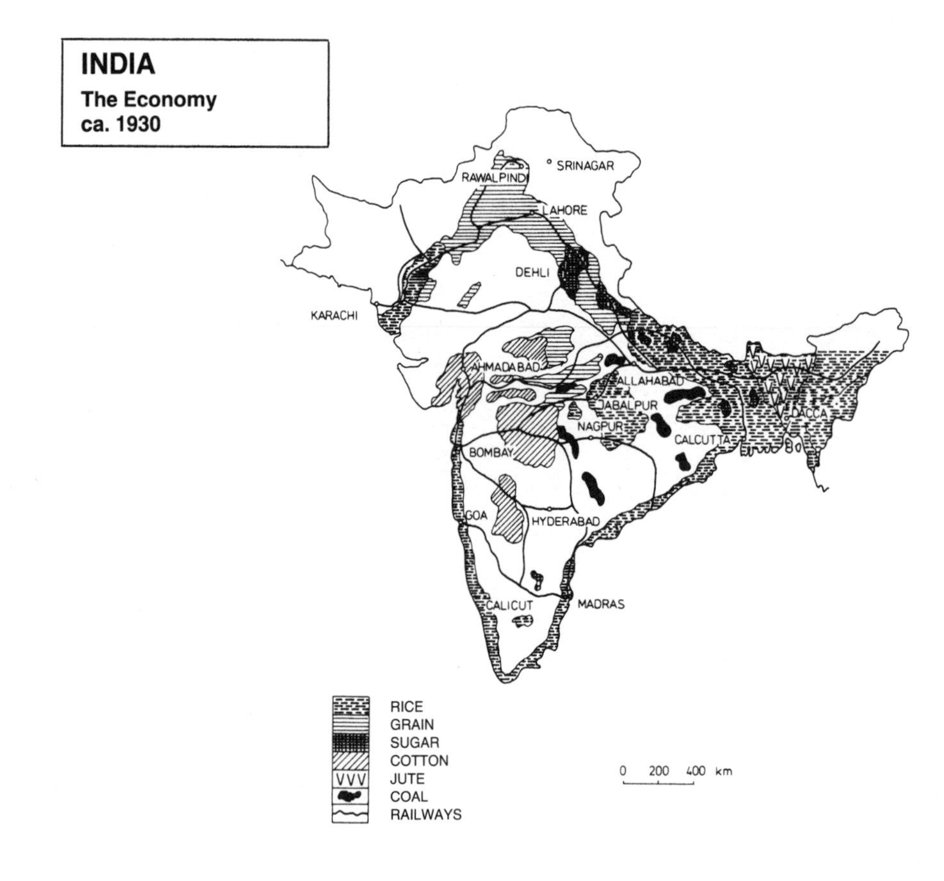
INDIA
The Economy
ca. 1930
SRINAGAR
RAWALPINDI
LAHORE
DEHLI
KARACHI
AHMADABAD
ALLAHABAD
JABALPUR
NAGPUR
CALCUTTA
DACCA
BOMBAY
GOA
HYDERABAD
CALICUT
MADRAS
RICE
GRAIN
SUGAR
COTTON
JUTE
COAL
RAILWAYS
0 200 400 km

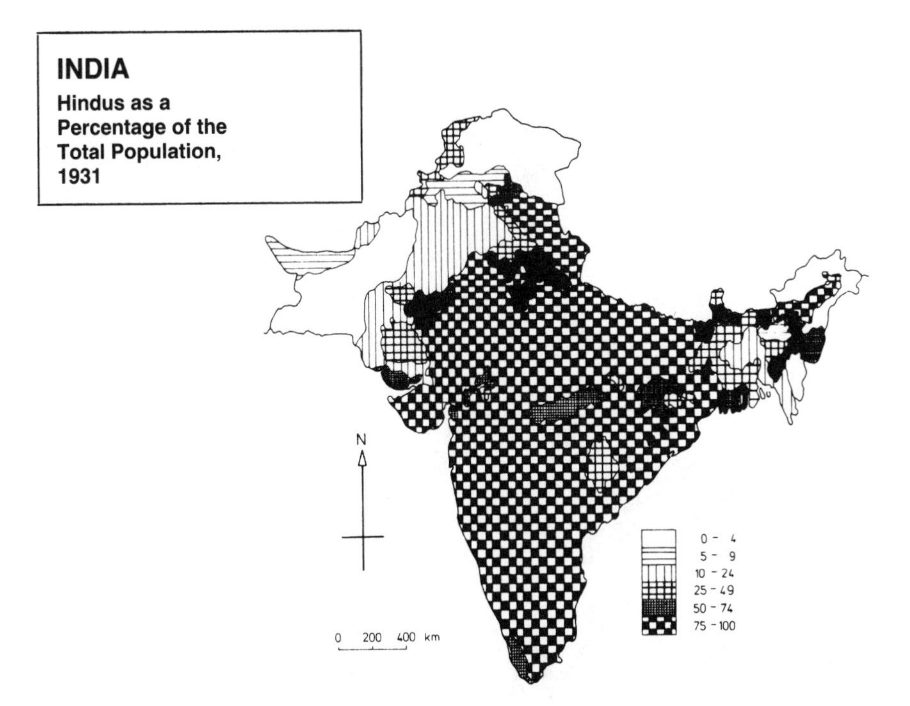
INDIA
Hindus as a
Percentage of the
Total Population,
1931
N
0 - 4
5 - 9
10 - 24
25 - 49
50 - 74
75 - 100
0 200 400 km

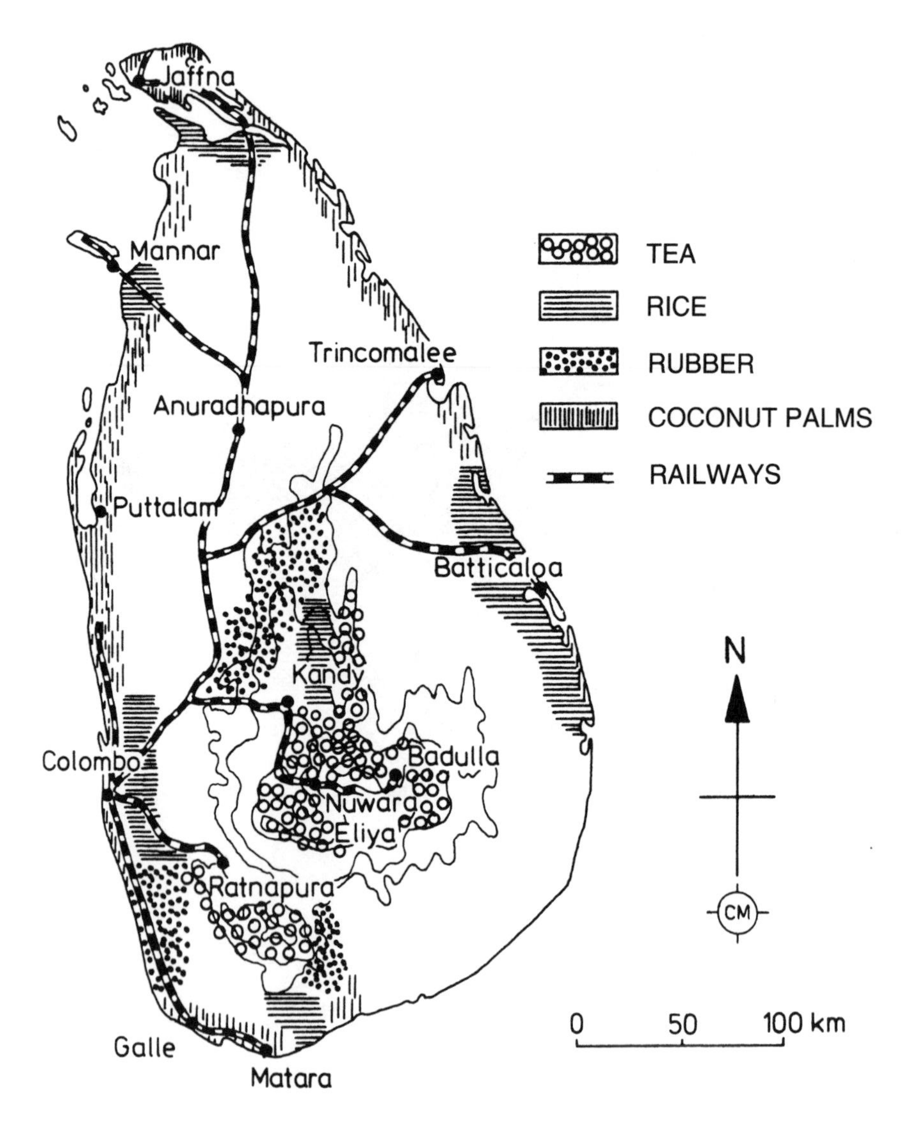
CEYLON
Jaffna
Mannar
Trincomalee
Anuradhapura
Puttalam
Batticaloa
Kandy
Colombo
Badulla
Nuwara
Eliya
Ratnapura
Galle
Matara
TEA
RICE
RUBBER
COCONUT PALMS
RAILWAYS
N
CM
0
50
100 km

BURMA

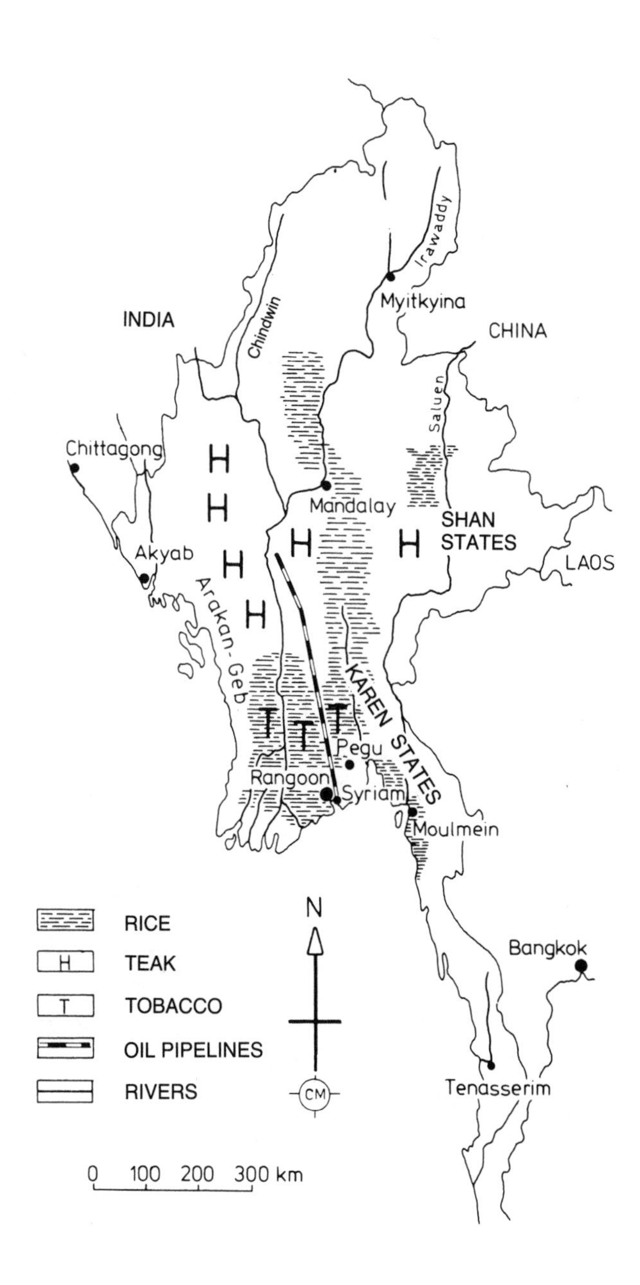
Irawaddy
Myitkyina
INDIA
CHINA
Chindwin
Saluen
Chittagong
Mandalay
SHAN
STATES
Akyab
LAOS
Arakan-Geb
KAREN STATES
Pegu
Rangoon
Syriam
Moulmein
RICE
TEAK
TOBACCO
OIL PIPELINES
RIVERS
N
CM
Bangkok
Tenasserim
0 100 200 300 km

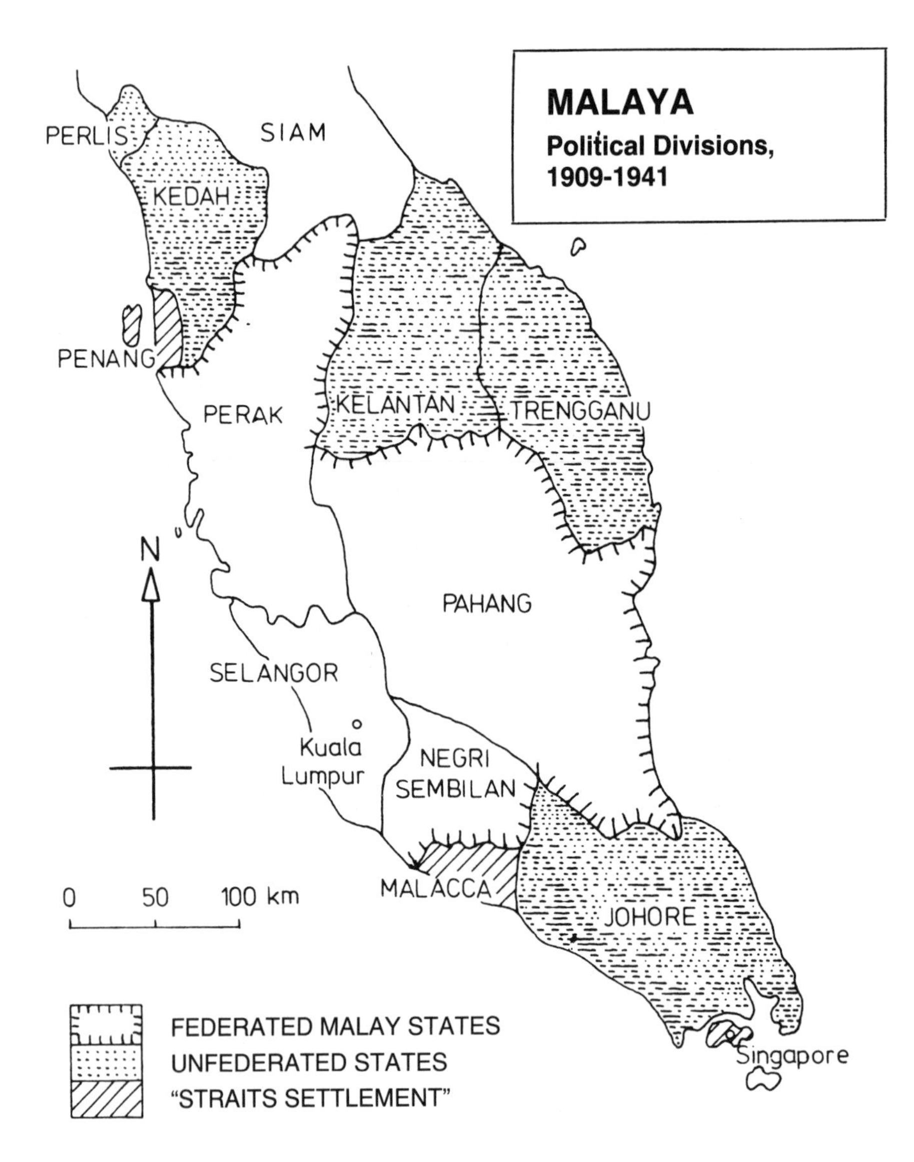
MALAYA
Political Divisions,
1909-1941
PERLIS
SIAM
KEDAH
PENANG
PERAK
KELANTAN
TRENGGANU
PAHANG
SELANGOR
Kuala
Lumpur
NEGRI
SEMBILAN
MALACCA
JOHORE
Singapore
N
0
50
100 km
FEDERATED MALAY STATES
UNFEDERATED STATES
"STRAITS SETTLEMENT"

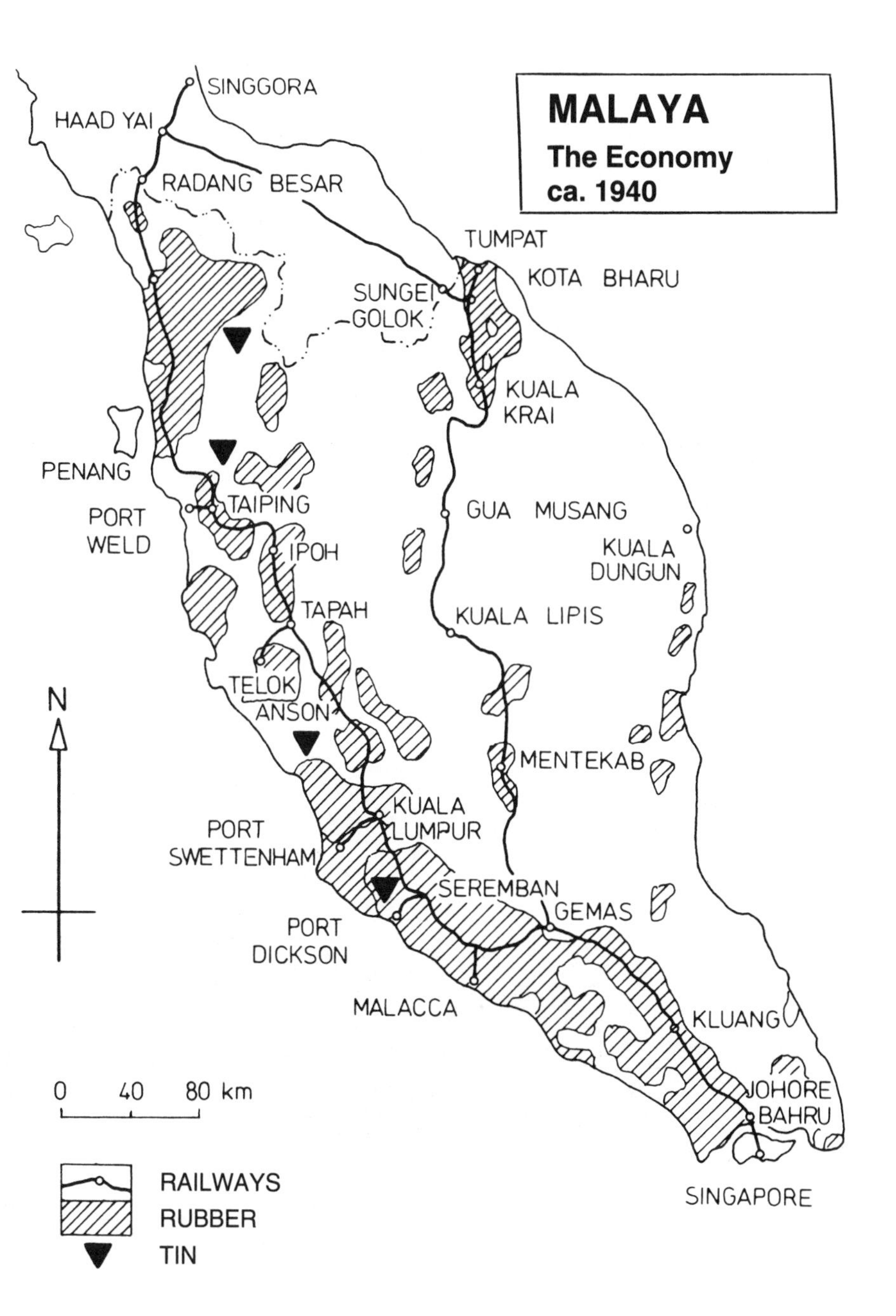
MALAYA
The Economy
ca. 1940
SINGGORA
HAAD YAI
RADANG BESAR
TUMPAT
KOTA BHARU
SUNGEI
GOLOK
KUALA
KRAI
PENANG
TAIPING
PORT
WELD
IPOH
GUA MUSANG
KUALA
DUNGUN
TAPAH
KUALA LIPIS
TELOK
ANSON
MENTEKAB
N
KUALA
LUMPUR
PORT
SWETTENHAM
SEREMBAN
GEMAS
PORT
DICKSON
MALACCA
KLUANG
JOHORE
BAHRU
0 40 80 km
SINGAPORE
RAILWAYS
RUBBER
TIN

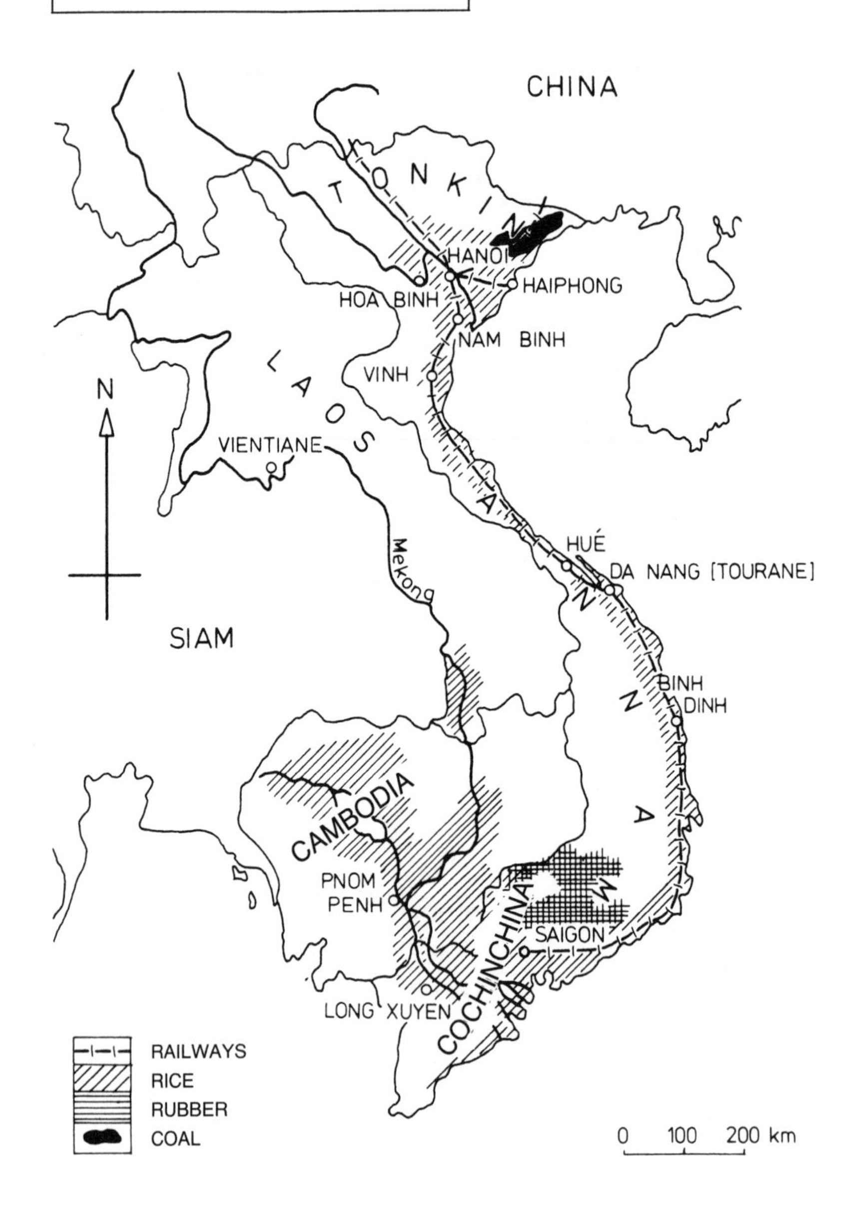
FRENCH INDOCHINA
CHINA
TONKIN
HANOI
HAIPHONG
HOA BINH
NAM BINH
VINH
LAOS
VIENTIANE
N
Mekong
SIAM
ANNAM
HUÉ
DA NANG [TOURANE]
BINH DINH
CAMBODIA
PNOM PENH
SAIGON
COCHINCHINA
LONG XUYEN
RAILWAYS
RICE
RUBBER
COAL
0 100 200 km

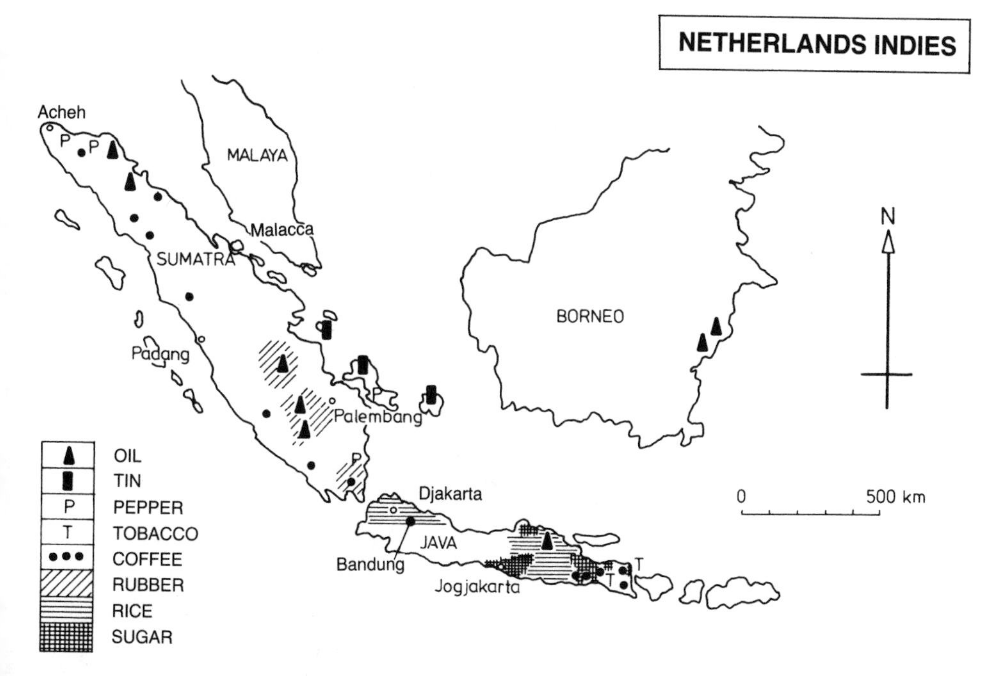
NETHERLANDS INDIES
Acheh
P
P
MALAYA
Malacca
SUMATRA
Padang
Palembang
P
BORNEO
N
0
500 km
Djakarta
JAVA
Bandung
Jogjakarta
T
T
OIL
TIN
P PEPPER
T TOBACCO
COFFEE
RUBBER
RICE
SUGAR

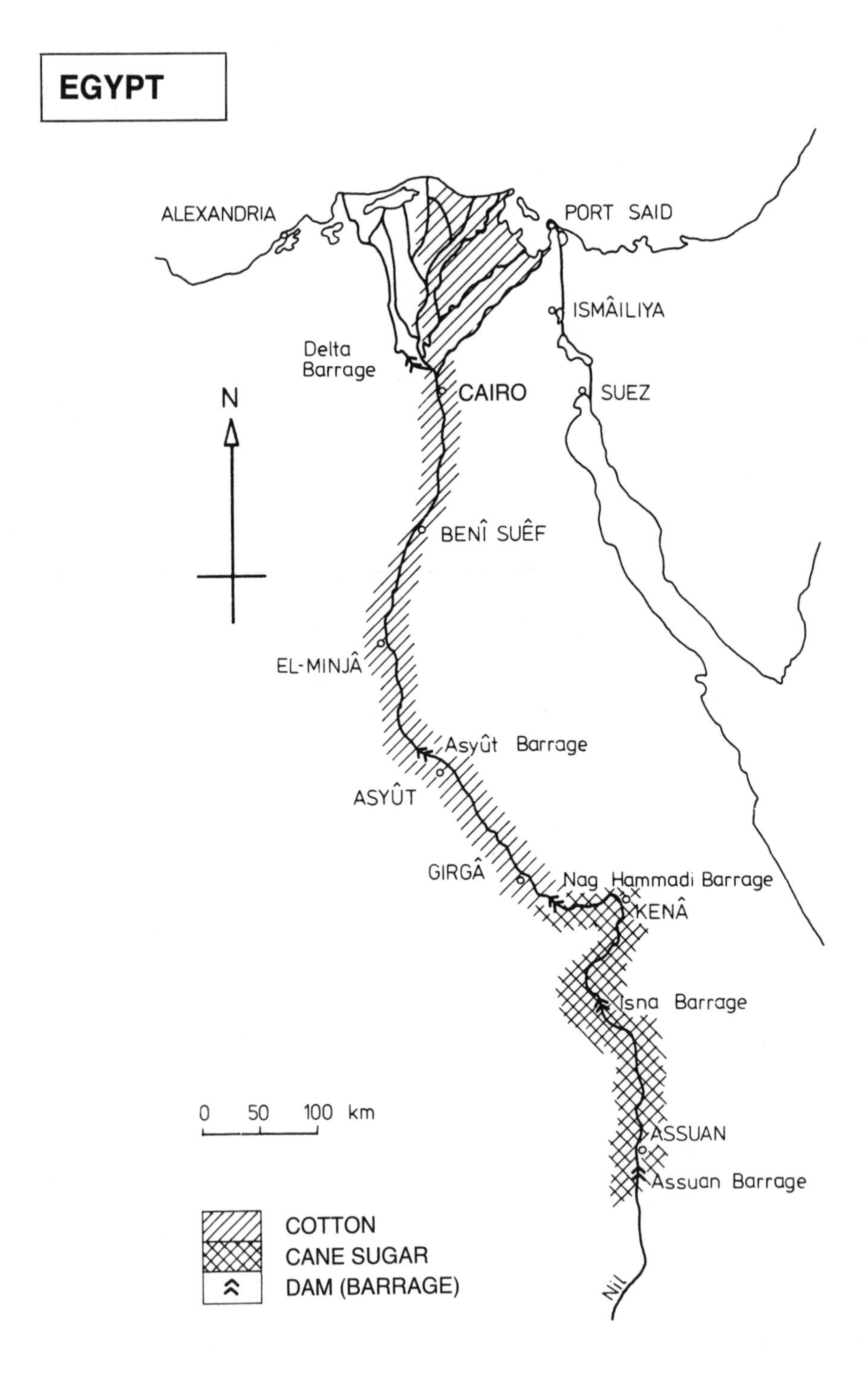
EGYPT
ALEXANDRIA
PORT SAID
ISMÂILIYA
Delta Barrage
CAIRO
SUEZ
N
BENÎ SUÊF
EL-MINJÂ
Asyût Barrage
ASYÛT
GIRGÂ
Nag Hammadi Barrage
KENÂ
Isna Barrage
0 50 100 km
ASSUAN
Assuan Barrage
COTTON
CANE SUGAR
DAM (BARRAGE)
Nil

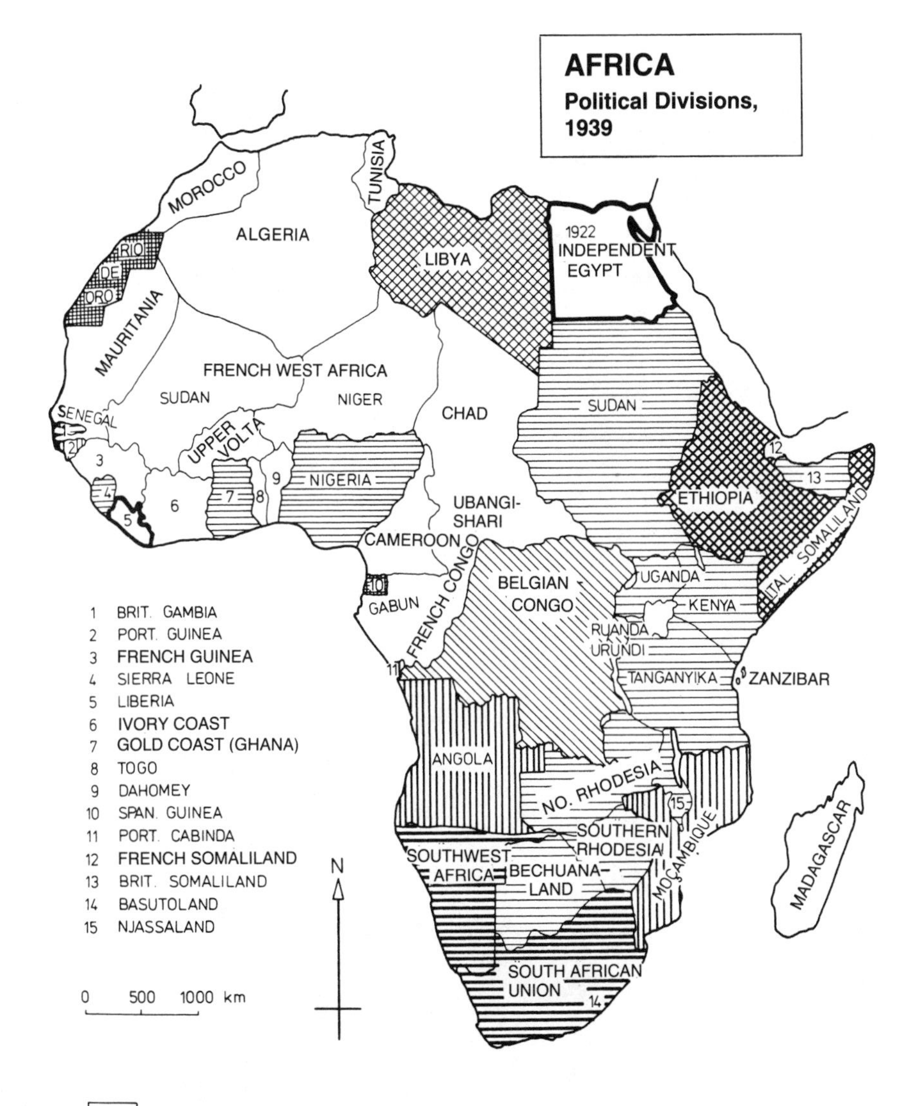
AFRICA
Political Divisions, 1939
MOROCCO
ALGERIA
TUNISIA
LIBYA
1922
INDEPENDENT
EGYPT
RIO
DE
ORO
MAURITANIA
FRENCH WEST AFRICA
SUDAN
NIGER
SENEGAL
UPPER VOLTA
CHAD
SUDAN
NIGERIA
ETHIOPIA
UBANGI-SHARI
CAMEROON
ITAL. SOMALILAND
GABUN
FRENCH CONGO
BELGIAN CONGO
UGANDA
KENYA
RUANDA
URUNDI
TANGANYIKA
ZANZIBAR
ANGOLA
NO. RHODESIA
SOUTHERN RHODESIA
MOÇAMBIQUE
MADAGASCAR
SOUTHWEST AFRICA
BECHUANA-LAND
SOUTH AFRICAN UNION
1 BRIT. GAMBIA
2 PORT. GUINEA
3 FRENCH GUINEA
4 SIERRA LEONE
5 LIBERIA
6 IVORY COAST
7 GOLD COAST (GHANA)
8 TOGO
9 DAHOMEY
10 SPAN. GUINEA
11 PORT. CABINDA
12 FRENCH SOMALILAND
13 BRIT. SOMALILAND
14 BASUTOLAND
15 NJASSALAND
N
0 500 1000 km

FRENCH POSSESSIONS
BRITISH POSSESSIONS
ITALIAN POSSESSIONS
BELGIAN POSSESSIONS
PORTUGUESE POSSESSIONS
SPANISH POSSESSIONS

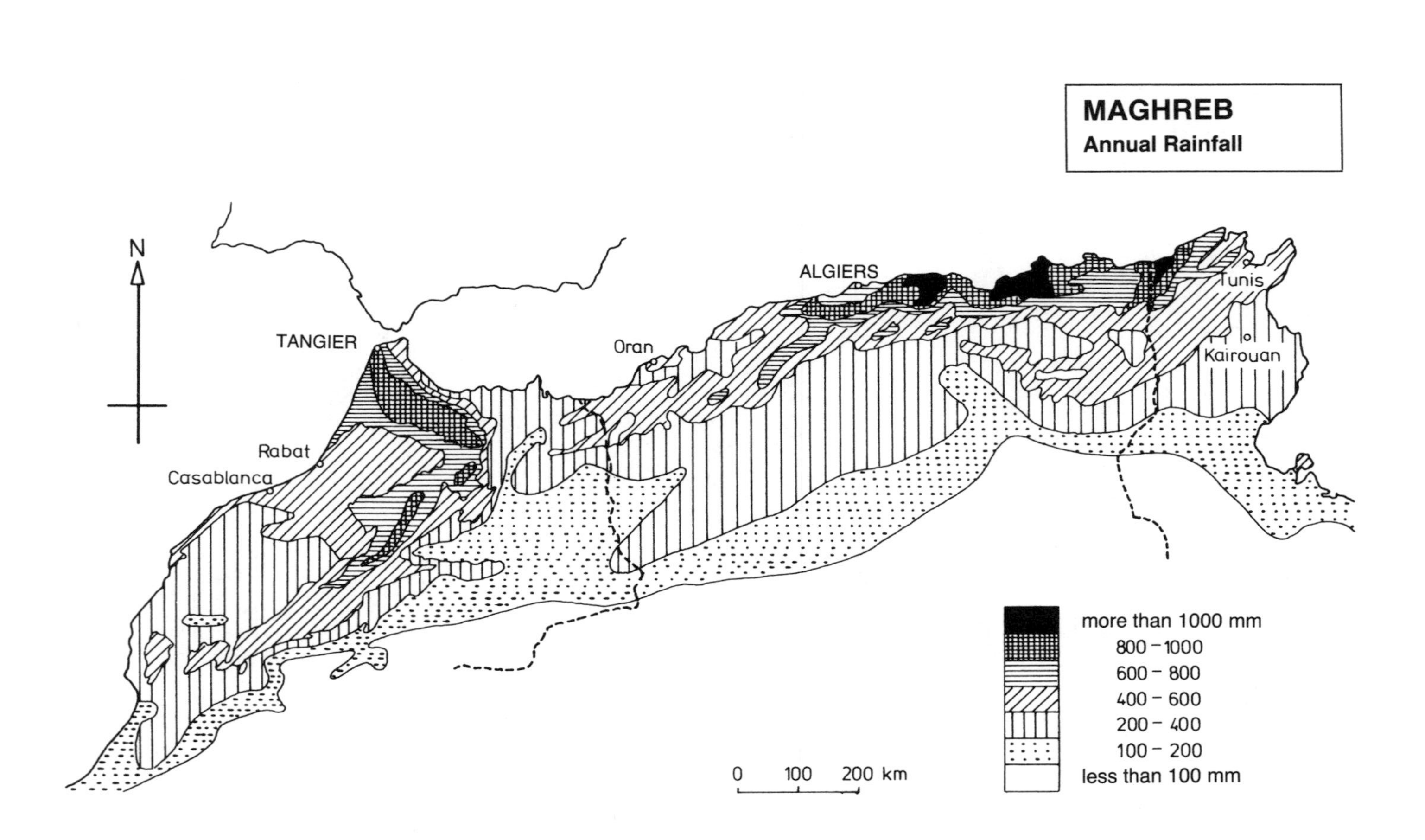
MAGHREB
Annual Rainfall
N
TANGIER
Rabat
Casablanca
Oran
ALGIERS
Tunis
Kairouan
more than 1000 mm
800 – 1000
600 – 800
400 – 600
200 – 400
100 – 200
less than 100 mm
0
100
200 km

MAGHREB
Agriculture and Industry

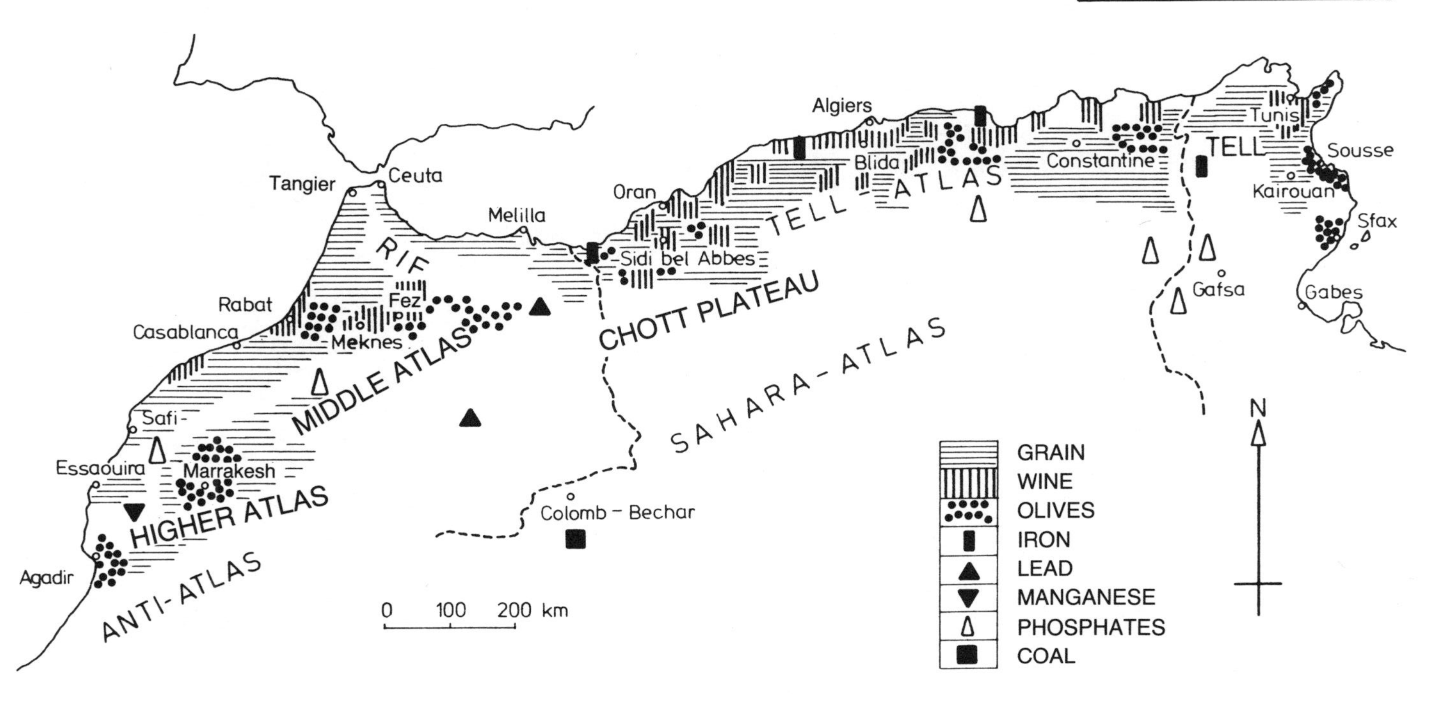
Tangier
Ceuta
Melilla
Oran
Algiers
Blida
Constantine
Tunis
TELL
Sousse
Kairouan
Sfax
Gabes
Gafsa
RIF
Fez
Rabat
Casablanca
Meknes
Sidi bel Abbes
TELL - ATLAS
CHOTT PLATEAU
SAHARA - ATLAS
MIDDLE ATLAS
Safi
Essaouira
Marrakesh
HIGHER ATLAS
Agadir
ANTI-ATLAS
Colomb - Bechar
0
100
200 km
GRAIN
WINE
OLIVES
IRON
LEAD
MANGANESE
PHOSPHATES
COAL
N

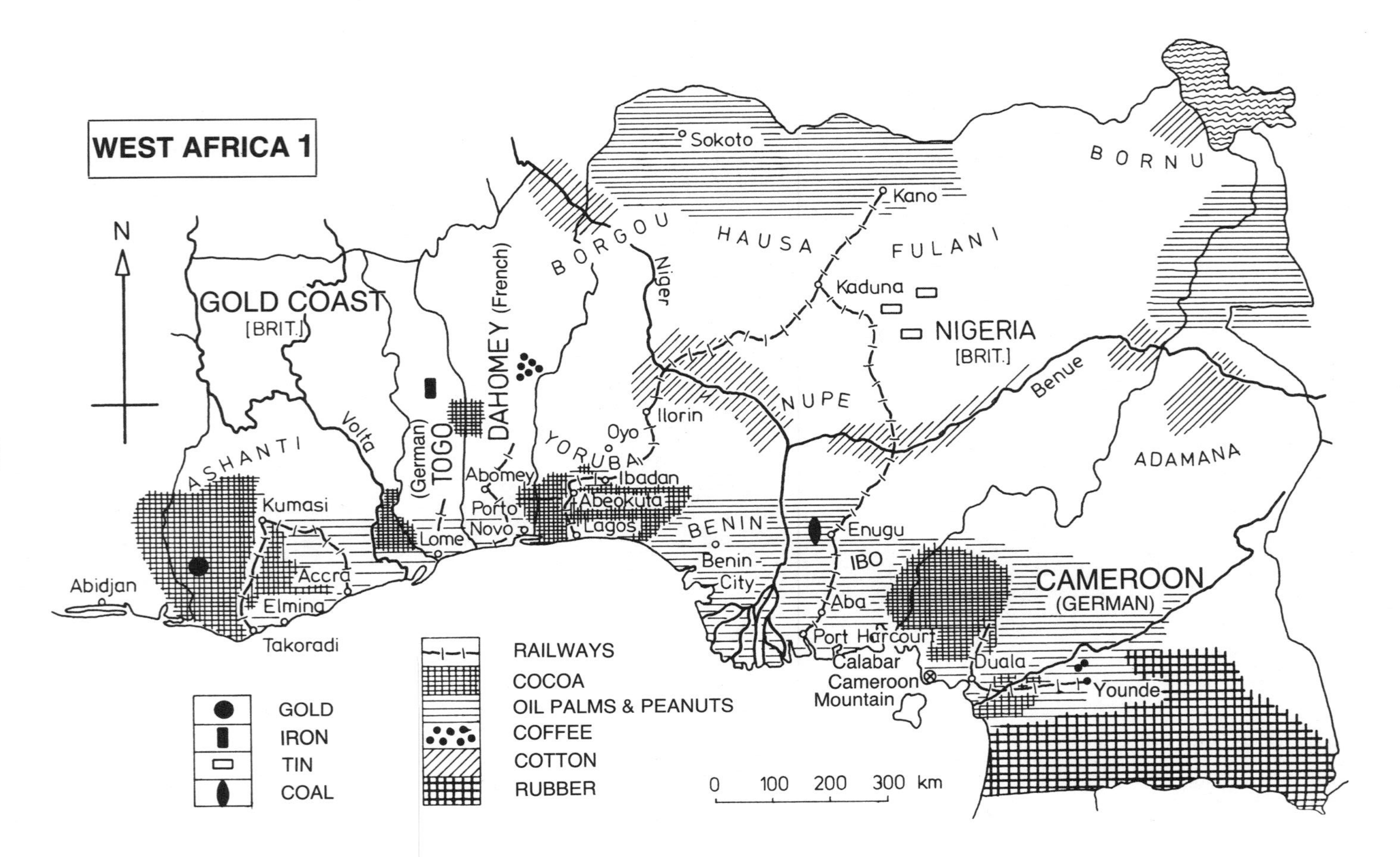

WEST AFRICA 1
N
GOLD COAST
[BRIT.]
A S H A N T I
Kumasi
Accra
Elmina
Takoradi
Abidjan
Volta
(German)
TOGO
Lome
DAHOMEY (French)
Abomey
Porto
Novo
B O R G O U
Y O R U B A
Oyo
Ibadan
Abeokuta
Lagos
Ilorin
Niger
Sokoto
H A U S A
Kano
Kaduna
F U L A N I
N U P E
NIGERIA
[BRIT.]
B E N I N
Benin City
IBO
Enugu
Aba
Port Harcourt
Calabar
Cameroon Mountain
Duala
Benue
B O R N U
ADAMANA
CAMEROON
(GERMAN)
Younde
GOLD
IRON
TIN
COAL
RAILWAYS
COCOA
OIL PALMS & PEANUTS
COFFEE
COTTON
RUBBER
0 100 200 300 km

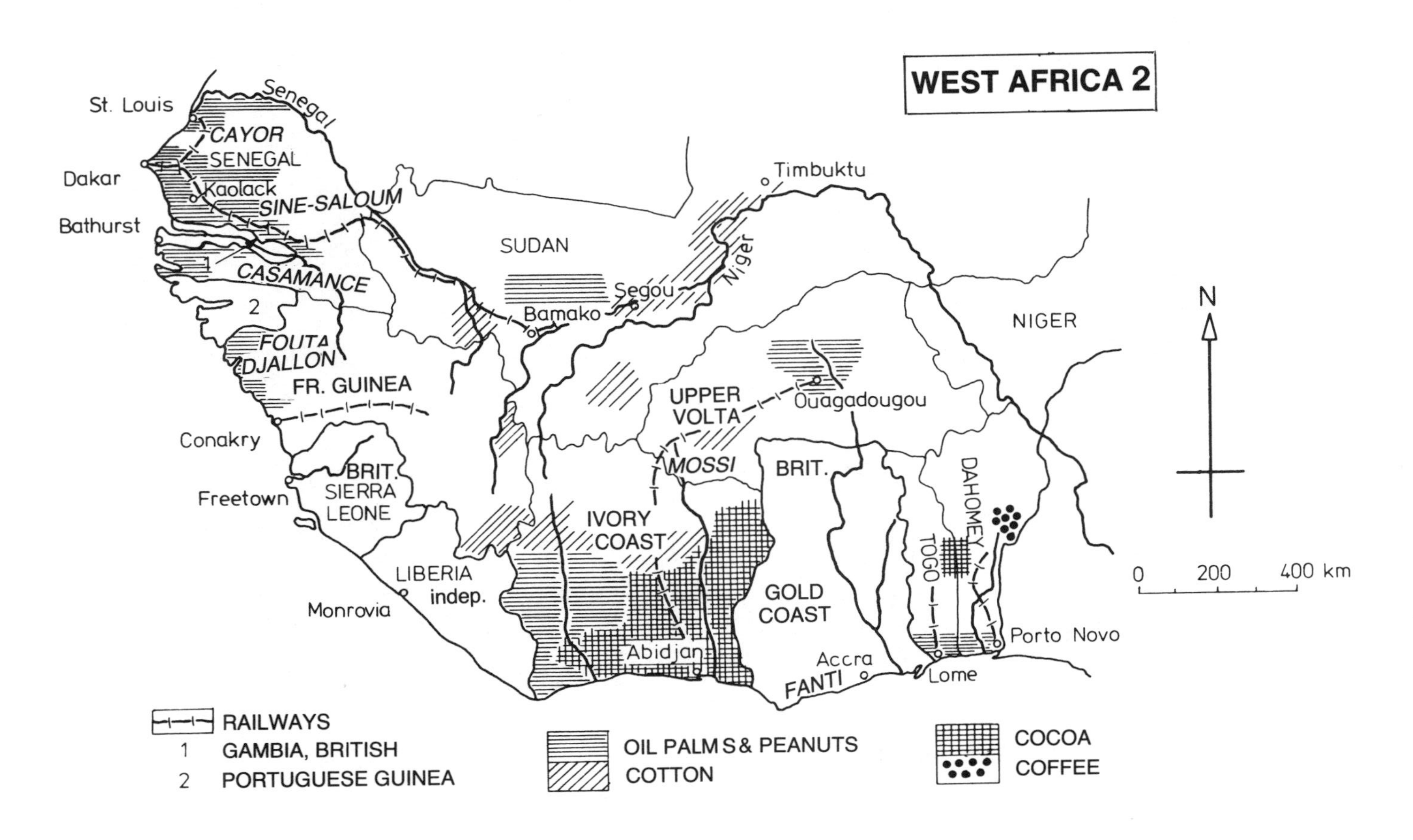
WEST AFRICA 2
St. Louis
Senegal
CAYOR
SENEGAL
Dakar
Kaolack
SINE-SALOUM
Bathurst
1
CASAMANCE
2
FOUTA
DJALLON
FR. GUINEA
Conakry
BRIT.
SIERRA
LEONE
Freetown
LIBERIA
indep.
Monrovia
SUDAN
Segou
Bamako
Timbuktu
Niger
NIGER
UPPER
VOLTA
Ouagadougou
MOSSI
IVORY
COAST
Abidjan
BRIT.
GOLD
COAST
Accra
FANTI
TOGO
DAHOMEY
Lome
Porto Novo
N
0
200
400 km
RAILWAYS
1 GAMBIA, BRITISH
2 PORTUGUESE GUINEA
OIL PALMS & PEANUTS
COTTON
COCOA
COFFEE

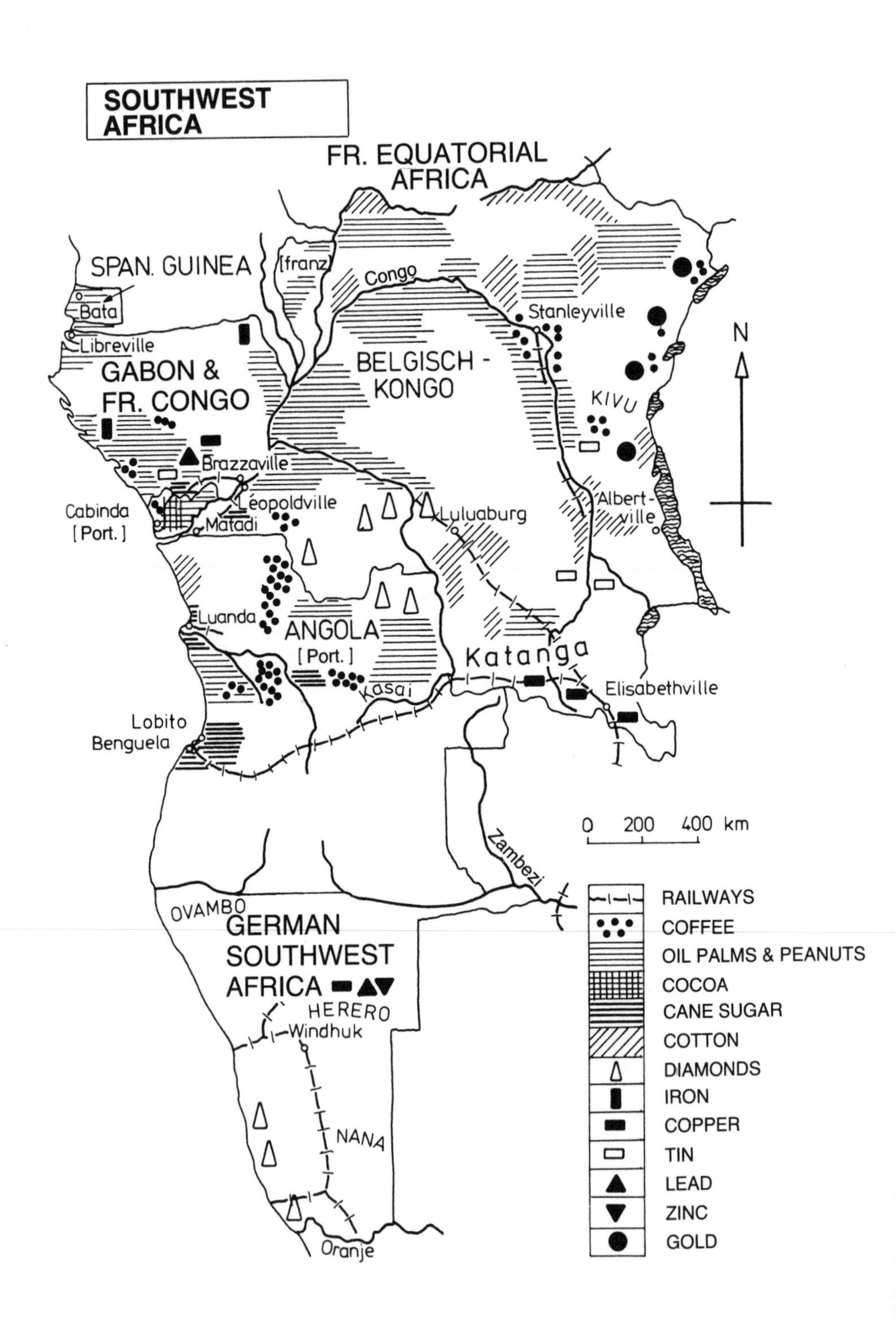
SOUTHWEST AFRICA
FR. EQUATORIAL AFRICA
SPAN. GUINEA
[franz]
Congo
Bata
Libreville
GABON & FR. CONGO
BELGISCH - KONGO
Stanleyville
KIVU
Brazzaville
Léopoldville
Cabinda [Port.]
Matadi
Luluaburg
Albert-ville
Luanda
ANGOLA [Port.]
Katanga
Elisabethville
Kasai
Lobito
Benguela
0 200 400 km
Zambezi
N
OVAMBO
GERMAN SOUTHWEST AFRICA
HERERO
Windhuk
NANA
Oranje
RAILWAYS
COFFEE
OIL PALMS & PEANUTS
COCOA
CANE SUGAR
COTTON
DIAMONDS
IRON
COPPER
TIN
LEAD
ZINC
GOLD

RHODESIA AND MOZAMBIQUE

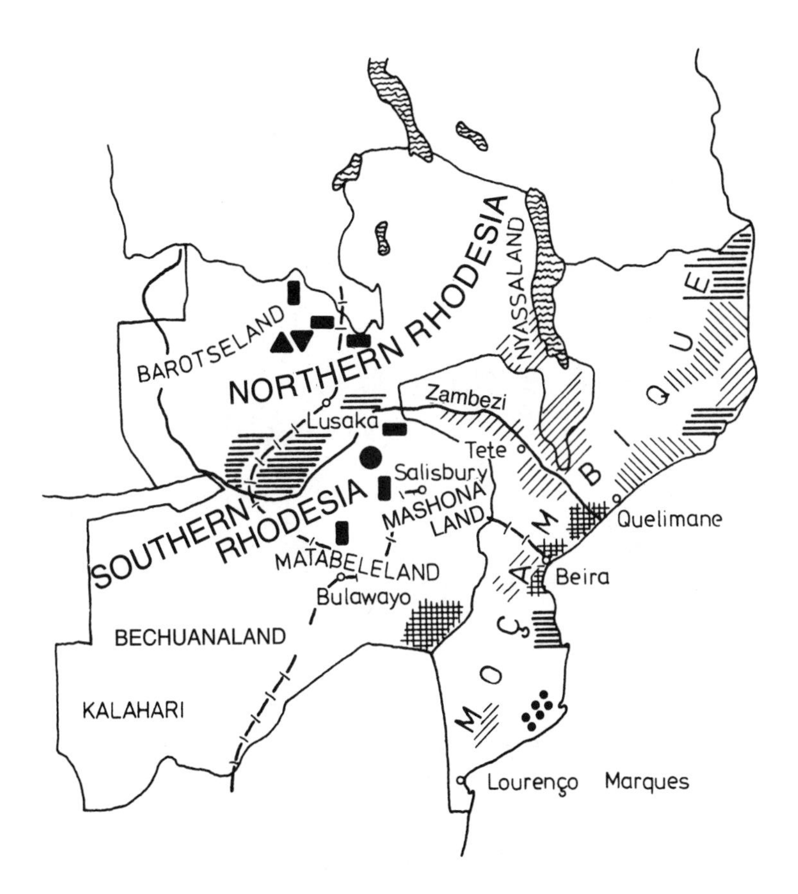

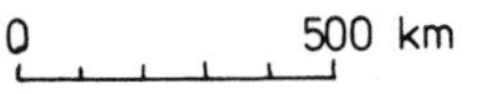

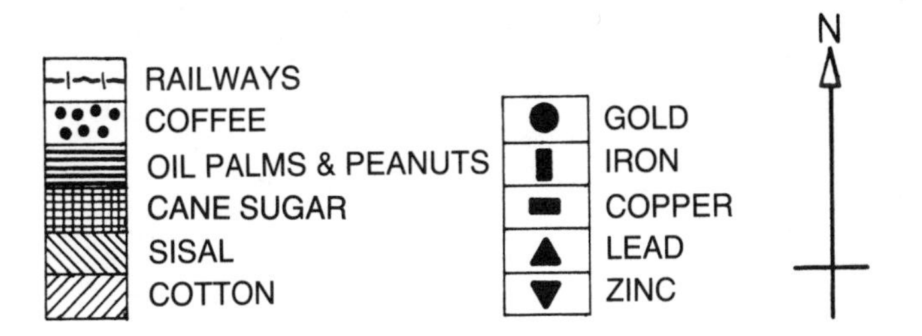

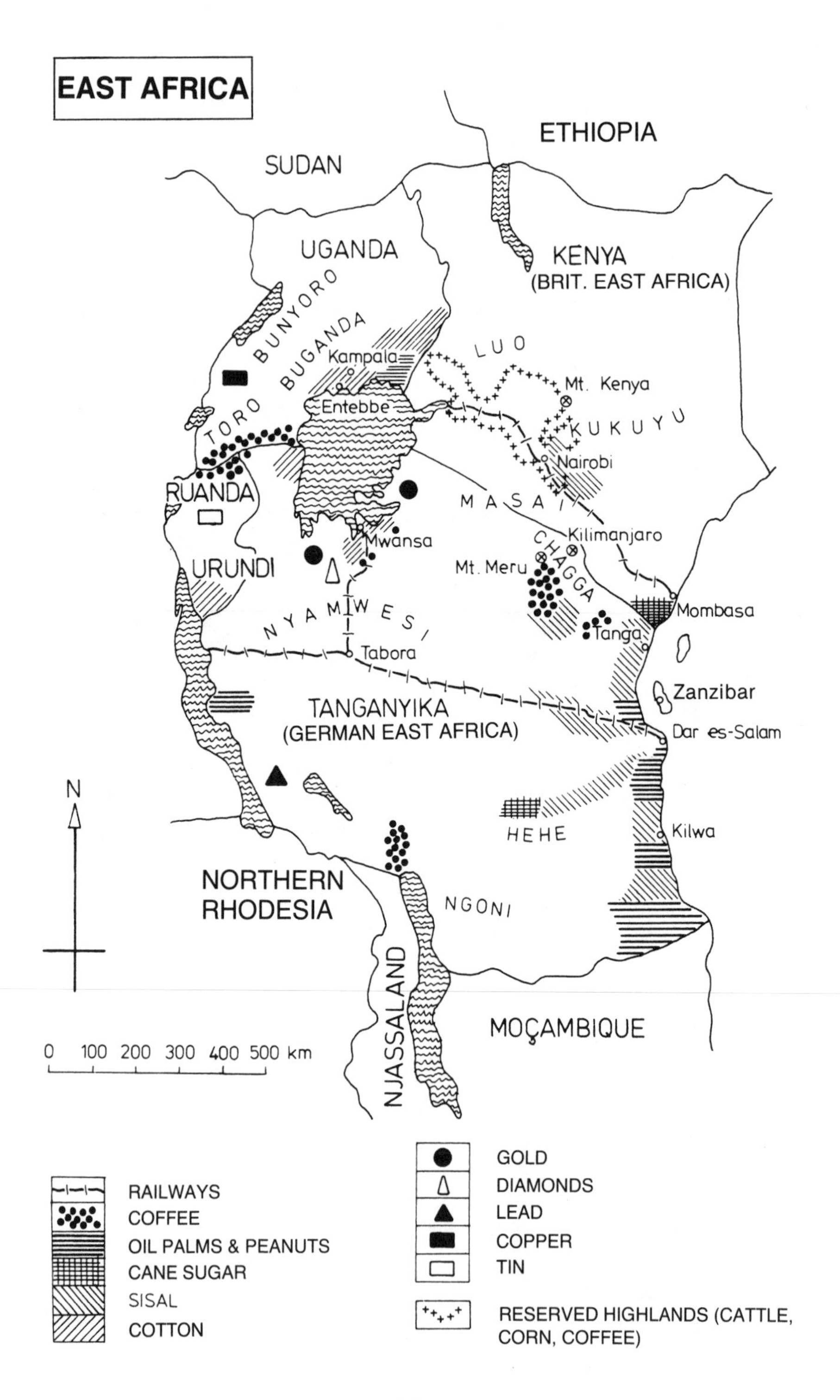
EAST AFRICA
ETHIOPIA
SUDAN
UGANDA
KENYA
(BRIT. EAST AFRICA)
BUNYORO
BUGANDA
TORO
LUO
Kampala
Entebbe
Mt. Kenya
KUKUYU
Nairobi
RUANDA
MASAI
Mwansa
Kilimanjaro
CHAGGA
URUNDI
Mt. Meru
NYAMWESI
Mombasa
Tanga
Tabora
Zanzibar
TANGANYIKA
(GERMAN EAST AFRICA)
Dar es-Salam
N
HEHE
Kilwa
NORTHERN
RHODESIA
NGONI
NJASSALAND
MOÇAMBIQUE
0 100 200 300 400 500 km
RAILWAYS
COFFEE
OIL PALMS & PEANUTS
CANE SUGAR
SISAL
COTTON
GOLD
DIAMONDS
LEAD
COPPER
TIN
RESERVED HIGHLANDS (CATTLE, CORN, COFFEE)

LIST OF WORKS CITED

This listing gives short titles and references to full citations for all works cited in the notes or tables. When the proper entry is by title rather than by personal name (e.g., *History of East Africa*) a "see" reference is usually provided under the name of the editor or compiler. Similarly, short titles of government documents give "see" references to the proper corporate entries (e.g., *Pim Report*, see Gt. Brit., Col. Off., Col. 145). The parenthetical reference after the short title gives the chapter abbreviation and note number for the full citation. Chapter abbreviations used are: B (Burma), BC (Belgian Congo), BCEA (British Central and East Africa), BI (British India), BPE (British Protectorate over Egypt), BWA (British West Africa), C (Ceylon), FM (French Maghreb), FV (French Vietnam), FWEA (French West and Equatorial Africa), GC (German Colonies in Africa), M (Malaya), NI (Netherlands Indies), P (Preface), PA (Portuguese Africa), SU (Summing Up).

Abbott, G. C., "A Re-Examination of the Colonial Development Act" (SU, n40)
Abdallah, R., "Le Néo-Destour" (FM n126)
Adas, M., "Immigrant Asians and the Economic Impact of European Imperialism" (B, n7)
Afigbo, A. E., "The Native Treasury Question under the Warrant Chief System in Eastern Nigeria" (BWA n31)
———, "Revolution and Reaction in Eastern Nigeria, 1900-1929" (BWA, n31)
———, "The Warrant Chief System in Eastern Nigeria" (BWA, n31)
Ageron, C. R., *Les Algériens Musulmans et la France* (FM, n1)
———, "L'Emir Khalêd, Petit-fils d'Abd el-Kader" (FM, n113)
———, "L'Evolution Politique de L'Algérie sous la Second Empire" (FM, n8)
———, "Gambetta et la Réprise de l'Expansion Coloniale" (FM, n18)
———, "Jules Ferry et la Question Algérienne en 1882" (FM, n12)
———, *Histoire de l'Algérie Contemporaine* (FM, n1)
———, "Le Mouvement 'Jeune Algérien' de 1900 à 1923" (FM, n109)
———, "Les Paysans Algériens du Constantinois devant la Fiscalité Française et la Crise Economique" (FM, n49)
———, "La Politique Berbère du Protectorat Marocain de 1913 à 1934" (FM, n129)
———, *Politiques Coloniales au Maghreb* (FM, n4)
———, "Premières Négociations Franco-Algériens" (FM, n4)
Ajalbert, J., *Les Destinées de l'Indochine* (FV, n17)
Ajayi, J. F. Ade, *Christian Missions in Nigeria, 1841-1891* (BWA, n88)
———, "Nineteenth Century Origins of Nigerian Nationalism," (BWA, n84)
———, and M. Crowder (eds.), *History of West Africa* (BWA, n3)
Albertini, R. von, *Decolonization* (P, n23)
———, ed., *Moderne Kolonialgeschichte* (P, n12)

L'Algérie Français (FM, n10)
Allen, G. C., "Industrialization of the Far East" (BI, n238)
———, and A. Donnithorne, *Indonesia and Malaya* (M, n12)
Allen, J. De V., "Malayan Civil Service" (M, n11)
Alsdorf, L., *Vorderindien* (BI, n277)
Amaral, I. de, *Aspectos do Povoamento Branco de Angola* (PA, n47)
Amin, S., *L'Afrique de l'Ouest Bloquée* (FWEA, n36)
———, *L'Economie du Maghreb* (FM, n99)
———, *Le Monde des Affaires Sénégalais* (FWEA, n39)
———, "La Politique Française a l'Egard de la Bourgeoise Commerçante Sénégalais" (FWEA, n39)
———, and C. Coquery-Vidrovitch, *Histoire Economique du Congo, 1880-1968* (FWEA, n63)
Amon d'Aby, F. J., *La Côte d'Ivoire dans la Cité Africaine* (FWEA n55)
Amphoux, M., *L'Evolution de l'Agriculture Européenne au Maroc* (FM, n89)
Andrus, J. R., *Burmese Economic Life* (B, n5)
Anene, J. C., *Southern Nigeria in Transition, 1885-1906* (BWA, n11)
Angola, Repartição de Estatística Geral, *Anuário Estatístico* (PA, n26)
Angoulvant, G. L., "Des Réformes en Endochine" (FV, n80)
———, *La Pacification de la Côte d'Ivoire, 1908-1915* (FWEA, n11)
Anlagen, see Germany, Reichstag (GC, n52)
AN Micro, see France, Archives Nationales (FWEA, n89)
Annuaire de Documentation Coloniale Comparée (BC, n31)
ANSOM, see France, Archives Nationales (FV, n57)
Ansprenger, F., *Politik in Schwartzen Afrika* (P, n1)
Anstey, R., *King Leopold's Legacy* (BC, n1)
Anstey, V. P., *The Economic Development of India* (BI, n76)
Antologia Colonial Portuguesa (PA, n30)
L'AOF (FWEA, n104)
Arasaratnam, S., "Die Inder in Malay in Geschichte und Gegenwart" (M, n31)
———, *Indians in Malaya and Singapore* (M, n31)
———, "Nationalism, Communalism and National Unity in Ceylon" (C, n31)
Archiv für Eisenbahnwesen (BI, n169)
Ardenne de Tizac, F. C. de, *Indochine S.O.S.* (FV, n57)
Argov, D. *Moderates and Extremists in the Indian Nationalist Movement* (BI, n307)
Arx, A. von, "L'Evolution Politique en Indonésie de 1900 à 1942" (NI, n76)
Aspects of Central African History (BCEA, n1)
Atanda, J. A., "The Iseyin-Okeiho Rising of 1916" (BWA, n30)
Atger, P., *La France en Côte d'Ivoire de 1843 à 1893* (FWEA, n9)
Austen, R. A., *Northwest Tanzania under German and British Rule* (GC, n58)
Autra, R., "Historique de l'Enseignement en AOF" (FWEA, n79)
Ayache, A., "Les Grèves de Juin 1936 au Maroc" (FM, n135)
———, *Le Maroc* (FM, n76)
Ayandele, E. A., "Background of the 'Duel' between Crowther and Goldie on the Lower Niger, 1857-1885" (BWA, n88)
———, *Holy Johnson, Pioneer of African Nationalism, 1836-1917* (BWA, n90)
———, *The Missionary Impact on Modern Nigeria, 1842-1914* (BWA, n9)
Aydelotte, W. O., *Bismarck and British Colonial Policy* (GC, n5)
Aye Hlaing, see Hlaing (B, n5)
Azevedo, J. M. C. de, *Subsídios para o Estudo de Economica de Angola nos Ultimos cem Anos* (PA, n52)
Azikiwe, N., *My Odyssey* (BWA, n101)
Aziz, V. A., "Land Disintegration and Land Policy in Malaya" (M, n33)

Bade, K. J., *Friedrich Fabri und der Imperialismus der Bismarckzeit* (GC, n7)
Baer, G. "The Dissolution of the Egyptian Village Community" (BPE, n58)
———, *A History of Landownership in Modern Egypt, 1800-1950* (BPE, n3)
———, "Social Change in Egypt" (BPE, n1)
———, *Studies in the Social History of Modern Egypt* (BPE, n5)
———, "Submissiveness and the Revolt of the Fellah" (BPE, n98)
———, "The Village Shaykh, 1800-1950" (BPE, n5)
Bagchi, A. K., "European and Indian Entrepreneurship in India, 1900-1930" (BI, n239)
———, *Private Investment in India, 1900-1939* (BI, n141)
Bairoch, P., *Diagnostique de l'Evolution Economique du Tiers-Monde*, 1900-1966 (SU, n9)
———, *Révolution Industrielle et Sous-Développement* (SU, n9)
Balandier, G., "Messianisme et Nationalisme en Afrique Noir" (FWEA, n107)
———, "La Situation Coloniale" (P, n12)
Bald, D., *Deutsch-Ostafrika 1900-1914* (GC, n66)
Baldwin, R. E., *Economic Development and Export Growth* (BCEA, n76)
Ballard, J. A., "Les Incidents de 1923 à Porto Novo" (FWEA, n106)
Ballhaus, J., "Die Landkonzessionsgesellschaften" (GC, n40)
Banerjea, S., *A Nation in the Making* (BI, n279)
Banerjee, A. K., *India's Balance of Payments* (BI, n254)
Baran, P. A., *The Political Economy of Growth* (P, n10)
———, *Politik und Ökonomie des wirtschaftlichen Wachstums* (P, n10)
———, *Über die politische Ökonomie der Rückständigkeit* (P, n6)
Bardin, P., "Les Débuts Difficiles de Protectorat Tunisien (Mai 1881-Avril 1882)" (FM, n20)
———, *La Vie d'un Douar* (FM, n74)
Baring, E., "Memorandum on the Present Situation in Egypt" (BPE, n88)
———, *Modern Egypt* (BPE, n28)
Barrier, N. G., "The Formulation and Enactment of the Punjab Alienation of Land Bill" (BI, n109)
———, *The Punjab Alienation of Land Bill of 1900* (BI, n109)
Barrows, L. C., "The Merchants and General Faidherbe" (FWEA n2)
Bastianpillai, B., "From Coffee to Tea in Ceylon" (C, n8)
Bastide, R., "Class Protest and Development in Brazil and Portuguese Africa" (PA, n24)
———, "Lusitropology, Race and Nationalism" (PA, n24)
Bastin, J., and R. Winks (comps.), *Malaysia* (M, n1)
Basu, A., "Indian Primary Education, 1900-1920" (BI, n276)
Bauer, P. T., "Some Aspects of the Malayan Rubber Slump 1929-1933" (M, n19)
Baxendole, A. S., and D. Johnson, "Uganda and Great Britain" (BCEA, n37)
Bayly, C. A., "Patrons and Politics in Northern India" (BI, n295)
Beaglehole, T. H., *Thomas Munro and the Development of Administrative Policy in Madras, 1792-1818* (BI, n41)
Bearce, G. D., *British Attitudes toward India, 1784-1858* (BI, n4)
Belal, A. A., *L'Investissement au Maroc (1912-1964)* (FM, n90)
Belchior, M. D., "Evolução Politica do Ensino em Moçambique" (PA, n27)
Belgium, Parlement, Senat, *Rapport de la Mission Senatoriale du Congo* (BC, n24)
Benda, H. J., "Christiaan Snouck Hurgronje and the Foundations of Dutch Islamic Policy in Indonesia" (NI, n67)
———, "Indonesian Islam under the Japanese Occupation, 1942-1945" (NI, n75)
———, "The Pattern of Administrative Reforms in the Closing Years of Dutch Rule in Indonesia" (NI, n73)
Bender, G. J., "Planned Rural Settlements in Angola, 1900-1968" (PA, n47)
Bengal, Land Revenue Commission, *Report*. . . (BI, n94)
Berger, E. L., *Labour, Race, and Colonial Rule* (BCEA, n76)

Berger, M., *Bureaucracy and Society in Modern Egypt* (BPE, n32)
Berkhuysen, A. P. H., *De drainagetheorie voor Indonesie* (NI, n49)
Bernard, Lt. Col. F., "La Réforme de l'Indochine" (FV, n11)
Bernard, P., *Nouveaux Aspects du Problème Economique Indochinois* (FV, n25)
———, *Le Problème Economique Indochinois* (FV, n25)
Berque, J., *L'Égypte* (BPE, n1)
———, *Le Maghreb entre les deux Guerres* (FM, n33)
Berrill, K., "Auslandskapital und Take-off" (SU, n13)
Besters, H., see *Entwicklungspolitik* (SU, n15)
Bhatia, B. M., *Famines in India* (BI, n67)
Bhutani, V. C., "Some Aspects of the Administration of Lord Curzon" (BI, n302)
Bidwell, R. L., *Morocco under Colonial Rule* (FM, n30)
Bigg-Wither, F., "Cleaning Up Burma's Murder Zone" (B, n4)
Birla, G. D., "Industrialization in India" (BI, n229)
Birmingham, D., "Themes and Resources of Angolan History" (PA, n1)
Blackett, Sir B., "The Economic Progress of India" (BI, n215)
Bley, H., *Kolonialherrschaft und Sozialstruktur in Deutsch-Südwestafrika, 1894-1914* (GC, n25)
Bloch, R., "Die französischen Colons im Protectorat Tunesien, 1923-1929" (FM, n26)
Blunt, W. S., "Ideas about India" (BI, n44)
Blyn, G., *Agricultural Trends in India, 1891-1947* (BI, n87)
Boeke, J. H., *Economics and Economic Policy of Dual Societies* (SU, n16)
———, *The Structure of the Netherlands Indian Economy* (NI, n20)
Bogorad, Y., "Tunesischer Nationalismus, 1934-1938" (FM, n126)
Bohnet, M., comp., *Das Nord-Süd Problem* (P, n6)
Boisson, J., *L'Histoire du Chad et de Fort Archambault* (FWEA, n70)
Borchardt, K., *Europas Wirtschaftgeschichte* (P, n19)
Borsa, G., "La Proprietà della terra in India sotto il dominio inglese" (BI, n92)
Bouche, D., "Autrefois, notre Pays s'appelait la Gaule" (FWEA, n81)
———, "L'Enseignement dans les Territoires Française de l'Afrique Occidentale" (FWEA, n79)
Bourdillon, *Memorandum*, see Nigeria, Governor-General. . .(BWA, n38)
Bourret, F. M., *Ghana, the Road to Independence, 1919-1957* (BWA, n3)
Bouvier, J., "Les Traits Majeurs de l'Impérialisme Français avant 1914" (SU, n52)
Bower, P. A., *Mining, Commerce, and Finance in Nigeria* (BWA, n51)
Braibanti, R. J. D. (ed.), *Asian Bureaucratic Systems Emergent from the British Imperial Tradition* (BI, n31)
Braun, R., et al., see *Industrielle Revolution* (SU, n13)
Brausch, G.E.J.B. "Le Paternalism" (BC, n12)
Brett, E. A., *Colonialism and Underdevelopment in East Africa* (BCEA, n1)
Brignon, J., et al., see *Histoire du Maroc* (FM, n83)
Britain and Germany in Africa (BWA, n1)
Brocheux, P., "Grands Propriétaires et Fermiers dans l'ouest de la Cochinchine pendant la Période Coloniale" (FV, n35)
Broomfield, J. H., *Elite Conflict in a Plural Society* (BI, n129)
———, "The Non-Cooperation Decision of 1920" (BI, n324)
Brötel, D., *Französischer Imperialismus in Vietnam* (FV, n4)
Brown, D. M., ed., *The Nationalist Movement* (BI, n308)
Brown, J. M., *Gandhi's Rise to Power* (BI, n317)
Brown, R., "Aspects of the Scramble for Matabeleland" (BCEA, n6)
Brun, E., and J. Hersh, *Kapitalismens udviklingssystem* (P, n10)
———, *Kapitalismus im Weltsystem* (P, n10)
Brunschwig, H., *L'Avènement de l'Afrique Noire du XIXe Siècle à nos Jours* (BWA, n1)

———, "De la Résistance Africain à l'Impérialisme Européan" (BWA, n1)
———, *L'Expansion Allemande Outre-Mer du XIXe Siècle à nos Jours* (GC, n1)
———, "French Exploration and Conquest in Tropical Africa from 1865 to 1898" (FWEA, n1)
Buchanan, D. H., *The Development of Capitalistic Enterprise in India* (BI, n167)
Bull, M., "Imperial Rule in Northern Nigeria, 1906-1911" (BWA, n25)
Bulletin de la Chambre, see Cochin China (FV, n48)
Burma, Land and Agriculture Committee, *Report. . . 1938* (B, n9)
"Butler Collection," see Gt. Brit., India Office (BI, n30)
Butler, H. B., *Problémes du Travail en Orient* (C, n13)
Büttner, F. (ed.), *Reform und Revolution in der islamischen Welt* (BPE, n87)

Cabral, A. C., *Unité et Lutte* (PA, n25)
———, *Unity and Struggle* (PA, n25)
Cady, J. F., *A History of Modern Burma* (B, n1)
Caldwell, J.A.M., "Indonesian Exports and Production from the Decline of the Culture System to the First World War" (NI, p. 168)
Callis, H. G., *Foreign Capital in South East Asia* (B, n20)
Calvelli, M.A.E., *Etat de la Propriété Rurale en Algérie* (FM, n39)
Cambon, H., *Histoire de la Régence de Tunis* (FM, n22)
Cambon, P., *Correspondance, 1870-1924* (FM, n21)
Cambridge Economic History (BI, n240)
Cardoso, F. H., "Brasilien" (SU, n35)
Cardozo, J., "Finance et Crédit" (PA, n38)
Carstairs, R., *The Little World of an Indian District Officer* (BI, n35)
Casely Hayford, see Hayford (BWA, nn86, 91)
Castro Lopo, J. de, *Jornalismo de Angola* (PA, n55)
Ceylon, Banking Commission, *Report* (C, n25)
———, Ministry of Labour, Industry and Commerce, *Bulletin* (C, n15)
Chailley-Bert, J., *Paul Bert au Tonkin* (FV, n9)
Challaye, F., "Le Congo Français" (FWEA, n67)
Chalux [pseud.], *Un An au Congo Belge* (BC, n20)
Chand, T., *History of the Freedom Movement in India* (BI, n11)
Chandra, B., "Reinterpretation of 19th Century Indian Economy" (BI, n86)
———, *The Rise and Growth of Economic Nationalism in India* (BI, n226)
Charlesworth, N., "The Myth of the Deccan Riots of 1875" (BI, n101)
Charney, J.-P., *La Vie Musulmane en Algérie* (FM, n51)
Chassaing, P., "La Naissance du Prolétariat en Indochine" (FV, n57)
Chaudhuri, B. B., "Growth of Commercial Agriculture in Bengal, 1859-1885" (BI, n152)
Chaudhuri, K. N., "India's International Economy in the Nineteenth Century" (BI, n258)
Cheng Siok Hwa, "The Development of the Burmese Rice Industry in the Late Nineteenth Century" (B, n5)
Chesneaux, J., *Contribution à l'Histoire de la Nation Vietnamienne* (FV, n1)
———, "Entwicklungsstufen der nationalen Bewegung Vietnams, 1862-1940" (FV, n76)
Chilcote, R., "Dependency" (P, n6)
——— (comp.). *Protest and Resistance in Angola and Brazil* (PA, n24)
Childs, G. M., *Umbundu Kinship* (PA, n3)
Chirol, Sir V., *Fifty Years in a Changing World* (BPE, n94)
———, *India Old and New* (BI, n314)
———, *Indian Unrest* (BI, n314)
Cochin China, Chambre d'Agriculture, *Bulletin de la Chambre d'Agriculture* (FV, n48)
Cohen, W. B., *Rulers of Empire* (FWEA, n20)
Cohn, B. S., "The British in Benares" (BI, n42)
Coleman, J. S., *Nigeria, Background to Nationalism* (BWA, n3)

———, and C. G. Rosberg (eds.), *Political Parties and National Integration in Tropical Africa* (FWEA, n108)
Collins, Sir C., "Ceylon" (C, n2)
Companhia de Diamantes de Angola, *A Short Report on its Work in Angola* (PA, n42)
Conference on the Modern History of Egypt, University of London, 1965, *Political and Social Change in Modern Egypt* (BPE, n1)
Congo: Revue Général de la Colonie Belge (BC, n13)
Congrès Colonial, Marseille, 1906, *Compte Rendu des Travaux* (FV, n8)
Contribution à l'Histoire, see Indochina, French, Direction des Affaires Politiques... (FV, n89)
Coquery-Vidrovitch, C., *Le Congo au temps des Grandes Compagnies Concessionaires, 1898-1930* (FWEA, n63)
———, "L'Echec d'une Tentative Economique" (FWEA, n63)
———, "French Colonization in Africa to 1920" (FWEA, n20)
———, and H. Moniot, *L'Afrique Noire de 1800 à nos Jours* (BWA, n1)
Corea, J.C.A., "One Hundred Years of Education in Ceylon" (C, n21)
Cornevin, R., "Les Divers Episodes de la Lutte contre le Royaume d'Abomey" (FWEA, n14)
———, "The Germans in Africa before 1918," (BWA, n1)
———, *Histoire du Congo* (BC, n1)
———, *Histoire du Dahomey* (FWEA, n14)
———, *Histoire du Togo* (GC, n49)
———, with M. Cornevin, *L'Afrique Noire de 1919 à nos Jours* (BWA, n1)
"Correspondence with Regard to Native Policy in Northern Rhodesia" (BCEA, n84)
Cosnier, H., *L'Ouest Africain Français* (FWEA, n45)
Cotter, M. G., "Towards a Social History of the Vietnamese Southward Movement" (FV, n2)
Couceiro, H. de P., *Angola* (PA, n35)
Courageot, P., *Les Communautés Agraires du Maroc et le Protectorat Français* (FM, n80)
Courrier d'Haiphong (FV, n59)
Cowan, C. D. (ed.), *The Economic Development of Southeast Asia* (B, n5)
Crane, R., *Aspects of Economic Development in South Asia* (C, n14)
Cromer, Lord, see Baring, E. (BPE, nn28, 88)
Crouchley, A. E., *Investment of Foreign Capital in Egyptian Companies and Public Debt* (BPE, n75)
Crowder, M., "Indirekte Herrschaft" (FWEA, n22)
———, *The Story of Nigeria* (BWA, n3)
———, *West Africa under Colonial Rule* (P, n8)
———, *West African Resistance* (BWA, n3)
———, and O. Ikime, see *West African Chiefs* (BWA, n20)
Cruise O'Brien, R., "Lebanese Entrepreneurs in Senegal" (FWEA, n39)
Cunha, J. M., da S., *O Trabhalho Indígena* (PA, n32)
Cunha Leal, F. P. da, *Caligula em Angola* (PA, n20)
Curtin, P., *The Atlantic Slave Trade* (PA, n3)

Dahm, B., *Emanzipationsversuche von kolonialer Herrschaft in Südostasien* (NI, n6)
———, *History of Indonesia in the Twentieth Century* (NI, n1)
———, *Sukarnos Kampf um Indonesiens Unabhängigheit* (P, n1)
Darkoah, M.B.K., "Togoland under the Germans" (GC, n49)
Darling, M. L., *The Punjab Peasant in Prosperity and Debt* (BI, n112)
Das, M. N., *India under Morley and Minto* (BI, n305)
Davis, K., *The Population of India and Pakistan* (BI, n58)
Deane, P., "The Long Term Trends in World Economic Growth" (SU, n25)
Deeb, M., "The 1919 Popular Rising" (BPE, n96)
Déherme, G., *L'Afrique Occidentale Française* (FWEA, n28)

Dekker, E. D., *Max Havelaar* (NI, n9)
Delavignette, R. L., *Les Paysans Noirs* (FWEA, n41)
———, *Service Africain* (FWEA, n24)
———, *Les Vrais Chefs de l'Empire* (FWEA, n19)
Demontès, V., *L'Algérie Agricole* (FM, n38)
Dernburg, B., *Koloniale Erziehung* (GC, n54)
———, *Zielpunkte des deutschen Kolonialwesens* (GC, n54)
Desai, A. R., *Social Background of Indian Nationalism* (BI, n103)
Deschamps, H. (ed.), *Histoire Générale de l'Afrique Noire* (BWA, n1)
———, "Und nun, Lord Lugard?" (FWEA, n22)
Devallée, J., "La Main de Oeuvre en Indochine" (FV, n53)
The Development of Indigenous Trade and Markets in West Africa (FWEA, n40)
Devilliers, P., *L'Asie du Sud-Est* (FV, n82)
Dewey, C., "The End of the Imperialism of Free Trade" (BI, n225)
———, and A. G. Hopkins (eds.), *The Imperial Impact* (BI, n225)
"Diamenten und Finanzen" (GC, n77)
Diehn, O., "Kaufmannschaft and deutsche Eingeborenenpolitik," (GC, n48)
Digby, W., *"Prosperous" British India* (BI, n108)
Dike, K. O., *Trade and Politics in the Niger Delta, 1830-1885* (BWA, n7)
Dobbin, C., "The Ilbert Bill" (BI, n44)
Donnison, F. S. V., *Burma* (B, n1)
Dorsenne, J., "Le Péril Rouge en Indochine" (FV, n96)
Doumer, P., *L'Indochine Français (Souvenirs)* (FV, n14)
Douwes Dekker, see Dekker (NI, n9)
Dresch, J., "Recherches sur les Investissements dans l'Union Français Outre-Mer" (FWEA, n75)
———, "La Situation Economique et Sociale de l'Afrique du Nord" (FM, n105)
Dreschler, H., *Südwestafrika unter deutscher Kolonialherrschaft* (GC, n10)
Drummond, I. M., *British Economic Policy and the Empire, 1919-1939* (BI, n190)
———, *Imperial Economic Policy, 1917-1939* (SU, n52)
Duclaux, P., "L'Annam et nous" (FV, n54)
Duffy, J., *Portuguese Africa* (PA, n1)
———, *A Question of Slavery* (PA, n32)
Dumont, R., *Paysanneries aux Abois* (C, n27)
Duncan-Johnstone, "Memorandum" (BWA, n34)
Dutt, R. C., *Economic History of India* (P, n10)
———, "Famines in India and Their Remedy" (BI, n73)
Dutta, A., "Interwar Ceylon" (C, n20)

Edwards, A. C., *The Ovimbundu under Two Sovereignties* (PA, n54)
Eggert, J., *Missionsschule und sozialer Wandel in Ostafrika* (GC, n63)
Ehrler, F., *Handelskonflikte zwischen europäischen Firmen und einheimischen Produzenten in Britisch-Westafrika* (BWA, n63)
Ehrlich, C., "Building and Caretaking" (BWA, n83)
———, "Some Social and Economic Implications of Paternalism in Uganda" (BCEA, n46)
Eisenstadt, S. N., "Social Change and Modernization in African Societies South of the Sahara" (SU, n1)
———, "Soziologische Aspekte der politischen Entwicklung in den Entwicklungsländern," (SU, n1)
Ekejuniba, F., "Omu Kwei, the Merchant Queen of Ossomari" (BWA, n79)
Ekundare, R. O., *An Economic History of Nigeria, 1860-1960* (BWA, n51)
Eli, B., "Paul Doumer in Indochina (1897-1902)" (FV, n10)
Elites in South Asia (BI, n241)

Emerson, R. *Malaysia* (M, n1)
———, and D. K. Fieldhouse, "Colonialism" (P, n11)
England, India Office, *Selections from Despatches*... (BI, n227)
Ennes, A., *Moçambique* (PA, n31)
Entwicklungspolitik (SU, n15)
Esquier, G., *Histoire de l'Algérie* (FM, n16)
Esquisses Sénégalaises (FWEA, n46)
Essays on Gandhian Politics (BI, n321)
Etienne, G., *L'Inde* (BI, n83)
"Etudes des Rapports entre les Propriétaires Fonciers et les Fermiers Métayers et Ouvriers Agricoles" (FV, n38)
Etudes Maghrébines (FM, n109)
Eyck, E., *Bismarck* (GC, n5)

Fajana, A., "Colonial Control and Education," (BWA, n50)
Fall, B. B., *The Two Vietnams* (FV, n58)
Fearn, H., *An African Economy* (BCEA, n30)
Fernando, P. T., "The British Raj and the 1915 Communal Riots in Ceylon" (C, n30)
Ferreira, V., *A Situação de Angola* (PA, n18)
Feyssel, P. de, *L'Endettement Agraire in Cochinchine* (FV, n43)
Fieldhouse, D. K., *The Colonial Empires* (P, n4)
Fischer, W., "Das Verhältnis von Staat and Wirtschaft in Deutschland am Beginn der Industrialisierung" (SU, n37)
Flint, J. E., "Nigeria, The Colonial Experience" (BWA, n5)
———, *Sir George Goldie and the Making of Nigeria* (BWA, n8)
Forde, C. D., and R. Scott, *The Native Economies of Nigeria* (BWA, n51
Fouquet, J., "La Traite des Arachides" (FWEA, n41)
France, Archives Nationales, Micro (FWEA, n89)
———, Archives Nationales, Section d'Outre-Mer (FV, n57)
———, *Journel Officiel* (FWEA, n16)
France and Britain in Africa (BWA, n1)
La France dans l'Afrique Occidentale, 1879-1883 (FWEA, n4)
Franck, L. (ed.), *Etudes de Colonisation Comparée* (BC, n13)
———, "Quelques Aspects de notre Politique Indigène au Congo" (BC, n13)
Frank, A. G., *Capitalism and Underdevelopment in Latin America* (P, n6)
———, "Die Entwicklung der Unterentwicklung" (P, n6)
Frankel, S. H., *Capital Investment in Africa* (BC, n21)
Freedman, M., "The Growth of a Plural Society in Malaya" (M, n29)
Freeman, D., "The Present Condition and Future Government of Malaya" (M, n13)
French-Speaking Africa (SU, n1)
Fritsch, B., *Die Vierte Welt* (P, n14)
Frochot, M., *L'Empire Colonial Portugais* (PA, n10)
Frykenberg, R. E. (ed.), *Land Control and Social Structure in Indian History* (BI, n98)
Furnivall, J. S. *Colonial Policy and Practice* (B, n1)
———, *Netherlands India* (NI, n1)

Gad, J., *Die Betriebsverhältnisse der Farmen des mittleren Hererolandes* (GC, n83)
Gadgil, D. R., *The Industrial Evolution of India in Recent Times, 1860-1939* (BI, n179)
Gadille, J., "L'Agriculture Européenne au Maroc" (FM, n87)
Gagzow, B., *Aussenwirtschaftsorientierte Entwicklungspolitik kleiner Länder* (C, n19)
Galbraith, J. S., *Mackinnon and East Africa, 1878-1895* (BCEA, n3)
Gallagher, J., "Congress in Decline" (BI, n346)
Gallissot, R., "Abd el-Kader et la Nationalité Algérienne" (FM, 3)

———, *Le Patronat Européen au Maroc* (FM, n96)
Galtung, J., "Eine strukturelle Theorie des Imperialismus" (P, n7)
Galvão, H., *Angola* (PA, n36)
———, *Santa Maria* (PA, n36)
———, and C. Selvagem, *Império Ultramarino Português* (PA, n11)
Gangulee, N., *The Indian Peasant and his Environment* (BI, n115)
Ganguli, B. N., *Dadabhai Naoroji and the Drain Theory* (BI, n250)
Ganiage, J., *L'Expansion Coloniale de la France sous la Troisième République* (FM, n18)
———, *Les Origins du Protectorat Français en Tunisie, 1861-1881* (FM, n18)
———, et al., *L'Afrique au XXe Siècle* (BWA, n1)
Ganier, G., "Lat Dyor et le Chemin de Fer d'Arachide, 1876-1886" (FWEA, n8)
Gann, L. H., *A History of Northern Rhodesia* (BCEA, n1)
———, and P. Duignan (eds.), *Colonialism in Africa, 1870-1960* (BWA, n1)
Geertz, C., *Agricultural Involution* (NI, n7)
———, *The Social History of an Indonesian Town* (NI, n20)
Geiss, I., "Das Enstehen der modernen Eliten in Afrika seit der Mitte des 19. Jahrhunderts" (BWA, n84)
———, *The Pan-African Movement* (BWA, n84)
———, *Panafrikanismus* (BWA, n84)
Gendarme, R., L'Economie de l'Algérie (FM, n44)
Germany, Reichstag, *Stenographische Berichte* (GC, n8)
———, Reichstag, *Stenographische Berichte...Anlagen* (GC, n52)
Gerschenkron, A., *Economic Backwardness in Historical Perspective* (SU, n31)
Gertzel, C., "Relations between African and European Traders in the Niger Delta, 1880-1896" (BWA, n10)
Ghali, I. A., "L'Egypte Nationaliste et Libérale" (BPE, n85)
Gifford, P., "Indirect Rule" (BWA, n20)
———, and W. R. Lewis (eds.), see *France and Britain in Africa* (BWA, n1)
Gold Coast (Colony), Legislative Council, *Debates* (BWA, n49)
Goldschmidt, A., "The Egyptian Nationalist Party" (BPE, n86)
Goldstein, D., *Liberation ou Annexion aux Chemins Croisés de l'Histoire Tunisienne 1914-1922* (FM, n22)
———, "Mise en Valeur et Mise en Marche Nationale" (FM, n22)
Gopal, R., *Indian Muslims* (BI, n352)
Gopal, S., *British Policy in India, 1858-1905* (BI, n300)
———, *The Viceroyalty of Lord Irwin, 1926-1931* (BI, n333)
Gordon, R., "Non-Cooperation and Council Entry, 1919-1920" (BI, n320)
Gosselin, C., *L'Empire d'Annam* (FV, n5)
Gourou, P., *Indochine Française* (FV, n28)
———, *Land Utilization in French Indochine* (FV, n26)
———, *Les Pays Tropicaux* (SU, n20)
———, *Les Paysans du Delta Tonkinois* (FV, n28)
———, "La Population Rurale de la Cochinchine" (FV, n26)
———, *L'Utilisation du Sol en Indochine Française* (FV, n26)
Gray, J., "Anglo-German Relations in Uganda, 1890-1892" (BCEA, n4)
Gray, R., *The Two Nations* (BCEA, n63)
Great Britain, Colonial Office, *Report by...Ormsby Gore...Malaya* (C, n13)
———, Col. Off., *Report by...Ormsby Gore...West Africa* (BWA, n56)
———, Col. Off., Col. 142, Commission on Higher Education in East Africa, *Report* (BCEA, n49)
———, Col. Off., Col 145, Commission Appointed to Enquire into the Financial and Economic Position of Northern Rhodesia, *Report* (BCEA, n75)
———, Col Off., Col 150, *Labour Conditions in Northern Rhodesia* (BCEA, n76)

———, Col Off., West Africa, "Report of an Investigation" (BWA, n44)
———, India Office, "Butler Collection" (BI, n30)
———, Parliament, House of Commons, *Sessional Papers* (BI, n51)
———, Royal Commission on Agriculture in India, *Report*. . . (BI, n82)
———, Special Commission on the Ceylon Constitution, *Ceylon* (C, n33)
Greenberger, A. J., *The British Image of India* (BI, n14)
Greenstreet, D. K., "The Guggisberg Ten-Year Development Plan" (BWA, n65)
Gregory, R. G., *India and East Africa* (BCEA, n22)
———, *Sidney Webb and East Africa* (BCEA, n26)
Grove, B. R., "Nature of Landrights in Moghul India" (BI, n89)
Gueye, L., *Itineraire Africain* (FWEA, n87)
Guggisberg, F. G., "Annual Address to the Legislative Council (1925)" (BWA, n48)
Guiral, P., "L'Opinion Marseillaise et les Débuts de l'Enterprise Algérienne" (FM, n2)
Gullick, J. M., *Indigenous Political Systems of Western Malaya* (M, n6)
———, *Malaya* (M, n1)

Habib, I., "Potentialities of Capitalist Development in Mughal India" (BI, n89)
Hailey, W. M., *An African Survey* (BWA, n1)
Hall, D. G. E., *A History of South-East Asia* (B, n1)
Halldèn, E., *The Culture Policy of the Basel Mission in the Cameroons, 1886-1905* (GC, n48)
Halstead, J. P. "The Changing Character of Moroccan Reformism, 1921-1934" (FM, n127)
———, *Rebirth of a Nation* (FM, n127)
Hammond, R. J., *Portugal and Africa (1815-1910)* (PA, n6)
———, "Uneconomic Imperialism" (PA, n29)
Handbuch der Dritten Welt (P, n6)
Hanna, A. J., *The Story of the Rhodesias and Nyasaland* (BCEA, n1)
Hardy, P., *The Muslims of British India* (BI, n306)
Hargreaves, J. D., *Prelude to the Partition of West Africa* (BWA, n5)
———, *West Africa* (FWEA, n1)
———, "West African States and the European Conquest" (FWEA, n1)
Harnetty, P. "Cotton Exports and Indian Agriculture" (BI, n154)
———, "The Imperialism of Free Trade" (BI, n185)
Harris, M., "Labour Emigration among the Moçambique Thonga" (PA, n37)
Harvey, G. E., *British Rule in Burma* (B, n1)
Hausen, K., *Deutsche Kolonialherrschaft in Afrika* (GC, n17)
Hauser, W., "The Indian National Congress and Land Policy in the Twentieth Century" (BI, n128)
Hayford, J.E.C., *Gold Coast Native Institutions* (BWA, n86)
———, *The Truth about the West African Land Question* (BWA, n91)
Heimer, F. W. (ed.), *Social Change in Angola* (PA, n47)
Heimsath, C. H., *Indian Nationalism and Hindu Social Reform* (BI, n278)
Helleiner, G. K., *Peasant Agriculture, Government, and Economic Growth in Nigeria* (BWA, n46)
Henderson, I., "The Limits of Colonial Power" (BCEA, n76)
Henderson, W. O., *Britain and Industrial Europe, 1750-1870* (SU, n24)
———, *Studies in German Colonial History* (GC, n6)
Henry, Y., see Indochina, French,. . . (FV, n29)
Hershlag, Z. Y., *Introduction to the Modern Economic History of the Middle East* (BPE, n1)
Heston, A. W., "Official Yields per Acre in India, 1886-1947" (BI, n142)
Heussler, R., *The British in Northern Nigeria* (BWA, n20)
Higgins, B., "The 'Dualistic Theory' of Underdeveloped Areas" (SU, n17)
Hill, P., *The Gold Coast Cocoa Farmer* (BWA, n53)
———, *Studies in Rural Capitalism in West Africa* (BWA, n57)

Histoire du Maroc (FM, n83)
History of East Africa (P, n8)
Hlaing, A., "Trends of Economic Growth and Distribution in Burma, 1870-1910" (B, n5.)
Hoffherr, R., *L'Economie Marocain* (FM, n86)
Holas, B., *Changement Sociaux en Côte d'Ivoire* (FWEA, n59)
———, *Le Séparatisme Religieux en Afrique Noire* (FWEA, n107)
Holland, W. L., *Asian Nationalism and the West* (M, n42)
Holmes, A. B., "The Gold Coast and Nigeria" (BWA, n51)
Holt, P. M., see Conference on the Modern History of Egypt (BPE, n1)
Hopkins, A. G., "Economic Aspects of Political Movements in Nigeria and the Gold Coast, 1918-1939" (BWA, n99)
———, *An Economic History of West Africa* (BWA, n51)
———, "Economic Imperialism in West Africa" (BWA, n12)
Horie, Y., "Capital Formation in the Early Stages of Industrialization in Japan" (SU, n32)
Hoselitz, B. F., "Ein Soziologischer Ansatz zur Theorie der Wirtschaftlichen Entwicklung" (SU, n33)
———, *Wirtschaftliches Wachstum und sozialer Wandel* (SU, n33)
Hourani, A., *Arabic Thought in the Liberal Age, 1798-1939* (BPE, n85)
Hutchins, F. G., *The Illusions of Permanence* (BI, n14)
Hutter, F. K., "Kamerun" (GC, n23)
"Huxley Papers" (BCEA, n24)
Huxley, E.J.G., *White Man's Country* (BCEA, n14)
Hymans, J. L., *Léopold Sédar Senghor* (FWEA, n88)

Ibingira, G. S. K., *The Forging of an African Nation* (BCEA, n50)
Ibrahim, I. I., "Der Aufstieg des Nationalismus" (BPE, n87)
Idowu, H. O., "Assimilation in 19th Century Senegal" (FWEA, n94)
Igbafe, P. A. "British Rule in Benin, 1897-1920" (BWA, n29)
Ikime, O., "Colonial Conquest and Resistance in Southern Nigeria" (BWA, n9)
Iliffe, J., "The Organization of the Maji Maji Rebellion" (GC, n34)
———, *Tanganyika under German Rule, 1905-1912* (GC, n32)
India, Famine Commission, *Report*... (BI, n161)
India, Industrial Commission, *Report*... (BI, n230)
Indian Annual Register (BI, n347)
Indochina, French, Direction des Affaires Politiques et de la Sûreté Générale, *Contribution à l'Histoire des Mouvements Politiques de l'Indochine Française* (FV, n89)
———, Inspection Générale de l'Agriculture, de l'Elevage et des Forêts, *Economie Agricole de l'Indochine* (FV, n29)
Industrialisation de l'Afrique du Nord (FM, n91)
Industrielle Revolution (SU, n13)
Ingham, K., *A History of East Africa* (BCEA, n1)
International Conference of Economic History, 2d, Aix-en-Provence, 1962 [*Proceedings*] (SU, n32)
International Congress of Historical Sciences, 12th, Vienna, 1965, *Rapports* (BI, n332)
———, 13th, Moscow, 1970 [*Reprinted Papers*] (BWA, n86)
International Encyclopedia of the Social Sciences (P, n11)
International Labor Office, Geneva, *Problèmes du Travail en Indochine* (FV, n39)
International Missionary Council, Department of Social and Economic Research and Counsel, *Modern Industry and the African* (BCEA, n76)
Isaacman, A. F., *Moçambique* (PA, n4)
Isnard, H., "Agriculture Européenne et Agriculture Indigène en Algérie" (FM, n46)
———, *La Vigne en Algérie* (FM, n53)
Isoart, P. *Le Phénomène National Vietnamien* (FV, n1)

Issawi, C. P., *Egypt in Revolution* (BPE, n13)
———, "Egypt since 1800" (BPE, n13)

Jack, J. C., *The Economic Life of a Bengal District* (BI, n156)
Jäckel, H., *Die Landgesellschaften in den deutschen Schutzgebieten* (GC, n39)
Jacoby, E. H., *Agrarian Unrest in Southeast Asia* (M, n30)
Jaeck, H. P. "Die deutsche Annexion" (GC, n9)
Johnson, G., "Chitpavan Brahmins and Politics in Western India" (BI, n283)
———, "Partition, Agitation and Congress" (BI, n303)
Johnson, G. W., "The Ascendency of Blaise Diagne and the Beginning of African Politics in Senegal" (FWEA, n95)
———, *The Emergence of Black Politics in Senegal* (FWEA, n95)
Johnson, S., *History of the Yorubas* (BWA, n86)
Johnson, W.A., *The Steel Industry of India* (BI, n213)
Jones, S. W., *Public Administration in Malaya* (M, n10)
Joshi, N. M., *Urban Handicrafts of the Bombay Deccan* (BI, n182)
Joshi, T. M., et al., *Studies in the Taxation of Agricultural Land and Income in India* (BI, n163)
Julien, C. A., *L'Afrique du Nord en Marche* (FM, n106)
———, "Colons Françaises et Jeunes Tunisiens (1882-1912)" (FM, n107)
———, *Histoire de l'Algérie Contemporaine* (FM, n1)
July, R. W., *The Origins of Modern African Thought* (BWA, n84)

Kaddache, M., *La Vie Politique à Alger de 1919 à 1939* (FM, n112)
Kaeselitz, R., "Kolonialeroberung and Widerstandskampf in Südkamerun" (GC, n50)
Kahin, G. McT., *Nationalism and Revolution in Indonesia* (NI, n50)
Kannangara, A. P., "Indian Millowners and Indian Nationalism before 1914" (BI, n304)
Kanya-Forstner, A. S., *The Conquest of the Western Sudan* (FWEA, n1)
"Kapitalanlagen und Bevölkerung der Schutzgebiete" (GC, n36)
Kartodirdjo, S., *Protest Movements in Rural Java* (NI, n19)
Katzenellenbogen, S. E., *Railways and the Copper Mines of Katanga* (PA, n46)
Kaunda, K. D., *Zambia Shall Be Free* (BCEA, n87)
Kaushik, P. D., *The Congress Ideology and Programme, 1920-1947* (BI, n344)
Kay, G. B. (ed.), *The Political Economy of Colonialism in Ghana*, (BWA, n48)
Kedourie, E., *The Chatham House Version and Other Middle-Eastern Studies* (BPE, n89)
———, "Saad Zaghlul and the British" (BPE, n89)
Keller, A., "Netherlands India as a Paying Proposition" (NI, n47)
Kennedy, J., *A History of Modern Malaya, 1400-1959* (M, n1)
Khérian, G., "Le Problème Démographique en Indochine" (FV, n27)
———, "La Querelle de l'Industrialisation de l'Indochine" (FV, n73)
Kilson, M. L., "Social Forces in West African Political Development" (BWA, n89)
Kimble, D., *A Political History of Ghana* (BWA, n3)
Kingsley, M. H., *Travels in West Africa* (BWA, n89)
———, *West African Studies* (BWA, n37)
Kirk-Greene, A. H. M. (ed.), *The Principles of Native Administration in Nigeria* (BWA, n20)
Ki-Zerbo, J., *Histoire de l'Afrique Noire* (BWA, n1)
Klein, H. S., "The Portuguese Slave Trade from Angola in the 18th Century" (PA, n3)
Klein, I., "Indian Nationalism and Anti-Industrialization" (BI, n226)
Klein, M. A., *Islam and Imperialism in Senegal* (FWEA, n47)
Knoll, A. J., *Togo Under Imperial Germany, 1884-1914* (GC, n49)
Köbben, A., "L'Héritage chez les Agni" (FWEA, n60)
———, "Le Planteur Noir" (FWEA, n55)
Koh, S. J., *Stages of Industrial Development in Asia* (BI, n184)

Köhler, O., "The Stage of Acculturation in Southwest Africa" (GC, n84)
Kon, W. L., "Western Enterprise and the Development of Malaya Tin Industry to 1914" (M, n12)
Koninklijk Institut voor de Tropen, *Indonesian Economics* (SU, n16)
Kopytoff, J. H., *A Preface to Modern Nigeria* (BWA, n4)
Körner, H., *Kolonialpolitik und Wirtschaftsentwicklung* (FWEA, n36)
Kotelwala, Sir J., *An Asian Prime Minister's Story* (C, n35)
Krauss, H., *Die Moderne Bodengesetzgebung in Kamerun, 1884-1964* (GC, n43)
Krishna, G., "The Development of the Indian National Congress as a Mass Organization, 1918-1923" (BI, n330)
Kritik des Bürgerlichen Anti-Imperialismus (P, n6)
Kulke, E., *The Parsees in India* (BI, n183)
Külz, W., *Die Selbstverwaltung für Deutsch-Südwestafrika* (GC, n78)
Kumar, D., "Caste and Landlessness in South India" (BI, n91)
———*Land and Caste in South India* (BI, n91)
Kumar, R., "The Bombay Textile Strike, 1919" (BI, n269)
———, "The Deccan Riots of 1875" (BI, n106)
———, "The New Brahmins of Maharashtra" (BI, n283)
———, *Western India in the Nineteenth Century* (BI, n102)
———, see *Essays on Gandhian Politics* (BI, n318)
Kunzu, H. N., "Defence of India" (BI, n20)
Kuznets, S. S. (ed.), *Economic Growth* (BI, n57)
———, "Underdeveloped Countries and Pre-Industrial Phase in Advanced Countries" (P, n19)
Kyaw, Yin, "The Problem of Crime and the Criminal and its Solution in Socialist Burma" (B, n4)

Labouret, H., "La Grande Détresse de l'Arachide" (FWEA, n52)
———, "Main d'Oeuvre dans l'Ouest Africain" (FWEA, n30)
Lacouture, J., *Ho Chi Minh* (FV, n93)
Lamb, H., "The State and Economic Development in India" (BI, n57)
Landes, D. S., *Bankers and Pashas* (BPE, n17)
Langlois, W. G., *André Malraux* (FV, n88)
Laroui, A., *L'Histoire du Maghreb* (FM, n36)
Lateinamerika, Faschismus oder Revolution (SU, n35)
Leach, E., and S. N. Mukherjee, see *Elites in South Asia* (BI, n239)
Leakey, L. S. B., *White African* (BCEA, n16)
Lefèvre, R., "Cacao et Café" (FWEA, n59)
Legge, J. D., *Indonesia* (NI, n1)
Lehmann, F., "Great Britain and the Supply of Railway Locomotives of India" (BI, n229)
Lemarchand, R., *Political Awakening in the Belgian Congo* (BC, n1)
Le Prévost, J., and H. Meyrat, "L'Admission des Indochinois dans les Cadres des Administrations et Services Publiques Françaises de l'Indochine" (FV, n77)
Leroy-Beaulieu, P., *L'Algérie et la Tunisie* (FM, n21)
Le Thanh Khoi, *3000 Jahre Vietnam* (FV, n1)
———, *Le Viet-Nam* (FV, n1)
Le Tourneau, R., *Évolution Politique de l'Afrique du Nord Musulmane, 1920-1961* (FM, n106)
Leubuscher, C., *Tanganyika Territory* (GC, n57)
Levin, J. V., *The Export Economies* (SU, n30)
Lewis, Sir W. A., *Aspects of Tropical Trade, 1883-1965* (SU, n9)
———, *Economic Survey, 1919-1939* (BI, n233)
——— (ed.), *Tropical Development, 1880-1913* (BI, n85)
Lewis, W. H., see *French-Speaking Africa* (SU, n1)

———, "Soziologische Aspekte der politischen Entwicklung in den Entwicklungsländern" (SU, n1)
Lidman, R., and R. I. Domrese, "India" (BI, n85)
Lim, C.Y., *Economic Development of Modern Malaya* (M, n12)
Lindequist, F. von, *Deutsch-Ostafrika als Siedlungsgebiet für Europäer* (GC, n68)
Lisbon, Universidade Técnica, Instituto Superior de Ciências Socièis e Politica Ultramarina, *Moçambique* (PA, n27)
Liversage, V., *Land Tenure in the Colonies* (BCEA, n41)
Livingston, D., and C. Livingston, *Narrative of an Expedition to the Zambesi and Its Tributaries* (PA, n5)
Londres, A., *Terre d'Ebène* (FWEA, n32)
Lonsdale, J. M., "Some Origins of Nationalism in East Africa" (BCEA, n11)
Lorey, R., "La Régie de l'Alcool en Indochine" (FV, n21)
Louis, W. R., "Roger Casement and the Congo" (BC, n10)
———, *Ruanda-Urundi, 1884-1919* (GC, n58)
Low, D. A., "Empire and Authority" (SU, n45)
———, "The Government of India and the First Non-Cooperation Movement" (BI, n328)
———, *Lion Rempant* (BI, n25)
——— (ed.), *Soundings in Modern South Asian History* (BI, n283)
Lugard, F.J.D., Baron, *The Dual Mandate in British Tropical Africa* (BWA, n22)
Lütt, J., *Hindu-Nationalismus in Uttar Pradesh, 1867-1900* (BI, n282)
Lyautey, L.H.G., *Paroles d'Action* (FM, n77)
Lynch, H. R., "Edward W. Blyden, Pioneer West African Nationalist" (BWA, n87)

Mabognje, A. L., and M. B. Gleave, "Changing Agricultural Landscape in Southern Nigeria" (BWA, n66)
McEwan, P. J. M., comp., *Twentieth Century Africa* (BWA, 89)
"McGregor Ross Papers" (BCEA, n100)
McIntyre, D., "British Intervention in Malaya" (M, n3)
McLane, J., "Peasants, Moneylenders and Nationalists at the End of the 19th Century" (BI, n295)
McPhee, A., *The Economic Revolution in British West Africa* (BWA, n73)
Macpherson, W. J., "Investment in Indian Railways, 1845-1875" (BI, n164)
McVey, R. T. (ed.), *Indonesia* (NI, n1)
———, *The Rise of Indonesian Communism* (NI, n71)
Maddison, A., *Class Structure and Economic Growth* (BI, n95)
Magnus, Sir P. M., *Kitchener* (BPE, n92)
Maher, C., "African Labour on the Farm in Kenya Colony" (BCEA, n36)
Malek, A. A., "La Formation de l'Idéology dans la Renaissance Nationale de l'Egypte (1805-1892)" (BPE, n85)
———, *Idéologie et Renaissance Nationale* (BPE, n87)
Malenbaum, W., *Prospects for Indian Development* (BI, n133)
Malik, H., "Sir Sayyid Ahmad Khan's Doctrines of Muslim Nationalism and National Progress" (BPE, n292)
Mamoria, C. B., "History and Growth of Cooperative Movement in India" (BI, n121)
Mandeng, P., *Auswirkungen der deutschen Kolonialherrschaft in Kamerun* (GC, n46)
Mangat, J. S., *A History of Asians in East Africa, 1880-1945* (BCEA, n22)
Mannoni, D. O., *Prospero and Caliban* (SU, n46)
———, *Psychologie de la Colonisation* (SU, n46)
Margarido, A., "Movimenti Profetici e Messianici Angolese" (PA, n57)
Marr, D. G., *Vietnamese Anticolonialism, 1885-1925* (FV. n5)
Martinelli, A., "Dualismus and Abhängigkiet" (SU, n18)
Marx, K., *Werke, Schriften, Briefe* (BI, n175)

Mascarenhas, R. A., "Norton de Matos" (PA, n17)
Masefield, G. R., *A Short History of Agriculture in the British Colonies* (BCEA, n28)
Mason, P., *The Birth of a Dilemma* (BCEA, n1)
———, ed., *India and Ceylon* (C, n31)
———, *The Men Who Ruled India* (BI, n4)
Matos, see Norton de Matos
Mehrotra, S. R., "The Politics behind the Montagu Declaration of 1917" (BI, n312)
Meillassoux, C., *Anthropologie Economique des Gouro de Côte d'Ivoire* (FWEA, n11)
———, see *The Development of Indigenous Trade and Markets in West Africa* (FWEA, n39)
———, *Le Monde des Affairs Sénégalais* (FWEA, n39)
"Memorandum on Native Agricultural Development in the Native Reserves, July 1937" (BCEA, n31)
"Memorandum Relating to Indians in Kenya" (BCEA, n26)
Merad, A., *Le Réformisme Musulman en Algérie de 1925 à 1940* (FM, n116)
Merlier, M., *Le Congo* (BC, n1)
Metcalf, T. R., *The Aftermath of Revolt* (BI, n4)
———, "The British and the Moneylenders in Nineteenth Century India" (BI, n100)
Metcalfe, G. E. ed., *Great Britain and Ghana* (BWA, n92)
Meynier, G. "Aspects de l'Economie de l'Est Algérien pendant la Guerre de 1914-1918" (FM, n111)
Michel, M., "Les Plantations Allemandes du Mont Cameroun, 1885-1914" (GC, n41)
Mills, L. A., *Britain and Ceylon* (C, n1)
———, *Ceylon under British Rule, 1795-1932* (C, n1)
———, *Malaya* (M, n44)
Milner, A., 1st Viscount, *England in Egypt* (BPE, n24)
Misra, B. B., *The Indian Middle Classes* (BI, n96)
Der moderne Imperialismus (P n4)
Moeller, A., "La Politique Indigène de la Belgique as Congo" (BC, n36)
Mommsen, W. J., *Imperialismus in Ägypten* (BPE, n19)
———, *Das Zeitalter des Imperialismus* (P, n4)
———, see also *Der Moderne Imperialismus* (P, n4)
Mondlane, E., *Kampf um Mozambique* (PA, n14)
———, *The Struggle for Mozambique* (PA, n14)
Monet, P., *Les Jauniers* (FV, n56)
Montagne, R., "La Crise Nationaliste au Maroc" (FM, n133)
———, "Naissance et Développement du Prolétariat Marocain" (FM, n91)
Monteil, V., "Lat Dior, Damel du Cayor, et l'Islamisation des Wolofs" (FWEA, n8)
———, "Une Confrérie Musulmane" (FWEA, n46)
Moore, B., *The Social Origins of Dictatorship and Democracy* (BN, n348)
Moore, R. J., "British Policy and the Indian Problem, 1936-1940" (BI, n342)
———, *The Crisis of Indian Unity, 1917-1940* (BI, n312)
Morgenthau, R. S., *Political Parties in French-speaking West Africa* (FWEA, n62)
Morris, M. D., "Caste and the Evolution of the Industrial Workforce in India" (BI, n257)
———, *The Emergence of an Industrial Labor Force in India* (BI, n258)
———, "Towards a Reinterpretation of Nineteenth Century Indian Economic History" (BI, n182)
———, "Values as an Obstacle to Economic Growth in South Asia" (BI, n167)
Mousinho de Albuquerque, J. A., *Moçambique, 1896-1898* (PA, n16)
"Moyne Report" (BCEA, n32)
Mozambique, Reportição Technica de Estatístia, *Anuário Estatístico* (PA, n28)
Mühlmann, W. E., "Die Mau Mau Bewegung in Kenya" (BCEA, n95)
Mukerjee, K. M., "Land Transfers in Birbhum, 1928-1955" (BI, n140)
Mukerjee, R. (ed.), *Economic Problems of Modern India* (BI, n117)

Müller, F. F., *Deutschland—Zanzibar—Ostafrika* (GC, n11)
Mungeam, G. H., *British Rule in Kenya, 1895-1912* (BCEA, n10)
———, "Masai and Kikuyu Responses to the Establishment of British Administration in the East African Protectorate" (BCEA, n15)
Mus, P., "Das Dorf im politischen Leben Vietnam" (FV, n3)
Musgrave, P. J., "Landlords and Lords of the Land" (BI, n126)
Mynt, H., "The 'Classical Theory of International Trade' and the Underdeveloped Countries" (SU, n4)
———, *Economic Theory and the Underdeveloped Coutnries* (SU, n4)
Myrdal, G. *Economic Theory and Under-Developed Regions* (SU, n38)
———, *Ökonomische Theorie und unterentwickette Regionen* (SU, n38)

Nanda, B. R., *Mahatma Gandhi* (BI, n308)
Naoroji, D., *Poverty and Un-British Rule in India* (BI, n250)
Narain, D., *Impact of Price Movements on Areas under Selected Crops in India, 1900-1939* (BI, n158)
Narayana Reddy, K., *The Growth of Public Expenditure in India, 1872-1968* (BI, n234)
———, "Indian Defense Expenditure, 1872-1967" (BI, 253)
Native Affairs Committee, *Report*, 1911 (BCEA, n67)
N'Diaye, F., "La Colonie du Sénégal au Temps de Brière de l'Isle (1870-1881)" (FWEA, n94)
Nehru, J. *The Discovery of India* (BI, n3)
———, *Jawaharlal Nehru* (BI, n54)
Neto, J. P., "Comércio externo de Moçambique" (PA, n52)
Nevinson, H. W., *A Modern Slavery* (PA, n31)
Newbury, C., comp., *British Policy Towards West Africa* (BWA, n2)
———, "The Development of French Policy on the Lower and Upper Niger, 1880-1898" (BWA, n8)
———, "The Formation of the Government General of French West Africa" (FWEA, n18)
———, "The Tariff Factor in Anglo-French Partition" (BWA, n6)
———, "Trade and Authority in West Africa from 1850 to 1880" (FWEA, n37)
———, and A. S. Kanya-Forstner, "French Policy and the Origins of the Scramble for West Africa" (FWEA, n1)
———, and Newitt, M.D.D., "The Portuguese on the Zambesi from the 17th to the 19th Century" (PA, n4)
Nicolson, I. F., *The Administration of Nigeria, 1900-1960* (BWA, n20)
Nigeria, Commission of Inquiry Appointed to Inquire into the Disturbances in the Calabar and Oweri Provinces, *Memorandum* (BWA, n31)
———, Education Department, *Annual Report* (BWA, n47)
———, Governor-General, 1935-1943 ([Sir Bernard] Bourdillon), *Memorandum on the Future Political Development of Nigeria* (BWA, n38)
———, Legislative Council, *Debates* (BWA, n42)
———, Legislative Council, "Minutes" (BWA, n67)
Nohlen, D., see *Handbuch der Dritten Welt* (P, n16)
Norton de Matos, J.M.R., *A Nação Uma* (PA, n18)
———, *Memórias e Trabalhos da minha Vida* (PA, n9)
———, *Província de Angola* (PA, n60)
Nouschi, A., *La Naissance du Nationalisme Algérian, 1914-1954* (FM, n50)
———, "Le Sens de Certains Chiffres" (FM, n118)
Nunes de Oliveira, J. N., *Moçambique* (PA, n17)
Nussbaum, M., *Vom "Kolonialenthusiasmus" zur Kolonialpolitik der Monopole* (GC, n37)
Nyi Nyi, "The Development of University Education in Burma" (B, n25)

O'Brien, P., "The Long-Term Growth of Agricultural Production in Egypt, 1821-1962" (BPE, p.237)

Ogot, B. A., "British Administration in the Central Nyanza District of Kenya, 1900-1960" (BCEA, n18)
Ohneck, W., *Die französische Algerienpolitik von 1919-1939* (FM, n1)
Oliver, R. A., see *History of East Africa* (P, n8)
———, and J. D. Fage, *A Short History of Africa* (BWA, n1)
Oloruntimehin, B. O., "The West African Sudan and the Coming of the French" (FWEA, n1)
O'Malley, L.S.S., *The Indian Civil Service, 1601-1930* (BI, n31)
Orde Browne, G. St. J., *Labour Conditions in Ceylon, Mauritius, and Malaya* (C, n13)
"Orde Brown Papers" (BCEA, n59)
Organisierter Kapitalismus (SU, n31)
Ormsby Gore, W. G. A., "Report," see Gt. Brit., Col. Off. (C, n14)
———, *Visit to West Africa*, see Gt. Brit., Col Off. (BWA, n56)
Orr, C.W.J., *The Making of Northern Nigeria* (BWA, n17)
Osborne, M. E., "The Debate on a Legal Code for Colonial Cochinchina" (FV, n13)
———, *The French Presence in Cochinchina and Cambodia* (FV, n13)
Osuntkun, J., "Post-First World War Economic and Administrative Problems in Nigeria and the Response of the Clifford Administration" (BWA, n95)
Owen, E.R.J., *Cotton and the Egyptian Economy, 1820-1914* (BPE, n7)
———, "Egypt and Europe" (BPE, n23)
———, "The Influence of Lord Cromer's Indian Experience on British Policy in Egypt" (BPE, n30)
———, "Lord Cromer and the Development of Egyptian Industry, 1883-1907" (BPE, n78)
———, and R. B. Sutcliffe, eds., *Studies in the Theory of Imperialism* (BPE, n23)
Owen, H. F., "Towards Nation-Wide Agitation and Organization" (BI, n310)

Paden, J. N., "Aspects of Emirship in Kano" (BWA, n23)
Pakeman, S. A., *Ceylon* (C, n1)
Palmier, L. H., "The Javanese Nobility under the Dutch" (NI, n4)
Panikkar, K. M., *Asia under Western Dominance* (BI, n2)
Papers on National Income and Allied Topics (BI, n131)
Parkinson, C. N., *British Intervention in Malaya*, 1867-1877 (M, n2)
Parmer, J. N., "Chinese Estate Workers' Strikes in Malaya in March 1937" (M, n26)
———, *Colonial Labor Policy and Administration* (M, n17)
The Partition of India (BI, n345)
Peerzada, S. S. (ed.), *Foundations of Pakistan* (BI, n352)
Pehaut, Y., "L'Arachide au Sénégal" (FWEA, n41)
Pelissier, P., "L'Arachide au Sénégal" (FWEA, n41)
———, *Les Paysans du Sénégal* (FWEA, n41)
Pelissier, R., "Campagnes Militaires en Sud-Angola 1885-1915" (PA, n7)
Pensa, H. (ed.), *L'Algérie* (FM, n12)
Perham, M. F., *Lugard* (BWA, n16)
———, *Native Administration in Nigeria* (BWA, n41)
———, "The System of Native Administration in Tanganyika" (BCEA, n53)
Person, Y., "Samori and the Resistance to the French" (FWEA, n5)
———, *Samori, une Révolution Dyula* (FWEA, n6)
Péter, G., *L'Effort Français au Sénégal* (FWEA, n47)
Peter, H.-B., *Sozioökonomische Grundprobleme der Entwicklungsländer* (SU, n18)
Peyer, H. C., "Leonhard Ziegler, Ein Zürcher in Indien, 1802-1846" (BI, n152)
"Pflanzungen" (GC, n49)
Philips, C. H. (ed.), *The Evolution of India and Pakistan, 1858 to 1947* (BI, n20)
——— (ed.), *Politics and Society in India* (BI, n342)
———, see *The Partition of India* (BI, n342)
Pike, J. G., *Malawi* (BCEA, n1)
Pim, Sir W. A., *The Financial and Economic History of the African Tropical Territories* (BWA, n51)

Pim *Report*, see Gt. Brit., Col. Off., Col. 145 (BCEA, n75)
Pinto, F. L. da V., *Le Portugal et le Congo au XIXe Siècle* (PA, n6)
Pinto, R., *Aspects de l'Evolution Gouvernementale de l'Indochine Français* (FV, n77)
Piquet, V., *L'Algérie Française* (FM, n39)
Platt, D. C. St. M., *Finance, Trade and Politics in British Foreign Policy, 1815-1914* (BPE, n23)
Plüss, W., "Friedliche Durchdringung oder militärische Unterwerfung?" (FWEA, n11)
Poncet, J., *La Colonisation et l'Agriculture Européenne en Tunisie dépuis 1881* (FM, n58)
———*Paysages et Problèmes Ruraux en Tunisie* (FM, n58)
Poquin, J. J., *Les Rélations Economiques Exterieures des Pays d'Afrique Noire de l'Union Française, 1925-1955* (FWEA, n36)
Portugal, Colonie de Moçambique, *Exposition Coloniale Internationale 1931* (PA, n38)
———, Instituto Nacional de Estatística, *Anuário Estatístico* (PA, n26)
Pössinger, H., "Interrelations between Economic and Social Change in Rural Africa" (PA, n54)
———, *Landwirtschaftliche Entwicklung in Angola und Moçambique* (PA, n13)
Potter, D. C., "Manpower Shortage and the End of Colonialism" (BI, n52)
Power, B. M. Le P., "Indian Labour Conditions" (BI, n267)
Prebisch, R., *The Economic Development of Latin America and Its Principal Problems* (SU, n7)
———, "Die Rohstoffexporte und die Verschlechterung der Terms of Trade" (SU, n7)
"Le Problème des Chefferies en Afrique Noire Française" (FWEA, n24)
Problèmes du Travail, see International Labour Office (FV, n39)

Queiroz Ribeiro, E. de, *O Algodão em Moçambique* (PA, n51)
"La Question Agraire en Indochine" (FV, n42)

Rajayatnam, S., "The Ceylon Tea Industry, 1886-1931" (C, n10)
Ranade, M. G., *Essays on Indian Economics* (BI, n296)
Randles, W. G. L., *L'Ancièn Royaume de Congo des Origines à la Fin du XIXe Siècle* (PA, n2)
Ranger, T. O., "African Attempts to Control Education in East and Central Africa, 1909-1939" (BCEA, n103)
———, "African Reactions to the Imposition of Colonial Rule in East and Central Africa" (BCEA, n9)
———, "Connections between 'Primary Resistance' Movements and Modern Mass Nationalism in East and Central Africa" (BCEA, n86)
———, "The Nineteenth Century in Southern Rhodesia" (BCEA, n6)
———, *Revolt in Southern Rhodesia, 1896-97* (BCEA, n9)
———, "The Role of the Ndebele and Shona Religious Authorities in the Rebellions of 1896 and 1897" (BCEA, n9)
———, see also *Aspects of Central African History* (BCEA, n1)
Ranis, G., "Die Finanzierung der wirtschaftlichen Entwicklung Japans" (SU, n29)
Rao, A. V. Raman, *Economic Development of Andhra Pradesh* (BI, n76)
Rattray, R. S., "Present Tendencies of African Colonial Government" (BWA, n36)
Raum, O. F., "Changes in African Life under German Administration, 1892-1914" (GC, n60)
Ray, R. K., "The Crisis of Bengal Agriculture, 1870-1927" (BI, n98)
Raychaudhuri, T., "Permanent Settlement in Operation" (BI, n98)
Reddy, see Narayana Reddy (BI, n234)
Reeves, P. D. "Landlords and Party Policy in the U.P., 1934-1937" (BI, n345)
"La Réforme des Impôts Personnels" (FV, n24)
"Reichszuschüsse" (GC, n19)
"Relatorio da Commissão de 1898" (PA, n30)
Report, 1938, see Burma, Land and Agriculture Committee (B, n9)
"Report on Cocoa" (BWA, n53)
"Report of an Investigation...on...Africanization" (BWA, n44)
"Report of the Royal Commission on Labour in India" (BI, n270)

Report, see also Gt. Brit., and the other areas in question.
Resnick, S. A., "The Decline of Rural Industry and Export Expansion" (B, n19)
Reynolds,E., "Economic Imperialism" (BWA, n18)
Rhodesia, Northern, Commission Appointed to Enquire into the Disturbances in the Copperbelt, *Report* (BCEA, n78)
Rhodesia, Southern, Native Affairs Committee of Enquiry, 1910-1911, *Report* (BCEA, n67)
Richards, A. I., *Land, Labour and Diet in Northern Rhodesia* (BCEA, n83)
Rita-Ferreira, A., *O Movimento Migratório Trabalhadores entre Moçambique e a Africa do Sul* (PA, n37)
Robequain, C., *The Economic Development of French Indo-China* (FV, n25)
Roberts, A. D., "The Sub-Imperialism of the Buganda" (BCEA, n38)
Roberts, M. W., "Indian Estate Labour in Ceylon during the Coffee Period (1830-1880)" (C, n9)
———, "Irrigation Policy in British Ceylon during the Nineteenth Century" (C, n16)
Robinson, K., and F. Madden (eds.), *Essays in Imperial Government* (BWA, n25)
Robinson, R., "Non-European Foundations of European Imperialism" (SU, n44)
———, and J. Gallagher, with A. Denny, *Africa and the Victorians* (BPE, n23)
Roeykens, A., *Léopold II et l'Afrique, 1855-1880* (BC, n2)
Roff, W. R., *The Origins of Malay Nationalism* (M, n37)
Rohdie, S., "The Gold Coast Cocoa Hold-Up of 1930-1931" (BWA, n62)
Rohrback, P., *Deutsche Kolonialwirtschaft* (GC, n80)
Rosberg, C. G., and J. C. Nottingham, *The Myth of the "Mau Mau"* (BCEA, n99)
Rosenbaum, J., *Frankreich in Tunesien* (FM, n20)
Ross, E. A., *Report on the Employment of Native Labour in Portuguese Africa* (PA, n34)
Rotberg, R. I., *A Political History of Tropical Africa* (BWA, n1)
———, "Psychological Stress and the Question of Identity" (BCEA, n91)
———, "Resistance and Rebellion in British Nyasaland and German East Africa, 1888-1915" (GC, n34)
———, "The Rise of African Nationalism" (BCEA, n86)
———, *The Rise of Nationalism in Central Africa* (BCEA, n77)
———, and A. A. Mazrui (eds.), *Protest and Power in Black Africa* (BWA, n1)
Rothermund, D., "Bewegung und Verfassung" (BI, n343)
———, "Freedom of Contract and the Problem of Land Alienation in British India" (BI, n107)
———, "Die historische Analyse des Bodenrechts als Grundlage für das Verständnis gegenwärtiger Agrarstruktur" (BI, n90)
———, "Nehru and Early Indian Socialism" (BI, n344)
———, *The Phases of Indian Nationalism and Other Essays* (BI, n306)
———, *Die politische Willensbildung in Indien, 1900-1960* (P, n1)
———, "Reform and Repression, 1907-1910" (BI, n306)
———, "Die Rolle der westlichen Bildungsschlicht in den politischen Massenbewegungen in Indien im 20. Jahrhundert" (BI, n329)
Roubaud, L., *Vietnam* (FV, n95)
Roy, N. C., "The Indian Civil Service" (BI, n54)
Royal Commission, *Report*, 1928, see Gt. Brit., Royal Commission on Agriculture in India (BI, n82)
Rudin, H. R., *Germans in the Cameroons*, 1884-1914 (GC, n17)
Rüger, A., "Die Duala und die Kolonialmacht, 1884-1914" (GC, n52)
———, "Die Entstehung und Lage der Arbeiterklasse unter dem deutschen Kolonialregime in Kamerun" (GC, n41)
Ryan, B., *Caste in Modern Ceylon* (C, n34)
Ryan, N. J., *The Making of Modern Malaya* (M, n1)
Ryckmans, P., *Dominer pour Servir* (BC, n15)
Ryland, S., "Edwin Montagu in India, 1917-1918" (BI, n315)

Sachse, F. A., "The Work of the Bengal Land Revenue Commission" (BI, n129)
Safran, N., *Egypt in Search of Political Community* (BPE, n85)
Saini, K. A.,"A Case of Aborted Economic Growth" (BI, n215)
Saintoyant, J. F., *L'Affaire du Congo 1905* (FWEA, n67)
Salomon, R. L., "Saya San and the Burmese Rebellion" (B, n28)
Samuels, M. A., *Education in Angola, 1878-1914* (PA, n27)
Sanderson, G. N., "The Anglo-German Agreement of 1890 and the Upper Nile" (BCEA, n4)
Santos, M. dos, *História do Ensino em Angola* (PA, n27)
Sarbah, J. M., *Fantis National Constitution* (BWA, n86)
Sari, D., "Le Demantèlement de la Propriété Foncière" (FM, n41)
Sarkisyanz, E., *Buddhist Backgrounds of the Burmese Revolution* (B, n27)
Saul, S. B., *Studies in British Overseas Trade*, 1870-1914 (BI, n199)
Sautter, G., *De l'Atlantique au Fleuve Congo* (FWEA, n73)
———, "Notes sur la Construction du Chemin de Fer Congo-Océan (1921-1934)" (FWEA, n32)
———, "Les Paysans Noirs du Gabon Septentrional" (FWEA, n73)
Savage, D., and J. F. Munro, "Carrier Corps Recruitment in the British East African Protectorate, 1914-1918" (BCEA, n23)
Sayeed, K. B., *Pakistan, The Formative Phase, 1857-1948* (BI, n289)
Scham, A., *Lyautey in Morocco* (FM, n29)
Schiefel, W., *Bernhard Dernburg 1865-1937* (GC, n20)
Schlunk, M., *Die Schulen für Eingeborene in den deutschen Schutzgebieten am l. Juli 1911* (GC, n63)
Schmidt, R., *Geschichte der Araberaufstandes in Ostafrika* (GC, n12)
Schmitt, H. O., "Decolonization and Development in Burma" (B, n37)
Schnee, H., see *Deutsches Kolonial-Lexikon* (GC, n19)
Schölch, A., *Agypten den Ägyptern*! (BPE, n2)
———, "Constitutional Development in Nineteenth Century Egypt" (BPE, n21)
———, "The 'Men on the Spot' and the English Occupation of Egypt in 1882" (BPE, n23)
———, "Wirtschaftliche Durchdringung und politische Kontrolle durch die europäischen Mächte im Osmanischen Reich" (FM, n18)
Schrieke, B.J.O., "The Causes and Effects of Communism on the West Coast of Sumatra" (NI, n72)
——— (ed.), *The Effect of Western Influence on Native Civilizations in the Malay Archipeligo* (NI, n20)
———, *Indonesian Sociological Studies* (NI, n4)
———, "The Native Rulers" (NI, n4)
Schröder, H. C., *Sozialismus und Imperialismus* (GC, n18)
Schuler, C., "Zu den Ursachen des 'rückständigen' Systems gesellschaftlicher Arbeit in der armen Welt" (P, n10)
Seal, A., *The Emergence of Indian Nationalism* (BI, n125)
Sebag, P., *La Tunisie* (FM, n22)
Sen, S. K., "Die Investitionen britischer Unternehmer in der Frühzeit der Industrialisierung Indiens, 1854-1914" (BI, n179)
———, *Studies in Industrial Policy and the Development of India (1858-1914)* (BI, n176)
Sen, S. P. "Effects on India of British Law and Administration in the 19th Century" (BI, n31)
Senghaas, D. (ed.), *Imperialismus und strukturelle Gewalt* (P, n6)
——— (comp.), *Peripherer Kapitalismus* (P, n6)
Sessional Papers, see Gt. Brit., Parliament, H. of C. (NI, n51)
Shaloff, S., "The Income Tax, Indirect Rule and the Depression" (BWA, n34)
Shephard, C. Y., *Report on the Economics of Peasant Agriculture in the Gold Coast* (BWA, n53)
Sidler, P., "Die 'Jeunes Tunisiens'," (FM, n107)

Sieber, H., *Die realen Austauschverhältnisse zwischen Entwicklungsländern und Industriestaaten* (BI, n153)
Sieberg, H., *Eugène Etienne und die Französiche Kolonialpolitik, 1887-1904* (FM, n27)
Sievers, A., *Ceylon* (C, n18)
Silver, A. W., *Manchester Men and Indian Cotton, 1847-1872* (BI, n144)
Simon, W., *Die britische Militärpolitik in Indien* (BI, n253)
Sinclair, K., "Hobson and Lenin in Johore" (M, n9)
Singer, H. W., "The Distribution of Gains between Investing and Borrowing Countries" ((SU, n7)
———, "Obstacles to Economic Development" (SU, n27)
Singh, S., and J. Landauer, "The Tax Bases of an Indian Land Tax" (BI, n162)
Singh, V. B. (ed.), *Economic History of India, 1867-1956* (BI, n77)
———, "Trade Union Movement" (BI, n268)
Sitsen, P. H. W., *Industrial Development of the Netherlands Indies* (NI, n38)
Skinner, E. P., *The Mossi of the Upper Volta* (FWEA, n10)
Smith, A. K., "Antonio Salazar and the Reversal of Portuguese Colonial Policy" (PA, n22)
Smith, R. B., "Bui Quang Chieu and the Constitutionalist Party in French Cochinchina, 1917-1930" (FV, n87)
———, *Vietnam and the West* (FV, n82)
———, "The Vietnamese Elite in French Cochinchina" (FV, n87)
Snodgrass, D. R., *Ceylon* (C, n22)
Sonntag, H. R. (ed. and trans.), see *Lateinamerika* (SU, n35)
Spear, P., *India* (BI, n1)
Spellmeyer, H., *Deutsche Kolonialpolitik im Reichstag* (GC, n18)
Spence, C. F., *The Portuguese Colony of Moçambique* (PA, n53)
Spillmann, G., *L'Afrique du Nord et la France* (FM, n97)
Stein, B., "Problems of Economic Development in Ceylon" (C, n14)
Stengers, J., *Belgique et Congo* (BC, n2)
———, "La Belgique et le Congo" (BC, n1)
———, "British and German Imperial Rivalry" (GC, n2)
———, "The Congo Free State and the Belgian Congo before 1914" (BC, n2)
———, "L'Impérialisme Coloniale de Fin du XIXe Siècle" (BS, n3)
———, "Léopold II et la Rivalté Franco-Anglaise 1882-1884" (BC, n2)
———, "La Place de Léopold II dans l'Histoire de la Colonisation" (BC, n2)
Steppat, F., "Nationalismus und Islam bei Mustafa Kemal" (BPE, n86)
Stewart, C. F., *The Economy of Morocco, 1912-1962* (FM, n76)
Stoecker, H. (ed.), *Kamerun unter deutsche Kolonialherrschaft* (GC, n9)
Stokes, E., "Traditional Resistance Movements and Afro-Asian Nationalism" (BI, n12)
———, and R. Brown (eds.), *The Zambesian Past* (BCEA, n1)
Sunthatlingam, R., "The 'Hindu' and the Genesis of Nationalist Politics in South India, 1878-1885" (BI, n286)
Suret-Canale, J., *L'Afrique Noire* (FWEA, n1)
———, "La Guinée dans le Système Colonial" (FWEA, n53)
———, "L'Industrie des Oléagineux en AOf" (FWEA, n76)
———, "Quelques Aspects de la Géographie Agraire au Sénégal" (FWEA, n41)
Susset, R. *La Vérité sur le Cameroon et l'Afrique Equatoriale Française* (FWEA, n74)
Symonds, R., *The British and their Successors* (P, n22)

Talbot, P., ed., *South Asia in the World Today* (NI, n47)
Tambiah, S. J., "Ethnic Representation in Ceylon's Higher Administrative Services, 1870-1946" (C, n6)
Tamuno, T. N., "Governor Clifford and Representative Government" (BWA, n95)
———, "Some Aspects of Nigerian Reaction to the Imposition of British Rule" (BWA, n5)

Tanganyika, Colonial Government, *Native Administration* (BCEA, n53)
———, Colonial Government, *A Report by Mr. E. C. Baker on the Social and Economic Conditions in the Tanga Province* (BCEA, n58)
———, Legislative Council, *Sessional Papers* (BCEA, n60)
Taylor, A. J. P., *Germany's First Bid for Colonies, 1884-1885* (GC, n4)
Taylor, J. C., *The Political Development of Tanganyika* (BCEA, n56)
Tetzlaff, R., *Koloniale Entwicklung und Ausbeutung* (GC, n33)
Thio, E., "The British Forward Movement in the Malay Peninsula" (M, n8)
Thompson, V. M., *French Indo-China* (FV, n1)
———, and R. Adloff, *Emerging States of French Equatorial Africa* (FWEA, n92)
———, and R. Adloff, *French West Africa* (FWEA, n105)
Thorner, D., "Great Britain and the Development of India's Railways" (BI, n164)
———, *Investment in Empire* (BI, n164)
———, "Long-Term Trends in Output" (BI, n149)
———, and A. Thorner, *Land and Labour in India* (BI, n139)
Tignor, R. L., *Modernization and British Colonial Rule in Egypt, 1882-1914* (BPE, n28)
Tillon, G., *L'Algérie en 1957* (FM, n52)
Tinker, H., *India and Pakistan* (BI, n37)
———, "Structure of the British Imperial Heritage" (BI, n31)
Tinthoin, R., "Les Trara" (FM, n47)
Tordoff, W., *Ashanti under the Prempehs, 1888-1935* (BWA, n35)
Tothill, J. D. (ed.), *Agriculture in Uganda* (BCEA, n40)
Trager, F. N., *Burma* (B, n1)
Tréchou, H., "Les Plantations Européennes en Côte d'Ivoire" (FWEA, n55)
Truong Buu Lam, *Patterns of Vietnamese Response to Foreign Intervention* (FV, n5)

U Ba Maw, *Breakthrough in Burma* (B, n32)
U Kaung, "A Survey of the History of Education in Burma before the British Conquest and After" (B, n25)
Das Überseeische Deutschland (GC, n23)
Udo, R. K., "The Migrant Tenant Farmer of Eastern Nigeria" (BWA, n66)
Uganda, Committee of Enquiry into the Grievances of the Mukama and the People of Toro, *Report* (BCEA, n42)
———, Protectorate, Committee of Enquiry into the Labour Situation in Uganda, *Report* (BCEA, n43)
Union Coloniale Française, Paris, Section de l'Indochine, *Les Problèmes posés par le Développement Industriel de l'Indochine* (FV, n71)
Urquhart, D. H., "Land Usage and Utilization in Southern Nigeria" (BWA, n66)

Vandenbosch, A., "The Netherlands Colonial Balance Sheet" (NI, n48)
Van der Kolff, G. H., "European Influence on Native Agriculture" (NI, n20)
Van der Kroef, J., "Dutch Colonial Policy in Indonesia, 1900-1950" (NI, n1)
———, "Economic Origins of Indonesian Nationalism" (NI, n47)
———, "The Eurasian Minority in Indonesia" (NI, n52)
———, *Indonesia in the Modern World* (NI, n1)
Van Deventer, C. T., "Een Eeresschuld" (NI, n16)
Van Eeghen, G. M., "The Beginnings of Industrialization in Netherlands India" (NI, n43)
Van Helsdingen, W. H. (ed.), *Mission Interrupted* (NI, 178)
Van Leur, J. C., *Indonesian Trade and Society* (NI, n2)
Van Niel, R., "The Course of Indonesian History" (NI, n8)
———, *The Emergence of the Modern Indonesian Elite* (NI, n16)
Varenne, A., *Discours pronouncé le 21 octobre 1927* (FV, n22)
Vatikiotis, P. J., *The Modern History of Egypt* (BPE, n1)
Verhandlungen, see Germany, Reichstag (GC, n8)

Vlekke, B. H. M., *Nusantara* (NI, n1)
Voigt, G., "Organisatorische Nachkriegsprobleme der Britisch-Indischen Eisenbahnen" (BI, n169)

Waley, Sir. S. D., *Edwin Montagu* (BI, n318)
Wallerstein, I. M., *The Road to Independence* (FWEA, n108)
——— (ed.), *Social Change* (M, n29)
Warhurst, P. R., *Anglo-Portuguese Relations in South-Central Africa, 1890-1900* (PA, n6)
Washausen, H., *Hamburg und die Kolonialpolitik des Deutschen Reiches 1880 bis 1890* (GC, n9)
Washbrook, D., "Country Politics" (BI, n36)
Wasserman, B., "The Ashanti War of 1900" (BWA, n19)
Wauters, A. J., *Histoire Politique du Congo Belge* (BC, n10)
Wehler, H. U., *Bismarck und der Imperialismus* (P, n3)
Weinstein, B., *Eboué* (FWEA, n91)
Wendt, J., *Economic Appeasement* (BI, n245)
Wertheim, W. F., *East-West Parallels* (NI, n1)
———, *Indonesian Society in Transition* (NI, n1)
———, "Social Change in Java, 1900-1930" (NI, n1)
West African Chiefs (BWA, n20)
Wheeler, D. L., "An Early Angolan Protest" (PA, n58)
———, "Gungunyane the Negotiator" (PA, n8)
———, "The Origins of African Nationalism in Angola" (PA, n58)
———, and René Pelisser, *Angola* (PA, n15)
Wilensky, A. H., *Tendências de la Legislación Ultramarina Portuguesa em Africa* (PA, n10)
Willcocks, Sir W., *Sixty Years in the East* (BPE, n35)
Williams, W. A., *The Tragedy of American Diplomacy* (P, n5)
Wills, A. J., *An Introduction to the History of Central Africa* (BCEA, n1)
Wilson, A. J., "The Creve-McCallum Reforms, (1912-1921)" (C, n29)
Winder, R. B., "The Libanese in West Africa" (FWEA, n38)
Winkler, H., "Das Kameruner Proletariat, 1906-1914" (GC. n46)
Winkler, H. A., *Bauern zwischen Wasser und Wüste* (BPE, n59)
———, see also *Organisierter Kapitalismus* (SU, n31)
, "Das Kameruner Proletariat, 1906-1914" (GC, n46)
Wipper, A., "Gusii" (BCEA, n94)
Wirz, A., *Vom Sklavenhandel zum kolonialen Handel* (GC, n22)
Wondji, C., "La Côte d'Ivoire Occidentale" (FWEA, n11)
Woolf, L., *Growing* (C, n5)
Wraith, R. E., *Guggisberg* (BWA, n43)
Wriggins, W. H., *Ceylon* (C, n1)
Wright, H. R., "Some Aspects of the Permanent Settlement in Bengal" (BI, n92)
Wrigley, C. C., "Buganda" (BCEA, n39)
———, "The Christian Revolution in Buganda" (BCEA, n37)
Wyndham, H. A., *Native Education* (C, n21)

Yacono, X., *Les Bureaux Arabes et l'Evolution des Genres de Vie Indigène dans l'Ouest du Tell Algérois* (FM, n5)
Young, C., *Politics in the Congo* (BC, n40)

Zacharias, C.W.B., *Madras Agriculture* (BI, n137)
Zapf, W. (comp.), *Theorien des sozialen Wandels* (P, n21)
Zenati, R., *Le Problème Algérien vu par un Indigène* (FM, n115)
Ziadeh, N. A., *Origins of Nationalism in Tunisia* (FM, n107)
Zinkin, M., *Asia and the West* (BI, n118)

INDEX

Abbas, Ferhat, 284-85, 291
Abbas II, Khedive of Egypt, 249
Abd el-Kader, 257
Abd el-Krim, 288
Abdel Aziz, Sultan of Morocco, 263
Abduh, Mohammed (Islamic reformer), 247
Aborigines Rights Protection Society, 1887 (Gold Coast), 330
Achimota College (Gold Coast), 319, 362
L'Action du Peuple (newspaper), 290
Action Tunisien (newspaper), 287
Acworth Commission, criticizes Indian railway management, 47
adat (Indonesian customary law), 161, 165, 183; *adat* class, 182
administrador (Portuguese official), duties, 422-23
administration, Belgian: under Leopold II, 375; under the *Charte*, 378-80
administration, British: in Burma, 118-19, 124-25; in Ceylon, 132-34; in Egypt, 235-36; in India, 12-21, under India Act of 1935, 88-89; in Malaya, 147-49; in East Africa, 448-50, 457-58, 462-64, 467, 471-72; and West Africa, 317-19, 331-32
administration, colonial: general considerations, xxi, 489-93; "dualism," 493
administration directe. *See* direct rule
administration, Dutch, in Indonesia, 164-67, 184-86
administration, French: in Algeria, 257-61; in Morocco, 263-65; in the Maghreb, 265-66; in Tunisia, 262-63; in Vietnam, 197-201; in West and Equatorial Africa, 346-54
administration, German, in Africa, 392-95
administration, Portuguese, in Africa, 422-26
Afgani, Jamal al-Din al (Islamic reformer), 247
Afghans, 3, 4; Afghan War, 117
African Association, 479
African Civil Servants Association, 479
African Orthodox Church, 478
Age of Consent bill (India), 75-76
agrarian structure: Ceylon, 135-37; Cochinchina, 204; Egypt, 229-31; 238-39; India, 27-28; Indonesia, 169-72; Maghreb, 269-77. *See also* native farming, plantations, *specific cash crops* (cotton, rubber, and peanuts)
agricultural revolution development, 504; and India, 44
Agriculturists' Relief Act, 1879 (India), 34
Ahmadou (African leader), 343-44, 345
Ainsworth, John, 451
Akbar, (Mughal emperor), 27-28
akida (Arab or Swahili sub-official) 397; role, 406; British take-over of, 463
Albuquerque, Mouzinho de, 424, 427, 432
Allenby, Gen. Edmund H. H., 250
Ambedkar, Dr. Bhimrao Ramji, leads untouchables, 88-89
Amery, Leopold S., 454
Amritsar massacre, 1919, 82
Anglo-American Corporation, 472
Anglo-Belgian Rubber Company, 376
Anglo-Oriental College, 1865, 73
Angoulvant, Gabriel Louis, 345
Anstey, Vera, 57
Antonetti, Governor General, 360
Arabi, Col. Ahmed, rebellion of, 233-34

arch land, defined, 258, 267
Archinard, Louis, 344
Ashanti (African people), 308-9
Ashanti Gold Fields Corporation, 325
askari troops, 391
assimilados (Portuguese Africa): 436; as protestors, 439-40
"*assimilation*": in French colonies, 256; implications, 258; in Portuguese colonies, "leveling," 424, "spiritual," 426; in West and Equatorial Africa, 362
Associacão Commercial de Loanda, pressure group, 423-24
"*association*": in French colonies, 258; as ideology, 362, 365
Association des Etudiants Musulmans Nord-Africains, 1927, 289
Association des Ulémas Algérians, 285
associations, voluntary: in British Africa, 332-35, 479-81; in Burma, 125-26; in French West and Equatorial Africa, 366; in India, 70-71; in the Maghreb, 282-85, 289-90; in Malaya, 156; and national liberation, 511; in Portuguese Africa, 439-40; in Vietnam, 214
Aswan dam, 237-38, 241
Ataturk, Kemal, 85
Atlee, Clement, 86
Aurangzeb, Mughal emperor, 3
Austen, Ralph, 463
Awolowo, Obafemi, 334
Azhar University, al (Cairo), 246, 247
Azikiwe, Nnamdi, 329, 334-35

Ba Maw, U, 127
Bach-Hamba, Ali, 282, 283, 286
Badis, Abdelhamid Ben (Islamic reformer), 284-85
Baer, Gabriel, 238, 239
Bagchi, Amiya Kumar, 67
Bairoch, Paul, 504
Baker Report, 1933, 465
balance of payments/trade: Burma, 124; for India, 53, 63-64; Indonesia, 174, 177-78; for the Maghreb, 280; Portuguese Africa, 433
Bamba (marabout), founds Mourides, 366
Bamberger, Ludwig, 391
Banda, Dr. Hastings, 481
Bandaranaike, S.W.R.D., 134, 141
Bandung Technical College, 186
Banerjea, Surendranath, 18, 70-71, 73, 77, 78
banks and banking: in Ceylon, 141; in Egypt, 232; and Indian development, 51, 61; in Indonesia, 172
Bantam (Javan state), 160-61
Bad Dai, emperor of Vietnam, 218
Bargash, sultan of Zanzibar, 444
Baring, Evelyn. *See* Cromer, Lord
Bataka Association, 479
Beau, Paul, 212-13
Bendjelloul, Dr. Muhammed Saleh, 284
Bengal, partition of, 77-78
Bengal Iron Works, 55
Bengal Land Revenue Commission, 1937, 38
Bengal Tenancy Act, 71, 75
Benguela Railway Company, 436
Bentinck, Lord William, 6, 10
Berlin Congress, 388, 419-20. *See also* Congo Conference, 1884-1885
Bernard, Paul, 209, 211
Berque, Jacques, 240
Bert, Paul, 197, 212, 213
Besant, Annie, 67, 79, 81
Binger, Louis Gustave, 345
Bismarck, Otto von, 375; colonial policy, 388-89; East Africa, 390, 391
Blantyre mission (Nyasaland), 478
Bledisloe Commission, 475
Bley, Helmut, 396
Blum, Léon, 285, 288
Blunt, Wilfred, 230
Blyden, Edward W., 329
Boeke, Julius Herman, 169; on "dual economy," 498-99
Bombay Presidency Association, 1885, 71
Borgnis-Desbordes, Gustave, 344
Borodin, Mikhail, 217
Bosch, Johannes van den, 162-63
Bose, Subhas, 90
Bourdillon, Sir Bernard, 315; *Memorandum on the Future Political Development of Nigeria*, 332
Bourguiba, Habib, 287-88, 291
Braganza monarchy, 424, 439
Brahmins, ch. 3 passim; in Burma, 116
Brahmo Samaj (religious movement), 18, 69-71, 75
Brazza, Pierre S. de, 346, 359-60, 374
Brévié, Jules, 218, 362
Brière de l'Isle, Louis A.E.G., 343
British Colonial Development Fund, 1929, 507
British Cotton Growing Association, 458
British East African Association, 445

British East India Company, 3-5, 13, 26, 28, 29, 41, 45, 49; and Burma, 116-17, 132, 145, 228, 389
British Indian Association, 36, 70, 71, 73
British South Africa Company, 433, 434, 447, 467, 468, 470-71
Bryce, James, 21
Buchka, Georg von, 399
Budi Utomo Union, 1908, 182
Buganda, 445-46; political organization, 457-58, 459
Bureaux des Affaires Arabes, 257-59
"Burghers," as class in Ceylon, 132
Burma Independent Army, 128
Burma Oil Company, 123
Burma Tenancy bill, 122-23

Cabral, Amilcar, 427
Cadbury, William, and Portuguese cocoa, 430
Cady, John, 125
"Cahier of Annamite Wishes," 215
caids (Arab officials): in Algeria, 260; in Morocco, 264-65; in Tunisia, 262
Caisse de Prêts Immobiliers du Maroc, 277
Caisse Mutuelles de Crédit Agricole (Morocco), 277
Calabar National Institute, 333
Calcutta University, 124
Cameron, Donald: West Africa, *Principals of Native Administration*, 312, 315; Tanganyika, 462-67; *My Tanganyika Service*, 466
cantonnement (Maghreb), 266; defined, 257-58
Cao Dai (religious movement), 219
capital formation and development, 504. *See also* investment
Caprivi, Gen. Leo von, 391
Carde, Jules G., 363
Carr, Henry, 317
Cartel des Gauches, and Vietnam, 215
Carter Commission, 1925, 480
Casely Hayford, Joseph E., 329-31, 333
Casement, Roger, 377
cash crops: importance assessed, 499-502; Belgian Congo lacking in, 381; British East Africa, 458; British West Africa, 321, 327; Burma, 120-21; Ceylon, 137; in India, 41-43; Indonesia, 169, 171-72; Egypt, 242; French West Africa, 355; 358-59; German colonies, 410-11; Portuguese colonies, 437-38. *See also* *specific cash crops* (coffee, cotton, cocoa, peanuts, rice, olives, rubber, tea, etc.)
caste: in Ceylon, 144; in Indian villages, 28, 34, 50, 70; and workforce, 48, 62, 65-66, 68; untouchables, 88-89
census, Indian, 22
Ceylon Indian Congress, 140
Ceylon National Association, 139
Ceylon National Congress, 140
Ceylon Reform League, 140
Chadbourne scheme, and sugar production, 173
Chagga (African people), as coffee growers, 465-66
Chamberlain, Austen, 79
Chamberlain, Joseph, 317; and Ashanti, 318
Chambre des Représentants du Peuple (Tonkin), 214, 216
Chandra, Bipan, 57
Charte Coloniale (Belgian Congo), 378
Charter of Restitution for the Algerian Muslim People, 1936, reform demands of, 285
Chau, Phan Boi, 214
Chaudié, Jean Baptiste, 353
chef de canton (African official), 349
chef de village (African official), 350
Chiang Kai-shek, 155
Chieu, Bui Quang, 205, 214-16
Chilembwe, John, 478
Chelmsford, Frederick, 20
chettyars (Indian moneylenders): in Burma, 121; Malaya, 154; and Vietnam, 205
Chinese: in Burma, 123; in Indonesia, 161, 168, 171-76, 179-80; in Malaya, ch. 4, passim; in Vietnam, 202, 204-5, 207
Chirol, Valentine, 58
churches. *See* religious movements
Churchill, Winston S., 452, 453, 470
circumscriptions (Portuguese Africa), basic administrative unit, 422
cigarette production: Egyptian, 244; Indonesian, 175-76
civil disobedience campaigns (Gandhi's), 82-84, 87-88
Civil War (U.S.), 42, 120, 230
Clarke, Andrew, 147
Clémenceau, Georges, 284
Clifford, Hugh, 330-31
Clive, Robert, 3-4; and Ceylon, 132
"closer union" movement, 434, 462

coal mining: in India, 54; in the Maghreb, 279; Vietnam, 210
cocoa: in British West Africa, 320-23; in the Cameroons, 410; in French West Africa, 357-58; "hold-ups" 322-23; in Portuguese Africa, 430
Code du Travail (Vietnam), 208
Coelho, Col. Manuel, 430
Coen, Jan Pieterzoon, 161
coffee: in British East Africa, 455, 464-65; in Ceylon, 134-36; in French West Africa, 357, 358; in German colonies, 400, 410; in Indonesia, 161, 163-64; in Portuguese Africa, 436
Cognacq, Maurice, 215
Colign, Hendrikus, 186
collaboration: in British West Africa, 333; and colonial rule, 509-510; in French West Africa, 344, 350; and Indirect Rule, 316; in Indonesia, 187-88; Portuguese Africa, 423; in Vietnam, 213, 216, 219
Collège Sadiki, 1875 (Tunisia), 261, 282, 287
"colonial condition," as Balandier defines, xxi; and Indian industrialization, 57
"colonialism," as Emerson defines, xxi; and dependency, xxi.
colonial policy. *See* administration
colonial scandals: Belgian, 376-77, 382-83; French, 207-8, 293, 296, 360; German, 404, 413; Portuguese, 430
colonial situation, 488-89, 510, 512; in Burma, 125; and Portuguese Africa, 439. *See also* colonial condition
colonization policy: Belgian, 380; British, in Kenya, 450, 455-56, in Rhodesia, 468; French, in Algeria, 257, 267-68, 272-73, in Maghreb, 280-81, in Morocco, 276-77, in Tunisia, 272-73, in Vietnam, 206-7; German, 396, 408-9; Portuguese, 435-36
colons, ch. 8, passim; in Vietnam, 204, 206; in West Africa, 352, 357-58. *See also specific colonies*, settlers
co-mat (Vietnam), 194; reorganized, 198
commandant du cercle (French official), role, 348
Committee for Trade and Industry, 1917 (Egypt), 249
Committee for Upper Congo Studies, and Congo exploration,.394
Communal Award (India), 92
communal representation, for Muslims in India, 78-81
communes de plein exercice, 259, 260, 263
communes mixte, 260
Communist party: Algerian, 285; Indian, 76; Indonesian (PKI), 184-85; Malay, 156; Vietnamese, 217-19
Compagne du Chemin de Fer du Congo, 376
Compagne du Sud-Katanga (CSK), 380
Compagne Française de l'Afrique Equatoriale, 306
Compagne Française de l'Afrique Occidentale, 1887, 354
Compagnie du Chemin de Fer du Bas-Congo au Katanga (BCK), 377
Companhia da Zambézia, 433-34
Companhia de Diamantes de Angola (Diamang), activities, 434-35
Companhia de Moçambique, 422, 433
Companhia do Nyassa, 422, 433-34
concession companies: Vietnam, 207; British, 307-8, Leverhulme refused, 320, 467-68; French Equatorial Africa, 359-60; Belgian Congo, 376-77, 381-82; German colonies, 389-91, 399-400, 411; Portuguese Africa, 422, 433-35
Conféderation Générale des Travailleurs Ouvriers (CGTU), 285
Conféderation Générale des Travailleurs Tunisiens (CGTT), 286
Conference of London, 1885, 236
Congo Conference, 1884-1885, 306-17; and Belgium, 375, 376. *See also* Berlin Congress
Congo Reform Association, 377
Congrès Indochinois, 218
Congress Party (India), 74-93; character of, 74; economic measures, 91; and elementary education, 69; founding, 70; and India Act of 1935, 89-91; membership, 84-85; and princely states, 13; program, 74; reorganized, 84; and zamindars, 38
Congress Socialist Party (India), 90
Conseil Colonial (Cochinchina), 199, reformed, 215
Conseil de Protectorat (Tonkin), 198
Conseil Générale (French West Africa), 365
Conseil Supérieur de l'Indochine, 198
Conseilleur du gouvernement chérifien (Morocco), 264
Constitutional Reform Party (Egypt), 246
Constitution of 1833 (Ceylon), 139-41
Constitution of 1923 (Egypt), 250

Constitution of 1925 (Netherlands Indies), 184
contrôleur: Dutch colonial official, 165; French official, 262
Convention of Associations, 1910, 453-54
Convention Peoples' Party (Gold Coast), 335
cooperatives: in British East Africa, 460-61, 466; in French West Africa, 356; in Gold Coast, 322; in India, 36; Indonesia, 175;
Cooperative Societies Act, 1904 (India), 36, 76
copper: in Belgian Congo, 377, 381-82; in Northern Rhodesia, 472-74
copra, 171
corn: in British East Africa, 545-55, 472, 474; in Egypt, 242; in Portuguese Africa, 438
Cornwallis, Lord (2nd Earl of, Charles Cornwallis), 4, 5; and administration, 16-17; and Muslims, 72; and Permanent Settlement, 29-30
Corporation of German Colonization, 390
corvée. *See* labor, compulsory
Cosnier, Henri, 355
Costa, Eustacio da, 424, 427
cotton: in Egypt, 229-30, 241-44; in French West Africa, 357; in German East Africa, 397-98, 404; in India, 42-43; in Portuguese Africa, 436-37; in Uganda, 458-61
Cotton, Sir Arthur, 26
Couceiro, Henrique Paiva, 431
Council for Improving the Education of the Natives, 212
Council of Notables (Egypt), 233, 234, 241
Crédit Foncier (bank), 238
Crewe, Robert, 80
Criminals Deportation Act (Egypt), 247
Cromer, Lord (Earl of Cromer, Evelyn Baring), 72; assessed, 247; in Egypt, 235-47; on Egyptians, 236
Crown Land Ordnance, 1896 (German Africa), 400-401
Crowther, Bishop Samuel, 329
cultivation, forced: in Belgian Congo, 381; in German Africa, 397-98; in India, 41-42; Indonesia, 161-64; in Portuguese Africa, 437. *See also* labor, compulsory, and taxation
Culture System (Indonesia), 162-64
Curtis, Lionel, 80-81
Curzon, Lord (Marquess Curzon of Kedlestone, George N. Curzon): and economic development, 41, 48, 55, 58, 68; and famines, 26; and India Council, 14; on Indians in ICS, 19-21; politics as viceroy, 76-77
customs policy: in British West Africa, 328; and development, 501, 506; in Egypt, 231; in French West and Equatorial Africa, 361; in India, 48, 51-52, 59-60; in Indonesia, 175-77; in the Maghreb, 256, 280; in Vietnam, 210

dacoity (Burma), 118
Daendels, Herman Willem, 162
dahir (Morocco), defined, 275
Dahir Berbère, 1930, 289-90
Dahm, Bernhard, 183, 512
Dalhousie, Lord (Marquis of, James A. B. Ramsay): and Burma, 117-18; developments under, 26, 45; of "forward school", 7
Damel of Cayor (African ruler), 344
Danquah, Joseph B., 334-335
Darling, Malcolm, 35-36
Das, C. R. Ram, 83, 85
Debt Protection Act, 1936 (India), 35
Deccan College, Poona, 76
Deccan riots of 1875, 33
Décret Crémieux (Algeria), 259
Décret des Tribunaux Indigènes (Belgian Congo), 378
De Gaulle, Gen. Charles, and Algerian reform, 285-86
de Graeff, Andries Cornelis Dirk, 186
de Jonge, Bonifacius Cornelis, 188
Dekker, Eduard Douwes, *Max Havelaar*, 164
Delamere, Lord (3rd Baron, Hugh Cholmondeley) 453, 480
Delavignette, Robert, 350, 422
Delcassé, Théophile, 263
Délégations Financières (Algeria), 259, 260, 263
Department of Agriculture, 1911 (Egypt), 242
dependency, colonial, discussed, xx, xxi-xxii
Depression, Great: and Algeria, 270; British East Africa, 466; in British West Africa, 328; and Burma, 122; in French West Africa, 356; and India, 60; and Indonesia, 172-73, 175-77; and Malaya, 151; in Vietnam, 211

Depius, Jean, 195
Dernburg, Bernhard, 393; and German colonial reforms, 404-405, 409, 411, 412
Dervieu, Edouard (private bank), 232
"de-stoolment," defined, 314
Destour Party (Tunisia), foundation and program, 286-87, 288
Deventer, Charles Theodor van: "A Debt of Honor," 166
Devonshire Declaration, 454, 475
Dhammathat (Buddhist law code), 119
Dia, Mamadou, 362
Diagne, Blaise, 364
diamonds: in Angola, 434-35; in German Southwest Africa, 411
Diem, Ngo Dinh, 218
Digby, William, *"Prosperous" British India*, 44
Dilke, Charles, on India, 9
Diouf, Galandou, 365
direct rule: French, and Indirect rule, 348-49; ideology, 349; Portuguese, 422
"distance," and British colonial rule, 8-9, 488
district commissioners (German), functions, 405
district officers: in India, 15-16; in West Africa, 311
diwani, defined, 3, 28, 29
djemaa (Morocco), tribal council, 276
Donoughmore constitution (Ceylon), 140-41
douars (Maghreb), defined, 260, 268
Doumer, Paul, 197-200, 206, 207; and railway construction in Vietnam, 208-9
Douwes Dekker, E.F.E., 182
Draft constitution of 1928 (India), 86
"drain of wealth" thesis: and Belgian Congo, 377; and Burma, 124; discussed, 497-98; and India, 62-65; and Indonesia, 177-78
Dresch, Jean, on social crisis in Maghreb, 281-82
"Dual Control" (Egypt), 232; ends, 234
dual economy: in Ceylon, 138-39; defined, xxiv; in general terms, 498-503; in India, 61; in Malaya, 149, 152; in Netherlands Indies, 177, 498-99; in Northern Rhodesia, 475
Dual Mandate in Tropical Africa, on Indirect Rule, 309
Du Bois, W.E.B., 440
Dufferin, Lord (Marquess of, Frederick T.H.—T. Blackwood): 72, 75, 118; and Egyptian situation, 234, 240
Durbar of 1901 (India), 76
Durham Report, 1839, 80, 140
Dutt, Romesh Chandra: "drain of wealth," 63; 70, *Economic History of India*, 75; and ICS examination, 18; *Open Letter to Lord Curzon*, 44; "re-ruralization," 49; and social crisis, 25
dyarchy; in Burma, 125; explained, 80-81; in India, 20; problems, 85, scope expanded, 89;
Dyer, Gen. Reginald, 82

East Africa Company, 450
East African Indian National Congress, 454
Eboué, Félix, 364
Ecole Coloniale (Paris), 348, 364
Ecole de Médicine (Dakar), 362
Ecole de Médicine Vétérinaire (Bamako), 362
Ecole des Fils des Chefs, 362
Ecole Primaire Supérieure et Professionelle (French West Africa), 363
Ecole William Ponty, 362
economic development: in British West Africa, 326-328; in Burma, 119-20; in colonial context, xxi-xxiv, 493-508; Egypt, 230-32, 244; in French West Africa, 361; in India, 21, 56-57; in Indonesia, 166-67, 175-77. *See also related topics* (customs policy, industrialization, etc.)
educational policy: Belgian, 383-84; British, Burma, 124, Ceylon, 133, East Africa, 477, 480-81, Egypt, 245, in India, 61, 68-69, Malaya, 154-55, West Africa, 318-19; Dutch, 175, 180-82; French, in the Maghreb, 260-61, 282, in Vietnam, 212-13, in West Africa, 363-66; German 407-408; Portuguese, 428
Ehrlich, Cyril, 461
Eisenstadt, S. N., 491
Elgin, Lord (9th Earl, Victor Alexander Bruce), 452
elites, new (or modern): in British West Africa, 316, 328-30, 333-35; in Ceylon, 139; in Egypt, 245-46; in French West Africa, 366; general role, 510; in India, 67-78; in Indonesia, 179-82; in Maghreb, 291-92; in Malaya, 155-56; in Portuguese Africa, 439; in Vietnam, 214, 216

elites, traditional: in the Belgian Congo, 378-79; in British East Africa, 449, 458, 459, 463-64, 466-67; in British West Africa, 309-18, 333; in Burma, 118-19, 125-26; in Ceylon, 132, 134; in Egypt, 227-29, 241, 246; in French West Africa, 350; in German Africa, 406-407; in India, 11-13, 27-29, 67-68, 72-73, 89; in Indonesia, 162-66, 178-79; in the Maghreb, 257, 261-66, 282; in Malaya, 147-49, 154-56; in Portuguese Africa, 422-23; in Vietman, 194, 196-98, 212-13
Elliot, Sir Charles, 450, 452
Elphinstone, Mountstuart, 5, 31
Elphinstone College, 70
Emerson, Rupert, defines colonialism, xxi
"enclaves" (economic): in British West Africa, 325; Burma, 123; in Ceylon, 138; discussed, 501-502; examples, xxiv; in India, 42, 54, 58, 65; in Indonesia, 174, 176, 180; Northern Rhodesia, 475
Enes, António, 424, 427, 429
entrepreneurs and entrepreneurial classes: and development, 505, 516; Egyptian, 244-45; Indian, 51-52, 61-62; Indonesian, 176, 180; Uganda, lack of, 461
Estado Novo, Salazar's Portugal, 425
"Ethical Policy" (Indonesia), 166-67, 172; "washed up," 188
Etienne, Eugène, 197, 263, 359
Etoile Nord-Africaine, 285-86
Eucharistic Congress, Carthage, 1930, 287
Eurasians, in Indonesia, 179

factory laws, Indian, 66-67. *See specific types of legislation for other colonies*
Fahmi, Mustafa, 247
Faidherbe, Gen. Louis, 343
famine, in India, 22-25
Famine Commission of 1880 (India), 24, 26, 33, 46
Farid, Muhammed, 247
Farmers' Union (Ashanti), 322
Fassi, Alal el, 289-91
Faure, Félix, 347
Fazhul Huq, Abdul Kasini, 91, 92
Fédération des Elus Indigènes, 1927 (Maghreb), 284
Ferry, Jules, 117; and French Algerian policy, 259-60, 261
Five Feddan Law, 1911 (Egypt), 239
Forah Bay College, 317, 318
Force Indigène (Vietnam), 200
Force Publique (Belgian Congo), 376
Forminière (Belgian Congo), 377, 380, 381, 435
Forster, E. M., and *Passage to India*, 9
Foundation de la Couronne (Belgium), 377
France, and India, 3-4; and Burma, 117
Franck, Louis, 378
Free trade. *See* customs policy
Freyeinet (French statesman), 117
Furnivall, J. S.: impact of capitalism on traditional societies, 121; and Indonesia, 163, 167; influence in Burma, 128

Gadgil, D. R., 49
Galliéni, Joseph, 196, 344
Galtung, Johan, xxi; and "bridgeheads, 505
Galvão, Henrique, 431-32, 435
Gambetta, Léon, 261
Gandhi, Mohandas K., 10, 21, 76, 77, 79; as leader of Indian nationalist movement, 81-93
Gangulee, Nagendranath, 33
Garnier, Francis, 195
Garvey, Marcus, 440
Geertz, Clifford: and alternatives, 171; "involution", 168-69, 500
General Council of Burmese Associations (GCBA), 126
Gerindo movement (Indonesia), 187-88
German Colonial Corporation for Southwest Africa, 390
German East African Company, 390
Gershenkron, Alexander, and industrialization, 505, 507
Gide, André, and *Voyage au Congo*, 360
Gladstone, Sir William E., 71, 77, 117, 147
al-Glaoui, Thami (pasha of Marrakesh), 265
Gokhale, Gopal Krishna, 75-76, 78-79, 81
Gold Coast Youth Conference, 334
Golden Stool (Ashanti), 309, 314
gold mining: in the Belgian Congo, 377; in British West Africa, 325; in Rhodesia, 447, 468
Gordon, Gen. Charles, 445
Gorst, Sir Eldon, 247
Götzen, Adolf von, 397, 405
Gourou, Pierre, 200, 204, 206
grain farming: in British East Africa, 455; in Egypt, 242-43; in the French Maghreb, 269, 273-74, 277-78
Grand Conseil (Tunisia), 263, 286-87
Grand Conseil des Intérets Financiers et Economiques (Vietnam), 184, 216

Greater Indonesian Party, 187
Greeks: in British East Africa, 464; in Egypt, 230, 239, 244-45
Grey, Sir Edward, 421
Grigg, Sir Edward S., 454
"grow-more-crops" campaign (Tanganyika), 466
guangs (Burmese officials), 119
Gueye, Amadou Lamine, 363, 365
Guggisberg, Sir Gordon (Gold Coast), 313-16; pushes localization and education 318-19; development program, 323, 332
guich lands (Morocco), 276
Gungunhama (ruler of Gaza), 421

Habib, Irfan, 57
habous (Maghreb), and administration, 262, 273; defined, 272
El-Hadira (Tunisian newspaper), 282
Hadj, Messali, 285
Haileybury College (England), 17
Hamilton, Lord George Francis, 55
Hardinge, Lord (Baron, Charles), 78, 79, 80
Hastings, Warren, 4, 29
Hatta, Muhammed, 186-87
Hausa (African people), 308
Henry, Yves, 205
Herero rebellion, 396-97, 412-13
El-Hiba (Moroccan marabout), 264
Hill, Polly, 221
Hindoo Patriot (newspaper), 70
Hindu College (Calcutta), 69
Hinduism, ch. 1, passim; and Ceylon, 131; in Indonesia, 160-61; and Malaya, 145; and modernist revival, 69-70; in Vietnam, 194;
Hlaing, Aye, 124
Ho Chi Minh, 217
Hopkins, A. G., 326
Hoselitz, Bert, 505
Houphouet-Boigny, Félix, 359, 362
Hume, A. O., 72
Hunter Report, on Amritsar massacre, 83
Hunter, William Wilson, 30-40

Ibos (African people), 312-13
Ibo Union, 333
Ilbert, Sir Courtenay, and Ilbert bills, 18, 72
imperialism, historiography of, xviii-xx, 513
Imperial Legislative Council, 77-78
imperial policy (the course of, and rationales for conquest): Belgian, 374-75; British, in India, 3-5, 7-8, 12, in Burma, 116-18, in Ceylon, 132, in East Africa, 445-48, in Egypt, 232-34, in Malaya, 145-48, in West Africa, 305-309; Dutch, 161-62, 165-66; French, in the Maghreb, 256-57, 261-64, in Vietnam, 194-96, in West and Equatorial Africa, 343-46; German, 388-91, 393; Portuguese, 418-20
Imperial Preference Duty, 136
indebtedness, agricultural, as social problem: in British West Africa, 321-22; in Burma, 121-23; in Egypt, 230; in the French Maghreb, 270; in India, 32-38; in Vietnam, 203, 205-206
Independent School Association (Kenya), 480
India Acts, 1773, 1784, 4, 13; 1935, 88-90
India Association, 70
India Council, 78
India Declaration, 20 August 1917, 80, 330
Indian Civil and Commercial Codes of Procedure, 16
Indian Civil Service (ICS), 16-20; examinations for, as political problem, 17-20, 71, 73, 74, 85, 124
Indian Jute Mills Association, 1884, 53
Indian Penal Code, 16
Indians, as expatriate minority: in British East Africa, 452-53, 465-66; in Burma, 121, 124; in Ceylon, 132, 136-37, 140; in Malaya, 151-55
Indian Universities Act, 1904, 68, 77
Indigénat, French statute controlling colonials, 260, 284, 365
indigo, 41-42, 161-63
Indirect Rule: and Belgian version, 378; Buganda as example, 457-58; contrasted with French direct rule, 348-49; discussed, 309-19; ends sought, 349; and German version, 406; in Maghreb, 265; Malaya as model, 147; and Northern Rhodesia, 473; and settler government in Kenya, 449-50; stultifying effects of, 461; in Tanganyika, 463
Indische Partij, 182
Indochine (newspaper), 215
Indochinese Union, 1887, 194, 197
Indonesian Association, 186
Indonesian Muslim Party, 188
Indonesian National Education Association, 187
Indonesian Social Democratic Union, 184
Indus dam, 26

Industrial Commission of 1916 (India), 59-60
Industrial Conciliation Act, 1934 (Southern Rhodesia), 471
industrialization: after 1882, 244-45; discussed, 502-507; in Egypt, 229-31; in India, 56-65; in Indonesia, 174-76; in the Maghreb, 278-80; in Vietnam, 209-211
industrial revolution: impact on modern colonialism, 4, 513; and India, 49-50
Inspection Générale du Travail, 1927 (Vietnam), 208
Institute of Science (Bangalore), 68
International Africa Society (Belgium), 346, 375
International Labor Organization (League of Nations), 351
investment, overseas, in colonies: in Burma, 123-24; discussed, 505, 507; in Egypt, 231-32, 234; in India, 46; in Indonesia, 168, 172, 175-77; in the Maghreb, 280; in Malaya, 150, 152; in Vietnam, 209-210
iron industry, Indian, 55-56; in the Maghreb, 279
Irrawaddy River Flotilla Corporation, 123
irrigation: in Ceylon, 131, 138; in Egypt, 229, 237-39; in French West Africa, 357; in India, 25-27, 76; in Indonesia, 160, 166; in Vietnam, 203-204
Irwin, Lord (Edward Wood), 14, 86-88
Islam and Islamic revival, as spur to national liberation: in Egypt, 245-46; in India, 73-74; in Indonesia, 182-83, 186; in Maghreb, 284-85, 289-92; in Malaya, 156
Ismail, Khedive of Egypt, 231-33
Issawi, Charles, 231-44

Jaffna Association, 139
Jaja, ruler of Opobo, 306
Jameson, Leander Starr, 447
Japan: and economic development, 500, 504-5; economic role of state, 57-58, 507; and education, 69; and Indian textiles, 51-52; and Indonesia, 175
Jauréguiberry, Adm. Jean B., 195, 306
Jaures, Jean, 214
Jehovah's Witnesses, in Congo, 385; in British East Africa, 478
Le Jeune Algérien (newspaper), 284
Jinnah, Mohammed Ali, 67, 85; and Muslim League, 92-93
jobbers (India), role explained, 66
Johnson, Rev. Samuel, 329
Johnstone, Harry, kidnaps Jaja, 306, 471
Joshi, T. M., 44
Jumel, Louis A. 230
jute, 43; industry, 52-54

"Kaffir farming," 453, 471
Kagwa, Sir Apolo, 457
Kamil, Mustafa, Islamic reformer, 246-47
Kamwana, Elliot, 478
Kanda Peasantry Commission (Ceylon), 137
kangany, defined, 151
Karachi Resolution, 1931, 90
Kaunda, Kenneth, 481
Kayser, Paul, 399
Kenya African Union, 481
Kenya Land Commission, 455
Kenyatta, Jomo, 479-81
Keita, Modibo, 362
Khaldounia (Tunisia), 282
Khaled, Emir, 284
Khama, ruler of Bechuanaland, 446
Khan, Gen. Ayub, 10
Khan, Syed Ahmad, 19-20
kharaj, land tax, 240
Khéréddine, Tunisian statesman, 282
Khérian, Grégoire, 211
Khilaphat movement, 82-83, 85
Kikuyu Association, 479-80
Kikuyu Land Commission, 1929, 455
Kikuyus (African people), 446, 449, 450-51, 453, 456
Kilimanjaro Native Planters Association, 466
Kimbangu, Simon, religious leader, 385; and Kimbangism, 439
Kimberly, Lord, 146-47
King Edward VII College for Medicine (Malaya), 155
Kings College (Nigeria), 318
Kirk, Sir John, 444-45
Kitchener, Gen. Horatio H., 77, 239, 248
Kivu National Committee (Belgian Congo), 380
Kotelwala, Sir John, 141, 144
Krishak Praja party, 91-92
Külz, Wilhelm, 411-12

labor. *See also* workers, expatriate and migrant, and working conditions
labor, compulsory: in the Belgian Congo, 376-77; in Ceylon, 131-32; in Egypt, 239-40; in French West Africa, 351-52, 357; German colonies, 401-05, 412-13; Portuguese Africa, 427, 429-32; in Vietnam, 203, 207

Labor Code for the Natives of the Portuguese Colonies of Africa, 1928, 431
Labor Law, 1899 (Portugual), 429-30
Labouret, Henri, 363
Lagos Youth Movement (Nigeria), 334
Lamb, Helen, 21
Land and Mortgage Company (Egypt), 228
Land Apportionment Act, 1931 (Southern Rhodesia), 470
Land Law, 1870 (Indonesia), 164
Land Ordnance, 1923 (Tanganyika), 464
land policy: Belgian Congo, 375, 380; British West Africa, 321; Buganda, 460; in Burma, 212-22; Ceylon, 135; Malaya, 150, 153; Egypt, 229, 239; French West Africa, 355; German colonies, 401, 403, 410; in India, 28-32; Indonesia, 162, 168; Kenya, 450-51; in the Maghreb, key role, 256, 266-67; Southern Rhodesia, 470-71; Tanganyika, 464; Vietnam, 203-4, 206-7; *See also* taxation
Land Reservation Act, 1913 (Malaya), 153
Lands Control Bill (British West Africa), 325
Landsdowne, Lord, (5th Marquess, Henry Charles Keith Petty-Fitzmaurice), 75
Laval, Pierre, 290, 364
law, Western, as applied in colonies: British West Africa, 330; Burma, 119; Egypt, 227, 230, 232; French West Africa, 355; India, 16, 30, 32; the Maghreb, 260, 268, 270, 272-73, 276, 289; Vietnam, 199; *See also* land policy, labor, compulsory, taxation
Law of Liquidation, 1880 (Egypt), 236
Lawrence, Henry, 5
Lawrence, John, 5, 46
League of Nations, and forced labor, 430, 462
Left Book Club, 127
Lenin, Vladimir I., 187
Léopold II, King of Belgium, 346: colonial aims, 374-75; and Congo, 375-78
Lettow-Vorbeck, Gen. Paul Emil von, 421
Leutwin, Major Theodor, and German Southwest Africa, 395-97
Levantines: British West Africa, 326; as expatriate traders, 501; in Egypt, 230; French West Africa, 356, 361
Leverhulme, Lord (Samuel Lever), 320, 380-81
Leys, Dr. Norman, 456
Liberal Party (India), 81
Liga Africana, 1919 (Portuguese Africa), 440
Liga Angola, 1913, 440
Liga National Africa, 440
Limburg Stirum, Count Johan Paul von, 184
Lindequist, Friedrich von, 405, 409
Linlithgow, Lord, (2nd Marguess, Victor A.J. Hope), 25
Livingston, David, 420, 445
Livingstonia mission, 477-78
Livre Foncier Marocain, 275
al-Liwa (newspaper), 246
Lloyd George, David, on ICS, 21
Lobengula, King of the Matabele, 446-47, 448, 468, 480
"local factor": in British East Africa, 446-47; in British West Africa, 305-8; in Burma, 118; in German Africa, 388-89, 393; in India, 4; in Malaya, 147; in Portuguese Africa, 421
"localization": in Belgian Congo, in economy, 383; in British West Africa, 316-18; in Burma, 124-25; in Ceylon, 133-34; defined, xxiv; in Egypt, 235-36; in French West Africa hardly attempted, 363-64; in general terms, 493; in India, 10, 19-21, 47; in Indonesia, 182; in Malaya, 155; in Portuguese Africa, 436; in Uganda, 461; in Vietnam, 213
Long, Maurice, 213
"lopsided" economic growth *See* economic development
Low, Donald A., 509
Low Country Producers' Association (Ceylon), 139
Lucknow Pact, 79-80
Lüderitz, Franz A. E., 388, 390
Lugard, Lord (Baron, Frederick J.D.): *Dual Mandate in Tropical Africa*; in East Africa 445-46; and Indirect Rule, 308-11; on Mandate Commission, 462; on new elites, 316
Lukiko (Bugandan legislature), 457
lumber, as export: Burma, 123; French Equatorial Africa, 360
Luo (African people), 451
Luo Union, 479
Lyall, Alfred, 11
Lyautey, Gen. Hubert, policies, 264-65, 275, 279, 284, 289
Lytton, Lord (2nd Earl of, Victor A.G.R. Bulwer-Lytton), 71

Macauley, Herbert, 332, 334, 335
Macauley, Thomas, "Minute on Education," 6, 68
MacDonald, Ramsay, 88
Mackinnon, William, 445
magharsa, explained, 274
Mahalwari Settlement (India), 31
Maherero, Samuel, policy, 395-96; rebellion, 396-97
Maine, Sir Henry, 11
Maize Control Board, 1936 (Northern Rhodesia), 474
Majapahit (Javan state), 161
Maji-maji rebellion (German East Africa), 397-98, 404
Makerere College (Uganda), 461-62
Malay Administrative Service, 155
Malay College, 147-48
Malay communist Party, 156
Malcolm, John, 31
Malenbaum, Wilfred, 65
Malraux, André, 215
Mamelukes, in Egypt, 227-28
managing agency system (India), explained, 50-51
mandarinate, ch. 6, passim; resistance to French, 196, 198-99, 212
Mandate Commission, 462
Manifeste Jeune-Algérien, 283
Mannoni, Dominique O., and colonial dependency complexes, 509
marabouts (Muslim holy men), political role, 257; and Mourides, 356
Marx, Karl, xx, xxiii, 48, 503
marxism, and Burma, 127-28; in Indonesia, 184, 186-187 *See also* Communist party, Socialist party, and Trotskyite party
Masai (African people), 446, 449-50
Mashona (African people), 446-48, 467
Matabele (African people), 446-48, 467-69, 480
Matabeleland Order in Council, 1894, 447
Mataram (Javan state), 160-61
Materi, Dr. Muhammed, 287, 288
Mattei, Antoine, 306
Mau-Mau (Kenya), 478
Max Havelaar, 164
Mayo, Lord, 46, 58
melk land (Maghreb), defined, 267, and Warnier Law, 268
Merlin, Martial Henri, 215, 350, 352
Messigny, Adophe, 201
Metcalf, Thomas, 34, 74
Michelin Rubber, and Vietnam, 217
military recruitment, British, in India, 9; in Burma, 118
Mill, James, *History of India*, 6; and ICS, 17
Mill, John Stuart, 30, 122, 170
Millerand, Alexandre, 284
Milner, Alfred: and Egypt, 234-235; Milner Commission, 250; and Northern Rhodesia, 471, 476
Minangkabaus (Indonesian people), 145, 171
Mindon Min, King of Burma, 117, 121
Minto, Lord (1*st* Earl of, Gilbert Elliot), 146
Minto, Lord (4*th* Earl of, Gilbert J.M.K. Elliot), 77-78
missionaries: in the Belgian Congo, 383; in British East Africa, 445, 449, 461, 477-78; in British West Africa, 305-6, 320, 328-29; in the German colonies, 407-8; in India, 6; in Vietnam, 194
Mitchell, Sir Philip, 461-62
mixed tribunals (Egypt), 230
Moçambique Convention, 1909, and migrant labor, 432
monopolies, salt; in India, 87; in vietnam, 200-201
Montagu, Edwin, 20, 80
Montagu-Chelmsford report, 20, 80, 140
Morel, Edward, 377
Morley, John, 58, and Morley-Minto reforms, 77-78
Moroccan Action Committee, 290
Morris, Morris D. 49, 66
Mouin, Paul, 215
Mountbatten, Lord Louis, 14
Mourides (Islamic brotherhood), 356, 366
Moutet, Marius, 211, 218
Mouvement Jeune Algérien, 282
Msiri, African king, murdered by Belgians, 377
Muhammadiyah, Islamic modernist movement, 180
Muhammed Ali, Khedive of Egypt, and modernization, 228-31, 237-38, 240, 243, 245
Müller, Max, 17
multazim (Egypt), tax farmers, 228
Mumbo cult, 478-79
Munro, Thomas, 5-6, 17; and ryotwari system, 31
Muslim Education Conference, 1886 (India), 74
Muslims in India: fear of Hindus, 73-74; impact of British rule on, 72-73;

intellectual revival, 73; Muslim League, 79-80, 82, 92-93; and Mutiny, 5
Mutiny, Indian, of 1857, impact on British rule, 5-13
Mwanga, King of Buganda, 457
Mynt, Hla, 327
myothugyis (Burmese officials), 119
myouks (Burmese officials), 119

não-civilizados (Africans), 427
Naoroji, Dadabhbai: and ICS, 20: as political moderate, 78; *Poverty in India*, 63-64, 75; on situation in 1850s, 70
Napoleon III, Emperor of France, 258
Narain, Dharm, 43
Nasser, Gamel Abdul, 229
National African Company, of George Goldie Taubman, 306
National Baptist Convention, 478
National Congress of British West Africa, 1920, 331; demands of, 333
National Democratic Party (Nigeria), 332
nationalism: in Burma, 125; in Malaya, 156-57; in Portuguese Africa, 439-40
National Mohammedan Association (India), 73
National Party for the Realization of Reforms (Morocco), 291
National Social Conference, 1887 (India), 75
Native Administration Ordinance, 1927 (West Africa), 314
native authorities: in British East Africa, 463, 473; under Indirect Rule, 311-314
Native Authority Ordnance, 1926 (Tanganyika), 463
native courts. *See also* native authorities
"native farming": in British East Africa, 459, 474; in British West Africa, 320-25, 327-28; in French West Africa, 354-58; in German colonies, 408, 410-11
Native Lands Trust Ordnance, 1938 (Kenya), 455
Native Passes Act, 1937 (Southern Rhodesia), 471
Native Registration Act, 1936 (Southern Rhodesia), 471
Natives Registration Ordnance, 1915 (Kenya), 453
navétanes (seasonal workers), 355, 358
Nederlandsche Handel-Maatschappij, 162, 172
"*Negritude*," and Senghor, 363
Nehru, Jawaharlal, 5, 7-8, 21; as Congress Party leader, 86-93
Nehru, Motilal, 67, 82, 85, 86
Neo-Destour party (Tunisia), 287-88, 292
Nevinson, Henry W., 430
Ngano, Martha, 480
Niger Company, 307-8
Nigerian Produce Traders Union, 334
Nigerian Youth Movement, 334-35
Nile Barrage (Egypt), 237, 241
Njoya (African ruler), 406
Nkrumah, Kwame, 335
Non-Brahmin party (India), 85
Non-Cooperation movement (India), 21, 82-84, 87-88
Northbrook, Lord (Earl of, Thomas George Baring), 51, 235
Northey, Sir Edward, 453
North Nyanza Native Association, 479
Northwest Cameroons Company, 400
Norton de Matos, José: "Caligula", 425; labor policy, 430, 436
Nu, U, 128
Nurbar Pasha, 235
Nyasaland African Congress, 481
Nyerere, Julius, 481

O'Dwyer, Governor, 82
Office du Niger, 357
Office du Riz (Vietnam), 203
Ofori Atta I, chief of the Fanti, 331
Oil River Protectorate, 1885, 306
olive growing, in Tunisia, 274-75
Onitsha Union (British West Africa), 333
Hermann Oppenheim (Egyptian private bank), 232
Oppenheimer, Ernest, 472
Ord, Sir Harry, 146
Orde Browne, Granville St. John, 465; *Report on Labour Conditions in Northern Nigeria*, 473
Ornelas, Ayres de, 422
Ottama, U, 126
Ottawa System, and India, 63
Ouezzani, Mohammad Hussan el-, 289
Ovimbundu (African people), 437-38
Owen, Edward R. J., 242, 243, 505
Owerri Union (British West Africa), 333

palm products: in the Belgian Congo, 380-81; in British West Africa, 319-20, 323-24; in Celyon, 137; in French

West Africa, 357; in Indonesia (copra), 171; in Malaya, 157; in Togo, 403, 411
Pan-African Congress, 1923 (Lisbon), 440
Pangkor Engagement, 1874 (Malaya), 147
Pan-Islamic movement, 183, 292
Pan-Lusitanianism, as ideology, 425-26
pantja sila (Indonesian nationalist ideology), 186
Paria (journal), and Ho Chi Minh, 217
Parsis (Indian class), as entrepreneurs, 50, 62
Partai Indonesia (Partindo), 187
Partai Nasional Indonesia, of Sukarno, 186-87
Parti Coloniale (France), 346
Parti Constitutionaliste (Vietnam), 205, 215, 216
Parti du Peuple Algérien, 1937, 286
Partindo Nacional Africano, 440
Parti Socialiste Sénégalais, 365
partition of Bengal, 77-78
Passfield Memorandum, 475
Patel, Vallabhai, 91
peanut farming: British West Africa, 324-25; in Senegal, 354-57, 361
pengulu (Malay chiefs), 148
Peninsular and Orient Line, 45
People's Union (Nigeria), 330
Pereira, José de Fontes, 439
Perham, Margery, 317-18, 491
Permanent Settlement (India), 15, 37, 44, 61; explained, 29-30
"personal status": in French West Africa, 364; in Maghreb, legal implications, 260, as political grievance, 284-85
Peters, Carl, 389-91, 445
petroleum production: in Burma, 123; in Indonesia, 174
phosphate mining (Maghreb), 279
Plan for Moroccan Reform, 1934, 290, 292
plantations: in the Belgian Congo, 380-81; in British East Africa, 454, 458, 464-65; in Ceylon, 134-37; in German Africa, 400; in India, 42, 66; in Malaya, 150-52; in the Netherlands Indies, 164-71; in Vietnam, 207-8. *See also specific plantation crops* (coffee, rubber, sugar, and tea)
Plassey, battle of, 3
plural societies: Burma, 120; Ceylon, 131-32, 140-41; Indonesia, 178-80; Malaya, 152-54
Political, Civil and Criminal Statute for the Natives of Guinea, Angola, and Moçambique, 1926, 426-27
pongyis (Burma), politicized monks, 126-27, 128
Ponty, William, 349, 350
Popular Front government: (France) in French West Africa, 352, 365; in the Maghreb, 285, 288, 292; in Vietnam, 211, 218-19
population: in British West Africa, 324; Ceylon, 137-39; Egypt, 237-38; in India, 22-23, 38-40; Java, 166; Kenya, 455-56; in the Maghreb, 281; Malaya, 153; Northern Rhodesia, 474; in Portuguese Africa, decreases, 431; in Vietnam, 202
Pössinger, Hermann (agricultural expert), 423
post-primary resistance: assessed, 508; in British East Africa, 448; in British West Africa, 308-309, 312-313; in Burma, 118, 126; in French West Africa, 366; in German Africa, 394, 396-98; in India, 7 (*see also* Mutiny, Indian); in Indonesia, 162, 165, 182; in the Maghreb, 257, 259, 261, 264, 288; and nationalism, 510; in Portuguese Africa, 421-22; in Vietnam, 196, 213-14, 217
Potter, David, 20
Prasad, Rajendra, 91
prazeiros (Portuguese landholders in Africa), 419
Prebisch, Raul, 496
Prempeh, King of the Ashanti, 309, 314
prestations, *See* labor, compulsory
prijaji (Indonisian aristocrats), 160, 180, 183
primary resistance (initial resistance to European conquest), 508. *See* imperial policy
princely states, of India, 12-13, 89
productivity, agricultural: in British East Africa, 459; in British West Africa, 325, 327; in Ceylon, 139; discussed, 500-501; in Egypt, 242; in French West Africa, 355-56; in India, 40-41; in the Maghreb, 269, 271, 274, 278, 281
productivity, industrial: in India, 52, 54; in Vietnam, 210
protection, *See* customs policy
Protectorat à trois (Tunisia), 261
Protectorate Treaty of 1884 (Vietnam), 196-97
Provincial Civil Service (India), 19, 125

Public Debt Administration (Egypt), 227, 232, 235-36
Punjab Alienation of Land Act, 1900, 34, 75-76
Punjab Relief of Indebtedness Act, 25
Puttkamer, Jesco von, 400, 405

"Quit India" campaign, 1942, 93

"races policy": in French West Africa, 349-350; in Vietnam, 196
racism: in Belgian Congo, 383; in British East Africa, 471, 473-74; in British West Africa, 317, 319; in Burma, 125; in colonial situation, 488; in Egypt, 247; in French West Africa, 365; in German colonies, 397, 412-13; in India, 8-9; in Indonesia, 179; in Maghreb, 259, 268; in Malaya, 156; in Portuguese Africa, 427, 439-40; and settlement colonies, 502; in Vietnam, 212-13
Raffles, Thomas Stamford, 145-46, 162, 163
Raffles College of Arts and Science, 155
Rahman, Tunku Abdul, 155
railroads: Belgian Congolese, 376, 382; British East African, 446, 449-50, 458, 467; British West African, 319-20, 325; Ceylonese, 135; French West African, 343-44, 354, 366; German Colonial, 396, 408-9; Indian, 44-48; Maghrebine, 278-79; Portuguese colonial, 434, 435; Vietnamese, 208-9
Ramanathan, Sir Ponnambalam, 139
Ramkrishna movement, 70
Ranade, M. G., 71, 75
Ranger, Terence O., 476, 479, 570
Rangoon Chamber of Commerce, 117
Rangoon College, 124
Rassemblement Démocratique Africain (French West Africa), 359
Rattray, Robert S., 314
Raum, Otto Friedrich, 407
Rawlinson, Lord (Baron, Henry Seymour Rawlinson), 10
Raynaud, Paul, 218
Reading, Lord (Marguess of, Rufus D. Isaacs), 86
Rechenberg, Baron von, 405, 408-9, 410
Reform Committee for India, 125
regedor (African official), 423
regedoria (Portuguese administrative districts), 423
regents (Indonesian officials), 161, 163-65, 178
Regeringsreglement, 1854 (Indonesia), 164
Régnier, Marcel, 284
régulo (African offical), 423
Reich Colonial Office, 404-5
religion, as basis for cultural reform movements: in the Belgian Congo, 384-85; in British East Africa, 477-80; in Burma, 125-26; common features, 510-12; in Egypt, 246; French West Africa, 266; German Africa, 413; in India, 69-73; in Indonesia, 182-83, 185-86; in the Maghreb, 282-86, 289-92; in Malaya, 156; in Portuguese Africa, 439; in Vietnam, 219
"reserved seats" (India), 73
Resident Natives Ordnance, 1918 (Kenya), 453
residents: in British West Africa, 310-11; in German colonies, 406; in Malaya, 147-49; in princely states, 12; in Tunisia, 262; in Vietnam, 197-98
Restriction of Credit to the Native Ordnance (Tanganyika), 466
Revue du Maghreb (journal), 286
Rhodes, Cecil, 374; in East Africa, 446-48; 467-68, 470
Rhodesia Bantu Voters Association, 1923, 480
rice farming: in Burma, 116, 119-24; in Ceylon, 137-38; in Egypt, 243; in India, 25, 41; in Indonesia, 160, 168, 173; in Malaya, 154; in Vietnam, ch. 6 passim, esp. 202-5, 208, 210
Ripon, Lord: (Marquess of, George F.S. Robinson), and industry, 55, 58; and political liberalization, 18-19, 71-72
Robequain, Charles, 211
Robinson, Ronald, 509
Rohrbach, Paul, 412
Rosebury, Lord, 446
Ross, W. McGregor, 456
Rotberg, Robert I., 476
Rothermund, Dietmar, 29, 83
Roume, Ernest, 354
route mandarine (Vietnam), 194, 209
Rouvier, Maurice, 347
Rowlatt bills, 81-82
Royal Botanical Garden, 136, 150
Roy, Ram Mohan, 69-70, 73
rubber: in the Belgian Congo, 375; in British East Africa, 444; in Ceylon, 137; in

French West Africa, 359-60; in the German colonies, 403; in Indonesia, 171, 173; in Malaya, 150-52; in the Portuguese colonies, 419, 437; in Vietnam, 207-208
Rudd, Charles, 447
ruling class, traditional. *See* elites, traditional
Russo-German pact, 1939, 219
Ryckmans, Pierre, on native chiefs, 379, 384
ryotwari system (India), explained, 31, 44

Said, Iman Seyyid, Sultan of Zanzibar, 444
Said, Khedive of Egypt, 231-32, 237, 243
Salafiyya (Morocco), 289-91
Salazar, Antonio de Oliveira, 425-26, 440
Salisbury, Lord (Marquess, Robert A. T. Gascoyne-Cecil), 235, 306, 420, 445, 446
Salvation Army, 385
Samory (African leader), 343-45
Sandhurst, and Indian officers, 10
Sang, Aung, 128
Sapru, Tej B., 83, 86
Sarbah, John Mensah, 329
Sarda Canal (India), 26
Sarekat Islam (Indonesia), organization and program, 182-84; 185
sarkar (Mughal administrative district), 15
Sarkisyanz, Emmanuel, 126
Sarraut, Albert, 212, 214-15, 507
Sarvjanik Sabha, 1870 (Poona), 71
Satyagraha, 82
Saul, S. B., 53
sawah land. *See* irrigation, in Indonesia
Saya San rebellion, 126-27
Sayyid, Ahmad Lutfi al-, 246-47
Schnee, Heinrich, 409
"School for Translations" (Egypt), 245
Schrieke, Bertram J. O., 171
Schuckmann, governor, 411
secteurs (Belgian Congo): basic administrative unit, 378-79
Seitz, Theodor, 405
Senanayake, D. S., 140, 141
Senghor, Léopold Sédar, 363
Serpa Pinto, A. du Rocha, 420
sertanejos, Portuguese traders, 437
Service de la Dette (Morocco), 263
settlers, European: in German colonies, 408-9, 412-13; in Kenya, 451-47; in Northern Rhodesia, 472, 475; in Portuguese colonies, 435, 440; in Southern Rhodesia, 467-470; in Tanganyika, 466. *See* colons for French colonies
"Settling up" treaty, 1890, 391
Shastri, Lal Bahadur, 151
shaykh (Arab official): in Egypt, 229, 240; in the French Maghreb, 294
"Short Declaration" (Indonesia) of submission, 165
silver, 419
Simon Commission, 85
Singapore, foundation of, 146; ch. 4 passim
Singer, H. W., 496
Sinhala Maha Sabha (Ceylon), 141
Sinha, S. P., 78
Sinhalese, *see* ch. 3, Ceylon
sisal, in East Africa, 400, 465
Sjahrir, Sutan, 187
slavery and the slave trade: in British East Africa, 444-45; in British West Africa, 306, 309, 311, 319; in French West Africa, 349; in German Africa, 394; in Portuguese Africa, 419-20, 429-430
Smuts, Jan Christian, 470
Sneevliet, Hendrik, 184
Société de l'Ouest Africain, 1906, 354
Société des Distilleries de l'Indochine, 201
Société des Huileries du Congo Belge, 380
Société Financière des Caoutchoucs, 207
Société Générale (Congo), dominant economic interest, 377, 381-82
Société Générale des Sucreries d'Egypte, 244
Société Marocain de Prévoyance, 278
Société Marseillaise de Crédit (Maghreb), 272
Sociétés Indigènes de Crédit Mutuel, (Vietnam), 206
Sociétés Indigènes de Prevoyance: in Maghreb, 270; in West Africa, 356
Soetardja (Indonesian statesman), 188
Snouck Hurgronje, Christiaan, 165, 186
Solf, Wilhelm, 413
South African Congress, 480
South Cameroons Company, 400
spice trade an spice production: in Ceylon, 134; in Indonesia, 160-64, 171
squatters, in East Africa, 453, 456, 471
Srivajaya (Sumatran state), 161
Stalin, Joseph, 185
Stanley, Henry Morton, 374, 445
Steeg, Théodore, 275, 289
Stengers, Jean, 374-77, 381
Stephen, Fitzjames, 19
Stephenson, George, 45
Stevenson Plan, 1922, 207

Strachey, John, 19, 58
strikes: in British East Africa, 473-74; Burma, 128; in French West Africa, 366; in India, 67; in the Maghreb, 286-87; in Malaya, 152; Vietnam, 208-18
"subimperialism": defined, 406; in Uganda, 458
Suez Canal, 55, 146, 250
Suez Canal Company, 232, 244, 248
sugar farming: in India, 43; in Indonesia, 168-72; in Malaya, 151
Sugar Law, 1871 (Indonesia), 164
Sukarno (Indonesian statesman), 186-87
Sultan Idris Training College (Malaya), 154, 165
Sun Yat-sen, 155, 217
Sûrété (French police), 217
Swadeshi movement, 77, 214
Swaraj Party (India): "swaraj" as slogan, 76, 85, 89; in Burma 127

Taalbi, Abdelaziz, 286, 288
Tagore, Rabindranath, family, 18, 70
talukdar (Indian landlord), 7, 28, 37-38
Tamils (Hindus), in Ceylon, 131, 136-37, 140-41
Tanganyika Concessions Company, 377
tariffs. *See* customs duties
Tata, Jamshed N., 48, 50, 55-56, 58, 61
Taubman, George Goldie, 306, 307, 310
Tawfiq, Khedive of Egypt, 234
taxation: in British East Africa, 451-52, 456, 469; in Ceylon, 133; in Egypt, 228, 230, 240; with the additional purpose of forcing black Africans to work, in French West Africa, 350-52; in German colonies, 402; in India, 3-4, 15-16, 25, 27-32, 44, 87; in Indonesia, 162, 192; in the Maghreb, 277; in Malaya; in Vietnam, 200-201
tea: in India, 42, 66; in Ceylon, 136-39
Technical School (Accra), 319
tehsil: Mughal administrative subdistrict, 15
Temple, Sir Charles, 311
tertib (Maghreb), agricultural yield tax, 277
tetzlaff, Rainer, 409
textile industry: Indian, 48-54; Indonesian, 174-75; Egypt, 230-31
Theosophical Society, 71, 79
Thibaw, kind of Burma, 117
Thorburn, Septimus, *Musalmans and Moneylenders in the Punjab*, 34
Throner, Daniel, 47
Thuku, Harry, 479-80
Thuyet, Ton That, 196
Tignor, Robert, 492
Tilak, Bal Gangadhar, 76, 78-79, 81, 83
tin: in British West Africa, 325; in Indonesia, 173-74; in Malaya, 149-50, 152; in Vietnam, 210
Tip, Tippo, 375
Tjokroaminoto, Umar Said, 186
Toffa, King (African ruler), 346
trade, balance of, *See* balance of payments/trade
trade, terms of: for British West Africa, 327; for Burma, 122; for Ceylon, 139; for Egypt, 243; in general terms, 496; for India, 57, 63; for Indonesia, 176
Trade Union Bill, 1926 (India), 67
trade unions. *See* unionization
transhumance, in the Maghreb, 266, 275, 277
Treaty of Bardo, 260
Treaty of La Marsa, 261
Treaty of Sevres, 83
Treaty of Versailles (the "*Diktat*"), 388
Treich-Laplène, Marcel, 345
Trevelyan, George O., 9
Trinh, Phan Chau, 214, 216
Trotha, Gen. Lothar von, 397, 406
Trotskyites, in Vietnam, 218-19
Tu-Duc, Emperor of Vietnam, 195
Tunisian Cartel, 1925, 287
La Tunisie martyr, ses revendications, 1920, 286
Turkish-Circassians: in Egypt, 227, 233, 234; in Algeria, 257
"Two Nations" resolution, 1940 (India), 93

Uganda National Congress, 481
Uganda Order in Council, 1902, 457
uhda (Egypt), explained, 229
ulema: in Egypt, 227, 228; in India, 73; in Indonesia, 165, 183; in the Maghreb, 285-86, 292; in Malaya, 156
Ulema Assembly, 292
Umar, El-Hajj, 343
umda (Egyptian village headman), 229, changing role of, 240-41
Umdah Law, 1895, 240
Ummah party (Egypt), 246-48, 250
underdevelopment, concept discussed, xxi-xxiii, xxvi, 495
Unilever (Belgian plantation company), 380-81

Union Coloniale, French colonial pressure group, 211
unionization: in India, 67; in the Maghreb, 286-87; in Malaya, 152; in Northern Rhodesia, 474; in Vietnam, 208
Union Minièr du Haut-Katanga, 377, 383
United Africa Company, 322
United East India Company (Netherlands), 132, 149, 160-61
University College, Colombo, 133
University of Hanoi, 215
University of Quarawiyin (Fez), 289
University of Rangoon, 125
ushr (land tax), 240
Usurious Loans Act, 1918 (India), 35
Utilitarianism and the Utilitarians in India, 6, 17, 31

Vaderlandsche Club, 188
Valery, Paul, 513
Varenne, Alexandre, 201, 206-8, 215
Verdier, A. (French trader), 345
Vernacular Press Act, 1878 (India), 71
Victoria, Queen of England, 447
Victoria Memorial (Delhi), 76
Viénot, Pierre, 288, 290
Viet Nam Duy Tan Hoi, 214-15
Vietnamese Nationalist Party (Viet Nam Quoc Dan Dang), 217-19
Vietor, J. K., 402
Village Headman Ordnance, 1902 (Kenya), 449
villages, under colonial rule: in Belgian Congo, 382; in British West Africa, 313; in Burma, 118-19; in Ceylon, 137; in Egypt, 240-41; in French West Africa, 345-46, 358; in India, 15-16, 27-28, 31-32, 49; in Indonesia, 163-64, 166-67, 169, 173; in Vietnam, 194, 198-201
Violette, Maurice, 284-85
Vivekanada (Indian religious reformer), 70
La Voix du Tuisien (newspaper), 287
Volksraad (Indonesia), 184-86, 188
Vollenhoven, Cornelis van, 186

Wafd party (Egypt), 247, 249-50
Warnier Law, 1873 (Maghreb), 268
"warrant chiefs," under Indirect Rule, 313
wars, colonial, 508. *See* primary resistance
Watu-wa Mungu (People of God) sect, 479
Wavell, Gen. Archibald, 14, 25
"We Burmans" society (Thakin party), 127-28
Wehler, Hans, Ulrich, xvii, 389
Wellesley, Lord (Marquess, Richard Colley Wellesley), 17
West African Pilot (Azikiwe's newspaper), 334
West African Victoria Plantation Company, 400
White Fathers, 445
Wickham, Sir Henry, 150
Widow Remarriage Act, 1856, 6
Wihowo Resolution (Indonesia), 188
Williams, William Appleman, xviii-xix
Willingdon, Lord (Marquess, Freeman Freeman-Thomas), 88
Wilson, Woodrow, 388, 413
wine industry in the Maghreb, 270-72
Wingate, Sir Reginald, 249
Witbooi, Hendrik, chief of the Nama, 295, 397
Witwatersrand Native Labour Association, 432
Wood, Sir Charles, 10, 68
workers, expatriate and migrant: in the Belgian Congo, 376, 379-83; in British East Africa, 455, 469, 473; in Burma, 124; in Ceylon, 135-37; in French West Africa, 350-51, 355, 358; in Malaya, 146, 150-52; in Portuguese Africa, 432-33; in Vietnam, 207-208

Yaba Higher College (Nigeria), 318-19, 334
Yorubas (African people), 307
Young Busag Association (Uganda), 460-61
Young Kavirondo Association, 1921 (Nyanza), 480
Young Malay Union, 165
Young Men's Buddhist Association (YMBA), 125-26
Young Tunisians, 282
Youssef, Salah ben, 388
Youssef, sultan of Morocco, 264
Yussuf, Side Muhammad ben, sultan of Morocco, 290

Zaghlul, Saad, 247-50
zamindars (Indian landlords), 7, 24, 27-30, 36-38, 67-68, 71, 73, 91
Zinkin, Maurice, 152

ABOUT THE AUTHOR

RUDOLF VON ALBERTINI is Professor of Modern History at the University of Zurich in Switzerland. Among his earlier works is *Decolonization: The Administration and Future of the Colonies, 1919-1960.*

Albert Wirz who teaches African history at the University of Zurich, is the author of *Vom Sklavenhandel zum kolonialen Handel: Wirtschaftsräume und Wirtschaftsformen in Kamerun vor 1914.*

John G. Williamson, Director of the Library of St. Mary's College of Maryland, is a specialist in German history and the author of *Karl Helfferich, 1872-1924: Economist, Financier, Politician.*